BOARD-SHAREHOLDER DIALOGUE

This book provides corporate law scholars and students and practitioners at law firms, advisory services firms and asset managers with a comprehensive and rigorous analysis of the financial, managerial, policy and legal issues arising from a key feature of today's corporate governance environment, namely, the dialogue between shareholders and corporate boards.

Bringing together top corporate law and corporate governance scholars from the world's leading academic institutions, the collection is characterized by a multi-dimensional approach that considers the particularities of some national legal systems and combines theoretical analysis with practical insights into various aspects of board-shareholder dialogue.

LUCA ENRIQUES is Professor of Corporate Law at the University of Oxford and a Research Fellow at the European Corporate Governance Institute.

GIOVANNI STRAMPELLI is Professor of Business Law and Director of the PhD in Legal Studies at Bocconi University, Milan.

INTERNATIONAL CORPORATE LAW AND FINANCIAL MARKET REGULATION

Corporate law and financial market regulation have major implications for how the modern economy is organized and regulated and for how risk is managed and distributed – domestically, regionally and internationally. This Series seeks to inform and lead the vibrant scholarly and policy debate in this highly dynamic area by publishing cutting-edge, timely and critical examinations of the most pressing and important questions in the field.

Series Editors

Professor Eilis Ferran, *University of Cambridge.*

Professor Niamh Moloney, *London School of Economics and Political Science.*

Professor Howell Jackson, *Harvard Law School.*

BOARD-SHAREHOLDER DIALOGUE

Policy Debate, Legal Constraints and Best Practices

Edited by

LUCA ENRIQUES

University of Oxford

GIOVANNI STRAMPELLI

Bocconi University

Assogestioni is the Italian Investment Management Association. Founded in 1984, the association's aims are to foster and disseminate the various forms of investment management in Italy, including retirement savings, and to promote the growth of its culture and values, in support of the development of the real economy and the financial market. Assogestioni is also focused on representing and protecting the collective interests of its members and their investor clients. Today its members manage more than €2.3 trillion on behalf of Italian households, corporates and public institutions.

CAMBRIDGE
UNIVERSITY PRESS

ASSOGESTIONI
associazione del risparmio gestito

CAMBRIDGE
UNIVERSITY PRESS

Shaftesbury Road, Cambridge CB2 8EA, United Kingdom

One Liberty Plaza, 20th Floor, New York, NY 10006, USA

477 Williamstown Road, Port Melbourne, VIC 3207, Australia

314–321, 3rd Floor, Plot 3, Splendor Forum, Jasola District Centre, New Delhi – 110025, India

103 Penang Road, #05–06/07, Visioncrest Commercial, Singapore 238467

Cambridge University Press is part of Cambridge University Press & Assessment, a department of the University of Cambridge.

We share the University's mission to contribute to society through the pursuit of education, learning and research at the highest international levels of excellence.

www.cambridge.org
Information on this title: www.cambridge.org/9781009360760

DOI: 10.1017/9781009360746

First published 2024

A catalogue record for this publication is available from the British Library

Library of Congress Cataloging-in-Publication Data
Names: Enriques, Luca, editor. | Strampelli, Giovanni, 1977- editor.
Title: Board-shareholder dialogue : policy debate, legal constraints, and best practices / edited by Luca Enriques, University of Oxford; Giovanni Strampelli, Bocconi University.
Description: Cambridge, United Kingdom ; New York, NY : Cambridge University Press, 2024. | Series: International corporate law and financial market regulation | Includes bibliographical references.
Identifiers: LCCN 2023058863 (print) | LCCN 2023058864 (ebook) | ISBN 9781009360760 (hardback) | ISBN 9781009360722 (paperback) | ISBN 9781009360746 (ebook)
Subjects: LCSH: Directors of corporations–Legal status, laws, etc. | Corporate governance–Law and legislation. | Stockholders–Legal status, laws, etc.
Classification: LCC K1328 .B63 2024 (print) | LCC K1328 (ebook) | DDC 346/.06642–dc23/eng/20240117
LC record available at https://lccn.loc.gov/2023058863
LC ebook record available at https://lccn.loc.gov/2023058864

ISBN 978-1-009-36076-0 Hardback

CONTENTS

CONTRIBUTORS

AFRA AFSHARIPOUR is Professor of Law at the University of California, Davis (UC Davis) School of Law.

TIM BOWLEY is a corporate law researcher at Monash University, Australia.

ANNA CHRISTIE is Departmental Lecturer in Law and Finance at the Faculty of Law, University of Oxford.

PAUL A. DAVIES KC, FBA is Allen & Overy Professor of Corporate Law Emeritus at the University of Oxford.

LUCA ENRIQUES is Professor of Corporate Law at Jesus College, University of Oxford.

LISA M. FAIRFAX is Presidential Professor of Law at the University of Pennsylvania Law School.

JILL FISCH is Saul A. Fox Distinguished Professor of Business Law at the University of Pennsylvania Carey Law School.

MATTEO GATTI is Professor of Law at Rutgers Law School.

OLIVER HART is the Lewis P. and Linda L. Geyser University Professor at Harvard University.

JENNIFER G. HILL is the inaugural Bob Baxt AO Professor of Corporate and Commercial Law, Monash University Faculty of Law.

MARCEL KAHAN is a professor of law at New York University School of Law.

DIONYSIA KATELOUZOU is Reader at the Dickson Poon School of Law, King's College London.

LARS KLÖHN is Professor of Civil and Commercial Law at Humboldt University, Berlin.

STEVE KOURABAS is a lecturer at Monash University Law School.

ANNE LAFARRE is an associate professor at Tilburg University Law School, The Netherlands.

LIN LIN is an associate professor in the Faculty of Law, National University of Singapore.

DOROTHY LUND is a professor of law at Columbia Law School.

COLIN MAYER CBE is Emeritus Professor at Saïd Business School, University of Oxford.

PETER O. MÜLBERT is Chair of Private Law, Commercial and Business Law, Banking Law, Faculty of Law and Economics, University of Mainz, Germany.

JENNIFER PAYNE is a professor of law and Warden of Merton College, University of Oxford.

WOLF-GEORG RINGE is Professor of Law and Finance at the University of Hamburg and Visiting Professor at the University of Oxford.

ADRIANA Z. ROBERTSON is Donald N. Pritzker Professor of Business Law at the University of Chicago Law School.

EDWARD ROCK is a professor of law at New York University School of Law.

ALEXANDER SAJNOVITS is Assistant Professor and Post-Doctoral Fellow, Chair of Private Law, Commercial and Business Law, Banking Law, Faculty of Law and Economics, University of Mainz.

GIOVANNI STRAMPELLI is Professor of Business Law, Bocconi University, Milan.

ANA TALESKA is a lecturer at the Faculty of Law, University of Cambridge.

MATTEO TONELLO is Managing Director at The Conference Board.

CHRISTOPH VAN DER ELST is a professor of law at Tilburg University Law School, The Netherlands.

LUIGI ZINGALES is a finance professor at Booth School of Business, University of Chicago.

FOREWORD

The practice of engagement between boards of directors and shareholders has become increasingly common around the world. Innovations in corporate governance, such as greater attention to environmental, social and governance (ESG) factors, more frequent and substantial activist investor campaigns, increased use of proxy advisory services, and a growing appreciation of the potential benefits of engagement, have prompted investors and corporate boards to reassess their approach to engagement with portfolio companies. Direct and transparent interaction between boards and investors is now seen as essential to promote better mutual understanding and to improve the overall quality of corporate governance, with the goal of achieving sustainable success in all financial markets. Increasing numbers of investors and directors are, respectively, requesting meetings with board members and accepting such requests, or even proactively initiating dialogue with investors.

Assogestioni, Italy's Investment Management Association, acknowledges that active and meaningful engagement between boards and shareholders has a key role to play in delivering sustainable corporate performance and building investor confidence. The members of Assogestioni are firmly committed to promoting best practices in governance and engagement. Since 1996, Assogestioni has provided technical and operational support to the Investment Managers Committee, a body made up of Italian and international institutional investors. The Committee engages with Italian-listed companies by electing minority independent directors through the "voto di lista" (slate voting system) and facilitates collective engagement initiatives in the form of direct dialogue with company boards. In 2013, Assogestioni adopted the Italian Stewardship Principles, and in 2022, it endorsed the Italian Shareholder-Director Exchange (I-SDX), a framework of best practices for the planning and execution of efficient and mutually beneficial engagements between shareholders and directors. Assogestioni is honoured to support the publication of *Board-Shareholder Dialogue:*

Policy Debate, Legal Constraints and Best Practices. This book is the first to explore the nuances of board-shareholder engagement in a comprehensive manner. It aims to be a valuable resource for practitioners, stakeholders and researchers. By examining the importance, challenges and best practices associated with this essential aspect of modern corporate governance, the book serves as a catalyst for informed discussion, policy improvements and more robust shareholder-board interactions. It provides a comprehensive analysis of key issues related to board-shareholder engagement and delves into critical aspects such as the legal and policy framework, the evolving landscape of ESG investment and shareholder stewardship, strategies for improving disclosure and communication channels, and the role of institutional investors in promoting engagement activities. A notable milestone of this initiative was the book conference held in Rome in October 2022 and hosted by Assogestioni. Chapter authors gathered to share insights and ideas with leading practitioners from around the world. Throughout the conference, the dialogue between academics and practitioners provided criticisms, insights and new perspectives that greatly enriched the book's contents.

The event took place in the prestigious and highly symbolic setting of the Museum of the Ara Pacis, the altar Augustus built and dedicated to Pax, the Roman goddess of peace. It marked the onset of the Pax Augustea, widely regarded by historians as a golden age. Inspired by this historic venue, we hope this remarkable publication will strengthen trust between investors and public companies, ultimately driving sustainable growth and value creation across the market.

Fabio Galli
Director General, Assogestioni

The Dialogue between Corporations and Institutional Investors

An Introduction

LUCA ENRIQUES AND GIOVANNI STRAMPELLI

I.1 Introduction

Institutional ownership of listed companies has grown significantly almost everywhere in the last three decades. Equity ownership has steadily moved from retail to institutional investors in that period.[1] With (minority) shares now concentrated in the hands of a relatively small number of institutions, the free-rider problem that prevented atomised individual shareholders of listed corporations from monitoring managers' (or controlling shareholders') actions and performance has become less daunting. In fact, institutional investors play an ever-increasing role in the governance of listed companies worldwide.

Not only are they capable of exerting influence on investee companies by using their voice through voting and engagement, but expectations that they do so have been growing considerably. In a context where sustainability-related issues are in the spotlight as they have never been before and legislators (especially in the EU) are nudging institutions into including ESG factors in their investment and stewardship strategies, institutions are called to engage with investee companies not only to monitor their financial performance but also to push them to pursue environmental and social goals.

However, the actual willingness of institutional investors[2] to engage with portfolio companies and to focus on ESG-related issues remains

We wish to thank participants in the Assogestioni Corporate Governance Conference 2022, and especially Maria Ortino for their helpful comments. Javier Paz Valbuena and Vasile Rotaru provided excellent research assistance.

[1] See for an overview Amil Dasgupta, Vyacheslav Fos, and Zacharias Sautner, 'Institutional Investors and Corporate Governance' (2021) ECGI Finance Working Paper N° 700/2020. https://papers.ssrn.com/sol3/papers.cfm?abstract_id=3682800 accessed 25 June 2023.

[2] The definitions of institutional investor and asset manager are not synonymous in the text. The term institutional investor (or institution) refers to any entity that invests money on

uncertain. Indeed, regardless of whether stewardship activities are conducted at the individual company level or at the portfolio level, holding stakes that are large enough to enable them to exert pressure over investee companies and capture potential economic benefits from stewardship activities is a precondition for institutions' engagement. But several economic and legal factors can affect the propensity of institutional investors towards engagement with portfolio companies, as well as the methods by which engagement is undertaken and the topics covered.

Against this backdrop, this chapter proceeds as follows. Section I.2 provides an overview of the institutionalisation of listed companies' ownership. Section I.3 illustrates asset managers' ownership and nationality in different jurisdictions. Section I.4 describes the shift to ESG-related engagement and discusses the relevance of end-clients' preferences as a main driver of this move as well as the potential regulatory backlash arising from increasing ESG engagement. Section I.5 provides the reader with a roadmap of the book contents.

I.2 The Institutionalisation of Listed Companies' Ownership

Institutional investors dominate the ownership of publicly listed firms worldwide. At the aggregate level, they are the largest category of shareholders.[3] They hold 41 per cent of global market capitalisation, accounting for more than USD 30 trillion invested in public equity markets.[4] This is three times the amount invested by public-sector owners and six times the value of investments by strategic individuals.[5] Institutional investors' presence in listed companies, while by far stronger in the US

behalf of its clients. In addition to asset managers, the definition of institutional investors includes asset owners such as pension funds, sovereign wealth funds, banks, endowments, and insurance companies.

3 Adriana De La Cruz, Alejandra Medina, and Yun Tang, 'Owners of the World's Listed Companies' (2019), www.oecd.org/corporate/Owners-of-the-Worlds-Listed-Companies.pdf, accessed 25 June 2023; Gur Aminadav and Elias Papaioannou, 'Corporate Control around the World' (2020) 75 Journal of Finance 1191.

4 According to the OECD, the reported percentage of 41 per cent is underestimated because institutional investors are not required to disclose their full ownership in most jurisdictions due to their overall size or the limited size of their stakes. See De La Cruz et al (n 3) 13 ff.

5 According to the definitions used by ibid 4, 9. Strategic investors are 'physical persons that are either controlling owners or members of a controlling family or block-holders and family offices'.

and the UK, where ownership is traditionally highly dispersed, is relevant also in countries, such as European ones, where the percentage of companies with a controlling shareholder (be it a private entity, a family, or the state) is common.[6] For example, as reported by the OECD, institutional investors hold 26.9 per cent of total market capitalization in Italy, 27.5 per cent in France and 28.3 per cent in Germany.[7]

Focusing on the asset management industry, the market is more concentrated in the US than elsewhere: since 1980, the top 10 institutional investors have quadrupled their holdings in US stocks[8] and, at the end of 2021, the five largest mutual fund and exchange traded fund sponsors – out of a total of 825 – accounted for 54 per cent of the industry's total assets.[9] While not as dramatic as in the US, concentration within the asset management industry is significant in the EU as well. At the end of 2021, the share of assets under management (AUM) held by the top 20 EU asset managers was 43.71 per cent.[10] Relatedly, in 2021, the share of the total AUM held by the world's top 20 asset managers (all from the US, the EU, and the UK) was 45.2 per cent.[11]

The concentration process that has taken place in the asset management industry over the past few decades has mainly been fuelled by the exponential rise of passive funds and ETFs. In the US, they accounted for

6 See online appendix of Aminadav and Papaioannou (n 3) providing percentage and identity of second and third largest categories.

7 OECD, 'OECD Capital Market Review of Italy 2020: Creating Growth Opportunities for Italian Companies and Savers' (2020) OECD Capital Market Series, www.oecd.org/corporate/OECD-Capital-Market-Review-Italy.htm, accessed 25 June 2023.

8 Itzhak Ben-David, Francesco Franzoni, Rabih Moussawi, and John Sedunov, 'The Granular Nature of Large Institutional Investors' (2021) 67 Management Science 6629.

9 See Steve Johnson, 'Passive fund ownership of US stocks overtakes active for first time', Financial Times (London, 6 June 2022), www.ft.com/content/27b5e047-5080-4ebb-b02a-0bf4a3b9bc08, accessed 25 June 2023.

10 See Detlef Glow, 'European Fund Industry Review 2021' (2022), https://lipperalpha.refinitiv.com/wp-content/uploads/2022/03/21-12-31-European-Fund-Industry-Review-2021-Awards-Edition-FINAL.pdf, accessed 25 June 2023, documenting that 2,239 promoters with at least one fund domiciled in a European fund domicile account for 56.37 per cent of the overall AUM.

11 Thinking Ahead Institute and Willis Towers Watson, 'The world's largest 500 asset managers, 2022' (2023), www.thinkingaheadinstitute.org/research-papers/the-worlds-largest-asset-managers-2022, accessed 25 June 2023. See also Robert G. Eccles, 'Concentration in the Asset Management Industry: Implications for Corporate Engagement' *Forbes* (New Jersey, 17 April 2019), www.forbes.com/sites/bobeccles/2019/04/17/concentration-in-the-asset-management-industry-implications-for-corporate-engagement/, accessed 25 June 2023, reporting that, at that time, the top five asset managers held 22.7 per cent of externally managed assets, and the top 10 held 34 per cent.

18 per cent of US stock market capitalisation at the end of 2022, surpassing the 14 per cent held by active funds.[12] Indeed, despite its continuous growth, the passive index fund industry remains highly concentrated. The market is dominated by Blackrock, Vanguard, and State Street Global Advisors (SSGA) – the 'Big Three' – which, overall, manage over 90 per cent of all AUM in passive funds.[13]

The combination of ownership reconcentration and asset management industry concentration dynamics has a direct impact on the ownership of listed companies and carries significant corporate governance implications. Indeed, although sectoral passive funds and personalised index funds that adopt active-like investment strategies and thus comprise more concentrated portfolios are increasingly widespread,[14] giant asset managers dominating the passive funds industry are heavily invested across all companies included in major stock indexes.[15] According to Lazard, at the end of 2021, Vanguard, BlackRock, and State Street together held on average 18.7 per cent of S&P 500 companies. Their ownership of smaller companies was even more concentrated as they held 22.8 per cent of the shares in the S&P MidCap 400 index and 28.2 per cent in the S&P SmallCap 600 index.[16]

The fact that the largest asset managers are large shareholders in an enormous number of listed companies is widely documented. To our knowledge, though, available studies mainly focus on the US and data on European markets are limited.

To fill this gap, we collected data on the shareholdings of the 25 largest institutional investors in each of the continental European companies

[12] See Investment Company Institute, 'Factbook' (2023), www.icifactbook.org/pdf/2023-factbook.pdf, 23.

[13] See generally, Jan Fichtner, Eelke Heemskerk, and Javier Garcia-Bernardo, 'Hidden Power of the Big Three? Passive Index Funds, Re-concentration of Corporate Ownership, and New Financial Risk' (2017) 19 Bus and Pol 298; Lucian Bebchuk and Scott Hirst, 'Index Funds and the Future of Corporate Governance: Theory, Evidence, and Policy' (2019) 119 Colum L Rev 2029. See also Lund & Robertson, Chapter 5 in this book.

[14] See Adriana Z. Robertson, 'Passive in Name Only: Delegated Management and Index Investing' (2019) 36 Yale J Reg 795; Paul G. Mahoney and Adriana Z. Robertson, 'Advisers by Another Name' (2021) 11 Harv Bus L Rev 311.

[15] Investment Company Institute (n 14) 106 noting that "Net assets of index equity mutual funds are concentrated more heavily in large-cap blend funds that target US large-cap indexes, such as the S&P 500".

[16] Lazard, '2021 Review of Shareholder Activism' (2022), on file with the authors. See also Scott Hirst and Lucian Bebchuk, 'Big Three Power, and Why It Matters' (2022) 102 Boston UL Rev 1547.

Table I.1 *Type of largest shareholders at top 65 European companies*

Type of largest shareholder	Asset managers	Government	Foundations and mutual entities	Families, insiders, managers	Strategic individuals, other companies
No. of companies	38	8	4	9	6

included in the Euro Stoxx 50[17] and the 15 largest UK companies in the FTSE 100 as of the end of April 2022.[18] We find that leading institutional investors rank among the largest shareholders in most companies comprised in the Stoxx 50 index. On average, the top institutional shareholder at these companies owns 6.54 per cent of the equity, the top three institutional shareholders own 14.09 per cent, and the top five institutional shareholders 18.50 per cent. We also look at the cumulative shareholding of the Big Three and the Big Four (BlackRock, Vanguard, State Street, and Fidelity). As far as the top 15 FTSE 100 are concerned, the corresponding figures are 13.42 per cent and 14.65 per cent. The percentage held by the Big Three and the Big Four in the Stoxx 50 companies amounts to 8.31 and 9.40 per cent, respectively.

To shed further light on the corporate governance role asset managers can play, we also look at the basic characteristics of the shareholder base of Stoxx 50 and top 15 FTSE 100 companies. Namely, we look at the type of entity the top shareholder qualifies as and the stake it holds.

Table I.1 classifies top shareholders at these 65 companies as asset managers, government (central or local government, a state-owned enterprise, or a sovereign wealth fund), foundations and mutual entities (four cases), insiders, managers and families, and strategic individuals and other operating companies and provides the number of companies with such shareholder at the top. Interestingly, only in three companies

[17] The EURO STOXX 50 Index covers 50 blue-chip stocks from eight Eurozone countries: Belgium, Finland, France, Germany, Ireland, Italy, the Netherlands, and Spain. Therefore, it is the most representative index of European larger-listed companies.

[18] Our analysis is based on data from CapIQ that is a widely used database (owned by S&P) in the financial industry (eg equity research, asset management) for its reliability and breadth. CapIQ collects the data on the shareholdings of the top 25 institutional investors in each of the companies in the sample.

does the largest shareholder account for the majority of the share capital. The stake of the largest shareholder exceeds 30 per cent or 20 per cent in four and six companies, respectively.

With regard to the size of the Big Three's shareholdings, it is worth mentioning that there is a significant difference in the size of the stakes of the Big Three depending on whether the company has a shareholder with a stake exceeding 30 per cent of the share capital or of the voting rights. Namely, the Big Three hold together, on average, 10.22 per cent of capital in non-controlled companies and 3.45 per cent in controlled companies. As the Big Three dominate the passive investment market and their AUM are largely represented by passive funds and ETFs, the fact that the Big Three's holdings in controlled companies are lower is also explained by the fact that the benchmark indices take into account the free float. For instance, the STOXX 50 index is weighted by companies' free-float market capitalisation.[19] As a consequence, controlled companies have a lower weight in the index than widely held ones with equal total capitalisation.

I.3 Asset Managers' Ownership and Nationality

In addition to the ownership structure of investee companies and the ownership stake held in them, the nationality and ownership structure of asset managers themselves may lead to divergence in the incentives structure and in the focus of shareholder engagement.[20]

We focus on ownership as it can affect asset managers' incentives structures and, in particular, can help explain potential conflicts of interests affecting asset managers' willingness to engage. As highlighted by the European Commission, 'conflicts of interest in the financial sector seem to be one of the reasons for a lack of shareholder engagement' and

[19] See STOXX/Qontigo, 'STOXX Index Methodology guide' (2023) www.stoxx.com/document/Indices/Common/Indexguide/stoxx_index_guide.pdf, 75, clarifying that 'All the stocks on the selection list are then ranked in terms of free-float market capitalization to produce the final index selection list'. Otherwise, the FTSE 100 Index is not weighted by free-float market capitalisation. To be included in the FTSE UK index series, a security must have a minimum free float of 10 per cent if the issuing company is incorporated in the UK and a minimum free float of 25 per cent if the issuing company is incorporated outside the UK. See FTSE/Russell, 'FTSE UK Index Series, v15.8' (2023), https://research.ftserussell.com/products/downloads/FTSE_UK_Index_Series.pdf, 15.

[20] For on overview of the corporate governance implications of investors' heterogeneity see Dasgupta et al. (n 1) 57–67.

'conflicts of interest often arise where an institutional investor or asset manager, or its parent company, has a business interest in the investee company'.[21]

It is widely recognised that also independent asset managers not belonging to conglomerate financial groups can be affected by conflicts of interests that can influence their stewardship and engagement decisions. Indeed, independent asset managers having financially significant business ties with investee companies and their managers may abstain from engaging with portfolio firms and from taking an adversarial stance for fear of losing corporate business.[22] For example, in the US, asset managers may be interested in obtaining, or maintaining, the substantial revenues they derive from managing defined contribution plans ('401(k) plans') of many of their portfolio firms.[23]

Nevertheless, it can be assumed that potential conflicts of interests are more relevant for asset managers belonging to multi-services banking and/or insurance groups. Where an asset manager is owned by one such group, in addition to potential conflicts of interests arising from asset managers' business ties with investee companies, a second layer of conflicts exists. In fact, it may happen that banks and insurance companies pressure their asset management arms to avoid antagonising the clients of another of the group's arms (for example, the investment banking arm) by voting against the board or conducting adversarial engagement initiatives.[24] Of course, the intensity of intra-group conflicts of interests depends on the weight of the asset management arm within

[21] European Commission, 'Green paper: The EU corporate governance framework (Communication from the Commission' COM (2011) 164 final.

[22] See eg Simon Wong, 'How Conflicts of Interest Thwart Institutional Investor Stewardship' (*Harvard Law School Forum on Corporate Governance*, 6 Nov 2011) https://corpgov.law.harvard.edu/2011/11/06/how-conflicts-of-interest-thwart-institutional-investor-stewardship/, accessed 25 June 2023.

[23] See Bebchuk and Hirst (n 18) 2059 ff.; Dijana Cvijanović, Amil Dasgupta, and Konstantinos E. Zachariadis, 'Ties that Bind: How Business Connections Affect Mutual Fund Activism' (2016) 71 Journal of Finance 2933, finding that investment managers are more likely to vote in support of portfolio company managers on closely contested proposals when the investment manager has significant business ties to the portfolio company. See also Benjamin Braun, 'Asset Manager Capitalism as a Corporate Governance Regime' in Jacob S. Hacker et al. (eds), *The American Political Economy: Politics, Markets, and Power* (CUP, 2021), 270.

[24] See eg Simon Wong (n 24); European Commission (n 23) 14, noting that in financial groups 'the asset management branch may not want to be seen to actively exercise its shareholder rights in a company to which its parent company provides services or in which it has a shareholding'. Along the same lines see Miguel A. Ferreira, Pedro Matos,

the group. The higher the asset management arm's contribution to the group's profits, the lower the influence of other group's branches over the asset management arm should be.

Moreover, asset managers belonging to banking and/or insurance groups could be less keen on conducting engagement initiatives because they can rely on a large base of group-captive clients and are less interested in winning over new clients. Hence, reputational (or marketing-related) incentives to engage with investee companies may be lower for such asset managers.

Nevertheless, available anecdotal evidence shows that European asset managers controlled by banking or insurance companies do conduct a significant number of engagements covering a wide range of ESG issues. For example, according to evidence provided by the London-based think-tank InfluenceMap,[25] European bank- and insurance-controlled asset managers, including BNP Paribas Asset Management, Legal & General Investment Management, UBS Asset Management, Aviva Investors, and AXA Investment Management, showed greater transparency around the targets of company engagements and the topics discussed, and engaged more intensively on climate-related issues than US independent peers. Relatedly, AXA, BNP Paribas, Legal & General, Aviva, and Allianz all supported 80 per cent or more of climate-relevant resolutions, while big US players, namely BlackRock, Vanguard, and Fidelity Investments, declined support for 75 per cent of them.

To shed light on asset managers' ownership and its potential impact on investors' approach to engagement we collected ownership data on the top 20 US asset managers and the top 20 European (EU and UK) asset managers[26] and tracked their weight in Stoxx 50 companies and the

and Pedro Pires, 'Asset Management within Commercial Banking Groups: International Evidence' (2018) 73 Journal of Finance, 2181.

25 InfluenceMap, 'Asset Managers and Climate Change 2021' (2022), https://influencemap.org/report/Asset-Managers-and-Climate-Change-cf90d26dc312ebe02e97d2ff6079ed87. Similar evidence is also provided by ShareAction, 'Voting Matters' 2022 (2023), https://shareaction.org/reports/voting-matters-2022/general-findings#finding5, finding that 'there is a clear regional divide. European asset managers, on average, backed 81% of proposals in 2022 compared to 69% in 2021. By contrast, we continue to find particularly poor performance from US asset managers. US managers backed on average less than half (43%) of the environmental and social resolutions on our list in 2022'.

26 We obtained data on AUM from the worldwide ranking provided by ADV Ratings (www.advratings.com/top-asset-management-firms#google_vignette) that includes the world's top 50 asset managers. Twenty of them are from the US. Only 17 are from Europe. To have the same number of asset managers from the two continents and to facilitate

top 15 FTSE 100 companies. Based on ownership data for the companies in our sample, we excluded the four US asset managers (Pimco, Prudential Financial, Edward Jones Investments, and TIAA) and the four EU and UK asset managers (Aegon, Insight, Generali, APG) which the CapIQ database does not capture, either because they do not invest in equity (Pimco) or because none of their stakes is among the top 25 holdings by institutional shareholders in any of the companies in the dataset. Therefore, our final sample includes 16 US asset managers and 16 European asset managers.

We grouped asset managers in the following categories: bank-owned; insurance-owned; publicly owned (including asset management companies listed on a stock exchange); independent and team-owned; others (including asset managers with peculiar ownership structures which do not fall in any of the above categories).[27] The independent and team-owned category includes asset management companies that are not listed and whose stakes are owned privately either by entities other than banks, insurance companies or other entities identified separately in the list (eg pension funds or sovereign wealth funds), or by their own workers and/ or management team.

We find that bank-owned asset managers make up the largest category among the EU's largest asset managers: nine out of the 16 of them are bank-owned, whereas in the US banks own six out of the 16 asset managers in the sample. By contrast, large publicly owned and independent asset managers are much more common in the US: nine out of the top 16 US asset managers included in the sample are listed or independent firms not belonging to banking or insurance groups. By contrast, there are only three listed companies among the top 16 European asset managers.[28]

comparisons, we have added the three European asset managers not already in the list that appear most frequently among the shareholders of the companies in our dataset (EuroStoxx 50 and top 15 FTSE companies), namely two German managers (Deka and Union AM) and a UK one (Baillie Gifford).

27 Namely, only two asset managers fall into this category: APG Asset Management, which is a wholly owned subsidiary of Stichting Pensioenfonds ABP ('ABP'), one of the largest pension funds in the world, and Norges Bank Investment Management that is the sovereign wealth fund of Norway.

28 Amundi is also a publicly traded company, but we classify it as bank-owned because Credit Agricole Group owns roughly 70 per cent of the share capital. It is also worth mentioning that Schroders, one of three listed companies among the top 17 European asset managers, is controlled by the Schroders family which owns 43.16 per cent of capital.

As far as US publicly owned or independent asset management companies are concerned, it is perhaps unsurprising but no less noteworthy that, with the exception of Vanguard,[29] they all have other top asset managers among their shareholders.[30] For example, Vanguard is the largest shareholder of BlackRock and SSGA, and Fidelity ranks among Vanguard's largest shareholders. Similarly, Vanguard, BlackRock, and SSGA are the three largest shareholders of T. Rowe Price and Northern Trust Global Investments Limited and rank among the largest shareholders of Invesco. Moreover, leading asset managers are large shareholders in some banks and insurance companies that have an asset management arm ranked among the top 20 investors.[31]

Whether cross-shareholdings among leading asset managers can affect their approach to engagement, especially regarding social and environmental matters, is controverted. On the one hand, as a recent op-ed in the Wall Street Journal contends, cross-shareholdings make leading asset managers non-independent actors.[32] According to this view, common ownership explains why major asset managers do share common ESG preferences and regularly engage on these topics. An alternative point of view is that common ownership in the asset management industry is too low to influence the preferences and behaviour of leading investors. It is in fact the case that the most influential shareholders of some asset managers do not hold significant stakes in their rivals. For example, the most influential shareholder at Fidelity Investments, FMR LLC (which is controlled by Fidelity's founder family), does not hold any stakes in other asset managers. Moreover, the fact that the Big Three and other major asset managers push on the ESG rhetoric and spend increasing sums in ESG-related engagements may support the view that they compete for investment flows by attracting clients who are more sensitive to ESG issues.[33]

[29] Vanguard's ownership structure is fairly unique as it is owned by its funds. Thus, Vanguard is owned by the people who invest in its funds and has no outside shareholders other than its clients.

[30] See Dan Morenoff, 'Break Up the ESG Investing Giants', *Wall Street Journal* (New York, 31 August 2022), www.wsj.com/articles/break-up-the-esg-investing-giants-state-street-blackrock-vanguard-voting-ownership-big-three-competitor-antitrust-11661961693, accessed 25 June 2023.

[31] See Gerald Epstein, 'The asset management industry in the United States', (2019) Financing for Development series 271, 12 ff., https://repositorio.cepal.org/bitstream/handle/11362/45045/1/S1900994_en.pdf, accessed 25 June 2023.

[32] Morenoff (n 32).

[33] We thank Martin Schmalz for his insights on this issue.

Our analysis also shows that the number of insurance-owned firms on the top asset managers' list has decreased in recent years, particularly in the United States, where only one insurance-owned asset manager is among the 16 included in the sample (whereas there are four out of 16 of them within the EU). According to consultancy Oliver Wyman, this decline can be attributed to the fact that, up until recently, persistently low interest rates pushed insurers to outsource more of their fund management needs to independent groups and, at the same time, insurance-owned asset managers have come under pressure from independent rivals, particularly from leading passive fund managers.[34]

To better assess whether asset manager ownership affects engagement, it is helpful to look into the distribution of AUM by asset manager ownership category. Data on the world's top 20 asset managers collected by the Thinking Ahead Institute show that 12 independent asset managers make up 70 per cent of total AUM, while eight bank- and insurance-owned asset managers account, respectively, for 22 per cent and 8 per cent of those assets.[35]

To shed further light on this, drawing from data collected from the CapitalIQ database, we provide evidence on the weight of each type of asset manager in the ownership of Stoxx 50 and top 15 FTSE 100 companies. We find that publicly owned and independent asset managers hold, on average, significantly larger stakes in companies included in our sample than bank and insurance asset managers. On average, publicly owned asset managers own 8.40 per cent, and independent asset managers own 6.99 per cent. Bank- and insurance-owned asset managers account, on average, for 4.11 per cent and 0.77 per cent of ownership of companies comprised in the sample, respectively. The average weight of publicly owned asset managers is significantly higher in the top 15 FTSE

[34] Julia Hobart and Anthony Bice, 'At a Tipping Point? The State of European Insurance Asset Management' (OliverWyman (2021)) 4, www.oliverwyman.com/our-expertise/insights/2021/oct/european-insurance-asset-management.html reporting that 'where insurer-controlled asset managers' share of AuM [asset under management] has fallen by nearly a third over the last ten years ... At the same time, the ten largest independent asset managers almost trebled their AuM during this same period.' See also Adrienne Klasa, 'Insurer-owned fund managers lose out in hunt for returns', *Financial Times* (London, 21 February 2022), www.ft.com/content/f4662b44-c0a2-4503-bbb5-bddaca500c36, accessed 25 June 2023, noting that '[t]he degree of interdependence between investors and their parents varies. Only about 10 per cent of Legal & General's assets are managed internally, and 30 percent of those at German group Allianz. In contrast, more than 70 per cent of the money overseen by Aviva Investors comes through its parent.'

[35] Thinking Ahead Institute and Willis Towers Watson (n 13) 34.

100 companies, where they account for 10.84 per cent, while holding, on average, 7.67 per cent in Stoxx 50 companies. Bank-owned (insurance owned) asset managers hold, on average, 5.45 per cent (2.13 per cent) in the top 15 FTSE 100 companies and 3.70 per cent (0.35 per cent) in the Stoxx 50 companies.

Ownership structure of asset managers is only one of several factors that together may influence investors' role in corporate governance.[36] As some studies show,[37] nationality is also key, as it can affect institutional investors' approach to engagement in at least four ways.

First, consider that social norms, legal rules and, perhaps more generally, clients' and beneficiaries' preferences and expectations and political pressures may impact the behaviour of institutional investors vis-à-vis investee companies.[38] In fact, the empirical literature reveals that nationality has an impact on stewardship concerning ESG issues, in relation to which investor preferences on the two sides of the Atlantic significantly diverge. Namely, based on voting records and stewardship policies, EU-based institutional investors have been found to pay greater attention to ESG issues than US competitors.[39]

Second, an institution can be expected to engage more with home portfolio companies than with foreign ones. The incentives to engage with the latter are intuitively weaker. First of all, cultural estrangement may justify caution, if not passivity, abroad, because a different corporate culture may yield a very different, and potentially counterproductive, reaction to the same active behaviour.[40] Next, to the extent that investors tend to favour domestic asset managers and so long as institutions use

[36] Dasgupta et al (n 1) 57 ff. [37] See for a literature overview ibid 66 ff.

[38] See, recently, Rob Bauer, Jeroen Derwall, and Colin Tissen, 'Legal Origins and Institutional Investors' Support for Corporate Social Responsibility' (2022), https://ssrn.com/abstract=4096769, accessed 25 June 2023, 5 arguing that 'legal origin captures difference in institutional investors' preferences for CSR beyond what is captured by these alternative sources of investor heterogeneity'; Anne Lafarre, 'Do Institutional Investors Vote Responsibly?' (2022) TILEC Discussion Paper No. DP2022–001, https://ssrn.com/abstract=4042907, accessed 25 June 2023.

[39] Lafarre (n 40), 19 ff.; Andrew Marshall, Sandeep Rao, Partha P. Roy, and Chandra Thapa, 'Mandatory Corporate Social Responsibility and Foreign Institutional Investor Preferences' (2022) 76 Journal of Corporate Finance 1, 4 arguing that 'firms belonging to civil law origin countries, particularly Scandinavian civil law, are engaged in higher levels of CSR activities compared to firms originating from common law origin countries'.

[40] See eg Lin Lin, Chapter 14 in this book.

engagement also as a marketing tool,[41] retail clients and beneficiaries will be more sensitive to domestic engagement than to engagement abroad, as they obviously care more about inequality, environmental protection, and social issues at home rather than abroad.

Third, there are greater political risks to engagement abroad, no matter whether the engagement is shareholder-oriented or ESG-focused: traditional as well as environmentally focused engagement may well have a negative impact on social aspects (for employees, local communities, suppliers). Other things equal, political backlash to protect local constituencies will be likelier against a foreign institution than a domestic one, because the latter may well be politically connected and the former is a more appealing target for a political campaign. That foreign investors can face more political pressure seems to be confirmed by the recent decision of the Texas Comptroller to include nine European asset managers in a list of 10 names (also including BlackRock) deemed to boycott fossil fuel companies, a designation that could lead Texas pension funds to stop trading with those asset managers.[42]

The political risk attaching to activism abroad can be expected to increase as a function of geopolitical tensions and the resurgence of nationalism: even assuming that geopolitical tensions will not just stop cross-border indirect investment altogether, governments with a tense relationship with the home country of an institutional investor will react harshly to any attempt from that investor to influence how local companies should be run. Having said that, it is also worth considering that, as suggested by the data on US asset managers' support for shareholder resolutions on environmental and social issues in both the US and the EU,[43] asset managers may well be more pro-ESG abroad than at home in cases where foreign legislation (as in the EU) is clearly more favourable to ESG factors than domestic legislation. Last but not least, foreign institutions wield less influence over politics when it comes to shaping the very laws that affect engagement.

Given the potential implications of asset managers' nationality, we track the shareholdings held by the 16 US investors comprised in our

[41] Michal Barzuza, Quinn Curtis, and David H. Webber, 'Shareholder Value(s): Index Fund ESG Activism and the New Millennial Corporate Governance' (2020) 93 Southern California Law Review 1243.

[42] See Patrick Temple-West and Brooke Masters, 'Texas accuses BlackRock of energy company boycott in ESG clampdown', Financial Times (London, 24 August 2022), www.ft.com/content/1fc2cc54-d364-48ad-aace-30625e5c61f6, accessed 25 June 2023.

[43] See n 70 and accompanying text.

sample at Stoxx 50 companies and the top 15 FTSE 100 companies. We focus on the US because investors domiciled there account for almost one-third of total cross-market equity investments globally and have a dominant position in EU and UK markets as well.[44]

We find that blocks held by top US investors are (by far, in many cases) larger than those held by the top European investors in all the companies included in our sample. Interestingly, US asset managers are among the largest shareholders also in two insurance companies included in the Stoxx 50 (Allianz, Axa), which control two of the top European asset managers. On average, the 16 US asset managers included in our sample own 15.56 per cent of the equity, while the 16 European institutional shareholders in the sample own a mere 5.71 per cent. While the average weight of the 16 European institutional shareholders in the top 15 FTSE 100 companies and Stoxx 50 companies is similar (5.93 per cent and 5.64 per cent, respectively), the average weight of the 16 US asset managers in the sample is significantly higher in top 15 FTSE 100 companies, where they account, on average, for 21.40 per cent, whereas their average holding in Stoxx 50 companies is 13.81 per cent.

I.4 The Shift towards ESG-Related Engagement: End-clients' Preferences and Potential Regulatory Backlash

The analysis above is not sufficient to draw any conclusion on the actual ability and willingness of institutional investors to engage with investee companies, as other factors can similarly affect asset managers' approach.

First, it must be considered that, as is widely recognised in the literature,[45] the propension of institutional investors to engage with investee companies may depend on the balance between costs and benefits arising from engagement initiatives. Resource and cost constraints are particularly pronounced for passive fund managers. In fact, costs associated with stewardship impinge much more significantly on asset managers' income, as passive funds have much lower fees. No performance fees apply for passively managed vehicles, but rather, if any at all, management fees proportional to the amounts invested in the fund: therefore,

[44] See De La Cruz et al (n 3) 15. The dominant position of US investors has been fuelled, over the last few years, by the rise of passive investing, as the market is dominated by a handful of investors domiciled in the US that hold relevant stakes in all companies included in major world stock market indices.

[45] See eg Bebchuk and Hirst (n 15) 1582.

the financial incentive for asset managers to allocate funds to stewardship activities with the aim of improving the fund's return appears to be nil. In addition, passive fund managers face significant collective action problems that can limit potential benefits arising from engagement activities. As each fund tracking the same index holds the same stocks in the same proportion, 'funds managed by other index fund managers will capture exactly the same returns from the stewardship activity'.[46] Therefore, index fund managers are able to capture only a small fraction of the benefits from stewardship, given the very low fees that they charge.[47] Indeed, sensitivity to the free-rider problem is particularly high within the asset management industry where fund managers compete to attract assets under management based on performance relative to alternative investment opportunities.[48]

While it is true that the cost issue remains a key constraint to engagement, the propensity of institutional investors towards engagement also largely depends on the preferences and priorities of their end-clients. Indeed, given their interest in preventing asset outflow and attracting new clients, there is growing reputational pressure for leading fund managers – chiefly the largest passive fund managers – to be active monitors.[49] In the light of this, it is also credible that creating the appearance of active ownership will help fund managers win over clients. Fund managers may see corporate engagement 'as a branding or marketing tool that provides them with another dimension on which to compete for assets'.[50]

[46] Bebchuk and Hirst (n 15) 1584, noting that 'a gain created by one manager will be shared by the funds of all managers tracking that index'.

[47] Bebchuk and Hirst (n 15) 2052–6.

[48] John C. Coates, IV and R. Glenn Hubbard, 'Competition in the Mutual Fund Industry: Evidence and Implications for Policy' (2007) 33 Journal of Corporation Law 151.

[49] Hortense Bioy, 'Passive Fund Providers Take an Active Approach to Investment Stewardship' (2017) 3 Morningstar, www.morningstar.com/articles/839337/passive-fund-providers-take-an-active-approach-to-investment-stewardship, accessed 25 June 2023. See also Marcel Kahan and Edward Rock, 'Index Funds and Corporate Governance: Let Shareholders Be Shareholders' (2020) 100 Boston University Law Review 1771, 1797 ff.

[50] Kahan and Rock (n 51) 1798, noting that '[i]n a world in which funds following the same index are largely indistinguishable, BlackRock may gain additional assets by appealing to investors with a "taste" for socially responsible investment'. See also Caroline Chambers, 'The role of stewardship in ESG and beyond' (3 June 2021), https://capitalmarketsblog.accenture.com/role-stewardship-esg-beyond, accessed 25 June 2023, noting that proactive, transparent investment stewardship could be a competitive differentiator and offering several other benefits for asset managers. Namely, they can strengthen their brand and attract more investors by weaving their stewardship approach and vision into

This seems to be especially true for ESG-related engagement. Indeed, despite signs of a slowdown in the demand for funds that incorporate ESG into their investment strategies due to a number of factors, including the ESG backlash in the US,[51] there is no doubt that there has been a significant shift in the preferences of a large part of end investors. In this respect, the incorporation of ESG issues into the investment strategies and engagement policies is intended – perhaps above all – to attract the increasing share of clients that give central attention to those aspects.

This has been the case not only for major investors such as large pension funds and sovereign wealth funds but also for a significant portion of retail investors, who have been redirecting their capital to sustainable investments at a steadily increasing rate in recent years. Indeed, it may well be the case that ultimate beneficiaries may prefer to see companies behave responsibly toward the communities with which they interact, even if profits suffer, an intuition upon which Oliver Hart and Luigi Zingales build upon in Chapter 1 to set out a new corporate governance paradigm. Moreover, this trend is set to increase as investment choices move into the hands of Millennials and GenZs, who are particularly attuned to such attitudes.[52] Acceptance by this increasing segment of the clientele of lower financial returns[53] and, even more

brand storylines; Bernard S. Sharfman, 'How the "Market Share Opportunism" of Investment Advisers Is Harming Investors and Public Companies' (*Promarket*, 18 April 2023), www.promarket.org/2023/04/18/how-the-shareholder-activism-of-investment-advisers-is-harming-america/, accessed 25 June 2023.

51 See Tommy Wilkes and Patturaja Murugaboopathy, 'ESG funds set for first annual outflows in a decade after bruising year' (*Reuters*, 19 December 2022), www.reuters.com/business/sustainable-business/esg-funds-set-first-annual-outflows-decade-after-bruising-year-2022-12-19/, accessed 25 June 2023; Morningstar, 'Global Sustainable Fund Flows: Q1 2023 in Review' (2023), www.morningstar.com/lp/global-esg-flows, accessed 25 June 2023.

52 Barzuza et al (n 43) 1283 ff.

53 See Roberto Boffo and Riccardo Patalano, 'ESG Investing: Practices, Progress and Challenges' (2020) 3, www.oecd.org/finance/ESG-Investing-Practices-Progress-and-Challenges.pdf, accessed 25 June 2023, highlighting that 'returns have shown mixed results over the past decade, raising questions as to the true extent to which ESG drives performance'; Sanjai Bhagat, 'An Inconvenient Truth about ESG Investing' (2022) Harv. Bus. Rev https://hbr.org/2022/03/an-inconvenient-truth-about-esg investing#:~:text=Unfortunately%20ESG%20funds%20don't,in%202%2C428%20non%2DESG%20portfolios, accessed 25 June 2023; Toni M. Barko, Martijn Cremers, and Luc Renneboog, 'Shareholder Engagement on Environmental, Social, and Governance Performance' (2022) 180 J Bus Ethics 777; Luc Renneboog, Jeroen Ter Horst, and Chendi Zhang, 'Is Ethical Money Financially Smart? Nonfinancial Attributes and Money Flows of Socially Responsible Investment Funds' (2011) 24 Journal of Financial Intermediation 562.

importantly, higher management fees,[54] may prompt asset managers to invest more in engagement activities, as the possible corresponding increase in fees charged does not necessarily lead to fund outflows. Furthermore, institutions can reduce engagement expenses by joining institutions, like the PRI and 100+, which are promoting an increasingly relevant number of ESG-focused collective engagement initiatives. Relatedly, signing up to the collective engagement initiatives promoted by these institutions can also help fund managers attract clients by demonstrating a commitment to ESG initiatives.[55]

Against this background, it seems credible that, insofar as an increase in their returns and/or assets under management may follow, asset managers can engage with companies on ESG matters to win over clients sensitive to social and environmental issues.

Yet, other factors can limit asset managers' willingness to engage with investee companies on ESG-related matters.

Engaging on environmental and social issues can bring a substantial risk of regulatory backlash.[56] While ESG-related engagements can help asset managers win over end clients sensitive to social and environmental issues, the same kind of engagement can draw criticism from a part of the client base and from public opinion. According to some conservative groups and commentators,[57] giant asset managers, like the Big Three, are using their power to play a political role that goes beyond institutional investors' duties and may undermine their legitimacy. Indeed, 'conservative critics decry the Big Three's effort to decide hotly contested questions

[54] Javier Carlos Matallín-Sáez, Antonio Soler-Domínguez, Sandra Navarro-Montoliu, and Diego Víctor de Mingo-López, 'Investor Behavior and the Demand for Conventional and Socially Responsible Mutual Funds' (2022) 20 Corporate Social Responsibility and Environmental Management 46, 56 finding that sensitivity of investors' redemptions to portfolio expenses is lower for ESG funds.

[55] For example, BlackRock reportedly joined the 100+ initiative after being criticized for greenwashing practices. See Richard Henderson, 'BlackRock joins climate action group after "greenwash" criticism', Financial Times (London, 9 January 2020), www.ft.com/content/16125442-32b4-11ea-a329-0bcf87a328f2, accessed 25 June 2023.

[56] See Benjamin Braun, 'Exit, Control, and Politics: Structural Power and Corporate Governance under Asset Manager Capitalism' (2022) 50 Politics & Society 630, 643 f.

[57] See eg Rupert Darwall, 'BlackRock's choice: Investment fiduciary or political activist?' (*The Hill*, 5 February 2020), https://thehill.com/opinion/energy-environment/495673-blackrocks-choice-investment-fiduciary-or-political-activist, accessed 25 June 2023; Tom Bailey, 'BlackRock's green guidelines raise profound questions about capitalism and democracy' (*CapX*, 25 March 2021), https://capx.co/blackrocks-green-guidelines-raise-profound-questions-about-capitalism-and-democracy/, accessed 4 January 2024.

of environmental and social policy outside the political arena'.[58] Institutional investors are seen as private regulators that bypass the democratic process of electing officials to political positions to pass laws and appoint regulators.[59] Such mounting criticisms can affect asset managers in several ways.

First, even though leading asset managers reiterate that stakeholder capitalism is not about politics and reject the accusation of 'wokism',[60] ESG backlash mainly inspired by conservative groups can harm asset managers' business by alienating conservative-minded clients.

Second, and perhaps more importantly, the belief that asset managers are increasingly using their power to impose a (supposedly, leftwing) ideological agenda has fuelled political initiatives aimed at limiting the influence of leading passive fund managers. For example, several commentators and organisations are calling for a breakup of the Big Three, or the introduction of ownership limits that would prevent the Big Three from owning more than a certain threshold (say, 10 per cent) in the equity of any portfolio company.[61]

In May 2022, a group of Republican Senators introduced the Investor Democracy Is Expected Act (Index Act) which would require passive investment-fund managers that own more than 1 per cent of a public company to collect instructions from their clients on how to vote their share.[62] In the light of this, while pass-through voting might also serve as a lever for offering an advantage to a firm's current and potential clients, it seems credible that the increasing regulatory pressure over investors' vast voting power was among the reasons behind BlackRock's decision to enable institutional clients, such as pensions and endowments, invested

[58] C. Boyden Gray and Jonathan Berry, 'The welcome pushback against politicized investment managers', The Wall Street Journal (New York, 19 May 2002), www.wsj.com/articles/politicized-passive-investment-index-funds-managers-blackrock-esg-energy-prices-larry-fink-proxy-voting-fracking-investor-democracy-is-expected-index-act-11652992438, accessed 25 June 2023.

[59] Darwall (n 60). See also Dorothy S. Lund, 'Asset Managers as Regulators' (2023) 171 University of Pennsylvania Law Review 77, 128 ff.

[60] See eg Larry Fink, 'Annual Letter to CEOs: The Power of Capitalism' (2022), www.blackrock.com/corporate/investor-relations/larry-fink-ceo-letter, accessed 25 June 2023.

[61] Morenoff (n 32); Graham Steele, 'The New Money Trust: How Large Money Managers Control Our Economy and What We Can Do about It' (2020) Working Paper Series on Corporate Power 8/2020 28 ff., www.economicliberties.us/our-work/new-money-trust/, accessed 25 June 2023. See also Bebchuk and Hirst (n 15) 2128 f.

[62] The text of the proposed bill is available at www.congress.gov/bill/117th-congress/senate-bill/4241/text?r=1&s=1.

in certain pooled vehicles managed in the US and the UK, to give vote-through instructions where legally and operationally viable.[63] Similarly, the aim to limit the potential negative consequences of a political and public backlash against their power may help explain why BlackRock and other leading asset managers have decided not to support climate-related shareholder proposals that are too prescriptive.[64]

The political controversy over (anti-)ESG investing is substantially limited to the US, where state laws having an impact on ESG investing significantly diverge depending on a state's political orientation.[65] Things are very different in the EU, where consensus is wide on the opportunity to integrate ESG factors in investing decisions and institutional investors are strongly nudged to play a role in the transition to a more sustainable economic model. Indeed, over the last few years, the European legislature has introduced several pieces of legislation that clearly promote the pursuit of ESG goals by institutional investors.

[63] On 13 June 2022, BlackRock announced it would be increasing the range of funds eligible for its 'Voting Choice' program in the UK and expanding the program to Canadian and Irish pooled funds. Nearly half (47 per cent) of the $ 4.9 trillion index equity assets are now eligible to participate in the firm's program. Following the changes announced, voting choice is available for 100 per cent of US pension plans, and 95 per cent of the firm's institutional index equity funds (amounting to about half of the firm's index equity assets and virtually all its index equity assets outside ETFs and retail mutual funds). In Europe and the UK, 80 per cent of BlackRock's index equity assets (other than ETFs) are eligible for the program. See BlackRock, 'BlackRock Expands Voting Choice to Additional Clients' (2022), www.blackrock.com/corporate/newsroom/press-releases/article/corporate-one/press-releases/2022-blackrock-voting-choice, accessed 25 June 2023. Blackrock also published a white paper outlining the firm's ambition to expand Voting Choice to all investors, including individual investors in funds: see BlackRock, 'It's All About Choice' (2022), www.blackrock.com/corporate/literature/publication/its-all-about-choice.pdf, accessed 25 June 2023. According to the firm, BlackRock clients have committed $ 530 billion – or a quarter of eligible assets – to voting their own preferences through Voting Choice. Of these, clients representing $ 120 billion of assets have elected to vote their own preferences in the five months since BlackRock introduced the program. See Jill E. Fisch and Jeff Schwartz, 'Corporate Democracy and the Intermediary Voting Dilemma' (2023) ECGI Law Working Paper No. 685/2023, https://papers.ssrn.com/sol3/papers.cfm?abstract_id=4360428, accessed 25 June 2023.

[64] See Cidney S. Posner, 'More prescriptive proposals, less support for 2022 proxy season' (*Harvard Law School Forum on Corporate Governance*, 22 August 2022), https://corpgov.law.harvard.edu/2022/08/22/more-prescriptive-proposals-less-support-for-2022-proxy-season, accessed 25 June 2023.

[65] See Ropes and Gray, 'State Regulation of ESG Investment Decision-making by Public Retirement Plans: An Updated Survey' (2022), www.ropesgray.com/en/newsroom/alerts/2022/August/Navigating-State-Regulation-of-ESG-Investments-by-Investment-Managers, accessed 25 June 2023.

To conclude, the different degree of political consensus over ESG investing on the two sides of the Atlantic and the backlash ESG is currently facing in the US are among the factors that contribute to explain why European asset managers are keener to engage on ESG issues and to support ESG-related resolutions than their US-based competitors. Indeed, the political risk arising from the ESG backlash (in addition to its potential impact on financial risk[66]) may affect the stewardship strategies of US asset managers by pushing them to adopt a less ESG-friendly approach. For example, amid the ESG backlash fuelled by conservatives, votes on environmental, social, and governance resolutions in the US fell by around a third in 2023 compared to 2022.[67] It is also worth noting that since 2017, BlackRock has voted in favour of shareholder proposals on environmental and social issues 87 per cent of the time in Europe, where there is a large consensus on ESG issues, while voting against such proposals 84 per cent of the time in North America.[68]

I.5 An Overview of the Book's Contents

This book's focus is on the dialogue between corporations, and boards more specifically, and their institutional shareholders. First, however, it sets the scene thanks to contributions, first, on the purpose of the corporation and, next, on the current landscape of engaged, ESG-sensitive asset managers, asset owners, and beneficiaries. Oliver Hart and Luigi Zingales' chapter presents their provocative vision of the shareholder-welfare maximising corporation as an alternative to the traditional shareholder value maximising one. They are followed by Paul A. Davies' critique of Colin Mayer's idea, popularised in his book *Prosperity*, of purpose statements as a key tool to ensure that companies create value for society rather than profiting from the creation of negative externalities. A response by Colin Mayer follows.

[66] Temple-West and Masters (n 44).

[67] Jeff Green and Saijel Kishan, 'Support for ESG Shareholder Proposals Plummets Amid GOP Backlash' (*Bloomberg*, 9 June 2023), www.bloomberg.com/news/articles/2023-06-09/support-for-esg-shareholder-proposals-plummets-amid-gop-backlash#xj4y7vzkg, accessed 25 June 2023; Patrick Temple-West and Attracta Mooney, 'Investors pull back support for green and social measures amid US political pressure', Financial Times (London, 8 June 2023), www.ft.com/content/28ea4f17-8a0b-4f82-b2e1-c10949a65250 accessed 25 June 2023.

[68] Braun (n 59) 644.

The book then shifts focus from corporations to their institutional shareholders, first with a chapter by Dorothy Lund and Adriana Robertson that explores the misconceptions and oversimplifications associated with the term the 'Big Three' to refer to the three largest managers of index funds: BlackRock, Vanguard, and State Street. Those three asset managers, together with the fourth giant one, Fidelity, are the epitome of universal owners, which some scholars consider suitable for engaging in 'systematic stewardship'. Kahan and Rock's chapter before this analyses the trade-offs and challenges faced by universal owners in adopting a systemic stewardship approach to tackle environmental externalities and systemic risks.

Dionysia Katelouzou's chapter also explores engagement and stewardship by institutional investors, tracing its historical development and examining the motivations behind micro-level shareholder stewardship. It discusses the engagement practices of various institutional investors, including hedge-fund-style activists, and the impact of engagement on corporate practices and shareholder proposals.

Subsequent chapters explore the phenomenon of ESG investment and engagement. Lisa Fairfax takes an optimistic perspective on shareholders acting as defenders of other stakeholders' interests, based on the available evidence in this regard. The intuition is that promoting such interests leads to higher returns in the long-term.

Wolf-Georg Ringe notices how ESG engagement relies on coalition-building even more than traditional activism and builds on this finding to recommend policies aimed to remove obstacles to investor collaboration. Such obstacles are then comprehensively described in the chapter by Peter O. Mülbert and Alexander Sajnovits.

One way to gauge the impact of any governance tool is to assess how it performs in the context of a merger or acquisition. Afra Afsharipour's chapter analyses how the consideration of ESG matters has affected the dynamics of the M&A market, including the dialogue between boards and shareholders in the context of an M&A transaction.

The remaining chapters examine the mechanics of the dialogue between companies and their boards from various angles and in different contexts. The chapter by Matteo Gatti, Matteo Tonello and one of us provides much needed empirical evidence on the reality of closed-door board-shareholder engagement through a survey of US public corporations, documenting the scope, contents, and perceived impact of initiatives for shareholder engagement.

Tim Bowley, Jennifer G. Hill and Steve Kourabas, in turn, survey the various engagement techniques that shareholders use, such as behind-the-scenes approaches, participation in shareholder meetings, public campaigns, and discussion boards and messaging apps oriented towards retail investors. They counter the idea that shareholder meetings are a relic of the past, arguing that they should instead be recognised as crucial when a company faces significant governance issues.

Anne Lafarre and Christoph Van Der Elst look into whether distributed ledger technologies (DLTs) can be the game changer in corporate governance that blockchain enthusiasts referred to them as only a few years ago. While acknowledging DLT's potential to tackle custody chain issues, improve the transparency of stock ownership records, and strengthen shareholder and stakeholder rights, the authors also question whether DLT is necessary to achieve outcomes that centralised systems with secure and transparent digital record-keeping may be sufficient to attain.

Hedge funds play a significant role in the dialogue between boards and shareholders, particularly in some countries. Lin Lin's chapter examines hedge fund engagement in China, Japan and South Korea and shows that, while hedge funds in these East Asian countries have similar objectives and strategies to their counterparts in the UK and the US, the patterns of hedge fund engagement within the three countries differ.

Anna Christie's chapter spotlights one of the most intense forms of shareholder engagement, namely the election of institutional shareholders' nominees on corporate boards. While in the experience of some countries, such as Italy, traditional institutional investors take advantage of mandatory minority shareholder representation on the board to appoint independent directors, in the US, it is hedge-fund activists that tend to express shareholder nominees as a lever to force change at target companies.

Shareholder proposals are the most traditional form of engagement by institutional investors. Jill Fisch and Adriana Z. Robertson focus on proposals requesting environmental and social disclosures. Their empirical analysis provides evidence of their frequency and support by institutions and should guide the SEC in its current attempts to extend the mandatory disclosure framework to include ESG matters.

While the law is mostly silent on the processes and mechanisms to facilitate meaningful dialogue between companies and their shareholders, corporate governance codes typically do provide guidance on how to structure the dialogue with shareholders. Ana Taleska's chapter provides an analysis of various such code provisions across Europe, finding that most of them add very little to the existing hard-law framework or just replicate the most diffused practices, while the few that also require companies to spell out their policies on shareholder engagement should serve as a model.

The final two chapters in this book focus on a formidable obstacle to board-shareholder dialogue, namely the broad-scope insider trading rules set out by the European Union's Market Abuse Regulation (MAR), which still applies in the UK as well. Lars Klöhn's analysis provides a detailed account of MAR's serious impact on board-shareholder dialogue but concludes that the case for a safe harbour permitting the selective disclosure of inside information to institutional investors would not be justified, suggesting that greater disclosure on the board-shareholder dialogue should be preferred.

In the final chapter, Jennifer Payne focuses her attention on MAR's market soundings rules and asks whether they could serve as a valuable template for board-shareholder engagement. She reaches a negative conclusion but also concurs with Lars Klöhn's view that a broader safe harbour would not be justified.

In addition to the book's contributors, we wish to thank the discussants that provided their views and comments on earlier versions of the chapters included in this volume at the Assogestioni Conference on Corporate Governance held in Rome in October 2022 namely, Mirza Baig (Aviva Investors), Alice Bordini (GLC Advisors), Amy Borrus (CII), George S. Dallas (ECGI), Anna Gatti (Intesa Sanpaolo), Claudia Kruse (APG Asset Management), Karina Litvack (Terna), Aeisha Mastagni (California State Teachers' Retirement System), Marco Maugeri (Università Europea di Roma), Robert McCormick (PJT Camberview), Massimo Menchini (Assogestioni), Chiara Mosca (Consob), Maria Ortino (Legal & General Investment Management), Valeria Piani (Phoenix Group), Daniel Summerfield (Pomerantz), Sachi Suzuki (HSBC Global Asset Management) and Michael Younis (State Street Global Advisors).

1

The New Corporate Governance

OLIVER HART AND LUIGI ZINGALES

1.1 Introduction

In the last few years, there has been a dramatic increase in shareholder engagement on environmental and social issues. Consider the following activity in 2021. Eighty-one percent of DuPont shareholders approved a proposal requiring the company to disclose how much plastic the company releases into the environment each year and to assess the effectiveness of DuPont's pollution policies.[1] Sixty-four percent of ExxonMobil shareholders approved a proposal requiring the company to describe "if, and how, ExxonMobil's lobbying activities (direct and through trade associations) align with the goal of limiting average global warming to well below 2 degrees Celsius (the Paris Climate Agreement's goal)."[2] Fifty-two percent of Duke Energy shareholders approved a proposal that requests disclosures on contributions to candidates, parties, committees, and 501(c)(4) organizations.[3] Ninety-five percent of Wendy's shareholders approved a proposal requiring the company "to disclose concrete evidence on the effectiveness of its Supplier Code of

We are grateful to Lucian Bebchuk, Ronald Gilson, Bernard Sharfman, Robert Sitkoff, Holger Spamann, David H. Webber, and participants at the University of Chicago Business Law Review Symposium for helpful discussions and feedback. We thank Jack Li for excellent research assistance. Oliver Hart gratefully acknowledges financial support from the Harvard-Radcliffe Institute. Luigi Zingales gratefully acknowledges financial support from the Stigler Center at the University of Chicago.

This chapter originally appeared in the *University of Chicago Business Law Review*, Vol. 1. It is reprinted with permission from the *University of Chicago Business Law Review* and the University of Chicago Law School.

[1] Kevin Crowley, *DuPont Loses Plastic Pollution Vote with Record 81% Rebellion*, BLOOMBERG (May 3, 2021), https://perma.cc/4HCR-2M5N.

[2] ExxonMobil Co., Amended Current Report (Form 8-K/A) (May 26, 2021).

[3] Andrew Ramonas & Lydia Beyoud, *Activist Shareholders Score Wins on Election Spending After Riot*, BLOOMBERG L. (July 14, 2021), https://perma.cc/L9LM-WDNA.

Conduct in protecting the human rights of workers at its produce and meat suppliers, with respect to COVID-19 in particular."[4]

It is hard to explain this behavior using the dominant corporate governance paradigm in economics, finance, and law. According to the traditional view, shareholders have a single objective: shareholder value maximization (SVM). There is no scope for any other goals, including social ones. But in each of the above examples, shareholders seem to be pushing companies to do things that might reduce value (most of which are opposed by management). Many scholars have criticized the SVM paradigm, arguing that managers should act in the interest of other stakeholders – workers, consumers, the community – or that companies should have a social purpose over and above making money.[5] These criticisms are normative. But a further powerful criticism is a positive one: the paradigm cannot explain what shareholders are actually pressuring companies to do.

Corporations are larger, more complex, and more powerful than they were in the 1970s and early 1980s when the traditional paradigm became established. In a more populous and interdependent world, the importance of externalities has also greatly increased, and many feel that governments are not dealing with them. The preferences of investors have changed too.[6] Investors, especially younger ones, are more sensitive to environmental and social issues. As a result, we think that the paradigm needs to change. This is true even if one accepts, as we do, the idea of shareholder primacy, that is, that companies should act on behalf of shareholders.[7] When externalities are important, and at least some

[4] The Wendy's Co., Current Report (Form 8-K) (May 19, 2021).

[5] *See, e.g.*, Colin Mayer, Prosperity: Better Business Makes the Greater Good (2018); Alex Edmans, Grow the Pie: How Great Companies Deliver Both Purpose and Profit (2020). *But see* Lucian A. Bebchuk & Roberto Tallarita, *The Illusory Promise of Stakeholder Governance*, 105 Cornell L. Rev. 91 (2020).

[6] For more on this, *see* Michal Barzuza et al., *The Millennial Corporation: Strong Stakeholders, Weak Managers* (Apr. 12, 2022) (unpublished manuscript), https://perma.cc/T22U-D7NN.

[7] The argument for this is standard. Shareholders, as residual income claimants, are the most vulnerable of the constituencies with which a company deals, and so they are allocated votes, and courts have determined that managers have a fiduciary duty to act in their interest. Whereas other groups – consumers, workers, creditors – are protected, at least partially, by contracts and/or have reasonable exit options (consumers or workers can quit), shareholders have weak, if any, contractual protection and can exit only by selling shares at the market price, which may be low if the company is not being run in their interest. *See, e.g.*, Frank H. Easterbrook & Daniel R. Fischel, *Voting in Corporate Law*, 26 J. L. & Econ. 395 (1983); Eugene Fama, *Contract Costs and Financing Decisions*, 63

investors are prosocial, we argue that shareholders will want companies to pursue shareholder welfare maximization (SWM), not SVM.

The purpose of this chapter is twofold. First, we reexamine the case for SVM, highlight the weaknesses of the case, and discuss why, in spite of these weaknesses, SVM has survived as a dominant paradigm. Second, we go into more detail about the meaning of SWM and how it can be implemented.

The chapter is structured as follows. We start, in Section 1.2, by reviewing the traditional case for SVM in a "perfect" world. We then turn in Section 1.3 to the weaknesses of the case when imperfections, including particularly externalities, are introduced. In Section 1.4, we discuss how and why SVM became an established norm in spite of its limitations. In Section 1.5, we suggest that SWM better represents the preferences of shareholders, explaining both how it should be interpreted and how it can be implemented. We argue that versions of SWM are actually being developed and used, as we write. Section 1.6 concludes.

1.2 The Case for Shareholder Value Maximization

We begin by reviewing the basic argument for SVM. Consider a perfectly competitive economy where no agent has an effect on prices. Suppose that there are no externalities and a complete set of (contingent commodity) markets. Each consumer maximizes utility subject to her budget constraint. An increase in the value of one firm increases the wealth of that firm's shareholders without affecting anybody else's wealth or prices. Thus, the shareholders are better off – their budget constraints move outwards, and they can spend their increased wealth on desirable goods and services – and nobody else is worse off (prices have not changed). It follows that shareholders unanimously favor SVM (even if they care about other people).[8]

J. Bus. S71 (1990); Henry Hansmann, The Ownership of Enterprise (1996). In some cases, other stakeholder groups are not well protected by contracts and company founders may choose to allocate votes to these groups. *See* Hansmann, *supra*. However, in most companies, votes are allocated to the residual income claimants, that is, the founders choose shareholder primacy.

[8] Under these conditions it is also the case that SVM leads to a socially (Pareto) efficient outcome. This is the first theorem of welfare economics. *See, e.g.*, Gérard Debreu, The Theory of Value: An Axiomatic Analysis of Economic Equilibrium (1959).

A similar logic applies if we think in terms of contracts rather than markets. Suppose that a firm has contracts with customers, workers, suppliers, creditors, etc., that perfectly insulate these groups from any change in the firm's production decision. Then a change in production that increases shareholder value makes the firm's shareholders better off (the pie is bigger) and nobody worse off. Again, such a change is unanimously favored by the firm's shareholders.

It is worth teasing out a further implication. Under the assumptions just described, shareholder value represents *precisely* a firm's contribution to society, in the sense that if it disappeared the shareholders would be worse off by this amount and nobody else would be affected (this is the no-surplus condition[9]).

1.3 Problems with the Case for Shareholder Value Maximization

In reality, competition is not perfect; markets are not complete; and externalities are important. Without giving too much away, we will argue that the issues raised by imperfect competition and incompleteness put a minor dent in the SVM edifice, based on shareholder unanimity, while the issues raised by externalities (and social considerations) bring the whole construction down.

1.3.1 Imperfect Competition

Suppose that a firm has monopoly power in the goods market (and cannot perfectly price discriminate). Some of the firm's shareholders may purchase and enjoy "consumer surplus" from its product. If their consumption is large enough, they may prefer the firm to increase output and lower price even if this reduces profit.[10] Or suppose that the firm has monopsony power in the labor market. Some of the firm's shareholders may be workers who would prefer the firm to employ more workers, thereby raising the wage, even if this is not profit-maximizing. Under these conditions, shareholder unanimity will not generally obtain.[11]

[9] *See* Louis Makowski & Joseph M. Ostroy, *Perfect Competition and the Creativity of the Market*, 39 J. ECON. LITERATURE 479 (2001).

[10] *See, e.g.*, Joseph Farrell, *Owner-Consumers and Efficiency*, 19 ECON. LETTERS 303 (1985).

[11] Of course, under imperfect competition, there is also no reason to think that SVM will lead to a socially efficient outcome.

1.3.2 Incomplete Markets

When markets are incomplete, a firm's profit is a random variable. Someone who holds shares may then enjoy a "consumption" benefit, to the extent that this random variable has risk-return characteristics that are not already available in the marketplace.[12] As a result, some owners may favor a production plan that provides a particular investment opportunity even if this does not maximize the firm's market value. However, Hart shows that this consumption effect (of a single firm) becomes negligible in a large economy.[13] The reason is that, if one investor enjoys a significant consumption benefit, so will many other similar investors, and competition by them will bid up the share price to the point where the benefit disappears. The consequence is that owners will continue to favor market value maximization.[14]

1.3.3 Common Ownership

These days, many shareholders hold diversified portfolios, often through indexed funds. Such shareholders will want the total value of their portfolio maximized rather than the value of a single firm. This may lead shareholders to push for firms to be less competitive and, at an extreme, engage in monopoly pricing since this increases total profit in an industry.[15] Common ownership does not necessarily destroy the unanimity

[12] *See, e.g.*, Jacques H. Drèze, Investment under Private Ownership: Optimality, Equilibrium and Stability, *in* Allocation under Uncertainty: Equilibrium and Optimality 129 – 66 (Jacques H. Drèze ed., 1974).

[13] Oliver Hart, *On Shareholder Unanimity in Large Stock Market Economies*, 47 Econometrica 1057 (1979).

[14] Even though shareholders may favor SVM, SVM will typically not lead to a (constrained) Pareto-optimal outcome in a multi-good/multi-period incomplete markets economy since firms' production decisions affect relative prices, which in turn can affect the degree of market incompleteness. *See, e.g.*, Oliver Hart, *On the Optimality of Equilibrium When the Market Structure Is Incomplete*, 11 J. Econ. Theory 418 (1975); John D. Geanakoplos & Heraklis M. Polemarchakis, Existence, Regularity, and Constrained Suboptimality of Competitive Allocations When the Asset Market Is Incomplete, *in* Uncertainty, Information, and Communication: Essays in Honor of Kenneth J. Arrow, Volume III (Walter P. Heller et al. eds., 1986).

[15] This was pointed out some years ago by Julio J. Rotemberg, *Financial Transactions Costs and Industrial Performance* (Alfred P. Sloan Sch. of Mgmt., Working Paper No. 1554-84, 1984), and Roger Gordon, Do Publicly Traded Corporations Act in the Public Interest?, Advances Econ. Analysis & Pol'y, June 12, 2003, at 1. It was emphasized recently by José Azar et al., *Anticompetitive Effects of Common Ownership*, 73 J. Fin. 1513 (2018).

result but does suggest that shareholders may favor something other than SVM.

1.3.4 Externalities and Social Considerations

The deviations from the unanimity result described in Sections 1.3.1 and 1.3.2 seem "second-order." As evidence, we are not aware of cases where shareholders have pushed firms to reduce prices because the shareholders consume the product, or to choose a production plan with risk-return characteristics that are not already available in the market. There is one important exception. Workers whose pension plans consist of shares have in recent years pushed companies to treat workers better, and this trend may grow.[16]

Concerning Section 1.3.3, the common ownership monopolization effect is hotly debated, and the jury is still out about its empirical significance.[17]

In this section we turn to a set of considerations and departures that we believe are of first-order importance. They are also ones that seem to underly the large and rapidly increasing shareholder activity that has occurred in recent years. They involve externalities and, in most cases, the idea that individuals care about others as well as themselves, that is, they are socially responsible.

Externalities do not alter the logic of Section 1.2 that shareholders will favor SVM as long as the government has implemented an optimal tax policy. Suppose firms cause environmental harm, for example, pollution, but that a firm must compensate each affected person by the (marginal)

[16] For an example of how labor union pension funds use their votes to pursue worker interests, *see* Ashwini Agrawal, *Corporate Governance Objectives of Labor Union Shareholders: Evidence from Proxy Voting*, 25 Rev. Fin. Stud. 187 (2012).

[17] Azar et al., *supra* note 15, find that prices of domestic airline tickets are 3 to 7 percent higher than they would have been if airlines had no common shareholders. José Azar et al., *Ultimate Ownership and Bank Competition*, 51 Fin. Mgmt. 227 (2022), document comparable results in the U.S. banking industry. The first paper has been challenged by Patrick J. Dennis et al., *Common Ownership Does Not Have Anti-Competitive Effects in the Airline Industry*, J. Fin. (forthcoming 2022), who document that the positive correlation between common ownership and ticket prices is driven by variation in airline market shares rather than variation in institutional ownership. The second paper has been challenged by Jacob Gramlich & Serafin Grundl, *Estimating the Competitive Effects of Common Ownership* (Bd. of Governors of the Fed. Rsrv. Sys., Finance and Economics Discussion Series Working Paper No. 2017-029, 2017), who document that the effects of common ownership on prices and quantities of deposits are fairly small.

damage incurred. Then the previous arguments go through. An increase in market value net of the tax makes shareholders better off and no one worse off, since everybody is compensated for the harm they experience.

But what happens if the government has not regulated optimally, a particular concern when an externality is global, as with climate change, and coordination by many governments is required for optimal mitigation?[18]

A dominant view over the last fifty years has been that even this does not disturb the SVM prescription. One might call this the Friedman separation theorem.[19] To understand the argument, suppose that, in the absence of an optimal tax policy, the Sierra Club is doing valuable work to preserve the environment. Assume that the shareholders of a firm care about the environment, either because environmental harm affects them directly or because they are socially responsible and care about the harm to others. Might the shareholders want their firm to reduce dividend payments and make a charitable contribution to the Sierra Club? The answer, at least according to Friedman, is no. The same outcome – a contribution to the Sierra Club – can be achieved if the firm pays out the higher dividend and each shareholder makes their *own* contribution to the Sierra Club. Given that individual shareholders can do anything the firm can do, it still makes sense for the firm to maximize profit, and for individual shareholders to engage in public welfare activities themselves (we revisit this argument in Section 1.5).

Unfortunately, the Friedman separation theorem is not general. Charitable contributions are a very special case. Charitable contributions are separable from a firm's other activities and a firm has no comparative advantage in making them relative to individuals.[20] But in many cases a firm's damage-inducing (or benefit-generating) activities are inseparable

[18] Even if the government does not regulate externalities optimally, an efficient class action system that allows all parties negatively affected by an externality to be compensated appropriately could achieve the same result. In practice, however, class actions are very expensive and cannot easily be organized across legal jurisdictions. In addition, informational asymmetries and limited liability make this system ineffective. *See* Roy Shapira & Luigi Zingales, *Is Pollution Value-Maximizing? The Dupont Case* (Nat'l Bureau of Econ. Rsch., Working Paper No. 23866, 2017), https://www.nber.org/system/files/working_papers/w23866/w23866.pdf.

[19] Milton Friedman, *A Friedman Doctrine: The Social Responsibility of Business Is to Increase Its Profits*, N.Y. Times (Sept. 13, 1970), https://perma.cc/TU2U-FJUE.

[20] Sometimes even charitable contributions are not easily separable from the business activities of a corporation. Consider, for instance, impact investment funds run by asset managers who are very knowledgeable about the areas in which gifts are made.

from its production activities, and under these conditions the separation theorem no longer holds.[21]

The following examples, two of which have already been mentioned in the introduction, help to illustrate the point.

(i) DuPont generates large quantities of plastic waste. Reducing the waste would improve the environment but reduce profit.
(ii) Costco uses antibiotics in raising chickens. This is profitable but is a major cause of the development of antibiotic resistance, a problem that costs human lives and billions of dollars in healthcare costs.[22]
(iii) Danco Laboratories LLC is the US distributor of the abortifacient drug Mifeprex (an abortion pill), better known as RU-486A.[23] Danco is privately held, but one can imagine some shareholders, who are anti-abortion, wanting Danco to scale back its activities even though this would reduce profit.
(iv) Duke Energy, like many companies, makes contributions or expenditures on behalf of political candidates and parties. Disclosing these contributions could be good for American democracy but might reduce share value.[24]

The first thing to notice about these examples is that separability does not hold: shareholders cannot easily replicate (or undo) the firm's decision. It would be very costly for individual shareholders to clean up the plastic waste produced by DuPont, and it is unclear how they can offset Costco's antibiotic usage, Duke Energy's political contributions, or Danco's distribution of RU-486A. In principle, a coalition of shareholders or other citizens could negotiate a desirable outcome with one of the firms, for example, a coalition could bribe DuPont to choose a technology that reduces plastic waste. But assembling such a coalition runs into serious free-rider problems: each person would prefer others to be in the

[21] Oliver Hart & Luigi Zingales, *Companies Should Maximize Shareholder Welfare Not Market Value*, 2 J.L., Fin., & Acct. 247 (2017).

[22] Stop Using Antibiotics in Healthy Animals to Prevent the Spread of Antibiotic Resistance, World Health Org. (Nov. 7, 2017), https://perma.cc/F76Z-ZZPN.

[23] Sharon Bernstein, *Persistence Brought Abortion Pill to U.S.*, L.A. Times (Nov. 5, 2000), https://perma.cc/629W-MKRX.

[24] See Saumya Prabhat & David M. Primo, *Risky Business: Do Disclosure and Shareholder Approval of Corporate Political Contributions Affect Firm Performance?*, 21 Bus. & Pol. 205 (2019); Christopher Poliquin & Young Hou, The Value of Corporate Political Donations: Evidence from the Capitol Riot (Jan. 11, 2022) (unpublished manuscript), https://perma.cc/3CZ3-CH3G.

coalition. In contrast, if DuPont itself chooses a less-polluting technology, all shareholders are forced to pay their pro-rata share of the cost, and the free-rider problem is eliminated.[25]

Second, in these examples, there is no reason to suppose that SVM is unanimously favored by shareholders. In (i), some shareholders may favor a less-polluting technology because plastic waste affects them directly or because they care about the effect of the waste on others; other shareholders may not be personally affected or may care less about the welfare of others, and so would like to stick to the current technology. In (ii), some shareholders may want to reduce the use of antibiotics because of the public health threat to them or others or because antimicrobial resistance reduces the profits of other companies in their portfolio;[26] others, being less concerned by the personal threat, putting less weight on others, and not having a diversified portfolio, may support the current strategy. In (iii), some shareholders may not care about the abortion issue, or may favor greater access to abortion, and will therefore support the wide distribution of RU-486A; others may be anti-abortion and regard the distribution of the pill as a sin. In (iv), some shareholders may care a lot about the threat to American democracy, while others may be more concerned about financial return.

There is also no reason to think that SVM achieves a socially efficient outcome among the group of shareholders as a whole (or for society). If the disutility that environmentally sensitive shareholders experience from DuPont's plastic waste exceeds the profit the waste generates, SVM leads to the production of the plastic waste even though it would be efficient for the shareholders as a group to eliminate the waste.[27]

It is very important to note that there is *no* neutral outcome in these examples. Friedman and others have suggested that a deviation from profit or value maximization imposes a tax on (some) shareholders.[28] For instance, in (i), if socially responsible shareholders persuade management to reduce the plastic waste, this imposes a tax on those who favor profit

[25] For more on this, see Eleonora Broccardo et al., Exit vs. Voice, 130 J. Pol. Econ., 3101 (2022).

[26] The idea that the shareholders of one firm may be concerned about the impact of that firm's externalities on the profitability of other firms the shareholders own is at the center of the growing literature on universal ownership. *See, e.g.*, Jeffrey N. Gordon, Systematic Stewardship, 47 J. Corp. L., 627 (2022); Ellen Quigley, *Universal Ownership in the Anthropocene* (Feb. 20, 2020) (unpublished manuscript), https://perma.cc/K43K-4UAC.

[27] And Coasian bargaining is unlikely to resolve the issue given free-rider problems.

[28] *See, e.g.*, Friedman, *supra* note 19.

maximization. This may be true, but it is equally true that, if less socially responsible shareholders persuade management not to reduce the waste, this imposes a tax on the socially responsible shareholders.

It is also worth noting that deviations from profit maximization are neither "left-wing" nor "right-wing". In (i), (ii), and (iv), the deviation may be regarded as left-wing, while in (iii) it may be thought of as right-wing. In the same way, profit maximization is neither right-wing nor left-wing. In (i), (ii), and (iv), it may be thought of as right-wing, while in (iii) it may be regarded as left-wing. Profit maximization is amoral, not immoral.

Our conclusion is this. To the extent that examples like these are widespread, and we believe that they are, there is nothing special about SVM: there is no reason to think that it will be unanimously favored or will deliver the right outcome among a firm's shareholders as a whole. What to put in its place? We believe that companies should pursue shareholder *welfare* maximization (SWM) not SVM, and that a shareholder vote on issues like those in examples (i)–(iv) is one way to implement this.[29] We consider this further in Section 1.5. But first we turn to why SVM, in spite of its defects, has become the norm.

1.4 Why Did Shareholder Value Maximization Become the Norm?

Consider a firm whose stock is 100 percent owned by an individual. Even if the firm is set up as a corporation with a board of directors, the firm will pursue the goal the only shareholder would want it to pursue. This goal is not necessarily the maximization of shareholder value or profit. In fact, Scott Morton and Podolny show that privately held wine producers maximize the utility of their major shareholders, not profits.[30] Similarly, Shive and Forester show that privately held companies curb pollution more than publicly traded ones, consistent with the idea that they are maximizing a different objective function.[31]

When the number of shareholders is more than one, however, there are two layers of agency problems that make it difficult for shareholders to get managers to maximize their welfare. The first agency problem is

[29] *See* Hart & Zingales, *supra* note 21; Broccardo et al., *supra* note 25.

[30] Fiona M. Scott Morton & Joel M. Podolny, *Love or Money? The Effects of Owner Motivation in the California Wine Industry*, 50 J. Indus. Econ. 431 (2002).

[31] Sophie A. Shive & Margaret M. Forster, *Corporate Governance and Pollution Externalities of Public and Private Firms*, 33 Rev. Fin. Stud. 1296 (2020).

between managers and shareholders. Corporate law delegates the business of running the corporation to directors. Directors have a fiduciary duty toward shareholders, but they also have enormous discretion provided by the business judgment rule. This discretion makes it easy for directors to pursue their own objectives. In contrast, there are two reasons why shareholders cannot force managers to pursue their own agenda. First, until very recently the SEC's "ordinary business" exception made it easy for the board to exclude from the proxy ballot any resolution that requires managers to run the business in a particular way. Second, even if such a resolution were put on the ballot and received majority approval, it would not be binding. A large individual shareholder can easily force management to pursue her own agenda by threatening to replace the board. It is much harder for dispersed shareholders to do this.

Today most dispersed shareholders own their shares through intermediaries such as BlackRock, Fidelity, and Vanguard. This is where the second agency problem comes in. Both the ERISA law regulating private pensions and standard practice have contributed to enshrining the idea that asset managers must support only shareholder resolutions that increase the long-run financial return of their clients.

Start with ERISA. To prevent abuses, the 1974 ERISA Law required that a fiduciary should discharge his duties "for the exclusive purpose of: (i) providing benefits to participants and their beneficiaries."[32] The law did not specify whether these benefits can also be non-pecuniary. Yet, in 2014 the Supreme Court stated that, "[r]ead in the context of ERISA as a whole, the term 'benefits' in the provision just quoted must be understood to refer to the sort of *financial* benefits (such as retirement income) that trustees who manage investments typically seek to secure for the trust's beneficiaries."[33]

The ERISA Law applies to the pension managers of 401k plans, for example, Harvard University, not to the fund managers themselves. Nevertheless, there is an indirect effect on fund managers. The fear of potential liability makes 401k plan managers reluctant to include in the

[32] Employee Retirement Income Security Act of 1974 (ERISA), 29 U.S.C. § 1104(a)(1)(A).

[33] Fifth Third Bancorp v. Dudenhoeffer, 573 U.S. 409, 420–1 (2014). Some legal scholars argue that SWM can be partially accommodated under current ERISA law. *See, e.g.*, David H. Webber, *The Use and Abuse of Labor's Capital*, 89 N.Y.U. L. Rev. 2106 (2014). For example, the Eleventh Circuit blessed a pension plan that offered below-market rate home loans to plan participants. Brock v. Walton, 794 F.2d 586 (11th Cir. 1986).

investment options available to plan participants a fund that explicitly states that it will pursue goals other than financial ones. Thus, any fund manager who wants to achieve economies of scale would have little incentive to offer a fund with a broader purpose since this runs the risk of being excluded from 401k plans.

In marketing themselves to investors, mutual funds face some of the same concerns ERISA law tried to address: how to commit credibly not to waste the investors' money. Given the lack of awareness of any possible interaction between a business purpose and a "philanthropic" one, mutual funds found it natural to commit themselves to the "long-term economic interests" of their clients, as the promotional material of BlackRock states.[34] BlackRock is not alone. We looked at the governance guidelines adopted by all the top five mutual fund families. Vanguard promises "to serve as a voice for our investors and to promote long-term value creation at the companies in which our funds invest."[35] State Street declares that it will "promote the long-term economic value of client investments."[36] JPMorgan asserts that its guidelines have been developed "with the objective of encouraging corporate action that enhances shareholder value."[37] It is only Fidelity that states that the corporate board must focus "on protecting the interests of shareholders" (without any qualification that the interest must be only economic).[38] When money has been raised under these premises, it is very difficult for an institutional investor to change course.

Besides the law and any existing contracts, a major role in enforcing SVM is played by business norms. Directors are routinely confronted with complex business decisions. Unless they are purely self-interested, they need some principle to guide them. Decades of academic thinking, both in the law and in finance, have enshrined the idea that the fiduciary duty owed to shareholders means the pursuit of shareholder value maximization. In other words, SVM has become the business norm.

34 *BlackRock Investment Stewardship*, BLACKROCK, https://www.blackrock.com/corporate/insights/investment-stewardship (last visited Apr. 22, 2022).

35 Vanguard, Global Investment Stewardship Principles (Nov. 2021), https://perma.cc/UZ4L-3PVK.

36 State St. Glob. Advisors, Proxy Voting and Engagement Guidelines (Mar. 2022), https://perma.cc/MN77-D8DS.

37 J. P. Morgan, Global proxy voting guidelines (Apr. 2022), https://perma.cc/6HAX-YH4M.

38 *Stewardship Principles and Proxy Voting*, FIDELITY, https://perma.cc/U2E4-RLS9 (last visited Apr. 22, 2022).

As an example of how legal rules about SVM have affected practice even outside the realm of their strict applicability, consider what Larry Fink, the CEO of BlackRock, declared in 2016:

> We live in a world where the Department of Labor gave us this guidance about what is our fiduciary responsibility as investors. We only have one responsibility as investors: to maximize return. That's it. So basically we can tell a company to fire five thousand employees tomorrow, and if that maximizes return for the company we did something well. We can tell that company to do something that maybe is bad for the environment. There is nothing right now that guides, other than a maximization of return behavior.[39]

1.5 Shareholder Welfare Maximization

In this section we describe the objective of shareholder welfare maximization (SWM) and discuss how it can be implemented.

1.5.1 The Meaning of Shareholder Welfare Maximization

To explore SWM, we follow Hart and Zingales and Broccardo et al. in the way we model socially responsible shareholders.[40] We suppose that, when making a decision, a shareholder puts weight $\lambda \epsilon [0, 1]$ on the welfare of others affected by the decision, where λ reflects her degree of social responsibility. Different shareholders may have different λ's, with some perhaps having $\lambda = 0$ (they are purely self-interested).

To see the implications of this, consider the Costco example of Section 1.3, where the issue is whether to stop the use of antibiotics in raising chickens in order to reduce the risk of antibiotic resistance in the human population. For expositional purposes start with a very simple scenario. Suppose that Costco has three shareholders, each of whom owns a third of the company, with social responsibility parameters λ_1, λ_2, λ_3, respectively. Assume that the additional cost of not using antibiotics is 120 and the monetary benefit attached to the reduced risk in humans is 180. Now imagine that these shareholders have the opportunity to vote on whether Costco should stop using antibiotics. Each shareholder votes her

[39] *Unusual Debate at Davos: Lobbying, Maximizing Shareholder Value and the Duty of CEO's*, ProMarket (April 1, 2016), https://perma.cc/2HEV-3QGW.

[40] Hart & Zingales, *supra* note 21; Broccardo et al., *supra* note 25.

preference, with the majority determining the outcome. Then, according to our formulation shareholder i (i = 1,2,3) votes to stop if

$$-40 + \lambda_i(180 - 80) > 0, \tag{5.1}$$

where the first term represents the capital loss the shareholder experiences herself if the extra cost of 120 is incurred, and the second term represents the impact on others – the environmental gain minus the capital loss incurred by her fellow shareholders – multiplied by her social responsibility parameter λ_i. We can rewrite (5.1) as

$$\lambda_i > 2/5. \tag{5.2}$$

Thus, if at least two of the shareholders have λ's above 2/5, the outcome of the vote will be to stop antibiotics, while if at least two of the shareholders have λ's below 2/5 the outcome will be to maintain the status quo.

In principle, shareholder welfare maximization can mean more than just majority rule. A natural approach is to follow Kaldor[41] and Hicks[42] and ask whether the winners could bribe the losers to support stopping antibiotic use. Suppose that shareholder i receives a monetary transfer t_i. Then (5.1) is replaced by

$$-40 + t_i + \lambda_i(180 - 80) > 0. \tag{5.3}$$

Given that the t_i's sum to zero, it is easy to see that (5.3) can be satisfied for all shareholders if and only if

$$\lambda_1 + \lambda_2 + \lambda_3 > 6/5, \tag{5.4}$$

which is just the sum of (5.2).

For future reference, it is useful to generalize the analysis. Suppose Costco has n shareholders, where shareholder i has a shareholding s_i. Let δ be the cost of dropping antibiotics and h be the value of the reduced risk to humans. Then, absent transfers, shareholder i will vote to stop if

$$-s_i\delta + \lambda_i(h - (1 - s_i)\delta) > 0, \tag{5.5}$$

where, as before, the first term represents the capital loss the shareholder experiences herself, and the second term represents the impact on others. (5.5) can be rewritten as

41 Nicholas Kaldor, *Welfare Propositions of Economics and Interpersonal Comparisons of Utility*, 49 ECON. J. 549 (1939).

42 J.R. Hicks, *The Foundations of Welfare Economics*, 49 ECON. J. 696 (1939).

$$-s_i\delta(1-\lambda_i)+\lambda_i(h-\delta)>0. \tag{5.6}$$

Since the first term is negative, (5.6) can only be satisfied if $(h-\delta)>0$, that is, shareholders will only vote for something that is socially efficient.

In this general formulation the Kaldor-Hicks criterion becomes

$$\sum_{i=1}^{n}\left[-s_i\delta+\lambda_i(h-(1-s_i)\delta)\right]>0, \tag{5.7}$$

which, by the same logic, can only be satisfied if $h>\delta$.

Returning to the numerical example, it is interesting to observe what happens to voting decisions when the number of shareholders increases. Suppose that there are 100 shareholders, each of whom owns 1 percent. Then (5.1) becomes

$$-1.2+\lambda_i(180-118.8))>0, \tag{5.8}$$

since each shareholder's personal capital loss is now only 1.2. As there are more and more shareholders, with each holding a smaller fraction of Costco – a situation that describes the world of diversified investors that we see today – the first term converges to zero and eventually all shareholders with a positive λ_i will vote to stop the antibiotics.[43] In other words a vote will lead to a socially efficient outcome as long as a majority of shareholders are socially responsible and have a small holding in the company.

The Costco situation may be one where, possibly with the help of management, fairly reliable estimates of the cost δ and the benefit h can be presented to shareholders. In other cases there may be more disagreement about the facts, and in politicized contexts disagreements about what should enter h. For example, in the case of Mifeprex, pro-choice shareholders might assign a very high positive value to h, the benefit of making the pill widely available, whereas anti-abortion shareholders may think that h is large and negative. Under these conditions, voting may not lead to a shareholder welfare maximizing outcome in the Kaldor-Hicks sense. Yet achieving the Kaldor-Hicks outcome would require shareholders to report truthfully their λ_i's and their views about h, something that they may not be willing to do. Whether incentive

[43] More generally, it follows from the results of Broccardo et al., *supra* note 25, that, as shareholdings converge to zero, each shareholder with a positive λ_i will vote to stop the antibiotics if and only if $h>\delta$, that is, doing so is socially efficient.

compatible mechanisms can be devised to elicit preferences is an interesting topic for future research. In the meantime, voting may be a reasonable second-best alternative, and we will focus on this in what follows.[44]

1.5.2 Which Topics/Decisions?

One concern with SWM is that the set of controversies corporations may be pushed to be involved in potentially explodes. Should corporations fight for animal rights, voting rights, gun rights, diversity, etc.?

As the discussion and examples in Section 1.3 make clear, SWM diverges from SVM when a company has a comparative advantage in achieving a social goal. Thus it seems reasonable to limit shareholder engagement on social issues to such cases. Here we provide the beginnings of a taxonomy concerning when comparative advantage is likely to exist and when it is not.

A natural case of comparative advantage occurs when a company controls a unique technology of production that cannot easily be reversed. We already described examples of this in Section 1.3: a company that produces plastic waste as a by-product of e-commerce, or a company that uses antibiotics in raising chickens. As another, in 1984 DuPont faced a choice between polluting the Ohio river with a toxic substance known as PFOA and investing in incineration. Dupont decided not to incinerate, an action that shareholders could not easily undo.[45]

A second case of comparative advantage occurs when a company has some market power. Along the lines of the Danco example in Section 1.3, consider a producer of a day-after abortion pill. Unless the market for these pills is perfectly competitive, a change in supply can have an effect on the price of the pill and thus on the number of people using it. It would be difficult, for free-rider reasons, to assemble a group to offset what the firm is doing by buying back pills in the marketplace (if the group wants to reduce abortions) or by subsidizing them (if the group

[44] For a different justification of the desirability of voting, see Adi Libson, *Taking Shareholders' Social Preferences Seriously: Confronting a New Agency Problem*, 9 U.C. IRVINE L. REV. 699 (2019). Libson argues that social decisions should be delegated to shareholders given that managers' human capital is nondiversified and as a result managers will not be inclined to promote social initiatives.

[45] *See* Shapira & Zingales *supra* note 18.

wants to increase access to abortion). In this sense, the producer has a comparative advantage in determining supply and influencing the price.

As another example in this category, consider a pharmaceutical company that produces a scarce vaccine. Profit maximation might lead to a very high price for the vaccine, but socially responsible shareholders may prefer that the company make the vaccine widely available at a lower price.

A third case of comparative advantage involves political pressure. In 2015 Indianapolis-based Angie's List announced it was canceling a $40 million headquarters expansion in protest against the passage of the Religious Freedom Restoration Act (RFRA), which opponents claim was targeted against LGBT people.[46] The protest led to an amendment of the RFRA that provided protections for LGBT customers, employees, and tenants. Individuals do not have the same power. Unless they can perfectly coordinate their actions, the threat of many small firms is not as powerful as the threat of a firm employing many people. Note that a large business can often exercise this threat at no cost since they get what they want and they do not have to move, something that a collection of small firms would find it very hard to achieve.

As a final example, let us return to corporate charitable donations. As noted in Section 1.3, this is often regarded as a slam-dunk case for Friedman's argument that companies should leave social matters to shareholders. In fact, the conclusion is not so obvious. Under classical economic assumptions, when an individual gives to charity – a contribution that, say, will save the life of a starving child – the individual trades off the marginal cost of giving against the marginal benefit she receives from saving the child, ignoring the marginal benefit others receive from there being one less starving child. But this leads to the undersupply of charity from a social perspective. In contrast, if a majority of shareholders vote for a company to give to charity, all shareholders are forced to make contributions. This amplification effect can push charitable contributions closer to the social optimum.

However, there is a countervailing force. Consider the founder(s) of the company at the IPO stage. Rather than setting up the company in such a way that it can make future charitable contributions, the founder

[46] Tim Evans, *Angie's List Canceling Eastside Expansion Over RFRA*, IndyStar (Mar. 28, 2015, 11:47 AM ET), https://www.indystar.com/story/money/2015/03/28/angies-list-canceling-eastside-expansion-rfra/70590738/.

can create two companies: one that does business but is prohibited from giving to charity and the other that is a charitable foundation. The charitable foundation would be funded by some fraction of the extra amount that investors are willing to pay for the shares of the first company given that there will be no outflows to charity (the fraction depends on how prosocial the founder herself is; if she is selfish she will pocket all of the extra amount). Under reasonable assumptions, one can show that the two-company alternative is at least as good as, and sometimes strictly better than, the one-company alternative for the founder. For this reason, preventing shareholders from voting on purely charitable activities can be justified.

While we have provided examples where a shareholder vote seems legitimate, we do not want to suggest that our views are sacrosanct. A company should be free to limit by charter which social issues are allowed on (or which ones are excluded from) the proxy ballot. Also, firms with political power or large market power are relatively rare. Thus, the vast majority of issues that would need to be voted on pertain to situations where there is a technological interaction between the prosocial and business activities of a corporation. We will discuss further possible restrictions in Section 1.5.4.

1.5.3 Voting in Practice

Most investors own stock via a financial intermediary, generally a mutual fund. Currently, these institutions vote on behalf of their investors, almost universally taking the view that they have a fiduciary duty to vote for the value-maximizing outcome. But shareholders can become more involved in the voting process, and that seems to be happening.

At least three approaches are possible. The first one is to push down the voting decision to the level of individual investors. This is a strategy that BlackRock is trying to implement now with its major investors. Thus, if the New York State Common Retirement Fund invests in BlackRock S&P500 ETF, it will have the right to vote pro-rata the shares it indirectly owns in all the S&P500 companies.

This strategy might work well for major pension funds and endowments, but it is unreasonable for individual shareholders. We cannot expect shareholders to express an opinion on all ballots of all the companies they own. This was hard to imagine in a world where investors owned just a few stocks. It is inconceivable today when most investors buy indexed mutual funds, which own hundreds if not thousands of stocks. Proxy ballot advisors employ an army of analysts to provide guidelines on how mutual funds should cast their votes in corporate ballots. It would be enormously inefficient to expect every single investor to duplicate that effort.

Fortunately, there is a solution. Today many institutional investors buy proxy advising services customized to specific needs. For example, Institutional Shareholder Services (ISS) has six sets of "specialty" proxy voting guidelines – each geared toward a specific special interest group: Taft-Hartley Advisory Services, Public Fund, Socially Responsible Investment (SRI), Catholic Faith-Based, Sustainability, Climate. Each set of guidelines is 70–80 pages long and describes in excruciating detail how the vote would be cast in different contingencies. In this sense, it is a much more detailed version of a party electoral platform. Thus, it would be relatively simple for each investor to choose one type of guideline and ask that her shares be voted accordingly. The main objection to this approach is that it limits investors' choice to the predetermined specialty policies available in the market. Yet, in the long run, if proxy advisors are paid on the basis of the number of clients who choose to follow their advice, competition is likely to lead to a broad range of "political platforms."

The second strategy would be for mutual funds to elicit investors' preferences and then cast their votes based on an aggregation of these preferences. As we have noted, this may be challenging since shareholders may not report their preferences truthfully. While it may be possible to develop incentive-compatible mechanisms to deal with this, a shortcut would be for mutual funds to ask their investors how they would vote and then aggregate these votes.

The third strategy is for mutual funds companies to offer investors funds with a very clear and predetermined voting strategy and let investors choose among them. For example, Vanguard could offer an S&P500 light green fund, ready to vote in favor of all shareholder resolutions that promote a greener economy, as long as their cost of reducing CO_2 emission does not exceed \$100 per ton. Vanguard could also offer an S&P500 dark green fund that votes in favor of all shareholder resolutions that promote a greener economy, as long as their cost of reducing CO_2 emission does not exceed \$200 per ton.

Voting strategies become more complex when one moves beyond simple Yes/No decisions. Consider Costco's use of antibiotics. Perhaps the issue is whether to eliminate them; moderate their use; or do nothing. We know from Arrow that preference aggregation runs into difficulties when there are more than two alternatives,[47] but political elections take place in spite of Arrow's result. Certainly, the current electoral system can be improved and many scholars have proposed valid alternatives, like ranked-choice voting, or methods to select the Condorcet winner.[48] These methods could also be applied in the corporate context.

1.5.4 Opening the Floodgates

One possible objection to SWM is that it would open the floodgates to thousands of shareholder resolutions that will dominate shareholder meetings and distract management from creating value. Before we address this concern it is important to review where we stand today. Tallarita analyzes all shareholder proposals on social and environmental issues for the period from 2010 to 2019 at companies included in the S&P 500 index.[49] He finds 2,410 proposals.[50] Thus, on average S&P500 companies receive less than half a proposal a year. Nineteen percent of the proposals are successfully excluded by the company, and so the average company in the S&P500 will have to vote on a shareholder proposal every three years.[51]

The distribution of proposals per company is not uniform. During the sample period, Exxon received on average seven and a half proposals a year, while companies in the bottom quartile of the distribution of proposals receive less than one proposal in ten years.[52] Companies outside the S&P500 index are likely to receive fewer proposals than the bottom quartile of the S&P500 index.[53] Thus, for the vast majority of companies shareholder propositions are not an issue. Consistent with Section 1.5.1, the issue is concentrated in a few companies that have disproportionate political or market power.

Filters for shareholder resolutions can also be employed. Currently, there are three. The first is the amount of stock required to file a proposal. Under Rule 14a–8 any shareholder who held at least $25,000 worth of the

[47] *See generally* Kenneth J. Arrow, Social Choice and Individual Values (3rd ed. 2012).

[48] *See, e.g.*, Eric Maskin, *Arrow's Theorem, May's Axioms, and Borda's Rule* (Mar. 2021) (unpublished manuscript), https://perma.cc/GZV4-LBR8.

[49] Roberto Tallarita, *Stockholder Politics*, 73 Hastings L.J. (2022). [50] Ibid.

[51] Ibid. [52] Ibid. [53] Ibid.

company's stock continuously for at least one year before the date the proposal is submitted (or $2,000 for three years) can file a proposal. If shareholder activism leads to too many proposals this requirement could be strengthened.

The second filter is that companies can request from the SEC a no-action letter if they exclude the proposal from the ballot. In Tallarita's sample, management tried to exclude the proposal from the proxy statement in 39 percent of the cases and it succeeded approximately half the time (49.6 percent).[54] Thus, the SEC does represent an important filter. The question is what it is filtering on. In the past, the principle has been that a proposal that involves "ordinary business" matters is inappropriate. Thus, a proposal advanced at Walmart to reconsider the sale of automatic weapons was blocked because it concerned the ordinary business decision: what to sell.[55] As we have seen, the most relevant proposals are precisely those that pertain to the business of a company and thus they risk being filtered out. But the SEC could adopt a different rule: allow only proposals that pertain to a company's comparative advantage.[56]

The third filter is represented by the fact that all these proposals are precatory. Thus, there is no legal obligation for companies to follow them.[57] In fact, one can think about these ballots as a way to elicit shareholders' preferences, leaving to management the final decision about what to do given those preferences. Our view is that it would be better to make shareholder resolutions binding since this would make it easier for shareholders to get managers to do what they want. However, if the main reason to oppose the SWM approach is the fear of making corporations ungovernable, having a transitory period where proposals remain precatory may make sense.

In sum, we believe that there are sufficient mechanisms available to prevent a dangerous floodgate of shareholder proposals in the future.

[54] Ibid.

[55] Clare O'Connor, *Walmart Beats Out Church in Court Fight over Gun Sales*, FORBES (Apr. 15, 2015, 1:35 PM EDT), https://perma.cc/F4YU-PCMF.

[56] On November 3, 2021, the SEC issued Staff Legal Bulletin No. 14L, providing a more nuanced interpretation of the ordinary business exception, which is likely to result in the exclusion of fewer shareholder proposals. We are grateful to Jill Fisch for alerting us to this change.

[57] As we stated above, shareholders could threaten to replace directors who do not implement their precatory proposals. Yet, this is much more easily done by large institutional investors than by individual investors.

1.6 Conclusions

Corporations are larger, more complex, and more powerful than they were in 1970. In a more populous world, the importance of externalities has also greatly increased. Finally, the preferences of investors have changed. Investors, especially younger ones, are more sensitive to social issues. In spite of all these changes, the view on the proper objective of a business enterprise does not seem to have adapted.

In this chapter, we have suggested that it should. We have argued that, when externalities are important and investors are at least somewhat prosocial, shareholder welfare maximization not value maximization is an appropriate goal. The standard defenses of SVM are untenable. SWM is what shareholders want and it is implementable. We outline several ways to achieve this. Interestingly, some of these are being adopted as we write. This is an area where practice is ahead of theory. In this chapter, we have tried to fill the gap.

2

Shareholder Voice and Corporate Purpose

The Purposelessness of Mandatory Corporate Purpose Statements

PAUL A. DAVIES

2.1 The Issue

In 2018, Colin Mayer, then Professor of Management Studies at the Saïd Business School of the University of Oxford, published a short book entitled *Prosperity*.[1] It has proved to be highly influential in business and broader policy circles and has been much debated around the world. It is a very ambitious book, which seeks to reset the goals of the management of large companies in all jurisdictions.[2] Mayer was reacting in particular against a dictum of Milton Friedman from 1970 that "there is one and only one social responsibility of business" which was "to increase [the company's] profits so long as it stays within the rules of the game".[3] There can be debate about what Friedman meant by "the rules of the game". In the sentence just quoted Friedman seems to have had in mind only competition and anti-fraud rules, but Mayer also quotes a sentence from elsewhere in the same article where Friedman refers more broadly to "the basic rules of the society, both those embodied in law and those embodied in ethical custom".[4] This latter

Iam grateful for comments on an earlier version of the chapter to Sir Geoffrey Owen, Alessio Pacces and participants in the Conference on Contemporary Corporate Governance held in Stockholm in May 2022 and in the Corporate Governance Conference 2022, held in Rome in October 2022, and especially to Colin Mayer.

[1] OUP 2018.

[2] The book is not clear on the exact range of companies to which it applies, but its prescription is most apposite for companies with multiple shareholders whose shares are traded on public markets. These will be the focus of this chapter.

[3] *Prosperity* p 2.

[4] M Friedman, "A Friedman Doctrine – The social responsibility of business is to increase its profits", *New York Times Magazine*, 13 Sept 1970. Nor, where directors were free of

formulation opens up a wider set of possible constraints on the profit-directed activities of companies.

However, as for Friedman, so for Mayer, the precise definition of the rules of the game is not central to the argument. Mayer's point is that a blunt version of Friedman's argument – that the purpose of business is to maximise (via profits) shareholder value without more than a passing reference to the rules of the game – has "defined business practice and government policies around the world" and has been "the basis of business education that has moulded generations of business leaders. Indeed, virtually every MBA course begins from the premise that the purpose of business is to maximise shareholder value".[5] Mayer is highly critical of this approach. In his view, it undermines the democratic legitimacy of private enterprise and deprives society of a powerful engine – the corporation – which has the potential to secure transformational benefits for society as a whole. Removing the Friedman doctrine from the place it currently occupies, in the view of *Prosperity*, is what one might term the negative goal of the book.

However, the ambition of *Prosperity* is demonstrated by its positive goal which is to substitute for profit maximisation the aim of "finding profitable solutions to the problems of people and the planet".[6] Indeed, the bulk of the book is devoted, correctly in my view, to the development of its positive goal. The Friedman doctrine is dealt with in some detail in the "Preface" of the book (really a substantial chapter) but thereafter comes in for only occasional bashing. It is clear that the negative goal of the book is achievable without resort to a mandatory purpose requirement. No corporate law system, to my knowledge, imposes a legal duty on the board to maximise the company's profits. If boards do view their role in the way *Prosperity* describes – and there is, of course, a good deal of evidence that they do – then that result flows from the pressures which shareholders and investors are able to apply to boards to behave in this way. There are various steps which could be taken to reduce those pressures, without removing shareholders from their position of ultimate control of the company. Looking at the UK, Professors Kershaw and

legal and ethical constraints, can Friedman be said to have advocated profit maximisation over any particular timeframe, ie he was not a "short termist".

5 *Prosperity* p 2. Cf B Cheffins, *Stop Blaming Milton Friedman!*, University of Cambridge, Legal Studies Research Paper 9/2020, who argues that the influence of Friedman's words was due, not to their novelty or innate persuasiveness, but to the adoption in the 1980s of high-powered executive pay arrangements in the US.

6 *Prosperity* p 12.

Schuster have advocated such a suite of reforms, which, they suggest, would operate to create a more neutral stance on the part of the law towards shareholder rights, compared with its currently strongly pro-shareholder orientation, and which would create a "zone of insulation" for the board from immediate shareholder pressure.[7]

The main focus of *Prosperity* is, then, on securing its positive and ambitious goal, that is, the adoption and implementation by companies of purposes which are both profitable and problem-solving for "people and planet". In its Chapter 7, purposes, and their coterminous commitments, are categorised into three types: self-regarding (the company is a main beneficiary of the commitment), communal (where the commitment relates to those who deal with the company but the company does not capture all the benefits of its commitment) and social (where benefits are conferred on those not in a contractual or analogous relationship with the company).[8] It is the communal and social purposes which are at the centre of the mandatory purpose rule.

As a corporate lawyer, my interest is in the implications of this shift for the configuration of corporate law. General corporate law changes are dealt with in *Prosperity*'s Chapter 7, entitled simply "Law".[9] This contains a surprisingly light treatment of corporate law, surprising for one might think that a fundamental shift in the goals of large companies would require quite a lot in terms of supporting corporate law or corporate governance reform. After all, a large part of corporate law and governance is about setting the incentives of those who control the central management of large companies and holding them accountable (and sometimes also liable) for their actions.

The answer to this initial puzzle is to be found in the book's central proposition that "the transformation of the corporation can be translated from a visionary ideal to a practical reality through an embarrassingly simple policy".[10] This policy is that "corporate law should prioritize purpose". More precisely, "corporate law is the means to achieving

[7] D Kershaw and E Schuster, "The Purposive Transformation of Company Law" (2021) 69 *American Journal of Comparative Law* 478. In the US, this set of policies is most strongly associated in academia with the work of Professor Stephen Bainbridge. See, for example, his "Preserving Director Primacy by Managing Shareholder Interventions", in *Research Handbook on Shareholder Power*, 231 (edited by J G Hill & R S Thomas, 2015).

[8] *Prosperity* p 152.

[9] Of the other implementation chapters, Chapter 8 deals mainly with the regulation of banks and capital markets and Chapters 9 and 10 deal with finance and investment.

[10] *Prosperity* p 22.

purposeful company ends . . . It should require companies to articulate their purposes, incorporate them in their articles of association, and above all demonstrate how they credibly commit to the delivery of purpose."[11] Once adopted, the chapter suggests, the purpose would control the contours of the directors' fiduciary duties, which is correct, and the configuration of the governance structure of the company, which is a more debatable claim. Beyond this, the book envisages that investors, suppliers and corporate (but not other) clients of the company would be required to commit to the purpose the company had adopted. This radical extension of the impact of companies' articles of association outside the company itself is mentioned briefly at the beginning of the book[12] but thereafter disappears from sight. The myriad legal questions it raises will be ignored by this chapter as well.

Prosperity was followed by a research/publicity/consultation exercise run by Colin Mayer under the auspices of the British Academy (BA). Its conclusions were published as *Policy and Practice for Purposeful Business* in September 2021.[13] This added a little to the company law implications of the book, but not a great deal. In the space of a single page, the BA Report put forward three different methods of implementing the purpose requirement in corporate law. It neither elaborated on any of them nor prioritised or ranked them.[14] The one closest to the implementation mechanism identified in *Prosperity* was put as follows: "Changing Section 172 of the Companies Act to require companies to state their purpose in their articles of association." An illustration was given of this reform: "Legislation would require companies to adopt purposes that aim to benefit people and planet as well as shareholders, and report on their success in so doing." This proposal reflects the suggestion in *Prosperity* that "if companies do not address communal and social commitments adequately" then "there may be obligations to enhance human, intellectual, natural and social capital beyond the levels that organisation would voluntarily choose."[15] This proposal is technically inept, since section 172 of the British Companies Act 2006 concerns the duties of directors

[11] Ibid p 23. [12] Ibid p 23.
[13] British Academy, *Policy and Practice for Purposeful Business*, 2021. [14] At p 22.
[15] *Prosperity* pp 158–9. This positive obligation appears as a separate requirement from the negative obligation to refrain from actions which "could be detrimental to the maintenance of these forms of capital" (p 159). In more recent writing, Mayer has placed more emphasis on the refraining element of his proposals than on the positive obligations. See C Mayer, *What Is Wrong with Corporate Law? The Purpose of Law and the Law of Purpose*, ECGI Law Working Paper 649/2022. The implementation of the negative

rather than the obligations of companies. This may appear to be a pedantic point, since the corporate obligation could clearly be placed elsewhere in the Act. However, the failure to observe the conceptual distinction between directors' duties and corporate obligations has consequences for other steps in the argument, as we see below.[16] A second proposal seemed explicitly to shift the duty to adopt the approved purpose away from the company and into the hands of the directors: "Company law emphasises duties of directors to *determine* and implement company purposes" (emphasis added). Finally, there was a proposal for governmental nudging which appeared not to have a mandatory element.

This chapter focuses primarily, not on the implementation of the chosen purpose, but on the first step in the process, which is the adoption by the company of a transformative purpose, either by the shareholders by amendment of the company's articles of association or by a directors' resolution. It will be suggested that shareholders or directors accountable to shareholders will not adopt purposes of the type envisaged by *Prosperity* without either substantial changes in corporate law beyond the mere adoption of a requirement to state a corporate purpose or a substantial alteration in the goals of investors from those the Friedman doctrine assumes (or some combination of the two). The purpose statement requirement envisaged in *Prosperity*'s Chapter 7 is not, it will be argued, "embarrassingly simple" but in fact complicated, perhaps even "embarrassingly" complicated if the goal is its quick implementation. A one-section addition to the Companies Act requiring companies to state a purpose of the required type in their articles of association will not by itself "transform business at a stroke".[17] Instead, it will be argued, it will either be a failure or be rescued by some non-simple changes in corporate law or by a transformation of investors' goals.

2.2 The Structure of This Chapter

This thesis will be explored in this chapter in relation to two contrasting shareholder worlds (which are taken in order to sharpen the analysis and not in order to argue that other worlds might not be conceivable or actually exist). In the first world, which was Friedman's starting point, shareholders wish to "make as much money as possible while

obligation raises different issues from that raised by the positive obligation, upon which this chapter is focused.

[16] See text attached to notes 108–12. [17] *Prosperity* pp 22–3.

conforming to the basic rules of the society". My argument here is that, in the current state of company law, any purpose statements which emerge in this world are not likely to constrain significantly the company's established modes of conducting its profit-making business. Profit-oriented shareholders will not favour purposes which impede their Friedmanite goal, whether those purposes are to be adopted by the shareholders (the normal rule for changes to the company's internal constitution) or by directors accountable to shareholders.

The chapter then explores two possible ways of securing transformative corporate purpose commitments, even in the face of shareholder opposition. Neither, it will be argued, is likely to be achievable or even desirable. The first strategy is to place the purpose-adopting duty on the board but then to re-configure company law so as to shield the directors from any adverse reaction from the shareholders to the board's decision. It will be suggested that this strategy, if implemented, would be unlikely to be wholly effective in achieving its goals, would come with considerable costs and, in any case, would be unlikely to obtain legislative endorsement. The second is to provide a counterweight to shareholder reluctance to adopt sufficiently transforming purposes by requiring regulatory or court approval of the shareholders' choice of corporate purpose, that is, corporate purpose ceases to be a matter of private ordering. This strategy blurs the boundary between the private and public sectors of the economy. It will be argued that this step would also be undesirable and, in any event, appears to run counter to the philosophy behind *Prosperity*.

The chapter then moves to the second corporate world, which is one where Friedman's description of shareholders' goals is no longer accurate. In short, I posit a change in the orientation of shareholders towards their investments. We are now in a world of ESG investing. Investors might change their views about what constitutes the best way of "making money" (a relatively limited shift) or, more boldly, they might come to share *Prosperity*'s views about the importance of communal and social goals for their investment strategies. In this world, investors evaluate the company's achievements along communal and social dimensions as well as along the financial one. The management of the company is not to be condemned even if it could be shown that a greater financial return would have resulted over a certain time period through the abandonment of the other goals. In practice, it might be difficult to disentangle the separate operation of these two developments. Either way, what might emerge in such a situation are some significant departures from current corporate behaviour, because shareholders themselves supported the adoption of corporate purposes which were communal or social. The core question here is not, however, about the rise of ESG investing as a general phenomenon, but about its potential to push companies in the direction of adopting corporate purposes of the type envisaged in *Prosperity*. Unlike the approaches discussed above, which are essentially top-down and rule-driven, the third is a bottom-up investor-driven approach. In this world the driver of change is not the adoption of a broad corporate purpose, but the transformation of investors' goals, which then expresses itself in the purpose statement or in some functionally equivalent way.

Of course, it does not follow that in this second world there is no space for corporate law to aid social change, for example, by making more credible the commitments that companies under shareholder pressure choose to make[18] or for the state to nudge companies in the direction of broad corporate purposes, as in the latest version of the UK Corporate Governance Code. However, the implications for the reform of corporate law in this second world are very different from those in the first. Far from aiming at shielding the board from the shareholders or subjecting its choices to review, the third strategy suggests that shareholder influence should be given full reign. Shareholders should be free to shape the broad contours of corporate strategy and behaviour and to remove directors who will not listen to shareholders' views on these matters.

Before proceeding with this analysis, it is worth making two additional points about *Prosperity*. The first is that it does not adopt the familiar shareholder/stakeholder frame of analysis. It is likely that stakeholders (however defined) would do better in the world envisaged by the book as compared with a Friedmanite world, but this result would appear to flow from the company's commitment to its stated purpose, not from a stakeholder framework of accountability. Both approaches are stated in *Prosperity* to be "misconceived". "There should be no presumption in company law of either shareholder primacy or stakeholder pluralism. One or other may sometimes be appropriate but never consistently so."[19] This underlines the novelty of the purpose proposal, and it is a refreshing change.

[18] Colin Mayer's previous book, *Firm Commitment* (2013), is enlightening on this matter. And see further n 115 below.

[19] *Prosperity* p 23. And see also C Mayer, "Shareholderism Versus Stakeholderism – A Misconceived Contradiction" (2022) 106 *Cornell Law Review* 1859.

Second, there is some ambiguity about how *Prosperity* conceives of the company and its governance. At places the book comes close to an entity theory of the company. Thus, one sentence reads: "The separation of the mind of the corporation from those of any individuals who comprise it confers an ability on it to demonstrate a quite different level of integrity from the individuals who comprise it."[20] However, this can be interpreted as meaning only that, once a company has adopted a binding corporate purpose of the type the book envisages, those involved in it will be required to implement that purpose, irrespective of their individual interests and goals – or else cease their association with it. In fact, the dominant conception of the company which the book adopts appears to be a managerialist one. As it is put early in the book, the company "is a vehicle for committing to the fulfilment of its stated purposes and once freed from the shackles of particular interest groups, be they shareholders, employees or governments, the corporation is capable of delivering substantial benefits to its customers and communities."[21] The inclusion of employees among the groups from whose shackles the company must be freed would be surprising from a stakeholder advocate, whilst the omission of managers from the list of "particular interest groups" fits with the idea that the managers are somehow above the fray and are there disinterestedly to discharge the responsibility of implementing the purposes the company has adopted – or perhaps even to adopt them in the first place.

2.3 Purpose Statements in a Friedmanite World

In this section, I proceed on the basis that shareholders' goals are purely financial and that they regard purpose statements, at least of the communal or social types, as inimical to the maximisation of the financial return on their investments. Although profit is still an essential part of corporate purposes under the *Prosperity* proposals, it is no longer the sole goal of the company. Where the adoption of a purpose statement is contrary to the perceived financial interests of the shareholders, one would expect either the statement not to be adopted or to take a form which does not in fact significantly constrain the company's capacity for pursuing profits. Following the current fashion, one might characterise weak purpose statements as "purpose-washing".

[20] Ibid p 14. [21] Ibid p 4.

The reasons for making this prediction are very straightforward. Given the posited goals of the shareholders, the analysis follows almost as a matter of definition where the purpose decision is in the hands of the shareholders, as in most jurisdictions it will be if the purpose is proposed to be embodied in the company's constitutional documents. Where the decision is in the hands of the board via a board resolution, then directors fearful of removal, whether by shareholder vote or a takeover, will be similarly unadventurous. It is useful to divide the analysis into two parts: first, where the adoption of purpose is formally voluntary for the company (even if subject to official encouragement) and where it is required by the law.

2.3.1 Voluntary Adoption of Purpose Statements

In this sub-section, I examine two pieces of evidence which support the proposition that, where purpose statements are not mandatory, they will either not emerge or will be formulated in a non-constraining way, even if companies are officially encouraged to adopt them. Those two pieces of evidence relate to practice in France and the United States, the French practice being particularly interesting. Since there is no reason to suppose that the shareholders in French and US companies are exclusively of the Friedmanite type, the conclusion I argue for would apply *a fortiori* in a Friedmanite world. It might be argued that this evidence is beside the point, since the proposal in *Prosperity* is that broad purposes should be mandatory, not voluntary. However, my argument is that the evidence of the antipathy of shareholders to constraining voluntary purpose statements and their accompanying commitments indicates that they would seek to minimise the impact of any mandatory obligation placed upon their company or its directors. Sub-section 2.3.2 gives an historical example of how easy such evasion will be, unless, to repeat the theme, the purpose requirement is accompanied by substantial additional changes in corporate law.

Under reforms of 2019, the French legislature created two optional ways for companies to commit to broad purpose objectives, one being stronger and one weaker than the other.[22] Under the stronger form, a company may choose to become a *société à mission* (which I shall refer to

[22] I am grateful to Alain Pietrancosta for discussion of aspects of these rules. The responsibility for what is said about them below is, of course, my own.

as a "committed company").[23] To achieve this status, the company must incorporate in its statutes one or more social or environmental purposes. The statutes must contain a statement of the methods (including resources) to be used to attain the stated purposes. A "purpose committee" must be created, containing at least one employee, whose role is to monitor the implementation by the company of the stated purposes. This committee reports annually to the shareholders, at the same meeting as that to which the company's financial statements are presented. It has unconstrained access to the company's records and full investigatory powers to discharge its supervisory function. In addition, the committee's report must have attached to it an independent third-party certificate verifying the company's progress. Finally, the company's status as a committed company is published in a public register. Apart from its voluntary characteristic, this appears to be a scheme which fleshes out what *Prosperity* advocates.

The weaker form of the purpose statement consists of the permission for companies to include in their statutes a statement of their *raison d'être*, consisting of a statement of the principles to which the company is committed and of its willingness to make expenditures to achieve these principles.[24] Quite apart from the absence of required internal and external monitoring mechanisms in the weaker mechanism, the types of principle the company must adopt in its *raison d'être* are not specified. Moreover, the better view is that inclusion requires directors only to take the principles into account; they are not obliged to prioritise them.[25] The *raison d'être* permission is, therefore, a significantly weaker approach to purpose statements than that which applies if the choice is made to become a committed company.

It is submitted that the evidence to date of the use of both mechanisms by companies in the SBF Index – the 120 most actively traded companies listed in Paris – supports the view that shareholders in publicly traded companies regard these mechanisms with extreme caution.[26] As of

[23] Article L210-10 of the *Code Commercial*.

[24] Article 1835 of the *Code Civil* (as amended). Since *raison d'être* appears in my English dictionary, I intend to leave that term as it is.

[25] A Pietrancosta, *Codification in Company Law of General CSR Requirements: Pioneering Recent French Reforms and EU Perspectives*, ECGI Law Working Paper No. 639/2022, para 43 (available at ssrn.com/abstract=4083398).

[26] The figures below are taken from Étude WEMEAN, *Raison d'être et société à mission : Où en est le SBF120 ?* (October 2021).

October 2021 only one had chosen to become a committed company.[27] This was Danone, which adopted the status in 2020, having pursued since 2014 a social and environmental business model. However, in 2021 activist shareholders forced out the person who had been CEO during this period on the grounds that shareholder financial interests had suffered during his tenure.[28]

With official encouragement,[29] much greater use has been made of the weaker form of the purpose commitment, but nevertheless the data provide evidence of companies not wishing to bind themselves to anything significantly constraining. A majority of SBF companies (68 or 57 per cent) had adopted a *raison d'être*, but only 14 (12 per cent) had taken advantage of the option provided by the law to place the purpose statement in their statutes (and five of those 14 had placed the purpose statement in the preamble to the statutes rather than in their main body). The remaining 54 (or nearly 80 per cent of the adopting companies) had placed the *raison d'être* outside the statutes. Arguably, this was something they were at liberty to do even without the legal reforms of 2019, though it seems overwhelmingly likely that these extra-statutory purpose statements were motivated by a desire to respond to the governmental policy of facilitating statutory purpose statements. Not placing the commitment in the statutes means it is not formally binding on the company and its directors. Thus, the directors cannot be sued on the ground alone that they have fallen short of what the purpose statement requires.[30] Where the statement is in the preamble to the statutes, it operate as an interpretative aid in relation to what is said in the body of the statutes. Finally, 51 of the SBF (42.5 per cent) had not adopted a *raison d'être*.

[27] Some further five large companies, not in the SBF 120 and some with strong state participation, have gone down the *société à mission* route, as have some 300 smaller companies, of which 70 per cent have fewer than 50 employees (Pietrancosta, above n 25, para 61).

[28] "The fall from favour of Danone's purpose-driven chief", *Financial Times*, 17 March 2021. At the time of its adoption of committed status, this step was hailed as a toppling of the statue of Milton Friedman.

[29] For an account of the political steps leading up to this reform, see A Pietrancosta, "Intérêt social et raison d'être" (2019) 4 *Annales des Mines: Réalités industrielles* 55.

[30] See Pietrancosta, above n 25, para 59 for an analysis of the duties placed on both directors and the companies when the purpose statement is incorporated in the statutes. However, even a *raison d'être* statement placed outside the articles might have indirect legal implications: since it is a public statement, it could provide or support an action by investors against the company based on misstatement to the market.

As important is the substantive content of the *raison d'être* statements actually adopted. Taking the ones embodied in the statutes, and which therefore had been approved by the shareholders, one can see that they in fact demonstrate little in the way of firm commitment to communal or social goals. Some are no more than short publicity glosses on the company's business model with no reference to specific communal or social policies.[31] Other statements do make some reference to such policies but only at such a high level of generality that departure from the policy would be capable of being demonstrated only in egregious cases.[32] The same analysis may be made about the non-statutory purpose declarations.[33] It is not clear what decision-making mechanism within the company was used to adopt the extra-statutory purpose statements. Some may have had no shareholder input and have been the result of a

[31] Orange: *Orange est l'acteur de confiance qui donne à chacune et à chacun les clés d'un monde numérique responsable.*

ADP (Aéroports de Paris): *Accueillir les passagers, exploiter et imaginer des aéroports, de manière responsable et à travers le monde.*

Nexity: *La vie ensemble.*

Soitec: *Nous sommes le terreau innovant de technologies intelligentes et économes en énergie, qui transforment durablement nos vies quotidiennes.*

[32] ENGIE (25 per cent owned by the French state): *Agir pour accélérer la transition vers une économie neutre en carbone, par des solutions plus sobres en énergie et plus respectueuses de l'environnement. Cette raison d'être rassemble l'entreprise, ses salariés, ses clients et ses actionnaires et concilie performance économique et impact positif sur les personnes et la planète. L'action d'ENGIE s'apprécie dans sa globalité et dans la durée.*

Worldline: *Nous concevons et exploitons des services de paiement et de transactions numériques pour contribuer à une croissance économique durable, renforcer la confiance et la sécurité dans nos sociétés. Nous les rendons respectueux de l'environnement, accessibles au plus grand nombre, tout en accompagnant les transformations sociétales.*

EDF (then majority state-owned, now fully): *Construire un avenir énergétique neutre en CO2 conciliant préservation de la planète, bien-être et développement grâce à l'électricité et à des solutions et services innovants.*

[33] The closest to a firm commitment that I found among these extra-statutory statements was part of a long declaration by Suez: *SUEZ s'investit pour la préservation et la restauration du capital naturel et ainsi l'avenir de la biodiversité sur mer comme sur terre. Partenaire engagé auprès des collectivités, des industriels et des citoyens, SUEZ mobilise les parties-prenantes pour réussir la transition environnementale, en développant des modèles d'économie circulaire et en innovant pour anticiper les exigences du futur. Fières de leurs métiers et fortes de leurs valeurs, les équipes de SUEZ ancrées sur tous les territoires façonnent un environnement durable, dès maintenant.* Even without legislative encouragement, purpose statements are widely adopted by publicly traded companies, but, not surprisingly, they too are more promotional than constraining. One author characterises the purpose statements of the DAX 30 companies in Germany as "increasingly crisp and catchy": H Fleischer, "Corporate Purpose: A Managerial Concept and Its Implications for Company Law" (2021) 18 *European Company and Financial Law Review* 161, 170.

board resolution. Their striking feature is that they are not more constraining in the round than statutory purpose statements.

It would be wrong to ignore the reputational risks created for companies by even general and non-binding purpose statements. Even if of little use in legal proceedings, civil society groups, employees and official bodies may be able to use them effectively to put pressure on companies over particular issues. However, it is suggested that none of the purpose statements put out by French companies is robust enough to carry by itself the weight of translating *Prosperity*'s proposals "from a visionary ideal to a practical reality".

The second piece of evidence comes from the United States and relates to proposals that public companies (i.e. those subject to the SEC's overview) convert to, or adopt goals analogous to those of, a public benefit corporation (PBC). The PBC has some affinities with the French *société à mission*. It aims to balance shareholder and stakeholder interests, and the non-shareholder interests it proposes to promote must normally be stated in the company's certificate of incorporation. These could include communal and social goals of the type envisaged in *Prosperity*. The delivery of the non-shareholder benefits is subject to reporting to the shareholders' meeting and may be required to be accompanied by third-party certification.[34] Jill Fisch analysed shareholder proposals in the period 2019–21 that companies convert to a PBC or take analogous steps. She found that none of the proposals secured the level of shareholder support necessary for adoption and indeed secured significantly less support than other types of shareholder proposal.[35] While Fisch sees these proposals as a potentially useful way of raising the purpose issue within companies, it is submitted that her data also indicate shareholder scepticism about robust forms of purpose adoption.

2.3.2 Mandatory Purpose Statements

The obvious way forward from this limited, but not encouraging, experience with voluntary purpose statements might seem to be to make them mandatory. Indeed, *Prosperity*[36] contemplates that the purpose statement would be mandatory and so it is arguable that the above experience with

[34] See, for example, Delaware General Corporation Law, §§361–8.
[35] J Fisch, *Purpose Proposals*, ECGI Law Working Paper 638/2022, especially Section IV and Tables 1 and 2.
[36] *Prosperity* p 23.

voluntary purpose mechanisms does not undermine what the book envisages. However, merely to require a purpose statement, whilst leaving its formulation to the board or the shareholders, is not likely to produce different statements from the ones emerging under a formally voluntary regime. Indeed, the overall quality of the purpose statements is likely to decline. This is because companies which, under the voluntary regime, choose not to adopt a purpose statement are, presumably, those which attach the least value to such statements. If required to make a statement, those companies now unwillingly within the net can be expected to adopt the least constraining formula they can devise. As *Prosperity* itself admonishes us: "stop believing that [laws and regulations] can constrain anything or anyone who is given a sufficiently strong incentive to violate them".[37] In the case of a requirement merely to state a corporate purpose, it would not even be necessary to violate the law, simply to discharge the legal obligation in a particular way.

The ease of circumvention of required purpose statements whose formulation is left to the company is surely the lesson from the history of required purpose statements as they appeared in the early UK Companies Acts. These required limited companies to specify in their founding documents "the objects for which the proposed company is to be established".[38] Of course, the aim of the nineteenth-century legislature was not the transformative goal envisaged by current advocates of purpose statements. On the contrary, fearing what this new-fangled, limited-liability company might get up to, the nineteenth-century legislature wished to constrain its areas of activity by requiring it to specify in its "objects clause" the scope of its commercial or other business. Nevertheless, the technique was the same both then and in the current proposals: the use of purpose clauses to shape the way in which the company conducts its business.

On the basis of this statutory provision, the courts built a fearsome set of restrictions, known as the *ultra vires* doctrine. Transactions outside the scope of the objects clause were of no legal effect (were void), while the directors' fiduciary duties required them to conduct the business of the company in accordance with its objects clause and directors were potentially liable to the company for the harm caused to it as a result of not so doing. No one within or dealing with the company liked the system, even

[37] Ibid p 9.

[38] This is the formula used in s 8 of the Companies Act 1862, but it was a routine part of statutory company law until the Act 1989.

if the legislature and the courts thought it performed a public purpose. Directors wished to be rid of risk of personal liability; third parties contracting with the company wished to be rid of the risk of an ineffective transaction – or the ex-ante cost of employing lawyers to crawl over the company's constitutional documents; and even existing shareholders did not like it because it hindered the organic growth of the company.[39]

In this situation, companies set their lawyers to work on drafting a way out of the problems. Objects clauses became longer and longer as drafters tried to anticipate all the areas where the company might wish to operate in the future. Eventually, bold drafters began to add at the end of the list of objects sweeping up clauses such as the following: anything "incidental or conducive" to the achievement of the specified activities or even "any other trade or business whatever which in the opinion of the board of directors can be advantageously carried on by the company" in connection with the specified objects. When the courts accepted these formulations,[40] the *ultra vires* doctrine was effectively dead – except for the unprepared – though it took a couple more decades before the legislature removed from the Act the requirement to state objects and to override the *ultra vires* doctrine.[41]

What does this history tell us? First, as with the *raison d'être* statements, it shows that companies will use their lawyers' drafting skills to navigate around required statements which they regard as inconvenient, especially if significant sanctions are attached to non-compliance with the statement. *Prosperity* does not deal in any detail with the legal consequences of failure to abide by the purpose clause, though it is clear that significant consequences are envisaged (which may, however, stop short of transactional invalidity).[42] Second, it shows that, if the law leaves

[39] Initially, the objects clause could not be altered and so a new business outside the objects clause requires a new company and a new capital; later the objects clause became alterable but only by supermajority vote of the shareholders.

[40] *Bell Houses Ltd v City Wall Properties Ltd* [1966] 2 QB 656 (Court of Appeal of England and Wales).

[41] For a brief history of the objects clause requirement and the *ultra vires* doctrine see *Gower's Principles of Modern Company Law* (6th ed, 1997; P L Davies ed.) pp 202–6.

[42] *Prosperity* floats two enforcement mechanisms (p 159). These would restrain the company from acting in breach of its purpose statement (ex-ante injunctions) and require it to restore "detriments where damage has been done" (ex-post damages). However, it is not clear whose "detriments" would be covered, who would be liable (only the company or the company and its directors and large shareholders?) or the range of parties who would be empowered to sue (all those who suffer a detriment?).

the formulation of the purpose statement wholly to the company, the courts and regulators will be ill-equipped to respond effectively to limit the corporate drafters' efforts.

2.4 Reviewing the Company's Choice of Purpose

One possible reaction by the lawmaker to the above analysis would be to subject the company's decision to a review, either by a court or a regulator. The initial formulation of the corporate purpose would be left with the company, but that choice would be open to review by an external tribunal. Apart from the delicate question of who would be empowered to trigger the review, it is suggested that there is an unresolvable tension between effective review and the company's commercial freedom: it is possible to have one or the other, but not both.

Review, whether by a court or a regulator, could be cast in more than one form. The least constraining would be a review standard analogous to the business judgement rule: the reviewer would check only that the company had acted in good faith and, perhaps, on the basis of adequate investigation. It would be possible to build a role for non-shareholder groups into the process of purpose formulation through either an ex-ante consultation requirement or an ex-post complaints procedure (either to the company itself or the court/regulator). However, the formulation of the purpose would remain principally in the hands of the company, with no legislative specification of the types of purpose which would be regarded as appropriate. How far this type of review would move the purpose statements beyond those generated by the voluntary mechanism is open to debate. The risk of having to demonstrate good faith and, possibly, adequate investigation might deter companies from adopting wholly vacuous statements of purpose. However, if the tribunal remains loyal to its remit, the fact that it or indeed most businesses or outside observers would regard the statement as inadequate would not lead it to overturn the company's choice.

Moving beyond the business judgement standard would be some form of a "range of reasonable responses" standard. Here, the law would specify, or the court/regulator would develop, a substantive standard for determining whether the purposes adopted by the company met the legislative requirement for a purpose statement. Purely self-serving or vacuous statements would no longer cross the bar for acceptability. However, the company's initial choice would still benefit from a level of protection against adverse review: the company would not have to produce a statement which the court/regulator thought was the most appropriate or "best" for its business. Provided the company had adopted a purpose the court/regulator thought suited its circumstances, this review standard would be met, even if the court/regulator would have formulated a different purpose statement, had it been permitted to impose it on the company. On this review standard the company makes a constrained choice from among a number of possible purposes assessed as reasonable by the law or its agents.

The third possible approach is one where the reviewer is given full power to revise the company's purpose statement. The company's choice would pass review only if the court/regulator agreed that it was the best fit for the company's circumstances. The reviewer would revise it if the company's choice did not accord with the court/regulator's view of what was appropriate for the company. Depending on how the reviewer sought to exercise its powers, the company on this standard might be left with limited choice as to the purposes it should adopt.

The second and third forms of review identified above have the potential to shift corporate behaviour away from the patterns disclosed by voluntary purpose statements. The law in conjunction with the reviewing agency would have a substantial role in setting corporate purposes. Since the goals that *Prosperity* seeks to promote are public (communal or social), a public role in specifying those goals might be welcomed by many. However, there are obvious downsides. Regulators (and governments acting through them) are not always more long-sighted than businesspeople or markets.[43] Even if regulators do a good job, concentrating decisions centrally may well reduce the rate at which solutions to problems emerge, because competitive experimentation is removed. Courts are more decentralised decision-makers than regulators but are less expert and so less able to deal effectively with the more demanding review standards. They are likely to be either non-interventionist, if they recognise their lack of expertise, or arbitrary in their interventions, if they do not – or possibly both at different times or in different parts of the judicial system. In effect, rigorous review by state organs to determine the acceptability of corporate non-social goals would mean overturning the principle that underlay the first modern UK Companies Act, the Joint Stock Companies Act 1844, that incorporation

[43] Is there anybody more short-termist than a politician seeking re-election?

for the purpose of carrying on business should not require the approval by the state of those business goals.

In any event, it appears that government/court control of the setting and implementation of corporate purposes would run against the philosophy underlying *Prosperity*. This is a book which leaves companies firmly in the private sector of the economy. It is not a book which promotes the pursuit of public purposes through state ownership or control – the traditional, if now somewhat tarnished, formula in the UK for safeguarding the public interest. As the book says: "[purpose] is not a theory of socialism or mutualism or stakeholder capitalism. . . . It is about . . . the purpose of business as producing profitable solutions to problems of people and planet."[44] This is not a prescription for state control of private sector companies via the backdoor of setting corporate purposes. Therefore, it is suggested that the book's underlying approach is inconsistent with anything other than light review of the company's choice of purpose.

Outside *Prosperity*, Professor Mayer has argued, with others, for a mandatory rule which would require large US corporations to incorporate as PBCs.[45] This could be regarded as another mechanism for reviewing the company's choice of purpose, since the law will not recognise a company as a PBC unless its purposes meet the specified statutory standards. However, at least under the Delaware version of the PBC, the constraints on the shareholders' choice of purpose (or public benefit) via provisions in the company's charter are light. Although a Delaware PBC could choose a demanding set of public purposes, it is required to have only a single one and that purpose may seek to promote "effects of an artistic, charitable, cultural, economic, educational, environmental, literary, medical, religious, scientific or technological nature."[46] The purpose, therefore, need not meet the transformative standard set out in *Prosperity*: established donations policies such as support for the local orchestra or university would apparently qualify.[47] The Delaware PBC provisions are drafted along the lines of encouraging corporate social responsibility rather than necessarily a transformative

[44] *Prosperity* pp 11–12.

[45] C Mayer, L Strine and J Winter, "50 years later, Milton Friedman's shareholder doctrine is dead", *Fortune*, 13 September 2020.

[46] DGCL §362(b).

[47] For example, a commitment to devote a small proportion (one per cent) of its annual profits to an identified worthy cause.

corporate purpose (though the latter would count as an example of the former). Nor is any particular level of commitment to the public benefit specified in the statute. Rather, the duty of the directors is to conduct the affairs of the company in a way which "balances the pecuniary interests of the stockholders, the best interests of those materially affected by the corporation's conduct, and the specific public benefit or public benefits identified in its certificate of incorporation".[48] Moreover, the directors' balancing decision is not open to easy scrutiny. The public benefit statement does not create a duty on the directors to non-stockholders in respect of its implementation and the duty owed to the stockholders requires the directors' balancing decisions only to be informed and to be free of conflicts of interest, that is, the statute applies a rationality rather than reasonableness standard.[49] To discourage non-shareholders from shifting easily into the shareholder category in order to initiate a derivative action, obstacles are put in the way of derivative actions to enforce the balancing obligation, in addition to those normally applicable to a derivative action. The claimants must hold the lesser of 2 per cent of the company's outstanding stock or shares with a market value of $2 million dollars.[50] Finally, monitoring is required only via a two-yearly report to the shareholders; there is no requirement for more demanding mechanisms, for example, by including a third-party verification requirement, unless the company chooses to include them in its certificate of incorporation or bylaws.

While a duty to operate as a PBC would deprive the shareholders of the choice not to become a PBC or to end that status, it is far from clear that the shift would produce a meaningful change in companies which adopt PBC status only under compulsion, and whose shareholders regarded the status as a drag on the achievement of their goals. One can predict that the shareholders' choice of public benefit in such cases would be unconstraining and that directors would readily understand how shareholders wished them to strike the balance among the corporate objectives, their understanding possibly aided by the formulation of the criteria for pay-outs under their performance-related pay schemes. Given the width of the purposes which are permitted to count as public and the limited enforcement mechanisms for the public duty (essentially

[48] DGCL §365(a) – this duty thus puts as much emphasis on a stakeholder approach as on the promotion of the purpose.

[49] DGCL §365(b).

[50] DGCL §367.

disclosure),[51] it appears that mandatory incorporation as a PBC is not a rule which escapes the above analysis.

To sum up the argument so far. In a Friedmanite world (as defined above) a requirement to state the corporate purposes does little or nothing to address the shareholder "shackles" on companies. So long as these are in place, the purpose requirement will not come anywhere near achieving the goals set for it in *Prosperity*. The assumption underlying the purpose proposal appears to be that a requirement to state a purpose will unshackle the company from the shareholders, because it will in some undefined way override the governance rights of the shareholders. As we have shown above, this is not the case, unless the purpose requirement is implemented together with a level of state control over the company's choice of purposes which is at odds with the vision set out in *Prosperity.* This is not the end of the discussion, however. One possible way forward, discussed in the next section is to complicate the corporate law reforms beyond the introduction of a purpose requirement, so as to reduce the influence of the shareholders on the board.

2.5 Shielding the Board from the Shareholders

Let us remain in the Friedmanite world for the time being but complicate the proposed purpose reform with bolder corporate law changes. Here, the aim would be to shield the directors from adverse shareholder reaction if, in response to a duty laid upon them, they chose to adopt a set of purposes with which the shareholders disagreed. Where there is a controlling shareholder in place (or a controlling small group of large shareholders),[52] there is no point in embarking on this exercise. The views of the controllers will ultimately prevail and, if they are Friedmanites, they will not countenance the adoption of purpose statements by their companies. Formally, it would be possible no doubt to strip shareholders of all their levers of control and influence over the company. This might be an effective way of destroying controlling shareholders as a class of investor: neither financial nor non-financial private benefits of control would be likely to survive the reform. However, the economic dislocation caused by this reform to an economy

[51] There are more constraining versions of PBC in some other states, but presumably unwilling corporations will choose the least constraining.

[52] Which is, worldwide, the dominant form of shareholding: A De La Cruz, A Medina and Y Tang, *Owners of the World's Listed Companies*, OECD Capital Market Series (2019).

built on financing corporate activity through controlling shareholders is likely to be huge. And controlling shareholders may be well-placed politically to resist the move.

However, it will be no easier to implement this reform today in dispersed shareholding jurisdictions, such as the US and the UK. The main targets of such reforms would be to reduce the impact of at least five powers which shareholders normally possess: (a) to appoint and remove directors; (b) to instruct the board how to act; (c) to convene meetings of the company; (d) to transfer their shares when a tender offer is made to them; and (e) to set profit-related pay. The aim would have to be to go beyond the "zone of isolation" envisaged by Professors Kershaw and Schuster.[53] Their goal might be said to be to preserve the capacity for directors to take actions which will pay off for the shareholders in due course but which the shareholders are not well-placed to evaluate accurately, that is, to reduce what are sometimes termed "principal costs".[54] Here, by contrast, the directors would have to be shielded from shareholder reaction when, on the hypothesis we are considering, the directors aim to run the company on a continuing basis in a way which hinders the achievement of the shareholders' goals in relation to their investment. This is a tall order indeed.

It might be said that a shielding strategy would need to aim to do no more than reproduce today a system of corporate governance which was not wholly unlike the one which in fact prevailed in the UK in the 1950s or until more recently in the US. But that is to indicate the nub of the difficulty. The move from dispersed and rationally apathetic investors to semi-concentrated shareholdings in the hands of institutional shareholders has created a politically influential set of incumbents with a strong interest in maintaining the present level of shareholder governance rights. Their opposition to the shielding strategy can be assumed but not their failure to defend it. Let us look briefly at the US and the UK in turn.

Until the end of the last century, the shareholders' position in the US was not totally removed from the position the shielding policy would put them in. This was the result mainly of private ordering via the company's constitution, in which the shareholders had acquiesced, though in the case of instructions to the board the SEC's proxy rules protected the

[53] Above n 7.

[54] Z Goshen and R Squires, "Principal Costs: A New Theory for Corporate Law and Governance" (2017) 117 *Columbia Law Review* 767.

board's managerial functions from intrusive shareholder intervention. For the rest, it was largely a matter of constitutional provisions on staggered boards, plurality voting and director control of the proxy machinery; confining the power of convening shareholder meetings other than the annual meeting to the board; and the board's power to adopt a poison pill in the face of an undesirable takeover.[55]

Although some may regret it,[56] this is not a division of powers between board and shareholders which any longer obtains. More than a decade ago Professors Kahan and Rock charted the decline of the system which protected the "imperial CEO" from shareholder influence.[57] As these authors put it, for the staggered board "the day is not far off when staggered boards will be the rare exception"[58] among the largest companies, with a consequential reduction in the effectiveness of the poison pill.[59] There had been a "meteoric rise" in the replacement of plurality

[55] Delaware corporate law deals with most of these issues via default rules, some of which are set in favour of the board and others in favour of the shareholders, but even the shareholder-friendly defaults may be changed if the shareholders acquiesce. Thus, §216 (3) DGCL sets plurality voting as the default, but that is alterable by the certificate of incorporation or the bylaws; the same is true of the power to convene an extraordinary meeting of the shareholders which §211(a)(2)(d) confines as a default to the board. On the other hand, annual election of directors is the default under §211(b) but §141 (d) provides for a shareholder choice of a staggered board. §141(k) provides an apparently mandatory rule that a simple majority of the shareholders may remove directors at any time, but the certificate of incorporation may require a supermajority for this action and until the clarification given in *Frechter v Zier* 2017 WL 345142 (Del. Ch. Jan. 24, 2017), it was thought the supermajority rule could be placed in the bylaws. The point here is that the company's certification of incorporation may, and usually does, give the board the power to amend bylaws without reference to the shareholders (§109(a)). The poison pill may be adopted unilaterally by the board under §157 unless, as is unusual, its powers over the issuance of options is restricted in the certificate of incorporation.

[56] For example, S Bainbridge, above n 7.

[57] M Kahan and E Rock, "The Embattled CEO" (2009–10) 88 *Texas Law Review* 987. This article also charts the greater control exercised over CEOs by boards, but I leave this part of their analysis on one side. On the issue of whether the poison pill is undergoing a revival as a tool against activist hedge funds, see J Gordon, "The Rejected Threat of Corporate Vote Suppression: The Rise and Fall of the Anti-Activist Pill" [2022] *Columbia Business Law Review* 206 and O Eldar, T Kirmsc and M Wittry, *The Rise of Anti-Activist Poison Pills*, available at https://ssrn.com/abstract=4198367.

[58] Kahan and Rock, above n 57 p 1008.

[59] In addition, it has been argued that incentive-based remuneration systems for directors and managers have been re-designed to give them an inventive not to block takeovers that are value maximising from the shareholders' point of view. The poison pill might thus have some impact on the distribution of gains from takeovers as between officers and shareholders, but not the incidence of takeovers. See M Kahan and E Rock, "How I Learned to Stop Worrying and Love the Pill: Adaptive Responses to Takeover Law"

voting by majority voting among S&P companies.[60] Finally, precatory resolutions adopted by shareholders, long thought to be ineffective, were increasingly implemented by companies.[61] Kahan and Rock put these changes down to the substantial re-concentration of shareholdings in the largest US companies from a multitude of individuals into the hands of a smaller number of institutional shareholders, notably public pension funds, mutual funds and hedge funds.[62] All have incentives, varying in strength and character from one type of institution to another, to exercise their governance powers so as to reverse the exclusionary constitutional rules in which they had previously acquiesced. These efforts were aided by some modest reforms by the SEC of the proxy rules, notably the one removing the need to file an (expensive) proxy statement where a shareholder wished to solicit votes on a resolution proposed by the company, an important step in a world of annual, majority voting on directors.[63]

There is little or nothing in subsequent developments which undermines Kahan and Rock's conclusion that "it is much more likely that CEOs, in the intermediate term (over the next ten years or so), will lose more power than that they will regain some of the power they have lost".[64] Of course, it would be possible formally to embody in corporate law or securities regulation rules which aimed to restore the protections US directors and officers had towards the end of the last century. However, given that these matters have been regarded by the public authorities in the US as ones appropriate for ordering primarily via the company's constitution, it would take considerable political pressure

(2002) 69 *University of Chicago Law Review* 871; J Gordon, "An American Perspective on Anti-takeover Laws in the EU" in G Ferrarini et al (eds), *Reforming Company and Takeover Law in Europe*, 2004, ch 9C.

60 Kahan and Rock, above n 57 p 1010. 61 Ibid p 1012. 62 Ibid §III.

63 Ibid §V. This helped shareholders seeking to deny re-election to an incumbent director – though not course shareholders seeking to put their own nominees on the board unless they could get their nominee onto the company's proxy statement. The shareholder friendliness of the SEC proxy rules tends to vary with the political composition of the US government. Although Kahan and Rock do not make this claim, it is likely that the SEC itself was responding to the desire of institutional shareholders to be increasingly influential in the world of corporate governance.

64 The principal example might be thought to be the rise of dual-class shares, but these are a mechanism for investing control, positive or negative, in a subset of shareholders, typically a visionary entrepreneur, rather than a mechanism for protecting corporate management against the shareholders as a whole. If the holder of the majority of the votes inhabits a Friedmanite world, as is assumed at this stage, then the analysis in Section 2.2 is undisturbed.

from directors and managers both to alter that commitment to private ordering and to introduce in its place corporate law rules that mandated the constitutional provisions which resulted from private ordering before the rise of the institutions. Above all, there would be fierce counter-lobbying from those institutions which perceived themselves as having benefitted from the new arrangements. Even Professor Bainbridge accepts that "in the near term, rolling back the gains made by shareholder activists and their academic proponents may not be politically viable"[65] and he confines himself to arguing against any further relaxations in favour of such shareholders.

The story in the UK is similar: from the (rational) apathy of dispersed shareholders to partial re-concentration of shareholdings in hands of institutions, initially pension funds and insurance companies, more recently mutual funds. There are two contrasts with the US experience. First, the process of re-concentration got under way some two to three decades earlier in the UK, probably because the incentives among moderately well-off people to save for retirement through institutional intermediaries, rather than through direct holdings, became strong somewhat earlier in the UK than the US.[66] Second, the story of dispersed shareholder apathy played out in the UK against not a background of managerial-inspired restrictions in the company's constitution on shareholder activism, but a background of strong positive shareholder governance rights in the companies legislation. Notable was the right, introduced in the Companies Act 1948, of a simple majority of the shareholders to remove at any time and for any reason any director of the company "notwithstanding anything in [the company's] articles or in any agreement between it and him".[67] In addition, since the theory of UK company law was, and still is, that the board's management powers

[65] Above n 7, p 247.

[66] P Davies, "Institutional Investors in the United Kingdom" in Baums, Buxbaum and Hopt (eds), *Institutional Investors and Corporate Governance*, 1994, ch 9.

[67] This provision was introduced into the Companies Act as a result of a recommendation made by a governmental committee at the end of the Second World War (*Report of the Committee on Company Law Amendment*, Cmd 6659, 1945). Surprisingly, the Committee put forward no rationale for its proposal other than that "it seems to us desirable to give shareholders greater powers to remove directors with whom they are dissatisfied than they have at present" (para 130). However, it seems likely they were reacting to a change in the judicial interpretation of the articles which occurred earlier in the century. Under this change, where the articles conferred management powers on the board, as would normally be the case, a shareholders' resolution could give the board instructions as to how to exercise those powers only if it was supported by a majority

derive from the articles of association, not the law, UK company law never had any doctrinal difficulty with shareholder resolutions which gave the board binding instructions about how to act within their managerial realm, provided the resolution had supermajority shareholder support.[68] Finally, the law has long provided that 10 per cent (today reduced to five per cent) of the shareholders may convene a meeting, whether the board wishes one or not, and five per cent may add a resolution to a meeting convened by the company.

The strategy of shielding management in the UK thus could not rely on changes to the company's articles, for these would normally be ineffective to override the shareholders' statutory rights. Instead, in the past, management had to rely principally on the high coordination costs which faced dispersed shareholders seeking to exercise those rights. Even five per cent was a high barrier for dispersed shareholders of a publicly traded company to cross. However, with the rise of the institutions these coordination costs were substantially reduced (though not eliminated). Relatively small coalitions of institutional shareholders could now access these long-standing governance rights and increasingly sought to do so.[69] Moreover, institutional shareholders now have sufficient influence to change both corporate practices and regulatory rules in their favour. The primary example of the former is the institutional investors' long-standing opposition to non-voting or weighted-voting shares, which have never been prohibited by the companies' legislation and were only recently banned by the listing rules, but which disappeared from corporate practice long ago when it became clear that the institutions would not buy such shares. The primary example of institutional investors' influence over regulatory rules is the presence of the mandatory "no frustration" rule at the heart of the UK takeover rules.[70]

equivalent to that needed to change the articles, ie three quarters of those present and voting. In the nineteenth century a simple majority was considered to be enough.

68 See previous note. The threat of the exercise of the removal power, requiring only a simple majority, reduced the need for shareholders to rely on the instruction power.

69 G Stapledon, *Institutional Shareholders and Corporate Governance* (1996), Part II.

70 On both these examples see P Davies, "Shareholders in the UK" in Hill and Thomas (eds), above n 7, ch 11; on the latter see P Davies, "Defensive Measures: The Regulation of Defensive Measures in the United Kingdom and the United States" in Hopt and Wymeersch (eds), *European Takeovers: Law and Practice*, 1992, ch 7 and J Armour and D Skeel, "Who Writes the Rules for Hostile Takeovers and Why?" (2007) 95 *Georgetown Law Journal* 1727.

As in the US, a rolling back of shareholder rights to the extent necessary to implement a shielding strategy is probably politically infeasible in the UK, which is not to say that some re-balancing of relations between shareholders and the board is not within the realm of practical contemplation.[71] A comprehensive rolling-back would entail a fundamental re-think of long-standing elements of UK company law which would generate strong opposition from those, in particular the institutional shareholders, who promoted them. Despite the limited setback for the domestic institutional shareholders entailed in the recent reform of the Listing Rules so as to implement a cautious acceptance of dual-class shares,[72] it is difficult to see them failing successfully to oppose a full-scale roll-back of their rights. In addition, the shielding strategy is inconsistent with the policy of "engagement" for institutional shareholders with their investee companies which has been heavily promoted by official bodies over the past decade.[73] The "stewardship" idea, however that term is defined, relies upon shareholders possessing significant governance rights over the company, though not necessarily the full suite which they currently possess in the UK.

Thus, neither in the US nor the UK is a comprehensive shielding strategy likely to be politically feasible. Nor is it obviously economically desirable. Shielded management may also be slack management. True, the shielding strategy is to be part of a larger set of reforms requiring company boards to adopt purpose statements. A tightly formulated and rigorously enforced purpose statement would reduce managerial slack in all probability, but corporate management is not likely to be any more favourable to such constraining statements than corporate shareholders. This would put the legislature back in the difficulty we analysed at the end of Section 2.3: either the legislature accepts weak, board-designed purpose statements or it engages in court or regulatory review and enforcement of those statements with the consequent reduction in the scope for private sector initiatives.

[71] See the proposals of Kershaw and Schuster, above n 7.

[72] E Lidman and R Skog, *London Allowing Dual Class Premium Listings: A Swedish Commentary*, ECGI Law Working Paper 580/2021, available at ssrn.com/abstract_id=3826174. All the recent reform did was to put the institutions back in the position they had been before 2014, ie reliant on their market power to regulate public companies' use of dual-class shares.

[73] P Davies, *The UK Stewardship Code 2010–2020: From Saving the Company to Saving the Planet?* ECGI Law Working Paper 506/2020, also available in D Katelouzou and D Puchniak (eds), *Global Shareholder Stewardship* (2022).

2.6 Shareholders in a Non-Friedmanite World

In this section, we relax the assumption that shareholders are stuck in a Friedmanite world or, perhaps better, in what convention understands to be the characteristics of that world. We analyse two forms of relaxation. The first, the more modest, is one in which investors hold to profit maximisation but take a more sophisticated and long-term view of the mechanisms through which profit is likely to be maximised. For example, they do not regard the quarterly earnings statement as the sole indicator of how well the company is doing to maximise the financial returns to the shareholders. The second relaxation is where shareholders are prepared to trade-off financial and non-financial goals, that is, profit maximisation no longer constitutes a full specification of the returns investors seek.

2.6.1 Sophisticated Profit Maximisation

Whether this form of shareholder action constitutes a significant shift from how Friedman contemplated shareholders would behave can certainly be debated. In the very article from which his famous quotation is drawn, he stated: "it may well be in the long-run interest of a corporation that is a major employer in a small community to devote resources to providing amenities to that community or to improving its government. That may make it easier to attract desirable employees, it may reduce the wage bill or lessen losses from pilferage and sabotage or have other worthwhile effects".[74] This is sophisticated profit maximisation at the firm level, sometimes referred to as "doing well by doing good". However, in terms of the goals of *Prosperity*, it probably does not need much analysis. The focus of the shareholders is still on the maximisation of their financial returns, even if they no longer adhere to a Gradgrind approach as how best to achieve their goal. Social and communal goals still have no place in their own right. And one might also think that existing corporate governance mechanisms should ensure, at least over time, that sophisticated profit maximisation is adopted at the firm level, if it is in fact an effective method of increasing profitability.

In terms of ESG investing, discussed further below, there is some evidence that sophisticated profit maximisation does drive institutional shareholder interventions at firm level and that such interventions have

[74] Above n 4.

some degree of success. A recent study by Professor Bauer and colleagues concentrated on non-public ESG-focussed engagements with investee companies carried out by an asset manager, both on behalf of itself and other funds, over the period 2007–2020.[75] Some of these engagements were on matters financially relevant to the company and some not.[76] The study found that three-quarters of the engagements were financially relevant and that material engagements were more likely to be successful (i.e. produce some appropriate response from the company) than non-material ones (suggesting that companies were more open to engagements which were financially relevant). After engagement, targeted companies' share price outperformed their peers, but this outperformance was particularly noticeable in relation to successful governance engagements. Engagements in the environmental and, especially, in the social categories had less impact of the performance of the stock.[77] Overall, these results suggest that the market attaches a higher value to the G element of ESG than to its other two elements and that this is so because they have the greater potential to improve the company's profitability.[78] *Prosperity* is right to conclude that sophisticated profit

[75] R Bauer, J Derwall and C Tissen, "Private Shareholder Engagements on Material ESG Issues" (forthcoming) *Financial Analysts Journal*, available at ssrn.com/abstract=4171496. See also P Krueger, Z Sautner and L Starks, *The Importance of Climate Risks for Institutional Investors*, ECGI Finance Working Paper 610/2019, showing significant institutional shareholder engagement with portfolio companies on climate change matters where climate change was thought to create risks of direct costs to the companies, of costs of dealing with climate change regulation, and of climate change-inspired technological changes which would undermine existing business models. Equally, climate change might open opportunities for new investments.

[76] How this categorisation was made is discussed in §2 of the paper. Reliance on the MSCI materiality framework suggests "financially relevant" equated with the impact of ESG factors on the company, not the impact of the company on the wider community.

[77] For literature supporting the importance of governance initiatives for financial performance see R Kräussl, T Oladiran and D Stefanova, *A Review on ESG Investing: Investors' Expectations, Beliefs and Perceptions*, Centre for Financial Studies Working Paper 694/2023 at 11 (available at ssrn.com/abstract=4123999), but contrast E Pollman, *The Making and Meaning of ESG*, ECGI Law Working Paper 659/2022 on the indeterminacy of the ESG term and, in consequence, the difficulties of measuring the impact of ESG investing accurately.

[78] Even non-G interventions might be financially relevant to a company in particular circumstances. For example, a company might announce a decision no longer to admit into its supply chain businesses which made use of child labour, provided that the benefits of a positive consumer reaction to this announcement exceeded the costs of finding alternative suppliers.

maximisation has limited potential to move companies towards social or communal purposes.[79]

However, an interesting recent discussion has emerged about the potential for sophisticated profit maximisation to generate at the level of an investment portfolio a trade-off between individual firm performance and overall returns to the portfolio. Professors Gordon and Coffee have developed, separately, a theory under which widely invested funds would have a financial incentive to pursue communal and social objectives at the portfolio level.[80] On this theory, a widely invested fund has succeeded in diversifying away idiosyncratic risk but is still exposed to systemic risk, that is, risks which affect the economy as a whole. Gordon focusses on three systemic risks in particular: climate change, financial crises and social disorder, the last possibly arising out of the first two risks but also arising independently out of the unequal distribution of gains and losses from globalisation. His theory is that such funds have an incentive to support actions by portfolio companies to mitigate these risks, even at the cost of reducing the financial returns to the companies taking this action. This would be the case if the actions reduced the systemic risks to the portfolio as a whole so that the risk/return ratio of the fund was improved by these actions, to the financial benefit of those invested in the fund. It would clearly be a matter of (complex) calculation in particular cases whether the costs of actions in terms of reduced returns at the individual company level exceeded their benefits at the portfolio level.

The above analysis suggests a way in which diversified and widely invested funds should approach the question of supporting or opposing firm-level initiatives aimed at reducing the identified systemic risks. It is not an analysis of how such funds do in fact conduct themselves at the moment, though the authors indicate some evidence pointing in this direction. Roberto Tallarita, however, has argued that the incentives for fund managers to act in this way are weaker than these authors suggest, though he considers only one of the risks, climate change, which Gordon analyses.[81] This is for two principal reasons. First, he argues that the

[79] *Prosperity* p 6.

[80] J Gordon, *Systematic Stewardship*, ECGI Law Working Paper 566/2021 (available at ssrn.com/abstract_id=3782814); J Coffee, "The Coming Shift in Shareholder Activism: From 'Firm-Specific' to 'Systematic Risk' Proxy Campaigns (and How to Enable Them)" (2021) 16 *Brooklyn Journal of Corporate, Financial and Commercial Law* 45.

[81] R Tallarita, "The Limits of Portfolio Primacy" (2023) 76 *Vanderbilt Law Review*, also available at ssrn.com/abstract=3912977. See also R Tallarita, "Fiduciary Deadlock" (2023)

market discounts the future benefits of climate change initiatives at a higher rate than most experts and governmental bodies think appropriate. Consequently, funds following market signals will invest less than is appropriate in climate change mitigation if the risk-reduction objective is to be realised. Second, he points out that many funds, while certainly diversified, do not hold (a proportion of) the whole economy, especially if the economy is defined in global terms. For example, many funds regarded as very widely invested are overweight in the developed world, which is likely to suffer relatively less from climate change than other parts of the world. Again, the consequence is an under-investment in (global) climate change mitigation, although arguably this is an appropriate level of investment for the particular fund.

The thrust of Tallarita's article is that it would be a mistake to rely heavily on market-driven corporate action to address climate change and he advocates instead a central role for external regulation. The conclusion must be that the prospects for portfolio-level policies of "doing well by doing good" to address effectively major social issues are uncertain. One indicator of the tensions at play is the recent rowing back by BlackRock from its famous CEO and client letters of 2020.[82] To the extent that these letters called for more than greater non-financial disclosure by investee companies, they can be seen as a call for the implementation of a portfolio level strategy of the type Professor Gordon contemplates. The 2020 CEO letter concluded as follows: "Companies must be deliberate and committed to embracing purpose and serving all stakeholders – your shareholders, customers, employees, and the communities where you operate. In doing so, your company will enjoy greater long-term prosperity, as will investors, workers, and society as a whole." However, it was reported that in the 2022 annual reporting season BlackRock's support for shareholder resolutions on environmental and social topics fell significantly. A spokesman for the fund manager explained that "Many climate-related shareholder proposals sought to dictate the pace of companies' energy transition plans with little regard to the disruption caused to their financial performance, given continued demand from consumers.

171 *University of Pennsylvania Law Review Online* 1, available at ssrn.com/abstract=4197225.

[82] Available at www.blackrock.com/corporate/investor-relations/2020-larry-fink-ceo-letter and www.blackrock.com/corporate/investor-relations/2020-blackrock-client-letter#:~:text=As%20Larry%20Fink%20writes%20in,and%20assets%20around%20the%20world.

Others failed to recognise the progress made".[83] The trade-off between short-term financial costs at individual company level and long-term portfolio benefits is clearly one which even the largest and most sophisticated fund managers find it difficult to assess consistently.

2.6.2 *Trading Off Maximum Financial Performance for Social or Communal Gains*

In this section we consider shareholders and investors who do not hold to the Friedmanite policy of profit maximisation. Certainly, they invest for a financial return – often they are investing for an income in retirement – but they are prepared to forego a portion of that return (it being unclear exactly how much) in return for the achievement of non-financial objectives (it being unclear what level of non-financial achievement or which type of achievement they will accept as compensation of the lower financial return). Such investors seem to be ideal candidates to support the purpose objectives which *Prosperity* advocates. But do such investors exist and are their incentives strong enough to bring about the adoption of social and communal goals by companies? If they do, then radical changes to current governance structures are hardly necessary since these are designed to reflect the shareholders' choices.

The argument that non-Friedmanite investors are already a significant force among investors and are about to become stronger has been put forward by Professor Ringe in terms of both demand and supply.[84] The demand, in his view, comes from the goals of the generation of investors entering or about to enter the investment market. This generation can be seen as having built up wealth earlier in their careers and now being poised to invest it for their future well-being. Possibly more important, they can be seen as likely soon to be the beneficiaries of substantial wealth which they have not themselves earned, that is, the wealth accumulated

[83] "BlackRock pulls back support for climate and social resolutions", *Financial Times*, 31 July 2022.

[84] Wolf-Georg Ringe, *Investor-led Sustainability in Corporate Governance*, (2022) 7 Annals of Corporate Governance 93. Cf S Haber et al, *ESG Investing: What Shareholders Do Fund Managers Represent?* available at ssrn.com/abstract=4267270, and S Hirst et al, *How Much do Investors Care about Social Responsibility?* ECGI Law Working Paper 674/2023 – both emphasising the diversity of attitudes towards ESG investing (including opposition) across the investor community.

by the parents during the Great Financial Moderation.[85] In either case, the argument is that their goals as investors depart from the Friedmanite model precisely because they define their aims in terms of a combination of financial return and social or communal goals.

No strong theory seems to have been advanced to explain the underlying drivers of this broadening of investment goals. It may be that the new generation of investors, used to a life of relative financial ease, are ready to admit non-financial goals into their investment strategies. Or it may be that a younger generation is more impressed by specific threats to their future well-being, such as climate change, than current investors with shorter time-horizons. However that may be, asset managers have a clear incentive to meet this demand by designing funds with the relevant characteristics. ESG funds usually involve an element of selection and thus command higher fees than passive non-ESG funds; even more so if the fund claims to produce a measurable impact on society. Apart from this, asset managers need to keep up with the predicted shift in investor goals for fear of losing out to competitors who do so. Hence, the extensive offerings of ESG funds which are now on the market.

Some scholars are not convinced by the supply and demand analysis based on new investor goals. Professor Schwartz has provided a political explanation for the growth of ESG investing, namely the incentive of funds to ward off regulation by showing commitment to ESG incentives.[86] Whilst it is the case that in some countries there is governmental pressure in this direction on asset managers,[87] the enthusiasm with which the asset management industry has embraced ESG funds is difficult to explain wholly on a political argument.[88] Kasey Wang has provided a more comprehensive historical account of mutual funds' ESG

[85] M Barzuza, Q Curtis and D Webber, "Shareholder Value(s): Index Fund ESG Activism and the New Millennial Corporate Governance" (2020) 93 *Southern California Law Review* 1243.

[86] J Schwartz, "Stewardship Theatre" (2022) 100 *Washington University Law Review* (forthcoming); "'Public' Mutual Funds" in A Laby (ed), *Cambridge Handbook on Investor Protection* (2022) (also available at papers.ssrn.com/sol3/papers.cfm?abstract_id=3821388).

[87] For example, the UK Stewardship Code (see Davies, n 73).

[88] As Professor Schwartz himself acknowledges in the *Cambridge Handbook* chapter (n 86 at p 32), some governmental agencies have expressed reservations about funds' commitment to ESG in relation to their fiduciary duties to end investors. See "BlackRock labels Texas 'anti-competitive' over ESG blacklisting', *Financial Times*, 25 August 2022.

activism, suggesting that funds have always responded to the goals of those important to them.[89] Thus, initially, ESG investing was confined to funds whose investors were limited to those with strong ethical concerns (often faith based). Later, ESG concerns spread to funds managed by public or trade union officials who needed to appeal to a public electorate to secure their continuance in office. Finally, ESG investing became important for at least a subset of general investors.

However, for the purposes of this chapter it is not enough to identify an increasing flow of funds into ESG vehicles. We need to assess the capacity of ESG investment to move companies in the direction of meaningful purpose statements. This turns, in part, on the methodologies which are used to implement ESG investing. For example, ESG investing which takes the form of excluding certain categories of investment opportunities from a portfolio are likely to have limited impact on moving companies towards the adoption of broad corporate purposes.[90] Even positive ESG strategies may not involve engagement with investee companies, especially if they are based on investment in an ESG index, though such funds may influence managerial policy indirectly, for example, through management's desire to maintain or improve the company's position in the index. It is now well established that both passive and active fund managers face disincentives in relation to the supply of engagement services to investors. Passive funds compete on cost, while engagement is expensive. Active funds are better resourced but find it virtually impossible to exclude competitors from the benefits of successful engagement.[91] However, in relation to low-cost forms of engagement, such as voting on propositions put up by others, the costs of engagement are not significant, especially where those costs can be

[89] K Wang, "Why Institutional Investors Support ESG Issues" (2021) *University of California Davis Business Law Journal* 129. This analysis is not inconsistent with the argument that political factors identified by Professor Schwartz have been important, but it does not attach primary importance to them.

[90] P Brest, R Gilson and M Wolfson, "How Investors Can (and Can't) Create Social Value" (2018) 44 *Journal of Corporation Law* 205. And see G Strampelli, "Can BlackRock Save the Planet? The Institutional Investors' role in Stakeholder Capitalism" (2021) 11 *Harvard Business Law Review* 1 on the costs faced by even negatively focussed index funds. This is not to say, however, that disinvestment strategies have no impact on the targeted companies. See M Becht, A Pajuste and A Toniolo, *Voice through Disinvestment*, ECGI Finance Working Paper 900/2023.

[91] L Bebchuk and S Hirst, "Index Funds and the Future of Corporate Governance: Theory, Evidence, and Policy" (2019) 119 *Columbia L R* 202.

spread over a number of funds.[92] Thus, the crucial question becomes whether there are entities with sufficiently strong incentives to incur the costs of designing and promoting ESG resolutions which other shareholders can then consider whether to support. In the area of non-ESG resolutions, scholarship attributes that role to activist hedge funds,[93] but their concerns focus on traditional operational and financial improvements to investee companies. The issue is whether there exist similar activists in the ESG space.

Much useful information about ESG activism has recently been provided by Roberto Tallarita.[94] Studying 2900 ESG proposals made in the United States between 2010 and 2021, he finds that a mere 25 organisations were responsible for submitting half of them and that a quarter of them were submitted by only four organisations.[95] These four were, in declining order of submissions, two public pension schemes (New York City Retirement Schemes and New York State Common Retirement Fund), one conservative think tank (the National Center for Public Policy Research and thus not an asset manager by principal focus[96]) and one a socially responsible asset manager (Trillium Asset Management[97]). Thus, of the four leading submitters, only one was an ESG asset manager, two were public pension funds which have been active traditionally in the submission area,[98] and one was a conservative

[92] E Rock and M Kahan, "Index Funds and Corporate Governance: Let Shareholders be Shareholders" (2020) 100 *Boston University Law Review* 1771; R Gilson and J Gordon, "The Agency Costs of Agency Capitalism: Activist Investors and the Revaluation of Governance Rights" (2013) 113 *Columbia Law Review* 863. For collaborative mechanisms to overcome the costs of intervention see P Mülbert and A Sajnovits, *Emerging ESG-Driven Models of Shareholder Collaborative Engagement*, ECGI Law Working Paper 668/2022.

[93] R Gilson and J Gordon, previous note.

[94] R Tallarita, "Stockholder Politics" (2022) 73 *Hastings Law Journal* 1617.

[95] Ibid, Table 9.

[96] Its website describes itself in the following terms: "*The National Center for Public Policy Research* is a communications and research foundation supportive of a strong national defence and dedicated to providing free market solutions to today's public policy problems. We believe that the principles of a free market, individual liberty and personal responsibility provide the greatest hope for meeting the challenges facing America in the 21st century." Presumably it buys shares in companies it wishes to influence purely for the purpose of exercising this influence.

[97] Described thus on its website: "*Trillium Asset Management* offers investment strategies and services that advance humankind towards a global sustainable economy, a just society, and a better world."

[98] See Wang, above, n 89.

think-tank which, one may guess, was opposed to ESG measures being taken by companies unless they were likely to improve profitability.

Besides identifying the "matchmakers", that is, those who put forward activist resolutions for consideration by ESG shareholders, Tallarita has interesting data on the substantive content of the resolutions and their success rate. Surprisingly for a non-US observer, 31 per cent of the submissions concerned political spending and lobbying and other political issues.[99] On this issue, the US is something of an outlier, for corporate political expenditures (not necessarily including lobbying) are often regulated by law in other countries,[100] whereas in the US the already limited legislative constraints on political expenditures have been weakened in recent years by the Supreme Court.[101] By contrast, 11.4 per cent of submissions related to climate change issues, 12.5 per cent to "sex, gender and race" – presumably often board composition matters; and 7.6 per cent to human rights. No other specific category of issues exceeded 3 per cent of the total.[102]

These percentages relate to the substantive content of shareholder resolutions over the 11-year period as a whole. It is possible that the substantive composition of the resolutions varied over time. For example, it might be that the political resolutions were over-represented at the beginning of the period (ie shortly after the *Citizens United* decision[103]) while climate change resolutions became more prominent towards the end of the period. There is some evidence of this from the article by Barzuza and colleagues.[104] Their focus is not on how resolutions are placed before the shareholders but on the level of support the "Big Three" asset managers give to the resolutions that are advanced by others. They rely on the ESG policy statements put out by and the voting records of

[99] Tallarita, above n 94, Table 3.

[100] See, for example, the Companies Act 2006 (UK), Part 14, requiring shareholder approval for corporate political donations and expenditure. The impact of requiring shareholder approval has been largely to shut off corporate political contributions (though not, of course, contributions by particular wealthy entrepreneurs or corporate lobbying).

[101] Notably in *Citizens United v Federal Election Commission* 558 US 310 (2010).

[102] "Other" environmental issues accounted for 5 per cent and "other" social issues for 8 per cent.

[103] Above n 101.

[104] Above n 85. See also M Gatti, G Strampelli and M Tonello, *How Does Board-Shareholder Engagement Really Work?*, in this book, at 20, reporting on non-public engagements to the effect that executive compensation, climate change and board diversity were the most common topics of engagement and that "the category of strategic issues . . . did not gather much attention".

these managers towards the end of the previous decade. They identify a strong move by these asset managers from 2017 onwards towards supporting two principal categories of shareholder resolutions, namely, those dealing with board diversity and those dealing with climate change. This may also help to explain Tallarita's finding of an increased success rate for shareholder resolutions over the period he studied. At the beginning of the period, only 1 per cent were approved by a majority whereas by 2021 the figure was 19 per cent. If withdrawn proposals are added in, on the basis that withdrawal indicates some level of acceptance of the resolution by the company, then the success rate in 2021 climbs to 40 per cent.[105] Equally, the overall support rate for resolutions voted on increased from 18 per cent at the beginning of the period to 35.4 per cent at the end.

It is clear that, at least in the United States, ESG activism is an established feature of shareholder activity. The question for this chapter is whether it has the potential to push companies towards the adoption of broad social and communal purposes, as envisaged in *Prosperity*. To date, the range of issues encompassed by ESG activism in the US has been limited, principally to diversity and climate change issues, with some degree of support for human rights issues. Even on climate change, Barzuza and colleagues analyse the concerns of the Big Three as driven by the impact of climate change on the company rather than the company's contribution to climate change.[106] Outside the Big Three, recent evidence suggests that institutional investors focus disproportionately on the governance element of ESG, to the detriment of the environmental and social elements, perhaps because governance is more closely related to financial returns than the other elements.[107]

The question thus has to be about the *potential* of ESG activism to move companies beyond individual topics in the direction of the broad communal and social goals advocated by *Prosperity*. Whilst not amounting to a purpose statement in form, shareholder resolutions on a sufficient range of ESG matters and formulated in a sufficiently

[105] Above n 94, Figure 2.

[106] Above n 85 at 1275. The impact on the company includes the impact of complying with regulation aimed at reducing the rate of climate change and not just the direct impact of climate change on the company's operations.

[107] F de Silanes, J McCahery and P Pudschedl, *Institutional Investors and ESG Preferences*, ECGI Law Working Paper 631/2022; S Gomtsian, "Different Visions of Stewardship: Understanding Interactions between Large Investment Managers and Activist Shareholders" (2022) 22 *Journal of Corporate Law Studies* 151.

constraining manner could operate functionally in a similar way. At this stage of the development of ESG activism, the answer to the question of whether this potential will be realised must remain open.

2.6.3 Shareholder Commitment without a Mandatory Purpose Requirement

If, however, investors' goals were to develop strongly in the direction of preferring companies which have committed themselves to communal or social goals, then the mechanisms of shareholder voice would operate to the benefit of the incorporation of these goals into the company's strategic choices, with or without an explicit purpose requirement in the law. In this situation, far from freeing the company from the shackles of its shareholders, the appropriate policy would be to maintain shareholder influence over the management of the company and, in particular, over the setting of its purposes. However, outside *Prosperity*, Professor Mayer has argued that a mandatory purpose provision still has a role to play in this situation, namely, to override a restriction which he finds in the current British companies legislation on the range of purposes a company is permitted to adopt. Referring in particular (again) to section 172 of the Companies Act 2006 (UK) he states: "At present, the law does not permit of commitment to objectives beyond the pursuit of the success of the company for the benefit of its members and it thereby fails to protect companies which seek to create long-term prosperity through committing to the interests of others."[108] This is not correct. In fact, section 172(2) explicitly recognises that the purposes of the company, as adopted by the shareholders, might be or include purposes which are not for the benefit of the members. In such a case, the sub-section provides that: "Where or to the extent that the purposes of the company consist of or include purposes other than the benefit of its members, subsection (1) has effect as if the reference to promoting the success of the company for the benefit of its members were to achieving those purposes."[109]

[108] C Mayer, above n 15, Abstract. On p 1 it is stated: "In . . . the UK, the success of the company is specified as being for the benefit of its shareholders (what are termed its 'members')." The relevant part of s 172(1) reads: "A director of a company must act in the way he considers, in good faith, would be most likely to promote the success of the company for the benefit of its members as a whole, and in doing so have regard (amongst other matters) to [a list of non-shareholder matters]."

[109] CA 2006, s 172(4).

It is not surprising that section 172 of the Companies Act takes a broad view of permissible corporate purposes. The role of this section is to define the directors' core duty of loyalty, not to stipulate the corporate purposes. The scheme of the Act is that the directors have a duty to promote whatever purposes the company has adopted. The specification of those purposes ("objects") is in the hands of the shareholders, in the company's articles on initial incorporation or by subsequent changes to them or possibly by a simple resolution of the shareholders adopted by supermajority vote, though there is a default of unrestricted business objectives.[110] Mayer's statement again displays analytical confusion between the duties of directors and the setting of the corporate purposes, but this time it leads to a wrong reading of the law. Get the purposes right (via provisions in the company's constitution) and the directors' duties (set by the Act) fall into place, not the other way around.[111] In the hypothesis we are discussing, of highly developed ESG strategies on the part of shareholders, the current formulation of the core duty of directors will work just fine to secure directors' adherence to the purposes the shareholders choose.

In short, UK corporate law does not prevent companies from adopting other-regarding purposes, but it does place the adoption of those purposes in the hands of the shareholders (through their control of the company's constitution). This is not an idiosyncratic approach of UK company law. Other jurisdictions proceed in the same way. There is no space here for a comparative survey, but we have already noted that the Delaware B-Corp legislation operates by placing the specification of the public benefits in the corporate charter (under the control of the shareholders) and then fashioning the directors' duties around what the charter says.[112]

A more realistic concern with shareholder-chosen social or communal purposes is the uncertain persistence of shareholders' commitment to those goals. What the shareholders decide to adopt, they can take away (albeit only by supermajority vote). The potential loss of commitment by the shareholders to the company's purposes is recognised in relation to charitable (eleemosynary) companies (where the whole purpose of the

[110] CA 2006, ss 21 and 31. [111] A point which *Prosperity* at p 23 gets exactly right.

[112] See text attached to n 47 above. Equally, French law requires the board(s) to "take into consideration" the company's *raison d'être* where one has been adopted in the company's statutes: French Commercial Code art L225–35 (board of directors) and L225–64 (board of management).

company is to benefit persons other than its members). Mandatory rules prevent the distribution of charitable company assets to its members, even in a winding up, and establish a regulator to police adherence to the charitable objectives when the company is a going concern.[113] This might be thought to be a heavy-handed solution in relation to companies which also have a commercial purpose. However, an effective, private-ordering solution is available. The company could make any alteration of its adopted purposes (as set out in the articles) conditional on the consent of the holder of a "golden" share (whose veto would be enforceable at a minimum by injunction) and then allocate that share to some appropriate guardian, while the ongoing faithfulness of the company to the stated objectives could be ensured by "green pills"[114] or a requirement in the articles for periodic validation by an external party, any alteration in the reporting requirements possibly also being subject to the consent of the holder of the golden share.[115] Private ordering gives the company flexibility as to how it organises its purpose arrangements. Nevertheless, for small companies there might be value in providing a separate corporate form, such as some form of public benefit corporation, which takes some of the design burden off the incorporators.[116]

[113] Charities Act 2011. Equally, the (non-charitable) UK Community Interest Company (CIC), whose assets are also locked in, is overseen by a CIC Regulator. In both cases, the absence of members of the company with an economic interest in its operations means that the members cannot be expected always to monitor the board effectively and the members may even have an interest in subverting the company's public purposes. Neither the charitable company nor CIC meets the design requirements promoted by *Prosperity* because of the severe constraints on distributions by these bodies.

[114] For an actual example of the use of a golden share in this way see "'Golden shares' to safeguard sustainability at Tony's Chocolonely", *Guardian*, 31 May 2023. (I am grateful to Luca Enriques for this reference.) For pills, see J Armour, L Enriques and T Wetzer, *Green Pills: Making Corporate Climate Commitments Credible*, ECGI Law Working Paper 657/2022, and O Perez and M Vandenbergh, *Making Climate Pledges Stick: A Private Ordering Mechanism for Climate Commitments*, 2023 (available at ssrn.com/abstract=4346020).

[115] For the importance of third party verification in relation to B-Corps, see DS Lucas, *Third Party Standards and Sustainability Reporting: The Case Of Minnesota Benefit Corporations* (available at ssrn.com/abstract=4232285); and for the potential of general mandatory reporting requirements, A Pacces, *Sustainable Corporate Governance: the Role of the Law*, ECGI Law Working Paper 550/2020 and V Knapp, "Sustainable Corporate Governance: A Way Forward" (2021) 18 *European Company and Financial Law Review* 216, esp §3.

[116] Cf S Shackelford, J Hillier and X Ma, "Unpacking the Rise of Benefit Corporations: A Transatlantic Comparative Case Study" (2020) 60 *Virginia Journal of International*

2.7 Conclusion

Establishing the purpose for which a company exists is clearly important. Without knowing it, it is difficult to see how the board and senior management can set the company's strategy optimally, investors decide whether to invest in it, shareholders work out how well it is doing, stakeholders decide whether to contract with it or society in general evaluates its worth. Nothing in this piece seeks to gainsay these points. Rather it is aimed at evaluating a further proposition, which is that the adoption of a stated purpose should be mandatory for (at least large) companies and that the chosen purpose should be required to contain a social or communal element (as these are defined in *Prosperity*). This step, it is argued in *Prosperity*, would "transform business at a stroke". This chapter has sought to argue, by contrast, that such a requirement, by itself, would bring about no such result. Rather, it has been argued that the mandatory, broad purpose requirement will be either (largely) ineffective or (largely) unnecessary. To be effective, it would need to be accompanied by either substantial changes in corporate law which would downgrade the governance rights of shareholders, almost to the point of elimination, or a substantial change in the investment goals of shareholders, coupled with some less far-reaching legal reforms. The former is undesirable on a variety of grounds; the latter is a possibility, but not a strong one, and in any event the transformation of corporate behaviour would then be driven, not by the mandatory purpose requirement, but the transformed behaviour of investors.

The defect in the analysis of the purpose requirement in *Prosperity*, it is suggested, is the characterisation of the reform as "simple". In formulation it is certainly simple, but in implementation it is not. *Prosperity* proceeds as if the purpose requirement were self-executing, but it is not. To require a company to do anything via an obligation contained in its internal rulebook, whether a purpose statement or anything else, requires a body within the organisation, which has the authority to bind it, to incorporate the required provision therein. Typically, this will be the shareholders in general meeting, but could be the board of directors in some cases. *Prosperity* mainly favours the board for the role of determining corporate purpose. "[T]he board is the custodian of corporate purpose. In contrast to a shareholder primacy

Law 698, reporting that, as of the end of 2015, there were 460 B-Corps incorporated in Delaware, of which 404 were newly formed entities.

view of the firm, corporate purpose does not reside with financial institutions or the market for corporate control."[117] But, this sentence contains a misleading contrast. Within the organisational structure of the company, it is the board or the shareholders in general meeting who can bind the company. Financial institutions (unless they are shareholders) or the market for corporate control (whoever that is) have no authority to take decisions binding on the company, no matter how much they may influence the decisions of those bodies which do take.

The weakness of *Prosperity*, it is suggested, is that it does not engage with the organisational structure of the company. To state for the last time the proposition this chapter advances: shareholders who do not like broad purpose requirements and directors accountable to them will not implement them in a meaningful way and those shareholders who do favour them are not dependent on the presence of a purpose requirement (though that requirement could perform a role in encouraging discussion of the issue within the company).[118] There are many ways in which the law reformer could seek to escape from this conundrum: state determination of corporate purposes or a reconstitution of the board along stakeholder lines are only the most obvious. But *Prosperity* does not engage with these implementation strategies and at times seems averse to some manifestations of them. This leaves us only with the uncertain potential of ESG investing, which again is not discussed in the book and at times is commented on unfavourably.

My goal in advancing the above analysis is not to suggest that the adoption of other-regarding corporate strategies might not be a social welfare-enhancing reform – that is a much bigger issue. Rather, it is to assert that the mandatory purpose requirement as envisaged in *Prosperity* launches, but does not conclude, a debate on the delineation and implementation of corporate purposes. The purpose proposal may constitute a principle (probably only one of a number) around which reforms could be assessed, but it is not a transformative reform in itself. As it stands, the arguments presented by *Prosperity*, even as developed in the British Academy report, do not constitute a watertight set of interrelated policy proposals for legal reform. Perhaps *Prosperity* can be thought to be a bit

[117] *Prosperity* p 121.

[118] Fisch, above, text following n 35. Taking this point further, Edmans has argued for a mandatory "say-on-purpose" vote for the shareholders: A Edmans, *Grow the Pie* (2020) at 206.

like the Coase theorem.[119] Coase did not suppose that in the real world there were no transaction costs, but starting from a position of no transaction costs allows one to analyse the real-world frictions which prevent bargaining over the allocation of damage. So, here, the assumption of no legal/organisational implementation problems allows one to examine why broad purpose statements are so rarely adopted in profit-seeking businesses in present circumstances and to analyse the conditions which might have to be met before there could be a significant change from the prevailing practice.

2.8 Postscriptum

This is a short rejoinder to Colin Mayer's response to my arguments, which appears as the next chapter in this book. The most salient point which he seeks to make is that my starting point, that *Prosperity* contemplates a legal obligation on companies to adopt social or communal purposes (as well as commercial ones), is incorrect. Readers of the Preface to and Chapter 7 of *Prosperity* are probably well placed to reach a conclusion about what a fair reading of those chapters can be taken to state or imply, without any further argument from me, beyond what I say in the body of this chapter.

In any event, Colin now asserts that the purpose of *Prosperity* should be understood in the following way:

> While Davies is focused on the front end of determination and adoption of purpose, that is not something of concern to *Prosperity*, which instead concentrates on the back end of commitment to and implementation of purpose. It is not concerned about the front end because it is not seeking to determine and adopt anything other than purposes which are supported by shareholders, namely *profitable* solutions for the problems of people and planet. (p 1)

In the face of the considerable evidence of shareholder reluctance to supplement the financial goals of the company with social or communal ones, this view of what *Prosperity* is about does substantially reduce the value of the book. Since the adoption of expanded corporate purposes is presented as a major reform, one would expect its advocate to devote attention to the mechanisms and incentives, within and without the law, for companies to adopt such purposes.

[119] R Coase, "The Problem of Social Cost" (1960) 3 *Journal of Law and Economics* 1.

After all, the principal problem with utopias is not imagining them, but working out how to bring them about – or some approximation of them.

In any event, Colin does accept that the British Academy Report,[120] the outcome of a study group which he chaired as a follow up to the book and of which he was the driving force, does contemplate the imposition of a legal obligation to adopt broader purposes via the company's articles. So, at a minimum, a legal obligation on companies to adopt broader purposes has been placed on the menu of policy choices as a result of Colin's activities, and it calls out for critical examination, which is what I have aimed to give it in my chapter. Colin identifies certain alleged defects in my arguments, but, again, I leave it to readers to judge whether these defects exist and, to the extent that they do, how important they are.

Colin seeks to explain what he regards as the "significant difference" (p 9) between what *Prosperity* and the British Academy Report say about mandatory, broad corporate purposes on the grounds that the Academy Report was addressing the additional topic of the "negative detriments" of corporate behaviour, not just the positive benefits of broader corporate purposes. As he puts it: "In contrast the British Academy introduces a second element to corporate purposes alongside 'producing profitable solutions to the problems of people and planet' and that is 'not profiting from producing problems for either'" (p 9).

This seems to me a post hoc rationalisation since, on the one hand, mandatory purposes are an incomplete legal response to corporate externalities. They do very little to provide redress to those outside the company who suffer from the company's behaviour in breach of the purposes.[121] That is the realm of tort law and regulation, not corporate

[120] Above n 13. In the acknowledgements in the BA Report, Colin is fulsomely thanked: "The report and the programme as a whole have benefited hugely from the insight and expertise of Professor Colin Mayer CBE FBA. Without his leadership and support, the programme would not have been possible."

[121] We know, sadly, that even non-profit organisations with the most elevated goals may find that their operations involve the infliction of negative externalities, if only because of the limitations of hierarchical control. Companies operating for profit are perhaps even more likely to be at risk of inflicting such harms, no matter how high the social value of their objects. Social and communal values at the top are always clearly not a guarantee of the absence of harmful behaviour and in all aspects of the organisation's activities. See BBC, *Oxfam: UK halts funding over new sexual exploitation claims*, 7 April 2021 (available at www.bbc.co.uk/news/health-56670162) and S Wheeler, *UN Peacekeeping has a Sexual Abuse Problem*, 2020 (available at www.hrw.org/news/2020/01/11/un-peacekeeping-has-sexual-abuse-problem).

law. On the other hand, broader purposes, whether voluntary or mandatory, cannot be said to lack all mitigating impact on corporate harms. For example, a company which has adopted voluntarily a purpose of reducing income inequality in society is less likely to lobby government against increasing the national minimum wage than one which has not. So, if Colin's argument is correct, *Prosperity* missed a trick by not examining the potential for corporate purposes to mitigate externalities.

However, in my reading, *Prosperity* did set out to deal with the negative elements of corporate behaviour as well as promoting the production of profitable solutions to the problems of people and the planet. This then explains the limitations of the British Academy's report. It was not setting out a general prospectus for dealing with corporate externalities but was rather taking further an issue already raised in *Prosperity*: how to deploy corporate law to promote the adoption of broad purposes on a mandatory basis where companies were unwilling to adopt them voluntarily. This is, after all, the only proposal to emerge from the "Law" chapter of the Academy's report (see its Table 1). Liability rules in favour of outsiders, whether directed at the company or its directors, are absent.

Prosperity in fact states that it does seek to address externalities. In its first pages, it lists among the problems the book seeks to fix that the company "is the source of inequality, deprivation and environmental degradation" and among the questions it seeks to answer is: "How can we ensure that we harness business as a source of societal benefits *and avoid its detriments*" (emphasis added).[122] Maybe the answer to the first part of this question is more fully developed in the book than the answer to the second, but it is clearly put on the agenda of the issues the book seeks to address.

As to the Academy Report, the adoption of broad purposes, whether voluntarily or in the shadow of the law, may be a way of formally binding directors to the company to pursue those purposes, but its practical efficacy in that regard is subject to limits, as a number of legal colleagues have argued.[123] The adoption of a purpose by the company in its articles

[122] *Prosperity*, pp 1–2.

[123] See Marco Ventoruzzo, "Brief Remarks on 'Prosperity' by Colin Mayer and the Often Misunderstood Notion of Corporate Purpose" (2020) *Rivista delle società* 65, and Klaus Hopt, *Corporate Purpose and Stakeholder Value – Historical, Economic and Comparative Law Remarks on the Current Debate, Legislative Options and Enforcement Problems*, ECGI Law Working Paper 690/2023, especially the reasoning supporting Conclusion 6.

or by board resolution increases directors' incentives to promote it but it is not guaranteed to ensure the directors' commitment to it in all circumstances or to remove from them all discretion in the interpretation of those purposes. The mandatory "purpose adoption" technique will probably need supplementation, for example, through "green pills".[124] I do not explore this issue in this chapter, because, as Colin would put it, I am writing about the front end. But it is undoubtedly an important consideration for those writing about the back end.

In short, the front-end/back-end distinction does not undermine my view that a reasonable reader of *Prosperity* would conclude that it had put on the agenda the issue of using corporate law to require the adoption of broad purposes – even if Colin now asserts that he did not intend this. So perhaps the aims of the book and of the report on this point are not so different after all.

The reader who has waded through my chapter, Colin's response and the present postscript may be a little impatient. After all, Colin does accept that the British Academy working party which he chaired did propose consideration of mandatory, broad corporate purposes. *Sub specie aeternitatis*, does it matter all that much whether this proposal was contained in Colin's book, his British Academy project or both? This gives rise to an intriguing question: where does Colin now stand – and where logically ought he to stand – on mandatory broad objects for companies? Has he abandoned this aspect of the British Academy's Report? Since his next book, which he trails, focusses on the topic of externalities, presumably we shall find out in due course. I look forward to reading it.

[124] See n 115 above.

3

The Purpose of Corporate Purpose Statements

A Response to "Shareholder Voice and Corporate Purpose: The Purposelessness of Mandatory Corporate Purpose Statements" by Paul A. Davies

COLIN MAYER

3.1 Introduction

In his chapter, "Shareholder Voice and Corporate Purpose: The Purposelessness of Mandatory Corporate Purpose Statements",[1] Paul A. Davies critiques my book, *Prosperity: Better Business Makes the Greater Good.*[2] He examines the legal foundations of my proposals regarding the role that law should play in promoting the notion of corporate purpose I advocate in the book. He finds them wanting in several respects and not practically relevant to the task at hand.

Davies' critique is highly insightful, and I am very grateful to him for paying such close attention to the legal aspects of the book. I am particularly grateful because I agree with and wholeheartedly support much of what he says in his chapter. Though he suggests otherwise, his arguments reinforce and strengthen rather than detract from or weaken the case presented in *Prosperity*. Where Davies' chapter in some respects falls short is in failing to identify the most substantial issues and problems that the book leaves unresolved.

Davies' chapter focuses on the determination and adoption of corporate purpose. He argues that only purpose statements which shareholders

Iam grateful to Luca Enriques, Jennifer Hill, Paul A. Davies, and Giovanni Strampelli for helpful comments on a previous version of the paper.

[1] Paul A. Davies (2022), "Shareholder Voice and Corporate Purpose: The Purposeless of Mandatory Corporate Purpose Statements", ECGI Working Paper Series in Law, No. 666/2022.

[2] Colin Mayer (2018), *Prosperity: Better Business Makes the Greater Good*, Oxford: Oxford University Press.

wish to and can determine will be adopted. Anything else will be infeasible in not being supported by shareholders or unnecessary in being implementable by them in any event.

I wholeheartedly agree with this. However, *Prosperity* and Davies' critique of it are like ships passing in the night. While Davies is focused on the front end of determination and adoption of purpose, that is not something of concern to *Prosperity*, which instead concentrates on the back end of commitment to and implementation of purpose. It is not concerned about the front end because it is not seeking to determine and adopt anything other than purposes which are supported by shareholders, namely *profitable* solutions for the problems of people and planet. They can be equally self-regarding as communal or social.

That is not to say that the issue which Davies raises is without importance. It is very much so, but not in the context of *Prosperity* which is not seeking to drive a wedge between corporations and their shareholders. It is most relevant to issues concerned with avoidance of detriment rather than delivery of benefits, which, while not the subject of *Prosperity*, is central to my forthcoming book, *Capitalism and Crises: How to Fix Them.*[3]

I will begin in Section 3.2 by summarizing Davies' argument and then in Section 3.3 give my opinion on how his assertions relate to what I say in *Prosperity*. In Section 3.4, I discuss the role that corporate law should play in promoting corporate activity and what is required to give effect to this. Section 3.5 describes how *Prosperity*'s proposals can have transformative effects while leaving the existing nature and structure of the firm intact. Section 3.6 discusses the issues that the book does not address and what is required to take it forward from where it left off. Section 3.7 concludes.

3.2 The Purposeless of Mandatory Corporate Purpose Statements

Davies' concerns revolve around five areas. The first concern is what is perceived to be the fundamental objective of legal reform in *Prosperity*, namely that "the adoption of a stated purpose … be mandatory for (at least large) companies and that the chosen purpose … be required to

[3] Colin Mayer (2024), *Capitalism and Crises: How to Fix Them*, Oxford: Oxford University Press.

contain a social or communal element (as these are defined in *Prosperity*)".[4]

The second concern Davies raises is that "shareholders or directors accountable to shareholders will not adopt purposes of the type envisaged by *Prosperity* without either substantial changes in corporate law beyond the mere adoption of a requirement to state a corporate purpose or a substantial alteration in the goals of investors from those the Friedman doctrine assumes (or some combination of the two)."[5] He attacks the claim I make in *Prosperity* that "corporate law should prioritize purpose. It should require companies to articulate their purposes, incorporate them in their articles of association, and above all demonstrate how they credibly commit to the delivery of purpose."[6]

Davies instead repeatedly makes assertions to the effect of "(t)he purpose statement requirement envisaged in Chapter 7 [of *Prosperity*] is not . . . 'embarrassingly simple' but in fact complicated, perhaps even 'embarrassingly' complicated if the goal is its quick implementation. A one-section addition to the Companies Act requiring companies to state a purpose of the required type in their articles of association will not by itself 'transform business at a stroke.'[7] Instead, it will be argued, it will either be a failure or be rescued by some non- simple changes in corporate law or by a transformation of investors' goals."[8]

Third, Davies is concerned about the suggestion that the law be used "to shield the directors from any adverse reaction from the shareholders to the board's decision. It will be suggested that this strategy, if implemented, would be unlikely to be wholly effective in achieving its goals, would come with considerable costs and, in any case, would be unlikely to obtain legislative endorsement."[9]

He goes on to say that "[t]he assumption underlying the purpose proposal appears to be that a requirement to state a purpose will unshackle the company from the shareholders, because it will in some undefined way override the governance rights of the shareholders".[10] "The main targets of such reforms would be to reduce the impact of at least five powers which shareholders normally possess: (a) to appoint and remove directors; (b) to instruct the board how to act; (c) to convene meetings of the company; (d) to transfer their shares when a tender offer is made to them; and (e) to set profit-related pay. The aim would have to

[4] Davies (2022), p. 38. [5] Ibid., p. 7. [6] Mayer (2018), p. 23. [7] Ibid.
[8] Davies (2022), p. 7. [9] Ibid., p. 8. [10] Ibid., p. 19.

be to go beyond the 'zone of isolation' envisaged by Professors Kershaw and Schuster."[11]

Fourth, and related to this, Davies asserts that *Prosperity* "comes close to an entity theory of the company[:] . . . the dominant conception of the company which the book adopts appears to be a managerialist one; [. . .] managers are somehow above the fray and are there disinterestedly to discharge the responsibility of implementing the purposes the company has adopted – or perhaps even to adopt it in the first place."[12]

Fifth, Davies objects to the suggestion that there be "regulatory or court approval of the shareholders' choice of corporate purpose, that is, corporate purpose ceases to be a matter of private ordering. This strategy blurs the boundary between the private and public sectors of the economy."[13]

Davies' analysis progresses in stages by considering two worlds. The first is a "Friedmanite world" where Milton Friedman's assertion about the social responsibility of business being limited to the pursuit of profit prevails. The second is a world where shareholders may have objectives beyond the pursuit of just profits – "a world of ESG investing. Investors might change their views about what constitutes the best way of 'making money' (a relatively limited shift) or, more boldly, they might come to share *Prosperity*'s views about the importance of communal and social goals for their investment strategies. In this world, investors evaluate the company's achievements along communal and social dimensions as well as along the financial one."[14]

Davies concludes that in the first world "any purpose statements which emerge in this world are not likely to constrain significantly the company's established modes of conducting its profit-making business. Profit-oriented shareholders will not favour purposes which impede their Friedmanite goal, whether those purposes are to be adopted by the shareholders (the normal rule for changes to the company's internal constitution) or by directors accountable to shareholders."[15] Attempts to impose purpose statements will suffer the same fate and demise of the object clauses and *ultra vires* conditions of early UK Companies Acts, the significance of which was steadily eroded by the adoption of progressively less meaningful statements by companies.[16]

[11] Ibid., p. 21, citing David Kershaw and Edmund Schuster, "The Purposive Transformation of Company Law" (2021) *American Journal of Comparative Law*, 69, 478.
[12] Davies (2022), pp. 9–10. [13] Ibid., p. 8. [14] Ibid. [15] Ibid., p. 7.
[16] S. 8 of the UK Companies Act 1862.

In the second world, Davies concludes that "the implications for the reform of corporate law in this second world are very different from those in the first. Far from aiming at shielding the board from the shareholders or subjecting their choices to review, ... [this] strategy suggests that shareholder influence should be given full reign. Shareholders should be free to shape the broad contours of corporate strategy and behaviour and to remove directors who will not listen to shareholders' views on these matters."[17]

He continues: "shareholders who do not like broad purpose requirements and directors accountable to them will not implement them in a meaningful way and those shareholders who do favour them are not dependent on the presence of a purpose requirement".[18] In other words, in the first world, purpose statements and their embedding in corporate law are ineffective and infeasible; in the second world, they are unnecessary or undesirable in impeding shareholder engagement and stewardship. Either way they won't work.

3.3 The Relevance of the "Davies Critique" to *Prosperity*

I will begin by addressing the third, fourth and fifth concerns that *Prosperity* seeks to "shield the directors from any adverse reaction from the shareholders to the board's decision", "comes close to an entity theory of the company[,] [...] a managerialist one", and there should be "regulatory or court approval of the shareholders' choice of corporate purpose, that is, corporate purpose ceases to be a matter of private ordering". All three assertions are precisely contrary to what the book sets out.

The book is not seeking to shield directors from shareholders; on the contrary it is seeking to strengthen accountability. Second, it is not an entity theory of the firm in a managerialist sense. It is one where the objective of the firm is precisely aligned with that of shareholders. Third, it is most certainly not seeking to impose regulatory or court or government approval on corporate purposes. It is seeking exactly the opposite – diversity and freedom of choice.

In fact, Davies acknowledges these points when he states that "the bulk of the book is devoted, correctly in my view, to the development of its positive goal"[19] of producing profitable solutions; the propositions in the

[17] Davies (2022), p. 9. [18] Ibid., pp. 38–39. [19] Ibid., p. 4.

book appear to flow from "the company's commitment to its stated purpose, not from a stakeholder framework of accountability;"[20] and blurring "the boundary between the private and public sectors of the economy ... appears to run counter to the philosophy behind *Prosperity*".[21]

Davies continues by saying that "it appears that government/court control of the setting and implementation of corporate purposes would run against the philosophy underlying *Prosperity*. This is a book which leaves companies firmly in the private sector of the economy. It is not a book which promotes the pursuit of public purposes through state ownership or control – the traditional, if now somewhat tarnished, formula in the UK for safeguarding the public interest."[22]

The book is indeed about how to promote the interests of shareholders; it is not a stakeholder or managerialist theory; and it seeks to avoid limitations on corporate purpose and instead to promote plurality and multiplicity of purposes.

The problem with Davies' interpretation of *Prosperity* comes early in his chapter where he says: "In Chapter 7 [of *Prosperity*] purposes, and their coterminous commitments, are categorised into three types: self-regarding (the company is a main beneficiary of the commitment), communal (where the commitment relates to those who deal with the company but the company does not capture all the benefits of its commitment) and social (where benefits are conferred on those not in a contractual or analogous relationship with the company)." That is correct. But then he goes on to assert: "It is the communal and social purposes which are at the centre of the mandatory purpose rule." That is completely incorrect.

In fact, the chapter makes clear that there are benefits of commitments to all three categories. In relation to the first category, it states that: "Self-regarding commitment benefits the provider by giving the recipient sufficient assurance of its irreversibility to encourage them to do things and in particular make investments that otherwise they would be reluctant to undertake. For example, they encourage employees to make firm specific human capital investments in education and training that they cannot readily transfer to another corporation. They induce customers to make purchases from suppliers on whom they are then dependent for after-sales service. They are self-regarding in so far as they are reflected in

[20] Ibid. [21] Ibid., p. 8. [22] Ibid., pp. 18–19.

the benefits, either priced or reciprocal, that the provider derives. In other words, they are consistent with, not divergent from profit maximization in improving the terms on which the corporation can trade by lowering its cost of employment, purchases, and capital and raising the prices it charges its customers."[23]

What is being put forward in the book is therefore as applicable to companies which are seeking to profit maximize through conventional forms of private goods and services as it is to those that are seeking to profit from addressing communal and social problems. All of them are required by the definition of corporate purpose to be profitable and therefore shareholder value enhancing, and those that are self-regarding and purely profit maximizing are as valid as those that derive from communal and social problem solving.

The reason is straightforward. As *Prosperity* states: "commitments relate to those components of obligations that are not enforceable by contract. Some of them are promoted by an alignment of incentives between the recipient and provider and some by more general forms of well-being that the provider might derive. In some cases, they reflect broader principles for which there may not be a direct profit motive. Why are they needed? The significance of commitments derives from the fact that they are opportunity enhancing. In their absence, the range of relations that can be sustained is constrained by those that are enforceable by contract or promoted by incentives. Most relations cannot be sustained in this way because they are dependent on the trustworthiness of the individuals and institutions involved and the trust that others have in them."[24]

The importance of this in relation to Davies' critique is that he is assuming something that simply is not the basis of the book or the justification for purpose statements. As Chapter 7 makes clear, the problem that the book is trying to address is how to make purpose statements credible commitments. It begins by describing several purpose statements that companies made prior to them becoming fashionable over the last few years. It suggests that they lack credibility as authentic, meaningful assertions of corporate objectives and that most people will be highly cynical about the significance that should be attached to them.

This has nothing to do with whether a company is seeking to solve a private, communal, or social problem. In all cases, there is a credibility

[23] Mayer (2018), p. 152. [24] Ibid., p. 153.

gap about the commitments it is making to its customers, employees, suppliers, distributors, communities, societies, environment, and investors. That affects the terms and conditions on which it can negotiate and engage with them. In seeking to solve the commitment problem, Davies is presuming that *Prosperity* is seeking overtly or covertly to impose a requirement on companies to promote communal and social objectives.

That is not the case, but it is this presumption that pervades Davies' entire discussion and is the basis of the first concern described in Section 3.2 of this chapter that "the chosen purpose should be required to contain a social or communal element". That is not at all what is intended. The role of law is in lending credibility to firm's commitments whatever they are in terms of promoting private or social benefits. It is enabling not restrictive and that is why so much emphasis is placed in the book on the enabling not prescriptive aspect of corporate law.[25] It is also the reason why the second concern that Davies makes that the solution is "embarrassingly complicated" not "embarrassingly simple" is also without foundation.

3.4 The Law and Purpose

Davies expresses surprise about the "light treatment of corporate law" in Chapter 7 of *Prosperity*, "surprising for one might think that a fundamental shift in the goals of large companies would require quite a lot in terms of supporting corporate law or corporate governance reform." It is surprising for Davies because of the fundamental shift and heavy lifting that he believes is required to achieve the goals of *Prosperity*, of imposing social goals on companies that are averse to adopting them.

It is, however, not surprising if the objective is precisely what is set out at the beginning of Chapter 7 of lending credibility to the purposes that companies themselves espouse.[26] Far from seeking to thrust unwelcome objectives on companies, what the chapter attempts to identify is ways in which the law might further corporations' own goals. The most interesting part of Davies' chapter comes right at the end when he turns to this question because the dichotomy between the Friedmanite and

[25] Ibid., p. 157.

[26] The origins of this problem were pointed out in my earlier book: Colin Mayer (2013), *Firm Commitment: Why the Corporation Is Failing Us and How to Restore Trust in It*, Oxford: Oxford University Press, which identified lack of firm commitment as a source of erosion of trust.

non-Friedmanite worlds, which forms the bulk of his chapter, is of little significance.

In a Friedmanite world, corporations should stick to self-regarding objectives and use the power to commit to the extent to which it assists in achieving them. In a non-Friedmanite world, the commitments should relate to the problem-solving objectives which shareholders wish their companies to deliver in profitable ways. The power to commit should feature in both worlds in different forms depending on the specific objectives that are being pursued. Many flowers should bloom, and Davies' two worlds should co-exist to the extent to which shareholder preferences mirror those of the worlds they inhabit. This is very closely related to Oliver Hart and Luigi Zingales' notion of shareholders being concerned about their welfare as well as their wealth.[27]

More relevant is Davies' discussion at the end where he finally engages with the issue that *Prosperity* addresses. He correctly notes that "[a] more realistic concern with shareholder-chosen social or communal purposes is the uncertain persistence of shareholders' commitment to those goals. What the shareholders decide to adopt, they can take away (albeit only by supermajority vote). The potential loss of commitment by the shareholders to the company's purposes is recognised in relation to charitable (eleemosynary) companies (where the whole purpose of the company is to benefit persons other than its members). Mandatory rules prevent the distribution of charitable company assets to its members, even in a winding up, and establish a regulator to police adherence to the charitable objectives when the company is a going concern. This might be thought to be a heavy-handed solution in relation to companies which also have a commercial purpose."[28]

But now apparently the boot is on the other foot and, dare one say it, there appears to be "an embarrassingly simple solution". "The company could make any alteration of its adopted purposes conditional on the consent of the holder of a 'golden' share and then allocate that share to some appropriate guardian, while the ongoing faithfulness of the company to the stated objectives could be ensured by a requirement in the

[27] See Oliver Hart and Luigi Zingales, "Companies Should Maximize Shareholder Welfare Not Market Value" (2017) *Journal of Law, Finance, and Accounting*, 2, 247–274; Eleonora Broccardo, Oliver Hart, and Luigi Zingales (2020), "Exit vs. Voice", European Corporate Governance Institute, Finance Working Paper No. 694/2020; and Oliver Hart and Luigi Zingales, "The New Corporate Governance", in this book.

[28] Davies (2022), pp. 36–37.

articles for periodic validation by an external party, any alteration in the reporting requirements possibly also being subject to the consent of the holder of the golden share. Private ordering gives the company flexibility as to how it organizes its purpose arrangements. Nevertheless, for small companies there might be value in providing a separate corporate form, such as some form of public benefit corporation, which takes some of the design burden off the incorporators."[29]

Precisely. The reason why Chapter 7 is surprisingly light in its treatment of corporate law is that the problem is embarrassingly simple to solve. It requires no change in corporate law for companies to commit to a purpose. The means to do it are already in place without requiring a change in law to bring it about.

But now I am the one who, I am afraid, must protest a slight naivety in what Davies presumes to be the simplicity with which to achieve the desired objective – a naivety to account for the complexity of the accompanying structures and processes and of the legal procedure to ensure its enforcement.

The reason why *Prosperity* is a book not an article or a chapter of a book is that the adoption of a purpose is more than its determination and commitment to its fulfilment. It involves a coherent and consistent set of accompanying ownership, financial, governance, regulatory, measurement, and incentive arrangements – all of which raise serious challenges and changes to existing practices. The current forms of ownership, governance, measurement, performance, finance, and investment are a coherent way of delivering self-regarding objectives. Extending them to incorporate other-regarding problem-solving objectives as well requires an equally consistent and coherent set of structures and processes based on company law.

3.5 The Transformative Role of *Prosperity*

It is natural to seek to classify a study as falling into one of a few familiar categories – shareholder primacy versus stakeholder theory; proprietary versus entity view of the firm; principal-agent versus managerial; capitalist versus socialist, etc. Something that seeks to go beyond the

[29] Ibid., p. 37. This provides a persuasive critique of the concerns raised about enforcement of corporate purpose statements by John Armour, Luca Enriques, and Thom Wetzer (2022), "Green Pills: Making Corporate Climate Commitments Credible", European Corporate Governance Institute, Law Working Paper, No. 657/2022.

conventional view of the firm therefore has a natural tendency to be categorized as stakeholder, entity, managerial, and/or socialist in nature. That is how Davies perceives *Prosperity* and that is precisely what it is not supposed to be. It is firmly in the shareholder, proprietary, principal-agent, capitalist camp.

If that is the case, how could the book in any way be regarded as fulfilling its promise of being transformative in relation to the world we inhabit? Do we not remain locked into all its current defects? The answer is no because it makes credible what currently is correctly regarded as lacking credibility, namely assertions about the goodness, well-meaning, and enlightenment of corporations and those who own and run them.

Instead of berating companies such as the members of the Business Roundtable who apparently have failed to live up to their promises since *Prosperity* was published,[30] let us return to the ones that the book cited in Chapter 7 as being examples that lacked conviction and see what could be expected to change if companies can be held to account for what is otherwise just "cheap talk".

"This was Formica Group's statement about sustainability:

- reduce energy use throughout the life of our products;
- reduce carbon emissions by developing renewable energy sources, waste-to-energy technologies and fuel-efficient freight activities;
- work with suppliers to increase recycled and eco-friendly content in our raw materials, making mandatory the use of fibres from sustainable forests . . .

Lockheed Martin is able to attract, develop, and retain a diverse workforce that has the opportunity to showcase and develop their skills and abilities . . . We believe that all employees should have a safe and inclusive work environment –one in which everyone is treated fairly, with the highest standards of professionalism, ethical conduct, and full compliance with the law."[31]

What is needed to lend conviction to such statements? First, they should be formally approved by the board and supported by the corporations' shareholders.[32] Second, there should be a process of consulting

[30] Lucian Bebchuk and Roberto Tallarita, "The Illusory Promise of Stakeholder Capitalism" (2020) *Cornell Law Review*, 106, 91–177.

[31] Mayer (2018), pp 159–160.

[32] Some observers have suggested giving shareholders a "Say on Purpose", i.e., a right to express their opinion on the adoption or implementation of a corporate purpose

with the relevant affected parties – employees, environmentalists, nature conservationists, etc. – about the obligations and requirements associated with them. Third, a set of metrics to evaluate performance against delivery of those objectives should be determined and a system of external reporting against them established.

Fourth, the corporations should set out how their internal governance, culture, values, incentive, and remuneration procedures of everyone in the organization are aligned with the statements. Fifth, the current and capital costs involved in fulfilling the obligations, and the provisions needed to ensure that failures to deliver can be rectified, should be estimated and projected forward.

Sixth, the corporations should set out a compelling business case for the commitments and demonstrate how they are profitable and value enhancing once account is taken of the risks and costs to which the corporations and their investors would otherwise be exposed. Finally, the corporations should determine the party who will be responsible for holding their boards to account for delivery of its commitments, exactly along the lines of what Davies sets out at the end of his chapter and I mention in the previous section of this chapter.

This then establishes the commitments as binding obligations for which the corporations are liable. It is transformational for corporations, their employees, the environment, their investors, and the world we inhabit.[33] Anything less is cheap talk and irrelevant. And all this comes in the context of boards that remain solely accountable to their shareholders for fulfilling their obligations.[34]

Will it happen and why has it not happened? This brings us to another set of issues that go beyond those covered by *Prosperity* and come closer to the ones that should concern Davies in his paper.

analogous to that on climate policy or executive pay. See Alex Edmans and Tom Gosling (2020), "How to Give Shareholders a Say on Corporate Social Responsibility", *Wall Street Journal*, 6 December.

33 See John Armour, Luca Enriques and Thom Wetzer (2022) for supporting arguments as to why providing companies with the means to commit is so important in the context of the environment.

34 While the firm in this context remains solely accountable to its shareholders and therefore is proprietary in nature, the resolution of the time consistency problem through commitment introduces a possible division between the interests of different generations of shareholders. In that respect it is an entity that, while not distinct from its shareholders, has objectives that may be at variance with a particular group of shareholders.

3.6 Beyond Prosperity

At one stage in his chapter, Davies further confuses matters in referring to the British Academy Programme on the Future of the Corporation[35] by failing to note a substantial distinction that exists between the programme and *Prosperity*. He describes the British Academy programme as "add[ing] a little to the company law implications"[36] of *Prosperity* and mistakenly characterizes it as "technically inept" in failing to recognize the distinction between director duties and obligations of companies.

This is because Davies seems to be unaware of the significant differences in the corporate purposes that underlie the book and the programme, and the potential implications of these for director duties and corporate obligations. The reason why *Prosperity* is solely concerned with enabling not prescriptive legislation is that it deliberately framed corporate purposes as being about producing profitable solutions. It does not seek to constrain corporate conduct in any way because it is simply seeking to promote positively profitable outcomes.

In contrast, the British Academy introduces a second element to corporate purposes alongside "producing profitable solutions to the problems of people and planet" and that is "not profiting from producing problems for either". While businesses and investors predictably like to focus on the positive former objective, policymakers, regulators, and society are at least as, if not more, concerned about avoidance of the negative latter one.

Since *Prosperity* did not incorporate this in corporate purpose, it was able to and did park this in the conventional location of regulation and avoid any suggestion of corporate law as being restrictive. It therefore drew a sharp distinction between corporate law as promoting positive purposes and regulation in addressing negative detriments in a conventional form.

The British Academy project, on the other hand, at least had to acknowledge that there was a potential issue that its definition raised

[35] Davies incorrectly refers to it as a programme "run by Colin Mayer under the auspices of the British Academy" as against a programme run by the British Academy for which I acted as its academic lead.

[36] British Academy (2019), "Principles for Purposeful Business", the British Academy Future of the Corporation Programme, www.thebritishacademy.ac.uk/publications/future-of-the-corporation-principles-for-purposeful-business/; and British Academy (2021), "Policy and Practice for Purposeful Business: The Final Report of the Future of the Corporation Programme", www.thebritishacademy.ac.uk/publications/policy-and-practice-for-purposeful-business/.

which went beyond the enabling function of corporate law to include its potential prescriptive and restrictive role. It was not something that it attempted to expand, and it has only subsequently given attention to related issues of corporate legal responsibility.[37]

This raises questions about the distinction between director duties and corporate obligations that do not arise in *Prosperity*, where the duties of directors are as conventionally defined in relation to promoting the success of the company for the benefit of its members. It introduces the possibility of private law and ordering as well as public law and regulation, and director duties as well as corporate obligations, enforcing avoidance of detriment.

Furthermore, the negative aspects of detriments caused by corporate activities are potentially an explanation for why few, especially large, companies appear willing to commit to positive corporate purposes. Davies suggests that "none of the purpose statements put out by French companies is robust enough to carry by itself the weight of translating the *Prosperity*'s proposals 'from a visionary ideal to a practical reality'"[38] and that evidence on the adoption of public benefit corporations in the US indicates "shareholder scepticism about robust forms of purpose adoption".[39]

Even if these statements were true (and evidence from France at least suggests they may no longer be),[40] in the absence of a level playing field, it may be impossible for large companies to make positive commitments when competing in markets with firms that are willing to profit through inflicting negative detriments on others. Smaller firms operating in more innovative or locally less competitive markets may be less disadvantaged by such considerations and gain more from committing to purposes that confer benefits on others.

It is in this broader context of deterring detriments that Leo Strine, Jaap Winter and I also raised the question, in another publication to which Davies refers in his chapter, of whether the public benefit corporation "should be the universal standard for societally important corporations".[41]

[37] British Academy (2022), "Implications of the British Academy Future of the Corporation Findings for Corporate Legal Responsibility", Discussion Paper for the Standing International Forum of Commercial Courts (SIFoCC).

[38] Davies (2022), p. 14. [39] Ibid. [40] https://societeamission.com.

[41] Colin Mayer, Leo Strine, and Jaap Winter (2020), "50 Years Later, Milton Friedman's Shareholder Doctrine is Dead", *Fortune Magazine*, 13 September.

These are fundamental issues that are developed at length in my forthcoming book *Capitalism and Crises: How to Fix Them*,[42] where the role of law features much more prominently than in either *Prosperity* or the British Academy programme in seeking to address avoidance of detriments as well as promotion of positive benefits. I will not attempt to elaborate on this here but merely restate that Davies has misdirected his concerns and criticisms against a publication that did not seek to accomplish the task he assigns to it.

3.7 Conclusions

It is extremely helpful and important to see how a piece of writing looks through the eyes of someone who presumes a completely different world from the one intended by the author. The tremendously valuable contribution of Davies' careful and thoughtful review of the legal aspects of *Prosperity* has been to make me do exactly that and I am very grateful to him for going to such lengths in setting out his reflections so clearly.

The complexity, impossibility, and undesirability that Davies sees in *Prosperity*'s mission presumes an objective it did not have of forcing the unwanted on the unwilling. The fatal mistake that the architects of the original object clauses of nineteenth-century corporate law made was to attempt to do exactly that – to restrain companies to their stated purposes. *Prosperity* is at the other end of the spectrum in terms of seeking to promote the enabling aspects of corporate purposes and commitments to them.

The reason why *Prosperity* emphasized this was that, in the absence of such means of commitment, we would observe precisely what has happened since the publication of the book and that is the appearance of a plethora of purposes that amount to little more than cheap talk. Anticipating this, *Prosperity* sought to identify ways in which a company could demonstrate an authentic and credible commitment to a purpose that was a meaningful challenge for the business. The law is one component that can be helpful in this regard by allowing firms to demonstrate a commitment to their purposes.

However, it is only one part of a broader systemic reset that is required to effect the necessary changes. *Prosperity* did not attempt to address the restraints on negative detriments that are required beyond conventional

[42] Colin Mayer (2024), *Capitalism and Crises: How to Fix Them*, Oxford: Oxford University Press.

regulatory instruments. *Capitalism and Crises: How to Fix Them* does that and it will offer Davies a chance of a second bite at the cherry.

But I want to conclude with a more substantial message and concern. Like it or not, there is a problem with the way in which our capitalist system is currently formulated and functioning. It is simply not working. The matters that Davies raises, and to which I have attempted to respond, are of profound importance for the world we inhabit and its future. They are of necessity difficult and complex, and they are at the forefront of all our understanding of them.

To most people these are arcane and inaccessible issues, and it is all too easy for them to descend into navel-gazing discourse which does not address the substantive task at hand. We are in the privileged position of having at least some appreciation of them and, I believe, it is our duty to stand above the fray and work together in resolving them constructively, productively, and rapidly for the sake of all of us.

4

Systemic Stewardship with Tradeoffs

MARCEL KAHAN AND EDWARD ROCK

4.1 Introduction

In this chapter, we analyze the extent to which universal owners can and should be expected to induce a firm to sacrifice itself in order to increase a universal owner's overall portfolio value. We are quite pessimistic that universal owners have the ability or inclination to do so. This is for three reasons. First, universal owners would have to take into account the possibility that inducing some firms to mitigate risk or reduce externalities will generate a competitive response that will eliminate the benefits from these actions for their other portfolio companies. If that were to happen, universal owners would be stuck with the losses without receiving any corresponding gains.

Second, shareholders, even universal owners, do not manage companies. Rather, the business and affairs of a corporation are managed by a full-time senior management team under the general oversight of the board of directors within a framework created by corporate law. But corporate law, as it currently exists, has a strong "single firm focus" (SFF) that stands in sharp contrast to the potential "multi-firm focus" (MFF) of large portfolio investors. If universal owners were to work individually or collectively to protect their overall portfolios from systemic risk, it would clash with corporate law in a fundamental way that could create risks of liability. Indeed, the more effective universal owners are in collectively constraining portfolio companies, the greater the legal risk.

Third, the largest and most important universal owners are asset managers that manage a wide variety of different portfolios for different

Thanks to Rick Alexander, Madison Condon, John Galloway, Jeff Gordon, Zohar Goshen, Matt Mallow, Michael Simkovic, and participants in the NYU Institute for Corporate Governance and Finance Roundtable, the IOC Auxiliary Corporate Governance Conference, and workshops and conferences at Harvard Law School, Hebrew University, USC, and Bar Ilan University for helpful comments and criticisms.

This chapter originally appeared in the Journal of Corporation Law, Vol. 48. It is reprinted with their permission.

clients and owe fiduciary duties to each of them. A centrally executed "tradeoff" strategy that would benefit some firms at the expense of others – and hence, in all likelihood, some portfolios at the expense of other portfolios – would conflict with the core multi-client, multi-portfolio business model as well as with their fiduciary duties.[1] As a result, we expect that universal owners will not openly pursue an MFF strategy. Rather, if at all, they will act under the cloak of promoting single firm value. But because making substantial inroads on –controlling systematic risks and reducing externalities involves tradeoffs that cannot be ignored while pretending to further single firm value, we do not expect universal owners to have a significant impact.

4.2 The Potential Benefits of "Systemic Stewardship"

4.2.1 Universal Owners and Externalities

Universal owners are larger than ever. Often, the largest asset owners and managers, firms such as BlackRock, BNY Mellon, CalPERS, CalSTRS, Capital Group, Fidelity, Norges Bank, State Street, and Vanguard, will collectively hold more than 30 percent of the shares of even the biggest public companies.[2] Because of their scale and market-wide diversification, large universal owners, in principle, have financial incentives to induce firms to internalize intra-portfolio externalities – the effects of the actions by one firm on the value of other portfolio holdings – including environmental externalities.[3]

Rick Alexander, who was instrumental in developing benefit corporations and is the founder of "The Shareholder Commons," which pushes for systemic stewardship, argues that universal owners should seriously consider the cost of externalities generated by portfolio companies:

> For example, because the first interest of UOs [universal owners] is in preserving healthy systems, investment fiduciaries can account for

[1] Similarly, universal owners that own assets – such as CalPERS and other pension funds – typically hold those assets in different segregated funds for different sets of beneficiaries and utilize a variety of investing strategies over a variety of asset classes. *See, e.g.*, BlackRock, Inc., Annual Report (Form 10-K) 47 (February 25, 2021).

[2] *See* Robert G. Eccles & Svetlana Klimenko, *The Investor Revolution*, Harv. Bus. Rev. (May–June 2019), https://hbr.org/2019/05/the-investor-revolution.

[3] For an early treatment of this perspective with reference to externalities of all sorts, see Robert G. Hansen & John R. Lott, Jr., *Externalities and Corporate Objectives in a World with Diversified Shareholder/Consumers*, 31 J. Fin. & Quantitative Analysis 43 (1996).

> systemic costs when allocating capital or exercising control rights over it. Individual corporations that raid common resource pools or otherwise take actions that exploit social or environmental systems can be disciplined by fiduciaries representing UOs. The UO can be comfortable that if it persuades a portfolio company to act responsibly through engagement, and competitors of that company seek an advantage by continuing to act irresponsibly, the UO's relative returns will be protected by the overlap of its ownership with that of other UOs.[4]

Madison Condon has sharpened this perspective by providing a plausible and concrete hypothetical.[5] ExxonMobil alone is responsible for 2.1 percent of annual global emissions, while Chevron is responsible for another 1.4 percent.[6] Given the externalities from climate change to the rest of a market portfolio, she argues, it would make economic sense for universal owners to reduce ExxonMobil's and Chevron's carbon output significantly, even at the cost of lowering ExxonMobil's and Chevron's stock price:

> Consider the analysis BlackRock makes when weighing whether or not to intervene to take a measure to curtail production at two firms, Chevron and Exxon. Assume this investor intervention forces each company to reduce its emissions by 40%, and this commitment results in that company's share price falling by 20% .... If it loses 20% of the value of each of these assets, it will lose $6.3 billion total .... [B]y intervening to reduce 1% of annual industrial emissions each year, BlackRock could avoid damages to its portfolio with a net present value of $9.7 billion. Because this value of mitigated damages outweighs the loss of share value from diminished expected fossil fuel profits by $3.4 billion, it would be in BlackRock's rational economic interest to pursue this intervention and to internalize the intra-portfolio climate externalities.[7]

Condon suggests that universal owners should pursue a true portfolio-maximizing strategy by forcing the internalization of climate externalities.[8] By her calculations, universal owners may be leaving huge amounts of money on the table by failing to act.[9] Even more interestingly, she generates this strong result within a "shareholder value" paradigm

[4] Frederick H. Alexander, *The Benefit Stance: Responsible Ownership in the Twenty-First Century*, 36 Oxford Rev. Econ. Pol'y 341, 355–56 (2020).

[5] Madison Condon, *Externalities and the Common Owner*, 95 Wash. L. Rev. 1, 14, 66–68 (2020).

[6] Paul Griffin et al, The Carbon Majors Database, CDP 4 (2017), https://cdn.cdp.net/cdp-production/cms/reports/documents/000/001/800/original/Carbon-Majors-Dataset-1.0.pdf?1489055836.

[7] Condon, *supra* note 6, at 45–47. [8] Ibid. at 16. [9] Ibid. at 45–46.

without considering the effects on other corporate stakeholders or society at large.[10]

Similarly, a universal owner might push for strategies to reduce systematic risks from financial crises. Jeff Gordon explores such strategies in a recent paper and takes, as his paradigm, the reduction of the risk to the financial system posed by "systemically important financial firms" (SIFIs).[11] A universal owner concerned with such systematic risk might vote "in support of the management of a systemically important financial firm in a face-off with activist investors who want the firm to take greater risks to enhance shareholder returns."[12] As Gordon points out, one lesson of the 2007–2009 financial crisis is that "the failure of a … (SIFI) can indeed result in losses across an entire portfolio. In deciding whether to support the risk-loving activist, the index-fund advisor ought to consider not only the return proposition at a single firm but the systematic risk effects."[13] In Gordon's account, systemic stewardship is primarily a "reactive" strategy that merely asks shareholders to vote against a "risk loving activist" and hence is easier to implement than a proactive strategy of implementing a different risk profile, such as the strategy advanced by Condon.[14]

Condon's approach highlights the tradeoffs – in her hypothetical, the values of ExxonMobil and Chevron decline substantially – but similar tradeoffs are present in Gordon's focus on the risks posed by SIFIs as well. A bank taking on "excessive" but legally permissible financial risk – just like ExxonMobil pumping "excessive" amounts of oil – generates a conflict between maximizing firm value and maximizing portfolio value. In both cases, we face the hard question of potential action by universal owners that produces both a private and social good – reduction of environmental externalities or financial systemic risk – at the cost of sacrificing value in a portfolio company that complies with existing regulations.[15]

These arguments about universal owners reducing environmental externalities or systematic risks have interesting parallels with the recent

[10] Ibid. at 80.

[11] *See generally*, Jeffrey N. Gordon, *Systematic Stewardship*, 47 J. Corp. L. 627 (2022).

[12] Ibid. at 629. [13] Ibid. at 629, 635. [14] Ibid. at 629.

[15] *See generally* John Armour & Jeffrey Gordon, *Systemic Harms and Shareholder Value*, 6 J. Legal Analysis 35 (2014). Their argument can be extended to the governance of firms that generate climate externalities. Ibid. at 57.

debate about the anti-competitive effects of common ownership.[16] The starting premise of both instances is that institutional investors have the incentives and some power to increase the value of their entire investment portfolio even when doing so would reduce the value of some individual companies in their portfolio. In other respects, however, these arguments differ. First, universal owners taking steps to reduce environmental externalities or systematic risks would increase social welfare. By contrast, common owners taking steps to reduce competition in an industry – for example, by inducing an airline to cut capacity on certain routes – to generate positive externalities for competing airlines held by these owners (which could then raise their prices) hurts consumers and would reduce social welfare. Relatedly, universal owners embarking on the reduction of environmental externalities would have to be comparatively *less* concerned that their actions would expose them to certain legal liability – such as liability for violating antitrust laws. This would generate an adverse reputational impact or would prompt governmental regulation or even a breakup.[17] As a result, some of the barriers that may, in practice, prevent common owners from inducing anti-competitive effects do not apply with equal force in the environmental externalities and systematic risks context.[18] This being said, the true motives of owners may not always be clear. If, say, a large asset manager were to push airlines to reduce capacity, or oil companies to reduce output, with the natural effect of increasing prices, it would often not be clear whether they were acting to reduce the environmental harm from emissions or to make the industry more profitable. Moreover, even if they are acting to reduce environmental harm, they may nonetheless be

[16] José Azar, Martin C. Schmalz, & Isabel Tecu, *Anticompetitive Effects of Common Ownership*, 73 J. FIN. 1513, 1521–51 (2018); Andrew Koch, Marios Panayides, & Shawn Thomas, *Common Ownership and Competition in Product Markets*, 139 J. FIN. ECON. 109 (2020); Mohammad Torshizi & Jennifer Clapp, *Price Effects of Common Ownership in the Seed Sector*, 66 ANTITRUST BULL. 39 (2021).

[17] *See* C. Scott Hemphill & Marcel Kahan, *The Strategies of Anticompetitive Common Ownership*, 129 YALE L.J. 1392, 1434–39 (2020). Some legal and reputational risks, however, would remain. For example, universal owners would face the legal risk that their actions breached their fiduciary duties to shareholders in undiversified funds or that politicians less concerned about climate change would push for increased regulation.

[18] Ibid. at 1439–40. An additional difference is that anti-competitive effects of common ownership derive mostly from common ownership within a certain industry or in related industries, while the incentives for systemic stewardship are based on ownership across multiple, often unrelated, industries.

accused of "participating in climate cartels and other ill-advised ESG schemes."[19]

4.2.2 *The Limits on Potential Benefits*

The arguments by Alexander, Condon, and Gordon would seem to present grounds for optimism. To lay the groundwork for our analysis, however, it is important to put the incentives created by universal ownership into perspective. As we explain in this subpart, universal owners will have incomplete and heterogeneous incentives to induce firms to internalize environmental, systematic risk-based, and other inter-firm externalities. Nevertheless, their incentives are likely to be substantially stronger than those of large, undiversified owners or managers incentivized to maximize firm value.

First, many universal owners like BlackRock and Vanguard are not *owners* at all. Instead, they manage the assets for investors. Indeed, even entities that are technically asset owners, like CalPERS or CalSTRS, as distinguished from asset managers, are run by individuals for the benefit of the beneficiaries. As we and others have discussed elsewhere, the incentives of agents managing money differ from the incentives of the beneficiaries of those assets.[20] In particular, institutions like BlackRock and Vanguard do not benefit per se if the value of their portfolio securities increases; they benefit only to the much smaller extent that their management fees increase as a result of such value increase. While the incentives of institutions generally point in the right direction – their fees are based on the value of the portfolio securities they manage – they are much lower in scale and may sometimes be swamped by conflicting incentives.[21]

[19] *See* Letters from Senators Tom Cotton, Michael S. Lee, Charles E. Grassley, Marsha Blackburn, & Marco Rubio to 51 law firms (Nov. 3, 2022), www.grassley.senate.gov/news/news-releases/grassley-cotton-colleagues-warn-law-firms-about-esg-initiatives.

[20] *See* Marcel Kahan & Edward Rock, *Index Funds and Corporate Governance: Let Shareholders Be Shareholders*, 100 B.U. L. Rev. 1771, 1776–77 (2020); Lucian Bebchuk & Scott Hirst, *Index Funds and the Future of Corporate Governance: Theory, Evidence, and Policy*, 119 Colum. L. Rev. 2029, 2037 (2019); Ronald J. Gilson & Jeffrey N. Gordon, *The Agency Costs of Agency Capitalism: Activist Investors and the Revaluation of Governance Rights*, 113 Colum. L. Rev. 863, 896 (2013); Hemphill & Kahan, *supra* note18, at 1429–34.

[21] Hemphill & Kahan, *supra* note18, at 1429–34; Rock & Kahan, *supra* note 21, at 1781–1800, 1809–10.

Second, universal owners are, at most, universal owners of businesses and thus will lack incentives to internalize externalities that fall on individuals. This is true for externalities that directly affect individuals – say, health effects from environmental harms – and for externalities that initially affect businesses but that businesses can transfer to individuals through the pricing mechanism – say, climate-change-induced droughts that raise food prices.

Third, universal owners are not really *universal* owners of businesses. While some invest in private equity, private "pre-public" firms, and alternative asset classes like real estate,[22] most are primarily universal owners of *publicly traded* firms.[23] Moreover, U.S.-based institutional investors – the most important universal owners for potentially influencing firm behavior – own a significantly greater fraction of U.S. firms than non-U.S. firms. This is due to two factors. First, publicly traded firms play a more significant role in the United States than in other countries.[24] Second, U.S.-based institutional investors typically own a greater fraction of U.S. publicly traded firms than of non-U.S. publicly traded firms.[25] Institutional investors based in other countries tend to show similar local biases.[26]

Fourth, different universal owners have different allocations across different asset classes that create differing incentives. To start, the allocation of assets between debt and equity varies significantly among universal owners. Debt holdings, for example, are far less exposed than equity to climate change for at least three reasons: creditors get paid before shareholders; debt typically has a fixed return while equity receives a variable return; and debt has a limited, defined term while equity has an

22 *See, e.g.*, *Blackstone – What We Do*, BLACKSTONE (Mar. 9, 2021), https://www.blackstone.com/blackstone-investments-in-dutch-housing-market-explained/.

23 *See, e.g.*, *Mutual Fund Capabilities Overview*, NUVEEN (June 30, 2021), https://www.tiaa.org/public/pdf/2Q21_Mutual_Fund_Capabilities_Overview.pdf.

24 *See generally* Roberto Tallarita, *The Limits of Portfolio Primacy*, 76 VAND. L. REV. (2023).

25 Ibid. at 14.

26 Relatedly, publicly traded companies will account for varying market shares in different industries. For example, in the United States, four publicly traded companies account for virtually the entire domestic, commercial airline industry. *Domestic Market Share of Leading U.S. Airlines from January to December 2021*, STATISTA (Feb. 3, 2023), https://www.statista.com/statistics/250577/domestic-market-share-of-leading-us-airlines/. By contrast, other industries – accounting services, legal services, restaurants, and residential real estate – are dominated by privately held companies. As a result, universal owners would have an interest in promoting the value of industries like airlines – which are dominated by publicly traded firms – at the expense of industries like restaurants, even if doing so reduces overall business profits.

indefinite term. Because of these differences, a universal owner with more of its assets in "fixed income" securities will have different incentives regarding climate change than a universal owner mostly invested in equities.

In sum, the degree to which universal owners will have incentives to induce portfolio companies to internalize externalities will vary. It will vary by which industries are affected by the externalities, by whether the externalities are mostly local or global, and by whether the externalities affect individuals or businesses.

Nonetheless, universal owners hold highly diversified portfolios in which each individual firm constitutes only a small fraction. Given the scale of their holdings, even the comparatively small additional fee income from an increase in portfolio value would generate meaningful benefits if a universal owner could reduce the negative externalities that a portfolio firm imposed on other portfolio firms.[27] While their incentives in this regard are not perfect, universal owners have significantly stronger incentives to constrain such externalities than undiversified shareholders of a company generating those externalities or managers of such a company.

4.2.3 Externalities and Competition

The possibility that a given company's reduction of externalities may engender an offsetting competitive response poses a more severe challenge to the argument that universal owners stand to gain from inducing firms to reduce environmental externalities or systematic risks even if that generates tradeoffs. A competitive response can, depending on the circumstances, eliminate or greatly reduce any benefits from such reductions, leaving universal owners with a portfolio loss rather than the gain they had hoped to reap.

To see this, let us return to Condon's hypothetical.[28] Condon posits that, by inducing Chevron and ExxonMobil to reduce their emissions by 40 percent, BlackRock would increase the value of its other holdings by \$9.7 billion, leaving it with a \$3.4 billion net gain even though the value of its stake in Chevron and ExxonMobil would decline by \$6.3 billion.[29]

Buried in these numbers is an important assumption: that the actions that Chevron and ExxonMobil take to achieve a 40 percent reduction in

[27] *See* Kahan & Rock, *supra* note 21, at 1786.
[28] Condon, *supra* note 6, at 45.
[29] Ibid. at 45–47.

their emissions – a reduction that, in turn, generates benefits for BlackRock's other holdings to the tune of $9.7 billion – will not induce other companies to take actions that *increase* their emissions. Whether this assumption is correct depends on *how* Chevron and ExxonMobil would reduce their emissions and, specifically, whether this opens up competitive opportunities for other companies.

Consider three possibilities. First, ExxonMobil could reduce its emissions by selling assets to other oil companies, as Shell recently did with its Permian Basin assets.[30] While such a sale would reduce carbon emissions at the company level, it is unlikely to affect overall emissions as the buyer would likely generate emissions at a level equivalent to those of the selling company.[31] Indeed, a sale to a less environmentally responsible operator could even increase emissions.[32]

Second, ExxonMobil could lower its emissions by reducing production from existing reserves while also retaining ownership of those reserves. By hypothesis, ExxonMobil would have made profits by continuing production. If ExxonMobil cuts production, another oil company with a single firm focus could profitably raise production from one of its existing fields or start producing oil from a new field. And companies with a single firm focus abound in the oil industry. For one, there are many important foreign energy companies – Saudi Aramco, Russia's Rosneft and Gazprom, Kuwait Petroleum Corporation, Petróleos de Venezuela S.A., the Nigerian National Petroleum Corporation, and China's Sinopec – that are unlikely to fall under the sway of universal owners because they are state-owned or held by less diversified investors.[33] Even within the United States, there are about 9000 independent oil producers[34] who develop 91 percent of the wells and account for

[30] Cara Lombardo & Collin Eaton, *Shell to Sell Permian Assets to ConocoPhillips for $9.5 Billion*, WALL ST. J. (Sept. 20, 2021), https://www.wsj.com/articles/shell-near-deal-to-sell-permian-assets-to-conocophillips-11632168002?mod=Searchresults_pos13&page=1.

[31] Sarah McFarlane, *Shell Vows to Speed Up Emissions Cuts in Wake of Court Ruling*, WALL ST. J. (June 9, 2021), https://www.wsj.com/articles/shell-to-speed-up-emissions-cuts-in-wake-of-court-ruling-11623236932?mod=article_inline.

[32] Rachel Adams-Heard, *What Happens When an Oil Giant Walks Away*, BLOOMBERG (Apr. 14, 2021), https://www.bloomberg.com/graphics/2021-tracking-carbon-emissions-BP-hilcorp/.

[33] Clifford Krauss, *As Western Oil Giants Cut Production, State-Owned Companies Step Up*, N.Y. TIMES (Oct. 14, 2021), https://www.nytimes.com/2021/10/14/business/energy-environment/oil-production-state-owned-companies.html?smid=em-share.

[34] "The U.S. Internal Revenue Code section 613A(d) defines an independent producer as a producer who does not have more than $5 million in retail sales of oil and gas in a year or

83 percent of U.S. oil and 90 percent of U.S. natural gas production.[35] Moreover, active investors who hold less diversified portfolios than universal owners could accumulate sufficient shares in some of the publicly traded U.S. oil companies to induce them to expand their production or exploratory activities. Similarly, a third party could offer to buy a publicly traded company with the goal of increasing production and making the company more valuable. Over the longer term, the number of independent oil producers would probably increase if public companies forego profit opportunities and other entities do not take up the slack. To the extent that ExxonMobil's production cuts engender any of these competitive responses, BlackRock would suffer the $6.3 billion loss without obtaining the full, if any, portfolio benefits from a decline in annual industrial emissions.

Whether such competitive responses would fully offset ExxonMobil's reduction depends on the extent to which ExxonMobil enjoys competitive advantages in producing oil. ExxonMobil's costs may be lower than those of its competitors, for example, because the location of the field reduces transportation costs or because the terrain of the field reduces extraction costs. At the price for crude oil prevailing before ExxonMobil's cut, it would then be unprofitable for some competitors to produce oil. Otherwise, they would have done so before ExxonMobil cut its emissions. ExxonMobil's cut could thus generate an increase in price and a corresponding increase in production by ExxonMobil competitors, albeit an increase of less than the initial ExxonMobil cut.[36] To that extent, there would be a net decline in emissions, but a smaller decline than ExxonMobil's reduction in emissions, and a correspondingly smaller benefit to BlackRock's other holdings. On the other hand, Saudi Arabia, a dominant oil producer, may try to manage the global supply and increase production to make up for ExxonMobil's cut at the oil price prevailing before the cut. In this case, ExxonMobil's actions, while reducing its emissions and its value, would have no effect on annual industrial emissions.

who does not refine more than an average of 75,000 barrels per day of crude oil during a given year." *Who Are America's Independent Producers?*, INDEP. PETROL. ASS'N AM., https://www.ipaa.org/independent-producers/.

35 Ibid.

36 One study estimated the substitution at around 50 percent. Peter Erickson & Michael Lazarus, *Would Constraining US Fossil Fuel Production Affect Global CO2 Emissions? A Case Study of US Leasing Policy*, 150 CLIMATIC CHANGE 29, 35 (2018).

Third, ExxonMobil could reduce its emissions in ways that are unlikely to engender a competitive response. Rather than reducing its output, it could, for example, make its production more energy-efficient through changes in its operations. To illustrate with a trivial example, suppose that ExxonMobil chooses to reduce carbon output by installing energy-efficient windows in its offices.[37] If these windows are not cost-justified on their own, installing them would lower ExxonMobil's profits but would not (at least in the short term) create competitive opportunities for other firms.[38]

That a company's actions designed to reduce externalities (ExxonMobil's emissions cut in our example) may engender a competitive response that eliminates the gain from such a reduction for universal owners affects their incentives in two ways. First, to the extent that it is easy to predict how competitors would respond and to evaluate the response, universal owners would have incentives to induce a reduction in externalities only in the subset of cases when such a reduction does not elicit a strong competitive response. Thus, in our example and using Condon's numbers, it would no longer make business sense for BlackRock to push for a 40 percent emissions reduction if competitive responses reduced portfolio gains by more than 35 percent.

Second, to the extent that it is difficult to predict how competitors would respond or to evaluate their response, the tasks that universal owners like BlackRock face are far more complicated than Condon's hypothetical suggests. It would require not only a valuation of the economic benefit generated by a reduction in emissions for BlackRock's portfolio companies and the economic costs to ExxonMobil and Chevron. It would also require an understanding of how ExxonMobil and Chevron would cut emissions, the competitive dynamics in the oil industry, the cost structure under which ExxonMobil, Chevron, and their competitors operate, and the extent to which competitive opportunities

[37] To be sure, other firms may not follow ExxonMobil's footsteps by installing energy-efficient windows. If they do not, while other firms may be more profitable than ExxonMobil, they will not make more money by installing even less energy-efficient windows than before. Over the long term, ExxonMobil's reduced profitability may make ExxonMobil non-competitive and force it to scale down, and ExxonMobil may be replaced by another firm. But this may not happen for a long time, if ever.

[38] Even this response may generate lower benefits. ExxonMobil's actions, for example, could lead to an increase in the price of energy-efficient windows, which would, in turn, induce others not to install energy-efficient windows.

would be exploited by publicly held companies in which BlackRock holds a stake or other entities.

By contrast, strategies that cut emissions without reducing profits pose far fewer problems. To vary Condon's hypothetical, assume that ExxonMobil cutting emissions by 4 percent would have no effect on its profits or even raise profits by a small amount (e.g., because the projects cut are not profitable at the margin) while at the same time increasing the value of other BlackRock holdings by $970 million. Since ExxonMobil's value would not decline, it would not be necessary to evaluate whether its emissions cut would engender a competitive response. Even though the emissions cut would have no significant effect on ExxonMobil's profits, it could benefit BlackRock.

Universal owners thus have clear-cut incentives to induce portfolio companies to take actions that have no material impact on their value (or increase their value) but reduce negative externalities for other portfolio companies. Importantly, this task would be much easier than a tradeoff strategy for two reasons. First, and more obviously, they would have to assess only the direction, but not the magnitude, of externalities to determine whether the action is in their interests. Second, they would not have to worry about competitive reactions. But, of course, merely inducing companies to refrain from environmentally harmful actions that are not profitable offers far less potential for substantial reductions in environmental or other externalities.

4.3 The Deep Architecture of Corporate Law

Alexander, Condon, and Gordon each argue that an investor with a diversified portfolio has financial incentives to adopt a portfolio-wide or multi-firm focus, including when significant tradeoffs are required. Even when true, such an MFF is in tension with traditional corporate law principles in a variety of ways. These tensions are likely to inhibit universal owners from pursuing an MFF approach and to make that approach, if pursued, less effective.

In this Part, we first describe corporate law's single-firm focus. We then discuss how corporate law understands the interests of shareholders as the interests in a particular firm – unrelated to their extraneous interests – including interests derived from other holdings. Next, we summarize the board's obligation to manage for the benefit of *all* the shareholders, not just the most powerful ones. Finally, we review shareholders' general right to vote their shares selfishly and the traditional limits to that right. The single firm focus that emerges from these principles stands in the way of implementing systemic stewardship with tradeoffs.

4.3.1 *Corporate Law's Single Firm Focus*

The traditional description of the properties of the corporate form is that "[t]he objective of a corporation is to enhance the economic value of the corporation, within the boundaries of the law ... for the benefit of the corporation's shareholders."[39] This description includes two key aspects: first, the objective of a corporation is to promote the value of *this particular corporation*; second, promoting the value of this corporation is for the benefit of *all* its shareholders. The SFF of corporate law has not received nearly as much attention as the issue of whether corporations are managed for the benefit of the shareholders (sometimes referred to as "shareholder primacy") or for some broader group of stakeholders ("stakeholderism"), possibly because the SFF is so fundamental to corporate law and corporate governance that it is hardly noticed.

Here we describe just some of the ways in which SFF is a fundamental principle in corporate law. First, the critically important business judgment rule – the commitment that courts will not second-guess business judgments – is entirely SFF. As the Delaware Supreme Court explained in *Aronson v. Lewis*, the business judgment rule creates "a presumption that in making a business decision the directors of a corporation acted on an informed basis [i.e., with due care], in good faith and in the honest belief that the action taken was in the best interest of the company."[40]

Fiduciary duties are likewise single-firm focused. As expressed in numerous decisions, "directors owe fiduciary duties of care and loyalty to the corporation and its shareholders."[41] Similarly, the classic language from *Guth v. Loft, Inc.*[42] has a clear SFF:

> A public policy, existing through the years, and derived from a profound knowledge of human characteristics and motives, has established a rule that demands of a corporate officer or director, peremptorily and

39 Restatement of the L.: Corp. Governance § 2.01(a) (Am. L. Inst., Tentative Draft No. 1, 2022).

40 Aronson v. Lewis, 473 A.2d 805, 812 (Del. 1984). As discussed below, the best interest of the company intrinsically includes the interests of shareholders *qua* shareholders (or, from a stakeholder perspective, the interest of other stakeholders, *qua* stakeholders), but does not include the extraneous interests of shareholders.

41 *See, e.g.*, Mills Acquisition Co. v. MacMillan, Inc., 559 A.2d 1261, 1280 (Del. 1988).

42 Guth v. Loft, Inc., 5 A.2d 503 (Del. 1939).

> inexorably, the most scrupulous observance of his duty, not only affirmatively to protect the interests of the corporation committed to his charge, but also to refrain from doing anything that would work injury to the corporation, or to deprive it of profit or advantage which his skill and ability might properly bring to it, or to enable it to make in the reasonable and lawful exercise of its powers. The rule that requires an undivided and unselfish loyalty to the corporation demands that there shall be no conflict between duty and self-interest.[43]

The fiduciary duty of loyalty has been summarized as mandating "that the best interest of the corporation and its shareholders takes precedence over any interest possessed by a director, officer or controlling shareholder and not shared by the stockholders generally."[44] Indeed, the very definition of what counts as an "interested" director or controller distinguishes between the interest of a specific corporation and a fiduciary's extraneous interests. Generally, a director or controller is "interested" in a transaction or conduct involving a corporation if the director or controller is a party to the transaction or conduct or if the director or controller receives a benefit as a result of the transaction or conduct that is not shared pro rata according to the number of shares held.[45] "Interest" is thus relative to a particular corporation, with interests derived from other portfolio holdings – which could generate benefits to a director or controller that is not shared pro rata according to the number of shares – rendering a director or controller not disinterested.[46]

Definitions of "good faith" and the related concept of "bad faith" are also SFF. In Chancellor Chandler's detailed exploration of Delaware precedent in *In re Walt Disney Co. Derivative Litigation*,[47] he captured this SFF by noting the following:

- "Bad faith has been defined as authorizing a transaction 'for some purpose other than a genuine attempt to advance corporate welfare . . . .'"[48]
- "[B]ad faith (or lack of good faith) is when a director acts in a manner 'unrelated to a pursuit of the corporation's best interests.' It makes no

43 Ibid. at 510. 44 Cede & Co. v. Technicolor, Inc., 634 A.2d 345, 361 (Del. 1992).
45 *See* Cinerama, Inc. v. Technicolor, Inc., 663 A.2d 1156, 1169–70 (Del. 1995).
46 *See* ibid.
47 *In re* Walt Disney Co. Derivative Litig., 907 A.2d 693, 753 (Del. Ch. 2005).
48 Ibid. at 753 (quoting Gagliardi v. Trifoods Int'l, 683 A.2d 1049, 1051 n.2).

difference the reason why the director intentionally fails to pursue the best interests of the corporation."[49]

- "To act in good faith, a director must act at all times with an honesty of purpose and in the best interests and welfare of the corporation."[50]
- "The good faith required of a corporate fiduciary includes not simply the duties of care and loyalty ... but all actions required by a true faithfulness and devotion to the interests of the corporation and its shareholders."[51]

The outrage with which courts view fiduciaries with conflicting interests is another indication of the SFF of fiduciary duties. As the Delaware Supreme Court thundered in *Weinberger v. UOP*, "there is no 'safe harbor' for ... divided loyalties in Delaware ... There is no dilution of this obligation where one holds dual or multiple directorships ..."[52]

Finally, in the Delaware court's review of defensive tactics in control contests under the *Unocal/Unitrin* standard, there is a clear SFF. The board's power to act in response to a tender offer "derives from its fundamental duty and obligation to protect the corporate enterprise, which includes stockholders, from harm reasonably perceived, irrespective of its source."[53] When responding to a pending takeover bid, the board "has an obligation to determine whether the offer is in the best interests of the corporation and its shareholders."[54] Given "the omnipresent specter that a board may be acting primarily in its own interests, rather than those of the corporation and its shareholders," the court announced a threshold examination before the business judgment rule would apply.[55] In this examination, the first step is the identification of a "danger to corporate policy and effectiveness."[56]

The limit case – a company with wholly owned subsidiaries – highlights the single firm focus of the normal case. Wholly owned subsidiaries

[49] Ibid. at 754. [50] Ibid. at 755. [51] Ibid. at 755.
[52] Weinberger v. UOP, Inc., 457 A.2d 701, 710 (Del. 1983).
[53] Unocal Corp. v. Mesa Petroleum Co., 493 A.2d 946, 954 (Del. 1985). [54] Ibid.
[55] Ibid.
[56] Ibid. at 955. Indeed, the *Unocal* court's explicit rejection of Frank Easterbrook and Dan Fischel's "passivity" thesis described in Frank H. Easterbrook & Daniel R. Fischel, *The Proper Role of a Target's Management in Responding to a Tender Offer*, 94 HARV. L. REV. 1161, 1175–80 (1981), is, to a significant degree, a rejection of the MFF that formed the foundation of their argument. As they argued, the increased merger premium that defensive measures might secure was unimportant as it was largely a transfer among fully diversified shareholders, while the threat of hostile tender offers would increase the value of their overall portfolios. Ibid. at 1201–04.

present a special case because, by construction, there are no possible conflicts of interest among shareholders. While the law is clear that the directors of a solvent, wholly owned subsidiary should pursue the interests of the parent company,[57] in all other cases (e.g., a partially owned subsidiary), the directors must pursue the interests of the subsidiary itself.[58] Put differently, extraneous interests of shareholders – as to which shareholder interests may conflict – are problematic except in the special case in which there is no potential for conflicts of interest among shareholders because the company has only a single shareholder.

4.3.2 *Single Firm Focus, Shareholder Primacy, and Stakeholderism*

As noted above, in the traditional formulation, the corporation is managed "for the benefit of shareholders," and the articulation of various duties often talks about "the corporation and its shareholders."[59] This raises two important issues. First, how does corporate law understand shareholders' interests? Second, how does SFF relate to the ongoing debate over whether corporate law does, and should, enshrine "shareholder primacy?"[60]

In the traditional understanding, the focus is on shareholders *qua* shareholders of a particular firm, taking into account their interests only insofar as they relate to the shareholders' relationship with the company and, importantly, ignoring their "extraneous" or outside interests, including their portfolio interests.

The focus on shareholders *qua* shareholders of a given corporation – to the exclusion of shareholders' extraneous interests – is best illustrated

[57] Trenwick Am. Litig. Tr. v. Ernst & Young, L.L.P., 906 A.2d 168, 201 (Del. Ch. 2006) (citing Anadarko Petro. Corp. v. Panhandle E. Corp., 545 A.2d 1171, 1174 (Del. 1988).

[58] For an interesting discussion of these SFF principles as applied to directors appointed by a particular shareholder or group of shareholders, *see* J. Travis Laster & John Mark Zeberkiewicz, *The Rights and Duties of Blockholder Directors*, 70 Bus. Law. 33 (2015).

[59] Restatement of the L.: Corp. Governance § 2.01(a) (Am. L. Inst., Tentative Draft No. 1, 2022).

[60] "Shareholder primacy" refers to the principle that the corporation should be managed for the principal benefit of its shareholders, rather than for the benefit of multiple constituencies, such as employees and customers. David Millon, *Radical Shareholder Primacy*, 10 U. St. Thomas L.J. 1013, 1013, 1016 (2013). For some recent contributions on how SFF relates to the debate over whether corporate law should enshrine shareholder primacy, see Donald C. Langevoort, *The Effects of Shareholder Primacy, Publicness, and "Privateness" on Corporate Cultures*, 43 Seattle U. L. Rev. 377 (2020); Jeff Schwartz, *De Facto Shareholder Primacy*, 79 Md. L. Rev. 652 (2020); Ramsi A. Woodcock, *The Antitrust Case for Consumer Primacy in Corporate Governance*, 10 UC Irvine L. Rev. 1395 (2020).

by *Revlon, Inc. v. MacAndrews & Forbes Holdings, Inc.*[61] *Revlon* involved a bidding contest for Revlon between Forstmann and Pantry Pride, a company owned by Ronald Perelman.[62] In the contest, Revlon's board of directors accepted a bid by Forstmann that entailed a lockup and cancellation fee for the benefit of Forstmann valued at $125 to $200 million.[63] In exchange, Forstmann had promised to support the value of Revlon's Senior Subordinated Notes, which had declined after the Revlon board agreed to waive certain note covenants.[64] The court's opinion criticized the board's attempt to secure benefits for Revlon's noteholders, holding that "concern for non-stockholder interests is inappropriate" when a company is sold for cash.[65]

While *Revlon* is often cited as an endorsement of shareholder primacy,[66] its significance extends further. The Senior Subordinated Notes that Forstmann had promised to support had been issued by Revlon only one month earlier pursuant to an exchange offer for its own shares in which 87 percent of Revlon's shareholders participated.[67] When the exchange offer closed, the vast majority of Revlon's shareholders also became noteholders, and all noteholders were also Revlon shareholders.[68] In all likelihood, this picture had not changed fundamentally by the following month. As Revlon Senior Subordinated Noteholders were largely Revlon shareholders, supporting the price of the notes would have benefitted these shareholders. Nevertheless, the Delaware Supreme Court was clear that this type of benefit – which derives from shareholders' extraneous interests (the ownership of Senior Subordinated Notes by persons who also happen to be Revlon shareholders) rather than their interests *qua* shareholders – should have been ignored.[69]

While stakeholderism expands the range of interests that count to include non-shareholder constituencies, the single firm focus remains. In a stakeholder jurisdiction, the board is typically permitted to consider non-shareholder interests (e.g., the interests of employees or creditors), but the permission is in the context of "considering the best interests of the

[61] Revlon, Inc. v. MacAndrews & Forbes Holdings, Inc., 506 A.2d 173 (Del. 1985).
[62] *See* Jacob Bernstein, *The Debt King*, N.Y. Times (Jan. 7, 2022), https://www.nytimes.com/2022/01/07/style/ron-perelman.html.
[63] Revlon, 506 A.2d at 178–79. [64] Ibid. at 179. [65] Ibid. at 182.
[66] *See, e.g.*, Matthew T. Bodie, *AOL Time Warner and the False God of Shareholder Primacy*, 31 J. Corp. L. 975, 979 (2006).
[67] Revlon, 506 A.2d at 177. [68] Ibid. [69] *See* Ibid. at 180–84.

corporation. . ."[70] This clear SFF language implies that only the interests of shareholders *qua* shareholders of this company, the interests of employees *qua* employees of this company, or the interests of creditors *qua* creditors of this company should enter the company's calculus. Indeed, given the variety of extraneous interests that can arise as one considers additional stakeholders, a stakeholder approach may be even more SFF than a shareholder primacy view. As a result, the shareholder versus stakeholder debate is largely orthogonal to our concerns here: both approaches incorporate a deep SFF.

Because shareholder primacy remains the dominant framework under which most corporations operate, the discussion in this chapter is mostly premised on shareholder primacy. However, it bears noting that the arguments advanced by Alexander, Condon, and Gordon are weaker under stakeholderism than in a shareholder primacy setting. Their arguments rely on the existence of large, highly diversified *shareholders* with huge extraneous portfolio interests that swamp their interest in any particular firm.[71] For example, BlackRock's holdings in ExxonMobil account for less than 0.5 percent of its $3.6 trillion domestic equity portfolio.[72] Other corporate constituents – employees in particular – are not equally diversified and therefore hold comparatively smaller extraneous interests. A decision by ExxonMobil to cut its emissions by 40 percent – raising the prospect that many employees would lose their jobs or that the company would buy less from some of its major suppliers – may well not be in the interests of ExxonMobil's stakeholders even if it benefited ExxonMobil's universal shareholders.

4.3.3 *Corporate Law's "Egalitarian" Focus: For All the Shareholders*

When it is said that a corporation is managed "for the benefit of the shareholders," what exactly does that mean? For the benefit of which shareholders?

If shareholder interests are understood as the interests of shareholders *qua* shareholders of a given company – abstracting from the interests of the actual shareholders, who will often have "extraneous" interests – then the principal focus is on the interest that all shareholders have in common, namely, maximizing the value of the company. This results in a highly stylized conception of shareholders' interests that often

[70] 15 Pa. Cons. Stat. § 1715 (2022). [71] *See, e.g.*, Gordon, *supra* note 12.
[72] BlackRock, Inc., Quarterly Report (Form 13F) (Sept. 30, 2021). Form 13F excludes most debt securities and foreign equity securities.

departs from shareholders' actual interests and, in doing so, avoids all of the complex issues that arise in reconciling heterogeneous interests and preferences.[73]

Shareholders, of course, may have differing views on *how* a company should maximize its value. From the beginning, corporate law has embraced indirect majority rule, providing for the election of directors by a majority or plurality of the shares voting while tasking directors with the company's management.[74]

Giving power to holders of a majority of shares, however, generates a problem. Holders of a majority of shares may use their power not merely to resolve differences of opinion on how to maximize the corporation's value for shareholders at large but also to pursue their extraneous self-interest. This problem is most acute if a single shareholder, or a group of affiliated shareholders, owns a majority of the shares or otherwise controls the corporation.

One way to constrain this abuse is to require that the majority's power to decide must be deployed for the benefit of *all shareholders*. Thus, in *East Rome Town Co. v. Nagle*,[75] a court blocked the attempt of a majority shareholder to convert a toll bridge owned by the corporation into a free bridge (which would have advantaged the majority shareholder) on the grounds that the corporation must use the bridge franchise for the profit of the corporation and thus for all shareholders ratably.[76] Similarly, in *Ervin v. Oregon Railway & Navigation Co.*,[77] the court recognized the power of the majority to dissolve the corporation, but then required that the majority account to the minority for the fair value of the assets sold.[78]

This principle also has deep roots in Delaware corporate law. In *Allied Chemical & Dye Corp. v. Steel & Tube Co. of America*,[79] a seminal decision on the fiduciary duties of a controlling stockholder, the court stated that:

> The same considerations of fundamental justice which impose a fiduciary character upon the relationship of the directors to the stockholders will also impose, in a proper case, a like character upon the relationship which

[73] *See generally* Henry Hansmann, The Ownership of Enterprise (2000).

[74] *See generally* John P. Davis, Corporations (1905).

[75] E. Rome Town Co. v. Nagle, 58 Ga. 474 (Ga. 1877).

[76] Ibid. at 477–78.

[77] Ervin v. Or. Ry. & Navigation Co., 27 F. 625 (S.D.N.Y. 1886).

[78] Ibid. at 630. As D. Gordon Smith points out, this principle is the origin of what we now think of as the shareholder primacy norm. D. Gordon Smith, *The Shareholder Primacy Norm*, 23 J. Corp. L. 277, 279 (1998).

[79] Allied Chem. & Dye Corp. v. Steel & Tube Co. of Am., 120 A. 486 (Del. Ch. 1923).

> the majority of the stockholders bear to the minority. When, in the conduct of the corporate business, a majority of the voting power in the corporation join hands in imposing its policy upon all, it is beyond all reason and contrary, it seems to me, to the plainest dictates of what is just and right, to take any view other than that they are to be regarded as having placed upon themselves the same sort of fiduciary character which the law impresses upon the directors in their relation to all the stockholders. Ordinarily, the directors speak for and determine the policy of the corporation. When the majority of stockholders do this, they are, for the moment, the corporation. Unless the majority in such case are to be regarded as owing a duty to the minority such as is owed by the directors to all, then the minority are in a situation that exposes them to the grossest frauds and subjects them to most outrageous wrongs.[80]

The board's obligation to manage the corporation for the benefit of all the shareholders has, over time, extended to imposing limited fiduciary duties on controlling shareholders. Unlike officers and directors, shareholders do not automatically owe fiduciary duties to the corporation. Rather, shareholders take on fiduciary duties when they become controllers, whether as a result of owning a majority of the corporation's shares or as a result of exercising actual control. Corporate transactions or conduct in which a controller has an interest that is different from the general shareholder interest, thus trigger the duty of loyalty. Thus, for example, when a controller freezes out non-controlling shareholders in a going-private transaction, the controller must establish the fairness of the transaction unless it adopts procedures that cleanse the transaction of the taint of self-dealing.[81]

The use of majority power to oppress minority shareholders in closely held corporations developed into the "minority oppression" remedy,[82] but the underlying principle remains the same: the corporation must be managed for the benefit of all shareholders and not just the majority shareholder.[83]

[80] Ibid. at 491; *accord* Epstein v. Celotex Corp., 238 A.2d 843, 847 (Del. Ch. 1968).

[81] *See, e.g.*, Kahn v. M & F Worldwide Corp., 88 A.3d 635 (Del. 2014). But controllers' duties *may* extend further. As Chancellor William T. Allen explained, "when a shareholder, who achieves power through the ownership of stock, exercises that power by directing the actions of the corporation, he assumes the duties of care and loyalty of a director of a corporation." Cinerama, Inc. v. Technicolor, Inc., 1991 WL 111134, at *19 (Del. Ch. June 24, 1991) (Allen, C.), *aff'd in part, rev'd on other grounds sub nom*, 634 A.2d 345 (Del. 1993).

[82] Smith, *supra* note 79, at 310–22.

[83] The U.K. cases reflect a similar "abuse of majority" principle according to which majorities must use their power over the corporation for the benefit of all, at least in some circumstances. *See* Allen v. Gold Reefs of W. Afr. Ltd, [1900] 1 Ch 656 at 671.

4.3.4 Shareholders' Limited Duties: Selfish Voting

There are two respects in which corporate law bows to the right of shareholders to pursue their extraneous self-interest: any shareholder, including a controller, may generally vote and sell shares selfishly. In the leading Delaware case, *Bershad v. Curtiss-Wright Corp.*,[84] the plaintiff argued that the majority shareholder's policy against selling its controlled subsidiary breached its fiduciary duties.[85] Rejecting this claim, the Delaware Supreme Court provided the iconic statement that is typically cited for the proposition that shareholders, including controlling shareholders, may vote selfishly:

> Stockholders in Delaware corporations have a right to control and vote their shares in their own interest. They are limited only by any fiduciary duty owed to other stockholders. It is not objectionable that their motives may be for personal profit, or determined by whim or caprice, so long as they violate no duty owed other shareholders.[86]

In our context, what is so interesting about this statement is its limitations, namely that shareholders may vote selfishly "so long as they violate no duty owed to other shareholders." When applied to controllers, this imports the case law imposing duties on other shareholders when acting through the board.

The right to vote selfishly is conceptually most important when shareholders vote on board proposals *other than* the election of directors. Thus, shareholders are legally free to oppose and defeat a merger or a charter amendment for extraneous self-interested reasons even if they acknowledge that the measure would be valuable for the company. To be sure, shareholders may also cast votes for directors "for personal profit." But directors are not permitted to further the personal profits of some shareholders and at least controlling shareholders could be subject to personal liability if directors did so. While fiduciary duty law in these respects is surely not perfectly enforced, it imposes substantial constraints on the ability of most shareholders to benefit from selfish votes in director elections and practical limits on how shareholders and directors campaign for elections.

By contrast, when a controlling shareholder intervenes in the governance directly and not in response to a board proposal – for example, through the enactment of a bylaw – the limitation on *Bershad*'s

[84] Bershad v. Curtiss-Wright Corp., 535 A.2d 840 (Del. 1986). [85] Ibid. at 841–43.
[86] Ibid. at 845.

permission to vote selfishly becomes relevant: a shareholder-adopted bylaw may be held void if adopted for an inequitable purpose.[87] Thus, while the "right to vote selfishly" protects controllers from suffering a cost for the benefit of noncontrolling shareholders, it may not license a controller to use its voting power to impose costs on noncontrolling shareholders – for example, by amending the charter or adopting a bylaw that injures noncontrolling shareholders.[88]

Shareholders are also free to vote in their self-interest on precatory shareholder resolutions. Votes on precatory shareholder resolutions fall between votes on director elections and votes on bylaw amendments. On one hand, these resolutions are not self-effecting but are addressed to the board. And the board, of course, must consider its own fiduciary duties in deciding whether to heed them. On the other hand, directors themselves are not directly involved in these resolutions. This dual nature means that shareholders may sometimes campaign openly in favor of resolutions on the basis of goals other than the best interest of the corporation. But if such a resolution then obtains majority support, such campaigning would make it harder for directors to implement the resolution.

4.4 Implementing Climate Stewardship

Let us assume that Condon is correct that ExxonMobil and Chevron, by reducing their carbon production by 40 percent, would substantially increase the value of the portfolios of universal owners despite the fact that ExxonMobil's and Chevron's stock price would decline by 20 percent. How might universal owners induce ExxonMobil and Chevron to cut their carbon emissions? What legal and political risks would it entail? Are there alternative strategies with less legal risk? Would those alternative strategies significantly reduce carbon emissions?

4.4.1 Embracing the Hypo with Enthusiasm: A Hypothetical Campaign

Suppose that BlackRock, Vanguard, and State Street (BVS), the three largest universal owners, were to team up explicitly to elect new boards at ExxonMobil and Chevron committed to reducing their carbon output by

87 *See* Hollinger Int'l, Inc. v. Black, 844 A.2d 1022, 1080–82 (Del. Ch. 2004), aff'd 872 A.2d 559 (Del. Ch. 2005).

88 We owe this insight to Zohar Goshen. *See, e.g.*, IRA Tr. FBO Bobbie Ahmed v. Crane, No. 12742-CB., 2017 WL 7053964, at *7–8 (Del. Ch. Dec. 11, 2017).

40 percent, despite clear evidence that doing so would substantially reduce their stock prices.[89] Let us suppose, for instance, that they enter into a shareholders' agreement committing themselves to vote together for a jointly selected slate, jointly retain a proxy solicitor and other professionals, and campaign for their slate based on the portfolio benefits an emissions cut would generate. What regulatory or corporate law obstacles and risks would they run?

First, having formed a "group" for the purpose of voting their shares, BVS would no longer qualify to file Schedule 13G but would now have to file a joint Schedule 13D disclosing their holdings and amend that filing when holdings or intentions changed. While filing a Schedule 13D would not, by itself, be particularly burdensome, amendments would add to the burden and filing a Schedule 13D would necessitate a fundamental change in practice, as each adviser currently files only Schedule 13Gs.

Second, this group of universal owners collectively holding more than 10 percent would likely find itself subject to section 16 of the Securities Exchange Act.[90] Section 16(b) requires the disgorgement of any "short-swing" profit made or loss avoided from "any purchase and sale, or any sale and purchase," within six months.[91] This would be very burdensome for BlackRock, Vanguard, and State Street, as they constantly buy and sell shares as money flows into and out of their funds and thus engage in substantial short-swing trading.

Third, having shifted from being "passive" holders to being "active" holders, the Hart-Scott-Rodino Act would impose advanced notice and pre-clearance requirements on additional purchase of shares of either company.[92] In periods when additional funds are flowing into their index funds, this would increase tracking error and expenses.

89 The actual calculation required by Condon's hypothetical, with its tradeoff over various margins, is complex. It is unclear whether universal owners, as currently configured, have the expertise to calculate such tradeoffs accurately. Were this to become a major strategy, however, they could acquire the expertise.

90 Section 16 incorporates the section 13(d) concepts of beneficial ownership. Securities Exchange Act of 1934 § 16a-1(a)(1); CSX v. TCI, 654 F.3d 276, 290–94 (2d Cir. 2011) (Winter, concurring).

91 Securities Exchange Act of 1934 § 16(b), 15 U.S.C. § 78p.

92 Hart-Scott-Rodino Antitrust Improvement Act, Pub. L. No. 94-435, 90 Stat. 1383 (1976). On the limitations that the Hart-Scott-Rodino exemption of purchases "solely for the purpose of investment" imposes on active engagement by the largest institutional investors, *see* Letter from Edward Rock, Co-Director, Inst. for Corp. Governance & Fin. at NYU Sch. of Law, to Federal Trade Commission (Jan. 28, 2021), https://www.regulations.gov/comment/FTC-2020-0085-0005.

Equally concerning would be the risks under Delaware corporate law. Let us assume that BVS's campaign is successful, their slate of directors is elected, and the boards of ExxonMobil and Chevron commit to implementing a 40 percent emission cut, resulting in an immediate 20 percent drop in the stock price. In the wake of their boards' decisions and the drop in the stock price, litigation is brought on behalf of ExxonMobil and Chevron shareholders against the directors of each company and against BlackRock, Vanguard, and State Street both as a collective "controlling shareholder" and for "aiding and abetting" the directors' breaches of their fiduciary duties. The lawsuit alleges, with detailed support, that the decision to cut carbon emissions was made to benefit the extraneous interests of the universal owners of the companies rather than ExxonMobil and Chevron.

In this robust form of climate change activism – in which universal owners team up to elect a new board committed to a strategy with substantial tradeoffs – these would be very substantial claims. We will briefly work through the steps.

First, while the claims would be derivative – the harm to shareholders derives from the reduction in the value of ExxonMobil and Chevron by virtue of adopting BVS's low carbon emissions strategy[93] – demand would clearly be excused: by hypothesis, a majority of the directors intentionally pursued a strategy that reduces company value for the extraneous benefit of a group of shareholders and, as we will show, faces potential liability.[94]

Second, on the merits, the claims against the directors would be strong. This extreme hypothetical, unrealistically, comes close to a confession of disloyalty. After all, the BVS campaign, by its terms, seeks portfolio benefits for BVS while acknowledging that it will harm ExxonMobil and Chevron. With respect to the directors, corporate law's fundamental principles described above – the SFF and the "egalitarian" commitment to managing the corporation for the benefit of all the shareholders and not just the most powerful – would both condemn the conduct. The goal of benefiting the portfolio interests of powerful shareholders over the interests of the corporation is improper. Benefiting those powerful shareholders at the expense of the other shareholders is likewise off-limits. Similarly, the fact that some other, smaller shareholders may share BVS's

93 *See generally* Tooley v. Donaldson, Lufkin & Jenrette, Inc., 845 A.2d 1031 (Del. 2004).

94 *See generally* United Food & Com. Workers Union v. Zuckerberg, 262 A.3d 1034 (Del. 2021).

interests would be of no avail. Under Delaware case law, such conduct by directors would constitute a lack of "good faith" and, in doing so, would violate the duty of loyalty and expose directors to the risk of personal liability.[95] While directors could take steps to protect themselves by commissioning reports that purport to show how reducing carbon emissions would increase firm value, there would still be a substantial legal risk.

The claims against BVS are more complicated. After all, none of BlackRock, Vanguard, or State Street individually have sufficient power to control ExxonMobil or Chevron. Their liability, then, would depend on whether a court would find that they, together, constitute a "controller."

Delaware "law recognizes that multiple stockholders together can constitute a control group exercising majority or effective control, with each member subject to the fiduciary duties of a controller."[96] To establish group control:

> [The shareholder must be] "connected in some legally significant way' . . . to work together toward a shared goal." To show a "legally significant" connection, [one] must allege that there was more than a "mere concurrence of self-interest among certain stockholders." Rather, "there must be some indication of an actual agreement," although it need not be formal or written.[97]

Here, of course, the hypo's explicit agreement between BVS – memorialized in a shareholders' agreement – presumably establishes the requisite "legally significant connection."

If BVS constituted a group, there could be a decent argument that the group had effective control over the companies, depending on the relationship between BVS and the directors they nominated. For example, nominees who are all employees of BlackRock, Vanguard, or State Street would be strong evidence of control. Similarly, if the nominees, while not BVS employees, nonetheless had committed to implementing the "low carbon" strategy as part of their agreement to be nominated to the board,

[95] While Delaware law permits companies to exculpate directors from monetary liability for breach of fiduciary duties by charter provision, that provision may not eliminate or limit liability "for any breach of the director's duty of loyalty to the corporation or its stockholders" or "for acts or omissions not in good faith." Del. Code Ann. tit. 8, § 102(b)(7) (West 2022). For a similar argument, see J. Travis Laster, *Fiduciary Duties in Activist Situations*, 13 Va. L. & Bus. Rev. 75 (2019).

[96] Sheldon v. Pinto Tech. Ventures, L.P., 220 A.3d 245, 251 (Del. 2019).

[97] Ibid. at 251–52.

that would also provide some evidence that BVS were pulling the strings, at least as to the "low carbon" initiative. While collective ownership of around 20–25 percent is at the bottom end of what is typically considered sufficient to become a controller,[98] it could suffice when combined with control over the board of directors.

Even if a court remained unconvinced that BVS jointly controlled ExxonMobil and Chevron and that BVS thus did not have fiduciary duties as controllers, they could still face liability for "aiding and abetting" the directors' breaches of fiduciary duties. To establish "aiding and abetting" liability, one must show "(i) the existence of a fiduciary relationship, (ii) a breach of the fiduciary's duty, (iii) knowing participation in the breach by a non-fiduciary defendant, and (iv) damages proximately caused by the breach."[99] Here, the relevant fiduciary relationship would be that of the directors. The fiduciary's alleged breach would be the directors' breach of their duty of loyalty in pursuing a goal other than ExxonMobil's or Chevron's interests. "Knowing participation" in a fiduciary's breach requires that the alleged aider and abettor "act with the knowledge that the conduct advocated or assisted constitutes such a breach."[100] On the facts of the hypothetical, BVS formulated the low carbon emission strategy and ran a proxy contest to have directors elected who would implement it. The plaintiffs would have a strong case that, in doing so, they induced the board to make the decision at issue.[101] Finally, the resulting 20 percent decline in the stock price would constitute evidence of the damages proximately caused by the breach.

4.4.2 *Pursuing a Condon "Tradeoff" Strategy Would Conflict with Universal Owners' Business Model and Legal Obligations to Clients*

"Universal owners" are, in fact, not real owners but managers of money for the benefit of clients. The plausibility of universal owners pursuing an active climate risk mitigation strategy depends on these firms' businesses and legal obligations to these clients. BlackRock, for example, describes its business as follows:

[98] *See, e.g.*, Tornetta v. Musk, 250 A.3d 793, 801–02 (Del. Ch. 2019) (finding that it was reasonably conceivable that Elon Musk, who owns "approximately 21.9% of Tesla's common stock," was Tesla's controller).

[99] Malpiede v. Townson, 780 A.2d 1075, 1096 (Del. 2001); Firefighters' Pension Sys. v. Presidio, Inc., 251 A.32 212, 273 (Del. Ch. 2021).

[100] Malpiede, 780 A.2d at 1097.

[101] Ibid. at 1098.

> BlackRock, Inc. (together, with its subsidiaries, unless the context otherwise indicates, "BlackRock" or the "Company") is a leading publicly traded investment management firm with $8.68 trillion of assets under management ("AUM") at December 31, 2020 . . . BlackRock provides a broad range of investment management and technology services to institutional and retail clients worldwide.
>
> BlackRock's diverse platform of alpha-seeking active, index and cash management investment strategies across asset classes enables the Company to tailor investment outcomes and asset allocation solutions for clients. Product offerings include single- and multi-asset portfolios investing in equities, fixed income, alternatives and money market instruments. Products are offered directly and through intermediaries in a variety of vehicles, including open-end and closed-end mutual funds, *iShares*® exchange-traded funds ("ETFs"), separate accounts, collective trust funds and other pooled investment vehicles . . .
>
> BlackRock serves a diverse mix of institutional and retail clients across the globe. Clients include tax-exempt institutions, such as defined benefit and defined contribution pension plans, charities, foundations and endowments; official institutions, such as central banks, sovereign wealth funds, supranationals and other government entities; taxable institutions, including insurance companies, financial institutions, corporations and third-party fund sponsors, and retail intermediaries.[102]

While Vanguard pursues a different, consumer-focused strategy that emphasizes low costs, it too is a highly regulated fiduciary that runs dozens of different mutual funds, including both equity and fixed income products, with different goals and targeted to different customers.[103]

Any sort of "tradeoff" strategy of the sort proposed by Condon would wreak havoc on universal owners' business model.[104] While the "low carbon" strategy might be optimal for the investors in an S&P 500 index fund, as Condon argues, it will not be optimal for investors in an energy ETF in which ExxonMobil and Chevron are significant holdings. For example, a decline of 20 percent in the stock price of ExxonMobil and Chevron would be devastating to the investors in BlackRock's $2 billion U.S. Energy ETF (holdings: ExxonMobil 22.78 percent; Chevron 16.09

[102] BlackRock, Inc., Annual Report (Form 10-K) 1 (Feb. 25, 2021).
[103] *See generally* Vanguard, Investment Stewardship 2021 Annual Report (2022).
[104] *See generally* John Morley, Too Big to Be Activist, 92 S. Cal. L. Rev. 1407 (2019).

percent),[105] or Vanguard's $4.8 billion Energy ETF (holdings: ExxonMobil 22.34 percent; Chevron 15.72 percent).[106] The strategy could also negatively impact actively managed portfolios that are overweight in these companies. How would BlackRock or Vanguard explain to current or prospective investors in the Energy ETFs or other funds heavily invested in ExxonMobil and Chevron why they supported a strategy that sacrificed ExxonMobil and Chevron for the benefit of their index fund investors? Indeed, a business model that prioritized the interests of index fund investors over other funds would likely doom those other funds, as competitors would offer competing products that pledged loyalty to fund investors.

A tradeoff strategy would also present a significant risk of fiduciary liability to clients.[107] As BlackRock explicitly says in its securities filings, "[t]he Company is highly regulated and manages its clients' assets as a fiduciary."[108] Just as corporate law incorporates an SFF in mandating that directors owe fiduciary duties to "their" corporation for the benefit of "their" corporation's shareholders, trust law's duty of loyalty has a similar, narrow focus.[109] Under the traditional "sole interest" rule, "a trustee must 'administer the trust *solely* in the interest of the beneficiaries.'"[110] As Max Schanzenbach and Robert Sitkoff point out,

> Under this rule, "the trustee has a duty to the beneficiaries not to be influenced by the interest of any third person or by motives other than the accomplishment of the purposes of the trust." "The trustee," in other words, "is under a duty to the beneficiary in administering the trust not to be guided by the interest of any third person." Acting with mixed motives triggers "an irrebuttable presumption of wrongdoing," full stop.[111]

As they discuss in detail, "the sole interest rule is mandatory under ERISA and is the default in trust law."[112] But even the somewhat more permissive "best interest" standard – applicable when the "sole interest"

[105] *iShares U.S. Energy ETF*, iSHARES, https://www.ishares.com/us/products/239507/ishares-us-energy-etf.
[106] *Vanguard Energy ETF*, VANGUARD, https://investor.vanguard.com/etf/profile/portfolio/vde.
[107] *See* Morley, *supra* note 105, at 1417.
[108] BlackRock, Inc., *supra* note 103, at 1.
[109] *See* Max M. Schanzenbach & Robert H. Sitkoff, *Reconciling Fiduciary Duty and Social Conscience: The Law and Economics of ESG Investing By a Trustee*, 72 STAN. L. REV. 381, 399–425 (2020).
[110] Ibid. at 400 (citing RESTATEMENT (THIRD) OF TRUSTS § 78(1) (AM. L. INST. 2007)).
[111] Schanzenbach & Sitkoff, *supra* note 110, at 400–01.
[112] Ibid. at 401.

standard is waived and a standard roughly equivalent to corporate law's "entire fairness" test – would not permit any tradeoff strategy precisely because it involves sacrificing the interests of the beneficiaries for the benefit of some third party to that relationship.[113]

Given these fiduciary obligations, along with business considerations, universal owners like BlackRock, Vanguard, and State Street simply could not embrace a tradeoff strategy of the sort suggested by Condon.

4.4.3 *Controlling Legal Risk: Less Robust Strategies*

The "enthusiastic" version of the hypo, analyzed above, is obviously unrealistic. In the real world, because of the substantial legal risk under both federal and state law, no one would proceed in such an explicit way. And, in the absence of extreme facts, it would be hard to establish that directors were acting in bad faith.

But that is part of our point: each step away from an explicit joint campaign comes at a price of effectiveness. Indeed, because of the clash between universal owners' MFF and corporate law's SFF, there will be nearly a direct relationship between how effective a strategy is for MFF purposes and how much legal risk it entails. Because the success of even the explicit MFF tradeoff strategy is hardly assured – shareholders could easily vote down the BVS slate of directors, either because they had different financial interests or because they did not trust BVS's directors to run the company well – more legally defensible (and less effective) approaches are unlikely to result in significantly lower carbon emissions.

First, BlackRock, Vanguard, and State Street would never explicitly form a group because of the legal risks we describe above. In the real world, BlackRock, Vanguard, and State Street do not nominate directors, run proxy contests, coordinate, or even discuss their positions at specific firms. Instead, they allow others to launch proxy contests and then independently decide whether to support a slate in full or in part.

Second, because of corporate law's SFF – with directors owing fiduciary duties to their corporations and not to their investors' portfolios – campaigns will typically be framed in SFF terms. As long as a campaign is framed in SFF terms, climate-aware directors have great latitude under the business judgment rule to reduce a firm's own carbon emissions, even

[113] Ibid. at 401–02.

if doing so turns out to reduce the company's stock price. For an individual firm, substantial unilateral reductions in carbon emissions can be justified as rationally related to the long-term success of the firm either because of reputational concerns, as a way of repositioning the firm for a post-carbon economy, or because of a judgment that current investments in production are unlikely to be profitable due to anticipated changes in either demand or regulation. A board that chooses to reduce carbon emissions for one of these reasons would thus be unlikely to face any significant legal risk.

Finally, at the fund family level, because of the differing interests of different funds, voting on issues that may affect different funds differently will often be pushed down to the fund level, with a fund's portfolio manager casting the votes.

While each of these steps will reduce legal risk, they will also make accomplishing the MFF outcome of Condon's hypo less likely. Without coordinating with each other and with the other universal owners, coming up with a jointly acceptable MFF "low carbon" strategy will become far more difficult. Given the complexities of the calculation that Condon's hypo demands, different investors will likely come to different conclusions and, without coordination, those different conclusions will result in different voting decisions.

Similarly, nominating or, more likely, supporting climate-concerned yet independent board nominees will be far less effective than nominating a slate of candidates committed to a given low-carbon strategy, especially when that strategy sacrifices the interests of ExxonMobil and Chevron for universal owners' portfolio interests.

Further, the need to push decisions on potential tradeoffs to the fund level will both reduce the universal owners' voting power and make it less likely that they will support proposals that involve tradeoffs necessitating this more complex procedure.

Fifteen years of hedge fund activism have demonstrated the challenges of forming a consensus around a strategy for increasing single firm value. Forming a shareholder consensus around a tradeoff strategy is an even more daunting challenge. Indeed, to date, we cannot identify a single campaign that has proposed a tradeoff strategy, much less succeeded.[114]

[114] On the other hand, some high-profile battles over the approval of mergers may provide examples of MFF investors *defeating* an SFF campaign. When HP and Compaq agreed to merge, Walter Hewlett, with a large holding in HP, opposed the merger inter alia because, among other reasons, he thought the exchange ratio disfavored HP

4.4.4 *What You May (or May Not) Get Instead: Engine No. 1 at ExxonMobil*

As Condon discusses, ExxonMobil is an ideal target for climate-driven activism. As the largest publicly traded oil company, ExxonMobil's products comprise a significant proportion of carbon emissions on both a current and historical basis. According to one study, ExxonMobil's cumulative 1988–2015 share of global industrial greenhouse gas emissions is 2.0 percent, while its emissions in 2015 were 1.4 percent of global totals.[115] Currently, it is responsible for approximately 1.2 percent of annual global emissions.[116]

Moreover, ExxonMobil's financial performance over the 10 years preceding 2021 had been poor in absolute and comparative terms. Total returns were −18.9 percent (one year), −15.9 percent (three years), and −17.5 percent (five years).[117] Comparatively, ExxonMobil substantially trailed its peers over the same time periods by 12.5 percent (one year), 31.7 percent (three years), and 45.2 percent (five years). As an article in the Wall Street Journal put it in September 2020, after ExxonMobil was removed from the Dow Jones Industrial Index:

> It has been a stunning fall from grace for Exxon Mobil Corp. Just seven years ago, ExxonMobil was the biggest U.S. company by market capitalization. It has since lost roughly 60% of its value, with its market cap now at around $160 billion, after the pandemic crushed demand for fossil fuels.[118]

A sense that it had not been listening to its biggest shareholders made ExxonMobil even more vulnerable. Already in 2017, BlackRock and

shareholders. By contrast, for an investor like an S&P 500 index fund with equal shares of each company, the exchange ratio was irrelevant; all that mattered was whether the companies were worth more together than apart. Hewlett's campaign against the merger – an SFF campaign – failed at least in part because of the support for the merger by MFF investors.

115 Griffin et al, *supra* note 7, at 14–15. Other estimates are higher. Friends of the Earth International, Exxon's Climate Footprint: The Contribution of ExxonMobil to Climate Change Since 1882 (2004) at 5.

116 Condon, *supra* note 6, at 10.

117 Exxon Mobil Corp., Notice of 2021 Annual Meeting and Proxy Statement (Schedule 14A) 51 (Mar. 16, 2021); ExxonMobil, Corp., Annual Report (Form 10-K) 124 (Feb. 24, 2021).

118 Christopher M. Matthews, *Exxon Used to Be America's Most Valuable Company. What Happened?*, Wall St. J. (Sept. 13, 2020), https://www.wsj.com/articles/exxon-used-to-be-americas-most-valuable-company-what-happened-oil-gas-11600037243.

Vanguard had both made it clear to ExxonMobil that it was moving too slowly in assessing climate risk.[119] And in 2020, BlackRock voted against two ExxonMobil directors and in favor of separating the chair and CEO positions.[120]

Against this backdrop, Engine No. 1, a newly formed hedge fund, launched a proxy contest to elect four directors at ExxonMobil's 2021 annual meeting.[121] Engine No. 1's campaign was framed entirely in SFF terms.[122] In the summary slide, the investment thesis was simple: "[t]he industry is evolving, and so must ExxonMobil," and presented four key elements:

- ExxonMobil has significantly underperformed and has failed to adjust its strategy to enhance long-term value.
- A focus on chasing production growth over value has resulted in an undisciplined capital allocation strategy and has destroyed value even during periods of higher oil and gas prices.
- A refusal to accept that fossil fuel demand may decline in decades to come has led to a failure to take even initial steps towards evolution, and to obfuscating rather than addressing long-term business risk.
- A lack of successful and transformative energy experience on the Board has left ExxonMobil unprepared and threatens continued long-term value destruction.[123]

Having "diagnosed" the "problem," Engine No. 1 then made the case for its four board nominees. In the course of doing so, it explicitly disclaimed a tradeoff strategy. As one slide pointed out, "[the strategy is n]ot just a climate issue[, but is] a valuation issue for all long-term investors."[124] This theme continued as it focused on ExxonMobil's "lack of capital allocation discipline,"[125] with a series of supporting points, including:

[119] Bradley Olson, Sarah Krouse, & Sarah Kent, *Big Investors Weigh Rebuking Exxon on Climate*, Wall St. J., May 26, 2017, at B5.

[120] *See CORRECTED-BlackRock Says Voted to Split CEO, Chairman Roles at Exxon Mobil*, Reuters (May 27, 2020), https://www.reuters.com/article/exxon-mobil-agm-blackrock-idCNL1N2D91WI.

[121] Svea Herbst-Bayliss & Gary McWilliams, *Exxon Faces Proxy Fight Launched by New Activist Firm Engine No. 1*, Reuters (Dec. 11, 2020), https://www.reuters.com/business/energy/exxon-faces-proxy-fight-launched-by-new-activist-firm-engine-no-1-2020-12-11/.

[122] *See generally* Exxon Mobil Corp., Engine No. 1, Reenergize ExxonMobil // Investor Presentation (Schedule 14A) (May 3, 2021).

[123] Ibid. at 6. [124] Ibid. at 27. [125] Ibid. at 49.

- Returns on upstream projects (~75 percent of capex) have been falling for years, even during times of higher prices.
- Rising costs and falling capital productivity have fundamentally changed return profile.
- ExxonMobil and peers are far more exposed to risk of declining demand than National Oil Companies (NOCs).
- ExxonMobil's capital expenditures have outgrown cash generation, despite declining returns.
- Despite these dynamics, ExxonMobil has repeatedly committed to more aggressive spending than the industry.[126]

Engine No. 1's campaign was remarkably effective and three of its four nominees were elected.[127] They received support from the major index funds, most actively managed funds, large state pension funds, and both of the major proxy advisers (ISS and Glass Lewis).[128] Vanguard and State Street supported two of Engine No. 1's four nominees, while BlackRock supported three.[129] CalPERS and CalSTRS publicly supported Engine No. 1 prior to the vote. Indeed, Aeisha Mastagni, Head of Corporate Engagement in CalSTRS' Sustainable Investment and Stewardship Strategies Unit, provided active support from the outset, coming close to jointly sponsoring the initiative.[130] Engine No. 1's victory likely sent a signal that shareholders will not tolerate poorly performing management that ignores investors' concerns with the risks posed by climate change. Certainly, this is how activist-defense advisors have interpreted the victory.[131]

[126] Ibid. at 46.

[127] Jennifer Hiller & Svea Herbst-Bayliss, *Engine No. 1 Extends Gains with a Third Seat on Exxon Board*, Reuters (June 2, 2021), https://www.reuters.com/business/energy/engine-no-1-win-third-seat-exxon-board-based-preliminary-results-2021-06-02/#:~:text=June%202%20%28Reuters%29%20-%20Exxon%20Mobil%20Corp%20%28XOM.N%29,victory%20at%20one%20of%20America%E2%80%99s%20top%20energy%20corporations.

[128] Evercore, *The New World of Shareholders* (June 2021) at 2.

[129] *Vote Bulletin: ExxonMobil Corporation*, BlackRock 1 (May 26, 2021), https://www.blackrock.com/corporate/literature/press-release/blk-vote-bulletin-exxon-may-2021.pdf.

[130] Leslie Kaufman & Saijel Kishan, *CalSTRS's Crucial Phone Call Eased Path for Activist's Exxon Win*, Bloomberg (June 18, 2021), https://www.bloomberg.com/news/articles/2021-06-18/calstrs-s-crucial-phone-call-eased-path-for-activist-s-exxon-win?leadSource=uverify%20wall.

[131] Evercore, *supra* note 129.

But despite the fact that Engine No. 1's campaign was framed in traditional single firm "total shareholder value" terms, it could constitute a disguised example of Condon's tradeoff hypothetical. ExxonMobil tried to characterize it that way. Its "deck" accused Engine No. 1 of being motivated by climate concerns rather than value concerns and claimed that Engine No. 1 had backpedaled from earlier positions that aggressively pushed for a reduction in oil and gas investment, increased investment in wind and solar, and a "wind-down" strategy.[132] And regardless of Engine No. 1's intentions, diversified owners of ExxonMobil stock may have thought that electing Engine No. 1's nominees could reduce ExxonMobil's carbon emissions with beneficial effects for their other portfolio holdings. Thus, even if the Engine No. 1 strategy was framed as an SFF strategy, their nominees may have been elected by a coalition of shareholders with MFF concerns.

So, is Engine No. 1's campaign at ExxonMobil a paradigm for a viable strategy to achieve the aims of Condon's hypothetical? Will activists conduct successful campaigns that are nominally SFF and hence entail low legal risks but hold an MFF appeal to universal holders?

Even if that is what happened at ExxonMobil – and we do not know that it is – it is not clear that a similar approach would succeed in other companies, even ones with poor performance like ExxonMobil's. An investor's view of a tradeoff strategy like Condon's will depend, among other things, on the share of an investor's portfolio represented by the target firm. Condon's calculation assumes an investor that pursues an indexing strategy. Extending her analysis, an investor that is "overweight" will give greater weight to the effects on the target, and less to the benefits of reducing emissions, than an indexed investor. On the other hand, an investor that is "underweight" will give *less* weight to the effects on the target and *more* weight to the effects on the rest of its portfolio than an indexed investor. More generally, as a first approximation, investors that are overweight (underweight) will be more (less) SFF than investors that hold the market portfolio.[133] Because universal owners must create a winning coalition to implement a tradeoff strategy, the composition of the shareholder base will thus be important.

[132] ExxonMobil, Corp.., Proxy Statement: Growing Shareholder Value in a Lower-Carbon Future 68 (Schedule 14A) (Apr. 26, 2021).

[133] Whether an investor is overweight or underweight in a given stock, without considering an investor's full portfolio, is an imperfect proxy for an investor's SFF v. MFF incentives.

To provide a sense of the intra-shareholder politics at ExxonMobil, Table 4.1 looks at the votes of the 30 largest ExxonMobil shareholders, that together controlled 34 percent of the vote in ExxonMobil. Due to the complex regulatory scheme governing investor ownership and voting disclosure, uncovering how these holders of ExxonMobil stock voted is a non-trivial task. Table 4.1 contains data prepared for us by Proxy Analytics LLC, a new firm that provides data analytics and consulting services on matters relating to ESG trends and shareholder voting practices.[134] Each year, Proxy Analytics captures and analyzes nearly 20 million voting records that were gathered from SEC (Form N-PX) and web-based disclosures in order to generate profiles on how institutional investors vote.[135] It then performs additional analysis to develop a deeper understanding of the factors that influence voting decisions.[136] Information on beneficial holding and estimated voting authority was derived from quarterly 13F filings as of March 31, 2021, and then adjusted by Proxy Analytics using its proprietary methodology.[137]

Table 4.1 also provides, for each holder, information on the value of ExxonMobil common stock as a percentage of the total value of the holder's 13F securities. This percentage reflects the extent to which a holder is invested in ExxonMobil, relative to the market. For comparison, ExxonMobil stock at the time accounted for approximately 0.59 percent of the capitalization of all the companies in the Russell 3000 index.

There are several notable features. First, among the 30 largest holders, many more seem to be underweight in ExxonMobil (relative to the Russell 3000 index) than overweight. Thus, for example, ExxonMobil stock represents more than 1.18 percent of the value of 13F securities (twice the Russell 3000 percentage) for only two holders, while it represents less than 0.29 percent (half the Russell 3000 percentage) for four holders. This is particularly noteworthy as being underweight in

[134] *About*, Proxy Analytics, https://www.proxy-analytics.com/about.html.

[135] Proxy Analytics, https://proxy-analytics.com/. [136] Ibid.

[137] The record date for the shareholder vote was March 29, 2021. As of March 31, 2021, ExxonMobil constituted about 0.586 percent of the capitalization of all Russell 3000 companies. Column 4 of the Table then provides, for each institutional investor, the percentage of the value of that holder's 13F securities accounted for by ExxonMobil stock. A percentage above 0.586 percent would indicate that the holder is overweight with ExxonMobil stock. Since 13F securities include securities beyond Russell 3000 stocks, these figures are likely to understate somewhat the degree to which investors are overweight in ExxonMobil.

Table 4.1 *Votes of the 30 largest ExxonMobil shareholders*

Holder	Percentage Voting	Percentage Investment Power	Percentage of all 13F Securities	Vote
Vanguard	8.25	8.25	0.53	Dissident
BlackRock	5.94	6.68	0.47	Dissident
State Street	5.53	5.85	0.79	Dissident
FMR	1.78	2.01	0.41	Dissident
Geode Capital Management	1.49	1.49	0.54	Management
Northern Trust	1.21	1.21	0.53	Management
Norges Bank	0.92	1.01	0.58	Management
State Farm Information	0.79	0.79	1.99	No
Bank of New York Mellon	0.79	1.28	0.62	Split
Franklin Resources	0.78	0.83	0.80	Dissident
Charles Schwab	0.66	0.66	0.58	Dissident
First Eagle	0.58	0.61	3.85	Management
T Rowe Price	0.48	0.48	0.11	Dissident
Capital World Investors	0.44	0.44	0.19	Dissident
TIAA-CREF	0.43	0.43	0.32	Dissident
Dimensional	0.41	0.44	0.35	Dissident
Bank of America Information	0.39	0.82	0.22	No
Swiss National Bank Information	0.38	0.38	0.61	No
Sumitomo Mitsui Information	0.32	0.32	0.48	No
PNC Information	0.29	0.30	0.84	No
Amundi	0.29	0.39	0.71	Dissident
Legal & General	0.26	0.54	0.47	Dissident
CalPERS	0.23	0.23	0.41	Dissident
APG Asset Management	0.21	0.21	0.71	Dissident
Federated Hermes	0.21	0.22	1.01	Dissident

Table 4.1 (*cont.*)

Holder	Percentage Voting	Percentage Investment Power	Percentage of all 13F Securities	Vote
AllianceBernstein	0.20	0.21	0.22	Dissident
New York State Common Retirement Fund Information	0.18	0.18	0.48	No
California State Teachers Retirement System	0.18	0.18	0.58	Dissident
Fisher	0.17	0.19	0.32	Dissident
Parametric	0.17	0.22	0.30	Dissident

ExxonMobil makes it less likely for a holder to be included in the list of top 30 holders. Ordinarily, one would have expected that the largest holders of a firm are holders that are overweight in that firm.

Second, the exposure to ExxonMobil is correlated with the vote of the holder. Thus, all four holders who voted for management nominees had a greater than median exposure to ExxonMobil stock. By the same token, active institutional investors that are underweight at a company may be more attracted to an MFF strategy. The data in Table 4.1, while very limited, are consistent with the notion that Engine No. 1's campaign found more appeal with investors that had relatively low exposure to ExxonMobil.

In other companies, however, where a larger number of active institutional shareholders are overweight, an (explicit or implicit) MFF strategy may encounter more resistance and could be used to split apart a coalition of shareholders. For active managers, an MFF strategy that comes at the expense of a company in which the investor is overweight may be objectionable for two reasons. First, such a strategy is less likely to enhance overall portfolio value because the loss in the overweight company's stock is less likely to be outweighed by the gains in the rest of the portfolio than for an index investor. Second, even if the MFF tradeoff strategy enhances overall portfolio value, it may lower their fund's relative performance and hence result in fund outflows.[138] In those companies, an MFF tradeoff strategy that requires the support of less diversified actively managed mutual funds will have greater difficulty assembling a winning coalition.

It is unclear whether ExxonMobil shareholders supported Engine No. 1's campaign for SFF or for MFF reasons. For what it is worth, ExxonMobil's stock price barely moved when the results of the proxy vote were announced,[139] suggesting that shareholders did not believe that Engine No. 1's victory would lead to a decline in the stock price (and perhaps that Engine No. 1 was not pursuing a "tradeoff" strategy). To the extent that universal owners perceived that electing the Engine No. 1 nominees to be at least not harmful to the value of ExxonMobil, their decisions to support them would also have been relatively easy and, from a legal perspective, free of risk.

But even if the effect on other portfolio holdings was the reason why many holders of ExxonMobil voted for Engine No. 1's nominees, it is unclear whether Engine No. 1's success can easily be replicated at many companies. At companies in which the shareholder base tilts more strongly to less diversified investors, even a whiff of MFF may undermine the credibility of the activists and harm the campaign.

4.4.5 Can Universal Owners Rely on an Intermediary?

One response to the liability risks that arise out of the conflict between universal owners' MFF and corporate law's SFF might be to encourage the emergence of "intermediaries" that can further the collective interests of the universal owners without exposing them to legal liability. Intermediaries in the corporate governance space have already emerged,

[138] *See, e.g.*, Richard A. Ippolito, *Consumer Reaction to Measures of Poor Quality: Evidence from the Mutual Fund Industry*, 35 J. L. & Econ. 45, 67 (1992); Brad M. Barber, Xing Huang, & Terrance Odean, *Which Factors Matter to Investors? Evidence from Mutual Fund Flows*, 29 Rev. Fin. Stud. 2600, 2620–21 (2016); Jonathan B. Berk & Richard C. Green, *Mutual Fund Flows and Performance in Rational Markets*, 112 J. Pol. Econ. 1269, 1274–80 (2004); *see generally* Jonathan Lewellen & Katharina Lewellen, *Institutional Investors and Corporate Governance: The Incentive to Be Engaged*, 77 J. Fin. 213 (2022).

[139] *Exxon Mobil Corporation (XOM) Stock Historical Prices & Data*, Yahoo! Fin., https://finance.yahoo.com/quote/xom/history?period1=1546300800&period2=1627776000&interval=1wk&filter=history&frequency=1wk&includeAdjustedClose=true.

including the Investors Forum[140] and Climate Action 100+.[141] In principle (although not in practice), one can imagine ISS or Glass Lewis playing an intermediary role.

According to its website, "Climate Action 100+ is an investor-led initiative to ensure the world's largest corporate greenhouse gas emitters take necessary action on climate change."[142] It claims that "700 investors, responsible for over $68 trillion in assets under management," support their initiatives to engage with "companies on improving climate change governance, cutting emissions and strengthening climate-related financial disclosures."[143] Climate Action 100+'s engagement strategy "is spearheaded by a lead investor or investors, who work cooperatively with a number of collaborating investors."[144] Investors also engage on an individual basis but, when they do so, are supposed to "liaise with relevant network staff and/or lead investors to ensure engagement priorities and ambition are aligned with the goals of the initiative, as well as with the overall collaborative approach (as appropriate in each sector)."[145] Importantly, BlackRock, State Street, CalPERS, and CalSTRS are all members.[146]

Climate Action 100+ makes three principal demands of companies: "clear commitments to cut emissions, improve governance and strengthen climate-related financial disclosures."[147] The demands are justified on an MFF basis: "[t]o mitigate investment exposure to climate risk and secure ongoing sustainable returns for their beneficiaries, investors are ensuring the businesses they own cut emissions to help achieve the goals of the Paris Agreement and accelerate the transition to net-zero emissions by 2050 or sooner."[148]

[140] The Investor Forum, https://www.investorforum.org.uk/.
[141] *Climate Action 100+*, Ceres, https://www.ceres.org/initiatives/climate-action100?gclid=EAIaIQobChMI6YWfobSS8gIViJyzCh3z6gkeEAAYASAAEgJm0vDBwE.
[142] *About Climate Action 100+*, Climate Action 100+, https://www.climateaction100.org/about/.
[143] Ibid.
[144] *Engagement Process*, Climate Action 100+, https://www.climateaction100.org/approach/engagement-process/.
[145] Ibid.
[146] Morgan LaManna & Rob Berridge, *Acting on the Climate Crisis*, Proxy Monthly, July 2021, at 8, 8, https://www.proxyinsight.com/wp-content/uploads/dlm_uploads/2021/08/Proxy-Monthly-July-2021.pdf.
[147] *The Three Asks*, Climate Action 100+, https://www.climateaction100.org/approach/the-three-asks/.
[148] *The Business Case*, Climate Action 100+, https://www.climateaction100.org/business-case/.

Suppose that Climate Action 100+, concerned that the "supply response" described earlier threatens its carbon reduction strategy, targets *all* major oil companies worldwide, with several of its members spearheading the effort. In keeping with its approach, it strives to coordinate its members' actions, including their stewardship efforts, voting policies, lobbying, and public relations. Suppose, further, that the multi-prong campaign is successful with the result that worldwide production of oil declines, and prices rise.

Two types of legal risks would immediately emerge. First, for U.S. targets, reporting under Schedule 13D would now be a real concern. Climate Action 100+'s website trumpets the cooperative nature of the engagements and their signatories' many successes.[149] Moreover, the broad support of Climate Action 100+ members for the industry-wide output reduction campaign would provide evidence that Climate Action 100+ and its members had formed a group for the purpose of voting, thereby triggering 13D disclosure obligations. While the website's disclaimer, echoing 13D, states that "Climate Action 100+ does not require or seek collective decision-making or action with respect to acquiring, holding, disposing and/or voting of securities,"[150] the facts (and Climate Action 100+'s self-promotion) arguably would demonstrate otherwise.

Less obviously, the campaign could raise significant risks under Section 1 of the Sherman Act. An agreement to restrict output, like an agreement to fix prices, is a per se violation of Section 1 and exposes all members of the conspiracy to treble damages and criminal liability.[151] This is true whether the reduction in output is motivated by a desire to increase prices or for some other reason, such as climate change.[152] One classic scenario in which an "agreement" is formed for the purpose of Section 1 is a trade association representative who organizes the members to work together.[153] One alternative description of the

[149] *Successes*, Climate Action 100+, https://www.climateaction100.org/progress/successes/.

[150] Climate Action 100+, Progress Update 2022: Five Years of Climate Action 100+, at 2, https://www.climateaction100.org/wp-content/uploads/2023/01/CA-100-Progress-Update-2022-FINAL-2.pdf.

[151] *See, e.g.*, Edward B. Rock & Daniel L. Rubinfeld, *Common Ownership and Coordinated Effects*, 83 Antitrust L. J. 201 (2020).

[152] *See, e.g.*, Amelia Miazad, *Prosocial Antitrust*, 73 Hastings L. J. 1637 (2022).

[153] The classic example is American Column & Lumber Co. v. United States, 257 U.S. 377 (1921). Another clear example comes from a recent case in the EU involving a management consultant whose specialty seems to have been organizing cartels. Case C-194/14 P, AC-Treuhand AG v. Comm'n, ECLI:EU:C:2015:717 (Oct. 22, 2015).

hypothetical Climate Action 100+ campaign is that Climate Action 100+ and its signatories were a "cartel ringmaster" that organized a production cartel (with a resulting increase in prices). Alternatively, one could describe the campaign as a "hub and spokes" conspiracy, with Climate 100+ and its members acting as the "hub" and the individual oil companies as the spokes. Under either description, the more effective the campaign – the greater the reduction in output – the greater the participants' legal risk. At the same time, because oil companies that reduced output in response to Climate Action 100+'s pressure could likewise face liability under Section 1 as members of the conspiracy, the collective nature of the campaign could *increase* companies' resistance as their lawyers warn them of the legal risks of any collective action to reduce output.

Like the "enthusiastic" version of Condon's hypothetical, the legal risks created by an effective intermediary strategy make it unlikely that universal owners would embrace it. Were Climate Action 100+ to embark on such a strategy, universal owners would be well advised to sever their connections with the group.

4.4.6 *The Softer Forms of Activism: Shareholder Proposals*

Engine No. 1's campaign at ExxonMobil was unprecedented, and it is too early to tell how many similar campaigns will be launched and succeed. Much more common are climate-related shareholder proposals and engagement meetings.

During the 2020 proxy season, climate-related shareholder proposals did very well. Of the 14 proposals primarily focused on climate change that reached a vote, three received majority support, including one at Chevron.[154] An additional two related proposals received majority support, including a proposal at Phillips 66.[155] Both Chevron and Phillips 66 were targeted by Climate Action 100+, which has taken a leading role. Environmental shareholder proposals garnered even more support during the 2021 proxy season, setting a new record: 13 of the

[154] Georgeson, 2020 Annual Corporate Governance Review 33–36 (2020), https://www.irmagazine.com/research-reports/georgesons-2020-annual-corporate-governance-review.

[155] Ibid. at 34.

36 shareholder proposals that reached a vote (most of them relating to climate change) passed.[156]

To what extent do shareholder proposals and engagement meetings push companies in an MFF direction? While Climate Action 100+, as discussed above, takes an explicit MFF, BlackRock frames its engagement priorities and expectations with an SFF.[157] Between the lines, however, BlackRock may well be motivated by MFF concerns. Specifically, when it comes to emissions, BlackRock is quite demanding:

> Specifically, we expect companies to disclose scope 1 and scope 2 emissions and accompanying GHG reduction targets. Companies in carbon-intensive industries should also disclose scope 3 emissions. A significant portion of the transition to a low-carbon economy hinges on the eventual retirement of fossil fuels, and it is particularly important for investors to understand the scope 3 emissions profile of oil, gas, and coal companies as the primary source of fuel transitions from carbon-intensive solutions to cleaner alternatives. The viability of these fuel sources will also become diminished as companies within the transportation and energy value chain, such as original equipment manufacturers, auto-makers, and utilities, accelerate the design of battery, electric, and hydrogen powertrains to further mitigate emissions and prioritize clean energy use.[158]

Increased disclosure on emissions can always be justified as aiding investors' ability to price securities. But what about "GHG *reduction* targets" which, the statement implies, are desirable for all companies? At least some companies may find it in their interests to maintain or even increase emissions (within legal limits). If fossil fuels will be regulated out of the energy sector, oil companies, for example, may want to increase production now before their reserves become valueless and coal-fired power plant operators no longer want to upgrade their soon-to-be-mothballed facilities by installing filters.[159] While BlackRock never says outright that it favors emission targets even if they reduce profits of the company setting the targets and while its statements are vague enough

[156] Georgeson, 2021 Annual Corporate Governance Review 18 (2021), https://content-assets.computershare.com/eh96rkuu9740/c40283f5c88d4946947b26a773462b2f/8eb312e71591f2d4d8b2a408b058be4b/Georgeson-2021-ACGR.pdf.

[157] *See BlackRock Investment Stewardship*, BlackRock, https://www.blackrock.com/corporate/about-us/investment-stewardship.

[158] Ibid.

[159] *See Fathoming Filtration: Reducing Pollutants in Coal-Fired Power Plants*, Power Tech. (Dec. 16, 2010), https://www.power-technology.com/features/feature104857/.

for BlackRock to walk away from this implication, its references to GHG reduction targets is much more compatible with an MFF than an SFF.

BlackRock's "Climate Risk and the Transition to a Low-Carbon Economy" memo is consistent with this interpretation. BlackRock explains:

> Underlying our desire for greater disclosure on emissions baselines, GHG reduction targets, and transition plans, is our conviction that climate risk is investment risk. Solutions to climate change and the transition to a low carbon economy require concerted effort on the part of companies, including assessing their operations and adapting their businesses to remain resilient.[160]

It is, of course, entirely legitimate for BlackRock to take a portfolio perspective in its investment strategy, given BlackRock's duties to its clients with diversified portfolios "to deliver sustainable long-term financial returns."[161] From a portfolio perspective, obtaining information on emissions and transition plans that helps BlackRock evaluate a particular investment's climate risk, and even pushing companies to reduce their *exposure to* climate risk is sensible and consistent with an SFF.[162] Nonetheless, GHG reduction targets would seem to affect climate risk principally by lowering the climate-based *negative externalities* generated by emissions rather than by reducing the climate risk facing the emitting firm. Favoring GHG reduction targets because of a concern with climate risk – rather than, say, because reducing emissions is a good strategy for fending off more onerous regulation – thus indicates an MFF orientation.

As discussed, BlackRock and other shareholders may legally adopt an MFF perspective in voting on precatory shareholder resolution. Indeed, as investment fiduciaries, they may even be required to do so. The problem is that the board has a different set of duties and, under the directors' duty of loyalty, must consider whether the actions proposed by

160 Jessica McDougall & Danielle Sugarman, *Climate Risk and the Transition to a Low-Carbon Economy*, HARV. L. SCH. F. ON CORP. GOVERNANCE (Mar. 2, 2021), https://corpgov.law.harvard.edu/20 21/03/02/climate-risk-and-the-transition-to-a-low-carbon-economy/.

161 Ibid.

162 It would be consistent with an SFF since market participants may generally be concerned about the amount of systematic risk (including climate risk that is systematic) that a particular investment contributes to a portfolio and since therefore a reduction in risk may increase the value of a company. *See generally* Richard Brealey ET AL, Principles of Corporate Finance (14th ed. 2023).

a resolution are in the company's best interest. The more a precatory resolution is premised on MFF, the harder it will be for the board to act in accordance with the resolution.

But BlackRock and other shareholders taking an MFF perspective in their engagement meetings with a company's directors and executives raises additional issues. Urging a board in such meetings to take actions that are in the shareholders' extraneous interest but not in the company's interest carries a somewhat higher legal risk than a mere vote in favor of a precatory resolution. At some point, if directors heed these demands, the shareholder may be exposed to claims for aiding and abetting a breach of fiduciary duties.

However, whatever BlackRock proclaims in its public materials, we do not know what BlackRock actually says to board members and executives in engagement meetings. BlackRock may spend little time discussing emissions, focus on disclosure rather than GHG reduction targets, or push for reduction targets only in situations where such targets can be justified as enhancing firm value. BlackRock's engagement team is well aware that the board has a fiduciary duty to act in the best interest of the corporation, and we doubt that it would ask the board in an engagement meeting to take an action that reduces company value in order to enhance the value of other portfolio securities owned by BlackRock.

Thus, both shareholder resolutions and engagement meetings entail a tradeoff: the more one openly advocates for board action on an MFF basis, the more the risk that a board will violate its fiduciary duties if it undertakes the action, and hence that the board will decide not to undertake it. We would expect BlackRock to at least pretend that the course it advocates benefits the company. Just as BlackRock understands the fiduciary duty constraints under which the board is operating, the board understands that BlackRock has substantial extraneous interests. While the board may thus be skeptical of BlackRock's SFF arguments, it also has an interest in maintaining good relationships with its large shareholders. As long as both BlackRock and the board can maintain the facade that the objective is to maximize company value, the board is more likely to heed BlackRock's requests.

The recent ExxonMobil vote provides some evidence of such a kabuki theatre. In addition to voting on the contested director election, shareholders were asked to vote on a proposal by BNP Paribas Asset Management that asked the company to issue a report within the next year "describing if, and how, ExxonMobil's lobbying activities (direct and through trade associations) align with the goal of limiting average global warming to well below 2 degrees Celsius (the Paris Climate Agreement's goal)."[163] The evident purpose of this proposal, in our view, was to induce ExxonMobil to stop lobbying against the Paris Climate Agreement, with the ultimate goal of facilitating implementation of the accord for the benefit of the public and the benefit of other companies. But BlackRock, which supported the proposal, explained that it was concerned about "the reputational risk to the company of misalignment in public positions on key strategic policy issues" – a pure SFF rationale for the vote.[164] Indeed, the BNP Paribas proposal also asked the company to assess "the risks presented by any misaligned lobbying and the company's plans, if any, to mitigate these risks"[165] – an addition that gave some surface plausibility to BlackRock's explanation.

In short, one can interpret many of BlackRock's statements and actions as promoting MFF under the cloak of SFF. While expressed in terms of an SFF, BlackRock's goal, we surmise, is at least partially based on an MFF because, as a sophisticated universal owner, any other strategy would be irrational.

But the need to articulate a plausible SFF basis for proposals, even if these proposals are truly meant to further MFF goals, places significant constraints on universal holders. Returning to Condon's hypothetical, we do not think that it is possible for a universal owner to make a sufficiently plausible case that it is in ExxonMobil's interest to cut its emissions by 40 percent when doing so would result in a 20 percent drop in the company's value. Having to talk the SFF talk, thus, makes it harder to walk the MFF walk.

4.5 Can Corporate Law's SFF Be Changed to Promote an MFF?

Madison Condon and Rick Alexander have advanced intriguing proposals for robust systemic stewardship. Universal owners have better incentives than most to pursue policies that force the internalization of carbon externalities even (or especially) when doing so requires sacrificing highly polluting companies for the benefit of their overall portfolios. If current corporate law and practice interfere with pursuing these

[163] *Report on Corporate Climate Lobbying in Line with Paris Agreement (XOM, 2021 Res)*, CERES, https://engagements.ceres.org/ceres_engagementdetailpage?recID=a0l1H00000CjqZOQAZ.

[164] BLACKROCK, *supra* note 130, at 7.

[165] CERES, *supra* note 164.

economically and socially rational goals, then perhaps corporate law and practice should change.[166] Is doing so politically plausible?

We think the answer is no. An MFF approach remains second-best to direct governmental regulation. Direct governmental regulation would be more beneficial for the environment as it would apply not just to publicly traded companies with powerful universal owners but also to other business entities. As a result of the broader scope, direct governmental regulation would also reduce the risk of a competitive response that would reduce or eliminate the benefits from actions by individual companies. Indeed, adopting an effective MFF approach for public companies without direct regulation would, over time, lead to a change in industry composition from public to private companies, especially in industries such as energy, which would be the prime targets of an MFF approach. Thus, the longer-term benefits of an MFF approach would be limited.[167]

Second, while there would be powerful political forces and interests that may favor a move to an MFF approach, a move to an MFF would also garner substantial opposition. Employees and managers of carbon-emitting firms that would be sacrificed under such an approach would stand to lose a lot and would likely be strongly opposed. The media responses to Engine No.1's SFF campaign provide a taste of what an explicit "tradeoff" campaign would attract. In an editorial immediately after the ExxonMobil shareholders meeting, the Wall Street Journal viewed Engine No. 1's victory as "a reflection of the enormous political pressure and financial leverage of government pension funds, proxy advisers and asset managers like BlackRock that want to be seen as virtuous to the progressives who are now in power."[168] Moreover, the Journal characterized the campaign's goal: "make the biggest U.S. oil and gas company 'transition' out of its legacy business."[169] Its columnist, Holman Jenkins, Jr., was similarly unimpressed: "[w]hen you've failed to convince consumers to stop consuming oil, when you've failed to sway politicians to ban or even disincentivize its production, that's when you go to oil company boards and insist that they voluntarily refrain from

[166] *See* Armour & Gordon, *supra* note16, at 50–56.

[167] An MFF approach that did not affect private companies would also generate less political opposition than direct governmental regulation. But because an MFF approach is less effective due to competitive responses and shifts in industry composition, it is likely to have a stronger effect on the degree of support than on the degree of opposition.

[168] *The Proxy Coup at Exxon*, WALL ST. J. (May 26, 2021), https://www.wsj.com/articles/the-proxy-coup-at-exxon-11622066709.

[169] Ibid.

producing a legal product for which there is huge and inelastic demand."[170] New investment funds have emerged to push back against systemic stewardship.[171]

Third, an MFF approach entails adverse collateral consequences. Empowering universal owners to cooperate for privately and socially beneficial goals like reduction in carbon emissions can also empower them to cooperate for privately beneficial but socially harmful goals like raising airline ticket prices.[172] Line drawing between these goals would be difficult since achieving them often entails the same type of actions – a reduction in output – and since owners may have mixed motivations. Whether common ownership has already resulted in anti-competitive effects is the subject of an ongoing debate. But as the barriers against an MFF approach are eroded, the potential for such anti-competitive effects increases.

At the federal level, we see no reason why a push to change the SFF focus of corporate law would succeed when the push for direct climate regulation has failed. In light of the strenuous opposition that a shift to MFF would engender, the superiority of dealing with environmental and risk-based externalities through direct regulation, and the potential anti-competitive effects of embracing MFF, any coalition that stood a chance of succeeding would prefer to put its efforts into direct regulation.

Corporate law is, of course, state law. Would the differences in the state-level interest group dynamic make legal change more likely than at the federal level? If anything, the interest group dynamic in Delaware, the most important jurisdiction, makes legal change less likely.[173] Given the extent to which an SFF is fundamental to the deep structure of Delaware corporate law, a shift to MFF would be unlikely to appeal to the array of interest groups that have reached an equilibrium. First, a shift to an MFF would require a wholesale reconfiguration of corporate law and would be

[170] Holman W. Jenkins, Jr., *The Climate Yawns at Exxon 'Coup'*, WALL ST. J. (June 1, 2021), https://www.wsj.com/articles/the-climate-yawns-at-exxon-coup-11622586147.

[171] *See, e.g.*, Amrith Ramkumar, *Anti-ESG Activist Investor Urges Chevron to Increase Oil Production*, WALL ST. J. (Sept. 6, 2022), https://www.wsj.com/articles/anti-esg-activist-investor-urges-chevron-to-increase-oil-production-11662494769.

[172] *See* Azar, Schmalz, & Tecu, *supra* note17.

[173] *See generally* Roberta Romano, *Law As a Product. Some Pieces of the Incorporation Puzzle*, 1 J. L. ECON. & ORG. 225, 265–76 (1985); Jonathan R. Macey & Geoffrey P. Miller, *Toward an Interest-Group Theory of Delaware Corporate Law*, 65 TEX. L. REV. 469 (1987).

unlikely to appeal to two key interest groups – lawyers and judges – both of whom have substantial intellectual investments in the status quo.

Second, a shift to an MFF would not be in Delaware's economic interest: the interest of the Delaware fisc in franchise taxes from companies incorporated in Delaware and the interest of the Delaware bar in revenues from representing Delaware companies and litigating in Delaware courts.[174] To maximize franchise fees and lawyers' revenues, Delaware wants to attract public incorporations and thus has an interest in satisfying directors and shareholders, who jointly control where companies incorporate.[175]

While managers would tend to oppose shifting to an MFF, shareholders would be split, with a large and growing segment of highly diversified universal owners favoring an MFF. But even though the interests of current shareholders and managers may create some basis for relaxing its SFF, examining the interests of current shareholders and managers is too narrow an approach. Delaware cares not only about where the existing stock of public corporations is domiciled but also about how attractive it is to become – and remain – a public corporation. Facilitating an MFF would make it substantially less appealing to be a publicly traded company, under pressure from its universal owners to sacrifice its profits for the good of others, than a privately held company, which will face no such pressure itself but can free-ride on sacrifices of others.[176] From that perspective, Delaware's long-term interests are inconsistent with MFF.[177] Finally, "universal owners" are uniformly located outside of Delaware and thus are a relatively weak force in Delaware politics. We thus see

[174] *See generally* Marcel Kahan & Ehud Kamar, *The Myth of State Competition in Corporate Law*, 55 Stan. L. Rev. 679, 687–99 (2002).

[175] *See* Marcel Kahan & Ehud Kamar, *Price Discrimination in the Market for Corporate Law*, 86 Cornell L. Rev. 1205, 1225 (2001).

[176] Similarly, if Delaware adopted an MFF, some other state intent on getting a slice of the incorporation business could offer, as a differentiated product, a commitment to SFF. Public companies, at the IPO stage or when still held by undiversified owners, could incorporate in such a state with provisions (such as high voting requirements) that would make it difficult to reincorporate in Delaware once its shareholder profile changes and it becomes dominated by universal shareholders.

[177] In addition, were Delaware to shift to an MFF, some other state intent on getting a slice of the incorporation business could offer a commitment of SFF as a differentiated product. Public companies, at the IPO stage or when still held by undiversified owners, could incorporate in such a state with provisions (such as high voting requirements) that would make it difficult to reincorporate in Delaware once its shareholder profile changes and it becomes dominated by universal shareholders.

little chance that corporate law's deep-seated SFF will be changed either at the federal or the state level.

4.6 Conclusion

In the face of the arguments that universal owners should, through systemic stewardship and other means, induce firms to reduce externalities and curtail systematic risks even if doing so lowers the firm's value, it is worth reviewing the normative foundations for the traditional single-firm focus that is so deeply entrenched in corporate law and that poses substantial obstacles to strategies that impose material tradeoffs.

The traditional defense of an SFF and, within that, a focus on shareholder value, is that it ultimately leads to greater social welfare. This traditional approach assumes adequate regulation: effective antitrust to maintain competitive markets; environmental regulation to force the internalization of externalities; employment law to protect workers; and so on. With that assumption, corporate managers face a constrained optimization task: maximize firm value consistent with meeting regulatory obligations. Within this framework, corporate law has a narrow scope: create the corporate form, define its terms and ground rules, and constrain agency costs.

When markets are competitive and other areas of the law carry out their missions, maximizing single firm value will benefit shareholders and increase social welfare. On the other hand, under conditions of monopoly, shareholders may not agree on single-firm profit maximization because they have heterogeneous interests.[178] This implies that one cannot simultaneously achieve complete portfolio diversification, management that implements shareholders' preferences, and competitive markets.[179]

Even in a world of substantial portfolio diversification, the advantages of this traditional framework are many. First, setting SFF as a goal avoids the instability and indeterminacy that heterogeneous shareholder interests can produce and benefits competition. Second, corporate governance's narrow lane avoids confrontation with political forces. Firms need not take any position on social policy and need not engage in social and political tradeoffs. Third, the narrow focus promotes accountability of management to shareholders.

[178] *See* José Azar, *The Common Ownership Trilemma*, 87 U. Chi. L. Rev. 263, 273 (2020).
[179] Ibid.

The push for *systemic* stewardship starts with a critique of the traditional model. In fact, proponents of systemic stewardship and more aggressive strategies argue that other areas of the law do not carry out their missions: financial regulation does not adequately control the systemic financial risk; antitrust law does not adequately protect competition; environmental law does not force the internalization of the social cost of carbon; and employment law does not adequately protect employees. Moreover, political dysfunction in the face of climate change threatens investors' entire portfolios (and life on the planet) and creates an imperative to respond.

From this perspective, systemic stewardship is a clear second-best to well-implemented SFF. The substantial political obstacles to changing the status quo, outlined above, raise fundamental questions. If there is the political will to change corporate law's SFF to permit universal owners to intervene to address climate change risk on a portfolio basis, why isn't there sufficient political will to enact a carbon tax or some other regulatory intervention to force internalization? Absent political will to control or mitigate climate change, will universal owners pursuing MFF have any material welfare effect?

On the other hand, an optimist might note, getting universal owners – among the most powerful forces in the capital markets – to take climate change seriously enough to change their corporate governance strategies may be the most effective way *to develop* the broad political consensus necessary to enact adequate regulation. This could be true in two different ways. First, if elites become convinced that climate change poses an existential threat, they may succeed in convincing governments to act. From this perspective, a variety of environmental initiatives – from recycling to electric vehicles to carbon offsets – may be "ideologically" important even if they do not, in fact, reduce emissions, curtail energy use or waste, or achieve any of the other stated goals.

Second, inducing change at a firm level, even (or perhaps especially) if it engenders a competitive response, may transform the political landscape in ways that could be far more important than the direct economic effect. Suppose that, under shareholder pressure, ExxonMobil and Chevron are forced to factor the social cost of carbon in their exploration and production decisions. As a result, their production drops substantially along with their stock price while their competitors pump more oil. This would give ExxonMobil and Chevron powerful incentives to lobby Congress to enact legislation that would force their competitors to do the same thing. Indeed, it is hard to imagine a more significant change in the political landscape than ExxonMobil and Chevron becoming active supporters of, say, a carbon tax. The recent embrace of a carbon tax and other market-based mechanisms by the American Petroleum Institute, the U.S. Chamber of Commerce, and the Business Roundtable provides some evidence that this process is already underway.[180] The best argument in favor of systemic stewardship may thus be that it could act as a catalyst for political change.

[180] *See* Press Release, Am. Petrol. Inst., API Outlines Path for Low-Carbon Future in New Climate Action Framework (Mar. 25, 2021), https://www.api.org/news-policy-and-issues/news/2021/03/24/climate-action-framework; Martin Durbin, *An Update to Our Approach on Climate*, U.S. CHAMBER OF COM.: GLOB. ENERGY INST. (Jan. 19, 2021), https://www.globalenergyinstitute.org/update-our-approach-climate; *Addressing Climate Change*, BUS. ROUNDTABLE, https://www.businessroundtable.org/climate.

5

Giant Asset Managers, the Big Three, and Index Investing

DOROTHY LUND AND ADRIANA Z. ROBERTSON

5.1 Introduction

Within the world of corporate governance, there has hardly been a more important recent development than the rise of the "Big Three" asset managers – Vanguard, State Street Global Advisors, and BlackRock. Due to the popularity of index funds and ETFs, these asset managers have enjoyed steady inflows over the past decade and now represent some of the largest owners of U.S. public companies. As of 2021, the average combined stake in S&P 500 companies held by the Big Three was 21.9 percent, a proportion that has been steadily increasing for the last two decades.[1]

Because of their size and influence, a robust scholarly literature has identified the promises and perils of Big Three ownership. For example, some scholars have focused on potential advantages of large "universal owner" shareholders that exercise substantial influence over the market;[2] others have voiced concerns about antitrust problems[3] and stewardship challenges that can arise when the largest corporate owners are broadly diversified passive owners.[4] In this chapter, we do not weigh in on the

1 Lucian Bebchuk & Scott Hirst, *Big Three Power, and Why It Matters*, 102 Bos. U. L. Rev. 1547, 1556 (2022).

2 *See* Madison Condon, *Externalities and the Common Owner*, 95 Wash. L. Rev. 1 (2019); Jeffrey N. Gordon, *Systematic Stewardship*, 47 J. Corp. L. 627 (2022).

3 *See* Eric A. Posner et al., *A Proposal to Limit the Anticompetitive Power of Institutional Investors*, 81 Antitrust L. J. 669, 673 (2017); Einer Elhauge, *Horizontal Shareholding*, 129 Harv. L. Rev. 1267, 1291–92 (2016); *but see* Edward B. Rock & Daniel L. Rubinfeld, *Defusing the Antitrust Threat to Institutional Investor Involvement in Corporate Governance* (N.Y.U. L. & Econ. Rsch. Paper Series, Working Paper No. 17-05, 2017); José Azar et al., *Anticompetitive Effects of Common Ownership*, 73 J. Fin. 1513 (2018) (showing that active owners like Berkshire Hathaway also pose common ownership problems).

4 *See* Dorothy S. Lund, *The Case Against Passive Shareholding*, 43 J. Corp. L. 493 (2017); Lucian Bebchuk & Scott Hirst, *Index Funds and the Future of Corporate Governance:*

substance of these debates; our task is simply to identify a series of proxies, or shorthand terms, that first appeared in the foundational works in this literature. We further show how this shorthand, which has become commonplace in both scholarly articles and the financial press, can contribute to misperceptions and confusion.

The first shorthand is the use of the term "Big Three" to refer to three distinct asset managers.[5] Each of the Big Three manage vast amounts of money in indexed products – amounts that have grown dramatically thanks to the rising popularity of index-based investing. However, there are important differences between them, both in terms of the composition of the assets they manage and their own institutional structure and operations. As such, it does not always make sense to lump these institutions together. The focus on these three institutions has also limited scholarly focus in important ways. For example, the term excludes Fidelity, even though it is larger than State Street in terms of assets under management (hereinafter, "AUM")[6] and has also benefitted from a steady inflow of investor funds over the past several years.

The second shorthand is to equate the Big Three with "passive" funds. This misperception is widespread, with many papers – including prior work by one of us[7] – studying the Big Three's governance practices to better understand the incentives of passive fund managers.[8] Although this shorthand can be useful under certain circumstances, we show that it has important limitations. After all, each of the Big Three also manage large amounts of active money, and the index funds that they offer are themselves far from homogeneous.

This brings us to the final shorthand – the idea that "index funds" are all passive and interchangeable. We explore the limitations of this shorthand by showing that the concept of "passive investing" is undertheorized and that there is ample diversity across index funds. In other words,

Theory, Evidence, and Policy, 119 COLUM. L. REV. 2029 (2019); Lucian A. Bebchuk, Alma Cohen, & Scott Hirst, *The Agency Problems of Institutional Investors*, 31 J. ECON. PERSPS. 89, 95 (2017).

5 While we critique the casual use of the term "Big Three" in this chapter, we nonetheless use the term throughout because of its ubiquity in the literature, while also highlighting its limitations in Sections 5.2.1 and 5.3.1.

6 *See* Leo E. Strine, Jr., *Fiduciary Blind Spot: The Failure of Institutional Investors to Prevent the Illegitimate Use of Working Americans' Savings for Corporate Political Spending*, 97 WASH. U. L. REV. 1007 (2020) (describing the Big Four).

7 *See* Lund, *The Case Against Passive Shareholder Voting*, *supra* note 4.

8 *See infra* Section 5.3.

just as there are closet indexers, or active funds that are really quite "passive,"[9] index funds vary dramatically in terms of the discretion that is awarded to – and used by – portfolio managers, the fees that are levied, and the trading strategy that is used. As such, the active/passive dichotomy that is used both by scholars and portfolio managers to market their mutual funds obscures important features of this market.

The final section of our chapter discusses the implications of these observations for future scholarship. Taken together, they shed light on conversations about how the rise of "passive" investing affects corporate governance. Beyond scholarly relevance, these observations matter for policymakers seeking to respond to these market developments with legislative action. For example, the INDEX Act, a bill recently introduced in the Senate, would require investment advisers to pass through the votes of "passively managed funds," defined as any fund that tracks an index or discloses that it is a passive fund or index fund.[10] As we show, this definition sweeps "closet active" funds under its umbrella.

Our analysis also sheds light on other pressing corporate governance conversations, and in particular, those about the growth and appropriate role of large asset managers. Our last section charts these implications in further detail and highlights questions for future research.

5.2 The Shorthand

In this section, we introduce the pervasive shorthand used by scholars studying mutual funds. First, scholars generally focus on "the Big Three" when studying large asset managers. In doing so, they tend to treat these three entities as a homogeneous block while simultaneously overlooking other important players. Second, scholars generally refer to the Big Three asset managers as "passive" investors, even going so far as to use their practices as a stand-in for the incentives of index funds more generally. Finally, scholars have treated all index funds as "passive" and homogeneous. Together, the second and third shorthand have led to concerns about the stewardship practices of index fund managers, and in

[9] *See* Martijn Cremers & Quinn Curtis, *Do Mutual Fund Investors Get What They Pay For? The Legal Consequences of Closet Index Funds* (2015), https://papers.ssrn.com/sol3/papers.cfm?abstract_id=2695133.

[10] INDEX Act, S. 4241, 117th Cong. (2d Sess. 2022).

particular, the idea that they are likely to underinvest in stewardship and monitoring of portfolio companies.

5.2.1 The Focus on the Behavior of "the Big Three"

A first common shorthand involves the use of the term "the Big Three" to describe three asset managers: Vanguard, BlackRock, and State Street. As money poured into the index funds offered by these managers, academic attention turned towards these three institutions in the latter part of the 2010s. Professors Lucian Bebchuk, Alma Cohen, and Scott Hirst made an early contribution to this literature, pointing out that collectively, the Big Three dominated the index fund market.[11] A large literature focusing on the Big Three – more or less to the exclusion of other asset managers – followed, which often treated these three institutions as a homogeneous block. For example, scholars often describe the Big Three's size, and therefore governance power, in the aggregate. They have pointed out that the Big Three (1) constitute the largest owner of most S&P 500 companies,[12] (2) collectively cast an average of 25 percent of the votes at S&P 500 companies,[13] (3) can together determine the outcome of most shareholder proposals at Fortune 250 companies,[14] and (4) will someday cast a majority of the votes at public companies.[15]

Much of the literature also seems to operate with the implicit assumption that the Big Three operate in identical competitive environments, and with identical governance practices. Consider, for example, statements suggesting that the Big Three employ "centralized voting strategies."[16] While this statement holds true for some of the funds within

[11] Bebchuk et al., *The Agency Problems of Institutional Investors*, *supra* note 4, at 94. *See also* Jan Fichtner, Eelke M. Heemskerk, & Javier Garcia-Bernardo, *Hidden Power of the Big Three? Passive Index Funds, Re-Concentration of Corporate Ownership, and New Financial Risk*, 19 Bus. & Pol. 298 (2017) for a roughly contemporaneous piece describing the rise of these asset managers.

[12] *See, e.g.*, Fichtner et al., *supra* note 11; Lund, *The Case Against Passive Shareholder Voting*, *supra* note 4.

[13] *See* Lucian Bebchuk & Scott Hirst, *The Specter of the Giant Three*, 99 Bos. U. L. Rev. 721 (2019).

[14] *See* Caleb N. Griffin, *Margins: Estimating the Influence of the Big Three on Shareholder Proposals*, 73 SMU L. Rev. 409 (2020).

[15] *See supra* note 11.

[16] Fichtner et al, *supra* note 11; *see also* Lund, *The Case Against Passive Shareholder Voting*, *supra* note 4.

each institution's fund family, it is not universal.[17] And of course, the voting strategies are not the same across these asset managers.[18]

Or consider suggestions that "[t]he Big Three exist in a super competitive industry with extremely low management fees," rendering them unlikely to invest in stewardship.[19] There is no doubt that this is true for some of the products offered by each of the three asset managers, but there are also important differences in the products they offer and the markets they serve.[20] Collapsing them into a single aggregate "Big Three" misses these important differences.

Perhaps an even more significant consequence of this shorthand is the intense scholarly interest and focus that has been devoted to the governance practices employed by BlackRock, State Street, and Vanguard. While this focus has been extremely fruitful, it also means that other large asset managers have been largely overlooked.[21] This, in turn, has insulated important players outside of the Big Three from academic and regulatory scrutiny. We return to these consequences in Section 5.3.1.

5.2.2 *Index Funds and the Big Three*

A second shorthand is to equate the Big Three with "passive" investment. More specifically, because the Big Three dominate the market for index funds in terms of AUM, the terms "the Big Three" and "passive" or "index funds" have come to be used interchangeably.

Consider the following examples. First, in their influential paper, "Index Funds and the Future of Corporate Governance," Professors Lucian Bebchuk and Scott Hirst state: "We [] provide an empirical analysis of the full range of stewardship activities that index funds do and do not undertake, focusing on the three largest index fund managers, which we collectively refer to as the 'Big Three.'"[22] In a contemporaneous

[17] *See infra* Section 5.3.1.

[18] *See infra* Section 5.3.1; *see also* Ryan Bubb and Emiliano M. Catan, *The Party Structure of Mutual Funds*, 35 Rev. Fin. Stud. 2839 (2022).

[19] Bernard S. Sharfman, *Looking at the 'Big Three' Investment Advisers through the Lens of Agency*, Oxford Bus. L. Blog (Feb. 18, 2022), https://www.law.ox.ac.uk/business-law-blog/blog/2022/02/looking-big-three-investment-advisers-through-lens-agency.

[20] *See infra* Section 5.3.2.

[21] One notable exception to this is Leo Strine Jr., who has argued that Fidelity should be considered alongside these other large asset managers. *See supra* note 6.

[22] Bebchuk & Hirst, *Index Funds and the Future of Corporate Governance: Theory, Evidence, and Policy*, *supra* note 4, at 2030.

paper, one of us examined the Big Three's stewardship practices and concluded that these "largely passive institutions" were not active participants in governance.[23] Similarly, in their important response to these papers, Professors Edward Rock and Marcel Kahan "provide a systematic analysis of the incentive and information structures within which advisers to index funds operate" by studying the Big Three, their structure, and their governance practices.[24] In another thoughtful response, Professors Jill Fisch, Assaf Hamdani, and Steven Davidoff Solomon introduce a theory of passive fund incentives, and "demonstrate that the behavior of passive investors is consistent [with it]" by focusing on the stewardship practices of the Big Three.[25]

Like all shorthand, the use of "the Big Three" and "passive" or "index funds" as synonyms can sometimes be useful. But what began as a benign linguistic choice has had meaningful consequences for scholarship. First, it has contributed to the (incorrect) assumption, discussed in the previous section, that the institutions that make up the Big Three are homogeneous and largely interchangeable. And second, when later scholars analyzed whether the Big Three's voting policies were consistent with the preferences of their investors, their focus has been on whether any given policy is consistent with a broad-based indexing strategy, not on whether it is consistent with their investors' actual preferences, or even their holdings.[26]

A related consequence of this shorthand is that scholars and policymakers considering how the Big Three should discharge their duties to investors often begin from the premise that the assets in question are broadly diversified index funds.[27] This, in turn, has motivated academics

23 Lund, *The Case Against Passive Shareholder Voting*, *supra* note 4, at 515.

24 Marcel Kahan & Edward B. Rock, *Index Funds and Corporate Governance: Let Shareholders be Shareholders*, 100 B.U. L. Rev. 1771, 1771 (2020).

25 Jill E. Fisch, Asaf Hamdani, & Steven Davidoff Solomon, *The New Titans of Wall Street: A Theoretical Framework for Passive Investors*, 168 U. Pa. L. Rev. 17, 43 (2019).

26 *See, e.g.*, Caleb Griffin, *Margins: Estimating the Influence of the Big Three on Shareholder Proposals*, 73 SMU L. Rev. 409, 439 (2020) (arguing that "the Big Three's voting behaviors speak for themselves and in ways that are very likely to conflict with the views and values of their alleged principals" of index fund investors).

27 BlackRock, Inc., *Rule 14a-8 Proposal – Public Benefit Corporation Request*, The Shareholder Commons (Dec. 8, 2020), https://theshareholdercommons.com/wp-content/uploads/2021/02/BLK-Proposal-PBC.pdf ("These costs matter to our shareholders, the vast majority of whom are diversified."); *From Alpha to Beta: BlackRock and the ABCs of Sustainability*, The Shareholder Commons (Jan. 2020), https://theshareholdercommons.com/from-alpha-to-beta-blackrock-and-the-abcs-of-sustainability/ ("To see why this is so, consider a typical BlackRock client, such as a pension fund or

(as well as advocates) to push the Big Three to pursue stewardship policies tailored towards an investor who owns the entire market.[28] For example, Professor Jeffrey Gordon has eloquently argued that the Big Three should pursue "systematic stewardship," which entails urging portfolio companies to reduce systematic risk consistent with "the investment theory behind the creation of maximally diversified portfolios."[29] This shorthand becomes even more consequential when coupled with the third shorthand – that all index funds are passive and essentially identical. We turn to this shorthand now.

5.2.3 *Passive Investing and Index Funds*

Just as the Big Three have come to be equated with index funds, index funds have long been equated with passivity, and scholars often treat all index (or passive) funds as interchangeable with every other index (or passive) fund. Indeed, this shorthand is so entrenched that the terms "index fund" and "passive fund" are used interchangeably to the point of being treated as synonyms.[30] Indeed, some scholars have even coined a new term – "passive index funds"[31] – which reinforces the ubiquity of the idea that index funds are universally passive.

This perception starts from the premise that index funds and ETFs follow a low-cost investment strategy that involves tracking a broad market index as closely as possible and very little else. Accordingly, scholars employ the term "passive" in two separate (but related) ways: to say something about the fund's trading strategy, and to suggest

401(k) investor: they are almost certainly invested in broadly diversified portfolios."); Gordon, *supra* note 2; Condon, *supra* note 2.

[28] Gordon, *supra* note 2; Condon, *supra* note 2; John C. Coffee Jr., *The Future of Disclosure: ESG, Common Ownership, and Systematic Risk*, 2021 Colum. Bus. L. Rev. 602 (2021).

[29] Gordon, *supra* note 2, at 632.

[30] *See, e.g.*, Giovanni Strampelli, *Are Passive Index Funds Active Owners? Corporate Governance Consequences of Passive Investing*, 55 San Diego L. Rev. 803 (2018); Michael Barzuza, Quinn Curtis, & David H. Webber, *Shareholder Value(s): Index Fund ESG Activism and the New Millennial Corporate Governance*, 93 S. Cal. L. Rev. 1243 (2020); Fisch et al., *supra* note 25.

[31] *See* Strampelli, *supra* note 31; Fichtner et al., *supra* note 11; *but see* Pat Akey, Adriana Robertson, & Mikhail Simutin, *Closet Active Management of Passive Funds* (Univ. Toronto – Rotman Sch. Mgmt. Working Paper Series, Working Paper No. 3874582, 2021).

something about the fund manager's involvement in corporate governance as a consequence of this trading strategy.

The leap from trading strategy to governance strategy occurs as follows. Because a "passive" fund's investors want the fund to track the market as cheaply as possible (as opposed to trying to beat the market), index fund managers get no benefit from investing in corporate governance. This, in turn, causes them to be "passive" monitors of their portfolio companies. We unpack this chain of reasoning in the next section.

Combined with the first two, this shorthand has contributed to the common perception that the business model employed by the Big Three investors[32] is incompatible with informed and engaged stewardship of portfolio companies. That observation, in turn, has also led to legislative action. To take a prominent example, the press release supporting the INDEX Act, which would require investment advisers to pass through votes associated with a "passively managed fund,"[33] states that "because [] passive funds exist to track broad swaths of the market, the asset advisers are not truly invested in the governance or success of the hundreds or thousands of portfolio companies."[34]

Academics contributing to the common ownership literature, for their part, have taken this shorthand in a different direction: If the Big Three invest in broadly diversified portfolios that approximate the market, the thought goes, they have an incentive to use their governance rights to push companies to act anticompetitively. For example, a recent paper by Professor Jose Azar that charts the rise of passive investing and the Big Three and concludes that "[i]n an economy in which everyone holds the market portfolio, all companies have the same shareholders. If, in addition, firms act in the interest of their shareholders ... the equilibrium

32 Note that implicitly, this assumes that all three have *the same* business model, which is an echo of the first shorthand discussed in Section 5.2.1.

33 Under the bill, "passively managed fund" is defined as a fund that "(A) is designed to track, or is derived from, an index of securities or a portion of such an index; (B) discloses that the qualified fund is a passive fund or an index fund; (C) allocates not less than 40 percent of the total assets of the qualified fund to an investment strategy that is designed to track, or is derived from, an index of securities or a portion of such an index; or (D) discloses that an allocation described in subparagraph (C) follows an investment strategy that is passive or based on an index of securities." INDEX Act, S. 4241, 117th Cong. (2d Sess. 2022).

34 Press Release, INDEX Act, Dan Sullivan – U.S. Senator for Alaska (May 2022), www.sullivan.senate.gov/imo/media/doc/DCGA_051722.pdf.

outcome is equivalent to an economy-wide monopoly."[35] We return to this conversation in Section 5.4.2.

5.3 The Reality

In this section, we show that this shorthand misses important facts about the investing ecosystem. This is not to say that there are no circumstances under which this shorthand can be useful, only that it must be used thoughtfully. Moreover, as we discuss in Section 5.4, the ubiquity of shorthand in the passive investing literature has had important consequences for academic scholarship and policy. Before turning to those consequences, we demonstrate the ways in which the shorthand paints an incomplete picture of the mutual fund investment ecosystem.

5.3.1 The Focus on the Big Three Misses Important Features of the Market

The first shorthand is the common tendency to use the term "Big Three" when describing three distinct asset managers. This use leads to both improper lumping and incorrect slicing.[36] First, it has led commentators to lump BlackRock, Vanguard, and State Street together without paying enough attention to important differences between the three asset managers. Second, it has caused scholars to carve the Big Three off from the rest of the market, thereby overlooking or downplaying the role of other large asset managers.

We begin with the second of these observations. While it is indisputably true that each of BlackRock, Vanguard, and State Street manage

[35] José Azar, *The Common Ownership Trilemma*, 87 U. Chi. L. Rev. 263, 263 (2020). Other scholarship has clarified that the potential for anticompetitive harm is not necessarily caused by index funds. *See, e.g.*, Martin Schmalz, *Common Ownership and Competition: Facts, Misconceptions, and What to Do About It*, OECD Competition Committee Background Materials (Dec. 6, 2017), https://one.oecd.org/document/DAF/COMP/WD%282017%2993/en/pdf (stating that "the academic research finds that common ownership reduces competition, not that index funds reduce competition. Much of common ownership concentration is driven by actively managed portfolios . . ."); Martin Schmalz, *Recent Studies on Common Ownership, Firm Behavior, and Market Outcomes*, 66 Antitrust Bulletin (2021) (highlighting that "common ownership is by no means solely driven by 'passive' diversification by textbook index funds across industry rivals . . . but is in many cases the results of active portfolio choice.").

[36] *See* Lee Anne Fennell, Slices and Lumps: Division and Aggregation in Law and Life (2019).

mindbogglingly large amounts of investor money ($10T, $8.5T, and $4.1T, respectively),[37] they are far from the only game in town. Fidelity, for example, manages more capital than State Street (and even more capital in "passively managed" domestic equity mutual funds than State Street),[38] yet it receives only a fraction of the attention of the Big Three.

To be sure, not everyone has overlooked this reality. For example, Leo Strine, Jr. has included Fidelity in what he termed "the Big Four."[39] But our main point is not that the term "Big Four" should be used instead of the "Big Three," nor is it to propose a particular universe of giant asset managers that ought to be included on the list. The point is that a shorthand term (like the Big Three, or the Big Four, or something else entirely) might make sense at some point in time for some particular purpose, but given the dynamic nature of the market, any such term needs to be evaluated to ensure that it fits the particular context.

There are also important differences between these three (or for that matter, four) asset managers. Depending upon the particular context, these differences could have first order consequences. Take, for example, their ownership and corporate structures. Far from being homogeneous, these four entities are different in ways that can have important consequences for their approach to money management and corporate governance. It is noteworthy, in our view, that a literature that focuses on the effect that ownership structure can have on corporate behavior at the portfolio company level has largely ignored the ownership structure at the *asset manager* level.

BlackRock is, in some ways, the asset manager with the simplest (and most transparent) corporate structure. While Larry Fink, its current CEO and one of its seven founders,[40] is often treated as the personification of BlackRock,[41] BlackRock Inc. is a public company (and indeed, the only public company of the Big Three),[42] whose stock trades on the NYSE.[43] As of August 3, 3022, Fink owned about 0.3 percent of the company's

[37] *See infra* Table 5.1. [38] *See infra* Table 5.1. [39] *See* Strine, *supra* note 6.

[40] *Larry Fink*, BlackRock, www.blackrock.com/corporate/about-us/leadership/larry-fink#:~:text=Laurence%20D.,in%20investment%20and%20technology%20solutions (last visited Dec. 23, 2022).

[41] *See, e.g.*, Yun Li, *BlackRock's Larry Fink, Who Oversees $10 trillion, Says Russia-Ukraine War Is Ending Globalization*, CNBC (Mar. 24, 2022), https://www.cnbc.com/2022/03/24/blackrocks-larry-fink-who-oversees-10-trillion-says-russia-ukraine-war-is-ending-globalization.html.

[42] BlackRock, Inc., Annual Report (Form 10-K) (Feb. 25, 2022). [43] Ibid.

stock.[44] While there is no doubt that Fink plays an important role at BlackRock, it is fair to say that BlackRock is subject to the ordinary mechanisms of corporate governance at large public companies. For example, it has many other large owners – including fellow members of the large asset manager club. As of December 31, 2021, the top five owners of BlackRock were: The Vanguard Group, Inc. (7.8 percent), BlackRock Inc (6.5 percent), Capital World Investors (5.0 percent), State Street Corp (4.2 percent), and Temasek Holdings Ltd. (3.28 percent).[45] In aggregate, institutions represent over 75 percent of the asset manager's owners.[46] As is to be expected for a large public company,[47] BlackRock's governance structure is conventional – the company has only a single share class, lacks a staggered board, utilizes majority voting for director elections, and has instituted proxy access for shareholders.[48]

By contrast, State Street Global Advisors is a wholly owned subsidiary of State Street Corporation ("State Street Corp."). While State Street Corp. is itself a public company[49] (which like BlackRock, counts the typical set of large asset managers as its major shareholders[50]), it is not an ordinary operating company. Instead, it is a financial holding company regulated under the Bank Holding Company Act of 1956[51] and has been designated as a SIFI by the FSOC and a G-SIB by the BIS.[52] As a consequence of this, State Street Corp. is subject to extensive regulation by a variety of federal regulators, most notably the Federal Reserve. These include both prudential regulation and activity restrictions, which can, in

[44] Authors' calculations based on BlackRock, Inc., Statement of Changes in Beneficial Ownership (Form 4) (Aug. 5, 2022) and BlackRock, Inc., Quarterly Report (Form 10-Q) (Aug. 5, 2022).

[45] Authors' calculations made using Thomson Reuters Institutional (13f) Holdings - s34 Master File, obtained through the Wharton Research Data Service (WRDS) on August 18, 2022. We recognize the limitations of relying on 13F filings for empirical research. Nevertheless, we believe that this is broadly informative for our limited purposes.

[46] Ibid.

[47] *See* Dorothy S. Lund, *In Search of Good Corporate Governance*, 131 Yale L. J. Forum 854 (2022).

[48] BlackRock, Inc., Definitive Proxy Statement (Form DEF 14A) (Apr. 9, 2020).

[49] *See e.g.* State Street Corp., Annual Report (Form 10-K) (Feb. 17, 2022).

[50] As of December 31, 2021, the top five owners of State Street Corp. were: The Vanguard Group (9.7 percent), BlackRock Inc (7.7 percent), Dodge & Cox (6.4 percent), T. Rowe Price Associates, Inc. (6.2 percent), and State Street Corporation (5.3 percent). In total, institutional investors held almost 94 percent of its shares. Authors' calculations. Based on Thomson Reuters Institutional (13f) Holdings – s34 Master File, *supra* note 46.

[51] State Street Corp., Annual Report (Form 10-K) 10 (Feb. 17, 2022).

[52] Ibid. at 39.

turn, affect the business of the subsidiary, State Street Global Advisors. For example, in its most recent 10-K, State Street Corp. disclosed that "Volcker Rule compliance entails both the cost of a compliance program and loss of certain revenue and future opportunities" for State Street Global Advisors.[53]

Fidelity, for its part, is a privately held, family-controlled company. For these reasons, it does not make the same public disclosures about its corporate governance as would be required of a public company. For example, while its website foregrounds its commitment to its customers, it provides very little detail about its ownership structure or governance. Notwithstanding this, some basic facts about it have been widely reported in the financial press. These include the fact that the company continues to be controlled by the Johnson family, which owns 49 percent of the company through a combination of individual ownership and family trusts ownership.[54] The remaining 51 percent is owned by employees of the company.[55] Fidelity divides its voting shares into two classes – Series B (held by the family, subject to a voting agreement under which all shares will be voted in accordance with the majority[56]), and Series A (held by non-family employees). The current CEO, Abigail Johnson, is the granddaughter of the company's founder.[57]

Vanguard's corporate structure is different still. Like Fidelity, the company is privately held, but it is "structured as a client-owned company . . . The company is owned by its funds, which are then owned by the shareholders."[58] The ownership structure is divided in proportion to a fund's share of Vanguard Group Inc's "aggregate assets and share in the total expenses incurred by the funds in their operations;" therefore, if a fund represents 1 percent of the aggregate assets, then it would own 1 percent of Vanguard Group's shares and assume 1 percent of

53 Ibid. at 16–17.

54 Fidelity Advisor Series VII and Fidelity Select Portfolios, Definitive Proxy Statement (Form DEF 14A) (Mar. 18, 2013).

55 *Profile – Fidelity Investments*, FORBES, https://www.forbes.com/companies/fidelity-investments/?sh=6c6e105f370a.

56 Fidelity Advisor Series VII and Fidelity Select Portfolios, Definitive Proxy Statement (Form DEF 14A) (Mar. 18, 2013).

57 Kris Frieswick, *Who's Afraid of Abby Johnson?*, BOS. MAG. (Aug. 7, 2018), https://www.bostonmagazine.com/news/2018/08/07/abby-johnson-fidelity/.

58 *Who Owns Vanguard?*, https://investor.vanguard.com/investor-resources-education/news/who-owns-vanguard#:~:text=Unlike%20other%20investment%20management%20companies,30%20million%20Vanguard%20investors%20worldwide.

operating expenses.[59] The company has suggested that this structure insulates it from conflicts of interest because it need not cater to outside shareholders.[60]

Beyond these institutional differences, each asset manager structures its governance practices and procedures in different ways. Although each institution has a centralized corporate governance group, these groups are composed of different professionals with different backgrounds and areas of expertise. Moreover, the degree of governance centralization varies by institution – for example, Fidelity delegates voting responsibilities of its index funds to its subadvisor, Geode.[61] Substantively, there is variation between each asset manager in terms of its willingness to oppose management[62] or support ESG issues,[63] to take two examples.[64]

Again, this is not to suggest that these entities have nothing in common (although of course they also have some things in common with other asset managers). The point is that the use of a term that aggregates all three institutions obscures important differences between them.

5.3.2 *Index Equity Mutual Funds Represent Only a Portion of Assets Managed by the Big Three*

The second shorthand equates the Big Three with "the manager of broadly diversified passive equity mutual funds." Taking as given, for the time being, that funds can easily be divided between "active" and "passive," this notion, while widespread, misses a huge segment of each

[59] John C. Bogle, Remark, *A New Order of Things: Bringing Mutuality to the "Mutual Fund"*, 27 Rev. Banking & Fin. L. 471, 473 (2008).

[60] However, longstanding claims that the company operated without a profit component and at an "at-cost basis" were dropped in response to litigation. Joseph N. DiStefano, *Vanguard SEC Filings Drop "At-Cost," "No-Profit" Claims that Were Dear to Late Founder John Bogle*, Philadelphia Inquirer (Feb. 7, 2019) ("Indeed, company officials acknowledge that it is a for-profit company that earns profits and pays income taxes.").

[61] *See* Hortense Bioy, Jose Garcia-Zarate, & Alex Bryan, *Passive Fund Providers and Investment Stewardship*, Harv. L. Sch. F. on Corp. Governance (Dec. 21, 2017), https://corpgov.law.harvard.edu/2017/12/21/passive-fund-providers-and-investment-stewardship/; *see also* Sean J. Griffith & Dorothy S. Lund, *Conflicted Mutual Fund Voting in Corporate Law*, 99 B.U. L. Rev. 1151, 1170 (2019) (describing the many differences between stewardship groups and how they lead to different degrees of uniformity).

[62] *See* Bubb & Catan, *supra* note 18.

[63] *See* Dorothy S. Lund, *Asset Managers as Regulators*, 171 U. Pa. L. Rev. 77 (2022).

[64] These asset managers also differ along a number of other dimensions, including their approach to securities lending. *See generally* Fisch et al., *supra* note 25.

Table 5.1 *Assets under management (by selected asset type) December 31, 2021*

	BlackRock	Fidelity	SSGA	Vanguard
Panel A: AUM ($ Trillion)				
Total	10.0	4.5	4.1	8.5
Panel B: Mutual Fund Assets ($ Billion)				
All MF	5704	4178	1231	8570
Equity	3249	2506	955	6020
Domestic	2468	2131	905	5079
Passive	889	765	507	3002

of BlackRock, Vanguard, and State Street's business. While it is indisputably the case that the equity index funds that they manage represent tremendous amounts of investor money, their other offerings are also enormous. Table 5.1 illustrates this in a rough-and-ready way. In the first column, we present the total AUM value at each of the "Big Four" asset managers as of December 31, 2021. These values are taken from the company's 10-Ks (in the case of BlackRock[65] and State Street[66]), the company's website (in the case of Fidelity[67]), or a company press release (Vanguard[68]). These figures are consistent with the "traditional" account of the size and importance of these asset managers.

The remaining rows in Panel B, however, reveal a much more nuanced story. We use mutual fund data from CRSP to get a sense of where these assets are invested, and doing so reveals many interesting differences between asset managers. For example, BlackRock, Vanguard, and State Street are often referred to as the largest providers of passive funds in the market, but Panel B reveals that Fidelity's indexed mutual fund assets exceed State Street's. Not only that, Table 5.1 makes clear that each of these institutions also manages vast amounts of investor capital in *actively managed* mutual funds. In other words, referring to the "Big

65 BlackRock, Inc., Annual Report (Form 10-K) (Feb. 25, 2022).

66 State Street Corp., Annual Report (Form 10-K) (Feb. 17, 2022).

67 *Fidelity by the Numbers: Asset Management*, FIDELITY, https://www.fidelity.com/about-fidelity/our-company/asset-management (last visited Dec. 26, 2022).

68 *Vanguard Reports Expense Ratio Reductions for Active Equity and Bond Funds*, VANGUARD, https://corporate.vanguard.com/content/corporatesite/us/en/corp/who-we-are/pressroom/Press-release-VG-reports-expense-ratio-reductions-for-active-equity-and-bond-funds-020122.html (last visited Dec. 26, 2022).

Three" (or Four) as managers of passive money completely misses the point that a huge percentage of their mutual fund AUM (and a large proportion of their income[69]) is invested in actively managed funds.

More broadly, these figures make clear that these asset managers focus on different clients: while the overwhelming majority of the assets managed by Fidelity and Vanguard are in mutual funds, they represent less than a third of the assets managed by State Street, and less than 60 percent of the assets managed by BlackRock. The importance of this distinction cannot be overstated, as most retail clients invest though mutual funds; presumably, the non-mutual fund portion of the AUM is in other investment structures like separately managed accounts used by institutional investors like pension funds, corporations, and governments.[70] To the extent that scholars and policymakers are advancing arguments premised on the desires of these asset managers' underlying investors, this distinction is crucial. For example, it suggests that BlackRock and State Street should be more sensitive to the preferences of their institutional clients than Fidelity and Vanguard, which are more geared towards individuals (either directly or through defined contribution pension plans), an implication that we return to in the next section.[71]

Another important difference emerges when we concentrate on equity mutual funds. After all, while debt, commodities, and other asset classes are important, they do not carry the governance rights associated with common stock. Moreover, when discussing the size of these asset managers, comparisons are often made to the equity market. To compare apples to apples, we therefore focus on equity investments. And when we do this, BlackRock no longer looks like a giant: it remains larger than Fidelity, but the difference is not nearly as stark ($3.2T compared to $2.5T). Vanguard, in contrast, is almost as large as the other three

[69] See Griffith & Lund, *supra* note 62, at 1177 ("As a result of these higher fees, BlackRock's smaller share of active funds generates an equal amount of revenue as its passive funds – approximately $1.3 billion each quarter").

[70] To be clear, while retail money is overwhelmingly invested in mutual funds, some smaller institutional investors also invest in mutual funds and ETFs.

[71] *See also* Lund, *Asset Managers as Regulators*, *supra* note 64, at 4 n.31 (discussing how Vanguard generally targets individual investors, rather than institutions, and how this could affect their governance practices). Note that this distinction also matters for empirical scholarship: to the extent that scholars that study mutual fund voting practices are focusing on votes recorded on Form NP-X, this form does not reflect votes cast on the basis of the non-mutual fund assets (which, for BlackRock and State Street, represents trillions of dollars).

combined. If size matters for governance and incentives, scholars would be wise to use the right measure.

Finally, since the focus (implicitly or explicitly) of much of the literature is on the corporate governance of American public companies, we zoom in on domestic equity mutual funds, which again affects the four asset managers differently. In particular, nearly a third of BlackRock's equity mutual funds focus on foreign markets, while the other asset managers' funds focus much more on domestic equities.

In sum, breaking down the total AUM by these simple categories reveals many important differences between these asset managers. One implication of this is semantic: it is plainly incorrect to equate the Big Three with passively managed equity mutual funds, or to contend that they are uniquely important providers of index funds (to the exclusion of Fidelity). Normative implications also follow. For example, it is too simple to argue that the stewardship practices of these three asset managers should further the interests of their broadly diversified "passive" investors, to the detriment of their many other investors.[72] And, particularly when combined with the other two, this shorthand also has implications for scholarship examining these asset managers' incentives to participate actively in corporate governance, as the next section addresses in more detail.

5.3.3 *Index Funds Are Not Interchangeable or Necessarily Passive*

The last shorthand is the idea that all index funds are "passive" and are, for practical purposes, interchangeable with one another. Like the others, this shorthand can be useful in certain contexts, but it has important limits. Part of the challenge in correcting this misperception arises from the fact that "passive investing" seems to be more of a slogan than a

[72] Indeed, BlackRock made this very argument in response to a shareholder proposal filed by Shareholder Commons, which asked BlackRock to "adopt stewardship practices designed to curtail corporate activities that externalize social and environmental costs that are likely to decrease the returns of portfolios that are diversified in accordance with portfolio theory, even if such curtailment could decrease returns at the externalizing company." SEC Notice of Exempt Solicitation at BlackRock by Shareholder Commons, https://www.sec.gov/Archives/edgar/data/1364742/000121465922005689/b422225px14a6g.htm. In response, BlackRock explained: "In our view, shifting [our] policies . . . in order to benefit 'diversified shareholders' would be inconsistent with our responsibility to our clients, and our legal duties, and create legal risks for BlackRock and our shareholders." BlackRock, Inc., Definitive Proxy Statement (Form DEF 14A) (Apr. 14, 2022).

well-defined concept: as discussed in Section 5.2.3, it generally encompasses assumptions about the fund's trading strategy, but can also connote something about the fund's perceived involvement in stewardship. As we show here, those assumptions do not fully capture the breadth and diversity of the index fund market.

The term "passive" is sometimes used to denote funds that try to match a benchmark index rather than beat it.[73] Although this definition is consistent with an index fund's general trading strategy, it obscures an important point: someone has to create the underlying index, and doing so necessarily involves discretion.[74] Accordingly, this model simply tells us something about who is primarily responsible for selecting the fund's portfolio; it doesn't tell us anything about what that portfolio looks like. When a fund tries to match an index, the index provider in effect acts like a portfolio manager, with everything that entails. Indeed, the idea that the index provider is effectively the portfolio manager isn't just a metaphor: one of us has argued, in other work with Professor Paul Mahoney, that in many cases, the index provider is an investment adviser under the Investment Advisers Act,[75] something that the SEC discussed in a recent request for comment.[76]

Moreover, by this logic, any trading strategy that can be reduced to an algorithm, no matter how complex that algorithm, could qualify as "passive." For example, this definition would encompass not just an S&P 500 index fund, but also a quant hedge fund and a hedge fund specializing in high-frequency trading. While scholars and commentators might be concerned about the impact of quant hedge funds and high-frequency traders on the market, those concerns are probably quite different from the standard concerns about "passive" funds. And one need not look to specialized indices to find discretion: even the S&P 500,

[73] See supra Section 5.2.3.

[74] *See* Adriana Z. Robertson, *Passive in Name Only: Delegated Management and "Index" Investing*, 36 Yale J. on Regul. 795 (2019); *see also* Paul G. Mahoney & Adriana Z. Robertson, *Advisers by Another Name*, 11 Harv. Bus. L. Rev. 311 (2021); Gabriel Rauterberg & Andrew Verstein, *Index Theory: The Law, Promise and Failure of Financial Indices*, 30 Yale J. on Reg. 101, 114–20 (2013).

[75] *See* Mahoney & Robertson, *supra* note 76.

[76] *See* Press Release, SEC, SEC Requests Information and Comment on Advisers Act Regulatory Status of Index Providers, Model Portfolio Providers, and Pricing Services (Jun. 15, 2022), https://www.sec.gov/news/press-release/2022-109; Press Release, SEC, Request for Comment on Certain Information Providers Acting as Investment Advisers (Jun. 15, 2022), https://www.sec.gov/rules/other/2022/ia-6050.pdf.

the most well-known index tracked by over $7 trillion in investor capital[77] expressly leaves the decision of which companies to add and delete, subject to eligibility rules, in the hands of a committee.[78]

Layered on top of that reality is the non-trivial amount of discretion that fund managers generally have in tracking the index. As one of us has shown in other work with Peter Molk, S&P 500 funds – including the very largest funds – retain for themselves substantial discretion in portfolio selection and routinely exercise this discretion to deviate from the index.[79] As a result, the idea that an index fund portfolio manager mechanically tracks a benchmark index might be true for some index funds, but it is far from universal.

Second and relatedly, the term "passive" can encompass the idea that the fund tracks "the market" and is therefore maximally diversified and no different from any other index fund.[80] This characterization, however, fails to describe a large portion of the index funds available for sale in the United States. Research has shown that there is huge diversity in the types of indices that are tracked by index funds.[81] While some of these indices can plausibly be described as a proxy for "the market" (or at least the market for U.S. equities[82]) most of them cannot. For example, some in this latter group track some segment of the market, like large or small stocks,[83]

[77] *See S&P 500 Factsheet*, S&P Dow Jones Indices LLC (Dec. 30, 2022) ("According to our Annual Survey of Assets, an estimated USD 15.6 trillion is indexed or benchmarked to the index, with indexed assets comprising approximately USD 7.1 trillion of this total (as of Dec. 31, 2021)").

[78] *See* Adriana Z. Robertson, *The (Mis)uses of the S&P 500*, 2 U. Chi. Bus. L. Rev. 137 (2023). This discretion amounts to roughly 5 percent of the total value of the Index.

[79] Peter Molk & Adriana Z. Robertson, *Discretionary Investing by 'Passive' S&P 500 Funds*, 41 Yale J. on Reg. 248 (2024).

[80] *See* Ronald J. Gilson & Jeffrey N. Gordon, *The Agency Costs of Agency Capitalism: Activist Investors and the Revaluation of Governance Rights*, 113 Colum. L. Rev. 863 (2013). One of us is guilty of using this shorthand. *See* Lund, *The Case Against Passive Shareholder Voting*, *supra* note 4. *See also* Strampelli, *supra* note 31; Barzuza et al., *supra* note 31.

[81] *See* Robertson, *Passive in Name Only: Delegated Management and "Index" Investing*, *supra* note 76; Akey et al., *supra* note 32.

[82] Two examples of broad-based equity indices are the Russell 3000 and Wilshire 5000. *See Index Factsheet: Russell 3000 Index*, FTSE Russell (Nov. 30, 2022); *FT Wilshire 5000 Index Series Factsheet*, Wilshire Advisors LLC (Jun. 30, 2022).

[83] The most prominent large cap equity index is the S&P 500. *See S&P 500 Factsheet*, S&P Dow Jones Indices LLC (Dec. 30, 2022). The Russell 2000 and the S&P SmallCap 600 are two examples of small cap equity indices. *See Index Factsheet: Russell 2000 Index*, FTSE Russell (Nov. 30, 2022); *S&P SmallCap 600 Factsheet*, S&P Dow Jones Indices LLC (Dec. 30, 2022).

value or growth stocks,[84] or some industry segment like technology companies.[85] These indices, and the funds that track them, are already departing – sometimes quite considerably! – from conventional notions of "the market." Rather, these index funds are best understood as representing some investing style,[86] something that the funds themselves don't even deny.

Many other index funds follow strategies that are so bespoke that there is no meaningful notion of "the market" that would encapsulate them.[87] Some particularly colorful examples include the VanEck Social Sentiment ETF, which trades under the ticker "BUZZ" and tracks the BUZZ NextGen AI US Sentiment Leaders Index,[88] and the (regrettably now defunct) Global X GuruActivist Index ETF, which tracked the Solactive Guru Activist Index.[89] In other words, not only do index funds engage in a dizzying array of different investment strategies, many of them engage in strategies that are hard to distinguish from a traditional actively managed mutual fund.

Third and finally, the term "passive" often embodies the assumption that all index funds are not proactive when it comes to issuer level corporate governance. This belief is often grounded in assumptions about

[84] Prominent examples of this category include the Russell 1000 Value Index and the Russell 1000 Growth Index. *See Index Factsheet: Russell 1000 Growth Index*, FTSE Russell (Nov. 30, 2022); *Index Factsheet: Russell 1000 Value Index*, FTSE Russell (Nov. 30, 2022).

[85] The NASDAQ 100 Index is perhaps the best known of these indices. *See NASDAQ-100 Fact Sheet*, Nasdaq, Inc. (Dec. 30, 2022).

[86] Interestingly, they sometimes even describe themselves in style terms. One interpretation is that these funds want to "have it both ways": marketing themselves as passive while also being able to market themselves to investors interested in a particular investment style.

[87] *See* Robertson, *Passive in Name Only: Delegated Management and "Index" Investing*, *supra* note 76; Akey et al., *supra* note 32.

[88] This index, according to the fund's regulatory filing, "is designed to identify the U.S. common stocks with the most 'positive insights' collected from online sources including social media, news articles, blog posts and other alternative datasets. 'Positive insights' are a measure of the degree of positive company sentiment as well as the breadth of active discussion about each company by participants on online platforms." VanEck Vectors Social Sentiment ETF, Registration Statement (Form N-1A) (Feb. 25, 2021).

[89] According to the fund's regulatory filing, the index "is comprised of U.S. listed equity positions reported on Form 13F and Schedule 13D by a select group of entities characterized as premier activist investors, as defined by Solactive AG, [the "Index Provider"]. Activist investors are selected from a universe of investors that aim to buy securities to put public pressure on management to increase shareholder value, as defined by the Index Provider." Global X Guru Activist Index ETF, 2015 Summary Prospectus (Form 497) (Apr. 27, 2015).

the fund's trading strategy: if a fund is maximally diversified and tracking the same index as every other fund, it will have little incentive to monitor and engage with its portfolio companies.[90] It is also bolstered by the additional assumption that all index funds are "low-cost." If the funds charges very low fees, the portfolio manager will only reap a small fraction of the gains from stewardship while shouldering the full costs of its efforts. This strategy, according to this theory, leads to a classic underinvestment problem.[91] However, this assumption about uniformly low fees also turns out to be incorrect across the board. Akey, Robertson, and Simutin find that, among ostensibly passive index funds, there is a wide dispersion of fees (using an all-in measure of fund expense ratio), from the well-known ultra (or even zero) fee funds all the way up to the 200 basis points (i.e., 2 percent) more familiar from the active management context.[92] A substantial mass of these fund charge fees of around 100 basis points.[93]

In short, the term "passive" seems to mean many things to many people, none of which apply to all, or even most, index funds. Perhaps more importantly, index funds are not all the same: The explosion of index funds and ETFs means that the term now encompasses a vast array of different funds: from mega-funds representing hundreds of billions of dollars in capital to tiny $70 million funds. These funds encompass ultra-low fee funds tracking well known, broad-based market cap weighted indices, as well as funds tracking proprietary indices that execute hyper-specialized strategies. They also encompass explicit self-indexers – funds that track indices that are produced by an affiliate of the fund itself. The fund complexes that offer these funds are equally diverse, from the "Titans of Wall Street," to quant managers to new entrants. These funds are, in other words, anything but homogeneous or interchangeable, and not all should be considered "passive" in any sense of the word.

5.4 Implications

An important body of work – some of which was mentioned in Sections 5.2 and 5.3 – has examined the incentives and influence of three of the largest asset managers in the U.S. capital market. In doing so, it

[90] Mutual fund portfolio managers are rewarded on the basis on their relative performance, and the broad-based, highly diversified index fund that invests in stewardship will ultimately benefit rival funds that track the same index. *See* Gilson & Gordon, *supra* note 82; Lund, *The Case Against Passive Shareholder Voting*, *supra* note 4.

[91] Bebchuk & Hirst, *supra* note 4.

[92] Akey et al., *supra* note 32, at Figure 7.

[93] Ibid.

established a crucially important foundation for our understanding of these important issues, even as it often employed the shorthand discussed in Section 5.2.

The next phase of scholarship in this area should build on this foundation while keeping in mind that this shorthand is just that: a simple way of discussing complex entities and their investment products, which may or may not be useful in a particular setting. Section 5.3 discussed the limits of this shorthand and also hinted at the problems that come from their overuse. Here, we extend that analysis and sketch how unpacking the assumptions that underlie these assumptions can advance scholarship in this area. We begin by discussing implications for the relationship between investors and the giant asset managers and their investors. We then turn to the implications for the relationship between the giant asset managers and their portfolio companies they invest in.

5.4.1 *The Relationship between Beneficial Owners and Giant Asset Managers*

As discussed in Section 5.2, scholars have generally treated the "Big Three" as homogeneous providers of index funds. Section 5.3 showed the limits of this shorthand by highlighting some of the key differences between these asset managers. This Section further delves into the consequences of those differences and in so doing, sets an agenda for future scholarship studying the relationship between investors and giant asset managers.

5.4.1.1 Retail vs. Institutional Clients

Much of the literature currently assumes (often implicitly) that much of the Big Three's investment capital comes from retail investors.[94] This assumption has colored the scholarship studying the governance practices of these asset managers. For example, Michal Barzuza, Quinn Curtiss, and David Webber contend in a series of important papers that the Big Three's ESG initiatives are the product of pressure from their millennial retail investors.[95]

[94] *See* Lund, *Asset Managers as Regulators*, *supra* note 64, at 15 ("Beneficial owners sometimes invest directly with asset managers, and a robust literature considers the agency cost issues that arise from that single layer of intermediation.").

[95] Michael Barzuza, Quinn Curtis, & David H. Webber, *The Millennial Corporation: Strong Stakeholders, Weak Managers* (Working Paper, 2022), https://papers.ssrn.com/sol3/papers.cfm?abstract_id=3918443; Barzuza et al., *Shareholder Value(s): Index Fund ESG Activism and the New Millennial Corporate Governance*, *supra* note 31.

While there is no doubt that these asset managers count on retail investors, Table 5.1 makes clear that there is another important piece of the story. In particular, the extent to which these asset managers invest enormous amounts of capital for other large institutions has been either overlooked or brushed aside.[96] One of us has coined this phenomenon as "double intermediation," to indicate that two layers of institutional intermediaries often stand between beneficial owners and their portfolio company investments.[97]

As Table 5.1 indicates, the extent of double intermediation varies by institution. BlackRock and State Street count many institutions as their clients, whereas Vanguard and Fidelity rely on retail investors to a greater degree.[98] This difference in client base is more than just semantic: it matters for governance. In particular, retail investors likely exert influence over the asset manager in different ways than large institutions, which operate pursuant to their own fiduciary obligations.[99] This difference also matters when asking whether an institution's governance practices are consistent with the interests of the institution's investors. In particular, instead of worrying that BlackRock is, for example, engaging in ESG activism to the detriment of its investor clients, it might be more fruitful to focus explicitly on a triparty relationship: BlackRock, its institutional clients, and its retail clients.[100] We explore this implication further in the next Section.

5.4.1.2 Investor Preferences

The previous Section revealed how the Big Three's client base is not homogeneous in ways that matter for governance and beyond. This Section broadens this analysis to consider how and whether we can make generalizations about the preferences of a giant asset manager's investors.

Recall from Section 5.2 that scholars and policymakers often refer to the Big Three's investors as "broadly diversified indexed investors," and that this assumption leads to prescriptions about how these asset managers should use their governance power. But Section 5.3 revealed that this characterization often misses the mark – some of their investors are invested in index funds, others are invested in active funds, and some

96 Lund, *Asset Managers as Regulators*, *supra* note 64, at 15–16.

97 Ibid. at 15.

98 The fact that many of these retail investors are themselves investing through defined contribution pension plans, where the employer has significant influence over the set of available funds, is yet another important wrinkle.

99 Lund, *Asset Managers as Regulators*, *supra* note 64, at 15–16.

100 Ibid.

aren't invested in mutual funds at all. Compounding this problem is the fact that not all "passive" funds are the same – as Section 5.3 revealed, some track bespoke indices that look more active than passive, and even the relatively "passive" ones differ from one another. This lack of homogeneity is even more obvious when we remember that many investors are not individuals, but institutions like pension funds, which invest vast amounts of capital with, but also separately from, one of these asset managers.

All of this leads to an empirical problem: Because asset managers do not disclose how the capital in these separate accounts is invested (i.e., whether it tracks a standard index, a bespoke index, or is actively managed), it becomes particularly difficult to use publicly available information to determine what those clients would like, and therefore, whether an asset manager is acting in its clients' interests. This empirical problem is attenuated somewhat in the case of retail investors and smaller institutional clients, who do invest through registered mutual funds. At least in their case, we can observe the portfolios of both the active and index funds. This means that here, at least, there is hope: Assuming that one was comfortable abstracting away from the fact that investors might (and likely do) own other assets, and perhaps even other mutual funds, it is at least possible to analyze the (hypothetical) preferences of these investors. Doing so, however, requires moving beyond the assumption that indexed investors "own the market," and instead requires careful analysis of what these index funds actually hold, and the differences between them.

Even putting aside the fact that mutual funds typically represent only a portion of any client's portfolio, our analysis reinforces the fact that it is a mistake to focus on mutual fund offerings to understand the clients (and corresponding incentives) of these asset managers. While a focus on mutual fund offerings will do a good job of capturing how the asset manager invests on behalf of *retail* investors, it misses the separate accounts and pooled investment funds used by large institutions. Table 5.1 makes clear that these constitute trillions of dollars, not something that can be easily assumed away. While it is possible to back out the total equity holdings in these accounts,[101] doing so yields the aggregate across all these accounts, not what any particular portfolio looks like. And even if we were confident that a large portion of these assets are

[101] 13F filings can shed light on the total AUM and one can subtract off the mutual fund holdings leaving, to a first approximation, the assets of interest.

"indexed," that still doesn't tell us what those portfolios look like. As Section 5.3 revealed, there are many different indices, including a dizzying array of custom indices designed specifically for these large accounts. Layering on top of this reality is the fact that a substantial portion of giant asset manager capital is explicitly actively managed. Therefore, the idea that we can speculate about what their beneficial investors own – and further, what kind of decision-making would be beneficial to them – becomes implausible. Shedding light on this issue would represent an important contribution to the field.

5.4.2 The Relationship between Giant Asset Managers and Portfolio Companies

We now move beyond the implications for the relationship between beneficial owners and asset managers and focus on two sets of implications for the relationship between giant asset managers and their portfolio companies. The first are conceptual and the second are empirical.

5.4.2.1 Conceptual

As discussed, scholars have discussed many corporate governance issues raised by the popularity of index investing. In particular, scholars have voiced concerns that a larger fraction of "passive" investors in the marketplace will reduce the level of shareholder monitoring, which in turn will reduce issuer performance.[102] We have identified common shorthand that appears in this conversation – and specifically, the assumption that all index funds are passive in corporate governance – and we now address the limits of this shorthand in greater detail.

Researchers concerned by the rise of "passive" investing should be wary of the simple active/passive categorization offered by a fund sponsor. For some time now, research has pointed out that many active funds are actually "closet indexers": ostensibly actively managed funds that actually track an index quite closely.[103] Relatedly, we have described how many index funds more closely resemble the traditional conception of actively managed funds because they track a custom index or allow the

[102] *See, e.g.*, Bebchuk & Hirst, *supra* note 4; Lund, *The Case Against Passive Shareholder Voting*, *supra* note 4.

[103] *See* Cremers & Curtis, *supra* note 9. *See also* Martijn K.J. Cremers & Antti Petajisto, *How Active Is Your Fund Manager? A New Measure that Predicts Performance*, 22 Rev. Fin. Stud. 3329 (2009).

exercise of ample discretion in investment selection.[104] They may also charge fees that more closely resemble those levied by active managers.

There is no question that some index funds are very likely to underinvest in stewardship and monitoring. But those funds may advertise themselves as being passive, active, or something else.[105] Therefore, rather than point to a broad category of index funds as the appropriate targets for scrutiny and legislative proposals,[106] a much more tailored approach, which goes beyond the size of the manager and the branding of the fund, is needed. For example, scholars concerned about the impact of low-cost investment vehicles on stewardship could focus directly on funds that charge low fees. Alternatively, scholars concerned about the rise of anticompetitive conduct due to crossholdings could focus on the subset of funds – however they happen to be branded – that actually have disproportionate amounts of these types of holdings. For example, this feature may be more plausible for a fund (whether or not it tracks an index) focused on a particular industry segment than one that tracks a broad-based market index.

In addition to the substantial heterogeneity across "passive" funds, we have also flagged that each of the Big Three have a substantial fraction of their AUM invested in actively managed funds.[107] This, under any analytical framework, should affect their incentives. Our analysis has also revealed substantial heterogeneity across the "Big Three" in terms of their size, ownership, and governance structure. By lumping them together and describing them as a homogeneous block, scholars are less likely to identify issues (and therefore research opportunities) in how these asset managers wield their governance power. While it may sometimes make sense to lump large asset managers together, the ubiquity of the term obscures important differences between institutions in a fast-moving market. It also makes it less likely that subsequent changes in the market

[104] See discussion *supra* notes 75 to 95 and accompanying text. For additional research in the finance literature demonstrating the activeness of ETFs, see Itzhak Ben-David et al., *Competition for Attention in the ETF Space*, REV. FIN. STUD. (2022), David Easley et al., *The Active World of Passive Investing*, 25 REV. FIN. 1433 (2021).

[105] For example, quant funds also lack incentives to be engaged stewards, but they are excluded from the analysis when index funds are the proxy.

[106] *See* INDEX Act, S. 4241, 117th Cong. (2d Sess. 2022).

[107] *See also* Martin Schmalz, *Common Ownership Concentration and Corporate Conduct*, 10 ANNUAL REV. OF FIN. E. 7 (2018) (observing that "questions such as whether 'index funds' engage in corporate governance are moot – index funds may not engage, but their sponsoring families do, jointly with the power of the active part of the family").

will be identified. For example, we strongly suspect that the focus on the Big Three has helped to obscure Fidelity's growth.

These observations have implications for many important discussions involving asset managers and portfolio companies, including how the rise of giant asset managers might lead to anticompetitive conduct and the promise of systematic stewardship. They also matter a great deal for conversations about the stewardship potential of giant asset managers and their portfolio companies. For example, the very different governance structures across these giant asset managers cautions against making blanket assumptions about their incentives; moreover, the very different asset composition (beyond differences in "passive" investment vehicles) suggests differing incentives to serve as informed and engaged stewards. All these differences are worthy of significant scholarly attention.

5.4.2.2 Empirical

The second set of implications concern empirical analyses of the relationship between asset managers and the governance of their portfolio companies. Take something as basic as the relevant size of these asset managers. If we are interested in size for the sake of analyzing their influence on corporate governance, it is crucial to ensure that we are focusing on the right numbers. In this context, the top line AUM figures are misleading. After all, in the ordinary course, debt, commodities, and other asset classes do not have traditional corporate governance rights. While all corporate stakeholders can exercise some limited influence on management, at the end of the day only equity gets to vote. And to the extent that we are concerned with corporate governance at American companies, we also need to exclude foreign equities. Focusing on the top line AUM figures vastly inflates the amounts in question. While careful scholars can avoid this trap, it is easy, and common, to simply equate size with governance power.

Our analysis raises even more challenges when it comes to empirical analysis of asset manager stewardship activities. If one is primarily interested in the stewardship behavior of these asset managers, the standard voting data that empirical scholars rely upon is massively incomplete. These datasets are drawn from Form NP-X, which only registered investment companies – like mutual funds (including ETFs) – are required to file. As discussed, there is no requirement that the separate accounts and pooled investment products – which are often favored by large institutional clients (and that make up a large fraction of the AUM at each of BlackRock, Vanguard, State Street, and Fidelity) – report their voting decisions, and we are aware of no source that even purports to have access to this information on a systematic basis. As a result, these votes are unknown and unknowable to researchers. While some of these votes are likely cast in accordance with the stewardship group's recommendations (meaning that scholars can make an educated guess about how some of the shares are voted),[108] others are retained by the underlying institution and cast according to their instructions.[109] As these institutions gradually expand this type of option by implementing pass-through voting and other voting choice programs, the focus on available voting data will become even more incomplete. Simply put, it is impossible to know how these asset managers vote with respect to vast amounts of the equities that they hold on behalf of investors. Focusing only on mutual funds, the available voting data therefore vastly understates the corporate governance might that they wield and may lead to inaccurate conclusions.

5.5 Conclusion

This chapter has focused on three sets of shorthand common in the literature studying the giant asset managers and their role in corporate governance. While each shorthand can be useful in certain contexts, its overuse can lead to problematic misperceptions and distort the evolution of scholarly research. We discuss some examples of how relying on this shorthand can lead scholars astray. We hope that the observations we raise in this chapter will inspire future scholars to delve deeply into the issues we identify, to further enrich this important area of research.

[108] *See* Sandy Bass et al., *It's All About Choice*, BLACKROCK (2022), https://www.blackrock.com/corporate/literature/publication/its-all-about-choice.pdf.

[109] Ibid.

6

Something Old, Something New

Cultivating Institutional Investor Engagement through Shareholder Stewardship

DIONYSIA KATELOUZOU

6.1 Introduction

Shareholder engagement has been at the heart of the corporate governance debate for a very long time now.[1] Ranging from sporadic and incidental forms of managerial monitoring to more systematic and strategic forms of shareholder activism, including firm-specific and portfolio-level activism, shareholder engagement is considered as a key mechanism to enhance corporate governance, improve value and more recently to 'save the planet' or even to 'save capitalism'.[2] Institutional investors have always featured prominently in this debate. As a result of their increasing presence in global capital markets,[3] institutional shareholders' engagement or more systematic forms of activism have been an important point of discussion not only in companies with dispersed ownership but more and more often in companies with controlling shareholders too.[4] What is often overlooked, however, is that the role of institutional investors in corporate governance has been portrayed and debated differently in different time periods from 'passive risk-bearers' to

[1] For the more than 400-year-old history of shareholder engagement, also known as shareholder advocacy, see contributions to Jonathan GS Koppell (ed), *Origins of Shareholder Advocacy* (Palgrave Macmillan 2011).

[2] Tom Gosling, 'Can Shareholders Save Capitalism', https://us12.campaign-archive.com/?e=[UNIQID]&u=3d3003a2ba56f7fc2f7872148&id=78c10bc5a9.

[3] See Introductory chapter in this book.

[4] For shareholder activism in controlled companies, see Matteo Erede, 'Governing Corporations with Concentrated Ownership Structure: An Empirical Analysis of Hedge Fund Activism in Italy and Germany, and Its Evolution' (2013) 10 *European Company & Financial Law Review* 328; Kobi Kastiel, 'Against All Odds: Hedge Fund Activism in Controlled Companies' (2016) *Columbia Business Law Review* 60; Yu-Hsin Lin, 'When Activists Meet Controlling Shareholders in the Shadow of the Law: A Case Study of Hong Kong' (2019) 14 *Asian Journal of Comparative Law* 1.

'sleeping giants', from 'rationally reticent' investors to 'shareholder stewards' and from firm-specific to 'systematic', portfolio-, or even market-level shareholder activists.[5] Conceptually and normatively these varying portrayals of institutional investors as shareholders of public companies have taken shape within oscillations between the contractarian or 'nexus of contracts' paradigm of corporate governance and the neoliberal emphasis on shareholder value on the one hand, and more recent calls for stakeholderism and sustainability, on the other.

Against this background, this chapter troubles scholars and practitioners to critically consider the policy-driven development of *shareholder stewardship*, that is, institutional investors using their shareholder status to monitor and influence portfolio companies, and places it against older notions of institutional investor engagement. While shareholder stewardship is currently exercised at different levels, in this chapter I will concentrate on only one level, that of *micro-level shareholder stewardship.* Micro-level shareholder stewardship is about how institutional investors *qua* shareholders monitor and engage with *individual* portfolio companies to increase value.[6] This chapter makes three main contributions to the understanding of micro-level shareholder stewardship.

First, the main argument developed is that micro-level shareholder stewardship is a refinement and an extension of 'older' notions of firm-specific institutional investor engagement founded on a tripartite rationale of: (i) engaging (formally or informally) at the *firm-level* to improve long-term firm (and portfolio) value on the basis of the private agency paradigm of corporate governance, (ii) with a commitment to the ultimate beneficiaries' investment needs on the basis of the private trusteeship relationship that governs the investment funds' relationships with their beneficiaries, and (iii) with the overall aim to serve public interests, including the saver needs and more recently mitigation of climate and other externalities.

Second, this chapter is looking for the ideal, firm-specific shareholder steward. At first glance, 'hedge-fund-style' activists (a term I use to refer to the familiar activist hedge funds and other alternative asset management firms that act like them) can be prime candidates for micro-level shareholder stewardship. They engage at the firm-level with a commitment to their beneficiaries, thereby meeting two out of three criteria of

[5] See Section 6.2.

[6] However, I do not claim that firm value maximization is always an optimal goal from a social welfare perspective.

micro-level shareholder stewardship, but they mainly focus on alpha. In turn, unless the incentives of 'hedge-fund-style' activists are aligned with the stewardship goals, hedge-fund-style activists cannot qualify as stewards.

Third, on the practical front, not only do I provide fresh empirical evidence that 'hedge-fund-style' activism has continued to disproportionately dominate shareholder activism over the last decade (suggesting that there is great scope for micro-level shareholder stewardship), but also I empirically study stewardship disclosures and find evidence that there is indeed a breed of hedge-fund-style activists – the *activist shareholder stewards* – who can fill the 'stewardship bill'.

The rest of the text proceeds as follows. Section 6.2 revises the classic case for firm-specific shareholder engagement and traces how the passive risk bearer was slowly transformed to an initially reluctant but then reticent activist. The argument developed is that hedge-fund-style activists can fulfil the promise of firm-specific investor engagement and fresh empirical evidence is provided on the scale of hedge-fund-style activism. Section 6.3 articulates how the development of shareholder stewardship revamped the 'old' notion of shareholder engagement on the part of institutional investors and how it progressively twisted from a 'right' to a 'duty' and from the micro- to the market-level. Section 6.4 sheds some empirical light on how the activist shareholder stewards themselves understand and report on micro-level shareholder stewardship. Section 6.5 concludes.

6.2 Firm-Level Institutional Investor Engagement: Theoretical and Empirical Aspects

6.2.1 *The Classic Case for Firm-Level Investor Engagement*

Traditionally, the discussion about the role of shareholders in corporate governance has taken place at the level of individual firms. Since Berle and Means' 1932 book established the problem of the separation of ownership and control as central,[7] the core goal of corporate law has been to protect the interests of the *shareholder risk bearer*. This was translated into a simple rule, that of shareholder value maximization

[7] Adolf A. Berle and Gardiner C. Means, *The Modern Corporation & Private Property* (2009 edn, Transaction Publishers 1932) 297.

where shareholder value was equal to firm value.[8] Even though the goal of maximizing (firm-level) shareholder value was never uncontested,[9] by the 1970s it became widely accepted that the best means to achieve social welfare is to make management accountable to shareholders.[10] Law and economics scholarship played a key role in this regard. The contributions of the nexus-of-contracts theory of the firm are well-discussed,[11] but what is often neglected is that shareholder value maximization was defended by contractarians not on the basis of the superiority of shareholder monitoring and control vis-à-vis management but on the basis of economic efficiency.

The contractarian position can be summarized as follows. Management is understood as one of the firm's many production factors and does not hold any strategic position in the firm.[12] Shareholders are 'residual claimants' or 'residual risk bearers' with incentives to maximize the performance of the firm and to decrease managerial shirking.[13] When ownership is widely dispersed, market efficiency dictates that shareholders opt for diversification rather than firm-specific monitoring.[14] Dispersed shareholders, it is argued, will perform the monitoring function by selling their shares, thereby causing the company's stock price to fall.[15] Exit is, therefore, preferred to voice and agency theorists contend

[8] For a critical view as to why this goal of corporate law cannot be attained, see Luca Enriques and Alessandro Romano, 'Rewiring Corporate Law for an Interconnected World' (2022) 64 *Arizona Law Review* 51.

[9] For early criticism, see E. Merrick Jr. Dodd, 'For Whom Are Corporate Managers Trustees' (1931) 45 *Harvard Law Review* 1145. On the so-called heroic managerialism of the 1950s and 1960s, see Harwell Wells, 'Corporation Law Is Dead: Heroic Managerialism, Legal Change, and the Puzzle of Corporation Law at the Height of the American Century' (2012) 15 *University of Pennsylvania Journal of Business Law* 305, 339–344.

[10] Milton Friedman, 'A Friedman Doctrine – The Social Responsibility of Business Is to Increase Its Profits' *The New York Times* (13 September 1970) SM 17.

[11] The literature here is voluminous. *See, e.g.*, William W. Bratton, 'The "Nexus of Contracts" Corporation: A Critical Appraisal' (1989) 74 *Cornell Law Review* 407; Charles R. T. O'Kelley, 'Coase, Knight, and the Nexus-of-Contracts Theory of the Firm: A Reflection on Reification, Reality, and the Corporation as Enterpreneur Surrogate' (2012) 35 *Seattle University Law Review* 1247.

[12] Armen A. Alchian and Harold Demsetz, 'Production, Information Costs, and Economic Organization' (1972) 62 *American Economic Review* 777.

[13] Eugene F. Fama and Michael C. Jensen, 'Separation of Ownership and Control' (1983) 26 *Journal of Law & Economics* 301, 303. See also Eugege F. Fama, 'Agency Problems and the Theory of the Firm' (1980) 88 *Journal of Political Economy* 288, 291–292.

[14] Fama, Agency Problems, 295.

[15] Alchian and Demsetz, Production, Information Costs, and Economic Organization, 788; Fama, Agency Problems, 292.

that it is due to the disciplinary forces of various markets (capital, product, management and labour)[16] rather than direct shareholder participation in corporate affairs that the separation of ownership and control becomes a viable, efficient arrangement. It comes, therefore, as no surprise that institutional shareholders with widely dispersed portfolios remained *passive risk bearers* opting for liquidity and diversification for most of the twentieth century.[17]

A key turning point in the history of corporate governance was the rise of institutional ownership that took place against the lull in takeovers at the close of the twentieth century. Indeed, with increasing equity holdings some institutional investors transformed from passive risk bearers to engaged 'owners'.[18] However, such firm-level shareholder engagement mainly occurred on an ad hoc basis, and most institutional shareholders rationally refrained from getting involved with the corporation's management, mainly because of the market efficacy to control managerial discretion and a series of legal and extra-legal obstacles to shareholders' active involvement.[19]

For a while it seemed that institutional engagement was too much to hope for, but the situation changed rapidly after the turn of the century. The continuing rise of financial intermediation and the concentration of equity holdings in the hands of a relatively small number of the very largest institutions (mainly in the US and the UK) hallmarked an

[16] *See, e.g.*, Fama, Agency Problems, 294–295.

[17] Pervasive collective action problems among widely dispersed shareholders exacerbated passivity and rational apathy. See Edward B. Rock, 'The Logic and (Uncertain) Significance of Institutional Shareholder Activism' (1991) 79 *Georgetown Law Journal* 445, 453–463.

[18] *See, e.g.*, John C. Coffee, Jr., 'Liquidity versus Control: The Institutional Investor as Corporate Monitor' (1991) 91 *Columbia Law Review* 1277; Ronald J. Gilson and Reinier Kraakman, 'Reinventing the Outside Director: An Agenda for Institutional Investors' (1991) 43 *Stanford Law Review* 863; Michael P. Smith, 'Shareholder Activism by Institutional Investors: Evidence from CalPERS' (1996) 51 *The Journal of Finance* 227.

[19] For the US, see Stephen J. Fisch and Jill E. Choi, 'On beyond CalPERS: Survey Evidence on the Developing Role of Public Pension Funds in Corporate Governance Symposium' (2008) 61 *Vanderbilt Law Review* 315; Roberta Romano, 'Public Pension Fund Activism in Corporate Governance Reconsidered' (1993) 93 *Columbia Law Review* 795; Bernard S. Black, 'Shareholder Activism and Corporate Governance in the United States' in P. Newman (ed), *The New Palgrave Dictionary of Economics and the Law*, vol 3 (Palgrave Macmillan 1998), 459–460. For the UK, see Bernard S. Black and John C. Coffee, 'Hail Britannia? Institutional Investor Regulation under Limited Regulation' (1994) 92 *Michigan Law Review* 1997; Brian R. Cheffins, *Corporate Ownership and Control: British Business Transformed* (Oxford University Press 2008), 373–381.

important shift to what has been called 'investor',[20] 'fiduciary',[21] 'shareholder',[22] 'agency'[23] or, more recently, 'asset manager' capitalism.[24] This shift has been deeply jarring on many levels.

On the one hand, the growth of large diversified investors and the lengthening of the investment chain have led some to forcefully claim that 'universal owners' – as fiduciaries for most citizens who have become indirect holders of public equity through their savings or pensions – should focus on the long-term performance of the entire market rather than firm-specific value.[25] The argument originally referred to pension funds, but these remained at large the 'sleeping giants'[26] in US and UK markets and portfolio-wide, systematic activism took about two decades to gain some market acceptance.[27] Today the argument has been expanded to large passive fund managers, including the Big Three.[28] The debate on the corporate governance role of passive investing is fierce and ongoing with convincing arguments on both sides.[29] While this

[20] Michael Useem, *Investor Capitalism: How Money Managers Are Changing the Face of Corporate America* (Basic Books 1996).

[21] James P. Hawley and Andrew T. Williams, *The Rise of Fiduciary Capitalism: How Institutional Investors Can Make Corporate America More Democratic* (University of Pennsylvania Press, Inc. 2000).

[22] Gerald F. Davis, *Managed by the Markets: How Finance Re-Shaped America* (Oxford University Press 2009).

[23] Ronald J. Gilson and Jeffrey N. Gordon, 'The Agency Costs of Agency Capitalism: Activist Investors and the Reevaluation of Governance Rights' (2013) 113 *Columbia Law Review* 863.

[24] Benjamin Braun, 'Asset Manager Capitalism as a Corporate Governance Regime' in Alexander Hertel-Fernandez and others (eds), *The American Political Economy: Politics, Markets, and Power* (Cambridge University Press 2021).

[25] *See, e.g.*, James Hawley and Andrew Williams, 'Universal Owners: Challenges and Opportunities' (2007) 15 *Corporate Governance: An International Review* 415, 416.

[26] Sharon Hannes, 'Brave New World: A Proposal for Institutional Investors' (2015) 16 *Theoretical Inquiries in Law* 245, 248.

[27] See Section 6.3.2.

[28] Jan Fichtner and Eelke M. Heemskerk, 'The New Permanent Universal Owners: Index Funds, Patient Capital, and the Distinction between Feeble and Forceful Stewardship' (2020) 49 *Economy and Society* 493; Frederick Alexander, 'An Honorable Harvest: Universal Owners Must Take Responsibility for Their Portfolios' (2020) 32 *Journal of Applied Corporate Finance* 24.

[29] See e.g., Lucian Bebchuk and Scott Hirst, 'Index Funds and the Future of Corporate Governance: Theory, Evidence, and Policy' (2019) 119 *Columbia Law Review* 2029 and Jill Hamdani Fisch, Assaf Solomon and Steven Davidoff, 'The New Titans of Wall Street: A Theoretical Framework for Passive Investors' (2019) 168 *University of Pennsylvania Law Review* 17; Davidson Heath *et al.*, 'Do Index Funds Monitor?' (2021) 35 *The Review of Financial Studies* 91.

debate cannot be resolved here, what needs to be highlighted is that, from the perspective of firm-specific engagement, even if passive managers engage with portfolio companies, they do so with the aim to maximize portfolio-level rather than firm-level value. In the words of Enriques and Romano, most institutional investors today are 'portfolio value maximizers' rather than 'firm value maximizers'.[30] And, their contribution is in internalizing negative externalities rather than improving alpha.[31] By contrast, the long-sought-after shareholder champion who can monitor ill-advised management and maximize firm value can be found (at least for some) in unexpected places.

6.2.2 *Hedge-Fund-Style Activism: Fulfilling the Promise of Firm-Specific Investor Engagement*

Since the early 2000s, activist hedge funds and similarly alternative asset management firms – to which I refer together as *hedge-fund-style activists* – turned to firm-specific shareholder engagement as a profit-making investment strategy to generate excess returns or alpha.[32] Even though many of these firms may resist the categorization as activist hedge funds, they all share a common feature: they all engage in a similar type of shareholder activism (often described as 'offensive'), which involves proactively building up substantial equity positions (around 5 per cent) in underperforming companies and agitating for firm-specific changes that will yield absolute returns.[33] Hedge-fund-style activists use an array of friendly or more confrontational strategies to persuade target management to address operational/strategic shortfalls and sometimes corporate governance weaknesses.[34] Their

[30] Enriques & Romano, Rewiring Corporate Law for an Interconnected World, 55.

[31] Madison Condon, 'Externalities and the Common Owner' (2020) 95 *Washington Law Review* 1.

[32] For a broad definition of the term 'activist hedge funds', see Dionysia Katelouzou, 'Myths and Realities of Hedge Fund Activism: Some Empirical Evidence' (2013) 7 *Virginia Law & Business Review* 459, 468–473.

[33] For the distinction between 'offensive' and 'defensive' activism, *see* Brian R. Cheffins and John Armour, 'The Past, Present and Future of Shareholder Activism by Hedge Funds' (2011) 37 *Journal of Corporation Law* 51.

[34] Katelouzou, Myths and Realities of Hedge Fund Activism, 491–495; William W. Bratton, 'Hedge Funds and Governance Targets' (2007) 95 *Georgetown Law Journal* 1375; Alon Brav *et al.*, 'Hedge Fund Activism, Corporate Governance, and Firm Performance' (2008) 63 *The Journal of Finance* 1729, 1735–1736.

engagement is firm-specific and value-oriented and differs from control-oriented takeover activities.[35]

More recently, environmental and social (E&S) objectives (and especially the former) are becoming key tools in the arsenal of reputed hedge-fund-style activists. For instance, The Children's Investment Fund (TCI) – previously characterized as a 'locust' following its campaign against Deutsche Boerse in 2005 – is now a 'climate radical' bringing its offensive tactics to the fight against climate change.[36] Bluebell Capital Partners, a $250 million, London-based activist hedge fund, which has taken aim at Danone and Solvay, is now taking an activist stance against BlackRock and criticizes BlackRock's ESG push as a 'distraction' and a 'hypocrisy'.[37] In addition, new ESG-focused activists are set up, including Inclusive Capital Partners and the notorious Engine No.1, to meet the increasing ESG mandates.[38] While research on the effects of E&S activism is still niche,[39] and while many point to concerning forces at work in the rise of E&S activism and ESG more generally,[40] with hedge-fund-style activists relying on support from fellow institutional shareholders who are increasingly internalizing negative externalities,[41] E&S activism is a trend that cannot be ignored.[42]

Another important trend is the geographical expansion of hedge-fund-style activism. The US may still have the greatest concentration of both

[35] For empirical evidence on the ownership stakes amassed by activist hedge funds supporting this claim see Dionysia Katelouzou, 'Worldwide Hedge Fund Activism: Dimensions and Legal Determinants' (2015) 17 *University of Pennsylvania Business Law Review* 798, 840–841.

[36] Edward Robinson, *World's Most-Profitable Hedge Fund Is Now a Climate Radical*, Bloomberg News (22 January 2020).

[37] Andrew R. Sorkin *et al.*, An Activist Investor Takes on BlackRock Over E.S.G., *New York Times Dealbook* (7 December 2022).

[38] Patrick Temple-West and Ortenca Allaj, 'Investor Jeff Ubben questions ESG funds in second act as activist', *Financial Times* (20 January 2023). Associated to this trend is the increase of E&S activism by index funds which is driven by Millenial demands. See Michal Barzuza *et al.*, 'Shareholder Value(s): Index Fund ESG Activism and the New Millennial Corporate Governance' (2019) 93 *Southern California Law Review* 1243.

[39] *E.g.*, Yongqiang Chu and Daxuan Zhao (2019) 'Green hedge fund activists' Working Paper, available at https://ssrn.com/abstract=3499373.

[40] Lucian A. Bebchuk and Roberto Tallarita, 'The Illusory Promise of Stakeholder Governance' (2020) 106 *Cornell Law Review* 91; Dorothy S. Lund and Elizabeth Pollman, 'The Corporate Governance Machine' (2021) 121 *Columbia Law Review* 2563.

[41] Philipp Krueger, Zacharias Sautner and Laura T. Starks, 'The Importance of Climate Risks for Institutional Investors' (2020) 33 *The Review of Financial Studies* 1067.

[42] See also Anna Christie (2021) 'The Agency Costs of Sustainable Capitalism' 55 *University of California Davis Law Review* 875.

Table 6.1 *Activist demands by country and type of investor, 2013–2022*

	All	Hedge-fund-style activists	Fund managers	Pension funds	Other institutional investors
US	6,569	5276	477	441	375
Japan	800	723	16	8	53
Australia	570	469	36	5	60
Canada	566	434	29	5	98
UK	505	402	68	2	33
Germany	258	189	9	2	58
Korea, Republic of	190	130	1	19	40
France	153	116	16	8	13
Switzerland	146	119	26	0	1
Poland	129	29	58	36	6
Singapore	95	91	0	0	4
Hong Kong	89	73	1	0	15
China	82	66	0	0	16
Sweden	78	59	2	14	3
Italy	77	73	1	0	3
Netherlands	76	71	2	0	3
Israel	69	56	2	1	10
Ireland	58	51	5	0	2
Austria	54	53	1	0	0
South Africa	49	37	9	0	3
Rest of the world	601	449	70	32	50
All	11,214	8,966	829	573	846

activist hedge funds and activist campaigns, but latest data collected from the Insightia database confirm that hedge-fund-style activism has become a truly global phenomenon.[43] Table 6.1 lists the top twenty countries around the world being targeted by activist institutional investors in the period 2013–2022. Public activist demands by institutional

[43] See also Ruth V. Aguilera *et al.*, 'Gone Global: The International Diffusion of Hedge Fund Activism' in Douglas Cumming, Sofia Johan and Geoffrey Wood (eds), *The Oxford Handbook of Hedge Funds* (Oxford University Press 2021). On East Asia, see Lin Lin's chapter in this book.

investors targeting US companies comprise 58.6 per cent of the total sample, but institutional shareholder activism spans across 60 jurisdictions on six continents. Within Europe, the UK may be known for its tradition of private, behind-the-scenes, shareholder engagement,[44] but is the home of 27.2 per cent of public activist campaigns in Europe. Germany comes second but has less than half the number of UK activist campaigns (258). In the rest of the world, Japan, Canada and Australia attract a large number of public activist campaigns (17.3 per cent of the total).

Another important finding is that the overwhelming majority of institutional shareholder activism (80 per cent) is attributed to hedge-fund-style activists. With the exception of Poland, hedge-fund-style activists have a strong presence globally. In the UK they made 469 publicly identifiable demands between 2013 and 2022. This confirms prior research attributing to activist hedge funds a 'disproportionate influence' on corporate governance over the last two decades.[45] By contrast, fund managers and pension funds only account for 12.5 per cent of all activist demands worldwide.

Figure 6.1 shows the time series of the 884 public activist campaigns launched by hedge-fund-style activists in Europe between 2013 and 2022. An activist campaign is defined by Insightia as 'a continuous period of time a company is publicly subjected to activist demands by an investor or group of investors working jointly'.[46] The figure shows the campaigns by the year during which the activist engagement was announced. Hedge-fund-style activism in Europe hit a record high in 2018 with a total number of 108 public activist campaigns. Since then, however, it has trended down. 2021 saw a surge in the number of new activist campaigns, but this trend did not continue to 2022. Much of this increase is due to hedge-fund-style activism in the UK which accounts for 66.67 per cent and 76.74 per cent of all European hedge-fund-style activism in 2021 and 2022, respectively.

The dominance of hedge-fund-style activism is due to many factors. Chief among them are the high success rate of hedge-fund-style activism

[44] Marco Becht *et al.*, 'Returns to Shareholder Activism: Evidence from a Clinical Study of the Hermes U.K. Focus Fund' (2008) 22 *The Review of Financial Studies* 3093.

[45] Amil Dasgupta *et al.*, 'Institutional Investors and Corporate Governance' (2021) 12 *Foundations and Trends in Finance* 276.

[46] See https://one.insightia.com. See also Katelouzou, Myths and Realities of Hedge Fund Activism, 491 (differentiating between activist objectives/demands and activist campaigns).

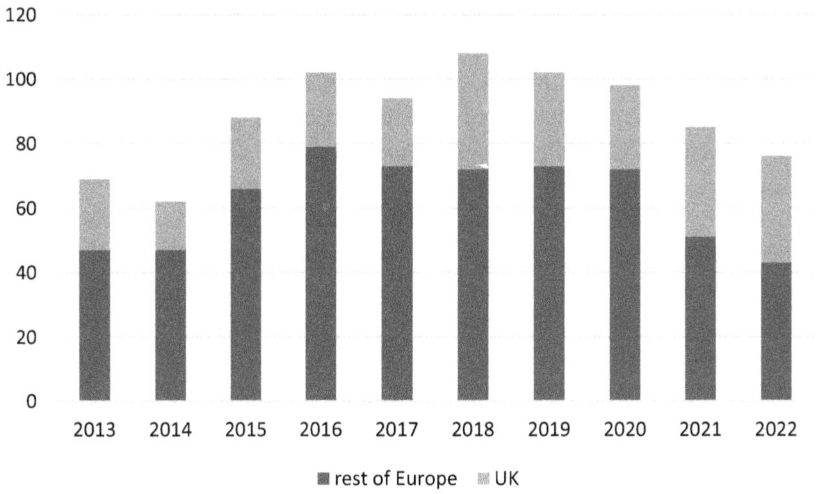

Figure 6.1 Hedge-fund-style activism in Europe, 2013–2022

in effecting firm-specific changes, the strong evidence of firm value creation along with some positive evidence on real effects, and the attractiveness of (implicit rather than explicit) coalition building.

There is a great deal of evidence that hedge-fund-style activists have been extremely successful in forcing their demands and generating above-market returns for their investors. They attain success in 40.6 per cent of the activist campaigns in the US and if one adds cases of partial success (where activists gain major concessions from the target company without achieving all their stated objectives) the success rate is reported to be as high as 66.4 per cent.[47] In addition, there is unequivocal evidence of abnormal stock returns around the activist events both in the US and abroad.[48] The positive effects of hedge-fund-style activism reach beyond target companies, as non-target companies are associated with improvements in governance and performance under the mere threat of

[47] Brav *et al.*, Hedge Fund Activism, Corporate Governance, and Firm Performance, 1744.

[48] For a review of the empirical literature in the US, see Alon Brav *et al.*, 'Hedge Fund Activism: A Review' (2009) 4 *Foundations and Trends in Finance* 185; John C. Jr. Coffee and Darius Palia, 'The Wolf at the Door: The Impact of Hedge Fund Activism on Corporate Governance' (2015) 41 *Journal of Corporation Law* 545, 551. For empirical evidence outside the US, see e.g., Marco Becht *et al.*, 'Returns to Hedge Fund Activism: An International Study' (2017) 30 *The Review of Financial Studies* 2933.

activism.[49] The empirical evidence on the long-term effects, however, is inconclusive. There is some empirical evidence suggesting that hedge-fund-style activism in the US, at least as of 2007, is able to achieve not only its investment objective of profiting from shareholder activism, but also a form of discipline, especially relating to the agency problems associated with free cash flows and to improve long–term performance.[50] Yet other studies find that firm value tends to decrease in the years following an activist campaign.[51] In terms of the real effects of hedge-fund-style activism and its impact on other stakeholders, several empirical papers link hedge fund activism in the US with improved productivity (including labour productivity), corporate innovation, bondholder wealth, and a reduction in firm's emissions, among others.[52] Outside the US, however, there is a lack of data on both the long-term and real effects of hedge-fund-style activism.

More importantly, for our purposes, hedge-fund-style activists triggered a modest, but significant, change in the behaviour of other (activist and non-activist) institutional investors. Even though it is well discussed that for most institutional investors firm-specific, hedge-fund-style shareholder engagement is not cost-effective,[53] many mainstream institutional investors (active funds, index funds and pension funds) support hedge-fund-style activists and fight against management to generate value. As Gilson and Gordon put it, institutions have been transformed from 'rationally apathetic' investors to '*rationally reticent*' in that they are increasingly willing to support activist demands, but are unlikely themselves to initiate them because competing funds will equally gain from their efforts.[54] In other words, institutional investors are 'responsive

[49] Nickolay Gantchev *et al.*, 'Governance under the Gun: Spillover Effects of Hedge Fund Activism' (2019) 23 *Review of Finance* 1031.

[50] Lucian A. Bebchuk, Alon Brav and Wei Jiang, 'The Long-Term Effects of Hedge Funds Activism' (2015) 115 *Columbia Law Review* 1085.

[51] Martijn Cremers, Saura Masconale and Simone M. Sepe, 'Activist Hedge Funds and the Corporation' (2016) 94 *Washington University Law Review* 261; Martijn Cremers *et al.* (2018) Hedge Fund Activism and Long-Term Firm Value, available at https://ssrn.com/abstract=2693231; and Mark R. DesJardine *et al.*, 'Why Activist Hedge Funds Target Socially Responsible Firms: The Reaction Costs of Signaling Corporate Social Responsibility' (2021) 64 *Academy of Management Journal* 851.

[52] For a literature review of this emerging literature, see Alon Brav *et al.*, 'Governance by Persuasion: Hedge Fund Activism and the Market for Corporate Influence' European Corporate Governance Institute – Finance Working Paper No 797/2021.

[53] See e.g., Dionysia Katelouzou, 'The Rhetoric of Activist Shareholder Stewards' (2021) 18 *New York University Journal of Law & Business* 665.

[54] Gilson and Gordon, The Agency Costs of Agency Capitalism, 867.

rather than initiatory'.[55] The reticence of pension funds and asset managers to make activist demands themselves is confirmed by Table 6.1. In addition, data on public collective action confirms the overall picture of rational reticence: there are only 332 public activist campaigns (out of 6,221) in the sample where institutional investors publicly acted together with hedge-fund-style activists.

Even though institutional investors may not be willing to publicly act together with hedge-fund-style activists, they tend to support them when the contested issue comes to a vote.[56] Several important links between activist funds and other institutional investors, including institutional investor investment in hedge-fund-style activists and the increasing mobility of corporate governance professionals across institutions, support such alliances.[57] To be sure, it is likely that institutional shareholders support hedge-fund-style activism only when firm value maximization is consistent with portfolio value maximization.[58] This is, for instance, the case when firm-specific activism generates 'governance externalities' that produce positive economic-wide effects from portfolio companies that want to avoid becoming activist targets.[59] The key point, therefore, from the perspective of firm-specific engagement is that hedge-fund-style activists play the role of 'governance intermediaries' or 'governance rights arbitrageurs' and their firm-specific activism is 'an endogenous response to the monitoring shortfall that follows from ownership re-concentration in intermediary institutions.'[60] Still, as Gordon notes, hedge-fund-style activists cannot be expected to internalize all externalities.[61] They can, however, serve the traditional objective of maximizing firm value and other investors may support this as long as firm value also serves or at least does not destroy portfolio value.

All in all, a growing clout of institutional investors ready to initiate or support firm-specific shareholder activism is taking shape. This growing

[55] Jeffrey N. Gordon, 'Systematic Stewardship' (2021) 47 *Journal of Corporation Law* 627, 660.

[56] See Alon Brav *et al.*, Governance by Persuasion, 69–79 (reviewing the literature on how other investors support hedge fund campaigns).

[57] Edward Rock, 'Institutional Investors in Corporate Governance' in Jeffrey N. Gordon and Wolf-Georg Ringe (eds), *The Oxford Handbook of Corporate Law and Governance* (Oxford University Press 2018).

[58] Alon Brav *et al.*, Governance by Persuasion, 6 (arguing that passive investors 'remain alert monitors in that their votes respond to firm performance).

[59] Gordon, Systematic Stewardship, 638.

[60] Gilson and Gordon, The Agency Costs of Agency Capitalism, 869.

[61] Gordon, Systematic Stewardship, 672.

clout has supported claims that hedge-fund-style activists can act 'like real owners',[62] or as a 'corrective mechanism'[63] in corporate governance. But the ability of those activists to promote firm-specific (and for some self-interested) agendas and to affect the structures and practices in national corporate sectors has given rise to questions about the activist funds' role and influence, especially following the 2008–9 global financial crisis (GFC) and the broader debate on short-termism. Post-GCF the 'dark side'[64] of hedge-fund-style activism has become a matter of concern for policymakers, executives, non-activist shareholders and other stakeholders alike, who pointed to the potential vulnerability of public corporations to short-term pressures in view of the increasing influence of activist shareholders and the likely negative impact on long-term corporate wealth in general.[65] At the same time, there has been a broad agreement that the public trust cannot be restored in the post-crisis market unless the dysfunctionality of shareholders' accountability is also addressed. This is what the policy development of shareholder stewardship aimed for, as the next Part will explain.

6.3 Shareholder Stewardship: Legitimizing 'Something Old'

6.3.1 The Policy Framework of Shareholder Stewardship: A Means to Awaken Institutional Investors

It is without doubt that the UK is the motherland of global shareholder stewardship. The UK Stewardship Code 2010, having its roots on the 2009 Institutional Shareholders' Committee (ISC) Code, established a 'comply-or-explain'[66] policy framework of seven principles dealing with

[62] Marcel Kahan and Edward B. Rock, 'Hedge Funds in Corporate Governance and Corporate Control' (2007) 155 *University of Pennsylvania Law Review* 1021, 1047.

[63] Paul Sharfman Rose, Bernard S., 'Shareholder Activism as a Corrective Mechanism in Corporate Governance' (2014) 2014 *Bringham Young University Law Review* 1015.

[64] Katelouzou, Myths and Realities of Hedge Fund Activism, 462. See also Mark J. Roe, 'Corporate Short-Termism – In the Boardroom and in the Courtroom' (2012) 68 *Business Lawyer* 977.

[65] Alan Dignam, 'The Future of Shareholder Democracy in the Shadow of the Financial Crisis' (2013) 36 *Seattle University Law Review* 639; Leo E. Jr. Strine, 'Can We Do Better by Ordinary Investors; A Pragmatic Reation to the Dueling Ideological Mythologists of Corporate Law Essay' (2014) 114 *Columbia Law Review* 449.

[66] It is noteworthy that for all UK-authorized asset managers the comply-or-explain approach has a more coercive effect as it is backed by the Financial Conduct Authority's Code of Conduct Handbook. Conduct of Business Rule 2.2.3. See http://fsahandbook.info/FSA/html/handbook/COBS/2/2. For a critical discussion of the

public disclosure and reporting of stewardship and voting policies, managing conflicts of interest, monitoring of investee companies, collective action and voting.[67] Along with its 2012 revision, the Code focused on shareholder engagement as the key means to exercise stewardship.[68] The two versions are therefore closely related, and I use the term 'first-generation' or '1G' UK Code to refer to both of them.[69] The 1G UK Code, likened to an 'Engagement Code',[70] contemplates the importance of firm-specific, micro-level institutional shareholder engagement that goes beyond the box-ticking exercise of governance mandates and financial metrics. Shareholder engagement on the part of institutional investors includes both formal and informal means. It is about 'purposeful' and 'active' dialogue, formal exercise of shareholder rights and informal engagement outside of the general meeting context (Principle 4), including collective engagement on the part of institutional investors (Principle 5).[71] Engaging involves listening as well as speaking – and specifically listening to explanations as to why a company chooses not to follow the UK Corporate Governance Code.[72] The 1G UK Code recommends relationships, not merely exercising rights (including voting), but it does not preclude escalation 'as a method of protecting and enhancing shareholder value'.[73]

The 1G UK Code inspired similar codes around the world, and today 21 more jurisdictions on six continents have introduced shareholder stewardship principles.[74] In addition, stewardship principles have been

coerciveness of the UK Code, see Dionysia Katelouzou and Peer Zumbansen, 'The New Geographies of Corporate Governance' (2020) 42 *University of Pennsylvania Journal of International Law* 1, 130.

[67] Financial Reporting Council, The UK Stewardship Code (July 2010) [hereinafter UK Code 2010], www.frc.org.uk/getattachment/e223e152-5515-4cdc-a951-da33e093eb28/UK-Stewardship-Code-July-2010.pdf. The ISC Code can be found in Appendix B of the FRC's consultation on a stewardship code for institutional investors (January 2010): https://media.frc.org.uk/documents/Consultation_on_a_Stewardship_Code_for_Institutional_Investors.pdf.

[68] Financial Reporting Council, The UK Stewardship Code (2012) [hereinafter UK Code 2012], https://media.frc.org.uk/documents/UK_Stewardship_Code_September_2012.pdf.

[69] See also Paul Davies, 'The UK Stewardship Code 2010–2020: From Saving the Company to Saving the Planet?' in Dionysia Katelouzou and Dan W. Puchniak (eds), *Global Shareholder Stewardship* (Cambridge University Press 2022), 44 (referring to the 2010 and 2012 versions together as the 'first version' of the UK Stewardship Code).

[70] Ibid. 47. [71] UK Code 2012, 6. [72] Ibid. 7. [73] Ibid. 8.

[74] See contributions to Dan W. Puchniak and Dionysia Katelouzou (eds), *Global Shareholder Stewardship* (Cambridge University Press 2022).

developed at the EU and international levels.[75] Even though there are differences between the various stewardship codes in terms of their formal design and content, their authorship, their enforcement mode and the functions they serve, they all share a common aim: to 'awake' passive institutional investors reflecting the view that engagement by institutional investors is an enforcer of good corporate governance.[76] The textual similarities uncovered by a previous empirical study supports this overriding objective and provide clear evidence of diffusion of the text of the UK Code 2012 especially among Asian common law countries.[77]

Building on earlier market-driven initiatives this UK-inspired policy promotion of institutional shareholder engagement through soft-law stewardship codes is rooted in the long-observed, economically grounded conception of the shareholder–management relationship analyzed above.[78] The 1G UK Code is ostensibly premised upon the idea that firm-specific shareholder engagement can overcome the agency problems between institutional shareholders and corporate directors and increase managerial accountability.[79] It focuses on firm-specific, micro-level shareholder stewardship and emphasizes the complementary capabilities and 'shared' responsibility of directors and institutional shareholders to monitor corporate governance and improve corporate performance not only in the short- but also in the long-term.[80] In turn, the 1G UK Code along with stewardship codes adopted in other jurisdictions provided a means of legitimation for the acceptable forms of (formal and informal) firm-specific institutional investor engagement which would be treated as *good* shareholder stewardship. The Code set up the expectations of 'proper' shareholder behaviour and only legitimized institutional investor

[75] *E.g.* Dionysia Katelouzou and Konstantinos Sergakis, 'When Harmonization Is Not Enough: Shareholder Stewardship in the European Union' (2021) 22 *European Business Organization Law Review* 203.

[76] Dionysia Katelouzou and Dan W. Puchniak, 'Global Shareholder Stewardship: Complexities, Challenges and Possibilities' in Dan W. Puchniak and Dionysia Katelouzou (eds), *Global Shareholder Stewardship* (Cambridge University Press 2022), 5–6.

[77] Dionysia Katelouzou and Mathias Siems, 'The Global Diffusion of Stewardship Codes' in Dan W. Puchniak and Dionysia Katelouzou (eds), *Global Shareholder Stewardship* (Cambridge University Press 2022).

[78] See Section 6.2.1.

[79] Iris H.-Y. Chiu, 'Turning Institutional Investors into "Stewards": Exploring the Meaning and Objectives of "Stewardship"' (2013) 66 *Current Legal Problems* 443, 457.

[80] UK Code 2012, 1.

engagement that contributes to long-termism. For instance, the reference to wider economic stress under Principle 5 which encourages collective action among institutional investors seems to have the effect of disavowing collective engagement in the interests of private, value-centred objectives and framing collective shareholder engagement within normative expectations that are consistent with wider public interests.[81] In this way, the form of shareholder activism carried out by hedge-fund-style activists, which is regarded with some scepticism in the UK and abroad, may have to conform to the standards in the Code if the activist insurgents wish to become Code signatories.

6.3.2 'Something New': Shareholder Engagement as a 'Duty' and the Ever-Widening Reach of Shareholder Stewardship

While the overall aim of the 1G UK Code – similarly to its ISC predecessor – was to promote institutional investor engagement at the micro-level as a valuable check on managerial abuses, a more careful look at the text of the two UK Codes reveals an important difference. As Table 6.2 reports, the words 'engagement/engage' and 'stewardship' appear with a quite similar frequency in the ISC Code and the UK Code 2010. This almost equal frequency in the use of the words 'engagement/engage' and 'stewardship' in the earlier codes is in sharp contrast to the text of the UK Code 2012 which refers to the words 'engagement/engage' nine times but 58 times to the word 'stewardship'. This is a remarkable textual change which illustrates an apparent contrast in the spirit and emphasis between the two early versions of the UK Code despite them having the same seven principles.

A closer look at the UK Code 2012 confirms this. The UK Code 2012 may still focus on institutional investor engagement as the crux of stewardship but it pushes stewardship beyond agency-based corporate governance to investment management as a tool to 'improve the functioning of the market for investment mandates.'[82] The 2012 version has brought a focus on the 'investment management' side of stewardship: the governance of stewardship within an organization and the relationship between the institutional investor – an investment intermediary – and their clients and ultimate beneficiaries. Shareholder stewardship is seen

[81] Ibid. 8–9. [82] UK Code 2012, 2.

Table 6.2 *Frequency of words engage/engagement and stewardship*

		Engage/engagement		Stewardship	
Code	Length of text in words	Times Appearing	Frequency (%)	Times Appearing	Frequency (%)
ISC Code	1504	10	0.66	6	0.40
UK Code 2010	1997	14	0.70	13	0.65
UK Code 2012	2954	9	0.30	58	1.96

as part of risk management and it thus needs to conform with the private trusteeship aspect that governs the investment funds' relationships with their clients/beneficiaries. It is because of this investment management dimension that the responsibility for stewardship does not rest with fund managers only but extends to asset owners themselves who 'should seek to hold their managers to account for their stewardship activities'.[83] Institutional investors 'cannot delegate their responsibility for stewardship' even though they can 'outsource to external service providers some of the activities associated with stewardship'.[84]

The UK Code 2012 sought to promote an efficient 'market for stewardship'[85] – or, in other words, a market for investment mandates – and tentatively expanded stewardship beyond firm-specific engagement to 'indirect' engagement through monitoring throughout the investment chain. Not only had the UK Code 2012 ushered in investor-led engagement to improve financial returns for the ultimate beneficiaries of those assets of which institutions are trustees, but Principles 1, 2, 6 and 7 of the UK Code 2012 dealing with the public disclosure of and periodic reporting on stewardship and voting policies specifically target the institutions' clients and beneficiaries. In addition, the UK Code 2012 extended the ambit of institutional investor engagement and assigned a sort of 'implicit social legitimacy'[86] to institutional investors' engagement and oversight. The UK Code 2012 states in its first paragraph that '[e]ffective

[83] Ibid. 1 and 2. [84] Ibid. 2.

[85] See Dionysia Katelouzou and Eva Micheler, 'Investor Capitalism, Sustainable Investment and the Role of Tax Relief' (2022) 23 *European Business Organization Law Review* 217.

[86] D. Walker, *A Review of Corporate Governance in UK Banks and Other Financial Industry Entities: Final Recommendations* (2009), 70.

stewardship benefits companies, investors and the economy *as a whole*'.[87] The assumption is that these wider benefits to the 'economy as a whole' can accrue as a result of a strong long-term performance of UK companies (to which shareholder engagement can contribute) and the ability of ultimate beneficiaries (savers) to benefit from this performance through returns to indirect (but also direct) ownership of shares in UK companies. The importance of shareholder stewardship is, therefore, not only a matter of achieving beneficiaries' private investment objectives through firm-specific shareholder engagement, but a matter of public interest.[88] This is in sharp contrast to previous private, agency-based understandings of shareholder engagement and resonates with universal ownership claims. The theoretical anchor of this argument is based on the stewardship theory of management and other social strands, including accounting, ethics, leadership and ecology.[89]

All in all, while both the 2010 and 2012 versions of the UK Code aspire to the model of micro-level shareholder stewardship, the UK Code 2012 places a stronger emphasis on the investment management side of stewardship and introduces (albeit tentatively) a stewardship 'duty' first and foremost to clients and beneficiaries (on the basis of the private trusteeship relationship that governs the investment funds' relationship with their beneficiaries) but also to the wider public.[90] A sceptic, however, may say that the FRC doubled its bet with the adoption of the 1G UK Code quickly sponsoring shareholder stewardship as a means to address the widespread post-GFC criticism that institutional investors failed in their role to call boards to account. A stronger critic may counter that the solution to the problems of poor corporate governance, excessive risk taking, and short-termism cannot be confined to shareholder engagement on the part of institutional investors and that other stakeholders must be

[87] UK Code 2012, 1 (emphasis added).

[88] Dionysia Katelouzou, 'Reflections on the Nature of the Public Corporation in an Era of Shareholder Activism and Stewardship' in Barnali Choudhury and Martin Petrin (eds), *Understanding the Company: Corporate Governance and Theory* (Cambridge University Press 2017), 117.

[89] *See, further*, Dionysia Katelouzou, 'Investor Stewardship: The State of the Art and Future Prospects' in Jeffrey N. Gordon and Wolf-Georg Ringe (eds), *The Oxford Handbook of Corporate Law and Governance* (2nd edn, Oxford University Press forthcoming) (developing a three-dimensional legal etymology of investor stewardship as (i) the exercise of power, (ii) on behalf of others, and (iii) for others).

[90] Iris H.-Y. Chiu and Dionysia Katelouzou, 'From Shareholder Stewardship to Shareholder Duties: Is the Time Ripe?' in Hanne S. Birkmose (ed), *Shareholders' Duties* (Wolters Kluwer 2017), 131.

mobilized.[91] To these one can add that problems along the investment chain are not for soft, policy-focused stewardship codes to solve but for a binding regulatory regime and that an increasing emphasis on outcomes rather than on processes and forward-looking policies is required.

It is because of these and other tensions[92] that the 1G UK Code failed to achieve its main objectives – to awaken passive institutional investors and promote an efficient market for stewardship. Perhaps one of its key flaws is that even though the Code conceptualized investor-led governance within a public-interest framing and is not merely a reiteration of a private agency-based concept of institutions as monitors, it continued to make overly optimistic assumptions about the motivations of different types of institutions and their alignment with socially beneficial effects in the long term.[93] The decreasing numbers of Code signatories after 2016 (which coincides with the introduction of the tiering exercise by the FRC) support the view that the model of micro-level shareholder stewardship promoted by the 1G Code mostly fell on deaf ears.[94]

This led to the introduction of the UK Code 2020 – the 'second generation' or '2G' UK Code – which overhauled how stewardship is understood.[95] The changes the UK Code 2020 brought about have been analysed elsewhere and will not be repeated here.[96] One key change, however, deserves our attention.

[91] *See, e.g.*, Janet Williamson, 'The Emperor's New Clothes – Enlightened Shareholder Value and the UK Stewardship Code' in Sigurt Vitols and Johannes Heuschmid (eds), *European Company Law and the Sustainable Company: A Stakeholder Approach*, Vol. 2 (European Trade Union Institute 2012), 253, 260.

[92] E.g. Brian R. Cheffins, 'The Stewardship Code's Achilles' Heel' (2010) 73 *The Modern Law Review* 1004; Arad Reisberg, 'The UK Stewardship Code: On the Road to Nowhere?' (2015) 15 *Journal of Corporate Law Studies* 217.

[93] See Section 6.4.1.

[94] The number of signatories to the 1G Code fell from a record high of 321 signatories in 2015 to 256 in 2017 but then increased to 295 in 2020. Data on file with the author. However, the FRC claims that the decrease in the number of signatories is not a matter of concern as the Code should not be used a reporting framework if stewardship is not relevant for an institution's business model. See Financing Reporting Council (January 2017) *Developments in Corporate Governance and Stewardship 2016*, at 26, www.frc.org.uk/getattachment/ca1d9909-7e32-4894-b2a7-b971b4406130/Developments-in-Corporate-Governance-and-Stewardship-2016.pdf.

[95] Financial Reporting Council, The UK Stewardship Code 2020 (2019), www.frc.org.uk/getattachment/5aae591d-d9d3-4cf4-814a-d14e156a1d87/Stewardship-Code_Dec-19-Final-Corrected.pdf [hereinafter UK Code 2020].

[96] See e.g., Davies, in 57–59; Bobby V. Reddy, 'The Emperor's New Code? Time to Re-Evaluate the Nature of Stewardship Engagement under the UK's Stewardship Code' (2021) 84 *Modern Law Review* 842.

The 2G UK Code marks an ambitious shift beyond micro-level shareholder engagement towards portfolio- and market-level engagement in recognition that asset owners and asset managers can act as 'guardians of market integrity' and work with other stakeholders, including regulators, associations and not-for-profits, in identifying and monitoring market-wide and systemic risks.[97] The 2G UK Code has expanded the remit of stewardship to *Environmental, Social, and Governance* (ESG) objectives.[98] ESG stewardship is not solely about micro-level shareholder engagement to advance ESG. Rather it serves two broader objectives: first, to incentivize the companies in which institutional investors invest to adopt an ESG agenda, and second, to provide the ultimate beneficiaries of institutional investors with the information and means to channel their funds towards ESG investments. Although this concept of stewardship was non-existent in the UK Code 2010 and received only a fleeting reference in the UK Code 2012, it is at the core of the latest version.[99]

This change is not merely the result of the increasing awareness of the importance of societal issues in corporate governance literature and practice.[100] More importantly, it is an attempt to align diversified investment strategies with the shareholder stewardship ideal – a problem at the heart of the 1G UK Code as elaborated elsewhere.[101] Exercising market- rather than micro-level stewardship is more consistent with the asset managers' mandate to maximize portfolio rather than firm value. In turn, passive as well as active investment strategies now clearly fall under the stewardship ambit. Even though this widening of shareholder stewardship beyond the micro-level expands the pool of potential activists, institutional investor engagement at the firm-specific level is still part and parcel of the 2G UK Code. Therefore, one of the questions still remaining is whether the original conception of micro-level shareholder stewardship has any champions. This is a complex question, and I cannot

97 UK Code 2020, 4. Principle 4.

98 Ibid. Principle 7.

99 It is also noteworthy that over the last decade ESG has found its way into stewardship codes around the world. Empirical evidence reveals that 84 per cent of the codes now refer 'at least once to ESG factors'. See Dionysia Katelouzou and Alice Klettner, 'Sustainable Finance and Stewardship: Unlocking Stewardship's Sustainability Potential' in Dionysia Katelouzou and Dan W. Puchniak (eds), *Global Shareholder Stewardship* (Cambridge University Press 2022), 561–563.

100 For the concurrent and larger-scale debate of 'corporate purpose' see Edward Rock, 'For Whom is the Corporation Managed in 2020? The Debate Over Corporate Purpose' (2021) 76 *Business Lawyer* 363.

101 Katelouzou, The Rhetoric of Activist Shareholder Stewards, 707.

hope to fully address it here.[102] Nevertheless, the next section will allude to part of the answer.

6.4 Are There Any Micro-level Shareholder Stewards Out There? Evidence from Stewardship Disclosures

6.4.1 *In Search of the 'Ideal' Shareholder Steward*

The analysis so far conceptualized the model of shareholder stewardship with a focus on the micro-level and exemplified its policy development through stewardship codes. This is where a paradox comes to light: the 1G UK Code was addressed to *all* asset managers and asset owners with equity holdings in UK-listed companies, but the model of micro-level shareholder stewardship – as originally envisaged by the 1G UK Code and carried on in the 2G Code – is by definition more suited to an undiversified investment strategy that entails firm-specific monitoring of operational and governance decisions, firm-specific engagement, and management oversight on a cost-effective basis.

Take, for instance, UK pension funds – which once were viewed as the archetype of universal owners. They now own just 1.8 per cent of UK equities,[103] but even if they owned as much public equity as they did in the 1980s and 1990s, most pension trustees have little incentives to engage in firm-specific shareholder engagement and monitoring and tend to play an 'indirect' form of stewardship through mandates to their fund managers.[104] A key stumbling block for this indirect type of stewardship has been the resistance of pension trustees to stewardship (especially to the 'enlightened' view discussed below) on the grounds that it entails considerations of broader benefits to third parties that extend beyond the financial interests of pension fund members and could therefore breach the fiduciary duty of loyalty to act solely for the interests of the beneficiaries.[105]

[102] For a fuller account, see Katelouzou, *The Path to Enlightened Shareholder Stewardship*.

[103] See Office for National Statistics, *Ownership of UK quoted shares: 2020* (2022), 4 (reporting a record low of 1.8 per cent in the equity shares of UK pension funds at the end of 2020, a further decrease from the 2.2 per cent in 2018).

[104] There are notable exceptions, however, such as The Church Commissioners for England, an £8.7bn investment fund managed in an ethical and responsible way, has a long history of active engagement with companies. See e.g., The Church of England Pensions Board, Stewardship Report 2021, www.churchofengland.org/sites/default/files/2022-10/5562_Stewardship%20Report_vFINAL.pdf .

[105] Anna Tilba and Arad Reisberg, 'Fiduciary Duty under the Microscope: Stewardship and the Spectrum of Pension Fund Engagement' (2019) 82 *The Modern Law Review* 456.

From the four categories of 'traditional' domestic institutional investors (pensions, insurance, unit trusts – or mutual funds – and investment trusts), only unit trusts – the British open-end mutual funds – are still significant players in UK-listed shares despite a recent fall in their ownership share.[106] Unit trusts together with other financial institutions, such as index funds and exchange traded funds which have an increasing presence in UK-listed equity, could, in theory, have the financial incentives to perform the role of the shareholder steward.[107] However, despite forceful scholarly debate on the stewardship role of passive investors, it is becoming clearer that index funds do not monitor the fundamentals of their portfolio companies, have very weak incentives to actively promote firm-specific governance improvements, and even if they were to do so their influence would be limited to their minority voting power.[108] Passive managers, therefore, can at best play a systematic, portfolio-level stewardship role.

This leaves us with active asset managers who can in theory undertake firm-specific engagement and stewardship. There are two instructive examples. First, when active asset managers *react* to corporate crises (such as excessive executive plans, acquisitions, poor succession plans or inappropriate capital increases) they align with the micro-level shareholder stewardship model. Second, when active asset managers address environmental and social issues engaging in ESG activism they align with the micro-level shareholder stewardship model.[109] But in the main, while active asset managers invest resources in stock-picking underperforming companies, their ability to actively engage to improve performance at the individual firm-level is limited due to their business model and resources.[110] This is why the firm-specific stewardship abilities of active managers are mostly reactive and incidental.

[106] Office for National Statistics, ONS 2022, 4 (reporting that unit trusts' proportions in the UK listed market have fallen sharply from a record high of 9.5 per cent in 2018 to 7.4 per cent at the end of 2020).

[107] Ibid (reporting that other financial institutions reached a record high of 12.8 per cent in 2020).

[108] But see John C. Coates, 'The Future of Corporate Governance Part I: The Problem of Twelve' (Harvard Pub. L., Working Paper No. 19–07, 2018) https://ssrn.com/abstract=3247337 (arguing that index funds have 'unsurpassed power' to control their portfolio companies).

[109] Elroy Dimson *et al.*, 'Active Ownership' (2015) 28 *The Review of Financial Studies* 3225 (empirically analysing ESG activism by a large active manager).

[110] Edward B. Rock and Marcel Kahan, 'Index Funds and Corporate Governance: Let Shareholders Be Shareholders' (2020) 100 *Boston University Law Review* 1771, 1806.

A neglected but important candidate for micro-level shareholder stewardship is the activist investor. This is not the one associated with aggressive US activist hedge funds but the one related to a 'softer' activist type mostly found outside the US context.[111] This type of activism is associated with hedge-fund-style activists that proactively – but also sometimes reactively – engage with companies mostly behind the scenes and on a long-term investment horizon.

From an investment management perspective, the business model of the so-called *activist shareholder stewards* is compatible with firm-specific engagement and the micro-level shareholder stewardship model aspired to by the UK Code.[112] A cautionary note is required here. As explained above, the UK Code legitimizes firm-specific engagement and activism only when long-term value improvement is aimed for and achieved. The investment style of activist funds can therefore fill the stewardship bill only if such activism is not used for the purposes of short-term value extraction. Many activists – especially outside the US – recognize 'attention to shareholder value . . . as a public good',[113] a view largely consistent with the model of micro-level shareholder stewardship. Nevertheless, there are some limitations in the conclusion that can be drawn on the value effects of hedge-fund-style activism from the existing empirical literature, which has mainly focused on value effects and thus has not adequately considered the market-wide impact of activist shareholders or their direct role in corporate governance.[114]

While reaching a conclusion about activist funds' net impact on corporate governance and social value is outside the scope of this chapter, the arguments presented so far support the thesis that the business model of activist shareholder stewards is in alignment – at least from a theoretical perspective – with the firm-specific shareholder stewardship model of the UK Code.[115] As for their incentives, as long as activists aim at

[111] See Section 6.2.2.

[112] For a comprehensive analysis see Katelouzou, The Rhetoric of Activist Shareholder Stewards, 707–716.

[113] John Buchanan *et al.*, *Hedge Fund Activism in Japan: The Limits of Shareholder Primacy* (Cambridge University Press 2012).

[114] See Section 6.2.2.

[115] For a more critical view of the stewardship role of activist hedge funds, see Roger M. Baker and Iris H.-Y. Chiu, *Corporate Governance and Investment Management: The Promises and Limitations of the New Financial Economy* (Edward Elgar Publishing 2017), 350.

protecting and enhancing the long-term value of investee companies, they can fill the stewardship bill.

6.4.2 *What Does the Language of Shareholder Stewardship Tell Us?*

An empirical analysis of the stewardship statements of activist asset managers corroborates the argument that activist shareholder stewards can fill the stewardship bill.[116] The full details of the empirical study are not discussed here. Instead, I present here those aspects of the empirical data that inform the understanding of micro-level shareholder stewardship. The application of natural language processing (NLP) techniques to a hand-collected corpus of 73,207 total tokens (that is, stemming abbreviations after pre-processing) confirms that activist signatories to the UK Code 2012 perceive exercising voting rights and engaging (formally and informally) as a key element of shareholder stewardship.

As Figure 6.2 reveals, the most frequently occurring word in the corpus is '*vote/ing*', while 'engage/ment' is the fifth most frequent word. The token '*proxi*' (proxy) is the 14th most frequently used word. This implies that the activist signatories perceive the proxy advisory firms as key counterparts in exercising shareholder voting and shareholder stewardship. '*Meet*' and '*board*' are also common words in the signatories' statements. Thus, it is evident that activist signatories understand shareholder stewardship in a broad way as including not only voting but also informal forms of monitoring and engagement, such as meetings and dialogue with the board of directors.

Examining the unigram distribution also confirms that engagement as a means to achieve better corporate governance ('*govern*') is a key component of shareholder stewardship. The frequencies of the words '*client*', '*conflict*' and '*interest*' are indicative of the investment management side of stewardship and highlight that institutional investors have a clear understanding of managing other people's money in expressing their stewardship policies. The token *respons*(ibility/ible) is the 16th most frequent word. This indicates that activist signatories understand stewardship as a key element of their responsibilities not only towards their clients and beneficiaries but also to a wider range of constituents as shareholders of public equity. '*ESG*' is the 27th most frequent unigram. This is reflective of the growing percentage of investors considering ESG

[116] See Katelouzou, The Rhetoric of Activist Shareholder Stewards, 717–744.

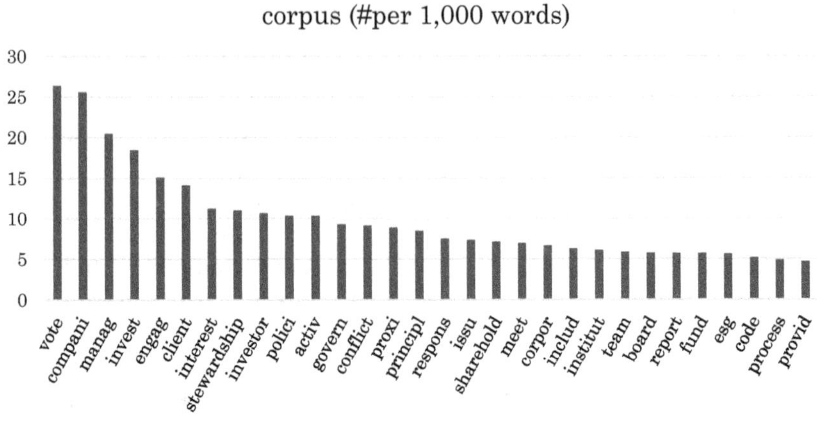

Figure 6.2 Most frequently occurring words in the corpus

investing as priority investment themes and the increasing emphasis worldwide stewardship codes place on ESG oversight.[117] Finally, among the top 30 most frequent words are '*issu*', '*report*', and '*inform*', which all reflect the emphasis of stewardship statements on publicly available information through issuing policy statements and reporting to clients and beneficiaries on voting, engagement and stewardship.

To analyse the rhetoric (thematic content) of shareholder stewardship as it is revealed in the activist signatories' statements, I adopted an *unsupervised* machine learning-based process. To conduct the analyses, I made use of an analysis technique named structural topic modelling. I implemented this technique via the *stm* software package for R programming language, which provides tools for machine-assisted reading of texts.[118] The analysis unveiled rich and intricate textual patterns. For the purposes of this chapter, four key findings require our attention.

First, activist signatories to the UK Code 2012 understand shareholder stewardship as including both corporate governance and investment management aspects; the so-labelled *Orthodox Stewardship* topic is the most frequent one across all disclosure statements. Tokens, such as '*nonexecut*' (non-executive directors), reveal the focus of stewardship disclosures on standard corporate governance topics. Monitoring and engagement, especially via formal means, such as voting ('*vote*'), feature

[117] See Sections 6.2.2 and 6.3.2.

[118] Margaret E. Roberts *et al.*, 'stm: An R Package for Structural Topic Models' (2019) 91 *Journal of Statistical Software* 1.

prominently in statements associated with this topic. Collective and collaborative action ('*collect*') with other shareholders is also an aspect of the shared understanding of shareholder stewardship. In addition to the corporate governance understanding of shareholder stewardship, the visual examination of the words associated with this topic reveals that conflicts of interest ('*conflict*' and '*interest*'), relationships with clients ('*client*') and proxy advisors such as the Institutional Shareholders Services ('*iss*'), and risk management ('*manag*') appear to be critical for the way stewardship is perceived by the signatories to the UK Code 2012. This suggests that statements in this topic understand that micro-level shareholder stewardship is not only about monitoring and engagement, but it has an investment management aspect which relates to the relationship between the investor–steward and its ultimate investors (clients or end beneficiaries) as well as other intermediated parties on the investment chain, such as asset managers, proxy advisors and investment consultants.

Second, while it is confirmed from NLP that micro-level shareholder stewardship is mainly about engagement on corporate governance issues via both formal and informal means to maximize the value of the target company,[119] an understanding which accords with the depiction of the 1G UK Code as an 'Engagement Code', it is important to note that statements emphasize that it is an unwavering commitment to the asset managers' clients ('*client*') and the beneficiaries ('*beneficiari*') of pension ('*pension*') funds that drives any firm-level shareholder engagement and monitoring. This confirms that micro-level shareholder stewardship is expected to be exercised only to the degree that serves the interests of the activists' clients and therefore any firm-specific value creation should have a materially positive impact on the activist's portfolio value for shareholder stewardship to be undertaken. This explains why micro-level shareholder stewardship cannot be a popular strategy for investors with large, diversified portfolios where any firm-specific value creation does not have any material impact on the total portfolio value.[120]

Third, it is clear from the statements of the activist signatories that shareholder stewardship cannot be understood – and more fundamentally cannot be effectively exercised – if the investors' own business

[119] The second most common topic, labelled as 'Monitoring & Engagement', focuses on shareholder engagement via formal and informal means.

[120] An exception would be when micro-level shareholder stewardship reduces negative externalities for other portfolio companies even though it does not materially improve their value.

models, incentives and abilities as well as regulatory constraints (including fiduciary duties) are not considered. Some activist stewards (mainly overseas and aggressive ones) tend to understand shareholder stewardship in an *instrumental* way which echoes a shareholder-centred, contractarian understanding of the role of investors–shareholders in corporate governance. On the other hand, friendly activist signatories and those who are PRI signatories appear to have a more sustainable and environment-friendly orientation in the way they perceive and communicate shareholder stewardship.[121] Their statements are mostly associated with the third most common topic (*Sustainability & Active Ownership*) and emphasize the notions of sustainability ('*sustain*') and active ownership ('*activ*'). Statements in this topic focus on environmental themes, such as climate change ('*climat*'), and general ESG factors ('*esg*'). This topic links stewardship to the broader literature of responsible ownership and sustainable investing and is more closely associated to the notion of 'enlightened' stewardship under which view shareholder stewardship is a means to create sustainable value for beneficiaries, investee companies, the economy and society, and address major societal goals that are not being met right now due to public companies' transgressions.

Finally, the empirical findings confirm that shareholder activism and micro-level shareholder stewardship are not incompatible. Shareholder stewardship may not be understood in the same way by all the activist stewards in the sample but there is encouraging evidence that activist signatories, especially the friendlier ones who are PRI signatories, recognize 'shared value' rather than monolithic shareholder value as the driver for their investment decisions and stewardship activities. Yet, stewardship-washing, that is overstatement or misrepresentation of investor engagement, can be an issue as stewardship-related disclosures do not necessarily mean that sufficient progress is achieved when it comes to stewardship outcomes.[122] Whether and to what extent the 'enlightened' rhetoric is translated to outcomes is open to further research, but the empirical findings confirm that the overhaul of the 1G UK Code and the introduction of the 2G UK Code was a step in the right direction and in alignment with the way many of the activist signatories were already perceiving stewardship.

[121] On the role of the PRI as a forum of collaborative engagement, see e.g., Elory Dimson *et al.*, 'Coordinated Engagements' ECGI, Finance Working Paper No. 721/2021, https://ssrn.com/abstract=3209072.

[122] Katelouzou, The Rhetoric of Activist Shareholder Stewards, 749.

6.5 Conclusion

Scholars, regulators and policymakers have held out hope that institutional investors, including hedge-fund-style activists, would use their voting power to collectively act as the 'real' or 'universal' owners', or 'good stewards' of public listed companies, thereby minimizing shareholder-manager agency costs, improving long-term corporate performance or even addressing negative externalities. This chapter offers some nourishment to such hopes. Focusing on the so-called micro-level shareholder stewardship, it identifies the canonical micro-level steward in funds which specialize in firm-specific engagements. Their business model is similar to hedge-fund-style activists: they aim to generate firm value through targeted activist interventions. But they differ from other activist hedge funds in their stewardship responsibility: they engage with companies with a sense of a duty, a responsibility to investors' beneficiaries and the wider public.

Micro-level shareholder stewardship, however, is no panacea. First, as the debate on the role of institutional investors in corporate governance evolves and shareholder stewardship is becoming more embedded across the investment chain, more attention should be placed on whether the activist shareholder stewards' model can operate at a large scale. In my sample, activist shareholder stewards make up about one-fifth of all the signatories to the UK Code so one needs to focus on whether their stewardship role is that of a safeguard for deeply undervalued and poorly governed companies and a 'stewardship arbitrageur' for other institutional investors to whom they turn for support. The interplays between different levels of stewardship, micro-, market- and macro- also need to be addressed. Second, even though the disclosure statements of activist shareholder stewards confirm that policy and practice go hand in hand and shape each other in continuing interaction, stewardship-washing cannot be ruled out. Future research should cast light on the extent to which activist stewards 'walk the stewardship talk'. Finally, the changes in what is socially acceptable for businesses and institutional investors and the growing need to internalize part of the negative externalities that affect investors' portfolios as a whole call for a reimagination of the 'old' notions of shareholder activism, shareholder engagement and shareholder monitoring.[123] The 2G UK Code supports this shift. It is now left to see whether and how the stewardship signatories will respond.

[123] Hart and Zingales' chapter in this book.

7

The Perils and Promise of Shareholders as Stakeholder Advocates

LISA M. FAIRFAX

Environmental, Social, and Governance ("ESG") and the corresponding focus on issues impacting non-shareholder stakeholders, has taken center stage in the U.S. corporate governance arena. ESG includes a wide array of (a) environmental issues, including climate change, renewable and greenhouse gas emissions, (b) social issues ranging from human capital management to addressing diversity, equity and inclusion ("DEI") issues, and (c) governance practices such as majority voting, board declassification, and proxy access.[1] These issues incorporate concerns around non-shareholder stakeholders, particularly employees, customers, and the broader community. These issues also have come to dominate corporate governance. Shareholders have prioritized ESG in their engagement efforts and voting policies.[2] Corporations not only are focusing more on ESG, but also are allocating an increasingly greater portion of their resources toward improving ESG.[3] Directors are devoting more time on oversight of ESG issues.[4] Executives and officers are more focused on incorporating ESG into their business, and taking steps to address ESG risks or take advantage of ESG opportunities.[5] There also

[1] *See* Gibson Dunn, *Shareholder Proposal Developments during the 2022 Proxy Season*, July 11, 2022, at 3–4 note 6, www.gibsondunn.com/wp-content/uploads/2022/07/shareholder-proposal-developments-during-the-2022-proxy-season.pdf [hereinafter Gibson Dunn, *2022 Shareholder Proposal Developments*].

[2] *See* EY Center for Board Matters, *2022 Proxy Season Preview* (Feb. 2022), at 2, 6, https://assets.ey.com/content/dam/ey-sites/ey-com/en_us/topics/board-matters/cbm-2022-proxy-season-preview-final-us-score-no-15036-221us.pdf [hereinafter EY, *2022 Proxy Season Preview*].

[3] *See* Lucy Perez, et al., *Does ESG Really Matter – and Why?*, McKinsey Q., Aug. 2022, at 1, www.mckinsey.com/business-functions/sustainability/our-insights/does-esg-really-matter-and-why.

[4] *See* EY, *2022 Proxy Season Preview*, *supra* note 2, at 4.

[5] *See* Governance Insights Center, *PwC's 2021 Annual Corporate Directors Survey: The Director's New Playbook, Taking on Change*, at 8 (noting that ESG has become part of

has been a substantial increase in the amount of money flowing into ESG-related investment funds.[6] Then too, the U.S. Securities and Exchange Commission ("SEC") has proposed the first-ever climate related disclosure rules and is contemplating disclosure rules associated with other ESG matters.[7]

Shareholders, particularly large institutional shareholders, have played an instrumental role in the recent effort to promote ESG and the interests of other stakeholders. It has now become common practice for the CEOs of BlackRock, Vanguard, and State Street Global Advisors ("State Street"), three of the world's largest and most influential shareholders and asset managers,[8] to publish open letters to CEOs outlining their ESG expectations for corporations and their boards.[9] Shareholders also have published engagement and voting guidance around a host of ESG issues in order to ensure that corporations more appropriately address those issues.[10]

business strategy and risk management policies), 16, https://www.pwc.com/us/en/services/governance-insights-center/assets/pwc-2021-annual-corporate-directors-survey.pdf.

6 *See* Perez, *supra* note 3, at 1 (noting that inflows into sustainable funds rose from $5 billion in 2018 to nearly $70 billion in 2021).

7 *See* Ibid. at 1; *see also* Proposed Rule: The Enhancement and Standardization of Climate-Related Disclosures for Investors, https://www.sec.gov/rules/proposed/2022/33-11042.pdf [hereinafter *SEC Rule Proposal*].

8 *See* Shaun Bisman & Felipe Cambeiro, *Big Three Institutional Investor Updates*, Harv. L. School Forum on Corp. Gov. (Apr. 13, 2022), https://corpgov.law.harvard.edu/2022/04/13/__trashed/#:~:text=Blackrock%2C%20Vanguard%2C%20and%20State%20Street,many%20U.S.%20publicly%20traded%20companies; Lucian Bebchuk & Scott Hirst, *The Specter of the Giant Three*, 99 B.U. L. Rev. 721, 723–24 (2019); Jan Fichtner et al., *Hidden Power of the Big Three? Passive Index Funds, Re-Concentration of Corporate Ownership, and New Financial Risk*, 19 Bus. & Pol. 298 (2017); Liam Kennedy, *Top 500 Asset Managers 2021*, IPE (June 2021), https://www.ipe.com/reports/top-500-asset-managers-2021/10053128.article.

9 *See e.g.*, Larry Fink, *The Power of Capitalism*, BlackRock (2022), at 4, https://www.blackrock.com/corporate/investor-relations/larry-fink-ceo-letter?cid=ppc:blk:ll:na:ol:goog:na:v2:bhv:tl&gclid=Cj0KCQjw94WZBhDtARIsAKxWG-EEMiwHJKi4kJjJh3f-FfCaFYHpjmE9LVAZ4kVUlpEwY2kS5dI6nIaAjc6EALw_wcB&gclsrc=aw.ds; Cyrus Taraporevala, *Capturing the Power of Diversity,* SSGA (Oct. 25, 2021), at 1, https://www.ssga.com/us/en/institutional/etfs/insights/capturing-the-power-of-diversity; William McNabb, *An Open Letter to Directors of Public Companies Worldwide*, Vanguard (Aug. 31, 2017), at 2, https://www.wlrk.com/docs/2017VanguardOpenLettertoBoards.pdf.

10 *See, e.g.,* State Street Global Advisors, *Guidance on Diversity Disclosures and Practices,* SSGA (Jan. 2022), at 5, https://www.ssga.com/library-content/pdfs/asset-stewardship/racial-diversity-guidance-article.pdf [hereinafter, *State Street Guidance on Diversity Disclosure and Practices*]; State Street Global Advisors, *Guidance on Human Capital Management Disclosures & Practices* (May 2023), at 1–2, https://www.ssga.com/library-content/pdfs/asr-library/proxy-voting-human-capital-disclosure.pdf [hereinafter *State Street Guidance on HCM Disclosures & Practices*]; BlackRock, *Our Approach to*

Moreover, shareholders have used the shareholder proposal process to encourage corporations to address critical ESG issues.[11] In the past few years, not only have shareholder proposals related to ESG issues come to dominate the shareholder proposal landscape, but also those proposals have garnered an increasingly larger percentage of shareholder support.[12] Shareholders' emphasis on ESG has dramatically altered the corporate governance landscape.[13]

Shareholders' prominent role in advancing ESG and other stakeholder interests has garnered considerable concern and criticism.[14] One prominent concern centers around the fact that shareholders' support for ESG is clearly linked to financial returns. Indeed, shareholders have been upfront in their conviction that their focus on ESG and stakeholders is linked to financial issues rather than any moral or ethical imperative to "do the right thing." In his 2017 open letter to public companies, then Chair and CEO of Vanguard, William McNabb, stated that Vanguard's stance supporting board diversity, is "an economic imperative, not an ideological one."[15] In his 2022 annual letter to CEOs, BlackRock CEO Larry Fink wrote: "We focus on sustainability not because we're environmentalists, but because we are capitalists and fiduciaries to our clients."[16] State Street's president and CEO similarly wrote that ESG issues of equity and inclusion "weren't merely matters of values to use as individuals – of what is morally right and wrong – but of value itself as investors."[17] According to critics, the fact that shareholders have linked ESG and stakeholder issues to profit begs the question about whether shareholders can be effective advocates for

Engagement with Companies on Human Rights (Feb. 2022), at 3, https://www.blackrock.com/corporate/literature/publication/blk-commentary-engagement-on-human-rights.pdf; Vanguard, *Global Investment Stewardship Principles* (Nov. 2021), at 3, https://corporate.vanguard.com/content/dam/corp/research/pdf/Global%20investment%20stewardship%20principles_final_112021.pdf.

11 *See* Sullivan & Cromwell, *2022 Proxy Season Review: Part I: Rule 14a-8 Shareholder Proposals* (Aug. 8, 2022), at 1, https://www.sullcrom.com/files/upload/sc-publication-2022-Proxy-Season-Part-1-Rule-14a-8.pdf [hereinafter Sullivan & Cromwell, *2022 Proxy Season Review*].

12 *See* Ibid.; Gibson Dunn, *2022 Shareholder Proposal Developments, supra* note 1, at 2.

13 *See* Sullivan & Cromwell, *2022 Proxy Season Review, supra* note 11, at 1; Gibson Dunn, *2022 Shareholder Proposal Developments, supra* note 1, at 2.

14 *See* Perez, *supra* note 3, at 2 ("As ESG has gone mainstream and gained support and traction, it has consistently encountered doubt and criticism as well.").

15 *See* McNabb, *supra* note 9, at 2.

16 *See* Fink, *The Power of Capitalism, supra* note 9, at 4.

17 *See* Taraporevala, *Capturing the Power of Diversity, supra* note 9, at 1.

stakeholders. Importantly, there is significant concern that tethering stakeholder interests to financial concerns could artificially limit or undermine the effort to advance stakeholder interests, increasing the likelihood that any embrace of ESG is rhetorical, or otherwise that corporations will focus on ESG and other stakeholders only when there is some clear and measurable economic benefit.[18]

While acknowledging these and other potential drawbacks, this chapter offers a more optimistic view. This chapter argues that available evidence around shareholder ESG efforts reveals that shareholders have been strong advocates for stakeholders, moving the needle around several critical ESG issues including disclosure, board oversight, and more specific ESG goals and initiatives. This chapter further argues that shareholders may be best positioned to ensure that corporations maintain a long-term focus on ESG and other stakeholders. Perhaps more importantly, this chapter posits that, rather than serving as a roadblock, the connection shareholders have made between ESG and financial returns may actually increase the likelihood that corporations pay appropriate attention to ESG in the long-term. In making these arguments, this chapter will draw primarily from the engagement practices, voting policies, and communications of the so-called Big Three institutional investors – BlackRock, Vanguard, and State Street.[19]

Section 7.1 of this chapter discusses the connection between shareholder value and ESG and some prominent concerns raised by that connection. Section 7.2 reveals that those concerns may have been overstated or misguided by highlighting the considerable effort shareholders have expended, and the considerable progress shareholders have made to ensure that corporations address vital ESG and stakeholder issues. Section 7.2 also demonstrates how the link between ESG and shareholder value may be the primary reason for both current and long-term progress on ESG and stakeholder concerns. Section 7.3 concludes.

7.1 The Perils of Profit

7.1.1 The Economics of ESG

Shareholders have been very transparent about the fact that their efforts to promote ESG and other stakeholders are driven by economic and

[18] *See e.g.*, Dorothy Lund & Elizabeth Pollman, *Corporate Governance Machine*, 121 Col. L. Rev. 2563, 2631 (2021).

[19] *See supra* note 8. See also Lund & Robertson, Chapter 5 in this book.

financial concerns. A recent survey by the EY Center for Board Matters found that shareholders' ESG expectations stem from their "conviction that more effective management of environmental, social and governance (ESG) issues will lead to better financial performance."[20] Shareholder statements abound highlighting this conviction. In describing its engagement priorities, BlackRock maintains that companies that focus on ESG issues will "enhance their ability to maximize long-term financial returns."[21] As BlackRock notes, "[w]e believe that companies that build strong relationships with their stakeholders are more likely to meet their own strategic objectives and deliver durable profits."[22] Similarly, State Street has emphasized its belief that ESG considerations have both positive and negative impacts on long-term financial performance.[23]

Shareholders have tied specific ESG issues to financial returns. For example, BlackRock characterized human rights as an investment issue when explaining its approach to engaging with companies on human rights.[24] Cyrus Taraporevala, State Street's then president and CEO, wrote that issues of equity and inclusion "weren't merely matters of values to use as individuals – of what is morally right and wrong – but of value itself as investors."[25] In its published guidance on diversity disclosures and practices, State Street stated: "[w]e remain focused on our fiduciary duty to maximize the long-term risk-adjusted returns of our clients' investments."[26]

With respect to the environment, Vanguard's McNabb noted that Vanguard's position on the importance of climate risk "is based on the economic bottom line for Vanguard investors."[27] State Street has referred

[20] *See* EY, *2022 Proxy Season Preview, supra* note 2, at 1.

[21] *See* BlackRock, *Engagement Priorities* (Feb. 2022), at 3, https://www.blackrock.com/corporate/literature/publication/blk-stewardship-priorities-final.pdf [hereinafter BlackRock, *Engagement Priorities 2022*].

[22] *See* BlackRock, *Our Approach to Engagement with Companies on Human Rights, supra* note 10, at 3.

[23] *See* State Street Global Advisors, *ESG Investment Statement* (June 2022), at 1, https://www.ssga.com/library-content/pdfs/esg-investment-statement.pdf [hereinafter State Street, *ESG Investment Statement*].

[24] *See* BlackRock, *Our Approach to Engagement with Companies on Human Rights, supra* note 10, at 2.

[25] *See* Taraporevala, *Capturing the Power of Diversity, supra* note 9, at 1.

[26] *See State Street Guidance on Diversity Disclosure and Practices, supra* note 10, at 5.

[27] *See* McNabb, *supra* note 9, at 2.

to climate change as a source of risk to the global financial system.[28] BlackRock's Fink wrote, "climate risk is investment risk,"[29] and: "We focus on sustainability not because we're environmentalists, but because we are capitalists and fiduciaries to our clients."[30]

These views are not isolated. Instead, according to a 2020 U.S. Government Accountability Office ("GAO") study, most shareholders believe that ESG factors could have a "substantial effect on a company's long-term financial performance,"[31] and most shareholders focus on ESG issues in order to monitor and evaluate the risks and opportunities that could impact a company's financial wellbeing.[32]

7.1.2 The Perils of the Shareholder Value of Stakeholder Interests

7.1.2.1 ESG as Rhetoric

Some opine that the fact that shareholders and corporations continue to cling to shareholder value as a core operating principle transforms their statements about advancing stakeholders into empty rhetoric.[33] Sung Hui Kim suggests that a commitment to engage around social issues based on economic self-interest is nothing more than a commitment in the abstract.[34] Others suggest that shareholders' focus on economic issues may be a form of, or lead to, greenwashing, which is a term used to

[28] *See* Ciara Horigan et al., *Making Sense of Sustainability: A Policy Perspective*, State Street (2022), at 15, https://www.statestreet.com/content/dam/statestreet/documents/Articles/state-street-making-sense-of-climate-sustainabilty-a-policy-perspective.pdf.

[29] *See* Larry Fink, *A Fundamental Reshaping of Finance*, Harv. L. School Forum on Corp. Gov. (Jan. 16, 2020), at 1, https://corpgov.law.harvard.edu/2020/01/16/a-fundamental-reshaping-of-finance/; Fink made the same statement in 2021; Larry Fink, *2021 Letter to CEOs*, BlackRock (2021), at 2, https://www.blackrock.com/corporate/investor-relations/2021-larry-fink-ceo-letter.

[30] *See* Fink, *The Power of Capitalism, supra* note 9, at 4.

[31] *See* GAO, *Public Companies Disclosure of Environmental, Social and Governance Factors and Options to Enhance Them* (July 2020), at 9, https://www.gao.gov/assets/710/707967.pdf.

[32] *See* Ibid., at 5.

[33] *See* Lucian A. Bebchuk & Roberto Tallarita, *The Illusory Promise of Stakeholder Governance*, 106 Cornell L. Rev. 91, 95–96 (2020); Jesse Fried, *The Roundtable's Stakeholderism Rhetoric Is Empty, Thankfully*, Harv. L. Sch. F. on Corp. Governance (Nov. 22, 2019), https://corpgov.law.harvard.edu/2019/11/22/the-roundtables-stakeholderism-rhetoric-is-empty-thankfully/. Andrew Winston, *Is the Business Roundtable Statement Just Empty Rhetoric?*, Harv. Bus. Rev. (Aug. 30, 2019), https://hbr.org/2019/08/is-the-business-roundtable-statement-just-empty-rhetoric.

[34] *See* Sung Hui Kim, *Diversity Double Standard*, 89 N.C. L. Rev. 945, 949 (2011).

describe behavior that falsely conveys alignment with ESG issues.[35] The fact that shareholders (and by extension corporations) may not be motivated by social or moral concerns may increase the possibility of greenwashing by increasing the likelihood that shareholders may be satisfied with performative actions related to stakeholders so long as those actions advance financial returns.[36]

Some research suggests that the focus on ESG could be merely rhetorical. Thus, some corporations engaged in behavior inconsistent with ESG even after making statements supporting ESG.[37] Studies of corporate governance documents reveal that almost all of the surveyed corporations that made ESG commitments made no changes to their governance documents to incorporate those commitments.[38] Instead, those documents continued to reflect a preference for shareholders and a strong link to shareholder value.[39] Moreover, in explaining their rationale for the lack of change to their governance documents, company executives stated that their ESG commitments did not require them to make any changes towards their treatment of stakeholders.[40] By confirming that the focus on ESG and other stakeholders does not negate the primacy of shareholders and financial performance, such statements – and the corresponding lack of changes in corporate governance documents – appear to legitimize the view that the focus on ESG and other stakeholders is merely rhetorical or "empty talk."[41]

7.1.2.2 Suboptimal ESG Strategies

There is also concern that ESG's link to profit increases the likelihood that shareholders and corporations will limit their ESG advocacy efforts

[35] In its climate change rule proposal, the SEC refused to define greenwashing, but instead noted that, while there is no universally accepted definition of greenwashing, the term is generally used to describe actions that falsely convey alignment with ESG issues. *See SEC Rule Proposal, supra* note 7, at 335.

[36] *See* Ibid., at 335; David Case, *Corporate Environmental Reporting as Information Regulation: A Law and Economics Perspective*, 76 U.Colo. L. Rev. 379, 395 (2005); Miriam Cherry, *The Law and Economics of Corporate Social Responsibility and Greenwashing*, 14 U.C. Davis Bus. L. J. 281, 289 (2014).

[37] *See* Dorothy S. Lund, *Corporate Finance for Social Good*, 121 Colum. L. Rev. 1617, 1619–20 (2021).

[38] *See* Lucian Bebchuk & Roberto Tallarita, *"Stakeholder" Talk Proves Empty Again: Two Years After Signing the Business Roundtable statement, Companies Still Prioritize Shareholders*, Wall St. J. (Aug. 18, 2021), https://www.wsj.com/articles/stakeholder-capitalism-esg-business-roundtable-diversity-and-inclusion-green-washing-11629313759.

[39] *See* Ibid. [40] *See* Ibid. [41] *See* Ibid.

to strategies deemed to benefit shareholders and their financial concerns, rather than the interests of other stakeholders. As Dorothy Lund and Elizabeth Pollman argue, the link between ESG and shareholder value may mean that "superior governance arrangements from a social welfare perspective may be discouraged or taken off the table."[42]

There exists research appearing to support this argument. In 2019, the Business Roundtable, the nation's leading nonprofit association of CEOS and directors, issued a statement signed by 181 CEOs, embracing a "fundamental commitment" to deliver value to all of the corporation's stakeholders.[43] However, Lucian Bebchuk and Roberto Tallarita found that while almost 100 of the Business Roundtable signatories updated their corporate governance guidelines after signing the Statement, those updates failed to add any language that focused on or elevated stakeholders.[44] Bebchuk and Tallarita also found that every corporation that signed the Statement opposed shareholder proposals designed to implement the stakeholder vision of the Statement.[45] Bebchuk and Tallarita's study supports the notion that ESG's focus on shareholder value may not result in an appropriate focus on stakeholders.

7.1.2.3 Stall Tactic?

Another concern with ESG's link with financial performance is that such a link may paralyze efforts to promote stakeholders by shifting focus to measurable outcomes or the pursuit of perfect empirical data. As Lund and Pollman note, ESG's focus on shareholder profits is problematic because it "favors activity that can be reduced to measurable metrics tied to risk or financial value."[46]

The experience with board diversity confirms the possibility that a focus on proving measurable economic outcomes may inappropriately hinder forward progress. Almost two decades ago, board diversity proponents intentionally shifted their advocacy efforts away from moral rationales and towards rationales associated with economic factors based

[42] *See* Lund and Pollman, *Corporate Governance Machine, supra* note 18, at 2566.

[43] *See* Business Roundtable, *Business Roundtable Redefines the Purpose of a Corporation to Promote 'An Economy that Serves All Americans'* (Aug. 19, 2019), https://www.businessroundtable.org/business-roundtable-redefines-the-purpose-of-a-corporation-to-promote-an-economy-that-serves-all-americans [hereinafter Business Roundtable Statement].

[44] *See* Bebchuk & Tallarita, *supra* note 38.

[45] *See* Ibid.

[46] *See* Lund & Pollman, *Corporate Governance Machine, supra* note 18, at 2631.

on a belief that such rationales would better ensure that corporate leaders would promote board diversity.[47] However, evidence suggested that the increased reliance on business rationales for board diversity had no impact on board diversity efforts.[48] Instead, board diversity efforts stalled despite such reliance.[49] Commentators indicated that the stagnation may have resulted from reliance on business rationales because such reliance focused outsized attention on proving empirical results – an inherently difficult process – instead of advancing effective diversity strategies.[50] In this regard, the shift towards embracing business rationales proved to be counterproductive.[51] This experience makes clear that reliance on economic rationales raises a real concern that such reliance could undermine rather than advance ESG efforts.[52]

7.2 Shareholders Keeping Their Promises?

This section provides a more promising assessment of shareholders to counteract the dire predictions about shareholders' role in ESG.

[47] *See* Lisa Fairfax, *Board Diversity Revisited: New Rationale, Same Old Story?*, 89 N.C. L. Rev. 855, 858 (2011); Lisa Fairfax, The Bottom Line on Board Diversity: A Cost-Benefit Analysis of the Business Rationales for Diversity on Corporate Boards, 2005 Wis. L. Rev. 795, 839–90 (2005); David Wilkins, *From "Separate Is Inherently Unequal" to "Diversity is Good for Business": The Rise of Market-Based Diversity Arguments and the Fate of the Black Corporate Bar*, 117 Harv. L. Rev. 1548, 1548–55 (2004).

[48] *See* Fairfax, *Bottom Line on Board Diversity, supra* note 47, at 858–59, 866–69; *see also* Heidrick & Struggles, *Board Monitor US 2020* (2020), at 4, 11, https://www.heidrick.com/Knowledge-Center/Publication/Board_Monitor_US_2020 [hereinafter Board Monitor 2020] (noting that "little progress" had been made with respect to racial and ethnic diversity on large boards); Peter Eavis, *Diversity Push Barely Budges Corporate Boards to 12.5%, Survey Finds*, NY Times (Sept. 15, 2020), https://www.nytimes.com/2020/09/15/business/economy/corporate-boards-black-hispanic-directors.html; Stefanie Johnson & David Hekman, *Women and Minorities are Penalized for Promoting Diversity*, Harv. Bus. Rev. (Mar. 23, 2016), https://hbr.org/2016/03/women-and-minorities-are-penalized-for-promoting-diversity (noting that numbers of executives and directors of color "hasn't budged for decades").

[49] *See* Ibid.

[50] *See* Fairfax, *Board Diversity Revisited, supra* note 47, at 859, 869; Robin Ely & David Thomas, *Getting Serious About Diversity: Enough Already with the Business Case*, Harv. Bus. Rev. (Nov–Dec. 2020), https://hbr.org/2020/11/getting-serious-about-diversity-enough-already-with-the-business-case.

[51] *See* Ibid.

[52] *See* Thomas Lee Hazen, *Diversity on Corporate Boards: Limits of the Business Case and the Connection Between Supporting Rationales and the Appropriate Response of the Law*, 89 N.C. L. Rev. 887, 890–91 (2011).

7.2.1 Beyond Rhetoric: The Shareholder Push for ESG

7.2.1.1 Shareholders' ESG Engagement

Shareholders have dramatically increased their engagement around ESG. Institutional shareholders have issued general voting and investment guidance in which ESG is prominently featured.[53] The CEOs of shareholders also have periodically posted open letters to public corporations emphasizing the importance of ESG.[54] Not only has BlackRock's Fink published an annual open letter since 2012, but also beginning in 2017, Fink's letters have increasingly prioritized expectations around ESG and other stakeholders.[55] With respect to specific topics, State Street has issued guidance on human capital management disclosures and practices, climate disclosures, and transition plans as well as diversity disclosures and practices.[56] BlackRock has issued guidance on human rights and diversity.[57] Each of BlackRock, State Street, and Vanguard have issued guidelines around board diversity.[58]

This emphasis on ESG engagement activity in general is mirrored in targeted engagement. Surveys show that ESG is the top issue shareholders want to discuss in their direct dialogue with directors.[59] For example, in their engagement with managers and directors, 71 per cent of shareholders prioritize engagement around climate while 60 per cent prioritize engagement around board and workforce diversity, equity, and inclusion.[60] BlackRock has made clear it uses direct dialogue with companies to explore important ESG topics from human rights to diversity initiatives and goals.[61] Similarly, State Street conducted over 185 engagements in 2021 around human capital management issues to help companies develop strategies around disclosure and best human

[53] *See* Vanguard, *Global Investment Stewardship Principles, supra* note 10, at 3; BlackRock, *Engagement Priorities 2022, supra* note 21, at 3; State Street, *ESG Investment Statement, supra* note 23, at 1.

[54] *See* McNabb, *supra* note 9.

[55] *See* Fink, *2021 Letter to CEOs, supra* note 29.

[56] *See e.g., State Street Guidance on Diversity Disclosure and Practices, supra* note 10, at 5; *State Street Guidance on HCM Disclosures & Practices, supra* note 10, at 1–2; BlackRock, *Our Approach to Engagement with Companies on Human Rights, supra* note 10, at 3.

[57] *See* BlackRock, *Our Approach to Engagement with Companies on Human Rights, supra* note 10, at 3.

[58] *See* Bisman & Cambeiro, *supra* note 8.

[59] *See PwC's 2021 Annual Corporate Directors Survey, supra* note 5, at 5, 7.

[60] *See* EY, *2022 Proxy Season Preview, supra* note 2, at 6.

[61] *See* BlackRock, *Our Approach to Engagement with Companies on Human Rights, supra* note 10, at 3.

capital management practices.[62] In 2020, State Street had over 275 engagements on the topic of diversity, equity and inclusion, and proactively reached out to 60 of the largest employers in its portfolio to engage around this issue.[63]

Institutional shareholders insist that engagement is a foundational aspect of their ability to impact corporate behavior.[64] As Vanguard puts it: "Engagement is a process, not an event, whose value only grows over time."[65] First, engagement enables shareholders to hear companies' views and gain a better understanding of how companies' views impact corporate policies and practices. Second, engagement allows shareholders to pinpoint their views and concerns around vital corporate policies and practices.[66] Third, engagement serves an important feedback function and ensures that shareholders can influence the views, behaviors, and ultimately practices of corporate directors and management.[67]

Finally, engagement plays a vital accountability role. Engagement not only allows shareholders to assess corporate progress against corporate goals and targets, but also allows shareholders to assess corporate goals and progress against shareholders' own principles and expectations.[68]

62 *See State Street Guidance on HCM Disclosures & Practices, supra* note 10, at 1–2.

63 *See State Street Guidance on Diversity Disclosure and Practices, supra* note 10, at 2.

64 *See* Vanguard, *Global Investment Stewardship Principles, supra* note 10, at 3 (referring to engagement as the "foundation" of their stewardship).

65 *See* McNabb, *supra* note 9, at 2. To be sure, in December 2022 Vanguard resigned from the Net Zero Asset Managers Initiative ("NZAM"), which is an industry-based initiative assumed at encouraging net zero goals. *See* Vanguard Corporate Statement, *An Update on Vanguard Engagement with Net Zero Asset Managers Initiative*, Dec. 7, 2022, https://corporate.vanguard.com/content/corporatesite/us/en/corp/articles/update-on-nzam-engagement.html. Some may view that decision as an indication of Vanguard's lack of commitment to climate risks and ESG considerations, and thus appearing to affirm the view that ESG commitments in general are mere empty talk. However, Vanguard made clear that its decision was based on its view that the Initiative was not advancing constructive dialogue. *See* Ibid. Indeed, like other public ESG policies and programs, the Initiative has been politicized and thus used to attack shareholders' ESG efforts. More importantly, Vanguard made clear that its decision did not negate its continued ESG commitment, including its commitment to continually engage and disclose around climate risks. As Vanguard emphasized, "This change in NZAM membership status will not affect our commitment to helping our investors navigate the risks that climate change can pose to their long-term returns." *See* Ibid.

66 *See* BlackRock, *Our Approach to Engagement with Companies on Human Rights, supra* note 10, at 3; BlackRock, *Engagement Priorities 2022, supra* note 21, at 8.

67 *See* BlackRock, *Engagement Priorities 2022, supra* note 21, at 3, 8; *State Street Guidance on HCM Disclosures & Practices, supra* note 10, at 1–2.

68 *See* McNabb, *supra* note 9, at 2.

Both State Street and BlackRock have noted the important role of engagement in board accountability, emphasizing that engagement enables BlackRock to lay important groundwork around expectations so that boards can be held accountable when they fail to meet those expectations.[69] As BlackRock stated, "we do not tell companies what to do."[70] Nonetheless, BlackRock went on to say: "However, when we do not see progress despite ongoing engagement or companies are insufficiently responsive on matters we believe contribute to long-term value creation, we would signal our concern by not supporting management in our voting."[71]

Shareholder engagement represents a core component of shareholder activity and an instrumental tool for understanding and impacting corporate behavior. The fact that shareholders have wielded that tool to advance ESG and stakeholder concerns reflects their prioritization of ESG as well as the fact that their ESG commitment extends beyond mere rhetoric.

7.2.1.2 Shareholder Proposals and the Coming of Age of ESG

ESG has come to dominate the shareholder proposal landscape. In 2021, for the first time in history, environmental and social proposals comprised the majority of submitted shareholder proposals.[72] In 2022, such proposals represented 63 per cent of overall submissions.[73]

The growth in ESG submissions was spurred by shareholder proposals focused on key environmental and social matters. The 2022 proxy season saw an increase in climate-related proposals, including proposals requesting climate targets and goals.[74] Driven by the racial reckoning and equity concerns sparked by the 2020 murder of George Floyd and

[69] *See* Fink, *A Fundamental Reshaping of Finance, supra* note 29, at 3; *State Street Guidance on HCM Disclosures & Practices, supra* note 10, at 2.

[70] *See* BlackRock, *Engagement Priorities 2022, supra* note 21, at 9.

[71] *See* Ibid.

[72] *See* Sullivan & Cromwell, *2022 Proxy Season Review, supra* note 11, at 1.; *see also PwC's 2021 Annual Corporate Directors Survey, supra* note 5, at 7 (noting that the 2021 proxy season saw more ESG-focused shareholder proposals than ever).

[73] *See* Sullivan & Cromwell, *2022 Proxy Season Review, supra* note 11, at 1; *see also* Gibson Dunn, *2022 Shareholder Proposal Developments, supra* note 1, at 2; *see also* Jamie Smith, *Four Key Takeaways from the 2022 Proxy Season*, EY (Jul. 27, 2022), at 2, https://www.ey.com/en_us/board-matters/four-key-takeaways-from-the-2022-proxy-season (noting that the 2022 proxy season was dominated by ESG shareholder proposals, with a record number of such proposals).

[74] *See SEC Rule Proposal, supra* note 7, at 26.

other unarmed Black people,[75] social proposals also witnessed a dramatic increase in 2022. Thus, as compared to 2021, there was an 81 per cent growth in the number of proposal submissions related to civil rights, human rights, and racial equity.[76]

On the one hand, in 2022 overall shareholder support for ESG proposals decreased.[77] Experts maintain that this decrease was based largely on the fact that shareholders shied away from supporting proposals that were too prescriptive.[78]

On the other hand, experts agree that shareholder support (or lack thereof) of particular ESG proposals is not necessarily indicative of the strength of their support for ESG issues.[79] Indeed, shareholders have made clear that their voting behavior with respect to shareholder proposals is based on company-specific circumstances, and the extent to which companies are making progress towards addressing the ESG issues underlying a given shareholder proposal.[80] As a result, shareholder votes against any given proposal is not an indication of shareholders' lack of concern with respect to the issues covered by the proposal.[81]

Moreover, many environmental and social proposals received record shareholder support in 2022.[82] For example, in 2022, eight shareholder proposals related to racial equity audits received majority shareholder support.[83] No such proposals received majority support in 2021.[84] In 2022, for the first time in history, two proposals calling for reports on gender/racial pay gaps received majority shareholder support.[85]

The shareholder proposal landscape has become an important mechanism for shareholders to communicate their priorities and expectations and to shape corporate behavior.[86] Corporations respond to shareholder

[75] *See e.g.*, Lisa Fairfax, *Racial Reckoning with Economic Inequities: Board Diversity as Symptom and Partial Cure*, 106 CORNELL L. REV. ONLINE 68, 68–69 (2021).

[76] *See* Sullivan & Cromwell, *2022 Proxy Season Review, supra* note 11, at 7; *see also See* EY, *2022 Proxy Season Preview, supra* note 2, at 7.

[77] *See* Gibson Dunn, *2022 Shareholder Proposal Developments, supra* note 1, at 6; Sullivan & Cromwell, *2022 Proxy Season Review, supra* note 11, at 1.

[78] Ibid.

[79] *See* Smith, *Four Key Takeaways from the 2022 Proxy Season, supra* note 73, at 3.

[80] *See* Ibid. [81] *See* Ibid.

[82] *See PwC's 2021 Annual Corporate Directors Survey, supra* note 5, at 7.

[83] *See* Gibson Dunn, *2022 Shareholder Proposal Developments, supra* note 1, at 7.

[84] *See* Ibid. [85] *See* Ibid.

[86] *See* Lisa Fairfax, The Shareholder-Stakeholder Alliance: Exposing the Link between Shareholder Power and the Rise of Corporate Social Purpose, *in* Research Handbook on Corporate Purpose and Personhood 14 (Elizabeth Pollman & Robert B. Thompson

proposals even when they are not the target of a given proposal because corporations use the shareholder proposal landscape as a barometer of shareholder priorities and preferences.[87] Corporations also respond to shareholder proposals even when they never come to a vote.[88] Importantly, shareholder proposals are often withdrawn as a result of negotiation between corporations and shareholders whereby corporations agree to address the issues that are the subject of the proposal.[89] Corporations also respond to shareholder proposals even when they do not receive a majority shareholder vote.[90] Research indicates that social and environmental proposals that receive a substantial percentage of shareholder support, even when they fall short of a majority, are often sufficient to capture the attention of management and thereby increase the likelihood that the board and managers will engage around those issues.[91] Finally, shareholders use the shareholder proposal process to hold corporations accountable for their progression on important ESG commitments.[92]

Given the impact of shareholder proposals on corporate behavior, shareholders' ESG activity in this area is yet another signal of the fact that their ESG commitments extend beyond mere rhetoric.

7.2.1.3 Shareholder ESG Voting

Shareholders have strategically used their voting power to influence corporate behavior related to ESG. While institutional shareholders agree

eds., 2021); Lisa M. Fairfax, *Making the Corporation Safe for Shareholder Democracy*, 69 Ohio State L.J. 53, 91 (2008).

87 *See, e.g.*, Fairfax, *The Shareholder-Stakeholder Alliance, supra* note 86, at 16–17; Fairfax, *Making the Corporation Safe, supra* note 85, at 91; Lisa Fairfax, *From Apathy to Activism: The Emergence, Impact, and Future of Shareholder Activism as the New Corporate Governance Norm*, 99 B.U. L. Rev. 1301, 1329 (2019).

88 *See* Fairfax, *The Shareholder-Stakeholder Alliance, supra* note 86, at 16–17; Fairfax, *From Apathy to Activism, supra* note 87, at 1329.

89 *See* Fairfax, *The Shareholder-Stakeholder Alliance, supra* note 86, at 16–17; Fairfax, *From Apathy to Activism, supra* note 87, at 1328.

90 *See* Lisa M. Fairfax, Shareholder Democracy: A Primer on Shareholder Activism and Participation 10 (2011); Fairfax, *The Shareholder-Stakeholder Alliance, supra* note 86, at 16–17; EY Center for Board Matters, *Five Takeaways from the 2019 Proxy Season* (July 2019), at 8, https://corpgov.law.harvard.edu/2019/08/08/five-takeaways-from-the-2019-proxy-season/ [hereinafter Five Takeaways].

91 *See* Fairfax, Shareholder Democracy, *supra* note 90, at 82; Fairfax, *The Shareholder-Stakeholder Alliance, supra* note 86, at 16–17; Five Takeaways, *supra* note 90, at 8.

92 *See* Smith, *Four Key Takeaways from the 2022 Proxy Season, supra* note 73, at 3.

that voting is not their first or sole engagement strategy, it nonetheless has a powerful impact on corporate behavior.[93] One survey found that 73 per cent of shareholders indicated that ESG oversight will be a more important factor in how they evaluate and vote on directors in the 2022 proxy season.[94] Another survey noted that in 2022 investors planned to use more proactive director voting strategies to hold boards accountable for their ESG matters.[95]

Shareholders have developed voting policies around specific ESG issues. Thus, a majority of shareholders indicated that corporate oversight of climate risk would play a more important role in how they elect directors in 2022.[96] As more shareholders have made net-zero and climate pledges, they have developed voting strategies commensurate with their pledges.[97]

Shareholders have used their voting power related to shareholder proposals to influence corporate behavior on ESG. Importantly, institutional shareholder support of a given shareholder proposal is not contingent on the issues associated with the proposal.[98] Instead, institutional shareholders will determine whether or not to support a shareholder proposal based on a company's progress on the issues associated with it.[99]

Shareholders have employed withhold-the-vote policies and practices to address ESG. In 2109, BlackRock withheld votes or voted against 4,800 directors at 2,700 companies who they believed were not addressing critical ESG issues.[100] BlackRock also announced that it may withhold the vote for inappropriate ESG disclosure, noting that "we will be increasingly disposed to vote against management and board directors when companies are not making sufficient progress on sustainability-related disclosures and the business practices and plans underlying them."[101] Vanguard has indicated that it would generally withhold its

[93] *See, e.g., State Street Guidance on HCM Disclosures & Practices, supra* note 10, at 2; BlackRock, *Engagement Priorities 2022, supra* note 21, at 9. *See also BlackRock Investment Stewardship Global Principles*, Harv. L. Sch. F. on Corp. Governance (Dec. 18, 2021), at 11, https://corpgov.law.harvard.edu/2021/12/18/blackrock-investment-stewardship-global-principles-2/ [hereinafter *BlackRock Global Principles*] (we "will express our concerns through our voting where a company's actions or disclosures are inadequate").

[94] *See* EY, *2022 Proxy Season Preview, supra* note 2, at 2.

[95] *See* Ibid., at 3.

[96] *See* Ibid., at 2.

[97] *See* Ibid.

[98] *See* Smith, *Four Key Takeaways from the 2022 Proxy Season, supra* note 73, at 3.

[99] *See* Ibid.; BlackRock, *Engagement Priorities 2022, supra* note 21, at 9; *State Street Guidance on HCM Disclosures & Practices, supra* note 10, at 2.

[100] *See* Fink, *A Fundamental Reshaping of Finance, supra* note 29, at 3.

[101] *See* Ibid.

vote against the chair of a committee responsible for overseeing material social and environmental risks, in cases where there is a risk of oversight failure involving ESG.[102] BlackRock may withhold support for directors if a company is not effectively addressing or disclosing material human rights-related risks or impacts.[103] BlackRock also may vote against directors responsible for human capital management decisions when there is insufficient disclosure related to oversight of such issues.[104] State Street may vote against directors of companies with insufficient human capital management disclosure.[105]

Shareholders have especially emphasized withhold-the-vote policies around board diversity. BlackRock announced its belief that boards should aspire to 30 per cent diversity and encouraged companies to have at least two directors who identify as female and one who identifies as a member of an underrepresented minority.[106] BlackRock may vote against members of the nominating committee for any perceived lack of commitment to board diversity.[107] Importantly, insufficient board diversity was a top reason why BlackRock withheld its vote against directors in 2022.[108] Vanguard may withhold the vote from the chair of the nominating committee when there is insufficient progress on board diversity or board diversity disclosures.[109] State Street may vote against the nominating committee chair when there is no disclosure on the board's racial and ethnic composition or the board does not have at least one director from an underrepresented racial/ethnic community.[110] State Street also may withhold votes against companies that do not have at least one female director.[111] Beginning in 2023, State Street may vote against the nominating committee chair of Russell 3000 companies if they do not have at least 30 per cent female directors.[112] To be sure, the fact that these entities have announced policies indicating that they "may" vote against board members for their lack of diversity means that

[102] *See* Gibson Dunn, *2022 Shareholder Proposal Developments, supra* note 1, at 4.
[103] *See* BlackRock, *Our Approach to Engagement with Companies on Human Rights, supra* note 10, at 3.
[104] *See* Bisman & Cambeiro, *supra* note 8. [105] *See* Ibid.
[106] *See* Gibson Dunn, *2022 Shareholder Proposal Developments, supra* note 1, at 2.
[107] *See* Bisman & Cambeiro, *supra* note 8.
[108] *See* Gibson Dunn, *2022 Shareholder Proposal Developments, supra* note 1, at 2.
[109] *See* Ibid., at 4.
[110] *See State Street Guidance on Diversity Disclosure and Practices, supra* note 10, at 2.
[111] *See* Gibson Dunn, *2022 Shareholder Proposal Developments, supra* note 1, at 8.
[112] *See State Street Guidance on Diversity Disclosure and Practices, supra* note 10, at 2.

their policies give them discretion to choose *not* to withhold-the-vote even when board diversity is lacking. On the one hand, this discretion may suggest that these policies are illusory or mere empty rhetoric. On the other hand, the fact that entities do not withhold their vote against every corporation with problematic board diversity does not negate the impact of these policies. This is because, as mentioned above with respect to shareholder voting, entities do withhold their vote in some circumstances. Moreover, these policies represent a starting point for engagement which can have a powerful impact on corporate behavior. As noted above, engagement is a process, not an event. These policies help ensure that board diversity and other ESG issues are a part of the routine engagement with corporations, thereby establishing an expectation that corporations must focus on board diversity and other ESG issues. In the absence of such policies, it is less likely that corporations would focus on these issues and begin the important work necessary to alter their behavior.[113]

Shareholder voting and the threat of shareholder voting is a powerful motivator of corporate behavior. The fact that shareholders have crafted voting policies around ESG therefore reflects the importance they have placed on ESG issues along with their serious desire to ensure that ESG concerns influence corporate conduct.

7.2.1.4 The Push for ESG Disclosure

Shareholders insist that disclosure around ESG is essential for addressing ESG. Disclosure increases the likelihood that boards and executives are paying appropriate attention to ESG issues. Disclosure ensures that shareholders and other stakeholders have the information they need to understand and assess corporate ESG activity.[114] Disclosure also ensures that corporations can be held accountable for their ESG commitments by giving shareholders and other stakeholders the ability to track ESG

[113] *See* Lisa M. Fairfax, *Racial Rhetoric or Reality?: Cautious Optimism on the Link Between Corporate #BLM Speech and Behavior*, 2022 Colum. Bus. L. Rev. 118 (2022) (finding that corporations that made commitments around racial equity were more likely to engage in behavior that supported those commitments, at least with respect to board diversity).

[114] *See SEC Rule Proposal, supra* note 7, at 7 (noting that mandated disclosure is aimed at providing "consistent, comparable, and reliable – therefore decision-useful – information to investors to enable them to make informed judgements about the impact of climate-related risks on current and potential investments").

performance from year to year and measure that performance against shareholder expectations and corporate ESG goals and targets.[115]

Given shareholders' belief in the importance of disclosure, shareholders have devoted considerable time and resources towards encouraging disclosure around ESG. Shareholders have produced considerable guidance around their expectation for ESG disclosure, insisting that companies align their strategy with ESG goals and continuously improve their ESG disclosures.[116]

Over 700 shareholders representing over $52 trillion in assets signed a statement emphasizing the need for more robust climate-related disclosure.[117] Both State Street and BlackRock have separate guidance around best practices for meaningful human rights disclosure.[118] Vanguard, State Street, and BlackRock all have provided considerable guidance on their expectations for board diversity disclosure.[119] In 2020 a group of shareholders representing $3 trillion in assets under management sent letters to companies on the Russell 3000 index asking them to disclose racial, ethnic, and gender data for their board.[120]

As the effort to promote board diversity disclosure has gained traction, and in the wake of the racial reckoning in the summer of 2020, shareholders have turned their sights on disclosure associated with workforce diversity.[121] While federal law requires many employers to submit so-called EEO-1 reports containing information about job

[115] *See State Street Guidance on Diversity Disclosure and Practices, supra* note 10, at 2; *see also* Vanguard, *Global Investment Stewardship Principles, supra* note 10, at 7–8.

[116] *See* Vanguard, *Global Investment Stewardship Principles, supra* note 10, at 4, 6; BlackRock, *Engagement Priorities 2022, supra* note 21, at 2; *BlackRock Global Principles, supra* note 93, at 11; *State Street Guidance on Diversity Disclosure and Practices, supra* note 10, at 2; Bisman & Cambeiro, *supra* note 8.

[117] *See SEC Rule Proposal, supra* note 7, at 319 n. 790 and *see also* Ibid., at 25–26.

[118] *See State Street Guidance on HCM Disclosures & Practices, supra* note 10, at 1; BlackRock, *Our Approach to Engagement with Companies on Human Rights, supra* note 10, at 2.

[119] *See* Vanguard, *Global Investment Stewardship Principles, supra* note 10, at 4, 6; *State Street Guidance on Diversity Disclosure and Practices, supra* note 10, at 2; Bisman & Cambeiro, *supra* note 8.

[120] *See* Kelsey Butler, *Investors Overseeing $3 Trillion Push for Board Racial Diversity*, BLOOMBERG (Oct. 28, 2020), https://www.bloomberg.com/news/articles/2020-10-28/investors-overseeing-3-trillion-push-for-board-racial-diversity.

[121] *See* EY, *2022 Proxy Season Preview, supra* note 2, at 6; Cyrus Taraporevala, *A Call to Lead on Racial and Ethnic Diversity*, STATE STREET (Feb. 16, 2021), at 2–3, https://www.ssga.com/us/en/institutional/ic/insights/a-call-to-lead-on-racial-and-ethnic-diversity.

categories and demographic workforce related to race, ethnicity, and sex, those reports are not required to be publicly disclosed.[122] However, in the last two years shareholders have strenuously pushed for such disclosure.[123] State Street not only has formally called on its portfolio companies to publicly disclose EEO-1 reports, but also joined a coalition of 14 other financial institutions who have collectively called for such disclosure and are engaging with other entities to do the same.[124] State Street insisted that the lack of data impedes the ability to address persistent challenges with the recruitment, retention, and promotion of diverse talent.[125]

Shareholders also have devoted significant attention to working with other shareholders and groups to develop best practices and frameworks for ESG disclosure and encouraging more standardization.[126] These disclosure efforts include encouraging companies to adopt specific ESG-related reporting frameworks.[127] By encouraging standardization of disclosure, shareholders have sought to play a vital role in improving ESG disclosure practices. Indeed, the fact that companies can rely upon different frameworks to disclose ESG information has meant that disclosures are inconsistent from company to company, undermining the ability to make cross-company comparisons and thus undermining the usefulness of ESG data.[128] Shareholders have responded to this concern by engaging in strategies aimed at creating more consistent ESG reporting.

Shareholders' considerable efforts regarding ESG disclosure reflect another example of the manner in which shareholders have sought to move the needle in favor of ESG and other stakeholders. Such disclosure plays a critical role in ensuring that corporations establish and maintain important ESG initiatives, while also ensuring more accountability.

[122] *See* 29 C.F.R. 1602.7-14; 41 C.F.R. 60-1.7(a).

[123] *See* EY, *2022 Proxy Season Preview, supra* note 2, at 6.

[124] *See* Taraporevala, *A Call to Lead on Racial and Ethnic Diversity, supra* note 121, at 2.

[125] *See* Ibid.

[126] *See* McNabb, *supra* note 9, at 2; *State Street Guidance on HCM Disclosures & Practices, supra* note 10, at 1; Taraporevala, *Capturing the Power of Diversity, supra* note 9, at 2; *State Street Guidance on Diversity Disclosure and Practices, supra* note 10, at 1.

[127] *See* Vanguard, *Global Investment Stewardship Principles, supra* note 10, at 6; *BlackRock Global Principles, supra* note 93, at 11; Fink, *A Fundamental Reshaping of Finance, supra* note 29, at 2–3.

[128] *See SEC Rule Proposal, supra* note 7, at 333.

7.2.1.5 Board Oversight of ESG

Shareholders also have pushed for disclosure around board oversight of ESG, making such disclosure a top engagement priority.[129] Shareholders have begun to outline detailed recommendations around best practices for effective board oversight.[130] As an example, State Street partnered with Russell Reynolds and the Ford Foundation to "create a playbook for effective board oversight of diversity."[131] These efforts include calls for corporations to alter their committee charters and governing documents to reflect board oversight of ESG.[132]

Shareholder focus on board oversight is a crucial component of their ESG advocacy. Board oversight of ESG ensures that corporations pay close attention to ESG issues and the related commitment to other stakeholders.[133] Such oversight also better ensures corporate accountability for ESG activities because shareholders have the ability to hold the board accountable for their actions. Thus, shareholder focus on board oversight of ESG is an important reflection of their considerable effort towards ensuring that corporations effectively address ESG.

7.2.1.6 Board Diversity

Shareholders' ESG efforts also have centered on encouraging board diversity.[134] Shareholder efforts include reaching out to hundreds of companies identified as having insufficient board diversity to call out their lack of diversity and encourage them to address such diversity.[135]

These board diversity efforts are intimately linked with ESG efforts because shareholders and other stakeholders believe that board diversity meaningfully contributes to a board's ability to effectively perform their responsibilities, including around ESG.[136] Shareholders insist that board diversity helps ensure that boards better understand how to oversee and

[129] *See State Street Guidance on HCM Disclosures & Practices, supra* note 10, at 1–2; Lisa Fairfax, *Board Committee Charters and ESG Accountability*, 12 Harv. Bus. L. Rev. 201, 221 (2022); EY, *2022 Proxy Season Preview, supra* note 2, at 3.

[130] *See* BlackRock, *Engagement Priorities 2022, supra* note 21, at 8.

[131] *See* Taraporevala, *Capturing the Power of Diversity, supra* note 9, at 2.

[132] *See* EY, *2022 Proxy Season Preview, supra* note 2, at 5; Smith, *Four Key Takeaways from the 2022 Proxy Season, supra* note 73, at 1.

[133] *See* Fairfax, *Board Committee Charters and ESG Accountability, supra* note 129, at 221–23.

[134] *See* McNabb, *supra* note 9, at 2; Bisman & Cambeiro, *supra* note 8.

[135] *See e.g., State Street Guidance on Diversity Disclosure and Practices, supra* note 10, at 2.

[136] *See* Vanguard, *Global Investment Stewardship Principles, supra* note 10, at 3.

address those concerns.[137] First, some have suggested that diverse board members can have an impact on workplace culture.[138] This includes promoting equitable policies and practices that increase the likelihood that people from all backgrounds and ethnicities will receive better treatment.[139] Second, some have suggested that board diversity better enables corporations to market their goods and services to the full range of consumers and customers, or otherwise better equips boards and corporations to identify and develop new products and services that address the needs of diverse communities.[140] Finally, some have suggested that board diversity counters groupthink on boards and thus better ensures that board decision-making incorporates a more robust range of potential problems and solutions.[141]

* * *

This section reveals that shareholders have expended considerable effort encouraging corporations to focus on ESG. As a result, this section rebuts the contention that shareholders' ESG pronouncements and commitments can be characterized as merely rhetorical.

7.2.2 Shareholders' ESG Results

Shareholder efforts have clearly garnered results. One recent survey concluded that companies have made significant efforts to address shareholder concerns and meet shareholder expectations around ESG priorities.[142] Thus, not only have companies made strides around ESG, but those strides are directly attributable to shareholder engagement. This section highlights some of the most notable areas impacted by shareholders.

7.2.2.1 Disclosure

Shareholders have dramatically influenced disclosure around ESG.[143] In 2020, 92 per cent of S&P 500 companies and 70 per cent of Russell

[137] *See* Russell Reynolds Associates (RRA), *The Board's Oversight of Racial and Ethnic Diversity, Equity and Inclusion* (July 13, 2021), at 16, https://www.russellreynolds.com/en/insights/articles/the-boards-oversight-of-racial-and-ethnic-diversity-equity-and-inclusion.

[138] *See* Fairfax, *The Bottom Line, supra* note 47, at 828–29.

[139] *See* Ibid.

[140] *See* Ibid., at 820.

[141] *See* Ibid., at 831–33.

[142] *See* Smith, *Four Key Takeaways from the 2022 Proxy Season, supra* note 73, at 4.

[143] *See* Federico Fornasari, *Knowledge and Power in Measuring the Sustainable Corporation*, 19 Wash. U. Global Study. L. Rev. 167, 190 (2020) ("more and more corporations report, because of investors' demand").

1000 companies publish a voluntary ESG report.[144] By contrast, in 2011 only 20 per cent of S&P 500 companies published such reports.[145] The significant surge in ESG disclosure has been driven by shareholder demand.[146] Then too, shareholder preferences have translated into a convergence around corporate adoption of the kinds of frameworks most recommended by shareholders. Such convergence helps ensure that ESG disclosures are more usable. Moreover, the SEC acknowledged that its decision to propose a first-ever mandate of climate-related disclosure was largely driven by shareholder demand.[147] To be sure, while there can be considerable disagreement around whether mandatory ESG disclosure is appropriate, there is no doubt that shareholders have played a pivotal role in helping to generate ESG disclosure.

7.2.2.2 Policies and Practices

Shareholder efforts also have led to sharp increases in corporate adoption of ESG initiatives. In 2021, almost all directors indicated that their companies were taking steps to address human capital and diversity issues.[148] In the 2022 proxy season, more than 90 per cent of *Fortune* 100 companies disclosed initiatives or commitments related to climate and workforce diversity while 68 per cent of companies disclosed goals related to greenhouse gas emissions reductions.[149]

Proxy analysts insist that the increase in ESG policies and practices results from shareholder influence. On the one hand, it is too soon to tell if these policies and practices will prove effective. However, any forward progress must begin somewhere and hence the emergence of these policies and practices is a notable development. Then too, the fact that more companies are establishing such measures increases the likelihood that companies can be held accountable for their ESG activities.[150] Hence, corporate action in this area is an important first step, and shareholders unquestionably played an instrumental role in encouraging that step.

144 *See* Perez, *supra* note 3, at 1; G&A Institute, *2021 Sustainability Reporting* (2021), at 2, https://www.ga-institute.com/2021-sustainability-reporting-in-focus.html.
145 *See* G&A Institute, *2021 Sustainability Reporting* at 3.
146 *See PwC's 2021 Annual Corporate Directors Survey, supra* note 5, at 9 ("investors are clamoring for more information on disclosure").
147 *See SEC Rule Proposal, supra* note 7, at 333.
148 *See PwC's 2021 Annual Corporate Directors Survey, supra* note 5, at 16.
149 *See* Smith, *Four Key Takeaways from the 2022 Proxy Season, supra* note 73, at 8.
150 *See* RRA, *supra* note 137, at 13.

7.2.2.3 Board Oversight

Companies also have answered the call for more board oversight. Thus, recent evidence demonstrates that companies not only have enhanced disclosure around board oversight of ESG, but also have increased committee level responsibility for board oversight.[151] Then too, boards have integrated ESG oversight into relevant charters.[152] My own survey revealed that 86 per cent of Fortune 50 companies have a board-level committee or committees with oversight of ESG.[153] A 2020 survey of the top 50 companies in the *Fortune* 100 revealed that 88 per cent of such companies have board oversight of ESG issues, and 44 per cent of such companies increased disclosure related to board oversight of ESG issues.[154] Board oversight is vital for corporate accountability around ESG.[155] Thus these board oversight changes ensure more appropriate attention on ESG. And such changes have resulted from shareholder engagement emphasis.

7.2.2.4 Board Diversity

Shareholder efforts related to board diversity also have resulted in significant change. First has been the dramatic change in board diversity disclosure.[156] State Street reports that its engagement efforts around diversity resulted in enhanced disclosures from 20 out of the 23 companies that initially had room for improvement in this area.[157] Surveys reveal that nearly all *Fortune* 100 companies (97 per cent) voluntarily disclosed the racial and ethnic makeup of their board.[158] A 2016 Deloitte survey found that only 18 per cent of large-cap and 9 per cent of medium-cap companies voluntarily disclosed race-related information for their directors.[159] As experts note, the current level of board diversity disclosure represents a "sea change in board diversity disclosures in

151 *See* Smith, *Four Key Takeaways from the 2022 Proxy Season, supra* note 73, at 6.

152 *See* Ibid., at 6–7. More companies also have begun to cite ESG in director qualifications. *See* Ibid., at 7.

153 *See* Fairfax, *Board Committee Charters and ESG Accountability, supra* note 129, at 205.

154 *See* Era Anagnosti, et al., *ESG Disclosure Trends in SEC Filings* (Aug. 13, 2020) 5, 9.

155 *See* Fairfax, *Board Committee Charters and ESG Accountability, supra* note 129, at 216–21.

156 *See PwC's 2021 Annual Corporate Directors Survey, supra* note 5, at 11.

157 *See State Street Guidance on Diversity Disclosure and Practices, supra* note 10, at 2.

158 *See* Smith, *Four Key Takeaways from the 2022 Proxy Season, supra* note 73, at 9.

159 *See* Deloitte, *2017 Board Survey: Seeing is Believing* (2017), at 7, https://www2.deloitte.com/content/dam/Deloitte/us/Documents/about-deloitte/us-about-board-diversity-survey-seeing-is-believing.pdf (citing 2016 survey).

recent years."[160] Second has been the significant increase in board diversity. State Street saw 862 companies, representing 60 per cent of the companies they identified as having all-male boards, add women to their board in the years following their targeted engagement efforts.[161] Recent surveys show that 93 per cent of surveyed directors say their board has taken action on diversity over the previous 24 months, while 69 per cent replaced a retired director with someone who brought diversity to the board.[162] Finally, director attitudes around board diversity have changed dramatically. In 2020, 71 per cent of directors agreed that no action was needed to increase board diversity because boards would naturally become more diverse without any intentional efforts.[163] In 2021, only 33 per cent of directors embraced such a belief, and directors are more supportive of almost all proactive measures aimed at achieving board diversity.[164] As a PWC survey notes "This represents a seismic shift and indicates an understanding of the fact that boards need to take deliberate actions in order to bring about changes."[165] Importantly, surveys reveal that boards are addressing diversity in new ways,[166] contradicting the contention that shareholder efforts may lead to limiting the strategies associated with addressing ESG issues.

Directors insist that the changes related to board diversity can be traced to shareholder efforts. While racial and ethnic diversity have been on the board agenda in the past, directors note that it "never had the focus it has now."[167] In addition, although the murder of George Floyd was clearly an inflection point, directors pinpoint enhanced pressure from institutional investors as one of the most important factors driving their increased focus on this issue.[168] Thus, even as some companies "bristle" at the influence of shareholders, directors acknowledge the role that institutional investors have played in increasing corporate focus on diversity, equity, and inclusion issues – and some even say that they appreciate the "huge impact" these investors have had.[169] Given the link between board diversity and

[160] *See* Smith, *Four Key Takeaways from the 2022 Proxy Season, supra* note 73, at 9.
[161] *See* Taraporevala, *Capturing the Power of Diversity, supra* note 9, at 2.
[162] *See PwC's 2021 Annual Corporate Directors Survey, supra* note 5, at 11.
[163] *See* Ibid., at 14. [164] *See* Ibid. [165] *See* Ibid. [166] *See* Ibid., at 11.
[167] *See* RRA, *supra* note 137, at 7.
[168] *See* Ibid. Directors rank investor pressure as the third most important motivator of enhanced attention on DE&I behind reputation and impact on financial performance. *See* Ibid., at 6–7.
[169] *See* Ibid., at 7.

appropriate attention to ESG and stakeholder matters, shareholder influence in this area is particularly notable.

7.2.3 Lingering Concerns

7.2.3.1 Paralysis Reconsidered

As the foregoing section highlights, ESG's link to economics has not led to paralysis around ESG efforts. To be sure, this link runs the risk that shareholders and corporations would focus too much effort on perfecting data rather than seeking promising solutions. However, this risk has not materialized. Instead, shareholders appear already convinced by the empirical evidence. Importantly, there is considerable evidence of a link between ESG and financial concerns.[170] Moreover, no evidence is infallible, and corporations routinely make decisions based on mixed or imperfect data.[171] Thus, it is entirely appropriate that shareholders and other ESG advocates do not allow the quest for unequivocal data to distract them from moving the needle on ESG. And it appears that shareholders have not been hindered by a hyper-focus on perfect data. Thus, while Vanguard CEO made clear that its stance in support of ESG issues was driven by a desire to enhance long-term shareholder value, it did not demand that such value be proven. Instead, after pinpointing research supporting its economic premise, Vanguard announced that it had recently joined the 30 per cent club, an organization focused on advocating for greater representation of women on boards and in leadership roles.[172] Similarly, State Street cited studies indicating that effective human capital management drives performance before detailing its efforts around promoting appropriate human capital management disclosures and practices.[173] State Street also referred to empirical studies revealing that diversity leads to innovation in the workforce while the lack of diversity harms a company's bottom line before discussing the many ways in which it has encouraged companies to engage around diversity.[174] These actions suggest that shareholders have already been

[170] *See* Chris Brummer & Leo Strine, *Duty and Diversity*, 75 VAND. L. REV. 1, 26–28 (2022) (citing studies); *see also* Lisa M. Fairfax, *Empowering Diversity Ambition*, 75 VAN. L. REV. EN BANC 131, 135 (2022).

[171] *See* Brummer & Strine, *supra* note 170, at 30–31.

[172] *See* McNabb, *supra* note 9, at 2.

[173] *See State Street Guidance on HCM Disclosures & Practices, supra* note 10, at 1–2.

[174] *See* Taraporevala, *Capturing the Power of Diversity, supra* note 9, at 1.

convinced of the economic link to ESG, and thus such link is not serving as a roadblock to progress in this area.

7.2.3.2 Stakeholder Voice

The link with shareholder profit also has not limited strategies to those focused solely on shareholders. As this chapter noted, the emphasis on shareholders and financial performance could translate into an undue focus on strategies that only benefit shareholders without consideration of stakeholder concerns. However, available information indicates that shareholders have instead been mindful of incorporating stakeholder voice into their ESG engagement efforts. Thus, one disclosure topic that has received special attention centers around the manner in which companies are giving voice to other stakeholders. For example, State Street's guidance notes that it expects disclosure around "How concerns and ideas from employees are solicited (and if appropriate, acted upon), and how the workforce is engaged in the organization."[175] With respect to diversity, State Street not only encouraged companies to evaluate the impact of their operations on communities of color, but also encouraged them to include the perspective of stakeholders in board discussions.[176] State Street's guidance states that in order to include the perspective of stakeholders, you must engage with employees and understand their experience, and you must "include impacted stakeholders from outside the organization who can speak to the role the company plays in the communities where it operates."[177] BlackRock also noted that companies should disclose how they identify their key stakeholders and how they consider their interests in business decision-making.[178] BlackRock also has noted its expectation that companies both engage with stakeholders impacted by human rights concerns and collaborates with other stakeholders on initiatives to address human rights issues.[179]

7.2.3.3 Our Best Option for the Long-Term?

Finally, rather than undermining progress around ESG, it is entirely possible that the connection between ESG and shareholder profit may

175 *See State Street Guidance on HCM Disclosures & Practices, supra* note 10, at 2.

176 *See* Taraporevala, *Capturing the Power of Diversity, supra* note 9, at 3; *State Street Guidance on Diversity Disclosure and Practices, supra* note 10, at 5.

177 *See* RRA, *supra* note 137, at 18.

178 *See BlackRock Global Principles, supra* note 93, at 13.

179 *See* BlackRock, *Our Approach to Engagement with Companies on Human Rights, supra* note 10, at 3.

be our best option for ensuring a long-term corporate focus on those issues. Experts have argued that "[t]he most critical part of tackling ESG is to embed these long-terms concerns into company strategy."[180] In fact, 69 per cent of shareholders have indicated that integrating ESG opportunities into a company's business strategy is core to ensuring long-term commitment to ESG issues.[181] As a result, shareholders have strenuously encouraged boards to align their business strategy with their ESG goals and commitments.[182] BlackRock expressed its hope that its engagement efforts would encourage companies to integrate ESG issues into sound business practices that "benefit relevant stakeholders over the long term."[183] This hope is rooted in their belief that a focus on other stakeholders is linked to long-term financial resilience and value creation.[184] Vanguard similarly notes that integrating ESG strategy into business strategy is vital for ensuring that companies are set up for success "today, next year, and well into the future."[185] "For Vanguard, sustainability is synonymous with long-termism."[186]

Surveys suggest that the fact that shareholders have highlighted the link between ESG and profit may be the primary reason why we experience success in the effort to ensure that corporations integrate ESG issues into their business strategy. Surveys demonstrate that directors increasingly believe that ESG has a financial impact on company performance.[187] Correspondingly, almost two-thirds of directors now say that their strategy is tied to ESG issues and that ESG is a part of their risk management discussions.[188] In this way, the belief in the financial relevancy of ESG appears to have motivated directors to integrate consideration of ESG factors into their business plans in a way that may increase the likelihood that ESG will remain an area of focus in the long run. This integration clearly stems from a belief that ESG is tied to long-term financial returns. In other words, shareholder emphasis on the link between financial concerns and ESG may serve to promote a more sustained commitment to ESG.

[180] *See PwC's 2021 Annual Corporate Directors Survey, supra* note 5, at 5.
[181] *See* EY, *2022 Proxy Season Preview, supra* note 2, at 8.
[182] *See* BlackRock, *Engagement Priorities 2022, supra* note 21, at 2.
[183] *See* BlackRock, *Our Approach to Engagement with Companies on Human Rights, supra* note 10, at 1.
[184] *See* BlackRock, *Engagement Priorities 2022, supra* note 21, at 5.
[185] *See* Vanguard, *Global Investment Stewardship Principles, supra* note 10, at 6.
[186] *See* Ibid. [187] *See PwC's 2021 Annual Corporate Directors Survey, supra* note 5, at 8.
[188] *See* Ibid.

7.3 Conclusion

It is important to remember not only that there has been a long-standing effort to encourage corporations to focus on other stakeholders and the issues underlying ESG, but also that such effort has been difficult to sustain over the long run. It is entirely possible that promoting these issues in alignment with shareholder power and interests has a better chance of impacting corporate behavior over the long haul, especially given the increased influence of shareholders. To be clear, this chapter does not mean to overlook the serious concerns with shareholders as stakeholder advocates, including the possibility that shareholders could encourage corporations to engage in actions antithetical to stakeholders under the guise of advancing ESG. However, no advocate, and no advocacy effort, is perfect. Then too, to date shareholders have managed to move the needle significantly around ESG. For this reason, while we should always be prepared to address potential downsides, we also should welcome shareholder engagement around ESG because of its many promises.

8

How to Facilitate ESG Investor Engagement

WOLF-GEORG RINGE

8.1 Introduction

Conventional wisdom has it that the transition to a more sustainable economy requires the incorporation of environmental, social, and governance (ESG) standards into corporate governance and finance. There is increasingly broad global consensus that the asset management sector has a vital role to play in helping society solve existential challenges such as the current climate crisis by allocating capital sustainably and thereby influencing the behaviour of investee companies.

The rise of ESG investing on capital markets has been recounted many times and does not have to be reiterated here.[1] It is only important for the present chapter to understand that there are principally two distinct strategies towards achieving a more sustainable securities market: (deliberate) investor engagement in the sense of investors pushing for the adoption of ESG criteria, and regulatory approaches where ESG objectives are prescribed by legislators and regulators.

To begin with the second option, many argue for achieving a sustainable market through modifying the legal regime governing the corporate organisation. For example, policy makers and courts toy with the idea of expanding the list of directors' duties by making corporate directors legally accountable for the promotion of ESG goals.[2] Another idea is to

This chapter draws on my previous paper 'Investor-led Sustainability in Corporate Governance' (Annals of Corporate Governance 2022).

[1] For further detail, see Wolf-Georg Ringe, 'Investor-led Sustainability in Corporate Governance' (2022) 7 Annals of Corporate Governance 93.

[2] In the US, litigation against corporate boards is increasingly relying on the *Caremark* duty for failing to exercise proper risk oversight. The European Commission even consulted on a proposed legal change in this direction: Public consultation on Sustainable Corporate Governance (26 October 2020–8 February 2021), https://ec.europa.eu/info/law/better-regulation/have-your-say/initiatives/12548-Sustainable-corporate-governance/public-consultation_en.

tie executive remuneration to certain sustainability criteria.[3] A third proposal, which has been gaining supporters worldwide, is the promotion of stewardship codes encouraging institutional investors inter alia to pursue ESG criteria in their investment decisions and disclose their engagement policies.[4]

The alternative strategy, investor engagement, offers a different, perhaps superior path towards achieving greater sustainability in capital markets. The past several years have seen an unprecedented surge in investor-led initiatives steered toward sustainability. This has been evidenced most prominently by the rise of ESG activists – hedge funds and other specialised investors who have been actively influencing the management of their investee companies to pursue more sustainable decision-making. But, perhaps more surprisingly, passive investment funds, index funds, and exchange-traded funds (ETFs) have also jumped on the bandwagon and are pushing for more responsible investment strategies, either with independent campaigns or by supporting the activist investors.

Some commentators are sceptical about such investor-led sustainability, possibly due to a general distrust in markets that has dominated the public discourse since the global financial crisis and that has continued into the ongoing Covid-19 pandemic.[5] However, this chapter argues that ESG engagement can be a very powerful driver towards a more sustainability-oriented future. I show that investor-led sustainability has many advantages compared to a more prescriptive, regulatory approach where legislatures are in the driver's seat.[6] For example, a greater focus on investor initiatives would follow a more flexible and dynamic pattern

[3] For example, in Germany, listed companies are required to adopt a remuneration structure which is to be geared 'towards a sustainable and long-term development' of the company (see Aktiengesetz § 87a). Thereby, social and environmental aspects should be taken into account when adopting remuneration packages.

[4] The paradigm example is the UK Code, which in its latest 2020 version also includes ESG criteria. See Financial Reporting Council, *The UK Stewardship Code 2020*, available at www.frc.org.uk/investors/uk-stewardship-code.

[5] For sceptical views, see Paul G. Mahoney and Julia D. Mahoney, 'The New Separation of Ownership and Control: Institutional Investors and ESG' (2021) Columbia Business Law Review 840; Paul Brest, Ronald J. Gilson and Mark A. Wolfson, 'How Investors Can (and Can't) Create Social Value' (2018) 44 Journal of Corporation Law 205; Jonathan R. Macey, 'ESG Investing: Why Here? Why Now?' (2022) 19 Berkeley Business Law Journal 256.

[6] I do not, however, argue against any additional regulatory initiative that seeks to curb externalities, such as a carbon tax.

rather than complying with pre-defined criteria that are slow to change. Moreover, investor-promoted assessments are not likely to impair welfare creation in the same way as ill-defined legal standards; they would also not trigger regulatory arbitrage and would avoid deadlock situations in corporate decision-making. Any regulatory responses should then be limited to a facilitative and supportive role.

This chapter proceeds as follows: I begin by exploring the different types of ESG-minded investors and their preferences (Section 8.2) and discuss their different strategies in Section 8.3. This allows me, in Section 8.4, to develop a set of regulatory tools to support investor engagement. Section 8.5 concludes.

8.2 Players and Motivations for ESG Engagement

It is apt to begin by disentangling the different types of investors who are pursuing ESG objectives and their motivations. This section explains how they differ and, at the risk of oversimplification, groups them into three broad categories: activists, passive institution, and retail investors. Section 8.3 will then outline their respective different strategies for implementation.

8.2.1 Activists

Recent years have seen a rise in specific activism for ESG objectives. Such activism differs markedly from classical activism which is pursued mostly for financial gains. There are mostly two distinct types of players: newly set-up vehicles that have been expressly created for activist campaigns; and secondly, traditional hedge funds that have turned their attention towards sustainability goals.

As an example, for the first category, the most prominent story of recent times in terms of ESG activism is that of Engine No. 1, an 'impact-focused fund' which launched an activist campaign at US oil giant ExxonMobil. Starting in December 2020, the tiny hedge fund initiated a proxy contest at ExxonMobil for its alleged failure to adequately respond to evolving energy needs and emissions standards. The following months saw increasingly strong pressure from Engine No. 1, which had urged Exxon to cut capital spending and to focus on accelerating rather than on deferring the transition to cleaner energy. This culminated in an epic shareholder meeting in May 2021, where Engine No. 1 was successful in installing three of its director nominees on the Exxon board – which, in effect, was a major defeat for the incumbent management.[7]

As an example for the second type of activist, the hedge fund TCI (The Children's Investment Fund) has recently shifted its attention to ESG objectives. In 2020, TCI launched a 'say on climate' campaign, calling for a shareholder vote on climate policy.[8] They filed resolutions at several US-listed issuers to annually disclose their greenhouse gas emissions, to produce a plan to manage those emissions, and to hold an annual advisory vote on the plan. In the case of Spanish airport operator Aena, TCI was successful in pushing for the introduction of the world's first 'say on climate' vote.[9] This push for an advisory vote on the climate plan was supported by BlackRock, which said in a voting bulletin it would be 'beneficial at Aena given the material risk to its business model and its need to accelerate its efforts'.[10]

The motivations for such ESG activism follow very heterogeneous patterns. It may either be fully rational in a sense of a pursuit of financial gains, as sustainable business decisions may be considered as a more profitable long-term strategy, or may at least provide a hedge against social and, in particular, climate change-related long-term risk.[11] Seen from this perspective, climate change is viewed as a significant source of financial risk, reflected in a return premium on assets with high climate risk exposure.[12] Relatedly, activists also care about the transition risks of stranded assets in individual firms.

[7] Derek Brower, 'ExxonMobil Shareholders Hand Board Seats to Activist Nominees', Financial Times (26 May 2021), www.ft.com/content/da6dec6a-6c58-427f-a012-9c1efb71fddf.

[8] Tim Human, 'TCI Goes Global With "Say on Climate" Campaign' (2 December 2020), available at www.corporatesecretary.com/articles/esg/32358/tci-goes-global-%E2%80%98say-climate%E2%80%99-campaign.

[9] Tim Human, 'Aena Adopts Annual Advisory Vote on Climate Plan', IR Magazine (5 November 2020), www.irmagazine.com/reporting/aena-adopts-annual-advisory-vote-climate-plan.

[10] BlackRock Investment Stewardship Group, *Voting Bulletin: Aena S.M.E. SA*, available at www.blackrock.com/corporate/literature/press-release/blk-vote-bulletin-aena-oct-2020.pdf.

[11] Philipp Krueger, Zacharias Sautner and Laura Starks, 'The Importance of Climate Risks for Institutional Investors' (2020) 33 Review of Financial Studies 1067.

[12] Robert Engle and others, 'Hedging Climate Change News' (2020) 33 Review of Financial Studies 1184; Stefano Giglio, Bryan Kelly and Johannes Stroebel, 'Climate Finance' (2021) 13 Annual Review of Financial Economics 15.

In the alternative, ESG activism may simply follow other, non-financial preferences and be motivated by the nonpecuniary goal of pursuing social, not necessarily profit-driven preferences. For example, the motivation of activists may be intrinsic, such as the pursuit of sustainability goals, frequently reflected in the preferences of specific wealthy individuals, pressure groups, NGOs, and other interest groups.

8.2.2 Traditional Institutions and Index Funds

Traditional institutional investors, such as pension funds, mutual funds (regulated by the UCITS Directive in the EU), and index funds, are historically more passive vis-à-vis their investee companies, for the most part due to a lack of resources, incentives to free-ride, and the remuneration of their fund managers. Specifically, index funds traditionally replicate a given index and are therefore normally passive in their relationship with investee companies, refraining from engagement activities. Recent years have seen a tremendous growth of passive investing. The 'Big Three' institutional investors, BlackRock, Vanguard, and State Street Global Advisors now control about 80 percent of all global indexed money, making them a dominant force in the governance of public companies around the world.[13] Together, these three giants now control a staggering 25 percent of the shares of all S&P 500 companies, and this share is growing.[14]

Despite their traditionally passive role, these funds do play an important role in the ESG context, for two reasons.

First, they frequently design and offer new products and portfolios, specifically oriented towards sustainability. This may be motivated by purely financial reasons. Promoting sustainable indices is a particularly lucrative business for many fund managers, especially index fund managers, as it allows them to charge higher fees. It is crucial to understand that the entire trend towards index investing was originally driven by the exact opposite consideration: the selling point of fees being significantly

[13] John C. Coates IV, 'The Future of Corporate Governance Part I: The Problem of Twelve', https://corpgov.law.harvard.edu/wp-content/uploads/2019/11/John-Coates.pdf. See also David McLaughlin and Annie Massa, 'The Hidden Dangers of the Great Index Fund Takeover', *Bloomberg Businessweek* (9 January 2020), www.bloomberg.com/news/features/2020-01-09/the-hidden-dangers-of-the-great-index-fund-takeover. See also Chapter 5 (Lund and Robertson).

[14] Lucian Bebchuk and Scott Hirst, 'Index Funds and the Future of Corporate Governance: Theory, Evidence, and Policy' (2019) 119 Columbia Law Review 2029, 2033.

lower has always been the main argument for the success of index funds over their actively managed rivals.[15] When index investing turned mainstream, it became a victim of its own success: when low fees are ubiquitous, profit margins shrink and index investing becomes intensely competitive. In the hunt for new business opportunities, specialised ESG indices provide an exit opportunity from this difficult situation in that they allow fund managers to charge higher fees that drive up revenues.[16] Rather than charging higher fees for their traditional, passive index fund (which might deter investors), a second, alternative market segment allows fund managers to cater for both fee-sensitive customers and those who are environmentally conscious. For example, BlackRock's 'iShares Global Clean Energy ETF', one of the largest ESG funds in the world, carries an expense ratio of more than 11 times that of BlackRock's plain vanilla S&P500 ETF.[17]

As a side effect, large asset managers may see an emphasis on ESG and a wide choice of different products as beneficial when it comes to attracting new customers by differentiating the firm from other, typically smaller index-portfolio specialists. Large institutional investors would thereby benefit from economies of scale in the course of bearing the costs of introducing such new products. This could give them a certain comparative advantage as first movers.

A related rationale for passive institutions' involvement in ESG objectives relies on the phenomenon of universal ownership. Over the past several years, this term has come to describe the phenomenon where a number of large diversified institutional investors dominating today's corporate landscape, such as the Big Three, are holding significant stakes in the vast majority of firms in many economies.[18] This trend has given universal owners greater incentives to favour policies and initiatives that support ESG values. The reason is that funds that have invested in

[15] Edwin Elton, Martin Gruber and Christopher Blake, 'Incentive Fees and Mutual Funds' (2003) 58 Journal of Finance 779; Marcel Kahan and Edward Rock, 'Index Funds and Corporate Governance: Let Shareholders Be Shareholders' (2020) 100 Boston University Law Review 1771, 1781–1801.

[16] These higher fees are partly necessary due to the costs of in-house research or licensing third-party sustainability research. See Harrison Hong, 'The Sustainable Investing Proposition' (2019) 2 NBER Reporter 23–26.

[17] Christopher Bancroft Burnham, 'BlackRock's ESG Strategy Plays Politics with Public Pensions', Barron's (28 May 2020), www.barrons.com/articles/blackrock-is-playing-politics-with-public-pensions-51590661589.

[18] See, for example, Lucian Bebchuk and Scott Hirst, 'The Specter of the Giant Three' (2019) 99 Boston University Law Review 721, 735, fig. 1.

virtually every firm in the market are less concerned with the performance of individual portfolio companies, and more interested in the state of whole economies, if not the world economy. Against this backdrop, scholars have argued that the trend towards universal ownership would increase their incentives to push for greater ESG commitment in investee firms, or at least favour general policies that support such efforts.[19] Seen in this light, funds that 'own the market' appear to be the ideal conduits for the internalisation of a large fraction of the negative externalities caused by environmental damage and social disparities. This prospect is even more promising in the ESG field than in the context of traditional corporate governance engagement, which predominantly relies on firm-specific analysis.[20]

8.2.3 Retail Investors and the Preferences of Millennials

Retail investors are normally not considered as relevant for questions of investor engagement as their share ownership is rarely significant and their incentives to engage are typically weak. Their power has become felt, however, in a number of salient campaigns around so-called meme stocks, where the saga around GameStop was the most prolific example.[21] Their role in the ESG engagement context is however important as they are the ultimate clients of many institutional investors and therefore indirectly influential for their decision-making.

There is considerable evidence that investors' preferences are shifting in that they become increasingly attracted to ESG investments over the last several years.[22] This phenomenon is best illustrated by the new set of values that dominate the investment interests of the so-called millennial generation.[23] Crucially, this new powerful generation markedly differs in

[19] See, for example, Madison Condon, 'Externalities and the Common Owner' (2020) 95 Washington Law Review 1, 17–18.

[20] See Michal Barzuza, Quinn Curtis and David Webber, 'Shareholder Value(s): Index Fund ESG Activism and the New Millennial Corporate Governance' (2020) 93 Southern California Law Review 1243.

[21] Dhruv Aggarwal, Albert Choi and Yoon-Ho Alex Lee, 'Meme Corporate Governance', forthcoming, Southern California Law Review.

[22] Samuel Hartzmark and Abigail Sussman, 'Do Investors Value Sustainability? A Natural Experiment Examining Ranking and Fund Flows' (2019) 74 Journal of Finance 2789; Marco Ceccarelli, Stefano Ramelli and Alexander Wagner, 'Low Carbon Mutual Funds' (2024) 28 Review of Finance 45.

[23] See William Strauss and Neil Howe, *Millennials Rising: The Next Great Generation* (Random House, 2000).

its values from previous generations, or is at least perceived to do so.[24] A recent Morgan Stanley study reports that 99 percent of millennials expressed interest in sustainable investing, in comparison to 79 percent of regular investors.[25] Generally speaking, it has long been documented that millennials are less interested in investment returns and more interested in investments reflecting their social values.[26] According to Fidelity, 43 percent of millennial investors are engaged in impact investing, compared to just 12 percent of baby-boomer and 22 percent of generation X investors.[27] Meanwhile, a study by Natixis revealed that 74 percent of millennials wanted to 'make a positive social impact' with their investments, a substantially higher percentage compared to other, older age cohorts.[28] Numerous other studies have confirmed this general trend.[29]

As these preferences are undergoing profound changes, it is obvious that the financial services sector would be offering products sought by the demand side.[30] In this light, many index fund managers have been strengthening their efforts to redefine corporate valuations from an ESG perspective, and offering new instruments and index products that focus on principles other than just shareholder returns. Furthermore, a wave of ESG activism has led funds to use their voting power to promote ESG values as well as widely reporting their efforts publicly to catch the attention of this new crop of investors.[31] Likewise, there is evidence that portfolio companies have strong incentives to do 'good' by serving a

[24] Gillian Tett, 'Millennials May Forever Change Investing', Financial Times (7 May 2021) 19.

[25] Morgan Stanley Institute for Sustainable Investing, *Sustainable Signals: Individual Investors and the COVID-19 Pandemic* (2021). They attribute this figure in part to the economic uncertainty and market volatility during the pandemic. Note further that the report refers to investor sentiment before ESG triggered the current political backlash in the Republican party.

[26] Barzuza and others (n 20) 1283 ff.; Amy Bell, 'Young Voices Grow Louder in Company Strategies and Values', Financial Times (24 May 2021) 10.

[27] Fidelity Charitable, *The Future of Philanthropy: The Evolution from Charitable Giving to Charitable Living* (2021), www.fidelitycharitable.org/insights/2021-future-of-philanthropy.html.

[28] The figure was 71 percent for Generation X, 68 percent for the Baby Boomers, and 65 percent for the Silent Generation. See Natixis, *2021 ESG Investor Insight Report*, www.im.natixis.com/us/research/esg-investing-survey-insight-report.

[29] See Tett (n 24).

[30] Richard Henderson, 'Funds Prepare for Future With Pitch to Millennials', Financial Times (25 July 2019) 19.

[31] Barzuza and others (n 20) 1250.

beneficial purpose and to attract financially sophisticated and dedicated investors.[32]

8.3 Patterns and Strategies

ESG-minded investors use their powers to influence investee firms in a variety of ways. On a general level, some will simply pick and only choose to invest in companies with high ESG ratings (thereby divesting from firms that have low ratings), while others invest in firms that do not (yet) engage in ESG issues, with a view to actively encouraging them to step up their efforts in the future (for example, through shareholder resolutions).[33] Both strategies have their merits: the former will improve the market position of investee companies that are complying with ESG ratings, while the latter promises to actively change corporate policy to embrace ESG.

It is however the latter strategy that is of particular interest for the present chapter. In the following, we will seek to disentangle different types of specific engagement.

8.3.1 Generic Campaigns

As we saw above, index investors rarely engage in company-specific initiatives – their incentives, cost structures, and benchmarking effects with respect to peers do not allow for such costly firm-level engagement. Rather, the Big Three and others tend to promote generic standards for the market as a whole. They vocally outline their priorities in open letters and public statements, threatening to use their influence to force change where companies are not responsive.[34] In particular, they have urged

[32] Claire Economidou and others, 'Is sustainability rating material to the market?' (2023) 52 Financial Management 127.

[33] Each type of ESG investment is associated with different financial performance. See Amir Amel-Zadeh and George Serafeim, 'Why and How Investors Use ESG Information: Evidence from a Global Survey' (2018) 74(3) Financial Analysts Journal 87, 94–96. On the economic benefits of specific target selection, see Tamas Barko, Martijn Cremers and Luc Renneboog, 'Shareholder Engagement on Environmental, Social and Governance Performance' (2022) 180 Journal of Business Ethics 777.

[34] BlackRock's CEO Larry Fink's annual CEO letters have become famous and are widely reported in the investment community. See Andrew Ross Sorkin, 'BlackRock Chief Pushes a Big New Climate Goal for the Corporate World', New York Times (26 January 2021), www.nytimes.com/2021/01/26/business/dealbook/larry-fink-letter-blackrock-climate.html.

firms to publicly disclose a plan for how their business model will be compatible with a net zero economy.[35] Given their share of the market, winning the voting blocks of passive investors in proxy situations is often pivotal to a voting outcome. Some activist investors recognise this and have begun to structure issues such as governance into their campaigns, to appeal to the core issues of concern to large passive voting blocks.

To be sure, the Big Three have been accused of greenwashing (i.e. claiming to pursue climate-oriented policies for marketing reasons).[36] But there is now evidence emerging to suggest that large institutions have genuinely encouraged their investee firms to reduce carbon emissions,[37] and even that their efforts have been successful in changing the behaviour of portfolio companies in this direction.[38] A recent study confirmed that, at least outside of the US, institutional investors which publicly commit to responsible investing principles do in fact exhibit better ESG performance.[39]

Other surveys go even further. A 2020 study, investigating the effects of carbon emissions in a cross-section of stock returns, found a 'carbon premium' charged on US and other capital markets, which conventional risk factors could not fully explain.[40] The carbon premium has been shown to have increased in the years after the adoption of the Paris Agreement, suggesting that investor awareness of climate issues is

[35] Blackrock, *Larry Fink's 2021 Letter to CEOs*, www.blackrock.com/corporate/investor-relations/larry-fink-ceo-letter.

[36] Anna Christie, 'The Agency Costs of Sustainable Capitalism' (2021) 55 UC Davis Law Review 875; Dana Brakman Reiser and Anne Tucker, 'Buyer Beware: Variation and Opacity in ESG and ESG Index Funds' (2020) 41 Cardozo Law Review 1921.

[37] See Gillian Tett, 'Passive Investing Goes Active', Financial Times (2 February 2018) 9.

[38] See José Azar and others, 'The Big Three and Corporate Carbon Emissions Around the World' (2021) 142 Journal of Financial Economics 674; Alexander Dyck and others, 'Do Institutional Investors Drive Corporate Social Responsibility? International Evidence' (2019) 131 Journal of Financial Economics 639; Condon (n 19) 1.

[39] Rajna Gibson Brandon and others, 'Do Responsible Investors Invest Responsibly?' (2022) 26 Review of Finance 1389. See also Anne Lafarre, 'Do Institutional Investors Vote Responsibly?', TILEC Discussion Paper No 2022-001 (April 2022); Krueger and others (n 11).

[40] Patrick Bolton and Marcin Kacperczyk, 'Do Investors Care about Carbon Risk?' (2021) 142 Journal of Financial Economics 517 (analysing the effect of corporate emissions on the cross-section of stock returns in the US between 2005 and 2017).

playing an ever more significant role, and that climate risk is generally impounded into asset prices at the firm level.[41]

Certainly, free-rider effects are present in generic rulemaking activity too. But three factors make this a more effective means of intervention than attempting to improve individual companies' governance. First, while divestment is a rational strategy with regard to particular investment objects, it is not rational with respect to market-wide rules. Hence, the choice is simply between intervention and free riding (rather than exit). Exerting influence over the content of ESG rules may yield positive returns, even in the presence of free-riding activity. Brocardo, Hart and Zingales have recently shown that, in competitive markets, voice is more effective than exit in pushing firms to act in a socially responsible manner: in other words, engagement trumps divestment.[42] Secondly, given that universal owners cannot easily exit the market, each institution recognises that if it is not involved in influencing a change, others might do so in a way that harms its interests. Hence, a prevalent strategy is one of coordinated lobbying for rules that were expected to maximise the joint welfare of institutional investors. Finally, coordinated efforts by the investor community may fend off any more interventionist government activity that might eventually entail hardcore regulation;[43] thus, self-regulatory standards and ESG campaigns are especially attractive for investors.[44]

As the influence of large index funds has been growing in recent years, their role is also evolving from being merely passive. The largest passive investors are now responding to calls for more active engagement with management. The Big Three recently expanded their corporate governance teams and made their interactions with management more transparent,[45]

[41] Darwin Choi, Zhenyu Gao and Wenxi Jiang, 'Attention to Global Warming' (2020) 33 Review of Financial Studies 1112; Irene Monasterolo and Luca de Angelis, 'Blind to Carbon Risk? An Analysis of Stock Market Reaction to the Paris Agreement' (2020) 170 Ecological Economics 106571.

[42] Eleonora Broccardo, Oliver Hart and Luigi Zingales, 'Exit versus Voice' (2022) 130 Journal of Political Economy 3101.

[43] John L. Campbell, 'Why Would Corporations Behave in Socially Responsible Ways?' (2007) 32 Academy of Management Review 946; David Vogel, 'The Private Regulation of Global Corporate Conduct' (2010) 49 Business & Society 68.

[44] Barzuza and others (n 20) 1272. See also Tett (n 37).

[45] Madison Marriage, 'BlackRock, Vanguard and State Street Bulk Up Governance Staff', Financial Times (28 January 2017), available at www.ft.com/content/657b243c-e492-11e6-9645-c9357a75844a.

while investment stewardship teams at large active and passive funds have significantly grown, with some doubling in size over the past 10 years.[46] A 2021 survey found that 85 percent of index funds were giving ESG more attention when exercising their right to vote.[47] In this way, the lines between what is passive and what is active engagement are blurring, and traditionally reticent investors are increasingly embracing activist tactics and engaging in activist campaigns.[48]

8.3.2 *Collaboration and Teambuilding*

The most important driver for successful engagement for sustainability relates to greater *collaboration* between different types of ESG-oriented investors, thereby supporting engagement and activism.[49] First observed in the context of traditional shareholder activism, the collaboration model is becoming increasingly important in the context of green activism.[50] Coalition-building, as we shall see below, has become a very valuable component of ESG engagement, not least through institutionalised platforms of collaboration.[51]

[46] Morrow Sodali, *Institutional Investor Survey 2021*, available at https://morrowsodali.com/insights/institutional-investor-survey-2021.

[47] Ibid.

[48] Richard Grossman and Neil Stronski, 'New Tactics and ESG Themes Take Shareholder Activism in New Directions', Skadden Arps memo (February 2021), available at www.skadden.com/insights/publications/2021/02/the-informed-board/new-tactics-and-esg-themes; Tett (n 37).

[49] William McNabb, Vanguard Chairman and CEO, stated that 'To understand the full picture, we often also engage with other investors, including activists and shareholder proponents': see Vanguard, 'An open letter to directors of public companies worldwide' (31 August 2017), available at https://global.vanguard.com/documents/investment-stewardship-mcnabb-letter.pdf.

[50] For shareholder proposals with a focus on environmental issues, see Robert Monks, Anthony Miller and Jacqueline Cook, 'Shareholder Activism on Environmental Issues: A Study of Proposals at Large US Corporations (2000–2003)' (2004) 28 Natural Resources Forum 317; Giovanna Michelon and Michelle Rodrigue, 'Demand for CSR: Insights from Shareholder Proposals' (2015) 35 Social and Environmental Accountability Journal 157; Erwin Eding and Bert Scholtens, 'Corporate Social Responsibility and Shareholder Proposals' (2017) 24 Corporate Social Responsibility and Environmental Management 648; Viju Raghupathi, Jie Ren and Wullianallur Raghupathi, 'Identifying Corporate Sustainability Issues by Analyzing Shareholder Resolutions: A Machine-Learning Text Analytics Approach' (2020) 12 Sustainability 4753.

[51] See on this also Peter Mülbert and Alexander Sajnovits, 'Emerging ESG-Driven Models of Shareholder Collaborative Engagement', Chapter 9 in this book.

Greater collaboration between institutional investors has been observed in traditional corporate governance for several years already.[52] It is now increasingly being observed in ESG activism, which is a promising sign for credible investor-led sustainability.

To illustrate, Engine No. 1 when taking on Exxon Mobile was only successful due to coalition-building with institutions such as US pension funds CalSTRS, CalPERS, New York State Common, and the Church of England. BlackRock and Vanguard, two of the largest Exxon shareholders, also voted to support at least three of the four director nominees on Engine No. 1's slate.[53] Together, this alliance proved critical in the campaign's victory and may herald a new era for shareholder activism.[54] The coalition of investors was therefore not only successful in shaking up Exxon Mobil, but it also handed a major victory to the ESG movement as a whole.

Other pertinent examples of shareholder team building abound. They have been documented in campaigns against Evergy[55] or Procter & Gamble.[56] Even IT giants, such as Apple, have become the target of shareholder coalitions led by activist fund Jana Partners.[57]

[52] Marcel Kahan and Edward B. Rock, 'Embattled CEOs', (2010) 88 Texas Law Review 987; Ronald J. Gilson and Jeffrey N. Gordon, 'The Agency Costs of Agency Capitalism: Activist Investors and the Revaluation of Governance Rights' (2013) 113 Columbia Law Review 863; Wolf-Georg Ringe, 'Shareholder Activism: A Renaissance' in Jeffrey N. Gordon and Wolf-Georg Ringe (eds), *The Oxford Handbook of Corporate Law and Governance* (2018) 387. See also recent evidence provided by Simi Kedia, Laura Starks and Xianjue Wang, 'Institutional Investors and Hedge Fund Activism' (2021) 10 Review of Corporate Finance Studies 1.

[53] Alastair Marsh and Saijel Kishan, 'Engine No. 1's Exxon Win Provides Boost for ESG Advocates', Bloomberg (27 May 2021), www.bloomberg.com/news/articles/2021-05-27/engine-no-1-s-exxon-win-signals-turning-point-for-esg-investors; Bernice Napach, 'BlackRock and Vanguard Played Key Roles in Exxon's Shareholder Proxy Vote', ThinkAdvisor (27 May 2021), www.thinkadvisor.com/2021/05/27/blackrock-and-vanguard-played-key-roles-in-exxons-shareholder-proxy-vote/.

[54] Matt Phillips, 'Exxon's Board Defeat Signals the Rise of Social-Good Activists', New York Times (11 June 2021), www.nytimes.com/2021/06/09/business/exxon-mobil-engine-no1-activist.html.

[55] David French, 'US Utility Evergy Adds Directors in New Agreement with Activist Firm Elliott', Reuters (26 February 2021), available at www.reuters.com/article/us-evergy-elliott-idUSKBN2AQ294.

[56] Alistair Gray and Patrick Temple-West, 'Investor Rebellion at Procter & Gamble Over Environmental Concerns', Financial Times (14 October 2020), www.ft.com/content/1dd92502-e95b-4c21-be1c-c18a598acf1a.

[57] Robert G. Eccles, 'Why an Activist Hedge Fund Cares Whether Apple's Devices Are Bad for Kids', Harvard Business Review (January 2018), https://hbr.org/2018/01/why-an-activist-hedge-fund-cares-whether-apples-devices-are-bad-for-kids.

8.3.3 *Institutionalised Platforms*

Moving beyond ad-hoc teambuilding, investor coalitions may become more institutionalised themselves. An extreme example is the initiative Climate Change 100+ which brings together more than 570 investors, responsible for over $54 trillion in assets under management.[58] The goal of the initiative is to engage firms on improving climate change governance, cutting emissions, and strengthening climate-related financial disclosures. It not only coordinates actions but also distributes leadership roles for individual campaigns and geographical areas of specialisation, thereby sharing the cost of activism.[59] In January 2020, BlackRock joined Climate Action 100+, adding itself to a long list of other prominent signatories (including CalPERS, CalSTRS, Fidelity, JP Morgan Asset Management, and the pension funds of the City and State of New York). The United Nations has identified Climate Action 100+ as one of the 'most consequential global initiatives to combat global warming'.[60]

But coalitions do not always need large numbers of participants to have a meaningful impact. In April 2021, two investor groups, BlackRock and Singaporean sovereign wealth fund Temasek, agreed on an institutionalised partnership called 'Decarbonization Partners', which committed $600 million to advancing decarbonisation solutions.[61] Furthermore, a broad range of international investor advocacy groups, like As You Sow, Follow This, Majority Action, the Shareholder Association for Research and Education, the Shareholder Commons, ShareAction, and Investor Advocates for Social Justice, represent both individual and institutional investors by filing shareholder resolutions on their behalf, tracking campaigns, and defending them against legal challenges that typically come from the corporate management of the investee company.[62] There is also

[58] https://www.climateaction100.org/about/.

[59] See, for example, Condon (n 20) 64; Christie (n 36) 22.

[60] Matteo Tonello, '2021 Proxy Season Preview and Shareholder Voting Trends', Harvard Law School Forum on Corporate Governance (11 February 2021), available at https://corpgov.law.harvard.edu/2021/02/11/2021-proxy-season-preview-and-shareholder-voting-trends-2017-2020/.

[61] Jonathan Shieber, 'Temasek and BlackRock form Decarbonization Partners with $600 million to create a zero-emission economy', TechCrunch (13 April 2021), https://techcrunch.com/2021/04/13/temasek-and-blackrock-form-decarbonization-partners-with-600-million-to-create-a-zero-emission-economy/.

[62] Jackie Cook and Lauren Solberg, 'The 2021 Proxy Voting Season in 7 Charts, Morningstar' (5 August 2021), www.morningstar.com/articles/1052234/the-2021-proxy-voting-season-in-7-charts.

a growing trend of several institutions simultaneously 'co-filing' shareholder resolutions.[63]

Several academic studies have established a notable increase in such collaborations over the last several years. Dimson and co-authors document a large number of coordinated engagements, conducted by a prominent international network of long-term shareholders who cooperate to influence target firms on ESG issues.[64] In particular, they show that investors tend to choose a two-tier engagement strategy, combining a lead investor (who spearheads the dialogue) with several supporting investors (typically major investment institutions). This strategy has proved highly effective in achieving the stated engagement goals and has also led to improved target performance. Their study is based on data from a collaboration platform provided by the UN's Principles for Responsible Investment (PRI). The PRI is a leading network and the largest initiative of its kind for investors committed to long-term, sustainable returns.[65]

Other researchers have confirmed this trend. Several studies have highlighted the role of 'investor-driven governance networks' (IGNs) as a key component of the infrastructure for private environmental governance: IGNs are coalitions or alliances led by investors, formed around a specific public good or issue such as climate, in which investors are the primary actors.[66] Such IGNs include the Carbon Disclosure Project (CDP), the Interfaith Center for Corporate Responsibility (ICCR), the Coalition for Environmentally Responsible Economies (Ceres), Investors Against Genocide, the Network for Sustainable Financial Markets, and the Institutional Investors Group on Climate Change (IIGCC). Such purpose-driven networks follow a particular mission, with varying rigour, and many tend to partner with classic institutional investors such

[63] Ibid.

[64] Elroy Dimson, Oğuzhan Karakaş and Xi Li, 'Coordinated Engagements', ECGI Finance Working Paper No. 721/2021, available at http://ssrn.com/abstract_id=3209072.

[65] See on the PRI platform also Section 8.4.5.

[66] Michael MacLeod and Jacob Park, 'Financial Activism and Global Climate Change: The Rise of Investor-Driven Governance Networks' (2011) 11(2) Global Environmental Politics 54; Aimei Yang, Nur Uysal and Maureen Taylor, 'Unleashing the Power of Networks: Shareholder Activism, Sustainable Development and Corporate Environmental Policy' (2018) 27 Business Strategy and the Environment 712. Network theory may help us understand the emergence of such coalitions: see Luca Enriques and Alessandro Romano, 'Institutional Investor Voting Behavior: A Network Theory Perspective' (2019) University of Illinois Law Review 223.

as pension funds and mutual funds.[67] Others have emphasised in greater detail the function that coalitions play in fostering shareholder engagement on ESG issues.[68] Pertinently, they disseminate information relating to their mission and propose strategies and tactics for action, while they also serve as rallying points for individual and institutional shareholders seeking to influence companies and facilitate cost-sharing for campaigns.[69]

Another emerging trend is collaboration between existing shareholder coalitions.[70] Thus, the recently launched 'Net Zero Asset Managers Initiative' is a 'network of networks' bringing together platforms such as Ceres, the PRI, and the IIGCC, who share a commitment to push the companies they invest in towards reducing their net greenhouse gas emissions to zero by 2050.[71] Among the signatories of this initiative are the Big Three and many other asset management firms from across the globe.

8.4 Regulatory Support

8.4.1 Current Regulatory Efforts

In parallel to these developments in the field of investor engagement, policymakers worldwide have been developing an array of activities, initiatives, and policy papers, with Europe spearheading the movement.[72] Investor engagement in its more traditional sense was promoted by the EU Shareholder Rights Directive II, which took up the stewardship idea first promoted by the UK Stewardship Code and imported it to continental Europe.[73] More recently, regulatory attempts sought to incorporate non-financial, ESG-oriented standards in the regulatory reporting

67 MacLeod and Park (n 66); Yang and others (n 66).

68 Gary Cundill, Palie Smart and Hugh Wilson, 'Non-financial Shareholder Activism: A Process Model for Influencing Corporate Environmental and Social Performance' (2018) 20 International Journal of Management Reviews 606.

69 Ibid 615.

70 David Grayson and Jane Nelson, *Corporate Responsibility Coalitions: The Past, Present, and Future of Alliances for Sustainable Capitalism* (Stanford University Press 2020).

71 https://www.iigcc.org/.

72 For a helpful review of the academic literature supporting disclosure standards, see Hans B. Christensen, Luzi Hail and Christian Leuz, 'Mandatory CSR and Sustainability Reporting: Economic Analysis and Literature Review' (2021) 26 Review of Accounting Studies 1176.

73 Wolf-Georg Ringe, 'Stewardship and Shareholder Engagement in Germany' (2021) 22 European Business Organization Law Review 87, 91.

framework: the EU was the first to do it with its adoption of the Non-Financial Reporting Directive (NFRD)[74] in 2014, and the UK extended its stewardship code to include ESG objectives.[75]

At the end of the last decade, the legislative machine really took off. A 2018 EU Action Plan entitled 'Financing Sustainable Growth' mandated agencies to report and advise on potential undue short-termism in financial markets.[76] The European Securities and Markets Authority (ESMA) then developed a number of proposals, including a revised disclosure framework for non-financial risk as well as reinforced monitoring of remuneration and engagement standards.[77] The Sustainable Finance Disclosure Regulation (SFDR) came into effect in March 2021 and is currently being implemented across the Union. It imposes sustainability-related disclosure requirements on financial institutions including banks and investment firms. Yet another directive, the Corporate Sustainability Reporting Directive (CSRD) entered into force in early 2023 and will significantly upgrade and expand the existing NFRD.[78] The CSRD will, inter alia, extend its scope of application to most large companies and all companies listed on regulated markets, except listed micro-enterprises. It introduces more detailed and more stringent reporting requirements, and a requirement to report according to mandatory EU sustainability reporting standards. It will also mandate companies to digitally 'tag' the reported information in a machine-readable form, feeding into the planned European single access point for corporate information.

Finally, the EU's Taxonomy Regulation is an important pillar of the EU regime in that it categorises and classifies types of investment, and provides common definitions and standards for what constitutes 'green' investment activities.[79] It thus has the clear objective of addressing the problem of greenwashing. Moreover, it obliges firms to disclose the ratio

[74] Directive 2014/95/EU of the European Parliament and of the Council of 22 October 2014 amending Directive 2013/34/EU as regards disclosure of non-financial and diversity information by certain large undertakings and groups [2014] OJ L330/1.

[75] Ringe (n 73) 92.

[76] European Commission, *Action Plan: Financing Sustainable Growth*, COM(2018) 97 final.

[77] ESMA, *Report: Undue Short-Term Pressure on Corporations*, ESMA 30-22-762 (December 2019).

[78] Directive (EU) 2022/2464 of 14 December 2022 amending Regulation (EU) No 537/2014, Directive 2004/109/EC, Directive 2006/43/EC and Directive 2013/34/EU, as regards corporate sustainability reporting [2022] OJ L322/15.

[79] Regulation (EU) 2020/852 on the establishment of a framework to facilitate sustainable investment [2020] OJ L198/13.

of their turnover that qualifies as environmentally sustainable.[80] The Taxonomy Regulation entered into force in July 2020 and was expected to create legal certainty for investors, to protect private investors from greenwashing, to help companies to plan their transition, to mitigate market fragmentation, and eventually to help shift investments toward where they are most needed.[81] The European Commission is currently adopting a number of delegated acts to put flesh on the Taxonomy Regulation's bones.

Most recently, the EU went further in seeking to implement changes to the internal checks and balances of the corporate governance system. A 2020 study on directors' duties and sustainable corporate governance, carried out by EY for the European Commission, had explored the need to redefine the legal catalogue of directors' duties and advocated a rethink in this area.[82] This move ultimately led to the proposed Corporate Sustainability Due Diligence Directive,[83] which shifted the focus somewhat from directors' duties to CSR due diligence in supply chains.

We do not claim to offer a complete overview here; it is enough to give the reader the general idea. What becomes clear is that lawmakers are exploring a motley set of initiatives, apparently without an overarching theory or based on a coherent intellectual framework. Some of the regulatory activity is genuinely specific, amounting to very prescriptive standards. In contrast, rules on institutional stewardship are seeking to stimulate investor engagement by harnessing transparency and market forces.

Genuine investor engagement towards sustainability has many advantages compared to a more prescriptive, regulatory approach where legislatures are in the driver's seat. For example, a focus on investor-led priorities would follow a more flexible and dynamic pattern rather than complying with inflexible pre-defined criteria. Where an EU legislative project may take years of discussion, drafting, and implementation time, investor preferences can be a much faster catalyst in the pursuit of a sustainable agenda. Further, once an EU piece of legislation has been

80 Taxonomy Regulation, Article 8.

81 European Commission, *What Is the EU taxonomy*, https://ec.europa.eu/info/business-economy-euro/banking-and-finance/sustainable-finance/eu-taxonomy-sustainable-activities_en.

82 EY, *Study on Directors' Duties and Sustainable Corporate Governance: Final Report* (July 2020), available at https://op.europa.eu/en/publication-detail/-/publication/e47928a2-d20b-11ea-adf7-01aa75ed71a1/language-en.

83 Proposal for a Directive on Corporate Sustainability Due Diligence, COM(2022) 71 final.

agreed, it is usually almost 'set in stone' for many years, in a way that makes it very difficult to revise and change afterwards.

Moreover, investor-promoted market developments are not likely to impair welfare creation in the same way as ill-defined legal standards as the former respond more adequately to consumers and investors' preferences, without having gone through tedious negotiations in the legislative process, which inevitably leads to lobbying and political constraints. What is more, investor engagement will not trigger regulatory arbitrage in the same way as regulation and would avoid deadlock situations in political decision-making.

For these reasons, any regulatory activity should be limited to a facilitative and supportive role that enables and empowers investor engagement and ensures that investor engagement reflects the true preferences of market participants. This can happen, for example, by enhancing transparency and comparability of sustainability criteria and thereby mitigating the problem of greenwashing. Further action should be oriented towards removing barriers to investor collaboration and to facilitate institutional engagement platforms.

For these reasons, it becomes obvious that specific additional modifications of the internal corporate governance regime governing for example corporate boards appear unwarranted. Worse still, modifying directors' duties may prove counterproductive in terms of investor-led sustainability. For example, corporate management may hide behind the guise of protecting stakeholders' interests by opposing institutional shareholders and their efforts, thereby becoming more entrenched.[84]

Efforts by rule-makers, in particular the European Commission,[85] to reform the regulatory regime governing corporate directors should therefore not be pursued further. As noted in a recent submission in response to EU proposals, these efforts need to be reconsidered in light of economic evidence and in light of the 'self-regulation' approach presented here.[86] The Commission's initiative as well as the underlying EY report

[84] Lucian Bebchuk and Roberto Tallarita, 'The Illusory Promise of Stakeholder Governance' (2020) 106 Cornell Law Review 91.

[85] European Commission, *Public Consultation on Sustainable Corporate Governance*, https://ec.europa.eu/info/law/better-regulation/have-your-say/initiatives/12548-Sustainable-corporate-governance/public-consultation_en.

[86] Alexander Bassen, Kerstin Lopatta and Wolf-Georg Ringe, *Feedback Statement on the Sustainable Corporate Governance Initiative* (October 2020), available at https://ec.europa.eu/info/law/better-regulation/have-your-say/initiatives/12548-Sustainable-corporate-governance/F594615_en. A summary featured on the Oxford Business Law Blog at www.law

have also drawn fierce criticism from different academic quarters.[87] The same is true for other, mostly mandatory attempts at prescribing sustainability criteria.[88]

Instead of pursuing such an overly prescriptive approach, regulation may be useful to streamline investor pressure, ideally filtered and vetted through the 'teaming-up' model, which will push firms to pursue sustainability initiatives out of intrinsic motivation. We have seen, however, that collaborative efforts also face challenges here. For example, the free-rider problem applies: costs may be borne by a small group of committed and resourceful investors, while benefits are shared by all investors in the firm. Furthermore, competition and rivalry between institutional investors makes collaboration difficult and frequently requires independent or mutual trust. Also, coordination is costly and time-consuming: it needs to overcome language and cultural barriers, so achieving agreement among many investors from diverse jurisdictions may prove difficult. Finally, some regulatory barriers persist. If anything, the regulatory framework should then address these concerns: its role should be to take a supportive and facilitative role to *enable* ESG engagement. There are several tools that may be employed to this end.

8.4.2 *Facilitation and Clarification*

Rather than *mandating* sustainability goals, the present analysis has identified the role of regulation in *facilitating* ESG investments. A good example on what regulation can sensibly do is exemplified by the recent reform of the US ERISA retirement plan framework, which clarifies the ability of retirement plan fiduciaries to invest in ESG funds.[89]

.ox.ac.uk/business-law-blog/blog/2020/10/ec-corporate-governance-initiative-series-eu-sustainable-corporate.

87 Mark Roe and others, 'The European Commission's Sustainable Corporate Governance Report: A Critique' (2021) 38 Yale Journal on Regulation Bulletin 133; The European Company Law Experts Group, 'A Critique of the Study on Directors' Duties and Sustainable Corporate Governance Prepared by Ernst & Young for the European Commission', Oxford Business Law Blog (14 October 2020), www.law.ox.ac.uk/business-law-blog/blog/2020/10/ec-corporate-governance-initiative-series-critique-study-directors.

88 Dirk Zetzsche and Linn Anker-Sørensen, 'Regulating Sustainable Finance in the Dark' (2022) 23 European Business Organization Law Review 47.

89 Department of Labor, *Final Rule on Prudence and Loyalty in Selecting Plan Investments and Exercising Shareholder Rights* (22 November 2022).

Prior to this reform, the Trump administration had caused considerable regulatory uncertainty regarding fiduciaries' ability to use ESG funds in their retirement plans. The new regime, in contrast, means that retirement plan sponsors can more confidently incorporate ESG funds into their plans. Although the fiduciary responsibilities of ERISA plan sponsors have remained consistent in previous ESG guidance documents, the continual issuance of guidance under different administrations had led to uncertainty for plan sponsors, resulting in a certain reluctance to include ESG funds in retirement plans.[90] This meant that ERISA-regulated fiduciaries were not able to follow common market practice.[91] Different from previous rules, however, the new rules now treat ESG funds no differently than any other investment fund. Although the core principles underlying ERISA – the duties of prudence and loyalty – remain of paramount importance, the revised framework recognises that ESG factors in investment selection can be 'financially material' and clarifies that the impact of an ESG factor may be an appropriate consideration when evaluating particular investment options. The use of ESG considerations as a 'tie-breaker' is also clarified, when choosing between investment alternatives that are otherwise equal with respect to return and risk over the appropriate time horizon.

These changes, technical as they may seem, have the potential to 'change the ESG game',[92] as they open up the ESG market for the vast funds of ERISA retirement plans. Crucially, however, the new rules are not prescriptive in mandating ESG investment; they simply clarify the position that fiduciaries *may* invest into ESG products if they wish to do so. Fiduciaries may not only consider them, but in some instances such products may even be warranted.[93]

[90] Melissa Kahn, 'The New DOL Proposal May Change the ESG Game', Harvard Law School Forum on Corporate Governance (8 December 2021), https://corpgov.law.harvard.edu/2021/12/08/the-new-dol-proposal-may-change-the-esg-game/.

[91] PRI, *Consultation Response – US Department of Labor: Prudence and Loyalty in Selecting Plan Investments and Exercising Shareholder Rights* (13 December 2021), www.unpri.org/download?ac=15663.

[92] Kahn (n 90).

[93] Thomas P. DiNapoli, State Comptroller of New York, *Consultation Response: Prudence and Loyalty in Selecting Plan Investments and Exercising Shareholder Rights* (9 December 2021), www.dol.gov/sites/dolgov/files/EBSA/laws-and-regulations/rules-and-regulations/public-comments/1210-AC03/00308.pdf.

8.4.3 *Disclosure and Standardisation*

Any attempt at self-regulation faces the difficulty of information asymmetry and of a lack of market standardisation. At the moment, a patchwork of standards exists around the globe, accompanied by poor data quality, which makes compliance challenging and undermines the efficacy of investor engagement, both for investors that invest directly and for those relying on intermediaries.[94] For companies operating in multiple jurisdictions, the widely varying rules and guidelines may impose extensive but differing disclosures, and make it harder for investors to compare and ascertain reliable and verifiable information.[95] At the same time, they invite regulatory arbitrage and greenwashing.[96] Worse still, diverging standards may ultimately result in a race to the bottom.[97] On a more practical level, the opacity of products, data, and standards makes it challenging for ultimate investors to put their funds to the most appropriate use, thus undermining the force of the investor-led model for sustainability.[98] It is therefore no surprise that institutional investors are increasingly calling for the adoption of more standardised and comparable reporting standards.[99]

Over the past several years, a number of ESG reporting frameworks have been adopted worldwide, such as the Sustainability Accounting Standards Board (SASB),[100] the Global Reporting Initiative (GRI),[101]

[94] Silvia Pavoni, 'The Search for the Meaning of Green', Financial Times (24 May 2021) FTfm 5, https://www.ft.com/content/71f57e02-8fdb-4680-a1f3-e65f47c9a0b1 (online version title).

[95] Sara Bernow and others, 'More Than Values: The Value-Based Sustainability Reporting that Investors Want', McKinsey & Company (7 August 2019), www.mckinsey.com/capabilities/sustainability/our-insights/more-than-values-the-value-based-sustainability-reporting-that-investors-want.

[96] Reiser and Tucker (n 36). See further the references at n 36.

[97] Jean Raby, 'Responsible Investment Should Improve and Outperform the Market, Not Become the Market', Financial Times (5 January 2021), www.fnlondon.com/articles/responsible-investment-should-improve-and-outperform-the-market-not-become-the-market-20210105.

[98] On the role of disclosure regulation for empowering the shift towards green finance, see Sebastian Steuer and Tobias Tröger, 'The Role of Disclosure in Green Finance' (2022) 8 Journal of Financial Regulation 1.

[99] PwC, *Global Investor Survey: The Economic Realities of ESG* (December 2021) 5, available at www.pwc.com/gx/en/corporate-reporting/assets/pwc-global-investor-survey-2021.pdf.

[100] The SASB standards are available for sector-specific download at www.sasb.org/standards/download/.

[101] Global Reporting Initiative, *Consolidated Set of GRI Sustainability Reporting Standards 2022* (2022), available at www.globalreporting.org/standards/download-the-standards/.

the World Economic Forum's (WEF) Metrics on Sustainable Capitalism,[102] and a framework adopted by the Task Force on Climate-Related Financial Disclosures (TCFD),[103] which was established by the G20 Financial Stability Board.[104] According to a recent survey, investors recommend the SASB (75 percent) and the TCFD (53 percent) as the best standards when it comes to communicating ESG information.[105]

At present, national and regional approaches differ significantly. In the US, the Big Three asset managers and others currently encourage companies to follow the SASB reporting standards and the TCFD regime. The SEC has proposed new rules to require specific ESG disclosures,[106] but they have not been finalised yet. In parallel to these efforts, the Financial Accounting Standards Board (FASB) has issued guidance to staff on the incorporation of ESG matters, including climate change, into financial statements.[107] At the same time, private institutions are pursuing their separate agendas. For example, Nasdaq has introduced changes to its listing standards that requires its listed companies to enhance their disclosures regarding board diversity and requires them to have, or to disclose why they do not have, a minimum of two 'diverse' board members.[108]

The EU regime is more advanced, yet still in flux. We explored the key elements of the 'alphabet soup' – the current stream of different directives and regulations that are adopted or planned – above.[109]

102 World Economic Forum, *Measuring Stakeholder Capitalism: Towards Common Metrics and Consistent Reporting of Sustainable Value Creation* (22 September 2020), available at www.weforum.org/reports/measuring-stakeholder-capitalism-towards-common-metrics-and-consistent-reporting-of-sustainable-value-creation.

103 TCFD, *Recommendations of the Task Force on Climate-Related Financial Disclosures* (June 2017), available at www.fsb-tcfd.org/recommendations/.

104 For an overview and comprehensive discussion, see Virginia Harper Ho, 'Modernizing ESG Disclosure' (2022) University of Illinois Law Review 277.

105 Morrow Sodali, *Institutional Investor Survey* (2021), available at https://morrowsodali.com/insights/institutional-investor-survey-2021.

106 SEC Proposes Rules to Enhance and Standardize Climate-Related Disclosures for Investors (21 March 2022), www.sec.gov/news/press-release/2022-46.

107 FASB, *FASB Staff Educational Paper: Intersection of Environmental, Social, and Governance Matters with Financial Accounting Standards* (19 March 2021), www.fasb.org/Page/ShowPdf?path=FASB_Staff_ESG_Educational_Paper_FINAL.pdf&title=FASB%20Staff%20Educational%20Paper-Intersection%20of%20Environmental.

108 See Securities and Exchange Commission, Release No. 34-92590 (6 August 2021), available at www.sec.gov/rules/sro/nasdaq/2021/34-92590.pdf.

109 See Section 8.4.

In the UK, the Financial Conduct Authority first adopted a new listing rule requiring premium-listed issuers to disclose, on a comply-or-explain basis, whether their climate-related disclosures are in line with TCFD recommendations.[110] Moreover, a recent reform makes climate-related financial disclosures mandatory for publicly listed companies, large private companies, and limited liability partnerships, also in line with TCFD standards.[111] Both instruments became operational in 2022.

This short overview demonstrates that the jungle of different regulatory instruments, standards, and obligations is hardly conducive to a transparent, global investment market seeking to promote investor-led sustainability. What is needed here is a truly global standard that makes investments and activities comparable. On the positive side, the ESG movement has already triggered the establishment of multiple initiatives and disclosure frameworks, although these are lacking coordination and consistency. A laudable initiative is the Corporate Reporting Dialogue (CRD), essentially a platform that is set up by the International Integrated Reporting Council to promote greater coherence, consistency, and comparability between international corporate reporting frameworks, standards, and related requirements.[112] Likewise, the new International Sustainability Standards Board (ISSB) recently published draft requirements for sustainability-related information, promising to yield a singular, global ESG disclosure framework for companies.[113] Whichever standard will play the leading role globally in the future would require the backing of a strong, independent, and, most importantly, credible institution.[114]

110 Financial Conduct Authority, *Proposals to Enhance Climate-Related Disclosures By Listed Issuers and Clarification of Existing Disclosure Obligations*, Policy Statement PS20/17 (December 2020), www.fca.org.uk/publications/policy-statements/ps20-17-proposals-enhance-climate-related-disclosures-listed-issuers-and-clarification-existing.

111 Department for Business, Energy & Industrial Strategy, *Mandatory Climate-Related Financial Disclosures by Publicly Quoted Companies, Large Private Companies and LLPs* (February 2022), www.gov.uk/government/publications/climate-related-financial-disclosures-for-companies-and-limited-liability-partnerships-llps.

112 https://corporatereportingdialogue.com/.

113 IFRS, *General Sustainability-Related Disclosures*, www.ifrs.org/projects/work-plan/general-sustainability-related-disclosures/.

114 Paul Brest and Colleen Honigsberg, 'Measuring Corporate Virtue – and Vice: Making ESG Metrics Trustworthy' in Neil Malhotra (ed), *Frontiers in Social Innovation: The Essential Handbook for Creating, Deploying, and Sustaining Creative Solutions to Systemic Problems* (Harvard Business Review Press 2022) 79.

8.4.4 *Removing Barriers to Collaboration*

We have seen above that the 'teaming-up' concept holds great promise for the future development of ESG activism, namely in that coalition-building gives engaged shareholders greater clout and also limits possibilities for abuse.[115]

Yet there are a number of regulatory barriers in place that limit the possibility of investor collaboration.[116] For example, US proxy solicitation rules make it very costly to initiate an investor campaign.[117] During the Trump administration, the SEC further toughened those requirements. Specifically, in 2019, the SEC adopted guidance on proxy advisors and proxy solicitation that made it more difficult and costly for investment advisers to exercise shareholder voting rights on behalf of their clients relying on independent proxy voting advice.[118] One year later, the SEC adopted new rules and additional guidance related to proxy advisors that imposed further cost and complexity into the voting process, and mandated greater issuer involvement in proxy voting decisions.[119] And most recently, regulatory reform of Rule 14a-8 has raised the thresholds and made it even more difficult for shareholders to adopt shareholder proposals for corporate general meetings.[120] This trend in policy making has been severely criticised, even from within the SEC, for obstructing shareholder engagement and in particular ESG initiatives.[121]

European and other jurisdictions' rules on 'acting in concert' limit the possibility of coalition-building: under EU disclosure rules, blocks of shares held by concerted parties would have to be counted together,

[115] See Section 8.3.2. For greater detail, see Ringe (n 1) 122 ff.

[116] See on this also Mülbert and Sajnovits (n 51).

[117] SEC Regulation 14A, Rules 14a-1 to 14a-7.

[118] See Commission Guidance Regarding Proxy Voting Responsibilities of Investment Advisers, Rel. No. IA-5325 (21 August 2019); Commission Interpretation and Guidance Regarding the Applicability of the Proxy Rules to Proxy Voting Advice, Rel. No. 34-86721 (21 August 2019).

[119] Exemptions from the Proxy Rules for Proxy Voting Advice, Rel. No. 34-89372 (22 July 2020); Supplement to Commission Guidance Regarding Proxy Voting Responsibilities of Investment Advisers, Release No. IA-5547 (22 July 2020).

[120] Procedural Requirements and Resubmission Thresholds under Exchange Act Rule 14a-8, Rel. No. 34-89964 (23 September 2020).

[121] Allison Herren Lee, 'Statement by Commissioner Lee on the Amendments to Rule 14a-8', *Harvard Law School Forum on Corporate Governance* (24 September 2020), available at https://corpgov.law.harvard.edu/2020/09/24/statement-by-commissioner-lee-on-the-amendments-to-rule-14a-8/.

which would require earlier disclosure.[122] A related problem is that investors acting in concert might have to make a mandatory bid under the EU Takeover Directive if they together are in 'control' of the company.[123] These rules have long been seen as a large barrier to more effective shareholder engagement as they trigger large financial consequences.[124] Finally, there is a certain tension and vast legal uncertainty concerning shareholder activism under existing insider dealing laws, which needs to be resolved.[125]

Regulators are beginning to realise that investor engagement should be facilitated, and not restricted, particularly when it is sustainability-driven. For example, former SEC Commissioner Allison Lee heavily criticised the 2020 regulatory changes and argued that the Commission should seek to facilitate greater ESG engagement rather than stifling it.[126] Also, ESMA maintains a White List of activities that would not count as 'acting in concert'.[127] It recently proposed a review of this list and explored whether it should include an explicit reference to coordination activities among institutional investors in the area of ESG, to stimulate engagement in this field.[128] Such initiatives are to be welcomed.

8.4.5 *Facilitating Investor Platforms*

We saw above that investor platforms, where they exist, greatly facilitate investor engagement.[129] Studies have revealed that such platforms – also

[122] Transparency Directive 2004/109/EC, Articles 9, 10(a).

[123] Takeover Directive 2004/25/EC, Article 5(1).

[124] See for example, the survey data reported by Joseph McCahery, Zacharias Sautner and Laura Starks, 'Behind the Scenes: The Corporate Governance Preferences of Institutional Investors' (2016) 71 Journal of Finance 2905, 2923. See also ESMA, *Report: Undue Short-Term Pressure on Corporations*, ESMA 30-22-762 (December 2019) 64; PRI, *Addressing System Barriers* (2022): 'Acting in concert is often perceived as a key regulatory barrier when institutional investors seek to engage collaboratively with companies'.

[125] See Ana Taleska, 'European Insider Trading Theory Revisited: The Limits of the Parity-of-Information Theory and the Application of the Property Rights in Information Theory to Activist Investment Strategies' (2020) 17 European Company and Financial Law Review 558, 580 ff. See also Lars Klöhn, 'Board-Shareholder Engagement and Insider Regulation', Chapter 18 in this book.

[126] Lee (n 121).

[127] ESMA, *Public Statement Information on Shareholder Cooperation and Acting in Concert under the Takeover Bids Directive* (8 February 2019), ESMA31-65-682.

[128] ESMA, *Report: Undue Short-Term Pressure on Corporations*, ESMA 30-22-762 (December 2019) 69, 70.

[129] See Section 8.3.3.

referred to as investor collective action organisations (ICAOs) – allow for easier interaction between investors, identifying lead investors, spreading information, and helping to share the costs of engagement.

One example is the PRI Collaboration Platform established by investors in partnership with the UNEP's Finance Initiative and the UN's Global Compact.[130] The PRI platform is the leading network and the largest initiative worldwide for investors with a commitment to responsible ownership and long-term, sustainable returns. It provides a significant database with records on ESG engagements worldwide. The platform allows lead investors to launch and market campaigns, with supporting investors either invited by the PRI or the leader to join an engagement, or allowed to join via the PRI's Collaboration Platform online.[131]

We have seen that several other specialised ESG-related platforms exist and play a vital role in facilitating investor engagements.[132] Successful examples here are the initiative Climate Action 100+ and Ceres, an NGO, among others.[133]

Outside of the ESG realm, investor platforms exist in various shapes and forms. An example is the Dutch corporate governance platform Eumedion, which represents the interests of institutional investors worldwide to have invested in Dutch-listed companies. The platform seeks to promote good corporate governance and sustainability policies at Dutch-listed companies and to promote engaged and responsible share ownership by its members. Eumedion, inter alia, supports its members by facilitating dialogue among them, and between the members and Dutch-listed companies.[134] A similar institution is the Canadian Coalition for Good Governance (CCGG), which bundles together institutional shareholders that invest in Canadian public equities.[135] The CCGG aims to promote good governance practices at Canadian public companies and coordinates engagement activities. It also claims to focus on topics related to the governance of environmental and social risks.[136]

130 The PRI platform is available at https://collaborate.unpri.org/.

131 Dimson and others (n 64) 14 ff.

132 See Section 8.4.

133 See Section 8.4.

134 Eumedion Corporate Governance Forum, *About Eumedion*, https://en.eumedion.nl/About-Eumedion.html.

135 On CCGG, see the important study by Craig Doidge, Alexander Dyck, Hamed Mahmudi and Aazam Virani, 'Collective Action and Governance Activism' (2019) 23 Review of Finance 893.

136 Canadian Coalition for Good Governance, *2021 Annual Report* (2022), available at https://ccgg.ca/annual-report/.

These and other networks and platforms are crucial in facilitating investor engagement, as well as overcoming free-rider incentives and collective action problems. Dimson and colleagues argued that they are paramount in helping investors to exploit the advantages and overcome the challenges of jointly pursuing shared objectives.[137] Related research has documented that institutional investors use such platforms to improve governance outcomes through collective action.[138] To be sure, such platforms may also be set up by business associations themselves and evolve by way of self-regulatory initiatives. However, the PRI platform, considered as the most effective platform promoting ESG objectives, draws a considerable part of its strength from the financial and reputational support stemming from the United Nations. Regulators may therefore be inclined to consider establishing or sponsoring further platform solutions in the field. The German Sustainable Finance Expert Group, in its final report, recommended the German government, in collaboration with institutional investors, to establish such a platform to facilitate collective engagement.[139]

8.5 Conclusion

This chapter makes the case for ESG investor engagement and favours a market-led approach over prescriptive regulatory intervention. I have argued that investors' initiatives and engagement are and should be the primary tool to promote sustainability orientation in the market. The need to build coalitions and to convince fellow investors of an initiative can then act as an in-built safety check, which would help mitigate the pursuit of merely idiosyncratic motives and would give support to only those campaigns that are supported by a majority of investors. In particular, institutionalised investor platforms have emerged over recent years to coordinate investor campaigns and to share costs. Accordingly, I conclude with the policy implication that lawmakers should take a supportive and facilitative approach that supports investor engagement and private ordering. By doing so, static and interventionist legal policies would become less justified.

[137] Dimson and others (n 64) 2. [138] See Doidge and others (n 135).

[139] Sustainable Finance Beirat der Bundesregierung, *Shifting the Trillions: Ein nachhaltiges Finanzsystem für die Große Transformation* (2021) 128, available at https://sustainable-finance-beirat.de/wp-content/uploads/2021/02/210224_SFB_-Abschlussbericht-2021.pdf.

9

Emerging ESG-Driven Models of Shareholder Collaborative Engagement

PETER O. MÜLBERT AND ALEXANDER SAJNOVITS

9.1 Introduction

The received view of shareholder engagement holds that the difficulties of collective action and the resultant rational apathy on the part of shareholders discourage effective (collaborative) engagement. In theory, recent fundamental transitions in ownership structures – in particular, the increasing concentration of investment capital within active and passive funds – should not alter shareholders' rational incentives to remain passive, particularly because funds compete on fees, and any engagement at the level of a single portfolio company brings with it an increase in costs. Free rider problems also contribute to shareholder passivity.

In practice, however, shareholder involvement has increased in recent years. This development is traditionally attributed to four main factors: (i) the "Big Three"[1] of the investment fund industry are too big to remain passive, (ii) institutional investors increasingly use proxy advisors, (iii) political pressure and stewardship considerations spur on proactive shareholder involvement, and (iv) institutional investors, in particular hedge funds, collaborate with each other ("wolf pack" activism) and institutional investors follow the lead of activist hedge funds.

In this chapter, we explore collaborative shareholder engagement as a way of overcoming collective action problems and high engagement costs. Considering the disincentives for shareholder engagement, collaboration between shareholders indeed is, on a theoretical level, a way to overcome, or at least mitigate, some of these disincentives. This is

A previous version of this chapter was presented at the Auxiliary Corporate Governance Conference organized by Assogestioni in Rome on October 12–13–14, 2022. The authors gratefully acknowledge the helpful comments of conference participants and especially Amy Borrus and the editors. The usual disclaimers apply.

[1] See *Lund/Robertson*, Chapter 5 in this volume, with further arguments on the limitations of referring to the "Big Three" only.

because: (i) voting rights and the associated informal influence can be bundled through collaborative interaction, (ii) collaboration may mitigate the free rider problem, (iii) collaboration can reduce information costs by sharing resources, skills, and expertise among collaborators, and (iv) collaboration contributes to risk-sharing among those who collaborate.

In this chapter, we understand collaboration as an active form of cooperation among people and/or institutions. Therefore, we distinguish collaborative behaviour from mere (coincidentally) simultaneous behaviour as well as from imitative behaviour without active cooperation or any kind of consultation between the parties. The nature of the collaboration, that is, whether it is formalized or merely informal, however, is immaterial, which is why we also analyse informal, non-binding exchanges of information between persons, or non-binding participation in certain platforms.[2]

Our focus is on collaboration among institutional investors, because they are the main players when it comes to engagement with listed public companies. Not only are institutional investors theoretically best placed to overcome the obstacles to effective collaboration, but collaborative engagement among institutional investors is also increasingly common in practice. In this regard, the focus has traditionally been on wolf packs, as well as on the interaction of large, diversified funds and/or their owners, with hedge funds. Since collaborative ES(G) engagement is becoming increasingly important, it will be a particular focus of our chapter.[3] Section 9.2 expands on the traditional micro picture of shareholder collaborative engagement. Here, we briefly touch on the (dis-) incentives for shareholder engagement in general (9.2.1), and the reasons traditionally put forward for why shareholder engagement still takes place despite these disincentives (9.2.2), before taking a closer look at collaborative engagement in particular (9.2.3). In Section 9.3, we introduce the nascent ES(G)-era as a potential game changer with regard to

[2] Cf. Dimson/Karakas/Li, The Review of Financial Studies 28 (2015), 3225, 3231 (distinguishing between hard and soft forms of collaboration). For a different view, see Fisch/Sepe, Texas Law Review 98 (2020), 863, 865 with fn. 7 (excluding mere exchanges of information).

[3] See Section 9.5. This chapter does not deal with the collaborative engagement of retail investors and the new forms of coordination collectively labelled as “swarm trading”. See Sajnovits, in Köhler/Korch, Schwärme im Recht, 2022, p. 197; Fisch, Boston University Law Review 102 (2022), 1799.

shareholder collaborative engagement and raise the question of whether increasing interest in E and S issues, in particular, might serve as an additional incentive for institutional investors to collaborate. Section 9.4 presents several new ES(G)-driven forms and strategies of collaboration. Section 9.5 discusses potential legal barriers to collaboration. The chapter concludes with a brief outlook as to what the future may hold in this regard (9.6).

9.2 Shareholder Collaborative Engagement: The Traditional Micro-picture

9.2.1 (Dis-)Incentives for Shareholder Engagement

US corporate law scholars have traditionally taken the view that a widely dispersed retail shareholder base is incapable of effectively monitoring management.[4] Shareholders have been characterized as "rationally apathetic",[5] with collective action problems, and excessive coordination costs discouraging them from taking a more active supervisory role.[6]

The concentration of share ownership among institutional investors, which was at first seen by optimists as a way of overcoming collective action problems,[7] did not initially prove in practice to pave the way for increased effective shareholder participation. With regard to owners and managers of *active funds*, the standard explanation is that of "rational reticence" of this type of investor.[8]

[4] Rock, in Gordon/Ringe, Oxford Handbook of Corporate Law and Governance, 2017, pp. 363, 374.

[5] Kraakman/Armour/Davies/Enriques *et al.*, The Anatomy of Corporate Law, 3rd ed. 2017, Chap. 2.1, p. 30; Christie, University of California Davis Law Review 55 (2021), 875, 898 with fn. 121; Clark, Corporate Law, 1986, pp. 390 et seq.; Black, Michigan Law Review 89 (1990), 520, 527.

[6] *Christie*, University of California Davis Law Review 55 (2021), 875, 898; *Enriques/Romano*, University of Illinois Law Review 2019, 223, 232; *Bowley/Hill*, Stewardship and Collective Action: The Australian Experience, ECGI Law Working Paper No. 491/2020, p. 13; see already *Rock*, Georgetown Law Journal 79 (1991), 445.

[7] Gilson/Kraakman, Stanford Law Review 43 (1991), 863; cf. also Rock, in Gordon/Ringe, Oxford Handbook of Corporate Law and Governance, 2017, pp. 363, 374.

[8] Gilson/Gordon, Columbia Law Review 113 (2013), 863; cf. also Barzuza/Curtis/Webber, Southern California Law Review 93 (2020), 1243, 1256 et seq.; Enriques/Romano, University of Illinois Law Review (2019), 223, 232 et seq.; already early on Coffee, Columbia Law Review 91 (1991), 1278, 1318 et seq.; Fisch, Ohio State Law Journal 55 (1994), 1009.

With regard to *passive funds*, especially index funds, the debate has seen the emergence of highly opposing schools of thought.[9] On the one hand, it is argued that the owners and managers of index funds theoretically have a very obvious interest in influencing the performance of portfolio companies, given that they do not have the exit option available to active funds.[10] On the other hand, *Lucian Bebchuk* and *Scott Hirst*, in particular, argue that index funds are exceptionally cost-averse and suffer from exactly the same problems as actively managed funds with respect to the free rider problem and incentives to underinvest in stewardship resulting, *inter alia*, from the remuneration of fund managers as a fixed percentage of assets under management.[11] As a result, rational reticence characterizes passive funds even more than active ones.

The incentives for *(value) hedge funds*, conversely, differ significantly.[12] Value hedge funds typically acquire a significant stake in a single company in the belief that they will be able to actively exert influence – that is, by influencing the corporate structure or strategy, or often by replacing the current management – to bring about an increase in the share price within a relatively short period of time.[13] Therefore, they have a clear interest in being informed and in influencing the company by exercising their participation rights or the resultant power of influence.[14]

9.2.2 *Traditional Reasons for Shareholder Engagement*

In practice, shareholder involvement has increased in recent years despite the disincentives described above. This development is typically

[9] See, e.g., Bebchuk/Hirst, Columbia Law Review 119 (2019), 2029; Bebchuk/Hirst, Boston University Law Review 99 (2019), 722 on the one side and Fisch/Hamdani/Solomon, University of Pennsylvania Law Review 168 (2019), 17, 27 et seq. on the other side. On engagement by passive funds, see *also* Strampelli, San Diego Law Review 55 (2018), 803; Lund, Journal of Corporation Law 43 (2018), 493; for empirical evidence, see Grove/Clouse/King, Corporate Governance and Organizational Behavior Review 4 (2020), 8; *Appel/Gromley/Keim*, Journal of Financial Economics 121 (2016), 111.

[10] Fisch/Hamdani/Solomon, University of Pennsylvania Law Review 168 (2019), 17, 27 et seq.; cf. Christie, University of California Davis Law Review 55 (2021), 875, 902 with further references in fn. 136.

[11] Bebchuk/Hirst, Columbia Law Review 119 (2019), 2029, 2050 et seq., 2053.

[12] Kahan/Rock, University of Pennsylvania Law Review 155 (2007), 1021, 1062 et seq.; *Enriques/Romano*, Rewriting Corporate Law for an Interconnected World, ECGI Law Working paper No. 572/2021, p. 19.

[13] Barko/Cremers/Renneboog, Journal of Business Ethics 180 (2021), 4; Barzuza/Curtis/Webber, Southern California Law Review 93 (2020), 1243, 1256 et seq.

[14] Kahan/Rock, University of Pennsylvania Law Review 155 (2007), 1021, 1069 et seq.

attributed to four factors:[15] (i) the "Big Three" of the investment fund industry because of their size are often targeted by political and public pressure not to remain passive,[16] (ii) stewardship considerations spur proactive shareholder involvement,[17] (iii) institutional investors increasingly use proxy advisors[18] and (iv) institutional investors collaborate ("wolf pack" activism) or follow the lead of other institutional investors, particularly activist hedge funds. We will turn to the latter aspect in greater detail in the following section.

9.2.3 Collaborative Engagement

Collaboration among shareholders is, at least in theory, an appropriate way to overcome or at least mitigate some of the disincentives to shareholder engagement described above.[19]

(i) First of all, voting rights and the associated informal influence over a company can be aggregated through collaborative interaction, thus creating greater potential for the exercise of influence than in the case of an investor acting individually.[20] In fact, several empirical studies showed that collaborative engagement is in any case more successful and usually also receives broader support from investors not directly involved in the collaboration.[21]

[15] Admittedly, other factors such as competition among asset managers may also play a role.

[16] Enriques/Romano, University of Illinois Law Review (2019), 223, 235 et seq. As to the present political backlash in the US, see Fn. 139.

[17] Balp/Strampelli, Ohio State Business Law Journal 14 (2020), 135, 159; *Hill*, Good Activists/Bad Activists: The Rise of International Stewardship Codes, ECGI Law Working Paper No. 368/2017.

[18] Enriques/Romano, University of Illinois Law Review (2019), 223, 236; see also Tuch, Boston University Law Review 99 (2019), 1459 (lack of institutional investor coordination led to the importance of proxy advisors).

[19] See Section 9.3.1. See also *Bowley/Hill*, Stewardship and Collective Action: The Australian Experience, ECGI Law Working Paper No. 491/2020, pp. 3, 13; Balp/Strampelli, Ohio State Business Law Journal 14 (2020), 135, 166; Christie, University of California Davis Law Review 55 (2021), 875, 907; Condon, Washington Law Review 95 (2020), 1, 61.

[20] *Dimson/Karakaş/Li*, Coordinated Engagements, ECGI Finance Working Paper No. 721/2021, pp. 2, 9 et seq.; Balp/Strampelli, Ohio State Business Law Journal 14 (2020), 135, 139, 185.

[21] Balp/Strampelli, Ohio State Business Law Journal 14 (2020), 135, 139 with further references to empirical studies. See Gillan/Starks, Journal of Financial Economics 57 (2000), 275; Dimson/Karakas/Li, The Review of Financial Studies 28 (2015), 3225; Kedia/Starks/Wang, Review of Corporate Finance Studies 10 (2021), 1; Doidge/Dyck/Mahmudi/Virani, Review of Finance (2019), 893, 894.

(ii) Second, collaboration may at least mitigate the free-rider problem since, by hypothesis, investors participating in the collaboration will not free-ride.[22] This reduces the *ex-ante* disincentives of those investors who have an interest in collaborative engagement.

(iii) Third, the costs of obtaining information may be lower than in the case of individual engagements, with collaborators being able to share resources, skills and expertise.[23] Furthermore, the expertise of the group may exceed the expertise of its individual members, which may also increase the overall value added of the engagement.[24]

(iv) Finally, collaboration contributes to risk-sharing among the collaborators.[25] For example, an individual investor may be deterred from engaging because of conflicts of interest, such as concerns about jeopardizing other business relationships with the target or its peers, and broader collaboration with other institutional investors could reduce this risk.[26]

Despite this potential mitigation of collective action problems and a reduction or sharing of information costs through collaborative action, the disincentives to engagement, especially among large, broadly diversified active and passive institutions, still work against – even collaborative – engagement.[27]

From an economic perspective, the first thing to note in this respect is that collaboration only eliminates the free-rider problem among the collaborating investors, but not for the group of collaborators vis-a-vis other investors.[28] The costs of collaboration and engagement are borne by a (potentially small) group while other investors equally benefit from the engagement of that group.[29] This can provide an incentive not to participate in the collaboration in the first place.

22 Balp/Strampelli, Ohio State Business Law Journal 14 (2020), 135, 166.

23 *Dimson/Karakaş/Li*, Coordinated Engagements, ECGI Finance Working Paper No. 721/2021, p. 2.

24 *Dimson/Karakaş/Li*, Coordinated Engagements, ECGI Finance Working Paper No. 721/2021, pp. 2, 9 et seq.; Balp/Strampelli, Ohio State Business Law Journal 14 (2020), 135, 191.

25 *Dimson/Karakaş/Li*, Coordinated Engagements, ECGI Finance Working Paper No. 721/2021, p. 10.

26 *Dimson/Karakaş/Li*, Coordinated Engagements, ECGI Finance Working Paper No. 721/2021, p. 9.

27 See Christie, University of California Davis Law Review 55 (2021), 875, 907.

28 *Dimson/Karakaş/Li*, Coordinated Engagements, ECGI Finance Working Paper No. 721/2021, p. 10.

29 *Ringe*, Investor-led Sustainability in Corporate Governance, ECGI Law Working Paper No. 615/2021, p. 33.

In addition, especially directly competing institutional investors, may refrain from collaboration at least as long as the potential financial gains of the collaboration are not clearly predictable *ex ante*. In addition, many investors or their management personnel may have a cultural reservation about working with competitors. Admittedly, this problem is less pronounced in the case of investors with very different business models, such as hedge funds and index funds.[30]

Moreover, collaborative engagement is time-consuming and costly, albeit less expensive than engagement on a stand-alone basis.[31]

9.3 ESG as a "Game Changer"?

Environmental, social, and governance-compliant investing ("ESG investing") has emerged as a major phenomenon in recent years,[32] with an almost exclusive focus on environmental and social aspects.[33]

While ESG investments to date represent only a small portion of the overall assets under management worldwide, and an even smaller portion of the total assets invested,[34] the sector is experiencing considerable

[30] *Dimson/Karakaş/Li*, Coordinated Engagements, ECGI Finance Working Paper No. 721/2021, p. 10.

[31] *Dimson/Karakaş/Li*, Coordinated Engagements, ECGI Finance Working Paper No. 721/2021, p. 10; *Ringe*, Investor-led Sustainability in Corporate Governance, ECGI Law Working Paper No. 615/2021, p. 33.

[32] Cf. BlackRock, Portfolio Perspectives, February 2020, Sustainability: The Tectonic Shift Transforming Investing, p. 3; *Ringe*, Investor-led Sustainability in Corporate Governance, ECGI Law Working Paper No. 615/2021, pp. 2 et seq.; Pedersen/Fitzgibbons/Pomorski, Journal of Financial Economics 142 (2021), 572; Friedman/Heinle, Review of Accounting Studies 21 (2016), 740, 741; Pastor/Stambaugh/Taylor, Journal of Financial Economics 142 (2021), 550; *Bowley/Hill*, The Global ESG Stewardship Ecosystem, ECGI Law Working Paper No. 660/2022; on the history of ESG investing, see Coffee, Columbia Business Law Review (2021), 602, 631 et seq.; Schanzenbach/Sitkoff, Stanford Law Review 72 (2020), 381, 392 et seq. On the origins of the term "ESG", see *Pollman*, The Origins and Consequences of the ESG Moniker, University of Pennsylvania Carey Law School ILE Research Paper No. 22–23.

[33] Because Governance aspects were already a major issue in the 1990s, the "G" in ESG – the modern "G", so to say – often relates to governmental features that facilitate or even support the implementation of the "E" and "S" aspects. Put differently, in contrast to the traditional G-features, for example independent outside directors, these modern G-features are not primarily designed with a view to improving a company's economic performance, but to support the introduction and effectiveness of the "E" and "S" features. A case in point is board gender diversity, which clearly demonstrates the interdependence with the S-aspect of gender equality in society at large.

[34] BlackRock, Portfolio Perspectives, February 2020, Sustainability: The Tectonic Shift Transforming Investing, p. 3, available at: www.blackrock.com/corporate/literature/whitepaper/bii-portfolio-perspectives-february-2020.pdf.

growth.[35] This development has been driven, in particular, by increasing demand. Key market observers expect that there will be a (re)allocation of capital on a massive scale to ESG-compliant investments in the near future as the result of fundamental social change.[36] In addition, regulatory measures are being, and will probably continue to be, introduced at the national, supranational and international level to further bolster this development.[37]

More specifically, shareholder engagement and collaborative shareholder engagement in favour of environmental and social (E&S) aspects is becoming increasingly common,[38] while shareholder engagement tackling governance issues has already been well under way since the 1990s. Environmental and social objectives together accounted for only about 10 per cent of all activist campaigns in 2016; this share had already risen to 20 per cent in 2021.[39] The US is clearly at the forefront of this trend, with 168 activist "E" or "S" campaigns in 2021, compared to only 25 in Europe, and 7 in Asia.[40]

On the other hand, more recently, politicians in the US and some activist fund managers have been complaining about "woke" companies;[41] a

[35] Global Sustainability Investment Alliance, Global Sustainability Investment Review 2020, available at: www.gsi-alliance.org/wp-content/uploads/2021/08/GSIR-20201.pdf; Capital Group, ESG Global Study 2022, available at: www.capitalgroup.com/content/dam/cgc/tenants/eacg/esg/global-study/esg-global-study-2022-full-report(en).pdf.

[36] BlackRock, Portfolio Perspectives, February 2020, Sustainability: The Tectonic Shift Transforming Investing, p. 3; cf. Barzuza/Curtis/Webber, Southern California Law Review 93 (2020), 1243.

[37] To date, the development in the EU has been driven much more by regulatory pressure than is the case in the US. Cf. Coffee, Columbia Business Law Review (2021), 602 (4, 8).

[38] For an overview, see, Condon, Washington Law Review 95 (2020), 1; Christie, University of California Davis Law Review 55 (2021), 875, 918; *Ringe*, Investor-led Sustainability in Corporate Governance, ECGI Law Working Paper No. 615/2021. For a critical assessment, see Mahoney/Mahoney, Columbia Business Law Review (2021), 840; Brest/Gilson/Wolfson, Journal of Corporation Law 44 (2018), 205. However, according to Lazard 2021 Review of Shareholder Activism, 43 per cent of activist campaigns in 2021 featured an M&A-related thesis.

[39] S&P Capital IQ, April 2022, available at: www.rbccm.com/en/insights/story.page?dcr=templatedata/article/insights/data/2022/04/esg_and_shareholder_activism.

[40] Insightia, ESG Activism Report 2022, available at: www.insightia.com/q12022/.

[41] See, for example, the complaint of *Vivek Ramaswamy* against Apple or Walt Disney (*Sorkin/Warner/Giang/Kessler/Gandel/de la Merced/Hirsch/Livni*, An Anti-E.S.G. Activist Takes on Apple and Disney, New York Times, 20 September 2022, available at: www.nytimes.com/2022/09/20/business/dealbook/anti-esg-campaign-fund-etf-disney-apple.html). So far, only a very few hedge fund leaders have taken up the call against "woke capitalism". But certain media outlets are giving them significant attention, which amplifies their message. On the issue, see *Bowley/Hill*, The Global ESG Stewardship Ecosystem, ECGI Law Working paper No. 660/2022, p. 33. The backlash is a potent

development that must be carefully observed as well and that may present companies and institutions with a number of new challenges.

9.3.1 *Why Might Institutional Investors Be Interested in ES(G)?*

Why might institutional investors – and, in particular, broadly diversified passive and active funds or their managers – be interested in E&S issues, and is it conceivable that the resultant incentives will lead to increased E&S engagement and collaboration? Irrespective of altruistic motivations[42] – the credibility of which is questioned by some, and the legal admissibility of which would also be highly questionable in light of fiduciary duties[43] – the following economic reasons, in particular, are put forward for such interest in E&S investing[44]:

- Prospect of higher returns[45]
- Reduction of systemic risk[46]

force in the current US political environment and could take root in Europe, too. For an overview on more recent state regulation of ESG investment decision-making by public retirement plans see https://corpgov.law.harvard.edu/2022/10/25/state-regulation-of-esg-investment-decision-making-by-public-retirement-plans/ (Harvard Law School Forum on Corporate Governance posted by *Joshua Lichtenstein, Michael Littenberg* and *Reagan Haas*, Ropes & Gray LLP, on 25 October 2022).

[42] Cf. *Azar/Duro/Kadack/Ormazabal*, The Big Three and Corporate Carbon Emissions Around the World, ECGI Finance Working Paper No. 715/2020, p. 2.

[43] Schanzenbach/Sitkoff, Stanford Law Review 72 (2020), 381; *Gosling/MacNeil*, Can Investors Save the Planet? – NZAMI and Fiduciary Duty, SSRN-Working Paper, Nov. 2022, available at: https://papers.ssrn.com/sol3/papers.cfm?abstract_id=4277960; for a comprehensive overview, see Freshfields Bruckhaus Deringer, A legal framework for the integration of environmental, social and governance issues into institutional investment: Produced for the Asset Management Working Group of the UNEP Finance Initiative, October 2005, p. 30 et seq., available at: www.unepfi.org/fileadmin/documents/freshfields_legal_resp_20051123.pdf.

[44] Cf. *Azar/Duro/Kadack/Ormazabal*, The Big Three and Corporate Carbon Emissions Around the World, ECGI Finance Working Paper No. 715/2020, p. 2; *Bowley/Hill*, The Global ESG Stewardship Ecosystem, ECGI Law Working paper No. 660/2022, p. 4 et seq.

[45] In empirical financial market research, the question of what, if any, effect the pursuit of ES(G) objectives by companies has on cash flows and the cost of capital is a source of great controversy, even though some studies do support the idea of the existence of theoretically plausible transmission channels. However, no unambiguous empirical evidence as yet exists with regard to a correlation between ESG factors and stock market performance. See, e.g., Zerbib, Review of Finance 26 (2022), 1; Albuquerque/Koskinen/Zhang, Management Science 65 (2019), 4451, 4452.

[46] Condon, Washington Law Review 95 (2020), 1, 18 et seq.; Coffee, Columbia Business Law Review 602 (2021), 13 et seq., 28 et seq.; Gordon, Journal of Corporation Law 47 (2022),

- Forestalling of regulation[47]
- Higher fees[48]
- Reputational concerns
- Rising demand (from millennials)[49]

9.3.2 *Incentives for Collaborative Engagement*

Irrespective of any lasting inconclusiveness as regards the incentives for ESG engagement in general, at least with regard to *collaborative* ESG engagement, some recent studies suggest (i) a higher success rate of collaborative engagements and (ii) a sustainable positive effect of collaborative ESG campaigns on share price performance.

In an empirical study on a total of 2,152 incidences of engagement by an investment company with US target companies published in 2015, *Dimson*, *Karakaş* and *Li* found that collaboration leads to a higher success rate for E&S engagements, in particular.[50] In addition, the authors found that successful engagement led to positive abnormal returns, improved performance and governance, and increased institutional ownership, while unsuccessful engagement led to zero abnormal returns.[51] Moreover, the authors show that, particularly with regard to "E" and "S" engagement, coordination is key, much more so than in the area of "G" engagement.[52] This would appear to be the case because E&S engagement requires the involvement of a greater number of investors in

627, 648 et seq.; see also *Ringe*, Investor-led Sustainability in Corporate Governance, ECGI Law Working Paper No. 615/2021, pp. 15 et seq. See, also, Enriques/Romano, Arizona Law Review 64 (2022), 51. For a critique, see Tallarita, Vanderbilt Law Review 76 (2023), 511.

[47] Davies, in *Katelouzou/Puchniak*, Global Shareholder Stewardship, 2022, pp. 44, 62 et seq.; Barzuza/Curtis/Webber, Southern California Law Review 93 (2020), 1243, 1280.

[48] *Ringe*, Investor-led Sustainability in Corporate Governance, ECGI Law Working Paper No. 615/2021, pp. 10 et seq.; *Azar/Duro/Kadack/Ormazabal*, The Big Three and Corporate Carbon Emissions Around the World, ECGI Finance Working Paper No. 715/2020, p. 2.

[49] See, in particular, Barzuza/Curtis/Webber, Southern California Law Review 93 (2020), 1243, 1249 et seq.; see also Christie, University of California Davis Law Review 55 (2021), 875, 910; *Ringe*, Investor-led Sustainability in Corporate Governance, ECGI Law Working Paper No. 615/2021, pp. 12 et seq.; *Azar/Duro/Kadack/Ormazabal*, The Big Three and Corporate Carbon Emissions Around the World, ECGI Finance Working Paper No. 715/2020, p. 8.

[50] Dimson/Karakas/Li, The Review of Financial Studies 28 (2015), 3225, 3241 et seq.

[51] Dimson/Karakas/Li, The Review of Financial Studies 28 (2015), 3225, 3252 et seq.

[52] Dimson/Karakas/Li, The Review of Financial Studies 28 (2015), 3225, 3228.

order to convince a portfolio company to tackle identified E&S issues rather than corporate governance issues.[53] Perhaps lack of collaboration was one reason why *Carl Icahn*'s campaign at McDonald's, which he ran alone, failed.[54] The general findings of the 2015 study were broadly confirmed by another study by *Dimson, Karakaş* and *Li* which also observed a significant increase in abnormal stock returns following *collaborative* engagement characterized by a clear lead figure among collaborating institutional investors.[55] In contrast, they observed no change in the financial performance of the target firms in the case of engagement without a lead investor.[56] Overall, these results suggest that coordinated engagement is value enhancing for shareholders and/or successful, especially when headed up by a lead investor.

Given these empirical findings, if institutional investors' interest in ESG were indeed motivated by some of the explanations outlined above, they should definitely think about collaborating with others. These studies indicate the achievement of significant abnormal returns with collaborative engagement with lead investors in particular, and, hence, may emphasize the real-world incentives to engage in, and even to organize, collaborative efforts. Whether the collaborative efforts will aim at engaging other hedge funds or, specifically, diversified funds, remains to be seen.

However, the increased success rate of collaborative engagement and the sizeable incentives, at least for lead investors within a collaboration, does not alter the fact that broadly diversified active and passive funds have no interest in increasing the financial performance of individual portfolio companies or in incurring costs for this purpose. In the absence of reliable signals as to the quality of the specialist funds, large institutional investors will be unable to determine which hedge fund is worth following without incurring additional costs (an information asymmetry problem, which could – absent a credible way to signal quality to the

[53] Dimson/Karakas/Li, The Review of Financial Studies 28 (2015), 3225, 3228.

[54] See *Mundy*, Carl Icahn Wades into the ESG Debate, FT-online, 29 April 2022. Carl Icahn had nominated two directors to the company's board as part of an animal rights campaign. When Icahn announced his campaign, he owned only about 200 shares of McDonald's, which has a market capitalization of more than $180 billion. In the end, he got just one per cent of McDonald's investors to back his campaign.

[55] *Dimson/Karakaş/Li*, Coordinated Engagements, ECGI Finance Working Paper No. 721/ 2021.

[56] *Dimson/Karakaş/Li*, Coordinated Engagements, ECGI Finance Working Paper No. 721/ 2021.

market – also become a "market for lemons" problem in an increasingly flooded market). Therefore, the prospect of achieving higher returns for individual companies particularly applies to specialist hedge funds and not to institutional investors in general, and as such can hardly be classified as a game changer.

However, as far as the incentives of large active and passive funds and their managers are concerned, the increasing *demand* for ESG-compliant investments and ESG-compliant behaviour will perhaps result in more than mere lip service and letters to CEOs. The current level of support for ESG initiatives by the Big Three – which in the US, for example, has declined in 2022 compared to 2021[57] – must not signify a fundamental change. The recent downturn in support for shareholder proposals in the US may well be due to the proponents' success in the previous year: the high support levels in 2021, along with more lenient SEC guidance, led to more proposals being filed for the 2022 proxy season, some of which pushed the line too far (too prescriptive) for many institutional investors to support.[58] On the other hand, political forces, particularly in the US, and to some degree even value hedge funds, increasingly complain publicly about "woke" corporations and a too heavy focus on E&S issues to the detriment of shareholder value.[59] The next few years will show whether E&S, in particular, can truly be a game changer.

9.4 Forms and Strategies of Collaboration

The E&S engagement that has been observed recently is characterized by the apparent proliferation of – to some extent novel forms of – collaboration between institutional investors.[60] In the following, we present several forms of collaborative shareholder engagement that have been observed in recent years.

[57] Insightia, ESG Activism Report 2022, available at: www.insightia.com/q12022/; *Masters*, BlackRock Pulls Back Support for Climate and Social Resolutions, FT-online, 26 July 2022.

[58] But see also *Briere/Pouget/Schmalz/Ureche-Rangau*, Do the Big Three Vote to Curb Climate Change? (21 April 2022), available at SSRN: https://ssrn.com/abstract=4245612, questioning the universal owner/reduction of systemic risk logic by showing that the Big Three support for shareholder resolutions tackling climate issues is lower than in other fund families.

[59] See Ibid at Fn. 92.

[60] *Ringe*, Investor-led Sustainability in Corporate Governance, ECGI Law Working Paper No. 615/2021, pp. 20 et seq.; *Bowley/Hill*, The Global ESG Stewardship Ecosystem, ECGI Law Working paper No. 660/2022.

In addition, we venture an outlook on potentially emergent types of collaborations. The increasing public concern for climate change leads us to expect a potential increase in collaborations between investors and environmental activists, such as *Fridays for Future*.

9.4.1 The Big Three

A special role in ESG engagement is attributed to the Big Three.[61] This is due to their special position (too big to be passive), the political and public pressure and the associated reputational effects to which they are subject, and possibly also to their special position as universal owners. To date, at least as far as collaborations are concerned, the Big Three have made their presence felt by supporting the campaigns of activist investors – especially ESG-funds. In contrast, not much is known about collaboration among the Big Three themselves, although at least in the context and aftermath of State Street's Fearless Girl campaign, there has been some talk of "concerted" action by the Big Three.[62] Independently of whether they had acted in concert or not, the pressure which has concurrently been exerted on portfolio companies in the US led to more than 300 public companies revamping their boards and electing at least one female director within just one year.[63] This shows that, unsurprisingly, the Big Three are able to exert even greater influence when they pursue certain goals jointly or at least in parallel.

9.4.2 Specialist Funds Taking the Lead: The Good Wolf Pack?

In the area of collaborative ESG engagement, we observe specialist funds increasingly working together, sometimes with specific, not exclusively financial, objectives. Unlike the traditional wolf packs, collaboration is more open here. The participating funds explicitly work together, exchange information – also via institutionalized platforms (V.4.) – and, like in traditional wolf packs, use their combined influence to bring about ESG-compliant behaviour on the part of portfolio companies.

[61] On the Big Three phenomenon, see *Lund/Robertson*, Chapter 5 in this volume. At least as far as shareholder resolutions are concerned, their special role is quite questionable. See *Briere/Pouget/Schmalz/Ureche-Rangau*, Do the Big Three Vote to Curb Climate Change? (21 April 2022), available at SSRN: https://ssrn.com/abstract=4245612.

[62] *Gormley/Gupta/Matsa/Mortal/Yang*, ECGI Finance Working Paper No. 714/2020, p. 1.

[63] *Ringe*, Investor-led Sustainability in Corporate Governance, ECGI Law Working Paper No. 615/2021, p. 7.

In this context, traditional value hedge funds have also participated in such "good"[64] wolf packs or even taken on a leading role.[65] However, after a very successful year for E&S engagement, especially on the part of hedge or ESG-funds, ESG engagement has decreased in 2022 – due to, among other things, the changes to the geopolitical landscape. Nevertheless, 2022 witnessed some spectacular instances of engagement by specialized activist funds.[66]

9.4.3 *Coalitions between Non-activist Institutional Investors and Non-activist Investors and Hedge or ESG Funds*

In the area of E&S engagement, large institutional investors ("mainstream" institutional investors[67]), especially pension funds and other mutual funds, are a major driving force.[68] Numerous – particularly successful – campaigns have been led by such collaborations in recent years. Examples include the Investors for Opioid and Pharmaceutical Accountability campaigns and the Human Capital Management Coalition. Such collaborations between institutional investors must – quite often – be supplemented by coordination with the respective asset managers of the institutional owners, which in practice means additional effort and often complications.

Besides, in E&S engagement (much like in traditional shareholder value engagement), the interaction between specialized (hedge) funds and large institutional investors is hugely important.

[64] Cf. also *Hill*, Good Activist/Bad Activist: The Rise of International Stewardship Codes, ECGI Law Working Paper No. 368/2017.

[65] One may recall, for example, Elliott Management's engagement against Evergy in early 2020, in which Elliott was supported by Bluescape Energy Partners. See also *Fletcher*, Ethical CSR Focus Triggers Hostile Investor Activism, Study Finds, Financial Times, 3 August 2020, available at: www.ft.com/content/2ab06d51-bb6d-4f41-88cf-b220b2a4bcd1.

[66] Among others, ThirdPoint's call for a split-up of Shell, and the engagements with Total, Standard Chartered and Sainsbury's, each of which was carried out by a collaboration of specialized funds coordinating with each other, deserve mention. See *Reed*, Third Point, an Activist Investor, Is Calling for a Breakup of Royal Dutch Shell, New York Times, 28 Oct. 2021, available at: www.nytimes.com/2021/10/28/business/third-point-shell-breakup.html.

[67] *Bowley/Hill*, The Global ESG Stewardship Ecosystem, ECGI Law Working paper No. 660/2022, pp. 7 et seq.

[68] See *Bowley/Hill*, The Global ESG Stewardship Ecosystem, ECGI Law Working paper No. 660/2022, pp. 7 et seq.; see, furthermore, PPI, Engaging with ESG: Climate Change, 2021, with a thorough investigation into the engagements of pension schemes available at: www.pensionspolicyinstitute.org.uk/media/0jejbvic/20210218-engaging-with-esg-climate-change-report-final.pdf.

In this respect, Engine No. 1's engagement with ExxonMobil has certainly received the most attention. The small ESG-hedge fund, with a share of only about 0.02 per cent of the voting rights, succeeded in gaining the support of huge institutional investors and, thus, in pushing through three of its four proposals for the board of ExxonMobil at the annual general meeting.[69] This was preceded by increased engagement by Engine No. 1, paralleled by numerous – mainly climate-related – criticisms and calls against ExxonMobil by other actors. Engine No. 1 was supported from the beginning by CalSTRS, which shows active collaboration between an ESG fund and a large institutional investor, especially in this still informal phase.[70]

Other cases of a successful collaboration between hedge (ESG) funds and large institutional investors in terms of E&S engagement include the cases of Green Century Equity Fund vs. Procter & Gamble,[71] the engagement on "say on climate" of The Children's Investment Fund (TCI) towards several large US companies,[72] the engagement against the management of Rio Tinto,[73] and the engagement of *Mike Cannon-Brookes* with AGL Energy. *Cannon-Brookes* was able to push through his climate-related goals – at least in part – and force important board members to resign, primarily with the backing of specialized funds and a large Australian pension fund.[74]

9.4.4 Institutionalized Platforms and Intermediaries

A special feature of ESG collaboration is certainly the establishment of institutionalized platforms for organizing collaborative engagement.[75]

[69] *Ringe*, Investor-led Sustainability in Corporate Governance, ECGI Law Working Paper No. 615/2021, p. 20.

[70] *Ringe*, Investor-led Sustainability in Corporate Governance, ECGI Law Working Paper No. 615/2021, p. 20.

[71] *Gray/ Temple-West*, Investor Rebellion at Procter & Gamble over Environmental Concerns, FT-Online, 14 Oct. 2020, www.ft.com/content/1dd92502-e95b-4c21-be1c-c18a598acf1a. See also in this regard *Ringe*, Investor-led Sustainability in Corporate Governance, ECGI Law Working Paper No. 615/2021, p. 22.

[72] *Ringe*, Investor-led Sustainability in Corporate Governance, ECGI Law Working Paper No. 615/2021, p. 22; *Bowley/Hill*, The Global ESG Stewardship Ecosystem, ECGI Law Working paper No. 660/2022, pp. 6 et seq.

[73] For a detailed assessment, see *Bowley/Hill*, The Global ESG Stewardship Ecosystem, ECGI Law Working paper No. 660/2022, pp. 19 et seq.

[74] For further details, see *Fernyhough/Fildes*, Tech Billionaire Wins Activist Fight Against Australia's Biggest Polluter, FT-online, 30 May 2022.

[75] *Ringe*, Investor-led Sustainability in Corporate Governance, ECGI Law Working Paper No. 615/2021, pp. 25, 42; *Dimson/Karakaş/Li*, Coordinated Engagements, ECGI Finance

These platforms allow their participants to organize collaborations of the kind described herein, while also drawing on the possibilities and resources of a third-party platform operator.

One of the most established platforms in this respect is the Principles for Responsible Investment (PRI) Collaboration Platform, which was created by investors in cooperation with, or with the support of, the United Nations Environment Programme's (UNEP) Finance Initiative and the United Nations Global Compact (UNGC).[76] The PRI Collaboration Platform is currently the largest platform[77] for organizing collaborative engagements – of varying intensity – and for sharing responsible investment-related issues.[78]

In their recent working paper, *Dimson*, *Karakaş* and *Li* examined a total of 31 PRI-coordinated engagement projects in the areas of ESG and (reflecting the UN origins of the PRI) work related to the UNGC and its sustainable development goals.[79] As has already been touched upon, they concluded that collaborative engagements are particularly successful when a lead investor leads the coordination and the investor group – unsurprisingly – has a larger voting stake in the target company.[80] Moreover, their research indicates that a significant incentive for involvement in an engagement stems from the location of the investors, in particular, from whether the potentially participating investors are located in the same country.[81] This finding is in line with an application of network theory. Since institutional investors are involved in a complex network of relationships, these relationships have a very decisive influence on their behaviour.[82]

Working Paper No. 721/2021, pp. 14 et seq.; Balp/Strampelli, Ohio State Business Law Journal 14 (2020), 135, 181.

[76] *Ringe*, Investor-led Sustainability in Corporate Governance, ECGI Law Working Paper No. 615/2021, p. 42; *Bowley/Hill*, The Global ESG Stewardship Ecosystem, ECGI Law Working paper No. 660/2022, pp. 12 et seq.

[77] In 2021, there was a total of 3,826 signatories to the Principles of Responsible Investment.

[78] For details, see *Ringe*, Chapter 8 in this volume.

[79] *Dimson/Karakaş/Li*, Coordinated Engagements, ECGI Finance Working Paper No. 721/2021, p. 1.

[80] *Dimson/Karakaş/Li*, Coordinated Engagements, ECGI Finance Working Paper No. 721/2021, p. 30.

[81] *Dimson/Karakaş/Li*, Coordinated Engagements, ECGI Finance Working Paper No. 721/2021, p. 26.

[82] Enriques/Romano, University of Illinois Law Review (2019), 223, 242 et seq.; cf. also *Bowley/Hill*, The Global ESG Stewardship Ecosystem, ECGI Law Working paper No. 660/2022, pp. 24 et seq.

Another growing platform is the Climate Change 100+ initiative, which has been joined by more than 600 institutional investors with a total of more than $65 trillion in assets under management,[83] including BlackRock, the California Public Employees' Retirement System (CalPERS), Fidelity, and J.P. Morgan Asset Management. Climate Change 100+ also provides a platform for collaboration.[84] Recently, however, criticism has been voiced about the sincerity of some of the signatories.[85]

In addition to communication platforms, there are also intermediaries that actively seek to organize ESG-driven collaborations, such as ShareAction, with participation by, or involvement of, private investors. Earlier this year, for example, a coalition of investors organized by ShareAction issued a shareholder resolution calling on Unilever to set ambitious targets for increasing the proportion of healthy food items in its product range. This resolution was supported by 11 key institutional investors (including Candriam, Dutch asset manager ACTIAM, US healthcare provider Trinity Health, the UK's Guy's & St Thomas' Foundation, asset manager CCLA Good Investment, and the Greater Manchester Pension Fund). In response to the resolution, Unilever has committed to disclosing the healthiness of its products measured on the basis of major government-endorsed nutrient profile models – as requested by the resolution – as well as their own internal metrics. It will also publish annual assessments of this data for 16 of its key strategic markets.[86]

9.4.5 *Investor Organizations*

Some investor organizations with a particular focus on ES(G) issues have been established in recent years. These include the Asia Investor Group

[83] *Mundy/Temple-West/Talman*, 'It's Greenwashing': Climate Action 100+ Members Let Standards Slip, FT-online, 2 February 2022; *Ringe*, Investor-led Sustainability in Corporate Governance, ECGI Law Working Paper No. 615/2021, p. 25; *Bowley/Hill*, The Global ESG Stewardship Ecosystem, ECGI Law Working paper No. 660/2022, pp. 24 et seq.

[84] For more details, see Chapter 8 by *Wolf-Georg Ringe* in this volume; moreover, *Ringe*, Investor-led Sustainability in Corporate Governance, ECGI Law Working Paper No. 615/2021, p. 25.

[85] *Mundy/Temple-West/Talman*, 'It's Greenwashing': Climate Action 100+ Members Let Standards Slip, FT-online 2 February 2022.

[86] For details, see https://shareaction.org/shareholder-resolutions/shareholder-resolutions-2022.

on Climate Change (AIGCC), an initiative with 49 members representing more than $11 trillion in assets under management; the Investor Group on Climate Change (IGCC), a collaboration of Australian and New Zealand institutional investors focused on the investment implications of climate change; and the Institutional Investors Group on Climate Change (IIGCC), a European membership organization for climate change investor collaboration with more than 270 members, mainly pension funds and asset managers, with over €35 trillion in assets under management.

9.4.6 *Collaboration between Institutional Investors and the Public, Climate Activists, and Environmental Organizations*

The increasing public focus and pressure on climate protection issues, in particular, leads us to expect entirely new forms of collaboration, namely the involvement of the public or environmental organizations as collaborators in shareholder engagement. We have already seen in the recent past that public pressure, also channelled through climate action initiatives – such as Fridays for Future – have been able to exert considerable pressure on companies. One example is the debate surrounding a coal mine in Australia supplied by Siemens, in the course of which the former Siemens CEO "offered" climate activist *Luisa Neubauer* a seat on the supervisory board of Siemens Energy.[87] If such climate protests are accompanied by pressure from investors, they can certainly have a considerable reinforcing effect on the attainment of their underlying objectives.

Moreover, investors, on the one hand, and environmental protection organizations, on the other, could in the future increasingly engage in work-sharing in the context of their activist endeavours.[88] One example of this would be the internal pressure by investors, accompanied by the filing of environmental complaints by external parties (as in the Shell case in the Netherlands[89]). In this respect, too, external pressure from environmental organizations and the public could significantly increase the clout of activist shareholders.

[87] See, e.g., *Connolly*, Climate Activist Turns Down Siemens' Offer of Seat on Energy Board, The Guardian, 13 January 2020, available at: www.theguardian.com/environment/2020/jan/13/climate-activist-turns-down-siemens-offer-of-seat-on-energy-board.

[88] Cf. Christie, University of California Davis Law Review 55 (2021), 875, 934 et seq.

[89] On the case, see, e.g., Mayer, Transnational Environmental Law 11 (2022), 407.

9.5 Obstacles to (Effective) Collaboration

In the following, we focus on legal obstacles, knowing full well that legal obstacles can also be economic ones, as they imply compliance risks. We only discuss obstacles that impede collaboration and not engagement more broadly. In the context of legal obstacles, the latter include fiduciary duties owed by institutional investors to end investors[90] or to the company or other shareholders, and proxy solicitation rules.[91]

Most of the legal obstacles described below are in place in the US, as well as in the EU and the UK. Nevertheless, there are certainly differences in substantive law and also in enforcement issues, particularly between the EU/UK, on the one hand, and the US, on the other. Our analysis focuses on the regulatory barriers that exist in the EU and, Brexit notwithstanding, still exist in the UK.

9.5.1 Acting in Concert

The focal point of the discussion on legal hurdles is the danger that the collaborative interaction will be classified as "acting in concert", which can have consequences both (i) for the disclosure of shareholdings and (ii) at least in the EU and in the UK, within the framework of takeover law.[92] ESMA has simplified matters in practice, at least as far as acting in concert under Directive 2004/25/EC of 21 April 2004 on takeover bids (Takeover Bids Directive) is concerned, by publishing a so-called White List.

(i) First, with respect to the *disclosure of shareholdings* and the obligation of parties acting in concert, pursuant to Art. 10(a) of the

[90] Schanzenbach/Sitkoff, Stanford Law Review 72 (2020), 381, 399 et seq. with further references; an overview over several jurisdictions is available in the report by Freshfields Bruckhaus Deringer, "A legal framework for the integration of environmental, social and governance issues into institutional investment: Produced for the Asset Management Working Group of the UNEP Finance Initiative", October 2005, pp. 30 et seq., available at: www.unepfi.org/fileadmin/documents/freshfields_legal_resp_20051123.pdf.

[91] Christie, University of California Davis Law Review 55 (2021), 875, 942; *Ringe*, Investor-led Sustainability in Corporate Governance, ECGI Law Working Paper No. 615/2021, p. 40.

[92] See Balp/Strampelli, Ohio State Business Law Journal 14 (2020), 135, 203; *Ringe*, Investor-led Sustainability in Corporate Governance, ECGI Law Working Paper No. 615/2021, pp. 40 et seq.; cf. Taleska, European Business Organization Law Review 19 (2018), 797; see also *Bowley/Hill*, Stewardship and Collective Action: The Australian Experience, ECGI Law Working Paper No. 491/2020, pp. 27 et seq. for the Australian perspective.

Transparency Directive, two or more persons will be deemed to be acting in concert where they have "concluded an agreement" "which obliges them to adopt, by concerted exercise of the voting rights they hold, a *lasting* common policy towards the management of the issuer in question". The requirement of a "lasting common policy" is intended, in particular, to rule out collaboration in individual cases.[93] Especially in the case of ES(G)-related activism, however, the line between an individual case and a "lasting common policy" is very thin. For example, where the commitment in question is aimed at bringing about a general change in corporate policy, even if it is limited to a one-off action against the company concerned, there is uncertainty as to whether it crosses the threshold to a lasting common policy. However, at least the German Federal Court of Justice (*Bundesgerichtshof*) understands the "individual case criterion" as being a purely formal one. The intensity of the influence exercised and the sustained nature of its effects are not decisive.[94] The German Federal Financial Supervisory Authority (BaFin) has just recently confirmed, that it follows this interpretation in its supervisory practice.[95] If more national supervisory authorities were to uphold this line of argument in their interpretation of Art. 10 of the Transparency Directive, this would considerably pave the way for (substantial) ESG engagement in particular.

(ii) These and other remaining doubts as to the interpretation of the term "acting in concert" under the Transparency Directive and also under the Takeover Bids Directive (Art. 2(d) of the Takeover Bids Directive) obviously create considerable legal uncertainty for the practice of collaborative engagement. For market players, such uncertainty is unfortunate to say the least. Even taking into account that it is rather difficult to show that companies have been acting in concert, at least under the current EU regime (in this respect, the

[93] See, in particular, German Federal Court of Justice (Bundesgerichtshof), BGHZ 169, 98, 107 = Neue Juristische Wochenschrift Rechtsprechungs – Report 2007, 1179, 1181 et seq.; Higher Regional Court (Oberlandesgericht) of Frankfurt Neue Juristische Wochenschrift 2004, 3716 on the German Securities Acquisition and Takeover Act.

[94] German Federal Court of Justice (Bundesgerichtshof) Neue Zeitschrift für Gesellschaftsrecht 2018, 1350 paras. 34 et seq.

[95] See BaFin, Collaborative Engagement, 20 March 2023, available at: www.bafin.de/SharedDocs/Veroeffentlichungen/DE/Fachartikel/2023/fa_bj_2303_Collaborative_Engagement.html.

TCI/Deutsche Börse case of 2006 might come to mind[96]), less risk averse investors should keep in mind that the ECJ has adopted a rather simplified approach to the discharging of the EU Commission's burden of proof under antitrust law with regard to the existence of agreements,[97] a practice which could conceivably also be extended to capital markets law.

Unsurprisingly, then, the European Commission had already stated in 2012 that clarification of the concept of "acting in concert" was required in order to reduce uncertainty for international investors who want to cooperate on corporate governance issues but feel deterred from doing so for fear of a mandatory offer.[98]

Following on from this, ESMA has drawn up a White List of collaborations or collaborative engagements that are generally not intended to constitute acting in concert within the meaning of the Takeover Bids Directive.[99] However, the "White List" is not legally binding for the interpretation of the relevant implementation provisions of the Takeover Bids Directive in the Member States and certainly not for the UK. Moreover, it does not, in principle, provide any guidance for the interpretation of the Transparency Directive. It does, however, provide some indication as to how ESMA would assess and evaluate collaborative engagements, which is helpful in practice. In addition, in its recently published "Sustainable Finance Roadmap 2022–2024", ESMA has indicated in its list of planned activities and deliverables that it will contribute to "developing further guidance in the area of stewardship and engagement to ensure acting in concert does not impede collaborative

[96] In 2005, TCI and other hedge funds engaged with Deutsche Börse to prevent it from taking over the London Stock Exchange. A subsequent investigation by BaFin did not find facts to prove "beyond reasonable doubt" that the hedge funds acted in concert within the meaning of the rules in force at the time. On the case, see Grant/Kirchmaier/Kirshner, EBOR 10 (2009), 233, 248.

[97] Cf. ECJ, judgment of 17 May 2013 – Trelleborg Industrie and Trelleborg v. Commission, Joint Cases T-147/09 and T-148/09.

[98] Cf. COM(2012)347; 2012 Action Plan on European Company Law and Corporate Governance.

[99] ESMA, Public Statement – Information on shareholder cooperation and acting in concert under the Takeover Bids Directive, ESMA/2014/677, 20 June 2014 (last updated: 8 January 2019), available at: www.esma.europa.eu/sites/default/files/library/esma-2014-677-rev_public_statement_concerning_shareholder_cooperation_and_acting_in_concert.pdf. See also Balp/Strampelli, Ohio State Business Law Journal 14 (2020), 135, 203; *Ringe*, Investor-led Sustainability in Corporate Governance, ECGI Law Working Paper No. 615/2021, p. 41.

engagement by investors around common sustainability goals".[100] BaFin has already taken the lead in this respect and recently issued specific guidance on collaborative ESG engagement.[101]

9.5.2 Insider Regulation

Another fairly significant obstacle to collaborative engagement in the EU is insider trading law.[102] In this context, one must distinguish from the outset between (i) inside information that individual investors obtain about the issuer or its financial instruments and (want to) exchange with other investors as part of the collaboration and (ii) inside information, the precise subject of which is the planned collaborative engagement and which is therefore "produced" by the collaborating investors themselves.

(i) As regards inside information which individual investors have obtained and which they intend to share with other investors for collaborative purposes, the relevant provisions in European Union market abuse law are Arts. 14 and 10 of the Regulation (EU) No 596/2014 of 16 April 2014 on market abuse (MAR). Pursuant to these provisions, inside information – regardless of how it was obtained – may not be unlawfully (selectively) disclosed to other persons, while Art. 10 of the MAR stipulates that a lawful disclosure is one "made in the normal exercise of an employment, a profession or duties".[103] Thus, MAR recognizes situations in which the interest in disclosure may outweigh the market's interest in containing the disclosure of information.[104] As regards the interests of the affected parties, the ECJ's Grøngaard and Bang decision clarified that the legitimate interest in disclosure can be based on national law, while the interest

[100] ESMA, Sustainable Finance Roadmap 2022–2024, ESMA30-379-1051, p. 29.
[101] See BaFin, Collaborative Engagement, 20 March 2023, available at: www.bafin.de/SharedDocs/Veroeffentlichungen/DE/Fachartikel/2023/fa_bj_2303_Collaborative_Engagement.html.
[102] Cf. Balp/Strampelli, Ohio State Business Law Journal 14 (2020), 135, 190; *Ringe*, Investor-led Sustainability in Corporate Governance, ECGI Law Working Paper No. 615/2021, p. 41; Taleska, European Company and Financial Law Review 17 (2020), 558, 580 et seq.
[103] For more details, see Mosca, in *Ventoruzzo/Mock*, Market Abuse Regulation, 2nd ed. 2022, Art. 10 note 10.46 et seq.; Gerner-Beuerle, in *Lehmann/Kumpan*, European Financial Services Law, 1st ed. 2020, Art. 10 MAR note 4 et seq.
[104] Cf. Klöhn in *Klöhn*, Marktmissbrauchsverordnung, 2nd ed. 2023, Art. 10 note 36.

in the confidentiality of information as well as the standards for balancing the interests are to be derived from EU law.[105]

The interest of an individual investor in sharing inside information with the collaboration partners may be justified, since it serves the investors' ulterior purpose of collaborative engagement, namely to facilitate their pursuit of certain legitimate (economic) objectives.[106] However, two limitations apply: (i) the individual investor may not already have obtained the information by way of a violation of the prohibition of disclosure by, for example, the issuer in the context of an impermissible selective disclosure of information to individual investors;[107] and (ii) the investor sharing the information may not be in violation of a confidentiality agreement.[108]

(ii) With respect to information about an imminent collaborative engagement or concrete activist plans of the collaborators, the legal position is even more uncertain. Indeed, such knowledge may also qualify as inside information within the meaning of Art. 7 of the MAR. This is because the rationale for prohibiting insider dealing in the EU regime – which follows a purely market-based approach rather than the fiduciary approach typical of the US system – is that if insiders can exploit their information advantage, uninformed outsiders risk systematically operating at an information disadvantage. Consequently, it is immaterial from whom the insider has obtained the relevant information and whether such person is in breach of a fiduciary duty. Even self-produced information, such as knowledge about one's own future actions, can be considered inside information. Therefore, knowledge of an imminent engagement qualifies as inside information, implying a prohibition both on trading (Art. 14(a) and (b) of the MAR) and on the selective disclosure of such information (Art. 14(c) of the MAR), in each case with an inhibitory effect on any intended collaborative engagement.

[105] ECJ judgment of 22 November 2005 – Case C-384/02, OJ 2005, I-09939 paras. 40, 44, 47 et seq., 50–52 (Grøngaard and Bang). For more details, see Klöhn in *Klöhn*, Marktmissbrauchsverordnung, 2nd ed. 2023, Art. 10 note 38 et seq.

[106] Cf. Mosca, in Ventoruzzo/Mock, Market Abuse Regulation, 2nd ed. 2022, Art. 10 note 10.88.

[107] See Klöhn, in Klöhn, Marktmissbrauchsverordnung, 2nd ed. 2023, Art. 10 note 187 et seq.; Hirt/Hopt/Mattheus, Die Aktiengesellschaft, 2016, 725; Bachmann, in Vereinigung für Gesellschaftsrecht Tagungsband, 2016, 135; Fleischer/Bauer/Wansleben, Der Betrieb, 2015, 360; Leyendecker-Langner, Neue Zeitschrift für Gesellschaftsrecht, 2015, 44.

[108] See Klöhn, in Klöhn, Marktmissbrauchsverordnung, 2nd ed. 2023, Art. 10 note 59 et seq.

It is true that Art. 9(5) of the MAR provides that the mere fact that a person uses their knowledge of their decision to acquire or dispose of financial instruments in acquiring or disposing of those financial instruments does not in itself constitute use of inside information. However, the exception provided for by Art. 9(5) of the MAR only applies to a person's own decision, and not to a collusive decision, which affects not only that person's own decision but also that of a third party.[109] In the Georgakis case before the ECJ, the main question posed – and answered in the affirmative by the Court – was whether inside information can also consist of a decision to "support" a share price by several members of a group who agree among themselves to artificially influence the price of securities.[110] Moreover, information about upcoming collaborative engagements is frequently not limited to one's own, or to joint *trading*, decisions, but also comprises information about other activist activities, such as the introduction of an agenda item at the AGM or the removal of a board member.

All in all, at least as long as the participants in the collaboration want to retain their ability to trade in the shares of the target, the MAR prohibitions substantially limit the exchange of information– and, hence, will hamper ESG collaborative engagement.

9.5.3 *Non-disclosure Obligations Generally*

Further statutory non-disclosure obligations may result from statutory law, in particular, from the organizational law of the legal entities of the institutional investors in question.

Moreover, confidentiality agreements concluded by individual investors with the issuer may have an inhibitory effect on institutional investors' ESG collaborative engagement. Pursuant to Art. 17(8) of the MAR, such confidentiality agreements are a basic prerequisite for an issuer to be able to pass on inside information selectively to individual investors,[111] which is why collective engagement initiatives based on inside information received from the issuer are rather unlikely.

[109] Klöhn, in Klöhn, Marktmissbrauchsverordnung, 2nd ed. 2023, Art. 9 note 133.

[110] ECJ, judgment of 10 May 2007 – Case C-391/04, ECLI:EU:C:2007:272 – Georgakis, paras. 33 et seq. Based on the old Insider Dealing Directive (89/592/EEC), however, the ECJ then denied that the members of such a group, in carrying out their plan, were exploiting the inside information they possessed within the meaning of Art. 2 of Directive 89/592/EEC.

[111] See, in more detail, Mülbert/Sajnovits, Wertpapier-Mitteilungen, 2017, 2041, 2044.

9.5.4 Competition/Antitrust Law

Very recently, it has been suggested that collaborative ESG engagement may violate antitrust law.[112] In this respect, the question at issue is not whether the concentration of share ownership, especially among the Big Three, can have anti-competitive effects on product and service markets,[113] but whether specific investors involved in collaborative (ESG) engagement could be deemed to be acting in violation of the prohibition against cartels pursuant to Art. 101 of the TFEU or corresponding national antitrust law.

While it may be unlikely that the European Commission or national antitrust authorities would initiate proceedings in matters involving ESG engagement, it is also doubtful that ESG collaborative engagement would generally be deemed to constitute a violation of Art. 101 of the TFEU.

Even though it is true that numerous cases of collaborative engagement will involve at least concerted practices, a prevention, restriction, or distortion of competition is not likely to take place in every case. Although the collaborating investors may well be in a competitive relationship with each other, this will not necessarily be affected by their collaboration regarding one or more portfolio companies. Rather, such investors will compete with each other in the market for the distribution of their collective investment schemes to end investors, but not in connection with their activism with regard to portfolio companies.

Even if an agreement or a concerted practice were to qualify as a restriction of competition – perhaps not generally but, for example, because it is part of the agreement not to invest in certain companies – an exception under the ancillary restraints doctrine[114] or an exemption under Art. 101(3) of the TFEU, may apply, in particular if the collaboration rectifies a market failure. In that case, the agreement must be one which "contributes to improving the production or distribution of goods or to promoting technical or economic progress", that is, it will be eligible for exemption under Art. 101(3) of the TFEU if the (economic) benefits provided by it at the

[112] *Brnovich* (Attorney General of Arizona), ESG May Be an Antitrust Violation, WSJ, 6 March 2022, www.wsj.com/articles/esg-may-be-an-antitrust-violation-climate-activism-energy-prices-401k-retirement-investment-political-agenda-coordinated-influence-11646594807; see also *Bryan/Mundy/Shimizuishi*, The Antitrust Threat to Climate Action, FT-online, 22 July 2022; *Temple-West/Bryan/Edgecliffe-Johnson*, Net Zero Group Cites Antitrust Threat – Legal Experts Don't Buy It, FT-online 29 July 2022.

[113] See Azar/Schmalz/Tecu, Journal of Finance 73 (2018), 1513; for the legal implications, see, e.g., Enriques/Romano, University of Illinois Law Review (2019), 223, 262 et seq.

[114] Cf. ECJ judgment of 19 February 2002 – Case C-309/99 – Wouters, para. 97 et seq., 107, 110.

level of the individual or, in the Commission's view, also at the level of all consumers, are greater than its adverse effects on competition.

In any case, the European Commission seems to take a favourable view of sustainability-related endeavours.[115] National antitrust authorities have also announced that they do not wish to stand in the way of collaborations aimed at achieving sustainability goals. For example,[116] the Dutch competition authority has issued guidelines that significantly expand the scope for companies to cooperate on sustainability initiatives, providing companies with interpretation criteria and demonstrating, in the spirit of a more sustainable economic approach, that antitrust law does not necessarily pose an obstacle to companies entering into joint commitments to foster greater climate protection, animal welfare, and the protection of human rights along the value chain.[117]

9.5.5 *Data Protection Law*

Another obstacle to collaborative engagement, or at least another aspect that should be taken into consideration in this context, arises out of data protection law. If investors process personal data for the purpose of planning collaborative engagements, they must also take the requirements of the General Data Protection Regulation[118] into account. This may become relevant, for example, in cases involving the processing of personal data of board members of portfolio companies.

9.6 Conclusion

Given the great potential of collaborations for effectively carrying out engagements, it is worth taking a closer look at the legal issues in this

115 See the proposed guidelines on the Horizontal Directive., Chap. 9 on Sustainability Agreements, available at: https://competition-policy.ec.europa.eu/public-consultations/2022-hbers_en.

116 *Andreas Mundt*, President of the BKartA, has emphasized that his authority "does not want to stand in the way of cooperations to achieve sustainability goals", 5. Cf. press release of the German Federal Cartel Office (Bundeskartellamt – BKartA) from 18 January 2022, available at: www.bundeskartellamt.de/SharedDocs/Meldung/DE/Pressemitteilungen/2022/18_01_2022_Nachhaltigkeit.html.

117 Autoriteit Consument & Markt, Guidelines Sustainability Claims, 2021, available at: www.acm.nl/system/files/documents/guidelines-sustainability-claims_1.pdf.

118 Regulation (EU) 2016/679 of the European Parliament and of the Council of 27 April 2016 on the protection of natural persons with regard to the processing of personal data and on the free movement of such data, and repealing Directive 95/46/EC.

context. Particularly in the context of E&S-related engagements, many see collaboration among institutional investors as an essential way to encourage companies to act responsibly.

Among the actions identified in this chapter for easing the way for E&S-driven collaboration, creating legal certainty regarding the admissible extent and content of collaborative engagement is of paramount importance. Specifically, ESMA should – as already indicated in its recent Sustainable Finance Roadmap 2022–2024[119] – update its Whitelist, and national regulators – BaFin has already taken the lead in this respect[120] – should also publish opinions on their interpretive practices.

Furthermore, one could consider guidance on insider regulation. However, we should not expect too much in that regard given that impediments from the insider regulation are not covered as an issue in ESMA's Sustainable Finance Roadmap 2022–2024. Therefore, for collaborators, organizing an effective framework for detecting inside information and dealing with such information seems to be key. The European Commission and the national antitrust authorities also have a role to play: They should explicitly extend the scope of the approach they have recently taken with regard to sustainability agreements between manufacturing companies, in particular, to include investor agreements.

[119] ESMA, Sustainable Finance Roadmap 2022–2024, ESMA30-379-1051, p. 29.
[120] See n. 117.

10

ESG and Board-Shareholder Engagement in M&A

AFRA AFSHARIPOUR

10.1 Introduction

Corporate governance debates have undergone a fundamental shift, with environmental, social, and governance ("ESG") issues coming to the forefront of decision-making by boards, executives, and shareholders.[1] Across a spectrum of shareholders, from institutional investors to retail investors, companies and their boards face pressure to incorporate ESG considerations into their business strategies, including strategies around fundamental merger and acquisition ("M&A") transactions. Other stakeholders, including employees and customers, are similarly demanding that companies factor ESG concerns in their decision-making.[2] And across the globe, there is a rising tide of regulatory reform focused on board oversight and disclosure of ESG risks. Many proponents of ESG advocate for its adoption, arguing that such considerations would provide information that could improve corporate decision-making, including M&A transactions.

This chapter analyzes the implications of this shifting landscape for M&A transactions. As ESG demands on companies accelerate, boards are

For helpful comments, I am grateful to participants at the Auxiliary Corporate Governance Conference organized by Assogestioni in Rome in October 2022 and to participants at the Organization of Social Impact Workshop held at UC Berkeley School of Law in November 2022. Evelynn Chun, Lauren Kim, and Kathryn Parsons provided excellent research assistance.

[1] The definition of ESG itself – and accordingly what is encompassed in ESG – is highly contested, with polarized views about the usefulness of ESG. *See* George Serafeim, *ESG: Hyperboles and Reality* (Harv. Bus. Sch. Rsch., Working Paper No. 22-031, 2021), https://ssrn.com/abstract=3966695; Elizabeth Pollman, *The Making and Meaning of ESG* (U. Pa. I. for L. & Econ. Rsch., Working Paper No. 22-23, 2022; Eur. Corp. Governance I. – L., Working Paper No. 659, 2022), https://ssrn.com/abstract=4219857.

[2] *See generally* Tom C.W. Lin, The Capitalist and the Activist (Berrett-Koehler Publishers, 2022); Jennifer S. Fan, *Woke Capital: The Role of Corporations in Social Movements*, 9 Harv. Bus. L. Rev. 441 (2019).

increasingly expected to consider ESG factors in both M&A strategy and board oversight of deals. For boards assessing M&A deals, ESG factors are emerging as critical to all aspects of dealmaking. For instance, given increased investor and regulatory scrutiny of ESG, advisors on M&A deals recommend in-depth ESG due diligence for both buyers and sellers. In addition to using ESG as part of deal selection, negotiation and execution, companies are also using ESG factors to influence shareholder – and stakeholder – support for deals.

The confluence of ESG and M&A presents boards with significant opportunities and challenges. This chapter's case study of Microsoft's acquisition of Activision Blizzard ("Activision") demonstrates how ESG pressures may both facilitate and spell trouble for a deal. Moreover, ESG considerations in M&A may not necessarily benefit stakeholders. While pressure to account for ESG issues in M&A is expected to grow, there is also concern that ESG can help mask interested decision-making by boards and managers. Such concerns are palpable in M&A where the potential for soft conflicts of interest is particularly acute.

The ESG movement may also complicate shareholder voting and activism related to M&A. To date, in many M&A transactions, even when shareholders have voting rights, their voice is muted – shareholders largely vote with or side with management. ESG activism may place a greater spotlight on how large institutional investors vote on M&A deals, revealing the tensions between their economic goals and their espoused ESG commitments. This, in turn, may result in greater institutional shareholder pressure on boards in connection with M&A.

10.2 The Rise of ESG in M&A

ESG has become increasingly important for companies and boards. Investors, regulators, and other stakeholders continue to demand ever-increasing ESG performance and disclosures. Accordingly, ESG issues are emerging as essential to M&A dealmaking, affecting both the logic of a deal and the procedural aspects of dealmaking. Section 10.2.1 discusses the shift in business norms toward ESG and examines how ESG has become a key concern for investors, other stakeholders, and regulators. Section 10.2.2 explores the implications of ESG for M&A. It uses a case study of Microsoft's acquisition of Activision to demonstrate the complexities of ESG for dealmaking.

10.2.1 Increasing Expectations for Companies to Address ESG

Corporate governance has experienced a fundamental shift, with issues of corporate purpose, sustainability and ESG coming to the forefront.[3] In what has been termed a "New Paradigm" of corporate governance, public corporations and their boards are urged to focus on broader stakeholder interests rather than just shareholder interests.[4] Demands to address environmental and social challenges are impossible to dismiss given the "growing sustainability imperative – widespread recognition that business as usual, despite the short-term returns generated, could undermine social and economic stability and even threaten our long-term survival, if we fail to grapple with associated costs."[5]

The pressures on companies to address environmental and social issues come from a diverse set of actors, including investors,

[3] *See, e.g.*, Martin Lipton & William Savitt, *Stakeholder Governance, Issues and Answers*, Harv. L. Sch. Forum on Corp. Governance (Oct. 25, 2019), https://corpgov.law.harvard.edu/2019/10/25/stakeholder-governance-issues-and-answers/; The British Academy, Principles for Purposeful Business: How to Deliver the Framework for the Future of the Corporation (2019), https://www.thebritishacademy.ac.uk/documents/224/future-of-the-corporation-principles-purposeful-business.pdf; The British Academy, Reforming Business for the 21st Century: A Framework for the Future of the Corporation (2019), https://www.thebritishacademy.ac.uk/documents/76/Reforming-Business-for-21st-Century-British-Academy.pdf; Klaus Schwab, *Davos Manifesto 2020: The Universal Purpose of a Company in the Fourth Industrial Revolution,* World Econ. Forum (Dec. 2, 2019), https://www.weforum.org/agenda/2019/12/davos-manifesto-2020-the-universal-purpose-of-a-company-in-the-fourth-industrial-revolution/. Issues of corporate purpose have long permeated corporate law, *see, e.g.*, William W. Bratton & Michael L. Wachter, *Shareholder Primacy's Corporatist Origins: Adolf Berle and The Modern Corporation*, 34 J. Corp. L. 99 (2008); John M. Conley & Cynthia A. Williams, *Engage, Embed, and Embellish: Theory Versus Practice in the Corporate Social Responsibility Movement,* 31 J. Corp. L. 1 (2005); C.A. Harwell Wells, *The Cycles of Corporate Social Responsibility: An Historical Retrospective for the Twenty-First Century*, 51 U. Kan. L. Rev. 77 (2002).

[4] Martin Lipton, Steven A. Rosenblum, Sabastian V. Niles, Sara J. Lewis & Kisho Watanabe, *The New Paradigm: A Roadmap for an Implicit Corporate Governance Partnership between Corporations and Investors to Achieve Sustainable Long-Term Investment and Growth*, World Econ. Forum (Sept. 2, 2016), https://www.wlrk.com/webdocs/wlrknew/AttorneyPubs/WLRK.25960.16.pdf; Martin Lipton, *It's Time to Adopt the New Paradigm*, Harv. L. Sch. Forum on Corp. Governance (Feb. 11, 2019), https://corpgov.law.harvard.edu/2019/02/11/its-time-to-adopt-the-new-paradigm/. For a survey of shareholder and stakeholder theories, see Cynthia A. Williams, *Corporate Social Responsibility and Corporate Governance, in The Oxford Handbook of Corporate Law and Governance* 664–77 (Jeffrey N. Gordon & Wolf-Georg Ringe eds., Oxford University Press 2018).

[5] Christopher M. Bruner, *Corporate Governance Reform and the Sustainability Imperative*, 131 Yale L. J. 1217, 1221 (2022).

stakeholders, governments, international and transnational institutions, academics, and even corporate managers themselves.[6] Even the Business Roundtable broke with its long-standing tradition of advocating for shareholder primacy to issue a new Statement on the Purpose of a Corporation.[7] The shift to take stakeholderism seriously is not surprising as companies are eager to attract the trillions of dollars funneled into ESG portfolios.[8]

Shareholders, especially institutional investors, have been at the center of efforts pressing corporate boards to incorporate sustainability and ESG considerations into their business strategies.[9] Leading global asset managers, such as BlackRock and State Street, argue that long-term sustainable value should be the primary goal of a company.[10] They claim that society and diversified investors are best served by companies that respect and "benefit all of their stakeholders, including shareholders, employees, customers, and the communities in which they operate".[11] As Professor Condon has argued, these "universal owners" – that is, institutional investors who hold large segments of the market – have strong economic incentives to address systematic environmental risks that affect their portfolios as a whole.[12] In a pair of papers, Professors Barzuza, Curtis,

[6] *See generally* Cynthia Williams, *Comparative and Transnational Developments in Corporate Social Responsibility, in Research Handbook on Comparative Corporate Governance* (Afra Afsharipour & Martin Gelter eds., Edward Elgar Publishing Ltd. 2021).

[7] *Business Roundtable Redefines the Purpose of a Corporation to Promote 'An Economy That Serves All Americans'*, BUSINESS ROUNDTABLE (Aug. 19, 2019), https://www.businessroundtable.org/business-roundtable-redefines-the-purpose-of-a-corporation-to-promote-an-economy-that-serves-all-americans.

[8] *See* Williams, *supra* note 6, at 97–99.

[9] *See generally* Stavros Gadinis & Amelia Miazad, *Corporate Law and Social Risk*, 73 Vand. L. Rev. 1401, 1408–09 (2020); Virginia Harper Ho, *Enlightened Shareholder Value: Corporate Governance Beyond the Shareholder–Stakeholder Divide*. 36 J. CORP. L. 59 (2010).

[10] *See, e.g.*, ST. STREET, 2016 CORPORATE RESPONSIBILITY REPORT 3 (2016), https://www.responsibilityreports.com/HostedData/ResponsibilityReportArchive/s/NYSE_STT_2016.pdf; Larry Fink, *Larry Fink's Annual Letter to CEOs: A Sense of Purpose*, BLACKROCK (2018), https://www.blackrock.com/hk/en/insights/larry-fink-ceo-letter.

[11] *See* Larry Fink, *2019 Letter to CEOs: Purpose and Profit*, BLACKROCK (2019), https://www.blackrock.com/corporate/investor-relations/larry-fink-ceo-letter.

[12] *See generally* Madison Condon, *Externalities and the Common Owner*, 95 WASH. U. L. REV. 1 (2020); *see also* Luca Enriques & Alessandro Romano, *Rewiring Corporate Law for an Interconnected World*, 64 ARIZ. L. REV. 51, 56–57 (2022); John C. Coffee, Jr., *The Future of Disclosure: ESG, Common Ownership, and Systematic Risk, 2021 Colum.* Bus. L. Rev. 602 (2022); *but see* Roberto Tallarita, *The Limits of Portfolio Primacy*, 76 VAND.

and Webber further argue that, in addition to such motivations, there will be increasing demand from a variety of institutional investors for sustainability-oriented disclosure and reforms as such firms themselves attempt to address the demands and capital of a new generation of investors and employees.[13]

Shareholder proposals on ESG-related matters, and support for such proposals, are regular features of the proxy season for public companies in the US.[14] The US Securities and Exchange Commission ("SEC") has made it easier for shareholders to file ESG-related proposals.[15] The 2022 proxy season yielded a record number of ESG proposals submitted to US publicly listed companies, with more "coordinated efforts between proponents and advocacy groups across the ESG spectrum."[16] Although such proposals garnered more muted support in 2022 than in prior years, that may not necessarily indicate that investors are less focused on ESG.[17] For instance, a large number of proposals were withdrawn as companies negotiated with investors on proposals, especially those related to environmental and social issues.

Companies also face increasing demands from regulators and investors to integrate ESG risks and opportunities into corporate disclosures.[18] For example, across jurisdictions, corporations are facing calls for mandatory corporate climate disclosure.[19] In the US, 2022 saw extended debate over the SEC's sweeping, and controversial, proposed climate

L. Rev. 511, 519 (2023) (arguing that "we should not expect portfolio primacy to become a meaningful tool in the fight against climate change"); Marcel Kahan & Edward B. Rock, *Systematic Stewardship with Tradeoffs*, Chapter 4 in this book.

13 *See generally* Michael Barzuza, Quinn Curtis, & David H. Webber, *Shareholder Value(s): Index Fund ESG Activism and the New Millennial Corporate Governance*, 93 S. Cal. L. Rev. 1243 (2020).

14 *See* Williams, *supra* note 6, at 97–99; Virginia Harper Ho, *Modernizing ESG Disclosure*, 2022 Ill. L. Rev. 277, 287 (2022).

15 *Shareholder Proposals: Staff Legal Bulletin No. 14L (CF)*, SEC (Nov. 3, 2021), https://www.sec.gov/corpfin/staff-legal-bulletin-14l-shareholder-proposals.

16 *See Early Look at the 2022 Proxy Season*, Georgeson, https://www.georgeson.com/us/insights/early-2022-us-agm-season-data (last visited Nov. 4, 2022).

17 *See* Jamie Smith, *Four Key Takeaways from the 2022 Proxy Season*, EY Center for Board Matters (Jul. 27, 2022), https://www.ey.com/en_us/board-matters/four-key-takeaways-from-the-2022-proxy-season; Jordan Wolman & Debra Kah, *Shareholder Activists Make Inroads*, Politico (Jul. 28, 2022), https://www.politico.com/newsletters/the-long-game/2022/07/28/shareholder-activists-make-inroads-00048445.

18 *See* Harper Ho, *supra* note 14, at 286–88.

19 For an overview, *see* John Armour, Luca Enriques, & Thom Wetzer, *Mandatory Corporate Climate Disclosures: Now, but How?*, 2021 Columbia Bus. L. Rev. 1085 (2022).

disclosure regime for public companies.[20] The proposal would require, among other disclosures, companies to describe the board's oversight and governance of climate-related risks.[21] The SEC's proposed rules follow growing global momentum toward standardized disclosure of climate-related risks.[22] For example, in 2022, the EU adopted the Corporate Sustainability Reporting Directive ("CSRD"), mandating enhanced disclosure standards to improve the coverage and reliability of sustainability reporting.[23] Institutional investors are also asking companies to provide ESG disclosure. BlackRock, for example, has stated that it may vote against directors that "failed to provide shareholders with adequate disclosure to conclude appropriate strategic consideration is given to [ESG risk factors] by the board."[24] State Street has made similar statements, noting that it "will start taking voting action against directors across applicable indices should companies not meet" climate-related disclosure expectations.[25]

[20] *See* SEC, Press Release, *SEC Proposes Rules to Enhance and Standardize Climate-Related Disclosures for Investors* (Mar. 21, 2022), https://www.sec.gov/news/press-release/2022-46. For an overview of some of the critiques of the proposal, *see* Jacqueline M. Vallette & Kathryne M. Gray, *SEC's Climate Risk Disclosure Proposal Likely to Face Legal Challenges*, Harv. L. Sch. Forum Corp. Governance (May 10, 2022), https://corpgov.law.harvard.edu/2022/05/10/secs-climate-risk-disclosure-proposal-likely-to-face-legal-challenges/.

[21] SEC, The Enhancement and Standardization of Climate-Related Disclosures for Investors 94 (2022), https://www.sec.gov/rules/proposed/2022/33-11042.pdf.

[22] *See The State of Climate Disclosure*, S&P Global (Apr. 15, 2022), https://www.spglobal.com/en/research-insights/featured/the-state-of-climate-disclosure.

[23] *See* Directive (EU) 2022/2464 of the European Parliament and of the Council of 14 December 2022 amending Regulation (EU) No 537/2014, Directive 2004/109/EC, Directive 2006/43/EC and Directive 2013/34/EU, as regards corporate sustainability reporting; *see also* Council of the European Union, Press Release, *Council Gives Final Green Light to Corporate Sustainability Reporting Directive* (Nov. 28, 2022), https://www.consilium.europa.eu/en/press/press-releases/2022/11/28/council-gives-final-green-light-to-corporate-sustainability-reporting-directive/. The scope of the EU's directive is significantly larger than that of the SEC's proposed climate disclosure rules. *See* Addisu Lashitew, *The Coming of Age of Sustainability Disclosure: How Do Rules Differ between the US and the EU?*, Brookings: Future Development (June 6, 2022), https://www.brookings.edu/blog/future-development/2022/06/06/the-coming-of-age-of-sustainability-disclosure-how-do-rules-differ-between-the-us-and-the-eu/.

[24] BlackRock, Blackrock Investment Stewardship: Proxy Voting Guidelines for U.S. Securities (Jan. 4, 2023), https://www.blackrock.com/corporate/literature/fact-sheet/blk-responsible-investment-guidelines-us.pdf.

[25] Cyrus Taraporevala, *CEO's Letter on Our 2022 Proxy Voting Agenda*, State Street Global Advisors (Jan. 12, 2022), https://www.ssga.com/us/en/institutional/ic/insights/ceo-letter-2022-proxy-voting-agenda.

In some jurisdictions, companies are facing a "regulatory hardening" on ESG issues.[26] For instance, the European Union's proposed Corporate Sustainability Due Diligence Directive sets forth mandatory human rights and environmental due diligence obligations for companies across their value chain, as well as a civil liability regime for companies that fail to conduct adequate due diligence.[27] Some jurisdictions have already imposed mandatory human rights diligence processes and disclosure.[28] In short, the scope of ESG regulation is rapidly expanding.

ESG engagement is not limited to investors and regulators. A changing workforce and customer base is similarly engaged in environmental and social activism.[29] Executives view ESG as critical for attracting employees, especially millennial and generation Z employees.[30] Consumers also express that ESG is important to them.[31] For instance, a 2021 survey by PWC indicated significant consumer expectations for companies to make and follow through on ESG commitments and actions.[32]

The rise of ESG and stakeholder capitalism has much appeal, as well as many detractors. Polarization around ESG is rising across stakeholders.[33] With respect to various ESG pronouncements, some argue that such

26 Virginia E. Harper Ho, Sustainable Finance & the Public Turn in Corporate Law, *in A Research Agenda for Corporate Law* (Christopher Bruner & Marc Moore eds., Edward Elgar Publishing Ltd., 2023).

27 *See* Press Release, European Commission, Just and Sustainable Economy: Commission Lays Down Rules for Companies to Respect Human Rights and Environment in Global Value Chains (Feb. 23, 2022), https://ec.europa.eu/commission/presscorner/detail/en/ip_22_1145; European Commission, Proposal For a Directive of the European Parliament and of the Council on Corporate Sustainability Due Diligence and Amending Directive (EU) 2019/1937 (2022), https://ec.europa.eu/info/sites/default/files/1_1_183885_prop_dir_susta_en.pdf.

28 *See* Clare Bartram, Marie-Anaïs Meudic-Role, Abigail Kyla Antonio, & Thiago Toste, *The Rapidly Changing World of Human Rights Regulation: A Resource for Investors* (2022), https://www.issgovernance.com/file/publications/iss-esg-the-rapidly-changing-world-of-human-rights-regulation.pdf.

29 *See* Michal Barzuza, Quinn Curtis, & David H. Webber, *The Millennial Corporation: Strong Stakeholders, Weak Managers* (2021), https://ssrn.com/abstract=3918443 (manuscript at 15–23).

30 *See* Ibid. at 18–20.

31 *See* Ibid. at 21–22; *see also* Michael O'Leary & Warren Valdmanis, *An ESG Reckoning Is Coming*, Harv. Bus. Rev. (Mar. 4, 2021), https://hbr.org/2021/03/an-esg-reckoning-is-coming.

32 *See* PWC, *Beyond Compliance: Consumers and Employees Want Business to do More on ESG* (2021), https://www.pwc.com/us/en/services/consulting/library/consumer-intelligence-series/consumer-and-employee-esg-expectations.html.

33 *See* Pollman, *supra* note 1, at 4–5.

pledges are not only generic and empty rhetoric, but that stakeholderism represents a power grab by already powerful CEOs.[34] Others express doubt that the ESG movement will actually benefit a company's stakeholders, and argue that a stakeholder orientation in corporate law is a weak mechanism for addressing income inequality, environmental protection, workers, and the like.[35] A growing number of commentators refer to ESG as a "marketing," "greenwashing," or a "scam."[36] Lastly, especially in the US, there is a growing and vocal anti-ESG movement that questions the legitimacy of ESG investing.[37] Conservative politicians have seized on the ESG backlash to make political inroads, adding fuel to the critiques.[38]

An important and significant concern with ESG is a lack of consensus on both definition and measurement.[39] Without a common set of agreement on what is included in ESG or how to effectively measure various factors encompassed by the E, the S, and the G, it will remain hard for companies to use information about sustainability in strategic and operational decisions or to devise metrics that accurately track their ESG

[34] *See* Lucian Bebchuk & Roberto Tallarita, *The Illusory Promise of Stakeholder Governance*, 106 Corn. L. Rev. 91, 97 (2020).

[35] *See, e.g.*, Ibid. at 94–97; Matteo Gatti & Chrystin D. Ondersma, *Can a Broader Corporate Purpose Redress Inequality? The Stakeholder Approach Chimera*, 46 J. Corp. L. 1, 60–63 (2020).

[36] *See* The Economist, *ESG Should Be Boiled Down to One Measure: Emissions* (July 21, 2022), https://www.economist.com/leaders/2022/07/21/esg-should-be-boiled-down-to-one-simple-measure-emissions; Matthew Goldstein & Emily Flitter, *Cracking Down on a Wall Street Trend: E.S.G. Makeovers*, N.Y. Times (Sept. 17, 2022), https://www.nytimes.com/2022/09/17/business/dealbook/esg-wall-street.html; David Gelles, *Another Culture War Front: Are Companies Too 'Woke' When It Comes to Climate?*, N.Y. Times (Sept. 19, 2022), https://www.nytimes.com/2022/09/19/climate/companies-conservatives-attack.html.

[37] *See* Witold Henisz, *How to Confront the Anti-ESG Campaign*, Knowledge at Wharton (Aug. 30, 2022), https://knowledge.wharton.upenn.edu/article/how-to-confront-the-anti-esg-campaign/; Andrew Ross Sorkin et al., *The Pushback on E.S.G. Investing*, N.Y. Times: Dealbook (May 11, 2022), https://www.nytimes.com/2022/05/11/business/dealbook/esg-investing-pushback.html.

[38] *See* Amrith Ramkumar, *Some GOP States Push Back Against ESG Investing Trend*, Wall St. J. (Aug. 30, 2022), https://www.wsj.com/articles/esg-backlash-at-odds-with-shift-by-companies-and-investors-11661825320.

[39] *See* Dambisa Moyo, *10 ESG Questions Companies Need to Answer*, Harv. Bus Rev. (Jan. 6, 2022), https://hbr.org/2022/01/10-esg-questions-companies-need-to-answer; David F. Larcker, Lukasz Pomorski, Brian Tayan, & Edward Watts, *ESG Ratings: A Compass without Direction* (Rock Center for Corp. Governance at Stan. U., Working Paper, 2022), https://ssrn.com/abstract=4179647; *see also* Pollman, *supra* note 1.

progress.[40] There is also substantial disagreement across rating agencies regarding what rating to give to individual firms.[41] Studies indicate that current ESG measurements may not have any direct correlation with achieving sustainable business practices.[42] While many companies now report on their sustainability or ESG practices, critics argue that "reporting is not a proxy for progress" as "measurement is often non-standard, incomplete, imprecise, and misleading."[43]

Despite the challenges with ESG, it is likely that sustainability and ESG issues will remain at the center of corporate governance concerns for some time to come.[44] Both companies and investors appear reluctant to abandon ESG, especially as a risk assessment tool.[45] And some argue that ESG has evolved from a "niche subfield into a mainstream practice" given its relevance to long-term firm value.[46]

10.2.2 ESG's Implications for M&A Dealmaking

Wachtell Lipton, one of the leading law firms advising on M&A, stated in 2020 that ESG's impact on M&A "cannot be underestimated" and predicted that "[a]ll aspects of M&A will be affected."[47] Corporate deal-makers, financial advisors and lawyers regularly report that ESG considerations "play a decisive role at every step of the M&A process, from

[40] *See* Jennifer Howard-Grenville, *ESG Impact Is Hard to Measure – But It's Not Impossible*, Harv. Bus Rev. (Jan. 22, 2021), https://hbr.org/2021/01/esg-impact-is-hard-to-measure-but-its-not-impossible.

[41] *See* Larcker et al., *supra* note 39, at 5–6.

[42] *See* Florian Berg, Julian Kölbel, & Roberto Rigobon, *Aggregate Confusion: The Divergence of ESG Ratings*, 26 Rev. of Finance 1315 (2022); Aneesh Raghunandan & Shiva Rajgopal, *Do ESG Funds Make Stakeholder-Friendly Investments?*, 27 Rev. Accounting Studies 822 (2022).

[43] Kenneth P. Pucker, *Overselling Sustainability Reporting*, Harv. Bus. Rev. (May-June 2021), https://hbr.org/2021/05/overselling-sustainability-reporting.

[44] *See* Allison Herren Lee, *Keynote Address at 2021 Society for Corporate Governance National Conference*, SEC (Jun. 28, 2021), https://www.sec.gov/news/speech/lee-climate-esg-board-of-directors.

[45] David Gelles, *Another Culture War Front: Are Companies Too 'Woke' When It Comes to Climate?*, N.Y. Times (Sept. 19, 2022), https://www.nytimes.com/2022/09/19/climate/companies-conservatives-attack.html.

[46] Alex Edmans, The End of ESG, 52 Fin. Mgmt. 3, 4 (2023).

[47] Andrew R. Brownstein, David M. Sil, & Sabastian V. Niles, *The Coming Impact of ESG on M&A*, Harv. L. Sch. Forum on Corp. Governance (Feb. 20, 2020), https://corpgov.law.harvard.edu/2020/02/20/the-coming-impact-of-esg-on-ma/.

target selection through to post-merger integration."[48] In other words, ESG factors are poised to impact both the logic of a deal and the procedural aspects of dealmaking. This greater focus on ESG performance and disclosure provides both opportunities and risks for M&A transactions, further complicating already complex M&A dealmaking.

10.2.2.1 ESG Considerations in M&A: From Target Selection to Integration

ESG-influenced dealmaking is on the rise, affecting M&A strategy for both buyers and sellers. As an example, throughout 2020 and 2021, sustainability and climate change concerns motivated many M&A deals, particularly among energy companies.[49] In the energy sector, some companies divested of so-called brown assets in favor of assets that would improve their ESG performance.[50] The acquisition of a target company with strong ESG ratings and performance can enable a buyer to improve its own ESG credentials.[51] For example, in its 2021 ESG report, The Hershey Company, a well-known candy bar and snack maker, prominently featured its 2021 acquisitions of Dot's Pretzels and Lily's Sweets, a maker of low-sugar products, as part of its strategy to offer consumers products that "support a healthy lifestyle."[52] Targets can also use M&A activity to cleanse themselves of ESG-related problems.[53] Moreover, ESG expertise and service itself has been an impetus for dealmaking. Across the globe, large firms, including BlackRock,

[48] Lindsay Patrick, *Eyeing a Merger or Acquisition? Keep ESG at the Top of Your Mind*, Fortune (Feb. 22, 2022), https://fortune.com/2022/02/22/mergers-acquisitions-deals-esg-investing/.

[49] Clare Connellan, Maia Gez, Seth Kerschner, Taylor Pullins, & Patrick Sarch, *ESG Enters M&A Mainstream in a Year of Change*, White & Case (Jan. 29, 2021), https://mergers.whitecase.com/highlights/esg-enters-ma-mainstream-in-a-year-of-change#.

[50] *See* Adam O. Emmerich & Trevor S. Norwitz, *2021's Most Interesting Developments in M&A*, The Int'l Comp. L. Guide: Mergers and Acquisitions (2022), https://ssrn.com/abstract=4088755.

[51] Renee Levin, *ESG: The Next M&A Frontier*, Fordham J. of Corp. and Financial L. Blog (Mar. 26, 2022), https://news.law.fordham.edu/jcfl/2022/03/26/esg-the-next-ma-frontier/.

[52] Hershey, 2021 ESG Report, https://www.thehersheycompany.com/content/dam/hershey-corporate/documents/pdf/hershey_2021_esg_report.pdf.

[53] *See, e.g.*, Emmanuel Yimfor & Heather Tookes, *Misconduct Synergies* (Oct. 13, 2021), https://ssrn.com/abstract=3942188 (finding "that disclosures of new disciplinary events in the combined firm drops by between 25 and 34 percent following mergers. This reduction is driven mainly by separations of high misconduct employees at the target firm.").

JP Morgan, and McKinsey, have acquired data analytics or consulting firms with ESG expertise.[54]

Companies report that ESG criteria are increasingly being considered in valuing and financing deals. Surveys of executives indicate that a target company's ESG leadership may justify higher valuation for the target.[55] On the flip side, surveys indicate that buyers reported reducing bid prices after ESG due diligence or even walked away from an M&A target due to negative ESG issues at the target.[56] As deal teams assign financial metrics to ESG criteria, some companies may use ESG credentials as "a key lever of value" in deal negotiations.[57] Moreover, with the rise in ESG investing, buyers may find more attractive financing terms if the parties to a deal have high ESG ratings.[58] Yet, experts caution that ESG measurement and risk are often very challenging to quantify in financial terms.

ESG considerations play a large role in M&A due diligence.[59] Risk assessment, including that related to non-financial factors, has long been an important focus of M&A due diligence. The emphasis on ESG heightens that focus.[60] Experts note that "a dedicated environmental and social lens opens up new opportunities to identify and quantify different types of risks and opportunities."[61] For example, with companies increasingly exposed to risks from climate change and extreme weather events, it is crucial to evaluate any real estate holdings for such risks.[62] Similarly, a target's supply chain may be severely disrupted due to

54 *See* Emmerich & Norwitz, *supra* note 50; Larcker et al., *supra* note 39, at 12.

55 *See* Bain & Company, Global M&A Report 2022 (2022), https://www.bain.com/globalassets/noindex/2022/bain_report_global_m_and_a-report-2022.pdf.

56 Baker McKenzie, Mitigating ESG Risks in M&A Transactions (2020), https://www.bakermckenzie.com/-/media/files/insight/publications/2021/05/mitigating-esg-risks-in-ma-transactionsv2_110521.pdf.

57 *See* Levin, *supra* note 51. 58 *See* Ibid.

59 *See* Andrew R. Brownstein, David M. Sil, & Sabastian V. Niles, *The Coming Impact of ESG on M&A*, Harv. L. Sch. Forum on Corp. Governance (Feb. 20, 2020), https://corpgov.law.harvard.edu/2020/02/20/the-coming-impact-of-esg-on-ma/.

60 *See, e.g.*, Global legal insights, Mergers & Acquisitions 2021 (2021), https://www.debevoise.com/insights/publications/2021/07/gli-mergers-acquisitions; Myron Mallia-Dare & Cindy Kim, *ESG: Creating Value and Mitigating Risk In Mergers & Acquisitions*, A.B.A. (June 15, 2022), https://www.americanbar.org/groups/business_law/publications/blt/2022/06/esg-ma/.

61 Lindsay Patrick, *Eyeing a Merger or Acquisition? Keep ESG at the Top of Your Mind*, Fortune (Feb. 22, 2022), https://fortune.com/2022/02/22/mergers-acquisitions-deals-esg-investing/.

62 *See* Liam Kelly, *Real estate: M&A preparations must address climate risk*, KPMG (2022), https://advisory.kpmg.us/blog/2022/real-estate-ma-preparations-address-climate-risk.html.

extreme climate events.[63] Additionally, human capital management has become a central issue in corporate governance.[64] For instance, M&A due diligence now regularly encompasses diligence on sexual harassment or misconduct issues at target companies.[65] With the increased focus on diversity and equity in the workforce, buyers are often advised to do significant diligence on workplace culture and workforce composition at a target company.[66]

Beyond valuation and pricing, some ESG factors are beginning to impact other terms included in deal documents. As ESG expands due diligence, there may be more disclosure on disclosure schedules and further calibration of representations and warranties.[67] Advisors typically recommend that buyers seek contractual protection for certain ESG risks.[68] For example, over the last few years, many buyers have come to insist on "Weinstein Clauses" in acquisition agreements that require targets to disclose allegations of sexual harassment or misconduct by senior executives.[69] Companies have also dealt with ESG-related liabilities through typical M&A contracting tools such as indemnification, holdbacks, and escrows.[70]

[63] *See* Annemargaret Connolly & Thomas Goslin, *Climate Change Considerations In M&A Transactions*, Lexis Nexis (Nov. 5, 2019), https://www.lexisnexis.com/community/insights/legal/practical-guidance-journal/b/pa/posts/climate-change-considerations-in-m-a-transactions.

[64] For an in-depth analysis, *see* George S. Georgiev, *The Human Capital Management Movement in U.S. Corporate Law*, 95 Tulane L. Rev. 639 (2021).

[65] *See* Barbara Borden et al., *ESG and M&A: Vetting a Target's ESG Strengths and Weaknesses to Assess Value, Go-Forward Risks and Disclosure Requirements*, Cooley (March 29, 2022), https://cooleyma.com/2022/03/29/esg-and-ma-vetting-a-targets-esg-strengths-and-weaknesses-to-assess-value-go-forward-risks-and-disclosure-requirements/.

[66] *See* Malcolm Lloyd, Colin Wittmer, & John Potter, *Global M&A Industry Trends: 2022 Mid-Year Update*, Harv. L. Sch. Forum on Corp. Governance (July 25, 2022), https://corpgov.law.harvard.edu/2022/07/25/global-ma-industry-trends-2022-mid-year-update/.

[67] *See* Kramer Levin, *ESG's Impact on M&A*, JDSupra (July 25, 2022), https://www.jdsupra.com/legalnews/esg-s-impact-on-m-a-7975911/.

[68] *See. e.g.*, George Casey, Doreen Lilienfeld, Marc Mezey, Paul Strecker, & Matthew Behrens, *ESG Considerations in M&A*, 24 M&A Law. 1 (2020), https://www.shearman.com/-/media/Files/Perspectives/2020/09/ESG-CONSIDERATIONS.pdf?la=en&hash=30B53E0F7976755FF0066DF1BBA77F04E2C2D818.

[69] *See generally* Anna Windemuth, *The #MeToo Movement Migrates to M&A Boilerplate*, 129 Yale L.J. 488 (2019); *see also* Amelia Miazad, *Sex, Power, and Corporate Governance*, 54 UC Davis L. Rev. 1913, 1980–81 (2021).

[70] *See* Kramer Levin, *supra* note 67. For an overview of such tools, *see* Afra Afsharipour, *Legal Transplants in the Law of the Deal: M&A Agreements in India, Research Handbook*

Parties are also using an ESG-rationale as part of their transaction announcement to influence shareholder and stakeholder receptivity to a deal. For example, when ConocoPhillips announced its $9.7 billion acquisition of Concho Resources in 2020, the company stated that a significant highlight of the deal was "[e]levated commitment to environmental, social and governance excellence with a newly adopted Paris-Aligned Climate Risk strategy" and repeatedly stressed "ESG excellence" and a "commitment to sustainability."[71]

Management and disclosure of ESG-related matters will undoubtedly affect post-deal governance, integration, and performance. Several studies have documented the impact of corporate social responsibility ("CSR") – arguably the precursor to ESG – on the success of M&A deals.[72] A 2013 study found that acquirers with stronger CSR policies earn higher short- and long-run stock returns and have better long-run profitability relative to those by companies with lower CSR.[73] A related study found that announcement returns are higher for deals involving target companies with stronger social and environmental risk management practices.[74] Furthermore, studies have found that cultural similarity between buying and selling firms is an important factor for deal success.[75] For example, a 2018 study found that firms with similarities in their CSR performance have a greater chance of deal completion and more success with post-deal integration.[76] Firms' greater ESG disclosure may make it easier for dealmakers to determine and assess cultural similarities between acquirers and target firms.

on Mergers and Acquisitions (Claire Hill & Steven Davidoff Solomon eds., Edward Elgar Publishing Ltd. 2016).

71 *ConocoPhillips to Acquire Concho Resources in All-Stock Transaction*, ConocoPhillips (Oct. 19, 2020), https://www.conocophillips.com/news-media/story/conocophillips-to-acquire-concho-resources-in-all-stock-transaction/.

72 For a review of these studies, *see* Luc Renneboog & Cara Vansteenkiste, *Failure and Success in Mergers and Acquisitions*, 58 J. Corp. Fin. 650, 671–72 (2019).

73 *See* Xin Deng, Jun-koo Kang, & Buen Sin Low, *Corporate Social Responsibility and Stakeholder Value Maximization: Evidence from Mergers*, 110 J. Fin. Econ. 87 (2013).

74 *See* Nihat Aktas, Eric de Bodt, & Jean-Gabriel Cousin, *Do Financial Markets Care about SRI? Evidence from Mergers and Acquisitions*, 35 J. Banking & Finance 1753 (2011).

75 *See* Renneboog & Vansteenkiste, *supra* note 72, at 667.

76 *See* Fred Bereskin, Seong K. Byun, Micah S. Officer, & Jong-Min Oh, *The Effect of Cultural Similarity on Mergers and Acquisitions: Evidence from Corporate Social Responsibility*, 53 J. Fin. & Quantitative Analysis 1995 (2018).

10.2.2.2 ESG Risks and Opportunities in M&A

Microsoft's $69 billion acquisition of leading game developer Activision exemplifies the opportunities and risks of ESG issues for a deal.[77] The transaction will make Microsoft the world's third-largest gaming company by revenue[78] and is the largest deal in Microsoft's history and the biggest all-cash acquisition in tech history.[79] Given the deal's size, and profile, regulators across the world, including the U.S. Federal Trade Commission ("FTC"), challenged the acquisition, citing concerns that the acquisition could substantially lessen competition in the videogame industry.[80]

ESG issues, particularly with respect to sexual harassment and workplace misconduct, play a prominent role in Microsoft's Activision deal. Since 2021, Activision has faced an avalanche of lawsuits and investigations related to sexual harassment, discrimination, and workplace misconduct, following a suit by a California regulatory agency alleging widespread sexual harassment at the company.[81] In response, Activision announced various reforms intended to "rebuild" employee trust.[82]

77 *Microsoft to Acquire Activision Blizzard to Bring the Joy and Community of Gaming to Everyone, across Every Device*, Microsoft, https://news.microsoft.com/2022/01/18/microsoft-to-acquire-activision-blizzard-to-bring-the-joy-and-community-of-gaming-to-everyone-across-every-device/ (last visited Jan. 29, 2022); Andrew Ross Sorkin, Jason Karaian, Sarah Kessler, Stephen Gandel, Michael J. de la Merced, Lauren Hirsch, & Ephrat Livni, *How Microsoft Bought Activision Blizzard*, N.Y. Times: DealBook (Jan. 19, 2022), https://www.nytimes.com/2022/01/19/business/dealbook/microsoft-activision-deal.html.

78 Karen Weise, Andrew Ross Sorkin, Kellen Browning, & Michael J. de la Merced, *Microsoft Will Buy Activision Blizzard, Betting $70 billion on the Future of Games*, N.Y. Times (Jan. 18, 2022), https://www.nytimes.com/2022/01/18/business/microsoft-activision-blizzard.html.

79 Anna Kaplan, *Microsoft Buying Activision Blizzard For Nearly $69 Billion – Will Be 3rd Largest Gaming Company*, Forbes (Jan. 18, 2022), https://www.forbes.com/sites/annakaplan/2022/01/18/microsoft-to-buy-troubled-activision-blizzard-for-nearly-69-billion/?sh=798ec11217c6.

80 Karen Weise & David McCabe, *F.T.C. Sues to Block Microsoft's $69 Billion Acquisition of Activision*, N.Y. Times (Dec. 8, 2022), https://www.nytimes.com/2022/12/08/technology/ftc-microsoft-activision.html; *Microsoft/Activision Blizzard Merger Inquiry*, Gov. UK Competition and Markets Authority Cases (Mar. 8, 2023), https://www.gov.uk/cma-cases/microsoft-slash-activision-blizzard-merger-inquiry.

81 Megan Farokhmanesh, *Activision Blizzard Employees Say HR Department Failed Them*, Axios (Aug. 3, 2021), https://www.axios.com/2021/08/03/activision-blizzard-harassment-lawsuit-hr.

82 Sara Ashley O'Brien, *Microsoft Makes a Big Bet That It Can Fix Activision Blizzard's Troubled Culture*, CNN (Jan. 27, 2022), https://www.cnn.com/2022/01/27/tech/activision-blizzard-microsoft-workplace-culture/index.html.

These reforms include leadership shakeups, adopting a "zero-tolerance harassment policy," expanding employee relations and compliance teams, and waiving the arbitration requirement for employees who want to bring sexual harassment or discrimination claims in the future.[83] Nevertheless, Activision employees have staged walkouts in response to what they perceive to be an inadequate response to overhaul a toxic workplace and called for the resignation of the company's CEO, Bobby Kotick.[84] Various reports allege that Kotick knew about various sexual misconduct allegations at the company, and himself engaged in mistreatment of women employees.[85]

Activision's ESG struggles, which led to a substantial drop in the company's stock price, prompted Microsoft to pursue the acquisition.[86] These struggles also affected Activision's receptivity to a deal. While Microsoft had long been interested in Activision and had discussed a potential acquisition in the past, Kotick was dismissive of such overtures until Microsoft opportunely offered him an exit from the company's ESG troubles.[87]

Activision's ESG struggles allowed Microsoft to pursue the deal, but they also pose ESG-related risks for Microsoft. Microsoft's CEO, Satya Nadella, has stated that corporate culture is his top priority and stressed the importance of redressing Activision's workplace.[88] Nevertheless, some labor experts caution that the acquisition could have a spillover effect by alienating some of Microsoft's existing employees.[89] Prominent politicians also urged the FTC to investigate the proposed acquisition, asserting that the deal runs the risk of undermining employees' calls for accountability over alleged misconduct at Activision.[90] Others have

[83] Sarah E. Needleman, *Judge Approves $18 Million Activision Settlement with EEOC*, Wall Street J. (Mar. 30, 2022), https://www.wsj.com/articles/judge-approves-18-million-activision-settlement-with-eeoc-11648644667?mod=article_inline.

[84] O'Brien, *supra* note 82.

[85] Kirsten Grind, Ben Fritz, & Sarah E. Neddleman, *Activision CEO Bobby Kotick Knew for Years About Sexual-Misconduct Allegations at Videogame Giant*, Wall Street J. (Nov. 16, 2021), https://www.wsj.com/articles/activision-videogames-bobby-kotick-sexual-misconduct-allegations-11637075680.

[86] Dieter Holger, *Microsoft's Activision Blizzard Deal Poses Sustainability Challenge*, Wall Street J. (Jan. 21, 2022), https://www.wsj.com/articles/microsofts-activision-blizzard-deal-poses-sustainability-challenge-11642785286.

[87] Kirsten Grind, Cara Lombardo, & Ben Fritz, *Activision Blizzard's Workplace Problems Spurred $75 Billion Microsoft Deal*, Wall Street J. (Jan. 18, 2022), https://www.wsj.com/articles/activision-blizzard-microsoft-deal-11642557922?mod=article_inline.

[88] O'Brien, *supra* note 82. [89] Ibid.

[90] Sarah E. Needleman, *Four U.S. Senators Cite Microsoft-Activision Deal Concern in FTC Letter*, Wall Street J. (Mar. 31, 2022), https://www.wsj.com/articles/u-s-senators-

called attention to the optics of Kotick – largely seen as responsible for and participating in Activision's culture of harassment – potentially receiving tens of millions as payout from the deal.[91] Concerns about Kotick's motivations in the deal have also led to shareholder litigation in Delaware, with shareholders claiming that Kotick negotiated Activision's sale to evade liability for misconduct at the company.[92]

The acquisition also risks creating vast ESG-related integration challenges for Microsoft. Experts contend that it could take years for Microsoft to bring Activision in line with its practices.[93] Microsoft has developed comprehensive ESG policies over many years, including various environmental and workplace-diversity disclosures, and plans to compensate for all its historical greenhouse-gas emissions. Activision, however, disclosed significantly less ESG information and had far fewer policies in place.[94]

10.3 Implications of the Rise of ESG for Board and Shareholder Engagement in M&A

The ESG pressure on M&A has important implications for corporate governance in M&A. Indeed, the M&A context magnifies the challenges that ESG presents for corporate governance. Large M&A deals affect virtually all constituencies of both the bidder and the target and directors face the challenge of considering the, at times, conflicting interests of these various constituencies.[95] This section addresses implications of the rise of ESG in M&A for boards and shareholders.

10.3.1 ESG and the Board's Role in M&A

Corporate law assigns responsibility for managing the corporation to the board of directors and defers to the business judgment of the board in

pressure-ftc-to-review-microsoft-activision-merger-11648741204?mod=Searchresults_pos3&page=1.

91 O'Brien, *supra* note 82.

92 Mike Leonard, *Activision's $69 Billion Sale to Microsoft Draws Challenge*, Bloomberg Law (Nov. 14, 2022), https://news.bloomberglaw.com/esg/activisions-69-billion-sale-to-microsoft-draws-court-challenge; Stephen Totilo, *New York City Sues Activision, Targeting CEO Bobby Kotick*, Axios (May 4, 2022), https://www.axios.com/2022/05/04/new-york-city-sues-activision.

93 *See* Holger, *supra* note 86.

94 *See* Ibid.

95 See Spencer J. Hazan, *Considering Stakeholders in M&A*, 16 NYU J. L. & Bus. 749, 756 (2020).

how it manages business decisions. The board's fiduciary duties of care and loyalty – including its obligation to act in good faith – provide the framework for the board's consideration of an M&A transaction. Directors have a fiduciary duty to act in the best interests of the corporation, and to exercise the care, diligence, and skill that a reasonably prudent person would exercise in comparable circumstances. So long as directors act in good faith and in the best interests of the corporation, the business judgment rule protects them from judicial second-guessing of their business decisions.[96] Thus, boards have wide discretion to make business decisions based on ESG factors if they reasonably believe that such actions are in the corporation's best interests. Experts argue "consideration of ESG factors and related metrics and the broader concepts of stakeholder governance and corporate purpose are entirely consistent with traditional conceptions of directors' duties" in M&A.[97]

Boards of most large public companies are dominated by independent directors who are charged with two broad, and often overlapping, roles: (i) directors serve as strategic advisors to management, with responsibility for approving or setting the strategy for the company; and (ii) directors serve as monitors of management on behalf of a firm's shareholders.[98] As ESG demands on corporations increase, boards must navigate their role vis-à-vis new stakeholder expectations as well as management control over much of M&A dealmaking.

10.3.1.1 ESG and the Board's Strategic Advisory Role in M&A

While the board's monitoring role is often heavily emphasized, its strategic advisory role is also critical to M&A.[99] Boards – especially bidder boards – are regularly advised to consider M&A activity as a strategic

[96] *See* Chris Brummer & Leo E. Strine, Jr., *Duty and Diversity*, 75 Vand. L. Rev. 1, 77–80 (2022).

[97] Andrew R. Brownstein, David M. Sil, & Sabastian V. Niles, *The Coming Impact of ESG on M&A*, Harv. L. Sch. Forum on Corp. Governance (Feb. 20, 2020), https://corpgov.law.harvard.edu/2020/02/20/the-coming-impact-of-esg-on-ma/.

[98] *See generally* Jeffrey N. Gordon, *The Rise of Independent Directors in the United States, 1950–2005: Of Shareholder Value and Stock Market Prices*, 59 Stan. L. Rev. 1465 (2007); *see also* Donald C. Clarke, *Three Concepts of the Independent Director*, 32 Del. J. Corp. L. 73, 81 (2007) (noting that a common function of directors is to serve as a "brain trust" or consultant).

[99] *See* PWC, A Corporate Director's Guide to Overseeing Deals (2022), https://www.pwc.com/us/en/services/governance-insights-center/assets/pwc-gic-overseeing-deals.pdf.

move for the company and to determine if a deal fits within a company's strategic plan.[100] As companies expand their own ESG goals, policies, and strategies, boards are increasingly advised to consider the ESG-logic of a deal.[101] Studies show that acquisitions of targets with better ESG performance can help buyers improve their own ESG performance and preserve stakeholder value.[102] Moreover, with rising demand for ESG disclosure, boards may need to consider how they will disclose and explain to shareholders the ESG risks and opportunities of a deal.

On the sell-side, boards are similarly involved in strategy. Consistent with their fiduciary responsibilities, Delaware law generally defers to the board's assessment about whether it is an opportune time to sell as company.[103] As the Delaware Supreme Court emphasized in the *Time Warner* case, in a non-sale M&A scenario, a board is under no duty to maximize short-term shareholder value and has discretion to select the appropriate timeframe for consideration of various alternatives.[104] Even when a decision to sell a company is made, Delaware law is generally deferential to a board's good faith and informed decision-making in assessing the strategic steps the company takes to maximize stockholder value in the sale.[105] Deal advisors increasingly note that boards of sellers should factor into their consideration of a deal a buyer's ESG performance and vulnerabilities. Boards of sellers are advised to evaluate whether and how ESG concerns may influence "shareholder decisions to support or reject a proposed transaction, particularly where the deal consideration includes shares of the acquiror."[106]

[100] *See* Alexandra R. Lajoux, *The Role of the Board in M&A*, HARV. L. SCH. FORUM ON CORP. GOVERNANCE (Sept. 7, 2015), https://corpgov.law.harvard.edu/2015/09/07/role-of-the-board-in-ma/.

[101] *See* Casey et al., *supra* note 68, at 6.

[102] *See* Ioannis Tampakoudis & Evgenia Anagnostopoulou, *The Effect of Mergers and Acquisitions on Environmental, Social and Governance Performance and Market Value: Evidence From EU Acquirers*, 29 BUS. STRATEGY AND THE ENV'T. 1865 (2020).

[103] *See, e.g.*, Paramount Commc'ns, Inc. v. Time, Inc., 571 A.2d 1140 (Del. 1989); Air Prods. & Chems., Inc. v. Airgas, Inc., 16 A.3d 48 (Del. Ch. 2011).

[104] *See* Paramount Commc'ns, Inc. v. Time, Inc., 571 A.2d 1140, 1150 (Del. 1990) (upholding board rejection of takeover offer that was based on a desire to protect Time's corporate culture).

[105] *See* Lyondell Chemical Co. v. Ryan, 970 A.2d 235 (Del. 2009); *see also* Charles R. Korsmo, *Delaware's Retreat from Judicial Scrutiny of Mergers*, 10 U.C. IRVINE L. REV. 55, 69–70 (2019) (noting the "retreat" of Delaware courts in reviewing boards' merger-related decisions).

[106] Emmerich & Norwitz, *supra* note 50.

While ESG may prove useful to a board's strategic decisions in M&A, the flexibility of ESG may also complicate the board's work. As Professor Pollman has argued, there is concern that the "constant expansion of sub-topics fitting under the big tent of ESG contributes to a sense that the term is too nebulous or so capacious that it is ultimately meaningless or will collapse under its own weight."[107] In the absence of a clear definition of ESG,[108] boards may overly focus on one set of factors for a deal – factors that may or may not be crucial for a successful M&A transaction – to the exclusion of other factors. The large breadth of topics encompassed by ESG also might be distracting in the deal context where speed, efficiency, and certainty regarding closing, are often paramount. Rather than helping a company make an informed business decision, a company's board and management, as well as their advisors, could get bogged down in the vast variety of ESG factors, without clear boundaries.[109]

Boards may also face challenges in evaluating the tensions between E and S that can arise in connection with M&A transactions. For example, some firms have used M&A to divest of "brown" assets. But while such a deal may benefit a company's environmental practices, it may also necessitate actions that do not benefit employees, including layoffs.[110]

10.3.1.2 ESG and the Board's Oversight Role in M&A

For many boards, their primary involvement in an M&A transaction is an oversight role to ensure "a reality check on management's plans."[111] Such an oversight role necessarily engages the board's core risk management responsibilities. ESG can both add to and complicate the board's risk management role in M&A.[112]

[107] Pollman, *supra* note 1, at 36.

[108] *See* Quinn Curtis, Jill Fisch, & Adriana Z. Robertson, *Do ESG Mutual Funds Deliver on Their Promises?*, 120 MICH. L. REV. 393, 402 (2021).

[109] *See* Hester Peirce, *Chocolate-Covered Cicadas*, SEC (July 20, 2021), https://www.sec.gov/news/speech/peirce-chocolate-covered-cicadas-072021?utm_medium=email&utm_source=govdelivery.

[110] *See* Alperen A. Gözlügöl, *The Clash of 'E' and 'S' of ESG: Just Transition on the Path to Net Zero and the Implications for Sustainable Corporate Governance and Finance* (SAFE, Working Paper No. 325, 2021; LawFin, Working Paper No. 25, 2021), https://ssrn.com/abstract=3962238.

[111] Lajoux, *supra* note 100.

[112] For an argument against extending the board's oversight obligations to ESG, see Stephen M. Bainbridge, *Don't Compound the Caremark Mistake by Extending it to ESG Oversight*, 77 BUSINESS LAWYER 651 (2022).

Over the past two decades, national legislation, corporate governance guidelines, and codes by leading international organizations have stressed the role of the board of directors in overseeing risk management.[113] Thus, the monitoring of risks has become a significant priority for corporate managers and boards.[114] Directors are not involved in the everyday management of risk – just as they are not involved in the day-to-day aspects of M&A dealmaking. However, they are often charged with setting the company's risk appetite and strategy. Moreover, the board is responsible for monitoring key risks and ensuring that a company's risk management framework achieves its business objectives.[115]

Some scholars, many investors and even companies themselves posit that ESG's value is as a risk management tool.[116] Professors Gadinis and Miazad found that at many companies "ESG has evolved into a separate corporate function, whose mission is to monitor and manage the risks facing the company due to environmental and social impact."[117] ESG has also become integral to the board's assessment of evolving risk. As the 2018 guidance by COSO and the World Business Council for Sustainable Development stressed, an ESG framework can help manage increasingly complex ESG risks – for example, climate change and sexual harassment scandals.[118]

ESG as a risk management tool can be useful to board oversight of M&A dealmaking.[119] For example, targeted ESG due diligence can help

[113] *See* OECD, Risk Management and Corporate Governance 10, 12 (2014), http://www.oecd.org/daf/ca/risk-management-corporate-governance.pdf; Virginia Harper Ho, *Board Duties: Monitoring, Risk Management, and Compliance, in Research Handbook on Comparative Corporate Governance* 4 (Afra Afsharipour & Martin Gelter eds., Edward Elgar Publishing Ltd. 2021).

[114] *See* Wachtell, Lipton, Rosen, & Katz, *Risk Management and the Board of Directors* 2–3 (Nov. 2019), https://corpgov.law.harvard.edu/wp-content/uploads/2019/11/Risk-Management-and-the-Board-of-Directors.pdf.

[115] *See* OECD, Risk Management and Corporate Governance, *supra* note 113, at 16.

[116] *See, e.g.*, Virginia Harper Ho, Sustainable Investment & Asset Management: From Resistance to Retooling, in *Investment Management, Stewardship and Sustainability* (Iris Chiu & Hans-Christoph Hirt eds., Hart Publishing 2023); Gadinis & Miazad, *supra* note 9; Virginia Harper Ho, *Risk-Related Activism: The Business Case for Monitoring Nonfinancial Risk*, 41 J. Corp. L. 647 (2016).

[117] *See* Gadinis & Miazad, *supra* note 9, at 1415.

[118] COSO & WBSCD, Enterprise Risk Management: Applying Enterprise Risk Management to Environmental, Social and Governance-Related Risks (Oct. 2018), https://www.wbcsd.org/erm.

[119] For a discussion of how boards can integrate compliance and ESG oversight, *see* Leo E. Strine, Jr., Kirby Smith, & Reilly Steel, *Caremark and ESG, Perfect Together: A Practical*

boards evaluate and plan for potential risks in the parties' operations and industry. As Microsoft's Activision deal demonstrates, boards can use ESG-related information to evaluate potential reputational risks connected to a deal or to question management on potential integration challenges. In addition to overpayment,[120] an acquisition may not achieve management's anticipated results due to a buyer's incomplete understanding of the business being acquired or due to cultural clashes between bidder and target.[121] Studies show that mergers of culturally similar firms are associated with greater synergies, superior long-run operating performance, and fewer write-offs of goodwill.[122] With companies identifying their risks more systematically and articulating their culture more clearly, such information can be valuable to boards as they evaluate management's assumption about a deal.

While ESG can be a useful risk management tool, it can also be difficult to assess and incorporate ESG risk analysis in M&A dealmaking. As discussed above, ESG itself does not have a common agreed-upon definition. A company may perform quite strongly on one aspect of ESG, but more poorly on another aspect of ESG. Tesla, for example, has faced numerous lawsuits alleging racial discrimination and sexual harassment at the company.[123] Given the lack of clear regulatory guidance on ESG, there may also be questions about the accuracy of a particular firm's ESG disclosure.[124] Moreover, many firms rely on ESG ratings to gain information about a target or bidder. Yet, measurement challenges abound with respect to ESG ratings.[125] Studies show that not only is there a wide

Approach to Implementing an Integrated, Efficient, and Effective Caremark and EESG Strategy, 106 IOWA L. REV. 1885 (2021).

120 For more on overpayment, *see* Afra Afsharipour & J. Travis Laster, *Enhanced Scrutiny on the Buy-Side*, 53 GA. L. REV. 443, 449–57 (2019).

121 *See* Michele Gelfand et al., *One Reason Mergers Fail: The Two Cultures Aren't Compatible*, HARV. BUS. REV. (Oct. 2, 2018).

122 *See* Bereskin et al., *supra* note 76, at 1995.

123 *See* Hyunjoo Jin, *Tesla Hit By New Lawsuit Alleging Racial Abuse Against Black Workers*, REUTERS (July 2, 2022), www.reuters.com/business/autos-transportation/tesla-hit-by-new-lawsuit-alleging-racial-abuse-against-black-workers-2022-07-01/; Michael Posner, *Does Tesla Deserve to Be Treated as an ESG Champion?*, ETHICAL SYSTEMS (Feb. 8, 2022), https://www.ethicalsystems.org/does-tesla-deserve-to-be-treated-as-an-esg-champion/.

124 *See* Jason Halper, Sara Bussiere, & Timbre Shriver, *"Sustainable" Companies Face Increased Pressure*, HARV. L. SCH. FORUM ON CORP. GOVERNANCE (Dec. 26, 2021), https://corpgov.law.harvard.edu/2021/12/26/sustainable-companies-face-increased-pressure/.

125 *See* Pucker, *supra* note 43; Larcker et al., *supra* note 39, at 2–4.

divergence across providers, but the measurement of the E, the S and the G also vary widely.[126] Furthermore, studies indicate that increased corporate disclosure of ESG may actually lead to less consistency in ESG ratings.[127] The divergence and measurement problems in ESG can make it challenging for a board – facing the pressures of time, speed, and costs in dealmaking – to effectively use ESG information to assess deal risks.

10.3.1.3 ESG and the Incentives of Boards and Managers

While corporate law and scholarship largely focus on the board and the interplay between the board and shareholders, for today's large public companies, senior executives – especially CEOs – dominate decision-making.[128] The domination of C-level executives in corporate decision-making is particularly acute in M&A deals where executives are the first among equals. In M&A, senior managers run the show. They typically control the initial conversations about a potential deal, engage in much of the diligence, negotiation and drafting, and control much of the flow of information to the board.[129]

Despite the board's power, there has long been concern that when it comes to serving as directors, even experienced businesspeople tend to be overly deferential to management.[130] As expressed by Delaware's former Chief Justice, directors "too often leave their business acumen, savvy, and, perhaps most important, skepticism, back home. Instead of pressing management for answers and learning the company's business deeply, directors sometimes act more like well-mannered season ticketholders to a stylized interactive theatre, in which performing managers shepherd

[126] *See* Berg et al., *supra* note 42. Not all see the divergence of ESG ratings as a concern, *see* Edmans, *supra* note 46, at 9; Anna Hirai & Andrew Brady, *Managing ESG Data and Rating Risk*, Harv. L. Sch. Forum on Corp. Governance (July 28, 2021), https://corpgov.law.harvard.edu/2021/07/28/managing-esg-data-and-rating-risk/.

[127] *See* Dane Christensen, George Serafeim, & Anywhere Sikochi, *Why Is Corporate Virtue in the Eye of the Beholder? The Case of ESG Ratings*, 97 The Accounting Rev. 147 (2022).

[128] *See, e.g.*, Megan Wischmeier Shaner, *Officer Accountability*, 32 Ga. St. U. L. Rev. 357, 367 (2016) (describing an "officer-dominated model of corporate governance, with officers exerting immense power and influence over the corporation"); Usha Rodrigues, *From Loyalty to Conflict: Addressing Fiduciary Duty at the Officer Level*, 61 Fla. L. Rev. 1, 1 (2009) (describing officers as the "true corporate decision makers").

[129] *See* Orit Gadiesh, Robin Buchanan, Mark Daniell, & Charles Ormiston, *A CEO's Guide to the New Challenges of M&A Leadership*, 30 Strategy & Leadership, 13, 13–14 (2002).

[130] *See* Gregory H. Shill & Matthew L. Strand, *Diversity, ESG and Latent Board Power*, 47 Del. J. Corp. L. 255, 272 (2022).

the audience through ritualized plays, listen to management give set piece reports, ask a few brief questions so as not to disrupt the actors' timing, and complete a series of management-driven acts."[131]

Concerns about board deference to management are intensified in M&A, where the board's judgment can be "contaminated by the interests of managers and advisors on whom directors rely."[132] Executives are incentivized to undertake M&A deals that will benefit themselves personally at the expense of the corporation.[133] Relatedly, prevalent cognitive and behavioral biases, such as hubris and overconfidence, may lead to value-destroying M&A deals pushed by executives and advisors.[134] Studies have found that executives may be overconfident about the value of a deal and, driven by their desire to win, they may be overoptimistic about their ability to successfully integrate the merged companies.[135] Executive decision-making in M&A has also been found to be tainted by other factors, such as extensive social ties between managers of bidders and targets, or a desire to keep up with peers undertaking acquisitions.[136]

Given Delaware's deference to boards and boards' deference to management, there are valid concerns that the ESG movement will expand the discretion given to managers and further insulate them from

[131] Leo E. Strine, Jr., *Documenting the Deal: How Quality Control and Candor Can Improve Boardroom Decision-Making and Reduce the Litigation Target Zone*, 70 Bus. Law. 679, 684–85 (2015).

[132] Afsharipour & Laster, *supra* note 120, 447–48.

[133] *See* Ibid. at 447, 470–73.

[134] For a comprehensive discussion of managerial biases in M&A, *see generally* Sanjay Dhir & Amita Mital, *Decision-Making for Mergers and Acquisitions: The Role of Agency Issues and Behavioral Biases*, 21 Strategic Change 59 (2012).

[135] *See* James A. Fanto, *Quasi-Rationality in Action: A Study of Psychological Factors in Merger Decision-Making*, 62 Ohio St. L.J. 1333, 1354–57, 1372–74 (2001); *see also, e.g.*, Vicki Bogan & David Just, *What Drives Merger Decision Making Behavior? Don't Seek, Don't Find, and Don't Change Your Mind*, 72 J. Econ. Behav. & Org. 930, 932 (2009) (noting that confirmation bias, "a situation in which an individual attaches too much importance to information that supports his views," impacts merger decisions); Deepak Malhotra, *The Desire to Win: The Effects of Competitive Arousal on Motivation and Behavior*, 111 Organizational Behav. & Hum. Decision Processes 139, 139 (2010) (examining "when and why potentially self-damaging competitive motivations and behaviors will emerge"); Deepak Malhotra, Gillian Ku, & J. Keith Murnighan, *When Winning Is Everything*, Harv. Bus. Rev. (May 2008), https://hbr.org/2008/05/when-winning-is-everything (identifying "three principal drivers of competitive arousal in business settings: rivalry, time pressure, and audience scrutiny").

[136] For an overview of this literature, *see generally* Afra Afsharipour, *Bias, Identity and M&A*, Wisc. L. Rev. 469, 477–79 (2020).

accountability.[137] Professor Roe has argued, for example, that when boards are encouraged or permitted to use stakeholder interests, it "could leave managers so much discretion that managers could easily pursue their own agenda, one that might maximize neither shareholder, employee, consumer, nor national wealth, but only their own."[138] Similarly, Professor Damodaran has stated that executives have actively encouraged and promoted ESG because of "the power it gives them to bypass shareholders and evade accountability."[139] In M&A deals where the potential for management conflict is particularly acute, concerns about too much discretion are palpable.

It is also unclear whether the ESG pronouncements of boards and executives result in any protection for stakeholders in M&A dealmaking. A recent study finds, for example, that in large M&A deals conducted during the COVID pandemic, managers of sellers focused on gains for shareholders, and of course for themselves, but failed to negotiate for any significant protections for stakeholders.[140] Similarly, in a study of private equity acquisitions of companies incorporated in states with constituency statutes that promote stakeholder interest, the study finds that corporate leaders "generally did not negotiate for any stakeholder benefits or any constraints on the post-deal power of the private equity buyer to make choices that would adversely affect stakeholders" including employees, customers, and local communities.[141]

10.3.2 ESG and Shareholder Engagement in M&A

The rising influence of ESG on M&A also complicates shareholder engagement with M&A deals. This section addresses the implications of ESG for shareholder voting and shareholder litigation in connection with M&A dealmaking.

[137] *See* Bebchuk & Tallarita, *supra* note 34, at 165.

[138] Mark J. Roe, *The Shareholder Wealth Maximization Norm and Industrial Organization*, 149 U. PA. L. REV. 2063, 2065 (2001).

[139] Aswath Damodaran, *The ESG Movement: The "Goodness" Gravy Train Rolls On!*, MUSINGS ON MARKETS (Sept. 14, 2021), https://aswathdamodaran.blogspot.com/2021/09/the-esg-movement-goodness-gravy-train.html.

[140] *See* Lucian A. Bebchuk, Kobi Kastiel, & Roberto Tallarita, *Stakeholder Capitalism in the Time of COVID*, 40 YALE J. ON REG. 60 (2023).

[141] Lucian A. Bebchuk, Kobi Kastiel, & Roberto Tallarita, *For Whom Corporate Leaders Bargain*, 94 S. CAL. L. REV. 1467, 1474–75 (2021).

10.3.2.1 Shareholder Voting and Voice

To date, in most M&A transactions, even when shareholders have voting rights, their voice is muted – shareholders largely vote with or side with management.[142] Studies indicate that passive index funds are less engaged in monitoring management in situations that would involve high-cost governance activities such as in M&A voting.[143] Moreover, large institutional investors often vote in favor of a deal because they are universal owners that frequently own shares in both the target and the bidder, as well as in competitors of the merging parties who may benefit from completion of a deal.[144]

ESG disclosure and engagement has the potential to make shareholder voting in and shareholder monitoring of M&A dealmaking more effective. Many studies find evidence of poor performance for large public company M&A transactions.[145] Several studies have found that shareholder voting and shareholder activism can positively impact M&A performance.[146] For example, studies find that shareholder voting can mitigate agency problems in acquisitions.[147] With more investors focused on ESG and with the rise in voting on ESG issues, it may be that such investors will similarly focus on voting on M&A deals in ways that lessen the impact of management biases and self-interest in M&A dealmaking.

ESG activism may also place a greater spotlight on how large institutional investors vote on M&A deals. Large institutional investors have backed ESG-related shareholder proposals and even voted against the reelection of directors at portfolio companies where ESG management

[142] *See* James D. Cox, Tomas J. Mondino, & Randall S. Thomas, *Understanding the (Ir) relevance of Shareholder Votes on M&A Deals*, 69 DUKE L.J. 503, 511–13 (2019); Sean J. Griffith & Dorothy S. Lund, *Conflicted Mutual Fund Voting in Corporate Law*, 99 B.U. L. REV. 1151, 1181 (2019); Giovanni Strampelli, *Are Passive Index Funds Active Owners? Corporate Governance Consequences of Passive Investing*, 55 SAN DIEGO L. REV. 803, 825–26 (2018).

[143] *See* Strampelli, *supra* note 142, at 823–26; Cornelius Schmidt & Rüdiger Fahlenbrach, *Do Exogenous Changes in Passive Institutional Ownership Affect Corporate Governance and Firm Value?*, 124 J. FIN. ECON. 285, 287 (2017).

[144] *See* Matt Levine, *Shareholders Like Any Old Merger*, BLOOMBERG (Feb. 14, 2022), https://www.bloomberg.com/opinion/articles/2022-02-14/shareholders-like-any-old-merger?leadSource=uverify%20wall.

[145] For a review of this literature, see Afsharipour & Laster, *supra* note 120, at 450–52.

[146] *See* Renneboog & Vansteenkiste, *supra* note 72, at 671–72.

[147] Kai Li, Tingting Liu, & Juan (Julie) Wu, *Vote Avoidance and Shareholder Voting in Mergers and Acquisitions*, 31 THE REV. OF FIN. STUDIES 3176 (2018).

was perceived as ineffective.[148] However, to date, their voting on M&A deals does not appear particularly aligned with their ESG pronouncements.[149] "[L]eading investors are generally unwilling to go beyond their standardized guidelines and to make significant investments in any company-specific analyses that may be required by engagement in more complex situations, such as ... M&A. ..."[150] With the greater focus on ESG, including the ESG activities of institutional investors, such investors may face pressure regarding their voting patterns in M&A deals. It is also possible that institutional investors' ESG focus may make engagement and voting in M&A deals more standardized and incentivize investors' monitoring of M&A deals.

The focus on ESG may also increase activism around M&A deals. Thus far, ESG activists have largely focused on shareholder proposals.[151] In 2021, however, ESG issues became key to a contested election when Engine No. 1 was able to secure three seats on the board of ExxonMobil. It does not seem out of the realm of possibility that ESG activists may partner with traditional activist investors to force a breakup or sale of the company, or to thwart a potential acquisition.[152] As an example, in fall 2021 a leading activist hedge fund, Third Point, launched a campaign against Royal Dutch Shell, calling for the breakup of the oil company into separate stand-alone companies, one of which, Third Point argued, could focus on renewable energy and other carbon-reduction technologies.[153]

[148] *See* Rodolfo Araujo & Garrett Muzikowski, *Boards Face Backlash as ESG Tips the Scales During 2021 Proxy Season*, Harv. L. Sch. Forum on Corp. Governance (Dec. 17, 2021), https://corpgov.law.harvard.edu/2021/12/17/boards-face-backlash-as-esg-tips-the-scales-during-2021-proxy-season/; Enriques & Romano, *supra* note 12, at 71.

[149] For an analysis of conflicts in institutional investor voting in M&A, *see* Griffith & Lund, *supra* note 142, at 1173–75. Many large institutional investors have relatively low incentives to engage with the active monitoring necessitated for M&A deals. *See* Enriques & Romano, *supra* note 12, at 62–65.

[150] Gaia Balp & Giovanni Strampelli, *Institutional Investor Collective Engagements: Non-Activist Cooperation vs. Activist Wolf Packs*, 14 Ohio St. Bus. L.J. 135, 190 (2020).

[151] *See* Marc S. Gerber & Raquel Fox, *Investors Press for Progress on ESG Matters, and SEC Prepares to Join the Fray*, Skadden Insights (Jan. 19, 2022), https://www.skadden.com/insights/publications/2022/01/2022-insights/corporate/investors-press-for-progress.

[152] *See* Andrew R. Brownstein & Carmen X.W. Lu, *ESG and M&A in 2022: From Risk Mitigation to Value Creation*, Harv. L. Sch. Forum on Corp. Governance (Jan. 24, 2022), https://corpgov.law.harvard.edu/2022/01/24/esg-and-ma-in-2022-from-risk-mitigation-to-value-creation/.

[153] *See* Stanley Reed, *Third Point, an Activist Investor, Is Calling for a Breakup of Royal Dutch Shell*, N.Y. Times (Oct. 28, 2021), https://www.nytimes.com/2021/10/28/business/third-point-shell-breakup.html.

Such campaigns may place significant pressure on institutional investors, and implicate tensions between the economic goals of investors and institutional investors' espoused ESG commitments.

10.3.2.2 Shareholder Litigation and M&A

M&A deals are often accompanied by shareholder litigation attacking the board's decision-making.[154] In response to an explosion of M&A-related deal litigation, the Delaware courts have increasingly constricted the ability of shareholders to bring M&A-related lawsuits.[155] The most significant shift in Delaware jurisprudence with respect to ex-post judicial review of board decisions in third-party takeovers has been the 2015 *Corwin* decision.[156] In *Corwin*, the Delaware Supreme Court held that the business judgment rule is "the appropriate standard of review for a post-closing damages action when a merger that is not subject to entire fairness has been approved by a fully informed, uncoerced majority of the disinterested stockholders."[157]

ESG-related diligence and integration efforts in connection with an M&A deal could provide useful avenues for shareholders to attempt to avoid *Corwin*. One way that plaintiffs can avoid *Corwin* is by bringing a claim about inadequate disclosures that would render the stockholder vote not fully informed. To satisfy the fully informed requirement, a board must disclose all material information within its control.[158] This has led plaintiffs to seek access to corporate records to craft viable inadequate disclosure claims in order to avoid the application of *Corwin*.[159] Plaintiffs have used inspection rights under section 220 of the Delaware General Corporation Law to show discrepancies between

[154] *See* Jill E. Fisch, Sean J. Griffith, & Steven Davidoff Solomon, *Confronting the Peppercorn Settlement in Merger Litigation: An Empirical Analysis and a Proposal for Reform*, 93 Tex. L. Rev. 557 (2015).

[155] *See generally* Afra Afsharipour, *Corporate Governance in Negotiated Takeovers: The Changing Comparative Landscape, in Research Handbook on Comparative Corporate Governance* (Afra Afsharipour & Martin Gelter eds., Edward Elgar Publishing Ltd. 2021).

[156] Corwin v. KKR Fin. Holdings LLC, 125 A.3d 304 (Del. 2015).

[157] *Corwin*, 125 A.3d at 305–06.

[158] *In re* Solera Holdings, Inc. S'holder Litig., 2017 Del. Ch. LEXIS 1, at *22 (Del. Ch. Jan. 5, 2017); *In re* Merge Healthcare Inc., S'holders Litig., 2017 Del. Ch. LEXIS 17, at *2, *26–27 (Del. Ch. Jan. 30, 2017).

[159] *See* Joel Friedlander, *Confronting the Problem of Fraud on the Board*, 75 Bus. Law. 1441, 1444 (2019–2020); *see also* Roy Shapira, *Corporate Law, Retooled: How Books and Records Revamped Judicial Oversight*, 42 Cardozo L. Rev. 1949 (2021).

the records and the provided disclosures.[160] Moreover, Delaware jurisprudence increasingly favors shareholders' ability to prove a proper purpose in accessing books and records.[161] Given the increasing importance of ESG factors to investor decisions, one could imagine shareholders using claims regarding inadequate ESG disclosure in connection with an M&A transaction.

An M&A transaction that conflicts with a company's pronounced commitments to ESG goals could also expose a buyer's board to potential shareholder action claiming that the board has failed to follow through on ESG commitments. For example, several companies have faced shareholder derivative litigation alleging that the board had failed to act on the company's commitment to diversity.[162] While courts have dismissed such cases, even unsuccessful shareholder derivative suits come with significant costs, particularly for M&A deals where such suits could undermine successful post-deal integration.

10.4 Conclusion

Demands on companies to systematically address ESG in their business decisions are poised to affect many critical aspects of M&A deals – from the logic of a deal to the procedural aspects of dealmaking. This chapter has provided an overview of the complex considerations that ESG poses for M&A dealmakers. The ESG pressures on M&A deals also influence corporate governance in M&A. As this chapter has explored, ESG has implications not only for board strategy and oversight in M&A, but also for shareholder engagement in M&A deals. In an ideal world, ESG information can help enhance board and shareholder decision-making around M&A. Yet, whether ESG considerations are likely to do so remains uncertain.

[160] *See* Friedlander, *supra* note 159, at 1472.

[161] *See* AmerisourceBergen Corporation v. Lebanon County Employees' Retirement Fund, 243 A.3d 417 (Del. 2020).

[162] For an overview of diversity-related shareholder suits, see Timothy Chow, Sharon Nelles, & Katharine Rodgers, Shareholder Derivative Actions in the United States, *in Diversity and Inclusion Practice Guide* (Timothy Chow ed., Law Business Research Ltd. 2021).

11

How Does Board-Shareholder Engagement Really Work?

Evidence from a Survey of Corporate Officers and from Disclosure Data

MATTEO GATTI, GIOVANNI STRAMPELLI AND MATTEO TONELLO

11.1 Introduction

Under a long-standing view, institutional investors are considered key actors in corporate governance of publicly listed firms.[1] Because such investors hold relevant stakes in thousands of corporations globally and, collectively, are often a corporation's major shareholders,[2] leading institutions are expected to perform an effective stewardship function and exert influence over portfolio companies.[3]

For helpful comments, we are grateful to Gaia Balp, Paul Davies, Doug Eakeley, Luca Enriques, Dionysia Katelouzou, Karina Litvack, Massimo Menchini, Wolf-Georg Ringe, Konstantinos Sergakis, and to participants at the Auxiliary Corporate Governance Conference organized by Assogestioni in Rome on October 13–14, 2022 and at the PhD Business Law Seminar at Bocconi University on October 18, 2022. Thanks to Thomas Daly for research assistance. All errors and omissions are our own. Support from the Rutgers Center for Corporate Law and Governance, the Schuchman Fund, The Conference Board, and ESGAUGE is gratefully acknowledged.

1 *See e.g.* John Coffee, Jr., *Liquidity versus Control: The Institutional Investor as Corporate Monitor*, 91 Colum. L. Rev. 1277 (1991); Bernard S. Black, *Agents Watching Agents: The Promise of Institutional Investor Voice*, 39 UCLA L. Rev. 811, 830 (1992).

2 Lazard, 2021 Review of Shareholder Activism, 19 January 2022, https://www.lazard.com/media/452017/lazards-2021-review-of-shareholder-activism_vff.pdf.

3 In the U.S., the Securities and Exchange Commission (SEC) "has indicated its support for increased communication between the board and its shareholders." Lisa M. Fairfax, *Mandating Board-Shareholder Engagement*, 2013 U. Ill. L. Rev. 821, 831 (2013) (citing Securities and Exchange Commission, Concept Release on the U.S. Proxy System, 75 Fed. Reg. 42,982, 42,998–99 (proposal July 22, 2010)). In the European Union, institutions are actually required to undertake stewardship efforts under various national stewardship codes and the shareholders rights directive. See Directive 2017/828, of the European Parliament and of the Council of 17 May 2017 amending Directive 2007/36/EC as Regards the Encouragement of Long-Term Shareholder Engagement, 2017 O.J. (L 132) 16.

In fact, institutions' appetite for engagement has grown over the last several years. Not only do institutional investors – especially larger ones – regularly vote portfolio shares at shareholders' meetings, but their active ownership playbook also largely relies on meeting the board, or management, of portfolio companies to discuss key issues, convey their concerns and views, and urge the corporation to collaboratively respond to investor demands.[4] Private dialogue with corporate directors that takes place "behind the scenes" has grown into one of the levers of engagement most popular among institutional shareholders[5] and, as this chapter shows, other types of investors.

The increasing relevance of board-shareholder engagement is also confirmed by the fact that a number of corporate governance actors and organizations have drafted protocols and recommendations concerning board-shareholder dialogue.[6] In 2014, for example, a working group of leading independent directors and representatives from some of the largest and most influential long-term institutional investors developed sets of guidelines (Shareholder-Director Exchange Protocol) to provide a framework for shareholder-director engagement.[7] Along the same lines, the Investor Stewardship Group (ISG) (a group of 38 U.S. and international institutional investors) has developed a framework for U.S. Stewardship and Governance comprising a set of stewardship principles for institutional investors and corporate governance principles for U.S.-listed companies.[8] Corporate Governance Principle No. 3.3, which deals with director-shareholder dialogue, established that "[t]he appropriate independent directors should be available to engage in dialogue with shareholders on matters of significance, in order to understand shareholders' views."[9] Nevertheless, in spite of this favourable trend, director-shareholder dialogue is in some aspects still tricky: for instance, public disclosure and insider trading rules may pose a hurdle to board-shareholder engagement.[10]

[4] *See generally* Matthew J. Mallow & Jasmine Sethi, *Engagement: The Missing Middle Approach in the Bebchuk-Strine Debates*, 12 N.Y.U. J. L. & BUS. 386 (2016).

[5] Joseph A. McCahery, Zacharias Sautner, & Laura T. Starks, *Behind the Scenes: The Corporate Governance Preferences of Institutional Investors*, 71 J. FIN. 2905, 2911–12 (2016).

[6] *See* Fairfax, *supra* note 3, at 836.

[7] Shareholder-Director Exchange Protocol (2014), available at https://www.sdxprotocol.com/what-is-the-sdx-protocol/.

[8] Investor Stewardship Group (ISG), Stewardship Framework for Institutional Investors, 2018, https://www.isgframework.org/stewardship-principles/.

[9] Ibid.

[10] *See generally* Giovanni Strampelli, *Knocking at the Boardroom Door: A Transatlantic Overview of Director-Institutional Investor Engagement in Law and Practice*, 12 VA. L. & BUS. REV. 187, 205 (2018).

The fact that private meetings with company directors and management can actually create value and have an impact on issuers' decisions, as some studies have suggested,[11] might explain the ever-growing relevance of board-shareholder engagement. Yet, while seeking to increase the amount and value of assets under management remains the primary and fundamental objective for many institutional investors, the focus of institutions' investment and engagement strategies has changed over time to include broader, non-financial objectives as well. Today, stewardship (and investment) strategies adopted by many institutional investors embrace not only governance standards but also environmental and social ones, to help incorporate the risk assessment of long-term environmental, social, and governance (ESG) challenges and developments, and to foster a more responsible conduct by portfolio companies that can positively impact the environment and society at large.[12]

Against this background, evidence on engagement practices is still limited: because it usually takes place behind the scenes, few details about it are reported. To fill the gap, this Chapter sheds light on board-shareholder engagement practices in the U.S. To that end, our study is based on a survey of SEC-registered corporations conducted in the spring of 2022 to investigate board-shareholder engagement. The survey was circulated among corporate secretaries, general counsel, and investor relations officers, and obtained 171 responses. We complement the survey with: (i) a review and analysis of data on corporate-shareholder engagement from disclosures by Russell 3000 and S&P 500 companies, and (ii) information on the 2022 proxy season.[13]

[11] *See* Marco Becht, Julian R. Franks, Colin Mayer, & Stefano Rossi, *Returns to Shareholder Activism: Evidence from a Clinical Study of the Hermes UK Focus Fund* 23 REV. FIN. STUD. 3093, 3108–18 (2010); Willard T. Carleton, James M. Nelson, & Michael S. Weisbach, *The Influence of Institutions on Corporate Governance through Private Negotiations: Evidence from TIAA-CREF*, 53 J. FIN. 1335, 1335 (1998).

[12] *See* Michal Barzuza, Quinn Curtis, & David H. Webber, *Shareholder Value(s): Index Fund ESG Activism and the New Millennial Corporate Governance*, 93 S. CAL. L. REV. 1243 (2020); John C. Coffee, Jr., *The Future of Disclosure: ESG, Common Ownership, and Systematic Risk*, 2021 COLUM. BUS. L. REV. 602 (2021) ; Madison Condon, *Externalities and the Common Owner*, 95 WASH. L. REV. 1 (2020); Riccardo Boffo & Robert Patalano, *ESG Investing: Practices, Progress and Challenges* 14, OECD Paris (2020), https://www.oecd.org/finance/ESG-Investing-Practices-Progress-Challenges.pdf.; Jeffrey N. Gordon, *Systematic Stewardship*, 47 J. CORP. L. 627 (2022); Elizabeth Pollman, *The Making and Meaning of ESG*, European Corporate Governance Institute – Law Working Paper No. 659/2022, https://papers.ssrn.com/sol3/papers.cfm?abstract_id=4219857; Caleb N. Griffin, Humanizing Corporate Governance, Fl. L. Rev. (forthcoming 2023), https://papers.ssrn.com/sol3/papers.cfm?abstract_id=4295710.

[13] THE CONFERENCE BOARD, SHAREHOLDER VOTING TRENDS (2018–2022) (2022) (on file with authors).

Our findings show that, while not ubiquitous, corporate-shareholder engagement is important and on the rise. Even though large-sized companies are more frequently engaged by institutional investors, board-shareholder engagement is extending to mid-sized companies as well, as ESG issues, traditionally affecting larger companies, are becoming crucial for a broader spectrum of issuers.

We find that, even though shareholder engagement is sometimes referred to as soft activism, roughly 60 percent of surveyed companies experience confrontational engagement. This is either because the shareholder has a history of activism or is adversarial to the board or management in the specific case. Hedge funds, the second-largest interlocutors of our respondents after private-sector asset managers, are mostly responsible for shareholder-initiated engagements. As the role of activists is more relevant for smaller companies, confrontational engagement becomes less frequent as the size of the company engaged increases.

Finally, we find that engagement can be consequential in terms of outcomes. Almost half of our survey respondents stated that engagement led to a change in corporate practice. Importantly, the responses show a very close link between voting and engagement, which often resulted in the withdrawal of a shareholder proposal and/or in a change in the proxy vote previously announced by the engaged shareholder(s), suggesting that engagement can sway voters to support a company's position in an election or shareholder resolution. Moreover, in three of 10 instances, engagement resulted in the inclusion of a director nominee proposed by the engaged shareholder(s) in the slate supported by management: an outcome especially relevant where hedge funds are involved.

This chapter is structured as follows. Section 11.2 describes the methodology we use to analyze engagement practices. Section 11.3 describes our findings on items such as: frequency and duration of engagement; typology of engaged shareholders; engagement initiated by the company; engagement initiated by shareholders and whether it was confrontational or not; topics of engagement; outcomes of engagement; director involvement and leadership; managerial involvement; factors preventing additional engagement; formal engagement policies; and Regulation FD liability risk mitigation measures. Section 11.4 analyzes certain main findings and Section 11.5 concludes.

11.2 Methodology

This study is based on data from three different sources: a survey, issuers' annual disclosures, and proxy season activity.

First, in the spring of 2022, we conducted a survey of SEC-registered corporations to investigate board-shareholder engagement and board members' involvement in the process. The survey was circulated among corporate secretaries, general counsel, and investor relations officers of SEC-registered issuers. We obtained 171 responses. Participants were asked to provide information based on board-shareholder engagement practices conducted either at the time of the survey or in the preceding 12 months. In addition to investigating topics and outcomes of the engagement, the survey inquired on the types of investors the company engaged with, the frequency of the engagement, whether the engagement was initiated by the company or the shareholder(s), and whether it was confrontational.

Survey data findings are categorized and analyzed according to (i) the company's inclusion in the S&P 500 and/or Russell 3000 indexes, (ii) the size of participating companies (by annual revenue), and (iii) three large business sector groups – manufacturing, financial services (including banking, insurance, and real estate companies), and nonfinancial services firms.

Second, we complement the survey analysis with a review of 2022 disclosure data on corporate-shareholder engagement from Russell 3000 and S&P 500 companies received from ESG data analytics firm ESGAUGE. Disclosure of shareholder engagement practices is more prominent among larger companies. In the S&P 500 index, 83.4 percent of companies made disclosures about their shareholder engagement practices, compared to 45.6 percent of Russell 3000 companies and 60.1 percent of S&P MidCap 400 companies. Such data provide important additional details, including for example on the number of shareholders with whom the company engaged, the percentage of shares held by such shareholders, and the disclosure of the specific involvement of board members in the engagement activities.

Finally, the discussion is corroborated with information on voting trends in connection with shareholder proposals during the 2022 proxy season. We collect such information from Shareholder Voting Trends (2018–2022), as published by The Conference Board at the end of the 2022 proxy season, in partnership with ESGAUGE and in collaboration with the Rutgers Center for Corporate Law and Governance and Russell Reynolds Associates.[14] References to proxy voting developments

[14] *See supra* note 13.

(including volume and topics of shareholder proposals, the level of support received by those proposals when put to a vote, and the types of proposal sponsors) at publicly-held shareholder meetings are used in this chapter to provide more context to the findings on the more private activities in connection with shareholder engagement.

11.3 Findings

11.3.1 Frequency and Duration of Board-Shareholder Engagement

11.3.1.1 Frequency

Corporate-shareholder engagement is important but not as ubiquitous as one would think: Four of 10 companies in the Russell 3000 sample and two of 10 in the S&P 500 sample did not engage with investors in the preceding 12 months (see Figure 11.1). The results suggest that investors can engage with only a limited number of their portfolio companies,[15] and can be argued that they tend to focus on larger and more prominent businesses. According to the survey, the larger the companies, the more frequent the engagement. Around 40 percent of survey respondents with annual revenue in the $1–10 billion bracket report they engaged between two and five times, while larger companies report even more frequency.[16] Nearly 9 percent of companies in the S&P 500 sample reported more than 12 episodes in the previous 12 months.

The data shows that engagement is still on the rise. Most companies across indexes and revenue sizes reported the frequency of their engagement has "somewhat increased" with respect to several categories, such as executive compensation issues, governance issues, environmental policy issues, human capital management issues, and other social policy issues (e.g., human rights, animal rights, political spending) (see Figure 11.2).[17] The survey also shows that ESG matters are increasing in importance also for medium sized firms: one out of six companies in the $1-to-$10 billion revenue bracket reported that ESG engagement significantly increased (six out of 10 responded that it somewhat increased).

[15] Lucian A. Bebchuk & Scott Hirst, *Index Funds and the Future of Corporate Governance: Theory, Evidence, and Policy*, 119 Colum. L. Rev. 2029, 2085–88 (2019).

[16] Companies with annual revenue between $100 million to less than $1 billion report less board engagement: half of them said their board never engaged shareholders, and almost one third reported only one episode.

[17] *See infra* Section 11.3.5.

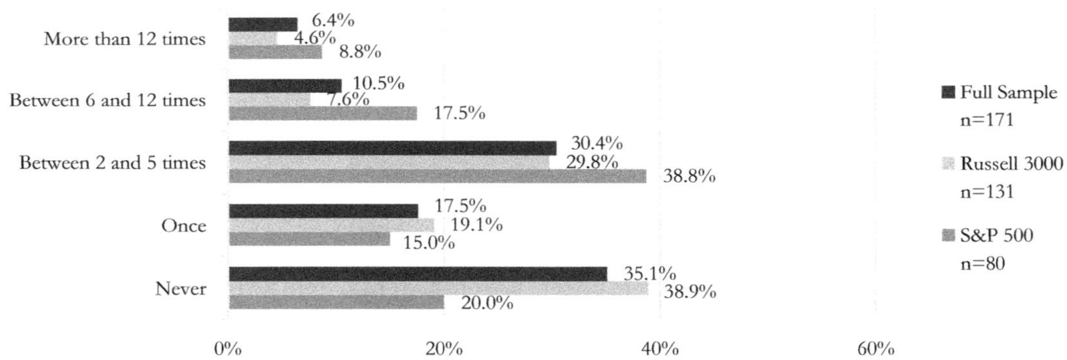

Figure 11.1 Frequency of board-shareholder engagement, *by index*

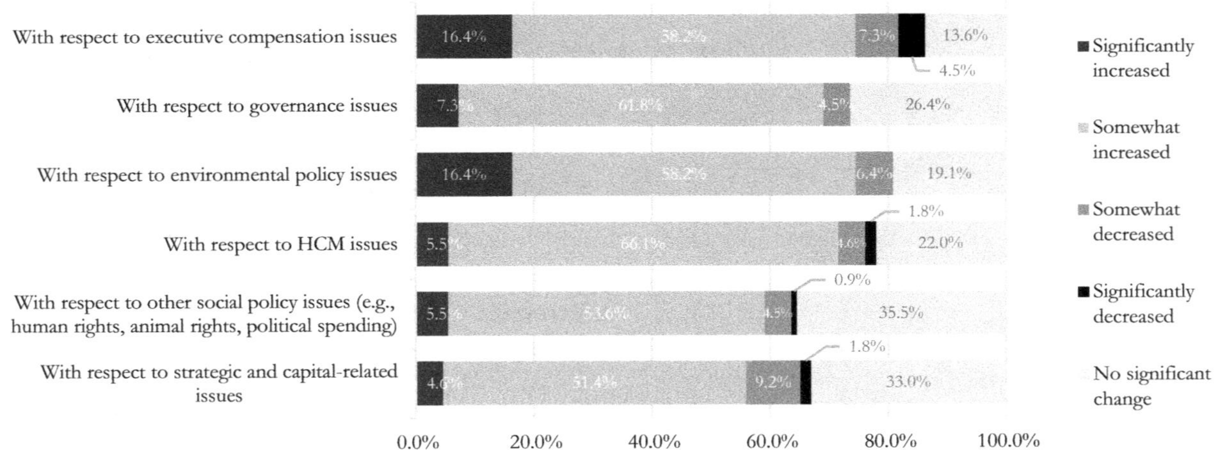

Figure 11.2 Frequency of board-shareholder engagements in the last three years, *full sample*

11.3.1.2 Duration

Engagement can last long: About seven of 10 surveyed companies responded that their longest engagement – the time between when an issue was first raised and the time when it was resolved – lasted more than a month, with nearly 40 percent of companies across the various samples responding that the longest instance of engagement lasted six months or longer.[18] Given the stewardship budget constraints mentioned above,[19] intensive and repetitive engagement involves only a small proportion of portfolio companies and is generally more common at the largest companies. On the other end of the spectrum, slightly more than 20 percent of S&P 500 companies responded that their longest engagement was only a one-time exchange (see Figure 11.3).

Conversely, upwards of 40 percent of companies across sectors reported that their *shortest* experience of board-shareholder engagement consisted of a one-time exchange between directors and investors on a certain issue. Yet roughly 10 percent of companies in the full sample and across the Russell 3000 and S&P 500 indexes reported that their shortest engagement lasted one to six months.[20]

11.3.2 Typology of Engaged Shareholders

11.3.2.1 Survey Data

As Figure 11.4 shows, *private-sector asset managers* (including the Big Three and other managers of mutual funds)[21] are the largest

[18] Companies use a variety of communication forms to facilitate the engagement of their boards with shareholders, including email and letter exchanges, phone (or video) calls, and individual (in-person) meetings. Generally, fifth analyst calls (i.e., a separate conference call with institutional investors dedicated to matters of corporate governance) and large town-hall meetings (whether in a public or private venue) are much less frequently deployed for this purpose. As a likely consequence of the pandemic, nearly all respondents had phone or video calls with their investors. Over half of the surveyed companies responded they had letter exchanges with investors and nearly half of them had individual in-person meetings (45.6 percent of Russell 3000 companies and 43.5 percent of S&P 500 companies) (note that the survey allowed for multiple answers and therefore the total exceeds 100 percent).

[19] *See supra* Section 11.3.1.

[20] According to the company size analysis, survey participants in the group of companies with annual revenue of at least $50 billion stated that their shortest experience of board-shareholder engagement either resulted in a one-time exchange (45.5 percent) or lasted less than a week (54.5 percent). As revenue decreased, companies saw their shortest engagements increase in time.

[21] *See* Dorothy Lund & Adriana Z. Robertson, *Giant Asset Managers, the Big Three, and Index Investing, in Board-Shareholder Dialogue: Policy Debate, Legal Constraints and Best Practices* (Luca Enriques & Giovanni Strampelli eds., Cambridge University Press 2024).

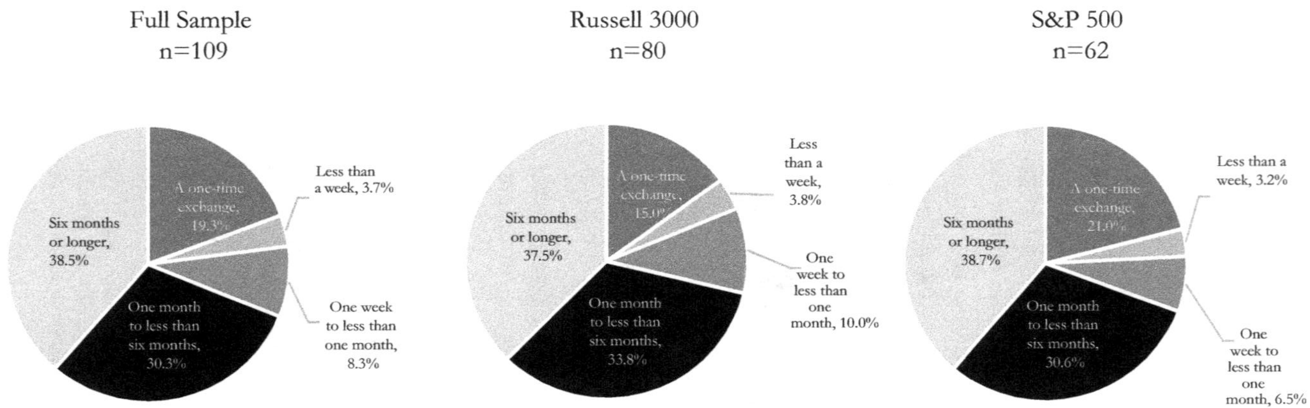

Figure 11.3 Longest experienced instance of board-shareholder engagement, *full sample*

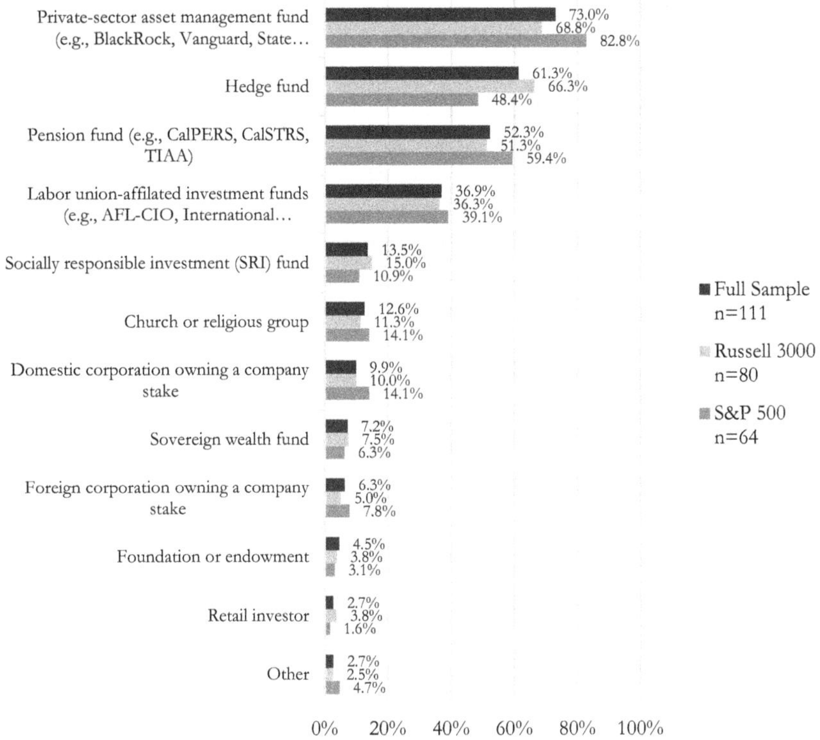

Figure 11.4 Engaged shareholder types, *by index*

interlocutors of our respondents (accounting for 73 percent of the whole sample, 68.8 percent of the Russell 3000 sample and 82.8 percent of the S&P 500 sample), followed by *hedge funds* (61.3 percent of the whole sample, 66.3 percent of the Russell 3000 sample, and 48.4 percent of the S&P 500 sample) and *pension funds* (52.3 percent of the whole sample, 51.3 percent of the Russell 3000 sample, and 59.4 percent of the S&P 500 sample). Labor union-affiliated funds were the interlocutor for more than one of three companies across the different samples. Socially responsible investment (SRI) funds (or funds adopting an investment strategy that aims at generating a combination of financial returns and social impacts), domestic corporations owning a stake in the underlying company, and churches or religious groups were each the interlocutor of around 10–15% of surveyed companies across the various samples. Retail investors were the smallest engagers (less than 5 percent across the various samples, except that when they engage, they generally pick very large companies: 9.1 percent of companies with revenue above $50 billion reported engagement with retail investors).

According to the company annual revenue segmentation, the larger the company the more likely for it to experience instances of private fund engagement: More than 90 percent of boards in the $50 billion-and-over revenue category reported meetings with private asset managers in their shareholder base in the previous 12 months. The prevalence of mainstream investors in large companies is in line with the increasing role of passive funds.[22] Indeed, larger companies tend to be weighted higher in the benchmark indices. On the other hand, companies with annual revenue between $100 million to less than $1 billion experienced more engagement by hedge funds (76.5 percent), followed by private funds (41.2 percent) and pension funds (29.4 percent).[23] SRI funds engage only with companies of larger size.[24]

11.3.2.2 Disclosure Data

The disclosure analysis brings additional insights into the type of shareholders companies engage with. Specifically, Figure 11.5 shows that, in the S&P 500, 60.6 percent disclosed the percentage of shares held by the shareholders with which the company engaged, while 9.4 percent disclosed the number of shareholders, and 10 percent discussed the extent of their engagement only in qualitative terms. The percentages for each of those categories are slightly smaller in the other two indexes, where a higher share of companies provided no disclosure whatsoever of the extent of their shareholder engagement.

[22] Similarly, companies with annual revenue between $10 billion to less than $50 billion also experienced private fund engagement most frequently (83.8 percent). These companies engaged pension funds second most frequently (62.2 percent), followed by hedge funds (45.9 percent). Companies with annual revenue between $1 billion to less than $10 billion had similar shareholder preferences.

[23] To be successful, hedge fund activism requires accruing a relatively large percentage of a company's shares, which is easier to do if the company has smaller capitalization and fewer shares outstanding. See Damien Park & Matteo Tonello, *The Shareholder Activism Report. Best Practices and Engagement Tools for Public Companies* 60, The Conference Board (2010). *See also* Alon Brav, Wei Jiang, Frank Partnoy, & Randall Thomas, *Hedge Fund Activism, Corporate Governance, and Firm Performance*, 63 J. Fin. 1729, 1746–49 (2008).

[24] 23.3 percent of companies in the $1–10 billion bracket reported engagement with SRI funds, and roughly 10 percent of companies above $10 billion of revenue.

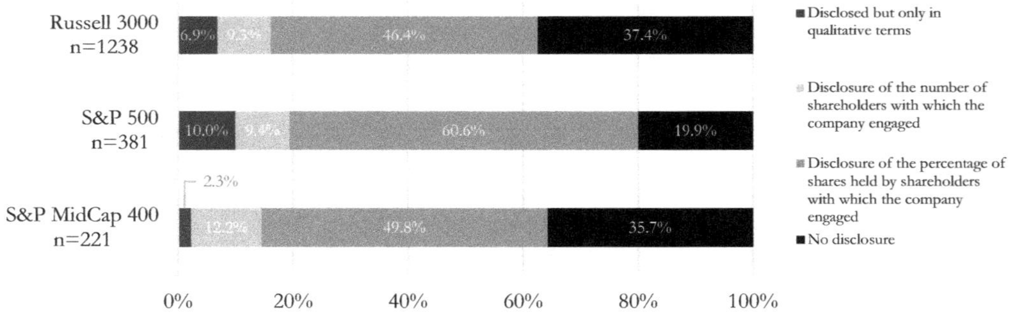

Figure 11.5 Disclosure of extent of shareholder engagement, *by index*

(a) *Number of Shareholders*. Many S&P 500 companies interact with several shareholders. What emerges from Figure 11.6 is that around 150 S&P 500 issuers indicated a number between 21 and 50 shareholders, while 30 of such issuers indicated a number between 51 and 100.

(b) *Holdings*. Near 20 percent of S&P 500 companies disclosed the percentage of outstanding shares held by shareholders they engaged with throughout the prior fiscal year. As Figure 11.7 shows, almost 30 percent of such disclosing companies reported that they engaged with shareholders holding an aggregate of more than half of the company's outstanding shares, while another 30 percent reported they engaged with more than 40 percent (but no more than 50 percent). All in all, 83 percent of the companies that reported aggregated holdings engaged with 30 percent or more of the outstanding shares.[25] To be clear, because each year companies experience multiple instances of engagement,[26] the percentages described in the distribution frequency in Figure 11.7 reflect aggregate holdings of shareholders that plausibly engaged *on different occasions*. Therefore, the data should not be interpreted as suggesting that the *average* episode of engagement draws the levels of holdings described in Figure 11.7.

11.3.3 Board-Shareholder Engagement Initiated by the Company

Most respondents reported that their board has initiated engagement; however, roughly 30 percent of companies in the sample have never initiated engagement in the preceding 12 months (approximately 35 percent of Russell 3000 companies and 24 percent of S&P 500 companies). There appears to be a direct correlation between boards' initiating engagement and revenue size. For smaller companies by revenue ($100 million to $1 billion), most boards never initiated shareholder engagement. As revenue increases, passive boards become less frequent. Less than a third of companies with revenue between $1 billion and $10

[25] Note that smaller companies engage with greater fractions of share ownership. For example, our data shows that half of Russell 3000 companies with annual revenue under $100 million engaged with investors holding an aggregate of 51 percent or more, compared to only 12.5 percent of companies with annual revenue of $50 billion or higher.

[26] *See supra* Section 11.3.1.

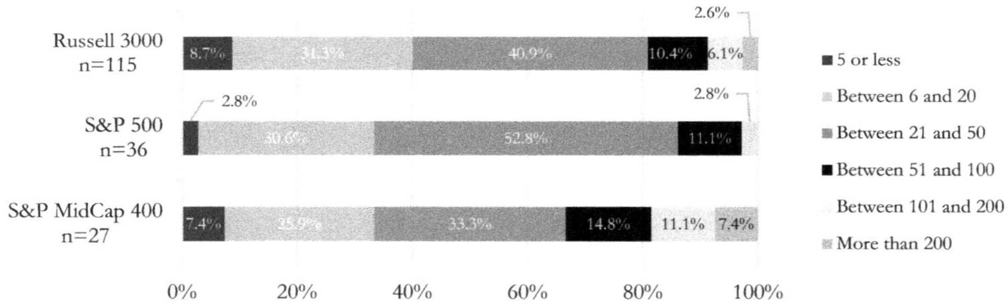

Figure 11.6 Number of shareholders the company engaged with, *by index*.

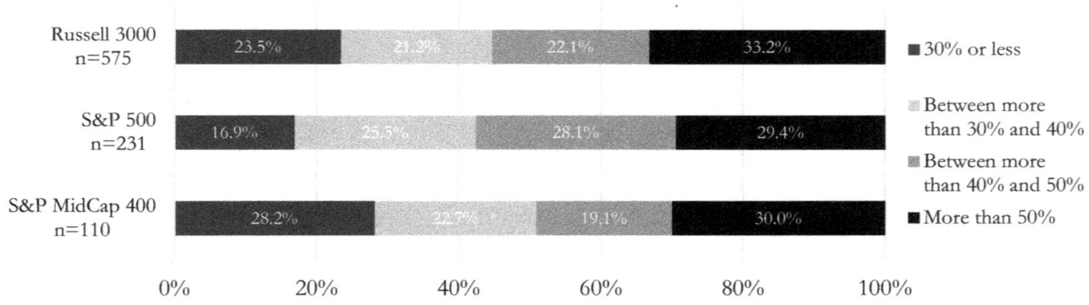

Figure 11.7 Shares held by shareholders the company engaged with, *by index*

billion indicated zero company-initiated engagements. 21.6 percent of respondents with annual revenue of $10 billion to less than $50 billion, and 18.2 percent of the largest companies by revenue, indicated the same.

11.3.4 Engagement Initiated by Shareholders: Confrontational v. Non-confrontational

We asked if engagement was confrontational – either because the shareholder had a history of activism or was adversarial to the board or management in the specific case. Although shareholder engagement is considered a softer form of interaction than activism,[27] as Figure 11.8 shows, only about four out of 10 engagements initiated by shareholders were non-confrontational (32.4 percent of the Russell 3000 sample and 48.4 percent of the S&P 500 sample). Roughly 60 percent of surveyed companies had confrontational engagements: around 40 percent of companies had both confrontational and non-confrontational engagements, and the remainder (around 20 percent) experienced only confrontational engagements. Activist hedge funds played a role in such episodes, with around one out of 10 companies experiencing engagement initiated by activists (engagement by activists is lower for S&P 500 and larger companies, in each case below 5 percent, confirming that the role of activists is greater at smaller companies).

11.3.5 Topics of Engagement

The survey inquired about the topics of discussion during engagement between directors and shareholders. The most common topics of engagement are executive compensation, climate and greenhouse gas emissions, and board diversity, while some hot topics are not a recurring subject of engagement. Only around 10 percent of respondents mentioned extraordinary transactions such as mergers and acquisitions, capital increases, share buybacks and only 13.8 percent mentioned corporate objectives.

To better grasp on what topics different types of shareholders engage, below we also report on responses from corporations that engaged only with hedge funds and those that engaged only with "Private-sector Asset Management Fund" and/or "Pension Fund" and/or "Labor-union Affiliated Investment Fund" (hereinafter, institutional investors).

[27] *See generally* Mallow & Sethi, *supra* note 4.

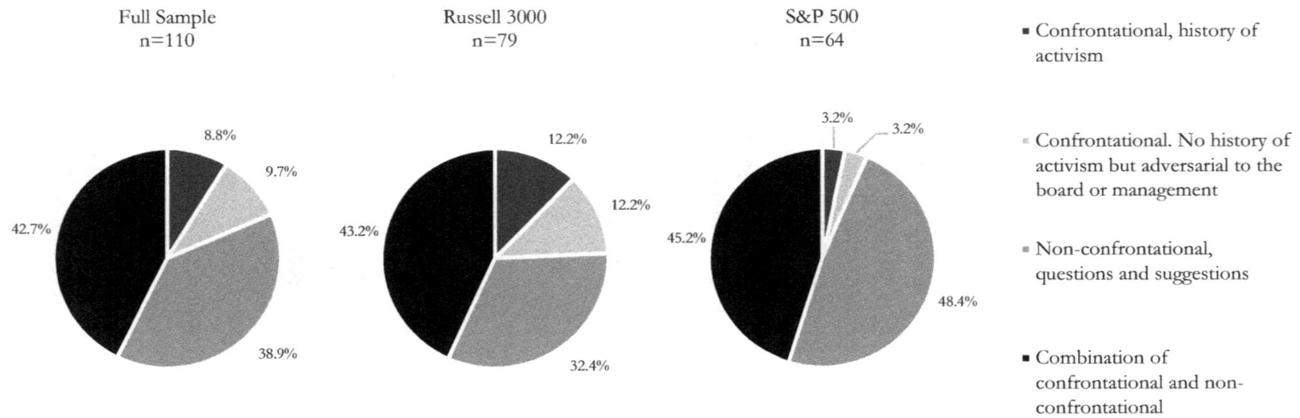

Figure 11.8 Board engagement with confrontational shareholders, *by index*

The analysis is further corroborated with information on shareholder resolutions that went to a vote in the 2022 proxy season. The comparison with survey findings helps underscoring how shareholder engagement is being used by corporations to preempt more public shareholder initiatives and to avoid the negative publicity that may follow a shareholder vote on a contentious issue such as gas emission reduction. To be sure, as we illustrate below, many of the successful proposals in 2022, especially on E&S-related matters, targeted large and prominent companies and made headlines – a tactic that is arguably used to maximize the publicity of the campaigns and influence corporate policies beyond the immediate target.

11.3.5.1 Executive Compensation

a) *Survey*. Under the category of executive compensation, the topic of incentive plan design issues (e.g., performance measures, targets, thresholds, maximum payouts) was most discussed across all indexes, sectors, and annual revenue.[28] Stock options and long-term incentive awards were mentioned by 31.2 percent of respondents, while each of annual bonus, pay for performance, and sustainability performance were mentioned by 25.7 percent of respondents. These issues appear to be less sensitive for hedge funds, which in turn pay more attention to annual bonus. See Table 11.1.

b) *Proxy Season*. In the last decade, shareholder resolutions on executive compensation issues have declined in volume, rarely reaching the majority support level. The introduction of say on pay has favored pre-season shareholder engagement on the company's pay policy for senior executives. In the 2022 proxy season, however, five resolutions regarding golden parachutes in severance agreements related to mergers or change-in-control transactions had a successful outcome.

11.3.5.2 Corporate Governance

a) *Survey*. As Table 11.2 shows, board diversity, and in particular racial and gender diversity, is the most recurring corporate governance issue. This is particularly the case for S&P 500 companies and as

[28] Companies that engaged with institutional investors only report even higher percentages (especially S&P companies: almost 60 percent).

Table 11.1 *Executive compensation,* by investor type

	Executive compensation issues (incl. CEOs and NEOs)		
	Full sample (%) n = 109	Hedge funds (%) n = 22	Institutional investors (%) n = 31
Annual bonus	25.7	36.4	16.1
Unrestricted stock awards	17.4	13.6	12.9
Stock options or other long-term incentive awards	31.2	13.6	41.9
Recoupment of incentive pay ("clawback")	21.1	13.6	16.1
Incentive plan design issues	45.9	45.5	54.8
Other issues on the link between compensation and financial performance	25.7	13.6	19.4
Other issues on the link between compensation and sustainability performance	25.7	18.2	32.3

revenue increases,[29] as well as for institutional investors, while these issues were mentioned by only 30 percent of respondents who dealt exclusively with hedge funds. Other issues that gathered investor attention are director over-boarding policies (restriction on number of multiple directorships), director qualifications and skills and retirement policy. Conversely hot button issues such as poison pills, proxy access, board declassification, proxy firm voting recommendation and CEO succession were mentioned by less than 10 percent of respondents: this is a possible consequence of companies having already taken substantial action in response to investor pressure in the last 10–15 years.

[29] Some conservative politicians have accused the Big Three of promoting "woke" politics despite being unelected to public office. In fact, almost two out of three companies that exclusively engaged with private funds cite racial and gender diversity as an engagement topic. Yet, if one looks at hedge funds, the ratio is almost one out of three for racial diversity and one out of four for gender diversity, which numbers are still quite substantial, if one considers that those were the two most discussed corporate governance topics for that type of investor.

Table 11.2 *Corporate governance,* by investor type

	Corporate governance issues		
	Full sample (%) n = 109	Hedge funds (%) n = 22	Institutional investors (%) n = 31
Board diversity (gender)	36.7	27.3	64.5
Board diversity (race or ethnicity)	44.0	31.8	64.5
Board diversity (sexual orientation)	15.6	18.2	12.9
Director qualifications and skills	19.3	13.6	25.8
Director retirement policy (e.g., based on tenure, term, or age limits)	19.3	13.6	16.1
Over-boarding policies (i.e., restriction on number of additional directorships)	35.8	13.6	38.7
Supermajority vote requirement	11.9	18.2	3.2

b) *Proxy Season.* Over the last few years, the focus of the proxy season has gradually shifted from issues of corporate governance to organizational policies regarding the environment, employees, and social impact. The 2022 season confirmed this trend. In the period from January 1 to July 15, 2022, shareholders of Russell 3000 companies granted majority support to only 30 corporate governance-related proposals, a sharp decline from the 50 recorded in the same period in 2021. Passed resolutions requested bylaw amendments to allow for shareholders to call special meetings, eliminate supermajority requirements, declassify the board, and transition from a plurality to a majority voting standard in uncontested director elections.[30]

[30] In 2022, investors filed 114 resolutions requesting their right to call special meetings of shareholders, or three times as many as those recorded in 2021 proxy statement filings. This proposal topic alone represented almost half (44.2 percent) of all governance-related proposal submissions in the season. Almost all special meeting proposals (109 proposals) went to a vote and nine (or 8.3 percent of the 109) passed. They were filed by individual shareholders at health care/medical equipment firm Becton, Dickinson, energy giant ConocoPhillips, and aerospace and defense technology company Northrop Grumman, among others. In 2022, investors also approved nine of the 11 voted proposals to

Table 11.3 *Environmental policy,* by investor type

	Environmental policy issues		
	Full sample (%) n = 109	Hedge funds (%) n = 22	Institutional investors (%) n = 31
GHG emissions	35.8	9.1	54.8
Energy consumption	21.1	13.6	25.8
Biodiversity	9.2	4.5	3.2
Waste management	14.7	13.6	12.9
Water and effluents	12.8	4.5	12.9
Climate change risk	49.5	27.3	51.6
Introduction of a say-on-climate vote by shareholders	10.1	9.1	3.2
Plastic pollution and material recycling	9.2	4.5	6.5
Other environmental issues	2.8	0.0	6.5

11.3.5.3 Environmental Policy

a) *Survey.* As Table 11.3 shows, within the category of environmental policy issues, climate change risk was most frequently discussed, regardless of sector or revenue segmentation, with larger respondents mentioning it more often. The related issues of GHG emissions and energy consumption were also more recurrently discussed and again, more frequently as company size increased. While data on engagement with institutional investors reinforce these observations, hedge funds appear much less focused on environmental matters.

eliminate supermajority vote requirements and apply a simple majority voting standard in the voting on any matter by shareholders. The most prominent firms where the resolutions were successful include The Southern Company, Goodyear, Netflix, and Fortinet. Finally, during the 2022 proxy season, shareholders granted majority support to five resolutions to declassify the board structure as well as four resolutions to change the standard for the election of directors from plurality to majority voting. Both practices are widely adopted by now, and the fewer resolutions now filed in these areas target smaller organizations.

b) *Proxy Season.* In 2022, shareholders filed a record number of environmental proposals, in most cases related to climate change. Typically, requests for disclosure on climate-related issues range from the company's current carbon footprint to the mitigation targets it set to align with the standards of the Paris Agreement; and from the impact that rising temperatures can have on business operations to the risks resulting from maintaining the current levels of gas emissions. Based on data from The Conference Board and ESGAUGE, there were 101 climate-related filings in the period from January 1 to July 15, 2022, up from 60 in 2021 and 50 in 2020. Of the climate-related proposals filed in 2022 – mostly by the investment vehicles of non-profit As You Sow or of religious groups such as Mercy Investment Services – 11 obtained majority support and passed.

11.3.5.4 Human Capital Management (HCM)

a) *Survey.* Under the category of HCM issues, equal employment opportunity issues such as data disclosure (so-called EEO-1 data disclosure), diversity and inclusion among senior management and the workforce at large, gender equity pay, and racial equity pay were the most common topics of discussion, as Table 11.4 shows. Worker

Table 11.4 *Human capital management,* by investor type

	Human capital management issues		
	Full sample (%) n = 109	Hedge funds (%) n = 22	Institutional investors (%) n = 31
Diversity and inclusion in senior management	21.1	9.1	35.5
Diversity and inclusion in the workforce (other than EEO-1 data disclosure)	22.9	9.1	38.7
EEO-1 data disclosure	30.3	13.6	38.7
Workplace and employee safety in conjunction with COVID-19	17.4	4.5	19.4
Gender pay equity	22.0	18.2	19.4
Racial pay equity	19.3	13.6	19.4

unionization and employee arbitration policies were among the least-frequent topics of discussion. Similar to what we observe on environmental matters, hedge funds engage at much smaller rates on these issues, whereas institutional investors confirm and reinforce the trends.

b) *Proxy Season.* In 2022, just like for the environmental area, shareholders filed a record number of HCM-related proposals (155, up from 136 in 2021), on issues ranging from board and workplace diversity to the concealment of sexual harassment and from workforce pay gaps to the audit of racial equity and/or civil rights. The 2022 proxy season, in particular, marked the spectacular rise of HCM-related proposals requesting companies to commission a third-party audit of the impact of their corporate policies, practices, products, and services on the civil rights of stakeholders, including ethnic and other minorities. As many as 31 of the record 43 civil rights audit proposals were voted and eight passed – among them, those filed at Altria, Home Depot, Johnson & Johnson, McDonald's, and Waste Management. The notion of civil rights violation is interpreted broadly: For example, the request at Altria focuses specifically on the impact that the company's investment in e-cigarette maker Juul may have on the civil rights of youth as a protected class in the US Constitution.

11.3.5.5 Other Social Policy Issues (Lobbying, Political Contributions)

a) *Survey.* As Table 11.5 shows, under the category of other social policy issues, lobbying activities were mentioned by 25.7 percent of respondents (around 30 percent for S&P 500 companies and 37.2 percent among non-financial services respondents), while political contributions were mentioned by 21.1 percent (27 percent among S&P 500 respondents). Discussions of lobbying activities and political contributions increase with company size, as do, albeit to a smaller degree, discussions of public health. Other issues such as animal rights and charitable giving were mentioned by fewer respondents. Interestingly, only 13.8 percent of respondents mentioned corporate purpose, a hot topic in academic and media circles.

b) *Proxy Season.* In the 2022 proxy season, shareholders voted on 53 political spending proposals – including requests for disclosure on monetary contributions offered to political campaigns and on

Table 11.5 *Other social policy issues (lobbying, political contributions)*, by investor type

	Other social policy issues		
	Full sample (%) n = 109	Hedge funds (%) n = 22	Institutional investors (%) n = 31
Corporate purpose	13.8	13.6	0.0
Political contributions	21.1	9.1	16.1
Lobbying activities	25.7	13.6	19.4
Public health	11.0	9.1	3.2
Racial equity audits	11.0	9.1	3.2

lobbying activities. Of those, four passed (two per category, down from six and four, respectively, in 2021). They were on the voting ballot at Dollar General, Netflix, Travelers Companies, and Twitter.

11.3.5.6 Strategic and Capital-Related Issues

a) *Survey*. The category of strategic and capital-related issues did not gather much attention, especially if compared to the categories discussed above. Changes in business strategy or operation were discussed by 14.7 percent of companies in the sample and 21 percent of companies in the S&P 500 index. Changes in management were mentioned by one out of 10 respondents. M&A activity, the sale of divisions or subsidiaries, and spin-offs, splits, and other break-up transactions were also mentioned by a limited number of respondents, as were share buybacks and other repurchase plans. Changes in business management and operation were mentioned by almost 15 percent of respondents, and so were R&D investments. See Table 11.6.
b) *Proxy Season*. Strategic and capital-related issues are seldom the subject of shareholder proposals. In the 2022 proxy season, shareholders voted on two capital-stock-related proposals (requesting the board to set up disclosure rules regarding insiders' trading plans

Table 11.6 *Strategic and capital-related issues,* by investor type

	Strategic and capital-related issues		
	Full sample (%) n = 109	Hedge funds (%) n = 22	Institutional investors (%) n = 31
Changes in business strategy or operations	14.7	4.5	19.4
Mergers & acquisitions (with company as acquiror)	12.8	18.2	9.7
Divestitures (i.e., stock or asset sales)	11.9	9.1	0.0
Investments in new products and services	12.8	4.5	9.7
Other R&D investments	14.7	13.6	3.2
Dividend payments	11.0	9.1	3.2
Share buyback or other repurchase plans	13.8	18.2	0.0

adopted by the company in accordance with insider trading laws); but none of them passed.

11.3.6 Outcomes of Board-Shareholder Engagement

Because corporations engage with multiple shareholders and on multiple issues, our survey allowed for multiple answers to this question. What emerges is that engagement is consequential. As Figure 11.9 shows, almost half of the respondents stated that engagement led to a change in corporate practice, while slightly more than half mentioned additional disclosure relating to the engaged topic.[31]

Importantly, the responses show a close link between voting and engagement. First, engagement resulted in the withdrawal of a shareholder proposal for 44.3 percent of companies in the whole sample, for 41 percent of Russell 3000 companies, and for 44.3 percent of S&P 500 companies. Second, approximately four out of 10 companies mentioned

[31] To be sure, additional disclosure may well be associated with other answers.

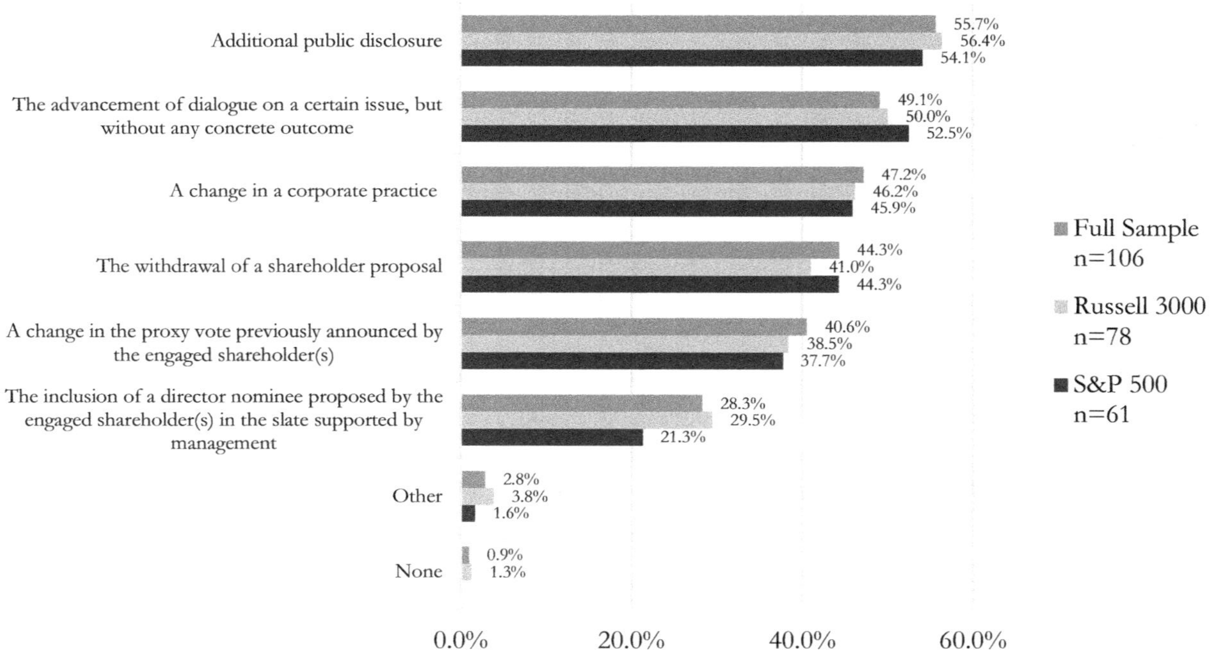

Figure 11.9 Outcome of board-shareholder engagement, *by index*

a change in the proxy vote previously announced by the engaged shareholder(s). These findings suggest that engagement can sway voters to support a company's position in an election or shareholder resolution. Third, engagement led a significant number of companies to include a director nominee proposed by the engaged shareholder(s) in the slate supported by management: almost three out of 10 in the whole sample and in the Russell 3000 sample and a little over two out of 10 in the S&P 500 (interestingly, this response peaked at 46.3 percent for companies in the $1 billion-to-$10 billion bracket).

Nonetheless, one out of two companies mentioned the advancement of dialogue on a certain issue, but without any concrete outcome – again, because companies may face multiple instances of engagement in the same year, it makes perfect sense that some outcomes are interlocutory.

Below we isolate responses from corporations that engaged only with hedge funds (see Figure 11.10) and those that engaged only with institutional investors (see Figure 11.11).

11.3.6.1 Outcomes with Hedge Funds

Among the respondents who reported engagement solely with hedge funds (n = 22), 45.5 percent reported that the engagement resulted in a change in a corporate practice, which is substantially in line with the overall sample. Importantly, 31.8 percent responded that the engagement resulted in the inclusion of a director nominee proposed by the hedge fund. In almost 60 percent of the cases the hedge fund withdrew a proposal (at a rate that is 15 percent higher than the average in the whole sample), while in 31.8 percent of the cases the hedge fund changed the vote it had previously announced (at a rate that is almost 10 percent lower than the average in the whole sample).

11.3.6.2 Outcomes with Institutional Investors

Among the respondents who reported engagement solely with institutional investors (n = 30), 73.3 percent reported that the engagement prompted additional public disclosure (significantly more than in the whole sample and in the hedge-fund segment), while 43.3 percent reported that the engagement resulted in a change in a corporate practice, which is substantially in line with the overall sample. Only 6.7 percent of engagements resulted in the inclusion of a director nominee proposed by the investor. In almost a quarter of the cases the institutional investor withdrew a proposal (at a rate that is 20 percent lower than the

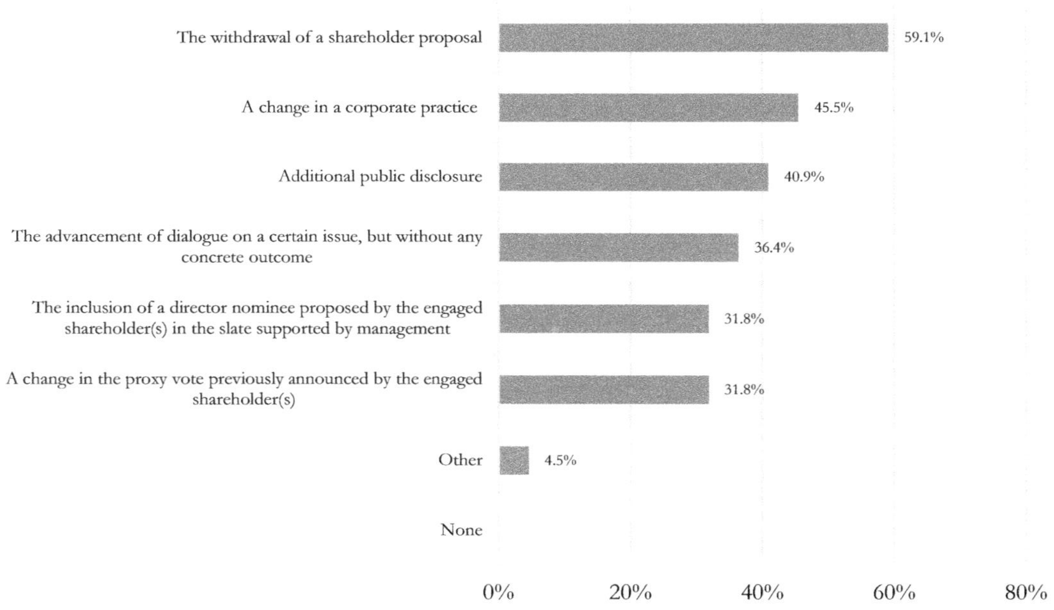

Figure 11.10 Outcome of board-shareholder engagement (hedge funds)

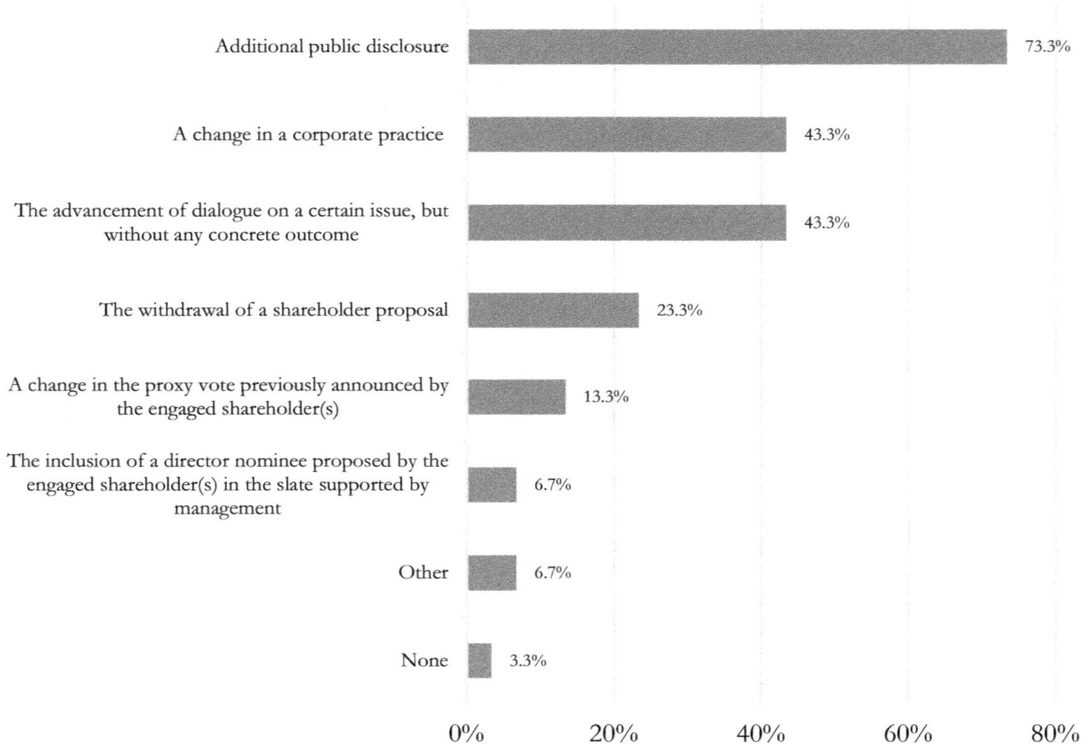

Figure 11.11 Outcome of board-shareholder engagement (institutional investors)

Table 11.7 *Board member involvement with board-shareholder engagement,* by index

	Index		
	Full sample (%)	Russell 3000 (%)	S&P 500 (%)
	n = 110	n = 80	n = 63
CEO	59.1	60.0	57.1
Board chair	37.3	36.3	33.3
Lead independent (or presiding) director	79.1	81.3	79.4
Audit committee chair	10.9	13.8	7.9
Compensation committee chair	40.9	42.5	41.3
Nominating/governance committee chair	40.9	43.8	41.3
Other executive directors	17.3	18.8	17.5
Other non-executive directors	5.5	6.3	6.3

average in the whole sample), while in 13.3 percent of the cases the mutual fund changed the vote it had previously announced (at a rate that is more than 25 percent lower than the average in the whole sample). 43.3 percent of the respondents said engagement with the institutional investor resulted in the advancement of dialogue on a certain issue but without any concrete outcome. Based on these responses, we observe that predictably the engagement with institutional investors occurs on much softer tones than that with hedge funds.

11.3.7 Director and Executive Involvement and Leadership in Board-Shareholder Engagement

Nearly 60 percent of respondents disclosed that their CEO was involved in the process, as Table 11.7 shows. Companies of all sizes reported high percentages of CEO participation, with only companies with annual revenue between $10 billion and $50 billion reporting CEO involvement less than half the time (48.6 percent). Yet, the most frequently involved board member for all company sizes was the lead independent director

(LID), who is generally present at least eight out of 10 times.[32] In fact, the LID is the most recurring leader of the engagement process: as Figure 11.12 shows, of the 216 companies in the S&P 500 index that disclosed their directors' involvement in the engagement process, 31 percent stated that engagement was led by the LID, while only 18.1 percent stated the leader was the CEO.

Turning to C-suite involvement, as Figure 11.13 shows, CEOs and general counsel were the most frequently involved members of management, across indexes and revenue volumes and with rates well above 70 percent (GCs of Russell 3000 companies were present 85 percent of the time, while their CEOs almost 75 percent).[33] Heads of IR were the third most present category involved (40–50 percent depending on index and revenue bracket), with corporate secretaries and CFOs to follow (from slightly below 30 percent to below 40 percent, depending on the index or revenue bracket).

11.3.8 Factors Preventing Additional Shareholder Engagement

Survey participants were asked about the three main impediments to further engagement between directors and investors. Across indexes, business sectors, and revenue, companies stated that the main factors preventing additional board-shareholder engagement were lack of shareholder interest, time constraints of shareholders, and staffing constraints of shareholders. With the caveat that the surveyed individuals were representatives of issuers, not of shareholders, these findings are in line with those showing that the board of directors is most often being proactive and initiating opportunities for engagement with investors.[34] The largest companies mentioned lack of shareholder interest as the number one impediment to additional engagement with investors, however they also frequently

[32] The board chair was present a little over one third of the time, with decreasing incidence for larger corporations.

[33] For manufacturing companies, 83 percent of respondents indicated the general counsel was the most involved officer; (76.7 percent for non-financial services companies and 64.3 percent for financial services companies). The next most frequently involved for each sector was the CEO, followed by the investor relations officer.

[34] The least relevant constraint varied by business sector: the manufacturing sector mentioned time constraints by the director(s) the least (22.7 percent), the financial services sector mentioned staffing constraints by the company the least (20 percent), and the non-financial services sector mentioned the expectation that shareholder engagement be conducted by senior management members (17.4 percent). Regulatory concerns were low across all sectors and indexes.

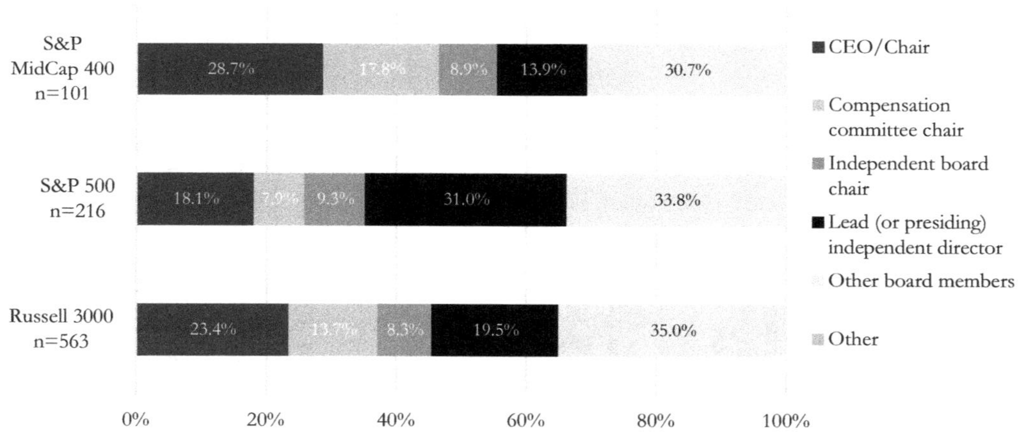

Figure 11.12 Stated leadership of board-shareholder engagement process, *by index*

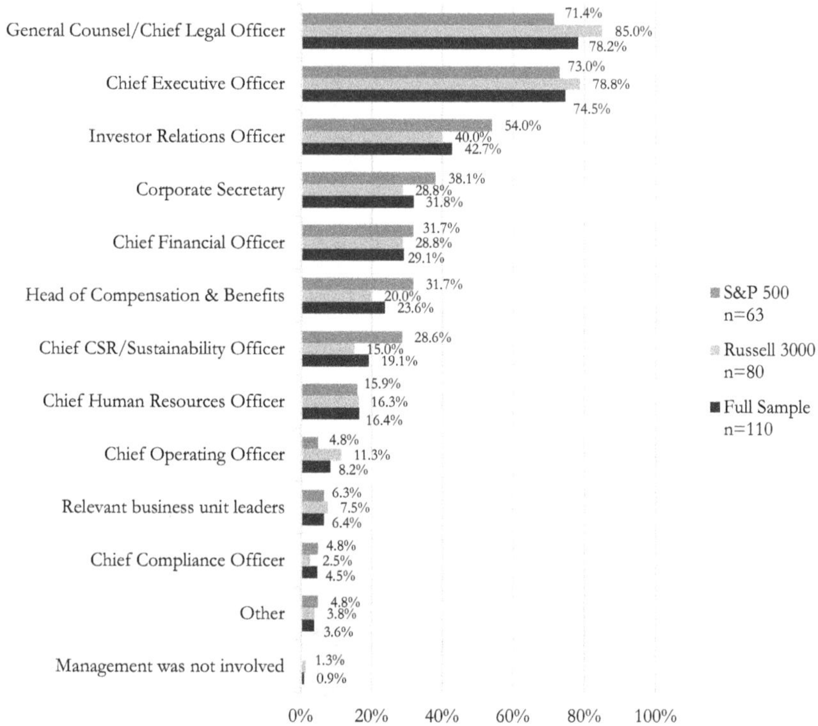

Figure 11.13 Management involvement with board-shareholder engagement, *by index*

mentioned time availability by their own board members. This factor ranked first for more companies as revenue increased. Among smaller firms in the financial sector, the main limitations are the time and staffing constraints for shareholders. Time constraints for directors was rarely a factor preventing engagement in the smallest companies. Interestingly, regulatory concerns were rarely mentioned.

11.3.9 Regulation FD Liability Risk Mitigation Measures

While regulatory concerns were seldom mentioned as impediment to engagement,[35] companies do take steps to mitigate Regulation FD

[35] *See supra* Section 11.3.1.

compliance risk.[36] The measure to mitigate Regulation FD liability risk that is more frequently used by companies is having legal counsel present during the engagement with shareholders; this was indicated by roughly one out of three respondents.[37] The second most frequent measure introduced is one that restricts the engagement agenda to public information only. The analysis by company size shows that many of the largest firms (46.2 percent of companies with $50 billion or more in annual revenue) adopt Regulation FD liability mitigation measures by limiting the agenda to the discussion of publicly available information, compared to their smaller counterparts (13.3 percent of companies with less than $100 million in annual revenue, and only 5.7 percent of companies with annual revenue from $100 million to less than $1 billion). The discrepancy may be indicative of the more extensive level of experience that large organizations have with Regulation FD compliance as well as deeper knowledge of the latitude the regulation provides to communicating with shareholders on issues of organizational and governance practices.[38] Signing a non-disclosure agreement prior to meeting with directors is a somewhat rare practice (4.7 percent for Russell 3000 companies and 6.5 percent for S&P 500 companies). See Figure 11.14.

[36] Relatedly, some companies also have formal, written policy regulating board-shareholder engagement policies in place, yet survey respondents were slanted more toward those who had not adopted one (only 23.8 percent in the Russell 3000 companies and 29.5 percent for S&P 500 companies reported to have one). Adoption of a board-engagement policy correlates with the size of the company. When adopted, these policies frequently provide on how investors can solicit an interaction with corporate directors (58.7 percent of companies in the sample) and the topics on which the engagement is permitted (50 percent of companies in the sample). On Regulation FD as a potential obstacle to boardroom engagement, *see* Lars Klöhn, *Board-Shareholder Engagement and Insider Regulation*, *in Board-Shareholder Dialogue: Policy Debate, Legal Constraints and Best Practices* (Luca Enriques & Giovanni Strampelli eds., Cambridge University Press 2024).

[37] The size group with revenue between $10 billion and $50 billion reports the highest share of companies requiring the legal counsel to be present at all board-shareholder interactions (39.6 percent). This is a notion commonly held across revenue sizes, though the largest companies implement this practice more frequently (38.5 percent of companies with more than $50 billion in annual revenue).

[38] *Cf.* Kobi Kastiel & Yaron Nili, *The Corporate Governance Gap*, 131 Yale L.J. 782 (2021) (noting that smaller and less scrutinized corporations tend to not follow their larger peers in adopting arrangements that are generally considered to foster better governance).

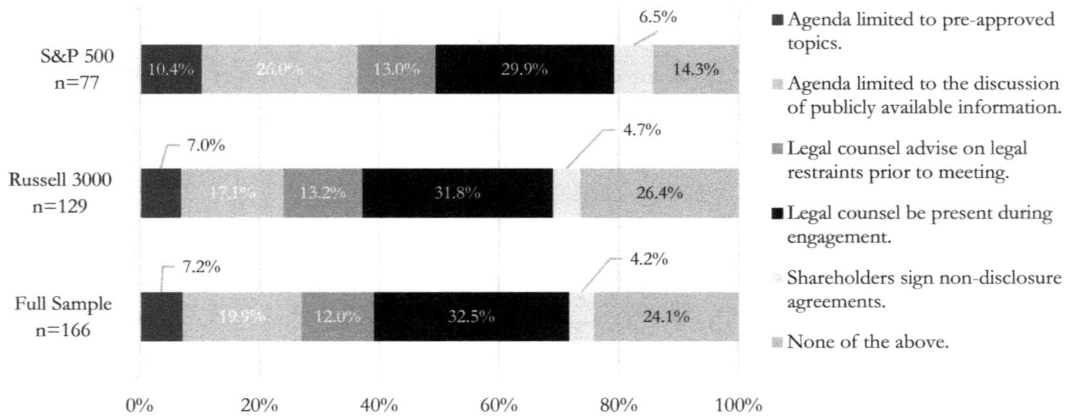

Figure 11.14 Regulation FD liability risk mitigation measures, *by index*

11.4 Analysis

The results presented above shed new light on several aspects of shareholder engagement.

a) *Size.* First, larger companies tend to be engaged most frequently. This makes sense from a financial point of view: All else equal, the larger the holding, the greater the incentive to engage.[39] The validity of this assumption is reinforced by the proliferation of passive funds and ETFs whose portfolio replicates the benchmark stock index, because in the portfolio of passive investors, larger companies necessarily have a higher weight. Also, larger companies are arguably preferred targets because engaging with them attracts more attention and brings more relevant reputational benefits. Although engagements are usually kept confidential, some of the larger asset managers and asset owners have begun to periodically disclose the list of engaged companies, the number of engagements with each company, and the subject matter of the engagement.[40] Another factor for the higher frequency of engagement with larger companies may be that, according to our survey results, these companies are more likely to initiate engagement initiatives. This may be because with scale come better resourced and efficient investor relations functions. But it may also be that larger companies expect to be more often engaged by institutional investors and therefore anticipate their initiatives, especially when they are likely to be confrontational, in an effort to control the agenda and steer any narrative.
b) *ESG Engagement at Smaller Corporations.* The survey results also show that smaller companies are increasingly engaged. While engagement with smaller companies tends to be shorter and less repetitive, it often relates to ESG issues. While such findings can be explained to some extent by the marketing and reputational benefits

[39] *See* McCahery, Sautner, & Starks, *supra* note 5. *See also* Bebchuk & Hirst, *supra* note 15, at 2051–52.

[40] However, it does not seem convincing that it is only for marketing or reputational reasons that investors engage with higher frequency with larger companies. *See* Tamas Barko, Martijn Cremers, & Luc Renneboog, *Shareholder Engagement on Environmental, Social, and Governance Performance*, 180 J. Bus. Ethics 777, 779 (2022) ("Our findings do not support the argument that the activist fund and the firm engage in CSR efforts only for marketing or reputational purposes.").

of ESG engagement,[41] they could also be consistent with the so-called systematic stewardship approach, whereby broadly diversified institutional investors seek to mitigate systematic risk at the portfolio level (rather than addressing company-specific issues), including in particular climate change, financial stability, and social stability risks.[42] Indeed, the fact that engagement on ESG issues with smaller companies is becoming more frequent, seems to indicate a focus on standard issues in line with the systematic stewardship approach.

c) *Tone.* Our study finds that roughly 60 percent of the companies surveyed experienced confrontational engagement. This can be explained in part by the fact that hedge funds, which are the second-largest category of our respondents after private-sector asset managers, do usually set the tone for shareholder-initiated engagements in a way far less collaborative, or soft, than mainstream institutions. Also, the data point confirms that, on some critical E&S matters, index funds can also be less forgiving.[43]

d) *Effectiveness of Engagement.* The survey data shows that shareholder engagement is effective in terms of outcomes. Almost half of our survey respondents stated that engagement led to a change in corporate practice. We also find that engagement closely affects voting behavior. Based on responses to our survey, engagement often led investors to withdraw a shareholder proposal submitted, and/or to change the proxy vote previously announced. Engaging with shareholders can thus be a tool for companies to sway voters to support a company's position, or to preempt more public shareholder initiatives. We also show that, especially where hedge funds are involved in board-shareholder interaction, engagement can sometimes enable shareholder-proposed director nominees to be included in the slate supported by management.

41 Barzuza, Curtis, & Webber, *supra* note 12, at 1283–303.

42 The term "sustainable stewardship" has been coined by Jeffrey Gordon (Gordon, *supra* note 12). *See also* Condon, *supra* note 12; Coffee, *supra* note 12. For a critical view of systematic stewardship theory, see the chapter by Marcel Kahan & Edward B. Rock, *Systemic Stewardship with Tradeoffs, in Board-Shareholder Dialogue: Policy Debate, Legal Constraints and Best Practices* (Luca Enriques & Giovanni Strampelli eds., Cambridge University Press 2024); Roberto Tallarita, *The Limits of Portfolio Primacy*, 76 VAND. L. REV. (2023), https://papers.ssrn.com/sol3/papers.cfm?abstract_id=3912977.

43 Barzuza, Curtis, & Webber, *supra* note 12, at 1267 (mentioning an account from BlackRock's head of global stewardship Michelle Edkins confirming that the fund's outreach to improve board diversity had a confrontational tone).

e) *The Fine Line between Activism and Engagement.* Some of our findings can help improve the evidence provided by empirical studies on hedge fund activism and its long-term effects. Hedge funds are in fact major engagers: more than 60 percent of respondents reported engagement with them. The data also show that the tone of engagement is often confrontational (only four out of 10 respondents did not experience confrontational engagement). While not all the instances of confrontational engagement come from hedge funds, the survey nevertheless confirms that engagement may be an initial phase of hedge fund intervention, and that in some cases the intervention may never emerge publicly.[44] This is because the percentage of respondents who stated they interacted with hedge funds (over 60 percent) is well above the percentages of corporations that are typically subject to activism on an annual basis.[45] It is therefore plausible that the existing empirical literature (which generally, but not uniquely, uses a 13D filing to track an activist's intervention) is undercounting hedge funds' interventions that do not become public. In addition, because such literature uses a matching technique to compare the performance of corporations experiencing activism against some similar, matched corporations that do not,[46] it may well be that some corporations in the control group of matched corporations were in fact subject to an intervention by a hedge fund, in the form of engagement, which never escalated to a public contest.

f) *Withdrawal of Proposals.* Our survey shows that engagement resulted in the withdrawal of a shareholder proposal by the engaging

44 *Cf.* Brav et al., *supra* note 23.

45 Andrew C. Baker, *The Effects of Hedge Fund Activism* 5 & 12 (2021), working paper, https://andrewcbaker.netlify.app/publication/baker_jmp/Baker_JMP.pdf (documenting at Fig. 1 less than 250 activist interventions per year in the period 2010–16 and at Fig. 3 that the sector that is typically most targeted over many eras of activism – business equipment/computers, software and electronics – does not exceed 25 percent of episodes per annum, while all other industries are below 15 percent with most below the 10 percent level).

46 Both sides of the empirical dispute on whether hedge fund activism has negative long-term effects use the matching technique. *Compare* Lucian A. Bebchuk, Alon Brav, & Wei Jiang, *The Long-Term Effects of Hedge Fund Activism*, 115 Colum. L. Rev. 1085 (2015) (finding no negative long-term effects) *with* K. J. Martijn Cremers, Erasmo Giambona, Simone M. Sepe, & Ye Wang, *Hedge Fund Activism and Long-Term Firm Value* 23 (working paper 2018), www.ssrn.com/ abstract= 2693231 (finding negative long-term effects of shareholder activism) and Baker, *supra* note 45 (not finding positive effects of activism).

shareholder in a significant number of cases. Data from the 2022 proxy season shows that, in the Russell 3000 index, as much as 23.6 percent of filed shareholder proposals were in fact withdrawn before the shareholder meeting.[47] Withdrawn proposals are mostly submitted by individual investors, stakeholder groups, and religious orders – all investor types that rarely escalate these matters to an outright proxy solicitation and would rather use the precatory proposal as a tool to gain the attention of their portfolio companies on issues of concern.[48]

g) *Proponents of E&S Resolutions.* The analysis of shareholder resolutions by type of proponent highlights the gradual rise to prominence of a category of proponent that has traditionally played a marginal role at shareholder meetings: non-financial proponents,[49] who seek to promote corporate change in the interests of stakeholder groups rather than mainstream institutional investors.[50] These organizations are now the main sponsors of resolutions on environmental and social policy,[51] with an involvement that has significantly increased over the years.[52] To get a sense of the prominent role they assumed, in the 2022 proxy season alone these proponents collectively filed around 36 percent of all environmental and social policy

[47] *See Shareholder Voting Trends in the Russell 3000 and S&P 500: Live Dashboard*, The Conference Board/ESGAUGE, in collaboration with Rutgers Center on Corporate Law and Governance, 2023, *available at* conferenceboard.esgauge.org/shareholdervoting.

[48] Ibid.

[49] *See supra* note 47. Such non-financial proponents include organizations such as the SRI fund Arjuna Capital or the non-profit organizations As You Sow, the National Center for Public Policy Research, the People for Ethical Treatment of Animals (PETA), and the Humane Society of the United States.

[50] Roberto Tallarita, Stockholder Politics, Hastings L.J. 1698, 1740–52 (2022) (defining such non-financial proponents "stockholder politics specialists"); Gordon, *supra* note 12, at 660–61; Anna Christie, *The Agency Costs of Sustainable Capitalism*, 55 UC Davis L. Rev. 875, 934–43 (2021).

[51] The resolutions filed by this type of organization cover a wide range of topics, including political contribution transparency, compliance with human rights, the adoption of a climate change policy, and disclosure on how the company plans on mitigating risks resulting from the current opioids epidemics in the United States. *Shareholder Voting Trends in the Russell 3000 and S&P 500: Live Dashboard*, *supra* note 47.

[52] Together, they filed 181 proposals at Russell 3000 companies in the 2022 proxy season (or 22.3 percent of the total – the highest volume ever recorded according to data compiled by ESGAUGE and The Conference Board for this category of sponsor), up from 120 proposals in 2020 (or 16.3 percent of the total for that year), and 86 in 2018 (11.7 percent). These figures were unimaginable just a few years ago: in 2013, for example,

resolutions at Russell 3000 companies.[53] Just like other proponents, they often seek management or board engagement on the issues of interest. In 2022, about one-third of the resolutions they filed were in fact withdrawn (60 out of 181 filings) – presumably because of concessions the proponents obtained in the engagement process.[54] That their strategy is to pursue corporate change through pre-proxy season engagement, rather than via an actual vote, is also evidenced by the relatively small percentage of proposals sponsored by these stakeholder groups that receive majority support; in 2022, only seven of the 108 voted proposals by these proponents (or 6.5 percent of the total) passed, as Table 11.8 shows.

11.5 Conclusion

Shareholder engagement plays an important role in corporate governance. In the last decade, investors have increasingly influenced business decisions and their activities have extended beyond the formal submission of shareholder resolutions for voting at annual meetings. On their part, directors and managers have kept an open channel of communication. Understanding the phenomenon is key, considering that engagement is expected to continue to evolve in the coming years, as mainstream investors increasingly take a stance on sustainability and ESG-related issues. Surely, by establishing a dialogue with shareholders, companies gain insights on market expectations relating to certain key matters. The knowledge that results from these interactions can inform business decision-making, help to mitigate risks, and ultimately contribute to new value creation. Yet, grasping the features of board-shareholder engagement – in terms of its frequency, content, process, and outcome – is not easy, as engagement consists of private interactions: as a result, few

there were only 28 proposals from these investors. *Shareholder Voting Trends in the Russell 3000 and S&P 500: Live Dashboard*, *supra* note 47.

53 *bis.*

54 *See* Jill E. Fisch & Adriana Z. Robertson, *Shareholder Proposals and the Debate over Sustainability Disclosure*, *in Board-Shareholder Dialogue: Policy Debate, Legal Constraints and Best Practices* (Luca Enriques & Giovanni Strampelli eds., Cambridge University Press 2024), finding that a substantial proportion of proposals were withdrawn, indicating that issuers and shareholders reached a resolution without putting the proposal to a vote. This may be due to the amendments to Rule 14a-8. In 2021, 41 percent of proposals were withdrawn without going to a vote; in 2022, 36 percent of proposals were withdrawn.

Table 11.8 *Voted, omitted, and withdrawn shareholder proposals, by sponsor (2022)*

Number of proposals (percent of total)

		Voted		Omitted		Withdrawn	
	n=	Number of proposals	Percent of total	Number of proposals	Percent of total	Number of proposals	Percent of total
Corporations	1	0	0,0	0	0,0	1	0,5
Hedge funds	22	22	4,0	0	0,0	0	0,0
Individuals	285	210	37,8	45	63,4	30	16,0
investment firms	4	1	0,2	0	0,0	3	1,6
Investment advisers	112	70	12,6	4	5,6	38	20,3
Labor unions	35	26	4,7	5	7,0	4	2,1
Other institutions	15	8	1,4	2	2,8	5	2,7
Other stakeholders	181	108	19,5	13	18,3	60	32,1
Public pension funds	40	22	4,0	1	1,4	17	9,1
Religious groups	68	38	6,8	1	1,4	29	15,5
Undisclosed	50	50	9,0	0	0,0	0	0,0
	n=813	n=555		n=71		n=187	

Source:
ESGAUGE, 2024.

details are reported. To shed new light on current trends in engagement, their determinants, and potential implications, in this chapter we surveyed corporate secretaries, general counsel, and investor relations officers at SEC-registered public companies, and investigated disclosure data on corporate-shareholder engagement from Russell 3000 and S&P 500 companies. Our chapter makes several contributions on various aspects of engagement including frequency, size, tone, topics, outcomes, and role of various players.

12

Shareholder Engagement inside and outside the Shareholder Meeting

TIM BOWLEY, JENNIFER G. HILL AND STEVE KOURABAS

12.1 Introduction

It is now more than 50 years since Albert O Hirschman published his groundbreaking book, *Exit, Voice and Loyalty*.[1] Hirschman argued that dissatisfied members of an organisation who are no longer prepared to support the status quo – or remain loyal, as Hirschman termed it – face a choice between 'exit' and 'voice'. That is, they must choose either to highlight their displeasure by leaving the organisation, or remain as members and encourage organisational change. As Hirschman showed, the choice between exit and voice is interrelated: the potential for meaningful exercise of voice could reduce the need to rely on exit.[2]

For a public company shareholder, the exit/voice choice is a choice between selling shares or remaining as a shareholder and encouraging the company's management to change the company's affairs. In contemporary corporate governance parlance, the voice option is often called 'engagement'.[3] Although exit via selling shares remains an option for

We would like to thank George Dallas for helpful comments and Abi Thillainadarajah for excellent research assistance. Thanks also go to Monash University, which provided funding for this project under a Network of Excellence grant on the topic, 'Enhancing Corporate Accountability'.

1 Albert O Hirschman, *Exit, Voice and Loyalty: Responses to Decline in Firms, Organizations, and States* (Harvard University Press 1972).

2 See Eleonora Broccardo, Oliver D Hart and Luigi Zingales, 'Exit Versus Voice' (2022) 130 Journal of Political Economy 3101 (for a more recent analysis of Hirschman's insight).

3 See, eg, Matteo Tonello and Matteo Gatti, 'Board-Shareholder Engagement Practices' (Harvard Law School Forum on Corporate Governance, 30 December 2019) https://corpgov.law.harvard.edu/2019/12/30/board-shareholder-engagement-practices/; Jeffrey Karp, Helena Grannis and Gaia Goffe, 'Cleary Gottlieb Discusses Shareholder Engagement Trends and Considerations' (*CLS Blue Sky Blog*, 24 January 2020) https://clsbluesky.law.columbia.edu/2020/01/24/cleary-gottlieb-discusses-shareholder-engagement-trends-and-considerations/; Australian Securities and Investments Commission, 'Shareholder Engagement' https://asic.gov.au/regulatory-resources/corporate-governance/shareholder-engagement/.

dissatisfied shareholders,[4] capital market, regulatory and technological developments have generated greater shareholder capacity and appetite for engagement.[5]

This chapter explores how shareholders today engage with public companies. Its starting point is the shareholder meeting which, in corporate law, is the principal formal mechanism for shareholders to engage with each other and with corporate management.[6] For some time, commentators have questioned the practical utility of the shareholder meeting, owing to concerns about managerial control of meeting procedure, rigid procedural rules which inhibit shareholder participation, and the limited incentives of dispersed shareholders to engage meaningfully in the governance of their company.[7] More recently, some commentators have also argued that the shareholder meeting is now redundant because technological developments have produced other more effective mechanisms for shareholder-company engagement.[8]

This chapter challenges such negative assessments and argues that the shareholder meeting is in fact a key engagement mechanism. The chapter highlights how different types of shareholders use the shareholder meeting in varying ways as an opportunity to highlight their concerns with corporate management.[9] However, although the shareholder meeting has practical significance, it is by no means the only, or even the main, engagement mechanism of public company shareholders today. Shareholders draw on other engagement techniques and mechanisms, including behind-the-scenes discussions and public campaigns. They also use mobile information and communications technologies, particularly where they seek prompt, iterative or direct engagement with corporate management. These other mechanisms are not, however, complete substitutes for engagement via the shareholder meeting and are often used in a complementary fashion to enhance shareholders' leverage at shareholder meetings. The chapter's analysis also highlights how much engagement, both inside and outside the shareholder meeting, is today undertaken collectively by shareholders, as another means of leveraging their corporate governance influence.

[4] Some investors, for example, consider that divestment of shareholdings in fossil fuel companies is a powerful strategy for compelling such companies to adapt their business models to a low carbon future: see, eg, University of Cambridge, 'Cambridge to Divest from Fossil Fuels with "Net Zero" Plan' (Media Release, 1 October 2020) www.cam.ac.uk/news/cambridge-to-divest-from-fossil-fuels-with-net-zero-plan.

[5] See Section 12.2. [6] See Section 12.3. [7] See Section 12.3.2. [8] Ibid.

[9] See Section 12.3.1.

In sum, contemporary shareholder-public company engagement is a multifaceted, dynamic and multilateral exercise, both inside and outside the shareholder meeting. We argue that this insight has important implications for understanding – and regulating – the governance of public companies.

The chapter proceeds as follows. Section 12.2 discusses important changes in public equity markets, corporate governance laws and norms, and communication and information technologies which underpin modern engagement practices. In Sections 12.3 and 12.4, we explore those practices. In Section 12.5, we reflect on the implications of our analysis for corporate governance and corporate accountability, and Section 12.6 concludes.

12.2 The Phenomenon of the Engaged Shareholder

Shareholder engagement has always been a central feature of closely held corporations.[10] However, in many jurisdictions, this was not historically true for larger companies, particularly public companies with a division between ownership and control. In their seminal text, *The Modern Corporation and Private Property*,[11] Berle and Means depicted public company shareholders as dispossessed owners or passive wealth-holders[12] who, as a result of dispersed shareholding and collective action problems, were powerless and in need of legal protection. This image of shareholders became hard-baked into corporate law and regulation in the United States and elsewhere. Concerns about the powerlessness of public company shareholders prompted law makers and regulators to focus on shareholder *protection*, rather than promoting shareholder *participation* in public company governance.[13] In this context, the shareholder meeting was perceived to have limited practical relevance. Berle later referred disparagingly to the shareholder meeting as 'a kind of ancient, meaningless ritual like some of the ceremonies that go with the mace in the House of Lords'.[14]

[10] See, eg, Abram Chayes, 'Madame Wagner and the Close Corporation' (1960) 73 Harvard Law Review 1532, 1533 (noting that 'the defining characteristic of the closely held business is that it is largely owner-operated').

[11] Adolf A Berle and Gardiner M Means, *The Modern Corporation and Private Property* (Macmillan 1932).

[12] Ibid xxxiv.

[13] See, eg, S Samuel Arsht, 'A History of Delaware Corporation Law' (1976) 1 Delaware Journal of Corporation Law 1, 9 (noting the theme of shareholder protection in early US case law, where directors were often described as trustees).

[14] Adolf A Berle, *Economic Power and the Free Society* (Fund for the Republic 1957), noted in *Blasius Industries Inc v Atlas Corp* 564 A 2d 651, 659 fn 1 (quoting Franklin Balotti, Jesse A Finkelstein and Gregory P Williams, *Meetings of Shareholders* (1987) 2).

The reality in many countries no longer reflects (or, in some cases, has never reflected) these negative assessments of shareholders' corporate governance potential. In some jurisdictions, public companies have long been dominated by controlling shareholders, such as founders, government investment entities, or trading companies, which exercise close oversight of corporate managers.[15] Moreover, in many markets, large institutional investors are now substantial public company shareholders.[16] Although these investors have constrained financial and commercial incentives to expend resources on corporate governance activities,[17] it is broadly accepted, even among more critical commentators, that they are capable of playing a significant role in public company governance.[18] Indeed, their capacity for engagement has been manifested in recent years by their increasing engagement with public companies regarding environmental, social and governance ('ESG') issues, such as climate change, social inequality and workforce diversity.[19] There is also one distinctive type of institutional investor – the 'activist' hedge fund – about whose capacity for exercising 'voice' there is little doubt. These

[15] See generally Dan W Puchniak, 'The False Hope of Stewardship in the Context of Controlling Shareholders: Making Sense Out of the Global Transplant of a Legal Misfit' American Journal of Comparative Law (forthcoming).

[16] OECD, *OECD Corporate Governance Factbook 2023* (2023) www.oecd-ilibrary.org/finance-and-investment/oecd-corporate-governance-factbook-2023_6d912314-en.

[17] See, eg, Ronald J Gilson and Jeffrey N Gordon, 'The Agency Costs of Agency Capitalism: Activist Investors and the Revaluation of Governance Rights' (2013) 113 Columbia Law Review 863.

[18] Ibid (arguing that, although institutional investors have limited incentives to proactively engage in corporate governance, they can be prompted by other market participants, such as hedge funds, to focus on issues of corporate performance). See also Lucian Bebchuk and Scott Hirst, 'Index Funds and the Future of Corporate Governance: Theory, Evidence and Policy' (2019) 119 Columbia Law Review 2029, 2042 ('[W]e believe that, despite the problems we identify . . . the concentration of shares in the hands of index funds produces substantially better oversight than would result [if shares held by index funds were] instead . . . owned directly by dispersed individual investors').

[19] See, eg, Jessica Strine, Marc Lindsay and Robert Main, 'The Age of ESG' (Harvard Law School Forum on Corporate Governance, 9 March 2020) https://corpgov.law.harvard.edu/2020/03/09/the-age-of-esg/ (arguing, inter alia, that investors' engagement on ESG issues heralds a 'true paradigm shift in the relationships between public companies and their investors'). Researchers have pointed out that institutional investors in fact have material financial and commercial incentives to focus their engagement activities on such issues: see, eg, Madison Condon, 'Externalities and the Common Owner' (2020) 95 Washington Law Review 1; John C Coffee, 'The Coming Shift in Shareholder Activism: From "Firm-Specific" to "Systematic Risk" Proxy Campaigns (and How to Enable Them)' (2021) 16 Brooklyn Journal of Corporate, Financial and Commercial Law 45; Jeffrey N Gordon, 'Systematic Stewardship' (2022) 47 Journal of Corporation Law 627.

are specialised investors whose business model involves investing in a public company and agitating forcefully for changes that will drive improvement in the company's share price.[20] Their targets have included some of the largest and most well-known public companies.[21]

Encouragement of shareholder engagement in public company governance has also occurred via regulatory or quasi-regulatory developments in a number of jurisdictions. Examples include 'say on pay' laws,[22] the requirement in the EU Shareholder Rights Directive for institutional investors to publicly disclose their approach to engagement,[23] and institutional investor stewardship codes which exhort investors to participate proactively in corporate governance, including by voting their shares and entering into dialogue with corporate managers.[24] Stewardship codes have in fact been a remarkably popular initiative and now exist in around 20 countries and are proposed in several others.[25] Even in the United States, where shareholder participation in corporate governance has been a contentious issue, commentators have noted a perceptible shift in both practice and norms in favour of shareholder engagement.[26] Reasons for this shift include rules and guidance which have mandated or emphasised the significance of voting by pension and mutual funds,[27] 'say on

[20] See, eg, Brian R Cheffins and John Armour, 'The Past, Present, and Future of Shareholder Activism by Hedge Funds' (2011) 37 Journal of Corporation Law 51; Marcel Kahan and Edward B Rock, 'Hedge Funds in Corporate Governance and Corporate Control' (2007) 155 University of Pennsylvania Law Review 1021.

[21] For a recent review of large companies targeted by activist hedge funds, see Rich Thomas, Christopher Couvelier and Leah Friedman 'Annual Review of Shareholder Activism' (Harvard Law School Forum on Corporate Governance, 26 January 2022) https://corpgov.law.harvard.edu/2022/01/26/annual-review-of-shareholder-activism-2/ (referring to companies such as General Motors, Allstate, Shell and Danone).

[22] See generally Randall S Thomas and Christoph Van Der Elst, 'Say on Pay Around the World' (2015) 92 Washington University Law Review 653.

[23] It has been said that the amended directive effectively imposes a 'duty to demonstrate engagement' on institutional investors: Iris H-Y Chiu and Dionysia Katelouzou, 'From Shareholder Stewardship to Shareholder Duties: Is the Time Ripe?' in Hanne S Birkmose (ed), *Shareholders' Duties* (Wolters Kluwer 2017) 131–52.

[24] See generally, Dionysia Katelouzou and Dan W Puchniak (eds), *Global Shareholder Stewardship* (Cambridge University Press 2022).

[25] Puchniak (n 15).

[26] See Chapter 11 in this volume. See also Matteo Tonello and Matteo Gatti, 'Board-Shareholder Engagement Practices: Findings from a Survey of SEC-Registered Companies' (The Conference Board, Director Notes, December 2019) 1–2; Lisa M Fairfax, 'From Apathy to Activism: The Emergence, Impact, and Future of Shareholder Activism as the New Corporate Governance Norm' (2019) 99 Boston University Law Review 1301.

[27] John C Coffee and Darius Palia, 'The Wolf at the Door: The Impact of Hedge Fund Activism on Corporate Governance' (2016) 41 Journal of Corporation Law 545, 557–58.

pay' laws prompting corporate managers to engage with shareholders to avoid negative votes,[28] the demise of staggered boards[29] and the rise of hedge fund activism.[30]

There have also been significant technological developments since the time of Berle and Means. Developments in computing, information technology and electronic communications assist shareholders to gather and analyse information regarding the performance of a company and to communicate instantly and cheaply with potential allies and supporters among a company's shareholder base.[31]

Significant demographic shifts in the investment market may even be transforming the small – or so-called retail – investor from their historical position of corporate governance 'bystander'[32] to a proactive governance participant. Generation Z and Millennials are projected to control collectively approximately $68 trillion in assets worldwide within the decade as a result of an intergenerational wealth transfer.[33] Data indicates that these generations are keen investors in public equities.[34] Such investors are generally regarded as more socially and environmentally progressive than older cohorts of investors[35] and, as this chapter will show, are adept at using new and potentially powerful mobile trading, information and communication technologies to make and manage their

[28] Tonello and Gatti (n 26). [29] Coffee and Palia (n 27) 557.

[30] Tonello and Gatti (n 26). [31] Cheffins and Armour (n 20) Pt III(C)(2).

[32] See Jennifer G Hill, 'Visions and Revisions of the Shareholder' (2000) 48 American Journal of Comparative Law 39, 47–51; Richard M Buxbaum, 'The Internal Division of Powers in Corporate Governance' (1985) 73 California Law Review 1671, 1683.

[33] Coldwell Banker, *A Look at Wealth 2019: Millennial Millionaires* (Report, 2019) 6–7; Remus Valsan, 'Social Media and Shareholder Activism' (*Edinburgh Centre for Commercial Law Blog*, 8 May 2014) [2]–[3] www.ecclblog.law.ed.ac.uk/2014/05/08/social-media-and-shareholder-activism. Cf Joseph Coughlin, 'Millennials are Banking on the Great Wealth Transfer, 4 Words Why You Shouldn't Cash That Check Yet' *Forbes* (16 November 2021) www.forbes.com/sites/josephcoughlin/2021/11/16/millennials-are-banking-on-the-great-wealth-transfer-4-words-why-you-shouldnt-cash-that-check-yet/?sh=2b56443c2dde (suggesting that the 'intergenerational wealth kinetics' are far from stable).

[34] Jack Caporal, 'Study: What Are Gen Z and Millennial Investors Buying in 2021?' (*The Motley Fool*, 3 August 2021). According to one US study, 73 per cent of Generation Z investors and 66 per cent of millennial investors own stocks, making equity investments the most common type of investment for both age groups. Bank of America, *Gen Z to the World: Watch Out, Here We Come*, archived at https://web.archive.org/web/20220125154245/https://www.privatebank.bankofamerica.com/articles/gen-z-defining-characteristics-understanding-impact.html.

[35] Michal Barzuza, Quinn Curtis and David Webber, 'The Millennial Corporation: Strong Stakeholders, Weak Managers' (2023) 28 Stanford Journal of Law, Business and Finance 255.

investments. Their significance as investors – and their potential for activism – has been highlighted in recent years by the controversy of 'meme' stocks, including the remarkable events at GameStop.[36]

In summary, important changes in equity markets, corporate governance regulation and norms, and communication and information technologies have created increased capacity and demand for engagement by public company shareholders. The next section explores how public company shareholders seek to undertake their engagement activities.

12.3 Shareholder-Company Engagement: The Shareholder Meeting

We start our discussion of contemporary shareholder engagement practices by examining the shareholder meeting. Under national corporate laws, such powers as shareholders hold must typically be exercised at a shareholder meeting by voting on resolutions.[37] The shareholder meeting also provides an opportunity for attending shareholders to interact among themselves and with corporate management. Although the shareholder meeting is by no means a perfect mechanism for shareholder-company engagement, the following discussion illustrates how the meeting nonetheless plays a key role in shareholders' engagement activities.

12.3.1 The Shareholder Meeting as a Forum for Engagement

There are two aspects of the shareholder meeting that are important in terms of engagement. First, the shareholder meeting is the forum where shareholder voting takes place. Voting typically relates to proposals that are material to a company's management and affairs, such as the appointment of directors, resolutions relating to the remuneration of directors and/or senior executives, and the approval of significant transactions.[38] The requirement for shareholders to approve such matters provides shareholders with a degree of governance leverage.

[36] See the discussion of the GameStop incident in Jill E Fisch, 'GameStop and the Reemergence of the Retail Investor' (2022) 102 Boston University Law Review 1799, 1806–16. For a sceptical assessment of the corporate governance significance of the meme stock phenomenon, see Dhruv Aggarwal and others, 'Meme Corporate Governance' Southern California Law Review (forthcoming).

[37] Reiner Kraakman and others, *The Anatomy of Corporate Law: A Comparative and Functional Approach* (3rd ed, Oxford University Press 2017) 49–50.

[38] Ibid ch 3.2 (discussion of appointment and decision rights of shareholders).

Public company shareholders increasingly seek to exercise this leverage. Voting data highlights increased rates of voting in a number of markets, primarily driven by increased levels of voting by institutional investors.[39] This trend is underpinned by the aforementioned growth of institutional investor share ownership and regulatory developments which have prompted institutional investors to exercise the significant voting power attached to their shareholdings.[40] The emergence of proxy advisers – specialised service providers that review companies' notices of meeting and provide recommendations about how to vote – has also significantly facilitated institutional investors' share voting.[41]

Public company shareholders commonly exercise their voting leverage in a reactive fashion. That is, shareholders who are dissatisfied with an aspect of their company's affairs will often choose to demonstrate their dissatisfaction by voting against or withholding votes on resolutions.[42] This practice is reflected in proxy adviser voting guidelines, which indicate, for example, that proxy advisers will recommend that their shareholder clients vote against the re-election of directors where a company has performed poorly.[43]

Activist shareholders, however, seek to harness voting power in a strategic and proactive manner. They table (or foreshadow the prospect that they will table) resolutions for consideration at a shareholder meeting as part of a broader campaign to drive change in a company's affairs. In the United States, this has been a long-standing tactic of individual

[39] See, eg, Tim Bowley, *Activist Shareholders in Corporate Governance: The Australian Experience and Its Comparative Implications* (Hart Publishing 2023) 73–75 (Australian data); Yaron Nili and Megan Wischmeier Shaner, 'Virtual Annual Meetings: A Path Toward Shareholder Democracy and Stakeholder Engagement' (2022) 63 Boston College Law Review 123, 145 (US data); Computershare, *2022 AGM Intelligence Report* (Report, 2022) 11 (UK data); Jun Usami and others, 'Japan 2022 Proxy Season' (*White & Case: Insight Alert*, 27 December 2022) www.whitecase.com/insight-alert/japan-2022-proxy-season (reporting emerging signs of a more activist stance to voting in Japan).

[40] See Section 12.2.

[41] See, eg, Andrew F Tuch, 'Proxy Advisor Influence in a Comparative Light' (2019) 99 Boston University Law Review 1459; Stephen Choi, Jill Fisch and Marcel Kahan, 'The Power of Proxy Advisors: Myth or Reality?' (2010) 59 Emory Law Journal 869.

[42] See, eg, Bowley (n 39) 75–81 (noting increased voting dissent in Australia); Jun Usami and others (n 39) (noting an increase in dissent levels in Japan).

[43] See, eg, Glass Lewis, *2022 Policy Guidelines: United States* (Policy Guidelines, 2022) 18 ('We typically recommend that shareholders vote against directors . . . with records of poor performance').

activist shareholders – so-called gadflies.[44] Activist hedge funds have also been adept at using the explicit or implicit threat of a proxy contest to apply pressure to corporate managers.[45] More recently, several jurisdictions have witnessed an increasing number of ESG-related shareholder proposals tabled by social activist organisations[46] such as ShareAction,[47] the Australasian Centre for Corporate Responsibility[48] and investor networks such as Climate Action 100+.[49] Evidence indicates that this form of activism operates as a significant catalyst for engagement. Hedge funds have been described as governance 'potentiators' whose proposals for change in a company trigger a tussle between the company's managers and the protagonist fund to engage with and win the support of the company's institutional investors.[50] ESG-related proposals filed by gadflies and social activist organisations can also catalyse shareholder-company engagement. Research indicates that the filing of such proposals can prompt company managers to engage with the activists and other shareholders regarding possible changes to address activists' concerns, thereby heading off the prospect of a negative vote.[51]

44 Kobi Kastiel and Yaron Nili, 'The Giant Shadow of Corporate Gadflies' (2021) 94 Southern California Law Review 569.

45 Coffee and Palia (n 27).

46 See, eg, Simmons & Simmons, 'More Hot News: Climate-Related Shareholder Resolutions' (Publication, 22 January 2021) (discussing the situation in Europe) www.simmons-simmons.com/en/publications/ckk8k0rnl1hik0918wl0w6qwr/more-hot-news-climate-related-shareholder-resolutions; Sullivan & Cromwell LLP, '2021 Proxy Season Review: Part 1 – Rule 14a-8 Shareholder Proposals' (*S&C Memos*, 27 July 2021) (discussing the situation in the United States); Lloyd Freeburn and Ian Ramsay, 'An Analysis of ESG Shareholder Resolutions in Australia' (2021) 44 UNSW Law Journal 1142 (discussing the situation in Australia).

47 ShareAction, 'Shareholder Resolutions 2022' (Web Page) www.shareaction.org/shareholder-resolutions/shareholder-resolutions-2022 (noting that '[s]hareholder resolutions are an essential tool in any investor's toolkit' and how they 'team up with institutional investors and individuals to call out some of the world's biggest companies for their role in fuelling environmental and social crises').

48 Australasian Centre for Corporate Responsibility (ACCR), 'Shareholder Resolutions' (Web Page) www.accr.org.au/resolution.

49 Climate Action 100+, 'Proxy Season & Flagged Shareholder Votes' (Web Page) www.climateaction100.org/approach/proxy-season.

50 Gilson and Gordon (n 17) 867 ('The role for activist [hedge funds] is to potentiate institutional voice'); Jennifer G Hill, 'The Trajectory of American Corporate Governance: Shareholder Empowerment and Private Ordering Combat' (2019) University of Illinois Law Review 507, 541–42 (describing institutional investors, when so activated by hedge funds, as 'the corporate equivalent of swing voters in politics').

51 See Chapter 11 (noting the engagement which follows the filing of such proposals and finding that this engagement commonly leads activists to withdraw their proposed

Moreover, those proposals that proceed to a shareholder vote are receiving significant levels of voting support from institutional investors due to the latter's increasing focus on ESG issues.[52]

Evidence from some markets indicates that the exercise (or threatened exercise) of voting power can be effective as an engagement tactic even where it will not result in a legally binding consequence. In the United States, where shareholder proposals are frequently 'precatory' (ie, non-binding) in nature,[53] research reports that such proposals can prompt corporate managers to make changes in their companies' affairs[54] even in cases where the level of voting support represents less than a majority of shares voted.[55] Research has also found that it is common for corporate managers to engage with proposal proponents ahead of the shareholder vote and that such engagement frequently leads to proponents withdrawing their proposals,[56] revealing the potential for precatory proposals to catalyse shareholder-company engagement.

Experience in other jurisdictions also highlights the governance potential of precatory shareholder resolutions. In Australia, shareholders' annual, non-binding 'say on pay' is generally regarded as one of shareholders' most effective mechanisms for applying pressure to corporate managers.[57] Australian research also indicates that non-binding proposals addressing ESG issues can affect corporate change.[58] Internationally, activists have attempted, with some success, to push prominent public companies to provide shareholders with a periodic, non-binding vote on a company's response to the challenges of climate change – otherwise known as a 'say on climate'.[59]

resolutions). See also Freeburn and Ramsay, 'An Analysis of ESG Shareholder Resolutions in Australia' (n 46) (Australia); Jun Usami and others (n 39) (Japan); Karp, Grannis and Goffe (n 3) (United States).

52 See, eg, the commentary in n 46.

53 Jill E Fisch, 'Purpose Proposals' (2022) 1 University of Chicago Business Law Review 113, 122.

54 Yonca Erimur, Frabrizio Ferri and Stephen Stubben, 'Board of Directors' Responsiveness to Shareholders: Evidence from Shareholder Proposals' (2010) 16 Journal of Corporate Finance 53; Kastiel and Nili, 'The Giant Shadow of Corporate Gadflies' (n 44) 573–75.

55 Kastiel and Nili, 'The Giant Shadow of Corporate Gadflies' (n 44) 594.

56 See Chapter 11. See also Kastiel and Nili, 'The Giant Shadow of Corporate Gadflies' (n 44) 582.

57 Bowley (n 39) 76–79.

58 Freeburn and Ramsay, 'An Analysis of ESG Shareholder Resolutions in Australia' (n 46).

59 Discussed in Tim Bowley and Jennifer G Hill, 'The Global ESG Stewardship Ecosystem' European Business Organization Law Review (forthcoming).

The second important feature of the shareholder meeting from an engagement perspective is that it provides shareholders with the opportunity for in-person engagement activities. Some activist shareholders, for example, use the shareholder meeting to confront directors and corporate management representatives in attendance at the meeting. ShareAction reports that it uses a company's annual shareholder meeting as an 'opportunity to quiz directors, and hold the company to account on a range of issues, from climate change to gender diversity, healthy food, the living wage and more'.[60] Gadfly activists have also long used shareholder meetings in a similar way. For example, notable US gadfly, Evelyn Davis, is reported to have attended up to 50 meetings a year[61] and to have commandeered shareholder meetings and driven discussion by asking questions that were uncomfortable for management.[62]

The shareholder meeting also provides shareholders with the opportunity to interact directly with one another – or engage in what Nili and Shaner term 'horizontal democracy'.[63] Activist shareholders can highlight their concerns to fellow shareholders and seek to shift sentiment among attending shareholders in their favour,[64] potentially increasing the pressure brought to bear on management representatives present at the meeting and also increasing the likelihood that contentious matters will be picked up by the financial press.

The significance of the in-person, deliberative aspect of the shareholder meeting came into focus during the Covid-19 pandemic. During this period, public companies in a number of jurisdictions held 'virtual' shareholder meetings; that is, meetings conducted exclusively online.[65] This development was welcomed by some

[60] ShareAction, 'What Is Shareholder Activism' (Web Page) www.shareaction.org/savers-resource-hub/agm-activism.

[61] Kastiel and Nili, 'The Giant Shadow of Corporate Gadflies' (n 44) 572.

[62] Leslie Bennetts, 'The CEO's Worst Nightmare' *Vanity Fair* (1 July 2002) www.vanityfair.com/news/2002/07/shareholder-activism-200207; Laurence Arnold, 'Evelyn Davis, Queen of Shareholder Activism, Dies at 89' *Bloomberg* (6 November 2018) www.bloomberg.com/news/articles/2018-11-05/evelyn-davis-feisty-queen-of-shareholder-activism-dies-at-89#xj4y7vzkg. See also Sarah Haan, 'Corporate Governance and the Feminization of Capital' (2022) 74 Stanford Law Review 515, 519–20 (discussing another well-known US shareholder activist, Wilma Soss).

[63] Nili and Shaner (n 39) 192.

[64] Lisa Fairfax, 'Virtual Shareholder Meetings Reconsidered' (2010) 40 Seton Hall Law Review 1367, 1394.

[65] See generally, Nili and Shaner (n 39); Lloyd Freeburn and Ian Ramsay, 'Virtual Shareholder Meetings in Australia' (2021) 32 International Company and Commercial Law Review 53.

commentators, who argued that virtual meetings are more efficient than in-person meetings[66] and facilitate shareholder participation as a result of the widespread use of mobile telecommunications technology.[67] However, considerable concerns have been raised by others, including the risk of technological malfunctions preventing shareholders from accessing and participating in meetings, management use of meeting technology to control debate and questioning by shareholders, and the risk that the absence of face-to-face interaction diminishes the capacity of the meeting to act as a mechanism for holding corporate managers accountable.[68] A recent Australian study, reflecting on the experience of virtual meetings during the pandemic, concludes that virtual meetings provide shareholders with a reduced opportunity to hold corporate managers accountable compared to in-person meetings.[69] The study's findings echo the aforementioned criticisms of virtual meetings, including that virtual meetings enable corporate managers to use online meeting technology to conduct choreographed and scripted presentations and question and answer sessions. Moreover, the study highlights how the lack of in-person interactions in a virtual meeting hinders shareholders' ability to use meetings to apply pressure to corporate managers. This is because managers do not need to provide a face-to-face account to shareholders or endure potentially hostile in-person questioning. It is also more difficult for shareholders in an online meeting to interact with each other. This reduces the ability of a concerned shareholder to generate support from the floor of a meeting and collectively apply pressure to corporate managers. In light of these concerns, the study concludes that permitting companies to continue to hold virtual meetings following the pandemic may adversely affect shareholder-company engagement.[70]

[66] Governance Institute of Australia, 'Governance Institute CEO Warns: "All Eyes Will Be on Your AGM This Year"' (Media Release, 31 August 2022) www.governanceinstitute.com.au/news_media/governance-institute-ceo-warns-all-eyes-will-be-on-your-agm-this-year-guidance-issued-as-peak-meeting-season-nears-under-updated-laws/ (noting that online meetings have created a 'newly flexible, digital landscape for . . . AGMs').

[67] Freeburn and Ramsay, 'Virtual Shareholder Meetings in Australia' (n 65) 67.

[68] Nili and Shaner (n 39) 189–92.

[69] Freeburn and Ramsay, 'Virtual Shareholder Meetings in Australia' (n 65).

[70] Ibid 79. Cf Nili and Shaner (n 39) 193 (who identify similar concerns with virtual meetings but conclude that the accessibility benefits of online technology 'is a benefit we cannot ignore' and that serious consideration should therefore be given to perfecting online meeting technology).

12.3.2 Limitations of the Shareholder Meeting

Nonetheless, the shareholder meeting has several limitations as an engagement mechanism. First, the meeting is typically a once-a-year event, follows a highly-structured agenda and takes place in the public glare, providing limited opportunity for shareholders to enter into fluid, interactive and candid discussions regarding a company's affairs.[71] The situation is compounded by the fact that information supplied at shareholder meetings typically repeats information already provided by companies to the market under securities law disclosure obligations,[72] and the extensive use of proxy votes means that the outcomes of items of business at the meeting are often a foregone conclusion.[73]

Second, a number of jurisdictions report low rates of attendance by shareholders.[74] In Australia, for example, the average proportion of a public company's shareholders who attended a company's annual shareholder meeting between 2012 and 2020 ranged 'from a low of 0.09 per cent in 2020 to a "high" of 0.18 per cent in 2018'.[75] These low attendance rates do not translate into low voting rates, as indicated by the voting data referred to earlier. However, low attendance rates potentially limit the impact of shareholders' attempts to use question and answer time to subject company managers to critical scrutiny.

Third, the exercise of voting power at a shareholder meeting can be an imperfect and impractical means of exerting influence over a company's affairs. Voting may send an ambiguous message to company managers as it will not necessarily be apparent from a voting tally why shareholders voted in the way they did. The act of voting only provides shareholders with an opportunity to signal approval or disapproval of the particular proposal reflected in the resolution put to the vote; it does not of itself allow for discussion or negotiation of the proposal or potential alternatives.[76] Shareholders who wish to enter into a substantive dialogue with

[71] In Australia, a 2012 government inquiry heard evidence that the formal and highly-structured nature of shareholder meetings limited their utility as an occasion for debate and inquiry: evidence presented to the Corporations and Markets Advisory Committee, *Inquiry into the AGM and Shareholder Engagement* (2012), cited in Bowley (n 39) 72–73, fn 10.

[72] Nili and Shaner (n 39) 153. [73] Ibid 146.

[74] Oliver Bampfield, 'Global AGM Trends in 2018' (2018) 70 Governance Directions 379; Nili and Shaner (n 39) 145 (noting that attendance rates in the US are 'abysmal').

[75] Bowley (n 39) 72, citing Computershare, *2021 AGM Intelligence Report* (Report, 2021) 5.

[76] Joseph A McCahery, Zacharias Sautner and Laura T Starks, 'Behind the Scenes: The Corporate Governance Preferences of Institutional Investors' (2016) 71 Journal of

corporate managers regarding the subject matter of a resolution will need to resort to one of the alternative engagement mechanisms described in Section 12.4.

Fourth, highly diversified investors, such as many institutional investors, experience significant challenges in focusing attention on the shareholder meetings of companies in their portfolios, particularly given that most annual shareholder meetings tend to be held within a space of a few months (sometimes called the 'AGM season' or 'proxy season').[77]

Fifth, unfavourable legal rules can also frustrate shareholders' ability to use voting at shareholder meetings to exert influence. For example, in some jurisdictions, the tabling of shareholder proposals is subject to detailed and/or restrictive rules.[78]

Lastly, the shareholder meeting, as currently constructed, does not provide an ideal engagement forum for many small – or so called retail shareholders. Voting turnout, as noted earlier, is driven largely by institutional investors[79] and retail shareholders tend not to attend meetings in person in material numbers.[80] This state of affairs is explained by a combination of the limited incentives of small shareholders to expend resources on corporate governance activities, collective action challenges, and the various limitations of the shareholder meeting noted above.[81] In markets where retail investors own a material proportion of listed equities, their non-participation means that the views of this significant class of investor are not reflected in shareholder decision-making, which is left largely in the hands of institutional investors. Commentators argue that this is suboptimal from a governance perspective because of

Finance 2905, 2913 (quoting a BlackRock executive who expresses a preference for behind-the-scenes dialogue over filing and/or voting on shareholder proposals because the former enables constructive dialogue with managers).

77 Australian Institute of Company Directors, *Institutional Share Voting and Engagement: Exploring the Links between Directors, Institutional Shareholders and Proxy Advisers* (Report, 2011) 3, 71.

78 See, eg, Paul Rose, 'Shareholder Proposals in the Market for Corporate Influence' (2014) 66 Florida Law Review 2179, 2186–89; Sofie Cools, 'Shareholder Proposals Shaking up Shareholder Say: A Critical Comparison of the United States and Europe' in Afra Afsharipour and Martin Gelter (eds), *Comparative Corporate Governance* (Edward Elgar Publishing, 2021) 302.

79 See Section 12.3.1.

80 Nili and Shaner (n 39); Kobi Kastiel and Yaron Nili, 'In Search of the "Absent" Shareholders: A New Solution to Retail Investors' Apathy' (2016) 41 Delaware Journal of Corporate Law 55.

81 Kastiel and Nili, 'In Search of the "Absent" Shareholders: A New Solution to Retail Investors' Apathy' (n 80); Nili and Shaner (n 39).

institutional investors' constrained incentives to participate in corporate governance and/or concerns that they engage in 'herding' behaviour, rather than adopting a suitably critical and informed perspective when engaging with companies.[82] Another concern is that retail shareholder non-participation undermines the representativeness and, therefore, the legitimacy of shareholder decision-making.[83]

In light of these limitations of the shareholder meeting, public company shareholders have developed alternative engagement mechanisms and techniques. As the next section shows, these alternatives are particularly favoured where shareholders seek prompt, direct, iterative or private interaction with corporate managers.

12.4 Other Engagement Mechanisms and Techniques

12.4.1 Behind-the-Scenes Engagement

Behind-the-scenes engagement involves private interactions between shareholder(s) and corporate managers. Such interactions may occur by way of meeting, telephone conversation or private correspondence and occur with company directors and/or senior executives.[84] Research and market data report that behind-the-scenes engagement is prevalent.[85] As corporate managers are not typically under any general legal obligation to enter into discussions with individual shareholders, behind-the-scenes engagement is generally only an option for prominent or strategically significant shareholders who have the leverage to secure private access to corporate managers. Consistently, research reports that behind-the-scenes engagement is a favoured engagement tactic of

82 Fisch, 'Gamestop and the Reemergence of the Retail Investor' (n 36).

83 Jill E Fisch, 'Standing Voting Instructions: Empowering the Excluded Retail Investor' (2017) 102 Minnesota Law Review 11, 14; Nili and Shaner (n 39) 187.

84 Governance Institute of Australia and Sandy Easterbrook, *Improving Engagement between ASX-listed Entities and Their Institutional Investors* (Backgound Paper, February 2014) 10; David A Bell, Ron C Llewellyn and Katherine K Duncan, 'Public Company Guide – Planning for Shareholder Engagement' (Harvard Law School Forum on Corporate Governance, 10 August 2021) https://corpgov.law.harvard.edu/2021/08/10/public-company-guide-planning-for-shareholder-engagement/; PriceWaterhouseCoopers, *PwC's 2022 Annual Corporate Directors Survey: Charting the Course through a Changing Governance Landscape* (Report, 2022).

85 See, eg, Tony Featherstone, 'Rise of the Active Investor' (2018) 34(3) Company Director 56 (discussing the prevalence of the practice in Australia); PriceWaterhouseCoopers (n 84) (US position); Jun Usami and others (n 39) (noting non-public discussions between investors and companies in Japan). See also n 86 below.

institutional investors.[86] Hedge funds also adopt this form of engagement with companies and with other major shareholders with a view to securing their desired changes without having to launch a public campaign against a company.[87] Activist organisations, like the Australasian Centre for Corporate Responsibility, also claim to undertake behind-the-scenes interactions with companies.[88] Behind-the-scenes engagement occurs throughout the year, although it will tend to intensify around key corporate events such as results announcements and the annual shareholder meeting.[89]

There are several reasons for the popularity of behind-the-scenes engagement. First, as there are typically no laws which mandate behind-the-scenes engagement,[90] investors have flexibility to determine the frequency and intensity of their engagement activities.[91] Given the constrained incentives and capacity of some investors to engage in corporate governance activities, this is a potentially important advantage of behind-the-scenes engagement. Second, the private nature of behind-the-scenes engagement may facilitate constructive interactions between shareholders and companies free from the glare of market scrutiny which might otherwise increase reputational pressures and encourage

86 McCahery, Sautner and Starks (n 76). Various other studies have explored the behind-the-scenes engagement practices of institutional investors: see, eg, Bernard S Black and John C Coffee, 'Hail Britannia?: Institutional Investor Behaviour Under Limited Regulation' (1994) 92 Michigan Law Review 1997; Marco Becht and others, 'Returns to Shareholder Activism: Evidence from a Clinical Study of the Hermes UK Focus Fund' (2009) 22 Review of Financial Studies 3093; Elroy Dimson, Oguzhan Karakas and Xi Li, 'Active Ownership' 28 Review of Financial Studies 3225, 3227 (2015).

87 Alon Brav and others, 'Hedge Fund Activism, Corporate Governance, and Firm Performance' (2008) 63 Journal of Finance 1729. Such interactions are not always initiated by hedge funds. It has also been reported that concerned institutional investors may sometimes approach hedge funds in private in an attempt to encourage them to launch a campaign at an under-performing company: Simi Kedia, Laura T Starks and Xianjue Wang, 'Institutional Investors and Hedge Fund Activism' (2021) 10 Review of Corporate Finance Studies 1, 9.

88 Australasian Centre for Corporate Responsibility, 'First Institutional Investor Group-led Climate Shareholder Proposals Filed in Japan' (Media Release, 11 May 2022) (claiming that the shareholder proposal filed in relation to J-Power 'follow[ed] months of engagement' with J-Power) www.accr.org.au/news/first-institutional-investor-group-led-climate-shareholder-proposals-filed-in-japan.

89 Karp, Grannis and Goffe (n 3).

90 Stewardship codes exhort investors to undertake discussions with companies, although they are typically 'soft law' instruments which apply on a 'comply or explain' basis: see generally Katelouzou and Puchniak (n 24).

91 Bowley (n 39) 103.

adversarial behaviour. Finally, when it takes the form of periodic interactions, behind-the-scenes engagement enables companies and their shareholders to explore and address issues iteratively.[92] These advantages of behind-the-scenes engagement contrast with the highly intermittent, public and formalistic nature of shareholder meetings.

Behind-the-scenes discussions are not simply a bilateral exercise between a single shareholder and their company. Institutional investors increasingly interact with their companies through representative bodies, investor networks and service providers that specialise in undertaking engagement assignments.[93] These organisations assist investors by undertaking behind-the-scenes discussions with companies on behalf of investors or by coordinating and supporting coalitions of investors to engage with companies.[94] Some of these organisations are substantial and undertake their activities on an international scale, such as Federated Hermes EOS, Climate Action 100+ and the PRI's Collaboration Platform.[95] Proxy advisers also engage with companies, helping to channel and convey their client shareholders' concerns about companies' voting proposals.[96]

Nonetheless, the utility of this practical form of engagement can be constrained by local norms and attitudes. Communication between US companies and institutional investors has traditionally been quite limited.[97] Expressing frustration at this state of affairs, the head of corporate governance at Calpers, the largest US pension fund, stated: 'It has been like pulling teeth to get the Exxon directors to talk to

[92] Black and Coffee (n 86) 2054–55; Matthew J Mallow and Jasmin Sethi, 'Engagement: The Missing Middle Approach in the Bebchuk-Strine Debate' (2016) 12 NYU Journal of Law and Business 385, 393–94.

[93] See, eg, Luca Enriques and Alessandro Romano, 'Institutional Investor Voting Behavior: A Network Theory Perspective' (2019) University of Illinois Law Review 223; Gaia Balp and Giovanni Strampelli, 'Institutional Investor Collective Engagements: Non-Activist Cooperation vs Activist Wolf Packs' (2020) 14 Ohio State Business Law Journal 135; Marco Becht and others, 'Outsourcing Active Ownership in Japan' (June 2021) European Corporate Governance Institute Finance Working Paper No 766/2021 http://ssrn.com/abstract_id=3864310; Tim Bowley and Jennifer G Hill, 'Stewardship and Collective Action: The Australian Experience' in Dionysia Katelouzou and Dan W Puchniak (eds), *Global Shareholder Stewardship* (Cambridge University Press 2022) 417.

[94] Ibid. [95] Bowley and Hill, 'The Global ESG Stewardship Ecosystem' (n 59).

[96] Bowley (n 39) 95–96.

[97] Gretchen Morgenson, 'At U.S. Companies, Time to Coax the Directors into Talking' *New York Times* (28 March 2015) www.nytimes.com/2015/03/29/business/time-to-coax-the-directors-into-talking.html.

investors'.[98] There is a much stronger engagement culture in other common law jurisdictions, such as the United Kingdom and Australia.[99] For example, in evidence given to a 2021 Australian parliamentary inquiry, the peak body for investor relations professionals referred to a survey of Australian and New Zealand public companies which indicated that corporate management typically spends between 10 and 15 per cent of their time speaking to shareholders 'in the normal course of business'.[100]

12.4.2 Public Campaigns

Shareholders who are dissatisfied with their company's affairs will sometimes openly reveal their dissatisfaction by speaking out in public against the company. Activist hedge funds are adept at using this technique to exert pressure on target companies; for example, by publicly releasing a highly-detailed written critique of the target company[101] or even mounting a broader public relations campaign involving features such as campaign websites and billboard and media advertising.[102] Research indicates, however, that hedge funds typically first seek to engage with target companies in private and only resort to public campaigns and other hostile tactics when such engagement fails to secure a satisfactory outcome.[103]

Some institutional investor stewardship codes also contemplate public criticism being used as an escalation strategy in the face of corporate

[98] Justin Baer, Dawn Lim and Cara Lombardo, 'Investors Give Exxon Payback for Frustrations on Strategy and Climate' *Wall Street Journal* (28 May 2021) www.wsj.com/articles/investors-give-exxon-payback-for-frustrations-on-strategy-and-climate-11622227480. See also PriceWaterhouseCoopers (n 84) 23 (reporting that 42 per cent of directors surveyed disclosed that their boards do not consider 'direct discussions between shareholders and boards are appropriate').

[99] Morgenson (n 97).

[100] Evidence to House Standing Committee on Economics, Parliament of Australia, Canberra, 22 September 2021, 47 (Ian Matheson, Australasian Investor Relations Association).

[101] Martin Lipton and Sabastian V Niles, 'Dealing with Activist Hedge Funds' (2015) www.wlrk.com/docs/DealingwithActivistHedgeFunds.pdf.

[102] Michael Jefferies, 'The Third Wave of Shareholder Influence and the Emergence of Informational Activism in Australia' (2019) 34 Australian Journal of Corporate Law 305 (describing the highly public campaign undertaken by the hedge fund, Elliott Management, against the Anglo-Australian resources company, BHP).

[103] See, eg, Alon Brav and others, 'Hedge Fund Activism, Corporate Governance, and Firm Performance' (2008) 63 The Journal of Finance 1729, 1732.

intransigence.[104] However, in practice, institutional investors tend to be reluctant to resort to public campaigns, although they may occasionally air their discontent in the financial press.[105] Commentators have previously attributed institutional investors' reluctance to undertake activism in the public domain to concerns about the reputational downside of adopting a public position or flagging their investment sentiment to their competitors who may exploit that information in their trading strategies.[106] Networks and organisations representing institutional investors are, however, more visible. For example, the Climate Action 100+ network of investors highlights the companies it is targeting on its website and in press releases.[107] This may reflect the fact that institutional investors are more comfortable with their intermediaries engaging in public activism on their behalf.[108]

Although public campaigns have the potential to apply considerable pressure to corporate managers, they can also be significant and costly undertakings and require investors to have the skill and resources to use the financial press and other public relations resources effectively. As the preceding examples demonstrate, public campaigns are generally, therefore, undertaken by well-resourced investors.

12.4.3 Tech-enabled Engagement

Our discussion of the preceding engagement alternatives has highlighted how significant shareholders, such as institutional investors, hedge funds and larger social activist organisations, predominantly utilise those alternatives. Reflecting on institutional investors' ability to secure more substantial engagement opportunities with companies, the well-known gadfly, Evelyn Davis, claimed: 'Institutional investors get treated like royalty, individual investors like peasants!'[109] Although this may have

[104] See, eg, Australian Council of Superannuation Investors, *Australian Asset Owner Stewardship Code* (2018) 11; Securities and Futures Commission (Hong Kong), *Principles of Responsible Ownership* (2016) 4, 5.

[105] McCahery, Sautner and Starks (n 76) 2913; Bowley and Hill, 'Stewardship and Collective Action: The Australian Experience' (n 93) 429.

[106] See, eg, Black and Coffee (n 86).

[107] Climate Action 100+, 'Companies' (Web Page) www.climateaction100.org/whos-involved/companies; Climate Action 100+, 'News' (Web Page) www.climateaction100.org/news/page/2.

[108] Bowley (n 39) 118 (noting how the interposition of an intermediary may lessen investors' concerns about competitive and reputational downside risk).

[109] Leslie Bennetts, 'The C.E.O's Worst Nightmare' *Vanity Fair* (1 July 2002) www.vanityfair.com/news/2002/07/shareholder-activism-200207.

been true at the time that Davis made the complaint, in recent years significant technological developments have started to transform how investors, particularly retail investors, engage with public companies.

Mobile trading, information and communication technologies are establishing an online ecosystem which is drawing smaller investors into the equities market and providing them with low-cost mechanisms to engage in corporate governance.[110] These technologies include chat forums and message boards, messaging applications, social media and online trading platforms. They are particularly favoured by younger investors – especially Millennial and Generation Z investors – who tend to be more comfortable than older investors using technology, including for investment activities.[111] Younger investors entered the stock market in large numbers during the Covid-19 pandemic[112] and they are forecast to continue growing as a major investor class as a result of intergenerational wealth transfer.[113] This demographic shift may see the use of mobile technologies become an embedded feature of public company corporate governance.

This online ecosystem has several components. First, low-cost and easy-to-use investment and trading apps make it easier (and, according to some commentators, more entertaining)[114] for small investors to participate in the public equities market.[115] Having acquired shares, investors then use social media platforms to access information relevant to their investments. For instance, investors aged between 25 and 45 who use the online trading platform 'Superhero' identified 'online news' and 'podcasts' as their most common sources for financial information.[116] Younger investors also appear to rely increasingly on posts made on

[110] See generally, Steve Kourabas, 'Shareholder (Dis)empowerment through Crowd-Sourced Equity Funding' (2023) 46(1) UNSW Law Journal 143.

[111] As the Australian Securities Exchange (ASX) notes, next generation investors are more likely than older cohorts of investors to seek information through sources such as YouTube, podcasts, social messaging, and social media platforms: ASX, *ASX Australian Investor Study 2020* (Report, 2020) 25–26, 40 www.asx.com.au/investors/investment-tools-and-resources/australian-investor-study. See also, Sergio Alberto Gramitto Ricci and Christina M Sautter, 'Corporate Governance Gaming: The Collective Power of Retail Investors' (2021) 22 Nevada Law Journal 51, 68–70.

[112] Fisch, 'Gamestop and the Reemergence of the Retail Investor' (n 36) 1817.

[113] See above n 33.

[114] Fisch, 'Gamestop and the Reemergence of the Retail Investor' (n 36) 1819 (discussing concerns that trading apps have 'gamified' investing).

[115] Gramitto Ricci and Sautter (n 111).

[116] Natalie Ann Hendry, Benjamin Hanckel and Angel Zhong, 'Navigating Uncertainty: Australian Young Adult Investors and Digital Finance Cultures' (August 2021) RMIT University and Western Sydney University Research Paper, 8 https://apo.org.au/node/

platforms such as Twitter, including posts made by celebrity figures such as Elon Musk, or on popular subreddits such as r/WallStreetBets.[117] In one survey, 34 per cent of retail investor respondents said that they had made at least one change to their investments as a result of announcements seen on social media, including Twitter, LinkedIn, Reddit and Instagram.[118] Tech-savvy investors also use communication and trading apps to facilitate their engagement with investee companies. Prominent activists, for example, have been quick to recognise the potential of social media as an engagement mechanism. In 2013–15, Carl Icahn used his extensive Twitter network to influence the value of Apple shares and the decision-making of Apple CEO, Tim Cook. A study conducted by Dinh, Kopf and Seitz found that Icahn's Twitter postings generated abnormal returns on Apple shares.[119] Icahn also claimed to have achieved his goal of convincing Cook to substantially increase Apple's share repurchases, after posting tweets urging Cook to take this course of action.[120]

Prominent actors like Icahn are not the only investors utilising technology in their engagement efforts. The role played by stock message boards highlights this point. These are internet forums providing discussion threads about particular shares or trading topics. Forums such as Stockaholics, Stockopedia and Trade Brains allow users to post information and ask questions at little cost in threads that are created on a particular topic.[121] They provide a means for individuals to aggregate and disseminate their knowledge, thereby potentially reducing the informational disadvantage they face relative to institutional investors.[122] These message boards also help investors to interact with and exert influence

313385. Further, young investors have also reported reading online news shared in finance-related Facebook groups as a source of information for investments.

117 Ibid.

118 Elana Dure, 'Social Media's Influence on the Investing Community', *JP Morgan* (13 September 2021) www.chase.com/personal/investments/learning-and-insights/article/social-medias-influence-on-the-investing-community. Many Gen Z investors report using TikTok and Instagram for financial information, while millennials turned to Facebook as a key source of advice.

119 Tami Dinh, Karla Kopf and Barbara Seitz, 'The Power of Social Media – Shareholder Activism via Twitter and a Firm's Market Value' (2017) 71 Swiss Journal of Business Research and Practice 50.

120 Ibid 69.

121 James Ang and others, 'Could Social Media Give Small Investors Greater Say in Corporate Governance?' (*CLS Blue Sky Blog*, 5 August 2020) https://clsbluesky.law.columbia.edu/2020/08/05/could-social-media-give-small-investors-greater-say-in-corporate-governance.

122 James S Ang and others, 'The Role of Social Media in Corporate Governance' (2021) 96 Accounting Review 1, 2.

over companies. A study by Ang and others explored the effect of stock message board postings on decisions by managers of Chinese companies regarding mergers and acquisitions.[123] Examining 303 firms facing potentially value-destroying acquisitions and 13,496 acquisition-related comments from a single stock message board, the authors found a correlation between a company's decision to withdraw from an acquisition and the extent of investor opposition to the acquisition on the message board forum in the 10 days following the acquisition's announcement.[124] The study also found that there was a link between the criticisms cited by users on the message board and subsequent managerial explanations for withdrawal decisions.[125] Interestingly, the authors found that information posted on the stock message board before any significant media coverage of the acquisition contributed significantly to managerial withdrawal decisions. This raises the possibility that the message board facilitated new and substantive analysis of the acquisition proposals, rather than just reflecting analysis or opinions generated and communicated elsewhere. However, even if the latter were true, the message board would still have served the function of disseminating information to investors and helping to coalesce investors' opinions regarding the acquisition proposals.

These technologies are enabling retail investors to engage in influential activism, including in relation to ESG issues. For example, Tulipshare, a start-up launched in 2021, identifies a company for intervention and encourages individuals to invest in that company. It then leverages those investments in support of an ESG-related campaign against the company – generally by filing a shareholder proposal.[126] At the time of writing, Tulipshare is seeking to compel Coca Cola to produce plastic bottles made from 100 per cent recycled material, Amazon to provide fair and safe working conditions for warehouse workers, and JPMorgan Chase to stop investing in fossil fuel projects.[127] The platform claims to have had a number of successes. In 2021, Tulipshare filed a shareholder resolution with Johnson & Johnson calling for the company to halt global

[123] Ibid. [124] Ibid 24.

[125] Ibid 4. In some cases, posts may be considered mere 'noise' with little impact on a firm's reputation or share price. In other cases, stock message board posts are seriously considered by investors and firms and consequently do have significant effects on financial markets: Hendry, Hanckel and Zhong (n 116).

[126] Tulipshare, 'How Does Tulipshare Work?' (Web Page) https://tulipshare.com/how-it-works.

[127] Tulipshare, 'Our Campaigns' (Web Page) https://tulipshare.com/campaigns.

sales of talc-based baby powder. Tulipshare claims that its activism prompted the company, less than one year later, to stop its sales of this product. Celebrating the outcome, Tulipshare founder and CEO, Antoine Argouges, pointed to Tulipshare's potential to invigorate the corporate governance influence of the individual:

> Today is a triumph in corporate governance and for the investors, consumers, and campaigners who all united under the umbrella of shareholder activism to make this happen. When individuals unite, their collective action really can overcome the power of companies. It is also a day of justice for over 38,000 victims who submitted claims to J&J after they developed cancer in the US and thousands more across the globe who have suffered unnecessarily.[128]

Tulipshare's activism is not limited to the shareholder meeting. After claiming that Tesla's management was 'sneaky' in quietly moving the date of its AGM so that shareholders could not file ESG-related resolutions, Tulipshare publicly stated that it would continue to seek meetings with Tesla management outside of the shareholder meeting to express its concerns.[129] The public posting of these claims on Tulipshare's website is itself a form of engagement that corporate management cannot easily control or restrict.

These technologies are marketed on the basis that they enable smaller investors to sidestep the hierarchically structured and intermediated process of investing in and engaging with companies through conventional investment and engagement channels. For example, the Robinhood trading app was established with the explicit aim of 'democratizing' finance through the removal of barriers to investment such as minimum balance requirements and complicated financial jargon.[130] In June 2022, Tulipshare added a further element to its activist shareholder approach when it began a partnership with As You Sow, a not-for-profit activist organisation that seeks to promote corporate

[128] Cited in Tulipshare, 'Johnson & Johnson are Stopping the Sale of Their Talc-Based Baby Powder around the World' (*Tulipshare Blog*, 12 August 2022) https://tulipshare.com/blog/JNJ-stop-sale-of-talc-based-baby-powder-after-calls-from-investors.

[129] Tulipshare, 'Tesla's Sneaky AGM Move and What It Means for Our Campaign' (*Tulipshare Blog*, 2 February 2023) https://tulipshare.com/blog/tesla-changes-AGM-date.

[130] United States Securities and Exchange Commission (SEC), 'Form S-1 Registration Statement: Robinhood Markets, Inc' (Registration Statement, 1 July 2021) www.sec.gov/Archives/edgar/data/1783879/000162828021013318/robinhoods-1.htm#ib5a32e8afc3b422193a2f2891a49e0c9_806.

responsibility through shareholder advocacy and legal strategy.[131] Tulipshare's press release heralded the partnership as a step-change in corporate governance because '[u]ntil now, investing for shareholder advocacy has largely been in the domain of large institutions'.

12.4.4 *New Technologies and the Disintermediation of Share Voting*

In spite of these developments, many investors are likely to continue to invest in listed equities through highly diversified intermediaries such as mutual and pension funds. This strategy can help investors achieve significant efficiencies, improve risk-adjusted returns and (in the case of retirement savings) may be required under retirement savings regimes.[132] In this situation, an intermediary will hold title to the shares and decide how governance rights attached to those shares are exercised, precluding underlying investors from exercising voice in the companies in which their savings are invested. Some commentators regard this as an unsatisfactory state of affairs, owing to institutional investors' constrained capacity and incentives to engage in the governance of their investee companies,[133] and have called for limits to be placed on intermediaries' ability to vote shares in investee companies. More recently, in light of institutional investors' increasing focus on ESG issues such as climate change, commentators have questioned the legitimacy of these large financial institutions engaging on such socially and politically salient issues without reference to the preferences of their underlying investors.[134]

Emerging technologies have the potential, however, to enable underlying investors in this situation to exert influence over how intermediaries engage with investee companies. For example, Tumelo, a fintech startup, has developed pass-through voting and expression-of-wish products to enable underlying investors to provide input into how

[131] As You Sow, 'As You Sow and Tulipshare Announce Strategic Partnership to Empower Global Retail Investors to Engage in Shareholder Advocacy' (Media Release, 22 June 2022) www.asyousow.org/press-releases/2022/6/22/as-you-sow-tulipshare-empower-retail-investors-engage-shareholder-advocacy.

[132] Gilson and Gordon (n 17) pt II (describing how these factors have underpinned the growth of intermediaries – or what the authors term 'agency capitalism').

[133] See, eg, Dorothy Lund, 'The Case against Passive Shareholder Voting' (2018) 43 Journal of Corporation Law 493.

[134] See, eg, Jill Fisch and Jeff Schwartz, 'Corporate Democracy and the Intermediary Voting Dilemma' (2023) 102 Texas Law Review 1.

intermediaries' approach their engagement activities. Tumelo's 'pass-through' product enables underlying investors to submit their vote instructions to an intermediary, which then aggregates and submits those instructions to the proxy agent for voting at a shareholder meeting.[135] The 'expression of wish' product leaves official voting power with the intermediary but allows it to engage with the underlying investors to capture their voting preferences in advance of a shareholder meeting.[136]

Prominent fund managers also have begun to embrace disintermediation in their share voting activities.[137] BlackRock, for example, announced its Voting Choice Initiative in 2021 which its CEO describes as 'a capability that leverages technology and innovation to give our clients . . . the option to engage much more directly in proxy voting'.[138] It has been suggested that, by transferring governance decisions to underlying investors, such technology will also allow large institutional investors to sidestep criticism of their role and influence in corporate governance, such as that which emerged in the common ownership debate[139] or more recent criticism questioning the legitimacy of their ESG activism.[140]

The impact of these developments on share voting practices remains to be seen. Proponents argue that they will catalyse 'shareholder democracy'[141] and there is some early evidence of this technology improving voting rates by small investors.[142] However, these developments also have the potential to fragment the considerable voting power currently exercised by institutional investors which, as discussed in Section 12.3

[135] Tumelo, 'Powerful Voting Technology That Wins You Clients' (Web Page) www.tumelo.com/fund-managers.

[136] Ibid.

[137] Brooke Masters, 'BlackRock Opens Door for Retail Investors to Vote in Proxy Battles' *Financial Times* (3 November 2022) www.ft.com/content/6446b81f-a1b4-492f-b335-62f0efe11e7c (referring to initiatives by BlackRock, Charles Schwab and Vanguard).

[138] Larry Fink, 'The Transformative Power of Choice in Proxy Voting' (Web Page) www.blackrock.com/corporate/about-us/investment-stewardship/blackrock-voting-choice/proxy-voting-power-of-choice.

[139] See generally, Jennifer G Hill, 'The Conundrum of Common Ownership' (2020) 53 Vanderbilt Journal of Transnational Law 881.

[140] Masters (n 137); Andrey Malenko and Nadya Malenko, 'Voting Choice' (April 2023) European Corporate Governance Institute Finance Working Paper 910/2023 https://papers.ssrn.com/sol3/papers.cfm?abstract_id=4390367 26.

[141] Tumelo, 'Get to Know Tumelo' (Web Page) www.tumelo.com/about-us.

[142] Rafe Uddin, 'Shareholder Participation on the Rise in the UK' *Financial Times* (11 January 2023) www.ft.com/content/8d5bacbd-2f70-4a13-bce7-971fa7c82e34?shareType=nongift.

above, is used to exert material influence in public company governance. Many underlying investors are small retail investors who have entrusted their retirement or other savings to intermediaries for investment and may not have the capacity or incentives to turn their mind to how intermediaries ought to vote shares in the numerous companies held in their portfolios.[143] This creates the risk that pass-through arrangements will simply result in large numbers of shares going unvoted or being voted on an uninformed basis.[144]

Moreover, these developments have the potential to complicate further engagement practices from the perspective of corporate managers. As the CEO of BlackRock has noted:

> Those of us who lead public companies will have a broader set of shareholders with whom to engage. Companies may need to develop new models of engaging with asset owners on their most important voting matters. This may take time to evolve.[145]

12.5 Shareholder-Company Engagement: A Multi-dimensional, Networked and Evolving Phenomenon

12.5.1 Engagement as a Multi-dimensional Phenomenon

Contemporary shareholder-company engagement is complex and evolving. Most strikingly, it is a multi-dimensional phenomenon. In addition to the shareholder meeting, shareholders also utilise, to varying degrees, behind-the-scenes engagement, public campaigns and a growing ecosystem of online trading, information and communication technologies. Whereas the shareholder meeting is typically a choreographed, once-a-year event whose agenda is largely determined by corporate management, these other techniques provide shareholders with greater scope to shape the timing, frequency, intensity and subject matter of their engagement activities.

Shareholders mix and match these various engagement techniques in a synergistic manner to leverage their influence. For example, online platforms like Tulipshare coordinate small investor activism in relation to shareholder voting proposals. Institutional investors use voting dissent at a shareholder meeting as a signalling device to indicate to a company that

[143] Gilson and Gordon (n 17); Fisch and Schwartz (n 134).
[144] Fisch and Schwartz (n 134). [145] Larry Fink (n 138).

it has not addressed concerns previously raised by shareholders in private discussions, and they rely on behind-the-scenes interactions to resolve investor concerns revealed through voting dissent.[146]

12.5.2 Engagement as a Networked Exercise

Another notable feature of contemporary shareholder-company engagement is the fact that it is not merely a bilateral interaction between an individual shareholder and a company. This chapter has highlighted how it is in fact a highly networked exercise, which involves shareholders employing engagement techniques in ways that mitigate collective action challenges traditionally faced by public company shareholders. The chapter has noted, for example, the synergistic interactions between institutional investors and activist shareholders such as hedge funds, gadflies and activist organisations and how these interactions enable institutional investors' substantial voting power to be employed as an offensive tactic at shareholder meetings. This chapter has also highlighted the important role played by investor organisations, investor networks and service providers such as proxy advisers and engagement firms. These organisations not only assist institutional investors with the substantial workload of engaging with the many companies in their diversified portfolios. By acting and advocating for multiple investors, these organisations also collectivise the influence of those investors. The technological innovations described in the previous section perform an analogous function. Commentators have pointed out that the current developments in online communication technology have facilitated a 'network of networks that connects all types of communication from one-to-one to many-to-many into a wider "space" of communication'.[147] At the most basic level, the communications revolution facilitates low-cost information sharing and the expansion of two-way, virtually instantaneous, and ongoing interaction in a way that was not previously possible.[148]

This networking does not simply increase the intensity of shareholder-company engagement. It also affects the content of corporate governance

[146] Bowley (n 39) 87.

[147] Nick Couldry, *Media, Society, World: Social Theory and Digital Media Practice* (Polity Press 2012) 2.

[148] See Pearlie Koh, 'Shareholder Empowerment in the Digital Age' in Andrew Godwin, Pey Woan Lee and Rosemary Teele Langford (eds), *Technology and Corporate Law: How Innovation Shapes Corporate Activity* (Edward Elgar Publishing 2021) 172–73.

discourse. Networked engagement, for example, is shaping the content of much contemporary ESG engagement. The interaction of gadflies, social activist organisations, ESG-conscious institutional investors, investor networks and international institutions such as the United Nations and its agencies is shaping and transmitting norms of ESG stewardship and coordinating ESG stewardship 'on the ground' in markets across the globe.[149] These engagement developments are, in turn, prompting companies to address environmental and social issues that were once considered the domain of lawmakers and governments.[150] For smaller investors, especially Millennial and Generation Z investors, social networking technology has created 'networked publics' that coalesce around issues not easily categorised as 'economic', 'social' or 'political', or defined by geographic reference. Rather, networked publics focus on social media-friendly issues that can be easily personalised and which bring attention to political identities and values.[151] Tulipshare's coordinated shareholder activism against prominent public companies in relation to producing bottles from recycled material, providing fair and safe working conditions for warehouse workers, and halting the production of talc-based baby powder highlights this development.

12.5.3 Implications for the Shareholder Meeting

The shareholder meeting has long been criticised as an engagement technique. Some of this criticism disputes the practical utility of the meeting, owing to rigid meeting formalities that limit the opportunity for shareholder engagement and low attendance rates.[152] A second, more recent, related criticism is that new forms of engagement, including online technology, have radically altered the relationship and engagement dynamics between shareholders and corporate management.[153] According to scholars such as Oranburg, engagement tools like Twitter are more effective at overcoming collective action problems that have

149 Bowley and Hill, 'The Global ESG Stewardship Ecosystem' (n 59).

150 Condon (n 19) (raising a concern as to whether it is legitimate for investors to be driving significant change on issues that were typically the domain of elected law makers).

151 See generally Eirik Vatnøy, 'The Rhetoric of Networked Publics: Studying Social Network Sites as Rhetorical Arenas for Political Talk' (DPhil thesis, University of Bergen 2017).

152 See, eg, Berle and Means (n 11) and Berle (n 14).

153 Seth C Oranburg, 'A Little Birdie Said: How Twitter Is Disrupting Shareholder Activism' (2015) 20 Fordham Journal of Corporate & Financial Law 695.

long plagued shareholder engagement through the shareholder meeting.[154] It is not a large leap to move from such critiques to a view that the shareholder meeting should be dispensed with in favour of alternative engagement mechanisms.

Although the shareholder meeting undoubtedly has its limitations as an engagement mechanism, it would be precipitous to dismiss it as redundant. The formal, in-person and public nature of the shareholder meeting sets it apart from the other engagement mechanisms described in this chapter and gives it unique potential as a forum for scrutiny and accountability. For corporate managers, providing a public and in-person account of a company's performance at a shareholder meeting can be an unsettling experience that 'focuses the mind' and imposes a level of discipline on how they account for that performance.[155] Shareholders are able to observe how corporate managers behave when subjected to the pressure of public scrutiny.[156] Activist shareholders can 'read the room', seek to build consensus and leverage the pressure brought to bear on managers from the floor of the meeting.[157] Low attendance rates, noted earlier, indicate that shareholders do not routinely avail themselves of these opportunities. However, these features of the shareholder meeting may prove significant when a company experiences material management problems and shareholders wish to exert concerted pressure on corporate managers. In this sense, the shareholder meeting is perhaps best conceived of as an engagement mechanism with 'contingent significance'. As the Delaware court has noted, 'a keen realization of the reality of the degree of deliberation that is possible [at a shareholder meeting], should make the preservation of residual mechanisms of corporate

[154] Ibid 696, 711.

[155] A point made in submissions made to a 2012 Australian government inquiry into the utility of the annual shareholder meeting. See, eg, Ashurst, *Submission on Future of the AGM and Shareholder Engagement* (20 December 2012) 2 (reporting results of a roundtable discussion involving representatives of 25 Australian public companies which noted that '[b]oards ... are conscious of the "discipline" which the AGM brings to the annual presentation of the company's activities, financial position and prospects'); Australian Institute of Company Directors, *Submission on Future of the AGM and Shareholder Engagement* (21 December 2012) 3; Business Council of Australia, *Submission on Future of the AGM and Shareholder Engagement* (February 2013) 4.

[156] Telstra Corporation Ltd, *Submission on Future of the AGM and Shareholder Engagement* (21 December 2012) 3.

[157] Freeburn and Ramsay, 'Virtual Shareholder Meetings in Australia' (n 65) 71–73; Nili and Schaner (n 39) 186.

democracy more, not less, important'.[158] It is also conceivable that shareholders who do not fully avail themselves of the governance potential of the shareholder meeting nonetheless value the opportunity which physical attendance at a meeting affords more activist shareholders to exert pressure on corporate management.[159]

This interactive public reckoning in a formal meeting setting cannot be fully replicated by alternative engagement mechanisms such as private shareholder-company meetings, public relations campaigns or online fora. The limitations of the latter, in particular, became apparent in light of the extensive use of virtual meetings in lieu of in-person meetings during the Covid-19 pandemic.[160]

One area where technological developments described earlier could potentially displace the shareholder meeting is in relation to share voting. Online technologies already facilitate share voting[161] and much voting today occurs in advance of meetings by proxy.[162] In these circumstances, it would not seem a major change, in practice, to undertake voting through a stand-alone plebiscite process, leaving the shareholder meeting as a forum purely for reporting, discussion and debate. In the authors' view, any such proposal should be approached with caution. An Australian government inquiry in 2012 raised the possibility of conducting voting pursuant to a plebiscite occurring following the close of a shareholder meeting.[163] Respondents to the inquiry pointed out that having share voting finalised at the shareholder meeting contributes to the meeting's capacity to act as a pressure point on corporate managers, especially where voting outcomes reveal material shareholder disquiet.[164]

158 *Hoschett v TSI International Software* 683 A 2d 43, 46.

159 See, eg, Bruce Goldfarb, 'Are Virtual Annual Meetings Good for Shareholder Democracy?' *Forbes* (5 May 2020) www.forbes.com/sites/brucegoldfarb/2020/05/05/are-virtual-annual-meetings-good-for-shareholder-democracy/?sh=3bda08fb27f3 (referring to the benefits for shareholders of observing the 'give and take' between dissidents and corporate managers at contested shareholder meetings).

160 See notes 65–70 and accompanying discussion.

161 Uddin (n 142); see also, Sharesies, 'Have Your Say with Shareholder Voting' (Webpage) www.sharesies.nz/blog/have-your-say-with-shareholder-voting (describing a facility for investors who acquire shares via Sharesies' online trading app to vote those shares using an interface in the app).

162 See, eg, Bowley (n 39) 72; Nili and Shaner (n 39) 146.

163 Corporations and Markets Advisory Committee, *The AGM and Shareholder Engagement* (Discussion Paper, 2012) 123–25.

164 See, eg, Hermes Equity Ownership Services, *Submission on Future of the AGM and Shareholder Engagement* (December 2012) 12 ('[W]e believe that [accountability] can

This is not to say that the shareholder meeting cannot be improved as an engagement mechanism. Possibilities such as hybrid meetings, improving the functionality of online meeting technologies, and streamlining the voting process for shareholders are all worthy of careful consideration.[165] However, reform initiatives need to recognise the fact that the shareholder meeting today forms part of a broader array of engagement techniques and mechanisms which shareholders use in a synergistic fashion. Whether changes to the format and structure of shareholder meetings are necessary or desirable and their likely impact on the quantity and nature of shareholder-company engagement will need to be assessed in light of the alternative mechanisms utilised by shareholders.

12.5.4 *Implications for Governance Accountability*

The engagement developments discussed in this chapter provide not only opportunities but also challenges. One important consequence of the varied engagement practices described in this chapter is that the process of corporate decision-making is now more diffuse and less transparent.[166] In these circumstances, we may need to consider what it means to move beyond reliance on strict hierarchies based on clear divisions of authority and responsibility towards greater acceptance of disaggregated, fragmented and networked models of influence-wielding and decision-making in corporate governance. In particular, accountability becomes a more complex issue in these circumstances. We must ask who is seeking to influence corporate policy and operations, what are their motivations, whether such influence is transparent, and whether there is an appropriate accountability mechanism to address such influence-wielding. This is particularly important when we consider that some aspects of contemporary shareholder engagement rest on the actions of a handful of key participants. In the United States, for example, a few individual gadflies are responsible for a disproportionate number of shareholder advisory

only be delivered by a meeting which combines the full range of reporting, questioning, deliberation and decision-making').

165 For a discussion of reform possibilities, see Nili and Shaner (n 39) Pt III.

166 Mark Fenwick and Erik PM Vermeulen, 'Technology and Corporate Governance: Blockchain, Crypto, and Artificial Intelligence' (November 2018) European Corporate Governance Institute Law Working Paper 424/2018, 5 https://papers.ssrn.com/sol3/papers.cfm?abstract_id=3263222.

proposals.[167] In some jurisdictions, a small number of proxy advisory firms play a vital role in supporting the voting activities of institutional investors at shareholder meetings.[168] Recent regulatory initiatives in relation to the regulation of proxy advisers in Australia[169] and the tightening of requirements for filing advisory proposals in the United States in 2020[170] can be seen as attempts to address such issues in light of the prominent roles played by proxy advisers and shareholder proposals in contemporary corporate governance.

12.6 Conclusion

Modern public company shareholder engagement is proactive, strategic, networked and collectivised. The shareholder meeting has not become redundant, as some critics would suggest. Nonetheless, it is by no means the only or even primary engagement mechanism and instead forms part of a broader constellation of engagement techniques. These developments entail both opportunity and risk from a corporate governance perspective. They hold the promise of establishing a more dynamic and responsive system of corporate accountability by providing multiple channels for shareholder influence-wielding. Yet, the disaggregated, informal and sometimes private nature of much contemporary engagement raises concerns about transparency and accountability of the various actors involved in this engagement ecosystem.

[167] Kastiel and Nili, 'The Giant Shadow of Corporate Gadflies' (n 44). See also, John Coates, *The Problem of 12: When a Few Financial Institutions Control Everything* (Columbia Global Reports 2023).

[168] Bowley (n 39) 203–4 (noting this situation in the Australian context).

[169] Josh Frydenberg and Jane Hume, 'Reforms to Bring Greater Transparency and Accountability to Proxy Advice' (Media Release, 17 December 2021) https://ministers.treasury.gov.au/ministers/jane-hume-2020/media-releases/reforms-bring-greater-transparency-and-accountability-proxy.

[170] Discussed in Kastiel and Nili, 'The Giant Shadow of Corporate Gadflies' (n 44) 619–21.

13

The Viability of Blockchain in Corporate Governance

ANNE LAFARRE AND CHRISTOPH VAN DER ELST

13.1 Introduction

Blockchain technology is often associated with volatile cryptocurrencies and speculation, leading to concerns about the need for new regulations.[1] Nevertheless blockchain (and distributed ledger technology, DLT[2]) can also significantly impact corporate governance. Several progressive ideas both inspire and question the existing corporate fundaments and paradigms.[3] For example, David Yermack inter alia explained the corporate governance impacts of issuing and trading corporate securities on blockchains, and voting in corporate elections.[4] Blockchain technology can enhance transparency of ownership, which in turn may impact shareholder activism and curb insider trading, and accelerate securities' trading and settlement processes leading to improved liquidity.[5] We ourselves were excited about the potential of blockchain for

[1] At the moment of writing, the European Union was working on a regulatory framework aimed at regulating cryptocurrencies and other crypto assets within the EU (Markets in Crypto-Assets Regulation or 'MiCA'). MiCA aims to provide legal certainty, consumer protection, and promote innovation in the crypto industry while mitigating the risks associated with crypto assets, such as money laundering and terrorist financing. The regulation proposal was released in September 2020, and Regulation (EU) 2023/1114 (OJ. L No. 150 of 9 June 2023) entered into force in June 2023.

[2] Blockchain technology can be considered an example of a distributed ledger technology (DLT) that uses a block structure to add data. DLT can be considered the umbrella term for distributed technologies like blockchain. Although it should be noted that several of the applications that are discussed in Sections 13.3 and 13.4 can also use another type of DLT, we mainly refer to blockchain technology.

[3] C.M. Bruner, 'Distributed Ledgers, Artificial Intelligence and the Purpose of the Corporation' 79 *Cambridge Law Journal* 431 (2020); L. Enriques & D.A. Zetzsche, 'Corporate Technologies and the Tech Nirvana Fallacy' 72 *Hastings Law Journal* 55 (2020).

[4] D. Yermack, 'Corporate Governance and Blockchains' 21(1) *Review of Finance* 7–31 (2017).

[5] *Idem*, section 3.

shareholder participation and decision-making in the blockchain-AGM.[6] Other contributions on the use of blockchain technology in corporate law have followed, even including fully decentralized companies in the form of blockchain-based Decentralized Autonomous Organizations (DAOs).[7]

It is questioned whether the use of blockchain technology for these and other corporate governance applications should be further encouraged, or whether it represents only a utopian vision that should be addressed with caution.[8] In particular, although blockchain technology may have the potential to facilitate corporate law and corporate governance in several ways,[9] there is often ambiguity regarding the true value and solutions of blockchain applications and their adherence to legal issues. This chapter delves into some of the present developments in the diverse applications of blockchain technology within corporate governance. After a brief introduction to blockchain and smart contracting technology in Section 13.2,[10] in Section 13.3, we first discuss the governance structures of DAOs that operate on the blockchain in a (fully) decentralized way. In addition, blockchain can also be used to strengthen the basic functions of corporate and financial law, such as facilitating secure and transparent shareholder voting in AGMs. Moreover, decision-making powers that are typically reserved for the board can potentially be shifted to shareholders or other corporate constituencies using blockchain technology. We discuss several of these (potential) applications in Section 13.3. Section 13.4 offers concluding remarks.

[6] C.F. Van der Elst & A.J.F. Lafarre, 'Blockchain and the 21st Century Annual General Meeting' 14(4) *European Company Law* 167–176 (2017).

[7] For example, M. Fenwick & E.P. Vermeulen, 'Technology and Corporate Governance: Blockchain, Crypto, and Artificial Intelligence' 48(1) *Texas Journal of Business Law* 1–15 (2019).

[8] Enriques & Zetzsche (2020), n. 4. See for a very critical analysis claiming that the blockchain potential is mostly imaginary, K. Low, E. Schuster and W.Y. Wan, 'The company and blockchain technology', LSE Law, Society and Economy Working Paper 18/2022, p. 22.

[9] I. H-Y. Chiu & E. W-K. Lim, 'Technology vs Ideology: How Far Will Artificial Intelligence and Distributed Ledger Technology Transform Corporate Governance and Business?' 18(1) *Berkeley Business Law Journal* (2021).

[10] This explanation involves a simplification of blockchain technology. For a more complete analysis, see for example P. De Filippi & A. Wright, *Blockchain and the Law: The Rule of Code*, Cambridge, Harvard University Press 2019, p. 312. Note that Yermack also provides an excellent and accessible explanation of (Bitcoin) blockchain technology in his 2017 article. Yermack (2017), n. 4.

13.2 Blockchain Technology and Smart Contracts

13.2.1 Blockchain Technology

The problem of double spending in electronic transactions, where messages can be duplicated easily, was addressed with the introduction of blockchain.[11] Traditionally, a central authority or intermediary is responsible for controlling and verifying all transactions to prevent double spending. Blockchain technology offers an alternative solution. Blockchain is a *distributed* ledger system that operates in a *peer-to-peer* network, where information is stored in a manner that makes it difficult or even impossible to change (*immutable*).

Distributed means that the information (including for instance the proof of each transaction) is stored in multiple locations (in network nodes). Each participant in the network has access to their own replica of the full ledger.

Peer-to-peer means that if a participant in the blockchain network wishes to make a transaction, the information is broadcast to the entire network. Participants verify the transaction in their own ledger and provide confirmation. As a result, the network can reach a consensus on the transaction. Participants (operators of a 'node') in the blockchain must be incentivized to verify transactions in a transparent and reliable manner. There are various consensus mechanisms that determine who can verify information and under what conditions. For example, in the Bitcoin-blockchain, miners group transactions into blocks and use computing power to find a correct random number (the *nonce*), a process referred to as *proof-of-work* (PoW). The nonce is a random number generated through computational effort and selected in such a way that, when combined with the other data in a block, produces a hash[12] that starts with a specific number of zeros. Once a miner finds this random number and completes the block, the blockchain network validates her solution. When consensus in the network is reached about the solution,[13]

[11] S. Nakamoto, 'Bitcoin: a peer-to-peer electronic cash system'. Available at: https://bitcoin.org/bitcoin.pdf (last accessed 29 March 2023).

[12] Hashing in a blockchain converts digital information into a unique and fixed-length string of characters. This ensures data integrity and security because even a small change in the input data will result in a completely different string.

[13] When multiple miners find a solution, the Bitcoin network determines with a simple majority which miner will receive the reward, typically the one who verified the most transactions. If nodes support different solutions, a 'fork' may occur in the blockchain, and miners will continue to work on the next blocks until one split becomes longer, at

the miner is rewarded and the miners start working on the next block. Another consensus mechanism is, for instance, *proof-of-stake* (PoS).[14] A blockchain participant is instructed to verify the information based on her stake, that is, the amount of cryptocurrencies, rather than computing power. More specifically, the blockchain protocol specifies that the network chooses the participant to verify the information based on the amount of cryptocurrencies she puts in a pool and the length of time they are held there.[15] Often, the authority to verify information is limited to particular stakeholders in the blockchain network.[16]

Finally, *immutability* means that once a file is created, it cannot be altered.[17] This is due to the block structure in the blockchain,[18] where hashed information is captured in a container data structure that aggregates transactions for inclusion in the blockchain. Particularly, each block within the blockchain contains data from the preceding block. Therefore, if a blockchain participant attempts to modify any information in a block, the information in the next and all subsequent blocks would change as well. The difficulty of this task explains why information on a blockchain is considered immutable.[19] Because multiple nodes have their own copies of the blockchain ledger, any inconsistency is immediately detected in the network.

In summary, blockchain enables participants to access information from all transactions immediately through their own replica of the ledger. The information is transparent, verifiable, and immutable, as transactions are added to the ledger in blocks in chronological order without overwriting previous transactions. These features of blockchain should enhance transparency and trust in the network.

which point all nodes will follow this longer chain. Miners essentially vote with their computing power to decide which block to continue working with.

14 Ethereum converted to PoS with ETH2.

15 The block hash now contains the signature of the participant responsible for building that block.

16 See for an extensive discussion of how consensus is reached under PoS; F. Saleh, 'Blockchain without Waste: Proof-of-Stake', 34(3) *Review of Financial Studies* 1156–1190 (2021).

17 In fact, it is very difficult to alter the information but not impossible.

18 Note that blockchain involves blocks, but DLT can also use other data structures.

19 One would need to control a majority of the mining power or have a much faster computer than anyone else in the blockchain network to be able to alter the information. Also see Yermack (2017), n. 4.

13.2.2 Smart Contracts

Smart contracts are computer programs that execute the conditions of a contract without an intermediary's involvement.[20] If all preconditions are noticeably met, the smart contract automatically executes the compliance ('when A, then B'). Blockchain technology is often used to execute smart contracts so that their terms are stored in a distributed way and cannot (easily) be altered. The consensus mechanisms that are used in the blockchain should ensure that smart contracts are executed correctly. In turn, smart contracts enable a large variety of applications for blockchain technology.[21] A simple example of a smart contract for a car purchase between a seller and a buyer is the following (written in Solidity[22]):

```
contract CarSale {
    address payable public seller;
    address payable public buyer;
    uint public price;
    bool public sold;

    constructor() {
        seller = payable(msg.sender);
        price = 100 ether; // Set the price of the car to
        100 ether
        sold = false;
    }
    function buyCar() public payable {
        require(msg.value == price, "The price of
        the car must be paid in full.");
        require(sold == false, "The car has not
        already been sold.");
```

[20] The proposal for a Regulation of the European Parliament and of the Council on harmonised rules on fair access to and use of data (Data Act) defines a smart contract as a computer program stored in an electronic ledger system wherein the outcome of the execution of the program is recorded on the electronic ledger (art. 2 (16) Interinstitutional File 2022/0047(COD) March 17, 2023, 7413/23).

[21] See for instance M. Raskin, 'The Law and Legality of Smart Contracts' 1(2) *Georgetown Law Technology Review* 305–341 (2017); R. O'Shields, 'Smart Contracts: Legal Agreements for the Blockchain' 21(1) *North Carolina Banking Institute* 177–194 (2017).

[22] Obtained with ChatGPT when asking the question to write a simple smart contract for a car purchase between two parties in Solidity (Ethereum blockchain).

```
            buyer = payable(msg.sender);
            seller.transfer(msg.value);
            sold = true;
     }
}
```

This example smart contract sets the car price at 100 ether and defines the seller and buyer addresses. The Boolean variable ('the sold variable') is set to false.[23] The buyCar() function checks if the buyer has paid the correct amount and if the car is still available. If both conditions are met, the function sets the buyer variable to the buyer's address, transfers payment to the seller, and updates the sold variable to true, indicating the car has been sold.

13.2.3 Public and Private Blockchains

Public blockchains, also known as 'unpermissioned' or 'permissionless' blockchains, are open to participation (including the creation and validation of new blocks) by anyone. There are also 'private blockchains' (also called 'permissioned' blockchains[24]) in which a central organization or a group of participants controls the blockchain and its access.[25] Private blockchains are widely used in various business applications, with IBM's Hyperledger Fabric being a prominent example of a private blockchain administered by the Linux Foundation.[26]

13.3 Applications in Corporate Governance

Several authors suggest that blockchain technology can revolutionize many aspects of companies and markets, especially in the domains of

[23] Booleans use 'true' and 'false' and can control a program's flow by checking conditions. In this smart contract, the boolean variable tracks whether the car has been sold.

[24] Sometimes a distinction is made between a *private* blockchain and a *permissioned* blockchain, where the latter is considered an intermediate form of the private blockchain and public blockchain. Note that commentators often suggest that these private and permissioned blockchains are not really a form of blockchain technology but fit into the broader range of DLT.

[25] In case a group of participants works with a consensus mechanism by means of a predefined system of approval, this is also called a *consortium blockchain*. V. Buterin, 'On public and private blockchain' (2015). Available at: https://blog.ethereum.org/2015/08/07/on-public-and-private-blockchains.

[26] Participation in Hyperledger Fabric requires approval from a Membership Service Provider (MSP). See: https://hyperledger-fabric.readthedocs.io/en/release-2.2/blockchain.html (last accessed 29 March 2023).

securities regulation and corporate governance.[27] The applications seem to leverage the technology's capability to generate decentralized tamper-proof records of transactions to ensure transparency and lower costs. Classical hierarchical governance structures may be avoided altogether with the use of peer-to-peer organizations operating on a blockchain and using smart contracts. These DAOs, may – according to some authors[28] – fundamentally reorganize the governance and structures of companies, but they also raise important legal and governance questions. How do DAOs differ from 'classical' corporations? Are these decentralized organizations truly decentral in terms of their ownership and decision-making structures? These questions are addressed in Section 13.3.1. Afterwards, we turn to the use of blockchain technology for issuing and trading of corporate securities. For instance, to solve existing issues in stock ownership records, digital tokens can be created to represent securities, potentially simplifying existing processes by increasing transparency and reducing time and costs. As its potential and the implications for corporate governance have been discussed elsewhere,[29] we focus on the latest (legal) developments and whether they are able to leverage this potential in Section 13.3.2. Finally, Section 13.3.3 explores how to use blockchain for corporate decision-making. How would shareholders be able to vote on a blockchain? Can shareholder (and stakeholder) rights be enhanced with blockchain technology? These and other questions are addressed in that section.

13.3.1 Decentralized Autonomous Organizations (DAOs)

Traditional corporate governance is based on centralized organizations with hierarchical relationships among shareholders, the board of directors, corporate management and employees.[30] Authority, responsibility

[27] Fenwick & Vermeulen (2019), n. 7; Yermack (2017), n. 4. For shareholder voting and intermediated securities, see in particular: Spencer J. Nord, 'Blockchain Plumbing: A Potential Solution for Shareholder Voting' 21 *University of Pennsylvania Journal of Business Law* 706 (2019); George S. Geis, 'Traceable Shares and Corporate Law' 113 *Northwestern University Law Review* 227, 227–278 (2018); A.J.F. Lafarre & C.F. Van der Elst, 'Shareholder Voice in Complex Intermediated Proxy Systems: Blockchain Technology As a Solution?' 4(1) *The Stanford Journal of Blockchain Law and Policy* 29–52 (2021).

[28] Including M. Fenwick. J.A. McCahery & E.P.M. Vermeulen, 'The End of "Corporate" Governance: Hello "Platform" Governance' 20 *European Business Organization Law Review* 171–199 (2019).

[29] Yermack (2017), n. 4.

[30] Fenwick, McCahery & Vermeulen (2019), n. 28.

and control flows downwards from the principals (the shareholders, via the corporate board) to the agents (the corporate management), while accountability flows in the opposite direction.[31] This delegated structure creates the risk of opportunistic behaviour by corporate management. This problem is exacerbated by information asymmetry and shareholder coordination problems. In recent decades, corporate governance experts have proposed a large variety of mechanisms to mitigate these agency problems and thus to ensure that agents do not pursue their immediate self-interests but perform their tasks and duties in line with the long-term interest of the company, its shareholders and other stakeholders. However, these mechanisms typically fall short.[32] Various authors have suggested that modern technologies like blockchain can bring forward new solutions to this classical problem.[33] Fenwick, McCahery and Vermeulen have proposed the idea of 'platform governance' and discuss 'community-driven' organizations as an alternative to existing corporate governance mechanisms, evaporating the principal-agent duality. In their model, platforms have an underlying technology like blockchain that offers peer-to-peer solutions and directly connects 'creators' and 'users'.[34]

DAOs are examples of community-driven blockchain-based organizations: novel types of technology-mediated social structures[35] in which smart contracts that operate together in a (blockchain) protocol are developed, used and controlled by their participants.[36] Setting up a DAO can be simple. An individual or (small) group develops an idea, like some kind of decentralized application, and establishes a community via social media and other channels to support this idea. With the help of DAO startup templates and tools like Aragon, the smart contracts that implement the idea are developed. These toolsets can also help with, for instance, creating and distributing tokens on the blockchain, authorizing the wallets of participants for participation in decision-making, and setting the governance conditions for voting and issuing proposals.[37]

[31] Ibid. [32] Enriques & Zetzsche (2020), n. 3. [33] Bruner (2020), n. 3.

[34] Fenwick. McCahery & Vermeulen (2019), n. 28.

[35] Call for Evidence for DAOs by the Law Commission for England and Wales of 16 November 2022, p. 9.

[36] P. De Filippi & S. Hassan, 'Decentralized Autonomous Organization' 10 *Internet Policy Review* 2–10 (2021); Coalition of Automated Legal Applications (COALA), *Model Law for Decentralized Autonomous Organizations (DAOs)*, p. 57 (2021).

[37] Aragon, for instance, recommends simple majority approval of the issued tokens for a proposal to be adopted with a minimum quorum of only 15 per cent or less, and an early execution rule, which means that the vote concludes at the moment a proposal reaches

Oftentimes, first a founding community is established that receives free tokens,[38] after which the first sales round of tokens starts. The tokens represent participation in the DAO, whose members operate according to the rules defined by the protocol.

The establishment process for DAOs highlights the existence of a governance structure that operates differently from a company's centralized decision-making body. In the founding phase of a DAO, its governance and its structure rely *ab initio* on the founding community participants. The smart contract defines the rules for participant collaboration, voting, distribution of voting rights, admission of new participants, issuance of tokens (NFTs), treasury allocation, addressing rule violations and other related matters. After the smart contracts and the DAO itself become operational, participants can only propose changes to the DAO's operation and functioning that are agreed upon and verified by other participants, as determined by the smart contract. Particularly, governance rights in DAOs are oftentimes distributed among participants who hold so-called *governance tokens*, enabling them to propose and vote on actions for the DAO to take. Smart contracts of the DAO execute those proposals that meet the pre-determined conditions, including the necessary number of votes.[39] Many DAOs have intricate voting processes, potentially impacting the decentralized governance structure's efficiency. For instance, *CityDAO*, a Wyoming-based LLC (*cf. infra*, Section 13.3.1.2), is developing a blockchain-native network city and allowing its token holders to suggest development projects and visit the site.[40] Its governance structure includes three platforms for communication and voting, two levels of decision-making (the entire DAO and subgroups that are called 'Guilds'), various quorum requirements, and objection mechanisms, as described in its charter.[41] To illustrate, CityDAO's charter outlines that token holders, referred to as 'citizens', can propose a CityDAO Improvement Proposal (CIP) that is posted on CityDAO's Forum and must receive 100 likes within three weeks to be

the appropriate threshold. See https://aragon.org/how-to/create-a-dao-on-polygon-with-the-aragon-app#7Selectgovernancesettings (last accessed 5 May 2023).

38 Usually, NFTs (non-fungible tokens) are utilized. Unlike fungible tokens such as Bitcoin, which are interchangeable, NFTs are unique and represent distinct underlying assets, giving them individual value.

39 Sarcuni v. bZx DAO, No. 22-618 (S.D. Cal. Mar. 27, 2023), I. Background.

40 See: https://city.mirror.xyz/OQ-VjksyKPgdswhN8vmnk3o_CNPym6PJ0EAFdX6h5TA (last accessed 20 January 2024).

41 Available at https://charter.citydao.io/ (last accessed 10 May 2023).

eligible for a vote via a tool called Snapshot. The vote is announced to token holders via an announcement channel on Discord and lasts for one week, and if the vote is unsuccessful, a one-month cool-down period is required before resubmitting the proposal.

13.3.1.1 A Decentralization Fallacy?

DAOs are decentralized in the sense that they bypass the board and management function and thus remove the agent from the corporate order.[42] DAOs avoid legal formalities and written contracts, rather relying on the 'rule of code'.[43] However, it seems that in practice, some sort of agent or centralization of control often remains,[44] meaning that the governance structure should ensure that the algorithm does not optimize the agent's goals, but that of the organization or platform.[45] First, the importance of founders' leadership in building platforms remains as signalled by Fenwick, McCahery and Vermeulen. For example, in many cases, a founding team establishes the DAO and sets the basic governance structure. In several DAOs, this founding team holds control in the startup phase, and only in a later stage delegate (some of) their powers and rights to token holders.[46]

Second, even when claimed that DAOs have no agent (and hence the participants are not principals), ownership is often centralized, de facto providing an agency structure. Notably, although open-source code in public blockchains allows any developer to contribute and propose changes and DAOs utilize various methods to determine voter eligibility and voting procedures,[47] in practice, centralization of control often

[42] Bruner (2020), n. 3.

[43] U. Rodrigues, 'Law and the Blockchain' 104(679) *Iowa Law Review* 707 (2019).

[44] N. Tse, 'Decentralised Autonomous Organisations and the Corporate Form' 51 *Victoria University of Wellington Law Review* 313–356 (2020); Enriques & Zetzsche (2020), n. 3.

[45] Enriques & Zetzsche (2020), n. 3.

[46] See for an example American CryptoFed DAO LLC addressing in its Constitution (www.sec.gov/Archives/edgar/data/1881928/000188192821000001/Exhibit1_ACFDAOConstitution.txt, last accessed 5 May 2023): '17.1 Voting Power of MShift Founding Team: Within 3 years beginning from the effective date of this Constitution, the MShift founding team will reduce its collective ownership to 15% or less out of the maximum authorized finite Locke tokens of 10 trillion. Furthermore, starting from the fourth anniversary of the effective date of this Constitution, MShift founding team's collective voting power out of the total Locke tokens outstanding will be reduced 1% annually until the cumulative voting power is reduced to 10% or less, independent of the founding team's total actual ownership of Locke tokens.'

[47] D. Qinxu, D. Liebau, W. Zhiguo & X. Weibiao, 'A Survey on Decentralized Autonomous Organizations (DAOs) and Their Governance' (2023). Available at SSRN. Available at:

appears to occur.[48] When the same group consistently holds the majority for decision-making in a DAO, they can be considered as a specific kind of agents for the larger group of DAO participants. Even large public blockchains exhibit oligarchical tendencies as key stakeholders program blockchain applications.[49] An analysis of major cryptocurrency repositories reveals that a significant proportion of code contributions come from a single author.[50]

Third, also decision-making processes within DAOs may exhibit a degree of centralization that may appear incongruous with the decentralized nature of these organizations. Research shows that in many Decentralized Finance (DeFi) protocols, less than 10 per cent of issued tokens participate in voting proposals, and in some DAOs the participation rate of the token holders is even lower than one per cent.[51] In 3 DAOs, a small number of participants (between eight and 18) have the power to dictate governance actions, despite the hundreds of thousands of token holders who authorized delegates to vote on their behalf.[52] The governance of DAOs encounters challenges such as a concentration of voting power, high costs associated with voting and delegation, and the possibility of voter coalitions further exacerbating the concentration of control. Specifically, 80 per cent of DAOs have high voting concentration

https://papers.ssrn.com/sol3/papers.cfm?abstract_id=4378966 (last accessed 22 January 2024).

48 A. Rajendra Sai, J. Buckley, B. Fitzgerald & A. Le Gear, 'Taxonomy of Centralization in Public Blockchain Systems: A Systematic Literature Review' 58(4) *Information Processing and Management* 102584 (2021). The authors describe in their taxonomy various layers, including the 'application layer', 'governance layer' and 'network layer'.

49 For instance, in the Ripple blockchain the resource allocations and direction of code developments is centralized. Following Y.-Y. Hsieh, J.-P. Vergne & S. Wang, 'The Internal and External Governance of Blockchain-Based Organizations', in M. Campbell-Verduyn (ed.), *Bitcoin and Beyond*, Routledge: Oxon (2018).

50 S. Azouvi, M. Maller & S. Meiklejohn, 'Egalitarian Society or Benevolent Dictatorship: The State of Cryptocurrency Governance', in A. Zohar et al. (eds.), *Financial Cryptography and Data Security*, Springer: Berlin (2019).

51 R. Feichtinger, R. Fritsch, Y Vonlanthen & R. Wattenhofer, 'The Hidden Shortcomings of (D)AOs- An Empirical Study of On-Chain Governance' (2023). https://arxiv.org/pdf/2302.12125.pdf (last accessed 29 March 2023).

52 R. Fritsch, M. Müller & R. Wattenhofer, 'Analyzing Voting Power in Decentralized Governance: Who controls DAOs?' Available at: https://arxiv.org/abs/2204.01176 (last accessed 29 March 2023). Also see: Y. Faqir-Rhazoui, J. Arroyo & S. Hassan, 'A Comparative Analysis of the Platforms for Decentralized Autonomous Organizations in the Ethereum Blockchain' 12 *Journal of Internet Services and Applications* 9, 1–20 (2021).

held by delegates representing a single token holder.[53] Furthermore, blockchain networks that utilize PoW consensus mechanisms may give rise to the formation of 'blockchain conglomerates'. These companies offer various blockchain-related services and products, such as high-performance computing equipment, and participate in mining pools to increase their influence on protocol proposals.[54]

Some research suggests that many proposals are being launched by participants in DAOs, which may signal a certain level of democracy. For example, *Compound DAO*, a DAO that generates returns on crypto holdings, receives an average of 2.3 proposals per month.[55] However, many of these proposals are initiated by individuals in founding roles, highlighting centralization issues. Research shows that DAOs experiencing centralization issues suffer from conflicts of interest that negatively affect the growth of the platform,[56] as well as issues related to responsibility and liability.[57]

13.3.1.2 DAOs and the Law

Over the past years, many thousands of DAOs have been formed in various forms and shapes,[58] dealing with substantial amounts of value and creating their own rules for decision-making.[59] When establishing a DAO, a legally recognized entity like an LLC is often wrapped around (part of) it.[60] If a DAO is operating for profit without any formal legal

[53] X. Sun, C. Stasinakis & G. Sermpinis, 'Decentralization illusion in DeFi: Evidence from MakerDAO' Available at: https://arxiv.org/ftp/arxiv/papers/2210/2210.11203.pdf (last accessed 29 March 2023).

[54] D. Ferreira, J. Li & R. Nikolowa, 'Corporate Capture of Blockchain Governance' 36 *Review of Financial Studies* 1364–1407 (2023).

[55] H. Axelsen, J.R. Jensen & O. Ross, 'When is a DAO Decentralized?' 31 *Complex Systems Informatics and Modeling Quarterly* 67 (2022).

[56] J. Han, J. Lee & T. Li, 'DAO Governance' (2023). Available at SSRN. Available at: https://papers.ssrn.com/sol3/papers.cfm?abstract_id=4346581 (last accessed 22 January 2024).

[57] Like the protocol changes breaching regulatory requirement. See for a preliminary analysis P. Østbye, 'Exploring DAO Members' Individual Liability' (2022). Available at SSRN. Available at: https://papers.ssrn.com/sol3/papers.cfm?abstract_id=4045799 (last accessed 22 January 2024).

[58] See for a concise overview of different kinds of DAOs https://tokenizedhq.com/list-of-daos/ (last accessed 29 March 2023).

[59] According to DeepDAO close to 13,000 DAOs with a treasury of more than $23 Billion with almost 7 million token holders of which 2.1 million are active voters and proposal makers existed early May 2023. See: https://deepdao.io/organizations (last accessed 5 May 2023).

[60] C. Brummer & R. Seira, 'Legal Wrappers and DAOs' (2022). Available at: https://papers.ssrn.com/sol3/papers.cfm?abstract_id=4123737 (last accessed 22 January 2024);

structure, its token holders are potentially general partners in a de facto general partnership (GP) when some conditions are met.[61] In many jurisdictions, a GP does not have legal personality separate from the partners who constitute it.[62] Its partners are jointly and severally liable. DAOs can have numerous anonymous members with transferable tokens, in contrast to GPs where partners know each other and share the collective risk.[63] As a result, the legal qualification of a DAO as a de facto GP can lead to undesirable outcomes.

Nevertheless, the *Sarcuni v. bZx DAO* ruling of 27 March 2023 by a US federal district court in California shows that – depending on their features and in absence of a 'legal wrapper' – DAOs can indeed be characterized as a GP. This case involved a DeFi application called 'bZx Protocol'.[64] Initially, bZeroX LLC controlled this bZx Protocol, but in August 2021, the control was transferred to bZx DAO. In November 2021, a 'hacker'[65] stole around 55 million USD in cryptocurrencies from bZx Protocol users. On 21 November 2021, bZx DAO approved a compensation plan for those impacted by the hack, but complete repayment under this plan would take 'thousands of years'[66]. As a result, in May 2022, the Plaintiffs (19 bZx Protocol users who

W. Edwards, 'Decentralised Autonomous Organisations: Unincorporated Companies by Another Name?' 3 *Journal of International Banking and Financial Law* 147 (2022). For the UK, see Law Commission, Decentralised Autonomous Organisations (DAOs) Call for evidence, November 2022, pp. 23–36; M.A. Schillig, 'Decentralized Autonomous Organizations (DAOs) under English Law' 16(1–2) *Law and Financial Markets Review* 68–78 (2023); B. Mienert, 'How Can a Decentralized Autonomous Organization (DAO) Be Legally Structured?' *Legal Revolutionary Journal LRZ* (2021). Available at: https://lrz.legal/de/lrz/how-can-a-decentralized-autonomous-organization-dao-be-legally-structured?highlight=WyJtaWVuZXJ0IiwibHJ6IiwyMDIxLCJtaWVuZXJ0IGxyeiIsIm1pZW5lcnQgbHJ6IDIwMjEiLCJscnogMjAyMSJd (last accessed 20 January 2024).

61 Or an unincorporated nonprofit association if the DAO is not operating for profit.

62 Therefore, in the event that a partner departs the partnership or a new individual becomes a member, the original partnership is legally dissolved and a new partnership is formed with the incoming partner(s) assuming the assets and debts of the dissolved firm while continuing its operations.

63 M.A. Schillig for the GP under English law. M.A. Schillig (2023), n. 60.

64 Sarcuni v. bZx DAO, n. 40, I. Background.

65 In the court decision, the hack is described in the following way: 'On or about November 5, 2021, an unknown hacker sent a phishing email to a bZx Protocol developer's personal computer [. . .] the hacker was able to access the developer's personal digital wallet, which in turn provided access to the developer's private key.' Ibid, I. Background.

66 Ibid, I. Background.

individually lost between 800 and 450,000 USD) filed a putative class action. The plaintiffs' negligence claim was premised on the existence of a GP among all participants holding BZRX tokens.[67] As regards the co-owners' requirement for a GP under the California Corporate Code,[68] the plaintiffs alleged that bZx DAO is controlled by those who hold BZRX tokens, and that these token holders have governance rights in the DAO, including the right to suggest and vote on governance proposals.[69] Although the defendants claimed that the governance rights of the token holders are too limited to establish the existence of a GP, the Court considered that a GP can still exist when individual partners only have limited governance rights.[70] The Court established that anyone holding BZRX tokens (that are considered *governance tokens*) is a partner in the partnership.

To limit legal uncertainty for DAOs, some jurisdictions have recognized DAOs as a legitimate legal entity, providing DAO token holders with limited liability. For example, Vermont allows for the creation of a Blockchain-Based LLC (BBLLC).[71] Similarly, Wyoming passed the 2021 Act on Autonomous Decentralized Organizations, with a 2022 amendment facilitating the establishment of a DAO as an LLC.[72] One important difference between these legislative initiatives is that Wyoming (like Tennessee) explicitly excludes members of DAOs from fiduciary duties that would exist under a 'normal' LLC.[73] Vermont, on the other hand, does not exempt members from a DAO from any other judicial, statutory or regulatory provision under Vermont law.[74]

67 Ibid., B. Negligence Claim. 68 Section 16202(a) California Corporate Code.

69 Sarcuni v. bZx DAO, n. 40, C. Partnership Liability.

70 Ibid. The court also finds the allegation that BZRX token holders may share profits weighs in favour of treating the DAO as a GP.

71 Subchapter 12: Blockchain-based Limited Liability Companies of Chapter 25 Limited Liability Companies of Title 11 Corporations, Partnerships and Associations of the Vermont Statutes. Also see P. Matera, 'Delaware's Dominance, Wyoming's Dare. New Challenge, Same Outcome?' 27(1) *Fordham Journal of Corporate & Financial Law* 73 (2022).

72 The Wyoming Decentralized Autonomous Organization Supplement. Hereinafter: Wyoming DAO Supplement or 'WDS'. Tennessee also allows for the creation of an LLC as a Decentralized Organization or 'DO' following section 48-250-103 (d) Tennessee Code (TC). Section 48-5 Utah State Code. In Utah an 'LLD' (Limited Liability Decentralized autonomous organization) may be used from 2024 onwards following Section 48-5 Utah State Code. In New Hampshire a similar bill is pending at the moment of writing (May 2023).

73 Section 17-31-110 WDS; and Section 48-250-109TC.

74 Section 4176 Vermont Statute. The law allows to reasonably restrict the fiduciary duties.

In addition, it seems that whereas Wyoming expressly mandates decentralization of management by stating that the DAO shall be 'managed by the members',[75] Vermont seems to require some human involvement in the DAO's organization and governance.[76]

The COALA 'Model Law'[77] for DAOs outlines that blockchain developers, members and others involved in DAOs should not have an implicit fiduciary status.[78] For instance, COALA argues that blockchain developers, like most open-source developers, do not have control over how their code is used or modified once released.[79] At the same time, the Model Law enables management by consensus as well as the appointment of 'administrator(s)'. An administrator is defined as 'a person, irrespective of title, that is appointed in a manner specified in the By-Laws to take discretionary decisions, either individually or collectively with other Administrators, with regard to specific, predefined operations of the DAO'[80]. COALA thus seems to explicitly acknowledge that, on the one hand, also DAOs in many cases need an agent, but on the other hand, the governance is always technically decentralized,[81] and administrators should not have fiduciary duties unless their fiduciary status is made explicit.[82]

The Model Law provides further possibilities for the governance structure of DAOs.[83] It allows for multiple classes of participation rights, and notes that only participants who hold governance tokens should be considered *members* of the DAO.[84] These governance rights include for instance the ability to propose, vote and veto proposals. Token holders with only financial rights are considered participants, but not members.[85]

75 Section 17-31-104(e) WDS. Section 17-31-109 WDS defines 'management' as follows: 'Management of a decentralized autonomous organization shall be vested in its members or the members and any applicable smart contracts.'

76 C.L. Reyes, 'Autonomous Business Reality' 21 *Nevada Law Journal* 437, 454–455 (2021).

77 'Coalition of Automated Legal Applications'. It considers itself 'the leading think tank on the legal and societal aspects of blockchain technologies'. See: www.legalico.io/author/coala. COALA states that the Model Law contains substantive and procedural rules that can be adopted in national laws. COALA Model Law (2021), nt. 36, p. 7.

78 COALA Model Law (2021), Article 15.

79 Ibid., Commentary to Article 15.

80 Ibid., Article 3(2).

81 Ibid., Commentary to Article 3.

82 Ibid.

83 Aside from the provisions discussed, the Model Law also covers proxy appointments (article 9).

84 COALA Model Law (2021), Article 7(1)–(2).

85 Similar to existing ways to delink shareholder capital and control rights, like the Dutch depositary receipts (article 2:118a Dutch Civil Code). However, less transparent voting methods without related capital interest can lead to empty voting. Yermack (2007) actually suggests blockchain as a solution to this problem. Yermack (2017), n. 5.

COALA also provides the example of crypto exchanges like Binance: participants that hold tokens via these exchanges do not have governance rights, and therefore are not considered members of DAOs.[86] In contrast to 'traditional' corporations, COALA claims that there should not be any default voting rights for DAOs, "because the distribution of voting rights must be proactively delineated when creating a DAO". This probably explains the complex voting procedures that are extensively outlined in the by-laws or operating agreement (and included in the smart contracts), like for CityDAO (*cf. supra*, Section 3.1). Transactions costs, however, may arise in DAOs as economic actors, including blockchain developers and other DAO participants, are boundedly rational and cannot anticipate all contingencies, leading to incomplete contracts.[87] Incomplete contract theory in the context of corporate governance suggests that contracts must therefore allow for some asset use discretion, with the owner of the firm retaining residual control rights.[88]

To conclude, DAOs present significant uncertainties in many jurisdictions regarding their legal status, liabilities, and complex governance features. Like all organizations, founding and managing a DAO seems to require at least one individual (agent). During its operational life, new governance questions should be addressed in a decentralized manner by its participants, as predetermined by the smart contract with intricate voting processes. This is fundamentally different from traditional corporations. However, in practice, DAOs appear to be more centralized than expected, including in terms of their ownership structures and (delegated) decision-making processes.

13.3.2 Issuing and Trading of Corporate Securities

The COALA Model Law suggests that DAO members receive their governance tokens directly from the DAO, which is usually not the case

86 COALA Model Law (2021), nt. 37, p. 31.

87 For a discussion of transaction costs in smart contracts resulting from 'the need for adaptation to mutable and unpredictable occurrences' and several possible solutions to this problem, see M. Vatiero, 'Smart Contracts vs Incomplete Contracts: A Transaction Cost Economics Viewpoint' 46 *Computer Law & Security Review* 105710 (2022).

88 S.J. Grossman & O.D. Hart, 'The Costs and Benefits of Ownership: A Theory of Vertical and Lateral Integration' 94 *Journal of Political Economy* 4, 691–719 (1986). For a discussion of this seminal work, including its criticism, one may refer to: P. Aghion & R. Holden, 'Incomplete Contracts and the Theory of the Firm: What Have We Learned over the Past 25 Years?' 25 *Journal of Economic Perspectives* 2 (2011).

for shareholders of (large) corporations. In fact, the situation for these corporations is often more complex due to custody chains that have arisen from market arrangements for issuing, trading, clearing and settling dematerialized securities, including shares. As a result of these chains, shareholders have less control over their shareholder rights and fewer opportunities for engagement, putting corporate governance at risk of being distorted.[89] Kahan and Rock have already noted that the US system is 'crude, imprecise, and fragile',[90] while European issuers and shareholders face similar challenges. Blockchain technology may offer a solution to the deficiencies created by custody chains in issuing, trading and stock ownership records. By continuously tracking ownership throughout the entire settlement cycle, blockchain can increase transparency and mitigate the risks associated with custody chains. Numerous studies have highlighted the benefits of using blockchain technology for these purposes, and present it as a promising solution to these challenges.[91]

Several developments in blockchain-based securities issuance, trading and settlement can be observed. In the United States, the SEC approved the BSTX stock exchange in early 2022. This allows for shares to be listed and traded with faster settlement times than the usual two days.[92] All

[89] '[. . .] despite their undoubted benefits, custody chains complicate shareholder participation in corporate governance by interposing several layers of intermediaries between companies and their end investors', E. Ferran, 'Shareholder Engagement and Custody Chains' 23 *European Business Organization Law Review* 507, 512 (2022).

[90] M. Kahan & E.B. Rock, 'The Hanging Chads of Corporate Voting' 164 *Faculty Scholarship at Penn Law* 1230–1231, at 1279 (2008).

[91] Lafarre & Van der Elst (2021), n. 27; F. Panisi, R.P. Buckley & D. Arner, 'Blockchain and Public Companies: A Revolution in Share Ownership Transparency, Proxy Voting and Corporate Governance?' 2 *The Stanford Journal of Blockchain Law and Policy* (2019); Geis (2018), n. 27. For a discussion of settlement services in a blockchain environment, see: H. Nabilou, 'Probabilistic Settlement Finality in Proof-of-Work Blockchains: Legal Considerations' (2022). Available at: https://papers.ssrn.com/sol3/papers.cfm?abstract_id=4022676 (last accessed 22 January 2024); Advisory Groups on Market Infrastructures for Securities and Collateral and for Payments, 'The use of DLT in post-trade processes' (2021). Available at: www.ecb.europa.eu/pub/pdf/other/ecb.20210412_useofdltposttradeprocesses~958e3af1c8.en.pdf (last accessed 29 March 2023); E. Micheler & L. von der Heyde, 'Holding Company Clearing and Settling Securities through Blockchain Technology Creating and Efficient System by Empowering Asset Owners' 31(11) *Butterworths Journal of International Banking and Financial Law* 652–656 (2016); P. Paech, 'The Governance of Blockchain Financial Networks' 80(6) *Modern Law Review* 1073–1110 (2017).

[92] BSTX reports T+1 (and aims at immediate settlement, T+0). See: https://rules.boxexchange.com/browse (last accessed 29 March 2023).

trading activities that take place on BSTX are recorded on a private blockchain. Participants can access their own trading activities as well as anonymized and aggregated trading activities with a delay of approximately five minutes.[93] Also the Depository Trust and Clearing Corporation (DTCC) introduced its Ion project, a blockchain-based alternative settlement platform that has been running alongside the traditional system since August 2022, processing up to 160,000 transactions daily.[94] Many stock exchanges closely monitored blockchain developments and were experimenting with its use,[95] but it seems that only the Australian Securities Exchange (ASX) has been undertaking a multi-year effort to fully replace their current settlement platform, 'CHESS', with a blockchain-based system. However, due to its complexity, the launch of the new system has been repeatedly postponed,[96] and eventually dropped in November 2022.[97] ASX explained that any technology must meet high standards and the market due to significant technology, governance and delivery challenges that need to be addressed, giving rise to serious doubts whether the current blockchain technology can digest the multi-billion trading activities of a large stock exchange.[98]

The experience of ASX demonstrates that transforming an existing settlement and trading platform into a blockchain-based system is 'a mammoth undertaking' that involves technical complexities, uncertain business cases, and the need to balance innovation with safeguards to protect the public welfare.[99] To ensure a gradual and smooth pace of change, new technologies can initially be adopted to enhance the performance and functionality of the current system. For instance, Regulation (EU) No 2022/858 permits the use of blockchain technology as a potential solution for the quick settlement of the registration and

[93] SEC 'Release No. 34-94092; File No. SR-BOX-2021-06', 27 January 2022, at 6.

[94] DTCC, 'DTCC's Project Ion Platform now Live in Parallel Production Environment, Processing over 100,000 Transactions per Day on DLT', 22 August 2022, available via: www.dtcc.com/news/2022/august/22/project-ion (last accessed 29 March 2023).

[95] Like the Deutsche Börse Group and the Deutsche Bundesbank. See: Schillig (2023), n. 60; as well as London Stock Exchange Group and Talinn Stock Exchange (Nasdaq). See: A. Andhov, 'Corporations on Blockchain: Opportunities and Challenges', 53(1) *Cornell International Law Journal* 1–40 (2020).

[96] J. Watkins 'ASX's post-trade blockchain project delayed once again', 4 August 2022, available via: www.thetradenews.com/asxs-post-trade-blockchain-project-delayed-once-again (last accessed 29 March 2023).

[97] See 'Australian stock exchange apologises for dropping botched blockchain upgrade', *Financial Times* 17 November 2022.

[98] Ibid. [99] Ferran (2022), n. 89, p. 534.

transfer of financial instruments.[100] The regulation mandates that the settlement date must not be later than the second business day after the transaction. However, this regulation upholds the centralized market mechanism and highlights that non-standardized provisions of registration and settlement persist.[101] At present, there are limitations on the size of the issuer and the value of the securities,[102] and strict requirements must be met by blockchain systems,[103] limiting the use of blockchain technology.[104] ESMA provided guidelines to finalize applications for the establishment of blockchain systems in accordance with this Regulation.[105]

Blockchain technology may also allow companies to register their (non-listed) shares and use tokens as digital securities on a permissioned blockchain. Smart contracts can record necessary consents and restrictions on share transfers, which is particularly helpful for private companies. For instance, with 'white listing', digital shares/tokens can only be transferred to parties listed in the blockchain, allowing issuers to not only verify the acquiring party's identity (KYC) and comply with AML rules,[106] but also with contractual shareholder rights like first refusal rights. Other measures, like correction mechanisms for statutory offer obligation violations or even approval schemes in a shareholder agreement, may also be considered.

Some jurisdictions have already developed legal frameworks for this use of blockchain technology. One example is Delaware, which was an

[100] Recital 14 Regulation (EU) 2022/858 of the European Parliament and of the Council of 30 May 2022 on a pilot scheme for market infrastructures based on distributed ledger technology and amending Regulations (EU) No 600/2014 and (EU) No 909/2014 and Directive 2014/65/EU, OJ. L No. 151 of 2 June 2022.

[101] Recital 45 Regulation (EU) 2022/858. See for a number of legal issues when operational activities take place in different jurisdictions and with nodes operating under different laws, D. Zetzsche, L. Anker-Sørensen, M. Passador & A. Wehrli, 'DLT-Based Enhancement of Cross-Border Payment Efficiency – a Legal and Regulatory Perspective', BIS Working Papers No 1015 (2022).

[102] See Article 3 of Regulation (EU) 2022/858.

[103] Articles 4 to 7 Regulation (EU) 2022/858.

[104] It appears that Euroclear is presently working on a DLT solution for bonds.

[105] ESMA, 'Report on the DLT Pilot Regime', ESMA 70-460-34, 111, 27 September 2022, and ESMA, 'Questions and Answers on the implementation of Regulation (EU) 2022/858 of the European Parliament and of the Council of 30 May 2022 on a pilot regime for market infrastructures on distributed ledger technology', ESMA 70-460-189, 3 February 2023.

[106] R. Badhwar, *The CISO's Next Frontier – AI, Post-Quantum Cryptography and Advanced Security Paradigms*, Springer: Cham 2021, p. 263.

early adopter and allows blockchain for the shareholders' register.[107] France established a *dispositif d'enregistrement électronique partagé* (shared electronic registration device, or DEEP) for issuing and trading securities.[108] Under French law there is no difference whether a shareholder holds the shares via a securities account or via a DEEP that meets certain conditions. The issuance and registration of securities in a DEEP is equivalent to the registration of financial instruments in a register kept by the issuer or intermediary.[109] Ownership of securities recorded on a blockchain (including those that are transferred[110]) is equivalent to a classic securities account. The French legislator also facilitates trading on a DEEP.[111] The conditions for a DEEP, however, inter alia include that the issuer must draw up a continuity plan, including an external system for the periodic storage of data.[112] Hence, the French legislator still uses external data storage as a backup.

An example of a company that uses blockchain technology to raise financial resources and trade securities digitally is Arca Capital Management that founded the *Arca US Treasury Fund* in April 2022, an American closed-end management investment company that invests in securities issued by the US government. Arca Labs LLC serves as the 'administrator' and holds responsibility for the development of services on the Ethereum blockchain, as well as the issuance of the digital securities, known as *ArCoins*. All transactions occur on the Ethereum blockchain and are recorded there. To invest in the fund, each investor must first be added to a pre-approved list. This requires undergoing KYC and AML procedures with a 'transfer agent', who then opens an account for the investor and records her Arcoin ownership. While it may appear that this investment fund relies on the transparency of the blockchain for the ownership record, the transfer agent maintains the official

[107] Section 224 DGCL. Starting from 2018, also Wyoming has allowed the shareholders' register to be facilitated on the blockchain, as long as it can be converted into a written form, as stated in Section 17-16-1601 (d) of the Wyoming Business Corporate Act.

[108] The ordinance 2016-520 of 28 April 2016 facilitated this for bonds and the law Sapin II increased this scope to financial instruments. Various laws, ordinances and decrees further supplemented these regulations.

[109] Article L.211-3, par. 2 *Code monétaire et financier.*

[110] Ibid., Article L. 211-17, I.

[111] Ibid., Article R. 211-5, par. 3 states that once registered in a blockchain, units or shares of a UCIT and debt securities can be traded on a trading platform without necessarily first being placed on a managed account.

[112] Ibid, Article R. 211-9-7. The DEEP must also be designed in such way to guarantee the registration and integrity of registrations and to allow, directly or indirectly, the identification of the owner of the titles, as well as the type and number.

shareholder register.[113] The prospectus indicates that Ethereum charges transaction costs for validating transactions in addition to the standard management and transaction fees.[114] As a result, it is uncertain whether the numerous benefits of using blockchain technology as described by Arca are realized.[115]

In conclusion, while blockchain technology may present a solution to the issues created by custody chains in issuing, trading and monitoring corporate securities and stock ownership records, practical examples and legal developments demonstrate that migrating an existing system to a new blockchain-based system is a complex process. The available applications are rather limited, and there is still some reluctance to fully rely on the technology.

13.3.3 Corporate Decision-Making

Custody chains complicate the relationship between the issuer and its shareholders: after all, for shareholder identification, information, communication and voting, issuers and shareholders depend on the transfer of information by intermediaries. In particular, shareholder votes are not always counted correctly. In Europe, these shortcomings have been acknowledged by the Shareholder Rights Directive (SRD) II.[116] The SRD II mandates confirmation to shareholders, at least upon request, that their votes have been correctly registered and counted.[117] The European Commission has suggested to encourage the use of 'modern technologies' for this.[118] Similarly, in 2016, Vice-Chancellor Laster of Delaware proposed blockchain as a potential solution for proxy voting in

[113] The process seems to proceed as follows. The transfer agent bears the responsibility for keeping an account of each potential counterparty of the shareholder who acquired the ArCoins. If the counterparty is not 'whitelisted', the transfer of the ArCoins fails. The transfer agent then has a correction possibility and can synchronize the blockchain with its own share register.

[114] The prospectus shows that the average transaction fee was $62, which is a very significant amount for small transactions.

[115] The benefits mentioned in the prospectus are: (i) the use of the peer-to-peer network, (ii) the reduced settlement time, (iii) the possibility of carrying out the transactions on the blockchain and (iv) the reduced costs (p. 15). However, the transaction costs are high, and one should note that the settlement period should take into account the registration process of the transfer agent.

[116] Directive (EU) 2017/828. Also see C.F. Van der Elst & A.J.F. Lafarre, 'Blockchain and Smart Contracting for the Shareholder Community' 20(1) *European Business Organization Law Review* 111–137 (2019).

[117] Ferran (2022), n. 89. [118] Implementing Regulation (EU) 2018/1212, Preamble 4.

the American context.[119] The use of blockchain technology can facilitate shareholder decision-making by enabling direct and simple exercise of voting rights, which can result in increased shareholder engagement with corporations.

Panisi, Buckley and Arner describe how increased transparency in shareholder voting with the use of blockchain provides substantial benefits, including (i) reducing errors and costs in shareholder voting; (ii) increasing the legitimacy and quality of the shareholder voting process and therefore enhance 'shareholder democracy' and (iii) enhancing 'fairness' between different stakeholders.[120] Our 2021 paper highlights an additional advantage, namely the potential for direct communication between an issuer and its shareholders.[121] Davies explains that UK proxy agents receive voting instructions shortly after meeting notices, but withhold submission until close to the deadline. Issuers prefer receiving this information when proxies are cast, rather than at the last minute, as the late submission offers issuers little value and is unlikely to influence policies or voting decisions.[122] However, research suggests that more transparency in blockchain markets may also lead to less shareholder involvement, discouraging activists and raiders from investing in firms, as they seem to prefer building share positions secretly to avoid higher costs.[123]

13.3.3.1 Shareholder Voting on a Blockchain

A permissioned blockchain can be used for voting by shareholders, identifying shareholders and passing on information from the issuer to shareholders, for example using the following model.[124]

[119] Travis Slander, 'CII Keynote Speech: The block chain plunger: using technology to clean up proxy plumbing and take back the vote', 29 September 2016. Available at: www.cii.org/files/09_29_16_laster_remarks.pdf (last accessed 29 March 2023).

[120] According to the authors, heightened transparency will make it increasingly challenging to conceal practices like empty voting until voting. This will enable stakeholders to respond promptly and employ opposing strategies to prevent certain actions. Also see Yermack (2017), n. 5.

[121] Lafarre & Van der Elst (2021), n. 27. Our paper discusses an additional benefit of blockchain, which is the potential for an improved model for virtual-only AGMs. This is due to the heightened transparency, verifiability and immutability of recorded information. Virtual-only meetings have been criticized for directors' ability to avoid difficult shareholder questions, but blockchain technology may be able to address this issue.

[122] P. Davies, 'Investment Chains and Corporate Governance', in L. Gullifer & J. Payne (eds.), *Intermediation and Beyond*, Hart: London (2019).

[123] Yermack (2017), n. 4; Ferran (2022), n. 89.

[124] While there may be some differences in implementation, the fundamental element of such a blockchain-based shareholder voting model is the establishment of a secure and

The issuer convenes the AGM and uploads the documentation in a standardized form to the blockchain so that the information about the AGM is available to all participants in the blockchain (step 1).[125] In case all transactions are recorded on a blockchain, whereby shares are issued and stored in the wallets of the shareholders, the voting rights attached to the shares can be directly matched with the corresponding shareholders using a KYC process (step 2).[126] In the traditional intermediated model the intermediaries at each level of the intermediated securities chain need to upload a list of their beneficiaries so that the beneficial shareholders can be identified.[127] As a next step, the beneficial shareholders are given access to the documentation of the AGM and the corresponding voting right tokens (step 3). Subsequently, shareholders can use these tokens to vote themselves or to appoint a proxy to vote on their behalf who is added to the blockchain by the issuer (step 4). After the beneficial owners (or their proxies) have cast their votes, the shareholders can verify that their vote is correctly included in the voting results (step 5).[128]

In recent years, several initiatives were introduced to leverage the technology's potential for shareholder voting.[129] For instance, ASX planned to enable shareholders to cast votes on the blockchain. The Spanish company Iberdrola announced it has used blockchain technology for its 2022 AGM.[130] As a major international player, Broadridge has

transparent digital record of share ownership that facilitates the direct exercise of shareholder rights. Also see Panisi, Buckley & Arner (2019), n. 91, at p. 213.

125 The use of blockchain technology can enhance transparency regarding the sequence of events occurring between the notice of the meeting and the date of the AGM. Frequently, agenda items are withdrawn, and in numerous instances, the board seems to be cognizant of the development of voting that takes place before the AGM.

126 See Panisi, Buckley & Arner (2019), n. 91, at p. 212. The authors describe the e-voting project in Estonia led by Nasdaq and the Tallin Stock Exchange.

127 Every relevant intermediary can run a node. But of course, the ultimate goal of using blockchain in shareholder voting is to disintermediate the current system. See Lafarre & Van der Elst (2021), n. 27.

128 In order to guarantee privacy, shareholders should have access only to their own voting decisions and overall voting results. However, institutional investors may find it desirable to disclose their voting decisions due to various (voluntary and compulsory) requirements related to the disclosure of their active ownership behaviour.

129 We refer to previous work for an overview of these initiatives. See: A.J.F. Lafarre & C.F. Van der Elst, 'Legal tech and blockchain for corporate governance and shareholders', in *Research Handbook in Data Science and Law* (2018).

130 See: www.iberdrola.com/press-room/news/detail/iberdrola-first-company-to-use-blockchain-to-certify-shareholdings-general-shareholders-meeting (last accessed 29 March 2023). In addition Iberdrola has used Metaverse to let shareholders take a virtual tour along its latest projects.

already launched several initiatives, including the cooperation with the Tokyo Stock Exchange (TSE)[131] and Banco Santander.[132] In 2022, Broadridge has announced to provide *end-to-end confirmation* to all shareholders of the listed companies in the US of which Broadridge registers the votes.[133] To our knowledge, although there have been several examples, no issuer has utilized blockchain technology for their AGM more than once, and many of the initiatives that are announced fail to materialize.

13.3.3.2 Stakeholder Involvement

Blockchain technology can also present possibilities to engage stakeholders in corporate decision-making.[134] As previously mentioned, shareholders can utilize blockchain to exercise their voting rights, and this approach may be extended to other stakeholders who may, for instance, be provided an advisory role in certain decisions. It provides limitless possibilities to reconsider the distribution of decision-making powers within the corporation and the inclusion of stakeholders in the process. For example, different classes of stakeholders could submit and evaluate proposals within their respective groups or networks, like the 'Guilds' in the governance structure of CityDAO (*cf. supra,* Section 13.3.1). After a certain predetermined level of agreement is achieved within a specific class of stakeholders, for example through a vote of that stakeholder class with predetermined majority and quorum requirements, the proposal can be presented to the corporate board and/or the AGM, or even to other stakeholder classes. Corporate boards can also consult their stakeholders directly on issues they are dealing with, such as sustainability

[131] See: www.broadridge.com/intl/press-release/2019/icj-and-broadridge-execute-the-proxy-voting-process (last accessed 29 March 2023).

[132] See: www.broadridge.com/intl/press-release/2018/santander-and-broadridge-completed-practical-use-of-blockchain (last accessed 29 March 2023).

[133] See: www.broadridge-ir.com/news/news-details/2022/Broadridge-Enhances-Trust-in-Proxy-Voting-Results-with-Extension-of-End-to-End-Vote-Confirmation-Services/default.aspx (last accessed 29 March 2023). Broadridge and the SEC have had end-to-end confirmation on their agenda for many years. See: Broadridge, 'Report of Roundtable on Proxy Governance: Recommendations for Providing End-to-End Vote Confirmation', August 2011, available via: www.broadridge.com/_assets/pdf/broadridge-report-on-roundtable-on-proxy-governance.pdf; SEC 'End-to-End Vote Confirmation Announcement: Conclusions from the Securities Industry End to End Vote Confirmation Steering Committee' 2016, available from: www.sec.gov/comments/4-681/4681-6355043-196249.pdf. At the time of writing this contribution, Broadridge has not yet reported on the results of these vote confirmations of the 2022 AGM season.

[134] Chiu & Lim (2021), n. 9.

issues. Stakeholder dialogue is an important pillar of corporate sustainability (human rights) due diligence,[135] and seems to become more embedded in corporate governance. For instance, the Dutch Corporate Governance Code 2022 indicates in Principle 1.1.5 that companies should discuss with relevant stakeholders about the sustainability aspects of the strategy and its implementation. Albeit interesting, the discussion of whether stakeholders should have voting rights and, if so, which ones, is not within the scope of this chapter. Blockchain technology and the decentralized governance structures of DAOs with their various token classes and (complex) voting procedures can perhaps inspire corporate law and governance scholars and regulators to rethink current corporate governance models and the division of powers in corporations.

Finally, blockchain technology can also be used in the relationship between institutional investors and ultimate beneficiaries. For example, research has led to the beneficiaries of Dutch pension fund *Pensioenfonds Detailhandel* being able to participate in the decision-making process about whether to add a SDG to the sustainability policy of this institutional investor.[136] By means of a technology such as blockchain, beneficiaries could regularly advise or co-decide on the investment and voting policy of institutional investors. Institutional investors, in turn, would also be able to communicate their voting preferences directly and in a transparent manner to their asset managers via the blockchain. Asset managers like BlackRock nowadays allow (part of) their clients to directly exercise their stewardship preferences through pass-through voting platforms.[137] Blockchain technology can offer the required transparency and reliability to guarantee asset owners that their shares are correctly voted, thereby enabling them to make credible claims about their engagement strategies to their beneficiaries. However, like with every blockchain application, it is essential to critically evaluate the necessity of blockchain technology itself, as centralized systems with secure and transparent digital record-keeping might offer comparable outcomes in these cases.

[135] For instance, see the OECD Due Diligence Guidance for Responsible Business Conduct on meaningful stakeholder engagement.

[136] R. Bauer, T. Ruof & P. Smeets, 'Get Real! Individuals Prefer More Sustainable Investments' 34(8) *The Review of Financial Studies* 3976–4043 (2021).

[137] See, for example, BlackRock's announcement: www.blackrock.com/corporate/newsroom/press-releases/article/corporate-one/press-releases/2022-blackrock-voting-choice (last accessed 29 March 2023).

13.4 Concluding Remarks

Advocates widely recognize blockchain technology and distributed ledger technologies (DLT) as transformative influences in corporate governance. They believe that these technologies enable the creation of decentralized autonomous organizations (DAOs) that operate fully decentralized, without hierarchical structures. Additionally, literature suggests that DLT can address inefficiencies arising from intermediated securities models by providing transparent shareholder identification and end-to-end verification of shareholder voting. The technology also holds the promise of enhancing shareholder participation and offers opportunities for stakeholder involvement.

However, despite the initial hype, serious questions remain about the practicality and viability of DLT-based corporate governance initiatives. The emergence of DAOs operating on the blockchain has garnered significant attention, but challenges and uncertainties persist regarding their legal status, complex governance structures, and liability features. Practical implementation often reveals elements of centralization and the presence of agents despite their intention to decentralize decision-making and ownership.

This chapter also examined the impact of blockchain and DLT on corporate governance, focusing on how they can strengthen various corporate functions, such as share issuance, trading and decision-making processes. While blockchain technology has the potential to address custody chain issues and enhance transparency in corporate securities and stock ownership records, the transition from existing systems to blockchain-based ones is complex, as evidenced by the ASX CHESS Replacement program. Although blockchain technology has the potential to provide advantages in the realm of shareholder and stakeholder rights, it is essential to consider the significant caveats and practical limitations. In addition, centralized systems with secure and transparent digital record-keeping might provide similar outcomes in various cases, raising doubts about the necessity of blockchain technology.

In conclusion, while blockchain technology offers significant advantages for corporate governance, understanding its limitations and legal implications is essential. The ongoing development of blockchain applications in corporate governance presents both opportunities and challenges in integrating this technology into existing frameworks.

14

Shareholder Engagement in East Asia

LIN LIN

14.1 Introduction

Shareholder activism is regarded as a way in which shareholders can assert their power as owners of the company to influence the company's behaviour.[1] Cheffins and Armour distinguish the type of activism that hedge funds engage in from that of "mainstream" institutional investors. "Mainstream" institutional investors, such as public pension funds and mutual funds, typically engage in "defensive" shareholder activism. They would hold a sizeable minority stake in the target company and lobby for change to enhance the value of their existing stake when the company is underperforming. On the other hand, hedge funds tend to adopt an *ex-ante* approach and engage in "offensive" shareholder activism. They first assess if the target company would benefit from activism, and then acquire and build up their stake strategically to influence management decisions. One distinctive feature of "offensive" activism is that hedge funds would acquire a minority stake only shortly before launching an activism campaign. Although hedge funds may obtain full voting control and launch a full-fledged takeover bid in some instances, they generally prefer to remain as a minority shareholder and engage the management and other shareholders to take action to improve investment returns.[2] Since its advent in the early 1990s, hedge fund activism has developed

I thank Gen Goto, Kyung-Hoon Chun, Virginia Harper Ho, Alexandros Seretakis, Xia Mian and Xu Sijia for valuable comments on earlier drafts of this article. I thank Rachel Goh and Anders Ong for research assistance in this project.

1 Dionysia Katelouzou, "Book Review on 'The Foundations and Anatomy of Shareholder Activism' by Iris HY Chiu" (2011) 11:2 *Journal of Corporate Law Studies* 551, at p. 551.

2 See e.g., Marco Becht, Julian Franks, Jeremy Grant and Hannes F. Wagner, "Returns to Hedge Fund Activism: An International Study" (2017) 30:9 *The Review of Financial Studies* 2933, at p. 2943, observing that even during engagements, the average stake held by hedge funds is 11 per cent.

into a niche area which combines investment with corporate governance goals using a mixed bag of activism strategies.[3]

The impact of hedge fund activism has been widely studied in the United States (US) and the United Kingdom (UK), although parts of this debate remain unsettled. One school of scholars is convinced that hedge fund activism brings a positive impact not only in terms of short-term shareholder returns but also in terms of long-term corporate governance and performance. Based on their extensive empirical research, Alon Brav and Wei Jiang contend that hedge fund interventions lead to improvement in target firms, both in terms of short-term metrics such as stock value appreciation, as well as long-term performance, including productivity, innovation and governance.[4]

Other scholars are more sceptical and have argued that profit-driven hedge fund activism brings a certain set of detriments to target companies. In this regard, John Coffee and Darius Palia argue that hedge fund tactics come at a cost.[5] Under the pressure to fund higher pay-outs to shareholders, companies targeted or at risk of being targeted by hedge funds have shown a significant reduction in their research and development expenditure.[6] Coffee and Palia further highlighted other downsides associated with the emergence of a short-term majority using the "wolf pack" tactic, where a loose network of activist investors act in parallel to acquire shares of a target company but usually avoid forming a group to circumvent securities disclosure requirements.[7]

Bearing these divergent views in mind, this chapter focuses on the distinctive features of hedge fund activism in East Asia. Regrettably little has been written in the legal literature about hedge fund activism in major East Asian markets such as China and South Korea. To fill this literature gap, this chapter aims to take an empirical and comparative approach to examining hedge fund activism in the three major East Asian markets of mainland China, South Korea and Japan. The structure of the rest of this chapter is as follows: Section 14.2 provides an overview of hedge fund activism in East Asia, with a focus on the characteristics of target companies, the objectives of hedge fund activists' campaigns, the

3 Alon Brav, Wei Jiang and Rongchen Li, "Governance by Persuasion: Hedge Fund Activism and Market-based Shareholder Influence" (2022) *European Corporate Governance Institute – Finance Working Paper No. 797/2021*, at p. 4.

4 Ibid.

5 John C. Coffee and Darius Palia, "The Wolf at the Door: The Impact of Hedge Fund Activism on Corporate Governance" (2016) 41:3 *Journal of Corporation Law* 545.

6 Ibid., at pp. 573–580.

7 Ibid., at pp. 561–568.

strategies adopted by hedge fund activists, the frequency of hedge fund activism, and the impacts of hedge fund activism on target firms; Section 14.3 analyses the distinctive features of hedge fund activism within the examined East Asian countries; and Section 14.4 concludes.

14.2 An Overview of Hedge Fund Activism in East Asia

To investigate the frequency of hedge fund activism, its practices and outcomes in East Asia, this study relies on hand-collected data on hedge fund activism events against listed companies in three representative East Asian jurisdictions. The three jurisdictions are mainland China, Japan and South Korea. They were chosen because of their vibrant economy and active capital markets. The three jurisdictions also have various similarities. They are all civil law countries that follow a German-centric civil law legal tradition. In recent years, they have also transplanted corporate governance mechanisms from the US, such as derivative actions and outside directors.[8]

Moreover, they share similar cultural characteristics in terms of the remnant influence of Confucianism, respect for hierarchy and preference for amicable rather than confrontational engagement, all of which have found their way into modern-day corporate governance.[9] Furthermore, the listed companies in these jurisdictions have a similarly concentrated

[8] See chapters 4, 5 and 6, in Dan W. Puchniak, Harald Baum and Luke Nottage eds., *Independent Directors in Asia: A Historical, Contextual and Comparative Approach* (Cambridge University Press, 2017); Chun Kyung-Hoon, "Korea's Mandatory Independent Directors: Expected and Unexpected Roles" in Dan W. Puchniak, Harald Baum and Luke Nottage eds., *Independent Directors in Asia: A Historical, Contextual and Comparative Approach* (Cambridge University Press, 2017), at p. 176. The concept of outside directors was first introduced in Japan in 2002, when Japan created the option of adopting a one-tier Anglo-American board structure to promote the appointment of outside directors to the boards of large companies. Gen Goto, Manabu Matsunaka and Souichirou Kozuka, "Japan's Gradual Reception of Independent Directors", in Dan W. Puchniak, Harald Baum and Luke Nottage eds., *Independent Directors in Asia: A Historical, Contextual and Comparative Approach* (Cambridge University Press, 2017) at p. 136. Korea's enhancement of board independence came in the aftermath of the Asian Financial Crisis, where Korea had to implement the requirements of the International Monetary Fund (IMF). Chun Kyung-Hoon, "Korea's Mandatory Independent Directors: Expected and Unexpected Roles", at p.1. The concept of independent directors was introduced in China in 1997, when the China Securities Regulatory Commission allowed listed companies to appoint independent directors.

[9] See for example, Lin Yu-Hsin, "When Activists Meet Controlling Shareholders in the Shadow of the Law: A Case Study of Hong Kong" (2019) 14:1 *Asian Journal of Comparative Law* 1–36, at p. 7; Tang Xudong, Gu Yan, Weng Ruoyu and

shareholding structure; even in Japan where the phenomenon is perhaps less so, ownership there is still more concentrated than in the US and the UK.[10] Their similarities aside, these three jurisdictions display a varying degree of openness to and regulatory control over hedge fund activists, adding to the scope and nuances of this study.

Like in other countries, there exists no official or standard database for hedge fund activism events in the three East Asian jurisdictions studied. Therefore, this study collected its own sample of hedge fund activist events. The main source of information comes from searches in newspaper archives, private research reports[11] and online search engines.[12] In terms of time span, this study focused on events that took place in recent years, that is, in the 2010s and the early 2020s. Although the activism events of listed companies can be traced using these sources, campaigns that started and ended with private negotiations between activists and target companies are generally inaccessible.[13] Information on such activist campaigns is usually not disclosed on public platforms due to the private nature of hedge funds, and thus could not be traced through the sources used in this study.[14]

Significantly, Japan ranked second globally in terms of the number of activist campaigns in 2022. According to Insightia, a global voting rights research firm, 107 Japan-based companies were publicly subjected to activist demands in a single year. Korea came in close at fifth place, with a total of 47 Korea-based companies publicly subjected to activist demands, most often via shareholder proposals.[15] In mainland China, activism declined sharply in 2022, with only two companies facing public

Ho Kungcheng, "Confucianism and Corporate Fraud" (2022) 17:6 *International Journal of Emerging Markets* 1425–1445.

[10] A. De La Cruz, A. Medina and Y. Tang, "Owners of the World's Listed Companies" (2019) *OECD Capital Market Series*, Paris, accessible at www.oecd.org/corporate/Owners-of-the-Worlds-Listed-Companies.htm, at p. 18.

[11] Insightia report which provides information on shareholder activism, investor voting and corporate governance.

[12] The news outlets entrusted to provide accurate information include Bloomberg, Reuters, the Financial Times, Nikkei and CNA, among others. The search engines deployed are mainly Google and Baidu. The searches in China were conducted in Chinese, while searches in the three other jurisdictions were mainly conducted in English.

[13] Including campaigns against non-listed companies. See also the chapter by Matteo Gatti, Giovanni Strampelli and Matteo Tonello in this book.

[14] In total, this study has identified 44 instances of hedge fund activism in China, Japan and South Korea as of the date of this chapter (on file with the author).

[15] Josh Black, "The Shareholder Activism Annual Review" (2023), *Insightia*, online: https://docs.insightia.com/issues/2023_02_16_Insightia_SAAR2023.pdf.

demands. This is down from eight and nine companies in 2020 and 2021, respectively.[16] Although the data does not elucidate which parties are responsible for initiating the public demands, it is found that most of the activist campaigns were launched by hedge funds and private equity funds.[17]

14.2.1 Target Companies

Broadly, based on my dataset and the reported cases, activist hedge funds in the three studied East Asian countries targeted companies that have one or more of the following characteristics: (1) relatively more dispersed ownership with no controlling shareholder,[18] (2) undervalued, (3) low profitability, (4) inefficient use of free cash flow in balance sheets, (5) under public criticism due to events such as ongoing criminal or administrative investigations and (6) controversial agenda pending, such as a restructuring.[19]

The target companies found in this sample are also mostly listed companies that are well-known, at least within their local markets, and

[16] Josh Black, "Corporate Governance in Asia" (2023), *Insightia*, online: www.insightia.com/asia2023.

[17] Author's interview with a Korean lawyer and a Japanese lawyer (anonymity required) dated 9 June 2023. (Most of the shareholder activists in Japan and Korea are done by hedge funds.) See also Sang Yop Kang and Kyung-Hoon Chun, "Korea's Stewardship Code and the Rise of Shareholder Activism" (2022) University of Oxford, Faculty of Law Blogs, online: https://blogs.law.ox.ac.uk/business-law-blog/blog/2022/05/koreas-stewardship-code-and-rise-shareholder-activism. See Lin Lin and Dan Puchniak, "Institutional Investors in China: Corporate Governance and Policy Channeling in the Market within the State" (2022), 35 *Colum. J. Asian L.* 74, at Appendix 2.

[18] In China, in our empirical study analysing 43 shareholder activist campaigns in Chinese companies conducted between 1994 and 2021, it was found that 76.7 per cent of the targeted companies lacked a dominant controlling shareholder holding over 50 per cent of the shares. See Lin Lin and Dan Puchniak, ibid., pp. 114–115. In South Korea, hedge fund activism also largely exists in firms with high foreign shareholding ratio that actively participate in the general meeting of shareholders. See Hyeon Deog Cho, Joon B Kim, Eun-Young Lee and Gun Woo Kim, "The Shareholder Rights and Activism Review: South Korea" (18 August 2022), *The Law Reviews*, online: https://thelawreviews.co.uk/title/the-shareholder-rights-and-activism-review/south-korea. In China, the dataset shows that the targets are generally the firms without major shareholders such as the state ownership.

[19] See Hyeon Deog Cho, et al., *supra* note 18. See also, Nga Pham, "Shareholder Activism in Japan" (2020), *Enterprising Investor CFA Institute*, online: https://blogs.cfainstitute.org/investor/2020/06/23/shareholder-activism-in-japan/#:~:text=Shareholder%20activism%20has%20been%20on,Monash%20Centre%20for%20Financial%20Studies.

command a respectable market presence. While activist campaigns have generally targeted large-cap firms, there has been a growing number of campaigns targeting small-cap and micro-cap firms in recent years.[20]

In Japan, recent activism events are associated with household names such as Sony,[21] Toshiba[22] and Seven & i Holdings (the parent company of 7-Eleven).[23] With regards to the target companies' industry, approximately two-thirds of the targeted companies in Japan were in the consumer goods, services and technology sectors.[24]

In South Korea, hedge fund activism has also caught well-established companies with strong ties to the *chaebols*, including Samsung, Hyundai Motor Company[25] and LG Corporation.[26] Elliott Management's campaign against Samsung, the largest *chaebol* in South Korea, sent shock waves not only to the business world but also to the political community, adding fuel to the impeachment of Park Geun-hye.[27]

Hedge funds targeted Korean companies across a wide range of industries, including the manufacturing, healthcare and entertainment industries, without a concentration in any specific sector.[28] KT&G

[20] Nga Pham, "Shareholder Activism in Japan" (2020), *Enterprising Investor CFA Institute*, online: https://blogs.cfainstitute.org/investor/2020/06/23/shareholder-activism-in-japan/#:~:text=Shareholder%20activism%20has%20been%20on,Monash%20Centre%20for%20Financial%20Studies.

[21] CNBC, "Hedge Fund Third Point Sells All of Its ADRs in Sony, Filings Show" (18 Aug 2020), *CNBC*, online: www.cnbc.com/2020/08/19/hedge-fund-third-point-sells-most-of-its-shares-in-sony.html.

[22] Francesca Regalado, "Toshiba Activist Investor Effissimo Wins Battle Over Management" (18 Mar 2021), *Nikkei Asia*, online: https://asia.nikkei.com/Business/Business-trends/Toshiba-activist-investor-Effissimo-wins-battle-over-management.

[23] Svea Herbst-Bayliss, "ValueAct Backs Seven & i Director Slate, Urges More Focus on 7-Eleven" (6 May 2022), *Reuters*, online: www.reuters.com/business/retail-consumer/valueact-backs-seven-i-director-slate-urges-more-focus-7-eleven-2022-05-05.

[24] Nga Pham, "Shareholder Activism in Japan" (2020), *Enterprising Investor CFA Institute*, online: https://blogs.cfainstitute.org/investor/2020/06/23/shareholder-activism-in-japan/#:~:text=Shareholder%20activism%20has%20been%20on,Monash%20Centre%20for%20Financial%20Studies.

[25] Byoung Kwon Park, et al., *infra* note_27.

[26] Joyce Lee and Shradha Singh, "US Hedge Fund Launches Activist Campaign against LG's Planned Spin-off" (15 Dec 2020) *Reuters*, online: www.reuters.com/article/us-lg-corp-restructuring-idUKKBN28P007.

[27] Byoung Kwon Park, Eun-Young Lee, Hyeon Deog Cho and Joon B Kim, "In Review: Recent Trends in Shareholder Activism in South Korea" (15 Oct 2020) *Lexology*, online: www.lexology.com/library/detail.aspx?g=ce71974f-f09e-4dec-96c4-4cb9c2868a98; BBC, "South Korean Authorities Raid Samsung in Park Geun-hye Probe" (23 Nov 2016) *BBC*, online: www.bbc.com/news/world-asia-38074082.

[28] Hyeon Deog Cho, et al., *supra* note_18.

Corporation, the world's fifth largest tobacco maker, has recently been targeted by two activist hedge funds, which called for improvements in corporate governance by electing more independent directors to the board[29] and increasing shareholder value through share buybacks.[30] Osstem Implant, South Korea's leading dental implant company has also recently been targeted by the Korea Corporate Governance Improvement (KCGI) Fund. The KCGI Fund is Osstem's third-largest shareholder with a 6.92 per cent stake and has called for the resignation of Osstem's founder and Chairman Choi Kyoo Ok in a bid to enhance the company's corporate governance after it was embroiled in the largest-ever embezzlement scandal for a Korean listed company.[31] SM Entertainment, one of the largest South Korean entertainment companies, also became the target of activist hedge fund Align Partners Capital Management (APCM), whereby APCM questioned payments made by SM Entertainment that unfairly benefitted the founder's private company, Like Planning, and called for the two to cut ties.[32]

In China, well-known names such as Gree Electric and FAW Car came under the activists' attention.[33] For instance. activist investors of Gree Electric managed to oppose the appointment of a director who was

[29] Dong-Hui Park, "Anda pushes for right to copy KT&G shareholder list" (10 Jan 2023) *The Korea Economic Daily*, online: www.kedglobal.com/shareholder-activism/newsView/ked202301100010.

[30] Flashlight Capital, "Flashlight Capital Comments on Outcome of KT&G's General Meeting" (28 Mar 2023) *Business Wire*, online: www.businesswire.com/news/home/20230328005919/en/Flashlight-Capital-Comments-on-Outcome-of-KTG%E2%80%99s-General-Meeting#:~:text=Sanghyun%20Lee%2C%20Managing%20Partner%20of,value%2Dcreating%20change%20at%20KT%26G.

[31] Ji-Eun Ha, "Activist fund KCGI to sell Osstem stake to UCK, MBK Partners" (2023), *The Korea Economic Daily*, online: www.kedglobal.com/shareholder-activism/newsView/ked202302100021.

[32] Bae Hyun-Jung and Sohn Dong-Joo, "Align Partners ending 'Korea discount' for fun and profit" (13 Feb 2023) *Korea JoongAng Daily*, online: https://koreajoongangdaily.joins.com/2023/02/13/business/industry/activist-fund-align-partners-sm-entertainment/20230213182012059.html; Kim Jaewon, "South Korean activist funds pick up steam on legal change" (31 March 2023) *Nikkei Asia*, online: https://asia.nikkei.com/Business/Companies/South-Korean-activist-funds-pick-up-steam-on-legal-change2.

[33] Du Zhixin, "Feng Jiyong: This is a Historical Day (冯继勇：这是具有历史意义的一天)" (28 May 2012) *Securities Times*, online: http://epaper.stcn.com/paper/zqsb/page/1/2012-05/28/B005/20120528B005_pdf.pdf; Xu Wei, "Chairman of Venus Investment: Will Bring Lawsuit if FAW Car Passes the Resolution on Delaying the Fulfilment of Commitment (明耀投资董事长：一汽若通过延期承诺将起诉)" (24 June 2016) *NetEase Finance*, online: www.163.com/money/article/BQADPSOI002534NV.html.

recommended by a state-owned majority shareholder which held close to 20 per cent of the total shares.[34]

Based on this sample, it appears that hedge funds operating in these East Asian markets have the incentive to make their name known by picking up a fight with giant corporations. This strategy seems to provide the added advantage of market publicity for the funds. On a related note, since there tends to be a greater amount of newspaper coverage on these household names, the funds also benefit from having more efficient channels to spread their message to other shareholders to rally their support.

In comparison, while such a David vs Goliath move is not unheard of in the West (e.g. Engine No. 1's successful campaign against Exxon Mobil),[35] studies have also shown that mid-and-small-cap corporations in the US and the UK are more common targets of hedge fund activism. For example, Alon Brav and Wei Jiang observe that hedge funds in the US tend to target firms with low to medium levels of market capitalisation.[36] They reported that the most represented target firms are those among the fourth quintile in terms of market capitalisation.

This observed difference in terms of the size of the target companies can be attributed to various factors. The hedge fund industries in these East Asian markets are still relatively young. They need high-profile interventions to attract attention and funding from investors. Furthermore, a majority of these interventions are launched by offshore funds. Comprehensive and in-depth information disclosure by the target companies is necessary for these offshore funds to conduct their research and analysis. In this sense, since large corporations are compelled by regulations and exchange rules to make more thorough disclosures in these markets whereas disclosures by smaller companies tend to be more elusive and obscure, large corporations are easier targets.

14.2.2 Activism Objectives and Trends on ESG

In general, hedge fund activist campaigns in East Asian markets seek similar objectives as their counterparts in the US and the UK. Alon Brav

[34] Yaqi Ding, "The Role of Institutional Shareholder Activism in Corporate Governance: A Comparative Study of the UK, US and China" (2017) University of Glasgow, at pp. 207–210.

[35] See, e.g., the chapter by Wolf-Georg Ringe in this book.

[36] Alon Brav, Wei Jiang and Rongchen Li, *supra* note_3, at pp. 31–37.

and Wei Jiang classified the motives of hedge fund activism in the US into five broad categories, namely, general undervaluation, capital structure, business strategy, sale of the target and corporate governance.[37] In the UK, Marco Becht et al. found the primary objectives of hedge fund activists to be corporate restructuring, board changes and financial and pay-out policies.[38] As will be seen in the following analysis, the objectives adopted by active hedge funds in the East Asian markets are largely congruent with those in the US and the UK.

In my sample, the common objectives of the activists are generally aimed at: (1) pay-out policies (e.g. special dividend, share buyback), (2) corporate governance and representation (e.g. dismissal of chairperson, directors or executives and/or appointment of their proposed candidates) and (3) business strategies (e.g. objection to a proposed merger, spin-off or diversification plans). In about one-third of the studied instances, the activists demanded some form of corporate governance and representation, including the dismissal of the chairperson and directors, replacement by their preferred candidates, and the establishment of an independent audit committee or remuneration committee. Sometimes, board representation is sought concurrently with other objectives. This is because with their candidates sitting on the board, the activists have greater room to advance their positions and gather support from other shareholders.

A study on over 450 shareholder demands in 130 Japanese companies revealed that most demands pertained to issues related to the firms' balance sheets and boards, with the top three concerns being dividend payments, board representation and director removal.[39] Returning cash to shareholders was an especially popular demand in 2022, with 63 cases in 2022 as compared to 24 cases in both 2021 and 2020.[40] This is because Japanese companies tend to retain a significant portion of cash on their balance sheets. Nearly half of the non-financial companies listed on the

[37] Ibid., at pp. 25–28.

[38] Marco Becht, Julian Franks, Colin Mayer and Stefano Rossi, "Returns of Shareholder Activism: Evidence from a Clinical Study of the Hermes UK Focus Fund" (2009) 22:8 *The Review of Financial Studies* 3093, at pp. 3111–3113.

[39] Nga Pham, "Shareholder Activism in Japan" (2020), *Enterprising Investor CFA Institute*, online: https://blogs.cfainstitute.org/investor/2020/06/23/shareholder-activism-in-japan/#:~:text=Shareholder%20activism%20has%20been%20on,Monash%20Centre%20for%20Financial%20Studies.

[40] Josh Black, "Corporate Governance in Asia" (2023), *Insightia*, online: www.insightia.com/asia2023.

Tokyo Stock Exchange held net cash of more than 20 per cent of their equity at the end of 2022.[41]

South Korean companies with idle cash have also been subject to activist campaigns calling for optimisation of capital structure through dividend increases and treasury stock acquisitions. For example, Elliott Management proposed in 2019 that Hyundai Motor Company should pay out a cash dividend of almost seven times higher than the dividend payment planned by the company,[42] on the grounds that Hyundai's cash reserves exceeded the industry average and were poorly managed.[43]

It is also fairly common for activists to raise objections to particular corporate actions such as a proposed takeover, merger or spin-off. The reason why this might be a particular concern for target companies in East Asia lies in the prevalence of the concentrated shareholding nature of the companies, controlling families, cross-shareholding and related party transactions.[44] A related party transaction not concluded at arms' length may undermine aggregate shareholder value and, in the latter case, by definition, hurt minority shareholders. In East Asian markets, this is further entangled with the issue of the tyranny of the controlling family and the potential damage to minority interests in times of business succession within the family. For instance, in November 2020, the founding Koo family of LG Corp announced its plan to spin off five affiliates into a new holding company to be controlled by the chairman's uncle.[45] This was widely perceived to serve the controversial purpose of resolving a family succession issue between the company's chairman and his uncle at the expense of minority shareholders' interests. Whitebox Advisors, the hedge fund that challenged this proposed spin-off, therefore accused the Koo family of treating minority shareholders as "second-class citizens".[46] Similarly, the issue of family succession also serves as a

[41] Ibid. [42] Hyeon Deog Cho, et al., *supra* note_18.

[43] Eun-Young Jeong, "Elliott Management Loses Hyundai Proxy Fight" (22 Mar 2019), *Market Watch*, online: www.marketwatch.com/story/elliott-management-loses-hyundai-proxy-fight-2019-03-22.

[44] Lin Yu-Hsin, *supra* note 9; John Buchanan, Dominic Heesang Chai and Simon Deakin, *Hedge Fund Activism in Japan – The Limits of Shareholder Primacy* (Cambridge University Press, 2012) at pp. 153–211.

[45] Kim Jaewon, "South Korea's LG Faces Challenge from US Hedge Fund" (25 Mar 2021) *Nikkei Asia*, online: https://asia.nikkei.com/Business/Companies/South-Korea-s-LG-faces-challenge-from-US-hedge-fund.

[46] Ibid.

contributing factor for hedge fund interventions in Samsung and Hanjin KAL (i.e. the majority owner of Korean Air).[47]

After years of making subtle appearances in activist campaigns, environmental, social and corporate governance- (ESG-) related demands have become increasingly prominent in recent years. In Japan, the Financial Services Agency mandated in 2021 that all Tokyo Stock Exchange Prime market-listed companies must make disclosures in line with the Task Force for Climate-related Financial Disclosure (TCFD) requirements.[48] Consequently, the number of climate change proposals subject to a vote at Japan-listed companies quadrupled in 2022 as compared to the previous year, with both domestic and foreign activist funds calling on target companies to ramp up their sustainability commitments.[49]

In Korea, there has been a spike in ESG-related campaigns partly due to regulatory changes in 2020 that require less disclosure and government scrutiny if investors exercise shareholder rights to improve the governance structure.[50] Similarly, in China, the first ESG disclosure standards came into effect in June 2022, with the China Securities Regulatory Commission urging companies to voluntarily disclose their oversight of ESG-related risks and opportunities.[51] Therefore, the slew of ESG reporting and disclosure requirements in these three East Asian markets will amplify the momentum of ESG-related activist campaigns.

14.2.3 Activism Strategies

There are a few different types of strategies deployed by hedge fund activists studied in this sample. These strategies are compared with those adopted by activists in the US and the UK to determine if there is, in fact,

[47] Se Young Lee, "Elliott Push for Samsung Makeover Puts Founding Family Plans under Microscope" (5 Oct 2016) *Reuters,* online: www.reuters.com/article/us-samsung-elec-elliott management-idUSKCN1251FA; Joyce Lee and Hyunjoo Jin, "FOCUS – No More Nut Rage: Activist Fund Takes on Family-controlled Korean Air" (13 Mar 2020) *Reuters*, online: www .reuters.com/article/southkorea-succession-korean-air-idUSL4N2B2538.

[48] Josh Black, "Corporate Governance in Asia" (2023), *Insightia*, online: www.insightia.com/ asia2023.

[49] Ibid.

[50] Jason Booth, "Activism Meets Politics in Seoul" (April 2022), *Insightia*, online: www .insightia.com/aginsightiamonthly0422.

[51] Josh Black, "Corporate Governance in Asia" (2023), *Insightia*, online: www.insightia.com/ asia2023.

any deviation from the Western practice in East Asia. The reasons that contribute to the distinctiveness of hedge fund activism in East Asia and any similarities and/or differences in the strategies adopted will be discussed in this section.

Firstly, hedge funds in East Asia generally adopt the plain vanilla strategy, which involves increasing their shareholding in the target and thereafter attempting to persuade the management of their objectives through private discussions with the added weight of their increased ownership. Secondly, they may exercise their voting rights at the shareholders' meeting, for example by opposing the board's proposal.[52] Nevertheless, hedge funds generally only acquire a minority stake. Therefore, voting rights alone do not guarantee that their agenda will be endorsed, especially in the presence of a clear controlling shareholder and in the absence of a veto right.[53] Thirdly, activist shareholders may also submit proposals at the general meeting of shareholders. In fact, activist shareholders in South Korea frequently exercise this right, making it the most commonly used activism strategy in South Korea.[54]

To further expand their persuasive power, hedge funds in this sample often issue public letters criticising the inefficiencies in corporate governance to push forward their demands for reforms. This strategy has multiple benefits. First, if the demand is in the form of greater information disclosure or access to corporate documents, the public letter will compel a certain level of compliance by the management, which is wary of appearing surreptitious in the public eye. For instance, when Oasis Management campaigned for an independent investigation into related party transactions between Fujitec and its president Uchiyama's family entities, they issued a public statement to challenge the bias in the investigation led by the company itself.[55] This exerted public pressure

[52] Kim and Chang, "In Review: Recent Trends in Shareholder Activism in South Korea" (2022), *Lexology*, online, www.lexology.com/library/detail.aspx?g=fd4b4b9c-aebf-4cca-ad01-15eda40588b0.

[53] Lin Yu-Hsin, *supra* note 9; John Buchanan, Dominic Heesang Chai and Simon Deakin, *supra* note 44, at p. 153.

[54] Eun-Young Lee, Gun Woo Kim, Hyeon Deog Cho and Joon B Kim, "In Review: Recent Trends in Shareholder Activism in South Korea" (19 Aug 2022) *Lexology*, online: www.lexology.com/library/detail.aspx?g=fd4b4b9c-aebf-4cca-ad01-15eda40588b0; Jeong Seo and Joo-young Kim, "Q&A: Shareholder Activist Strategies in South Korea" (18 April 2023) *Lexology*, online: www.lexology.com/library/detail.aspx?g=2f6a336f-56ce-4dcd-978e-56f5ffd91d0c. See also Sang Yop Kang and Kyung-Hoon Chun, *supra* note 22.

[55] Businesswire, "Oasis Statement on Fujitec AGM" (27 June 2022) online: www.businesswire.com/news/home/20220627005738/en/Oasis-Statement-on-Fujitec-AGM.

on Fujitec to ensure greater independence and transparency of its investigation.

Second, public statements are an effective way to gather support at the general meeting from retail shareholders and, more importantly, institutional investors and proxy advisors. In the Japanese case of Fujitec, Oasis Management also called for the removal of president Uchiyama and it successfully gathered support from proxy advisors, including ISS and Glass Lewis.[56] Similarly, Franchise Partners amassed the support of ISS and Glass Lewis when it issued public criticism to oppose the diversification plan into biotechnology, pharmaceuticals and cosmetics by Kirin Holdings.[57] The support from retail investors and proxy advisors helped these hedge funds win proxy contests and pass favourable resolutions at shareholders' meetings. Lastly, regular publication of such public letters helps these hedge funds build a stronger reputation as activists, which in turn nudges management teams into taking their advice more seriously.[58] In practice, target companies in China that faced public activist demands were on the rise from 2013 to 2017.[59] Nevertheless, studies have found that hedge fund activists avoid making aggressive public statements in the presence of a strong controlling shareholder and that campaigns relying on an "open letter only" strategy are prone to failure.[60]

In a few exceptional instances, hedge funds have applied to the local courts for injunctions or commenced actions against the target companies. At the peak of its campaign against the proposed merger between Samsung C&T and Cheil Industries, Elliott Management applied for an

[56] Oasis Management, "ISS and Glass Lewis Recommend Shareholders Vote against the Reelection of Fujitec President Takakazu Uchiyama" (8 June 2022) *Businesswire*, online: www.businesswire.com/news/home/20220608005670/en/ISS-and-Glass-Lewis-Recommend-Shareholders-Vote-Against-the-Reelection-of-Fujitec-President-Takakazu-Uchiyama.

[57] Isa Martinez and Apoorva Gupta, "Kirin Pushes for Diversification as Shareholders Reject Activist's Proposal" (27 Mar 2020), *S&P Global Market Intelligence*, online: www.spglobal.com/marketintelligence/en/news-insights/latest-news-headlines/kirin-pushes-for-diversification-as-shareholders-reject-activist-s-proposal-57784016.

[58] C.N.V. Krishnan, Frank Partnoy and Randall S. Thomas, "The Second Wave of Hedge Fund Activism: The Importance of Reputation, Clout, and Expertise" (2016) 40 *Journal of Corporate Finance* 296.

[59] Jan Holthuis and Li Jiao, "Shareholder Activism in China: Overview" (1 May 2022) *Thomson Reuters Practical Law*, online: https://uk.practicallaw.thomsonreuters.com/w-013-1127?transitionType=Default&contextData=(sc.Default)&firstPage=true.

[60] Lin Yu-Hsin, *supra* note 9, at pp. 11–12, 25–27. See also Lin Lin and Dan Puchniak, *supra* note 17, Appendix 2.

injunction against Samsung C&T to prevent the company from issuing a call for the general meeting of shareholders at which the approval of the merger was anticipated.[61] After the injunction was dismissed and the merger approved at the shareholders' meeting, Elliott Management further filed for an investor-state dispute settlement against the South Korean government, claiming that the government had improperly intervened in the merger of Samsung C&T and Cheil Industries in breach of the US–Korea Free Trade Agreement and caused it to suffer losses of at least USD 770 million. In June 2023, the International Center for Settlement of Investment Disputes (ICSID) partially accepted Elliott's claims and ordered the Korean government to pay a fraction of Elliott Management's compensation requests.[62]

For comparison, Alon Brav and Wei Jiang reported seven categories of tactics used in US hedge fund activist campaigns.[63] In increasing order of aggressiveness, these are: (1) private communication, (2) request for board representation without a proxy contest, (3) shareholder proposal or public criticism, (4) threat of proxy contest or lawsuit, (5) proxy contest, (6) lawsuit and (7) takeover bid. Private communication is reported to be the most common strategy and litigation is one of the rarest, as the latter tends to be used as a last resort after other tactics prove unsuccessful. Settlement agreements have also become more prevalent between activist hedge funds and target companies: their incidence has increased substantially from three per cent for campaigns that started in 2000 to 21 per cent for those that started in 2013.[64] The likelihood of settlement increases with public visibility[65] and for campaigns involving: (1) hedge funds with an above-median stake in the target company, (2) hedge funds with a track record of reaching settlements in past campaigns and (3) underperforming target companies.[66]

Similarly, Marco Becht et al. found that the primary strategy of UK hedge funds is to hold private discussions with the management, and sometimes also with other shareholders and relevant parties.[67]

[61] Byoung Kwon Park, et al., *supra* note 27.

[62] Jin-Seong Kim and Yong-Hoon Kwon, "Tribunal partially accepts Elliott's claims over Samsung merger" (20 June 2023), *The Korea Economic Daily*, online: www.kedglobal.com/shareholder-activism/newsView/ked202306200026.

[63] Alon Brav, Wei Jiang and Rongchen Li, *supra* note 3, at pp. 25–28.

[64] Lucian A. Bebchuk, Alon Brav, Wei Jiang and Thomas Keusch, "Dancing with Activists" (Aug 2019) *National Bureau of Economic Research Working Paper 26171*, at p. 9.

[65] Ibid., at p. 17. [66] Ibid., at p. 16.

[67] Marco Becht, et al., *supra* note 38, at pp. 3108–3111.

In exceptional circumstances where private communication fails, they may escalate the matter and put forward their proposals at the annual shareholders' meeting or even call for an extraordinary shareholders' meeting. Only in a few cases did the activists take a step further and attempt public interventions by filing a lawsuit or making a takeover bid.

In this regard, the findings in this study are largely similar to those conducted in the US and the UK. The first port of call for activist hedge funds in East Asia is private engagement. When that fails, they attempt to issue public letters criticising the alleged poor practices and gather support from other shareholders. Only in very exceptional circumstances would they resort to severe measures such as lawsuits or takeover bids. This is largely in line with industrial practices elsewhere.

14.2.4 Frequency of Activism and Trend on Stewardship Codes

For comparison, a comprehensive sample collected by Alon Brav and Wei Jiang reported 4,657 instances of hedge fund activism in the US between 1994 and 2018.[68] Other studies reported that only around 12 per cent of hedge fund engagements worldwide took place in Asia, compared to 22 per cent in Europe and 66 per cent in North America.[69] According to Insightia, in 2022, 218 activist campaigns were launched in Asia, which pales in comparison to the 882 activist campaigns launched in the US over the same period.[70]

Nevertheless, hedge fund activism is on a growing trajectory in East Asia. In Japan, there is a second wave of activism as a result of the Japan Revitalization Strategy. The promulgation of the Stewardship Code and the Corporate Governance Code signalled a greater desire for institutional investors to play a more active role in corporate governance, catalysing a wave of shareholder proposals from activist hedge funds.[71] The Japanese Stewardship Code defines "stewardship responsibilities" as the responsibilities of institutional investors to enhance the medium- to long-term investment return for their clients and beneficiaries [. . .].[72]

[68] Alon Brav, Wei Jiang and Rongchen Li, *supra* note 4, at p. 23.

[69] Marco Becht, et al., *supra* note 2, at p. 2941.

[70] Josh Black, *supra* note 16.

[71] Hiroaki Miyachi and Fumiko Takeda, "Hedge Fund Activism in Japan under the Stewardship and Corporate Governance Codes" (2021) 27 *International Advances in Economic Research* 119, at p. 120.

[72] Gen Goto, "The Logic and Limits of Stewardship Codes: The Case of Japan" (October 2018) The University of Tokyo Business Law Working Paper Series, at p. 7.

The 2017 revision further emphasises this aim by urging institutional investors to participate more actively in engagement and to vote with a mid-/long-term view.[73] The number of activist hedge funds focused on Japan has experienced a consistent upward trend, and has more than doubled from a decade ago. As of March 2023, there is a record high of 233 activist hedge funds operating in the Japanese market.[74]

Similarly, by calling on institutional investors to take on steward responsibilities and regularly monitor investee companies in order to enhance their mid-to-long-term value, the Korean Stewardship Code triggered greater shareholder activism.[75] Following the adoption of the Korean Stewardship Code in December 2016, the rate of institutional investors exercising their voting rights has significantly increased.[76] According to a study, the opposing rate of asset management firms that participated in the Korean Code more than doubled from 2017 to 2018.[77] Further, it has been observed that since the introduction of the Korean Stewardship Code, some institutional investors have begun to send opinion letters to the investee companies requesting to reform their corporate governance.[78] A notable instance was when KB Asset Management sent opinion letters to Gwangju Shinsegae, a company that is part of South Korea's leading retail *chaebol*, suggesting that it change the company's listing status, revamp the corporation's ownership structure and enhance its dividend payment level.[79] This growing trend of stewardship has gained even more momentum in recent years, with funds such as Align Partners launching eight activism campaigns in South Korea in the first quarter of 2023.[80]

Presently, shareholder activism in China is quite uncommon and much less frequent than in Japan and South Korea. Unlike Japan and South Korea, China has no stewardship code. Institutional investors have been seen as a mechanism for improving corporate governance within

[73] Gen Goto, "The Japanese Stewardship Code" in Dionysia Katelouzou and Dan W. Puchniak eds., *Global Shareholder Stewardship* (Cambridge University Press, 2022), at pp. 231–232.

[74] Caroline Rolle, *infra* note 99.

[75] Sang Yop Kang and Kyung-Hoon Chun, "Korea's Stewardship Code and the Rise of Shareholder Activism" in Dionysia Katelouzou and Dan W. Puchniak eds., *Global Shareholder Stewardship* (Cambridge University Press, 2022), at p. 246.

[76] Ibid. [77] Ibid. [78] Ibid. [79] Ibid.

[80] Ortenca Aliaj, "Boom time for boardroom raiders as activism hits record highs" (10 April 2023) *Financial Times*, online: www.ft.com/content/f8f6415e-2916-438f-a221-702eef4bb1fe.

the China model.[81] The Chinese Code of Corporate Governance makes it clear that the primary agency problem in China is regulating controlling shareholders.[82] Therefore, the role of institutional investors in China is to monitor corporate controllers, and not "steward" listed companies.[83] Nevertheless, an increase in activism may be seen in the coming years due to changes in regulations. In 2020, the Chinese Corporate Governance Code was amended to encourage institutional investors to engage more actively in the corporate governance of their investee companies.[84] My recent studies also show that there has been a growth of domestic institutional investors, both in terms of type and size in mainland China, through the relaxation of policies and law reforms to improve corporate governance and stabilise the stock market. There has also been a growing number of activist campaigns in China, including those spearheaded by hedge funds.[85]

14.2.5 Impact of Hedge Fund Activism on Target Firms

The impact of hedge fund activism on target firms in East Asia is varied. On one hand, some Japanese scholars find that activism brings about numerous long-term benefits for the target companies, such as serving as an effective check against inefficient management. An empirical study on the long-term impact of hedge fund activism on Japanese listed companies between 2000 and 2012 shows that target companies had generally improved Tobin's Q after activist intervention succeeded.[86] Beyond target companies, institutional activism has spillover effects on non-target companies as well. A study on over 500 listed South Korean companies indicates that announcements of institutional activism efforts gave rise to increased investment across the market, especially in non-target companies which grant fewer rights to outside shareholders. This

[81] Dan W. Puchniak and Lin Lin, "Institutional Investors in China" in Dionysia Katelouzou and Dan W. Puchniak eds., *Global Shareholder Stewardship* (Cambridge University Press, 2022), at p. 415.

[82] Ibid. [83] Ibid.

[84] *See* Part II (Principle 11 of the Chinese Corporate Governance Code).

[85] Lin Lin and Dan W. Puchniak, *supra* note 17.

[86] Wataru Tanaka and Gen Goto, "日本におけるアクティビズムの長期的影響 (Nihon ni okeru akuthibizumu no chokiteki eikyo) [The Long-term Effect of Hedge Fund Activism in Japan]" (2020), *Japan Securities Dealers Association (ed.), JSDA*キャピタルマーケットフォーラム(第2期)論文集 (JSDA Kyapitaru Maketto Foramu (Dai-2ki) Ronbunshu) [Collected Papers of the 2nd JSDA Capital Market Forum] 115, at pp. 158–159.

is because fewer rights granted to outside shareholders presently leave greater room for activism in the future.[87]

On the other hand, other scholars find that the impact of hedge fund activism on the target firms has been minimal. In China, as discussed in Section 3, there are much fewer hedge fund campaigns than in Japan and South Korea, and hence limited rigorous empirical evidence on the impact of hedge fund activism.[88]

14.3 Distinctive Features of Hedge Fund Activism in East Asia

This section examines the factors that contribute to the peculiar features of hedge fund activism in East Asia, highlighting both the similarities amongst the three East Asian countries and the distinctive dynamics at play in each country. The key similarity between the three countries is their shareholding structure, while the distinctive factor is the constraints on foreign hedge funds.[89]

14.3.1 Shareholding Structure

Compared to the UK and the US, the ownership of listed companies in East Asia is more concentrated.[90] Looking at corporate control and ownership concentration across the world in 2020, the mean percentage of voting rights held by the three largest shareholders in mainland China (52.7 per cent), Japan (41.2 per cent) and South Korea (47.7 per cent) is generally larger than that in the US (34.2 per cent) and the UK (37.4 per cent).[91]

China has a high concentration of shareholding in its listed companies, with the average shareholding of the largest shareholder in A-share[92] listed

[87] Dong Wook Lee and Kyung Suh Park, "Does Institutional Activism Increase Shareholder Wealth? Evidence from Spillovers on Non-target Companies" (2009) 15:4 *Journal of Corporate Finance* 488, at p. 503.

[88] See Weng Xiaochuan, Ni Rubing and Lu Ying, "The Pros and Cons of Hedge Fund Activism in Corporate Governance and Prospects in China" Zhengquan Fayuan, Vol.3 (2010), pp. 160–172.

[89] Lin Lin and Dan Puchniak, *supra* note 17.

[90] A. De La Cruz, A. Medina and Y. Tang, *supra* note 10.

[91] OECD, "Corporate ownership and concentration: Background note for the OECD-Asia Roundtable on Corporate Governance" (October 2022), online: www.oecd.org/corporate/Background-note-Asia-Roundtable-Corporate-ownership-and-concentration.pdf.

[92] A-shares are the shares of mainland China-based companies that trade on the two Chinese stock exchanges, the Shanghai Stock Exchange (SSE) and the Shenzhen Stock

companies exceeding 30 per cent.[93] This is noticeably higher than the average shareholding of the largest shareholder in the US, which is only 10 per cent.[94] Furthermore, according to statistics, as of 2015, the average stake of the largest shareholder in listed companies in China's Shanghai and Shenzhen Main Board, Small and Medium-sized Board and ChiNext was 35.7 per cent, 33.5 per cent and 31.3 per cent, respectively.[95]

In my empirical study analysing 43 shareholder activist campaigns in Chinese companies conducted between 1994 and 2021, I found that 76.7 per cent of the targeted companies lacked a dominant controlling shareholder holding over 50 per cent of the shares.[96] This shows that the ability of hedge funds to engage in shareholder activism is significantly curtailed when they are a minority shareholder in a company with a dominant controlling shareholder.

The observation above holds for Japan, where cross-shareholdings between companies are common, and for South Korea, where family-run *chaebols* dominate.[97] In Japan, many companies hold shares in each other's companies as a defence against hostile takeovers. For instance, Dai Nippon Printing, the largest printing company in the world, is backed by large domestic companies that are generally sceptical of activism by foreign hedge funds.[98] This has traditionally made it challenging for activist funds to obtain support from a majority of shareholders.

Exchange (SZSE). Historically, China A-shares were only available for purchase by mainland citizens due to China's restrictions on foreign investment.

[93] Li Jianwei, "How Courts Have Upheld Shareholders' Abstract Dividend Distribution Claims: A Typology of 197 Commercial Decisions (法院如何支持股东的抽象股利分配请求 来自 197 份商事裁决书的类型化分析)" (2021) 33:2 *Peking University Law Journal* 484, at p. 490.

[94] Zeng Bin, "Kangmei Pharmaceutical Case: A Few Thoughts on the Advent of the 'Strong Liability' Era for A-shares (康美药业案—A股"强责任"时代来临下的几点思考)" (17 Nov 2021) *Law and Economics Notes (WeChat official account)*, online: https://mp.weixin.qq.com/s/U8sjdadJPuElkZMWh_Wulg.

[95] Wu Xinchun, "Study on the Battle for Control in Listed Companies (上市公司控制权之争研究)" (2017) *Shanghai Stock Exchange Research Report No. 13*, online: www.sse.com.cn/aboutus/research/report/c/4306275.pdf, at p. 6.

[96] Lin Lin and Dan Puchniak, *supra* note 17, at pp. 114–115.

[97] See Hyeok-Joon Rho and Kon-Sik Kim, "Invigorating Shareholder Derivative Actions in South Korea" in Dan W. Puchniak, Harald Baum and Michael Ewing-Chow eds., *The Derivative Action in Asia: A Comparative and Functional Approach* (Cambridge University Press, 2012) at p. 188; John Buchanan, Dominic Heesang Chai and Simon Deakin, *supra* note 44, at pp. 153–211.

[98] Caroline Rolle, "Japan activist hedge funds ramp up campaigns" (6 Apr 2023) *Preqin*, online: www.preqin.com/insights/research/blogs/japan-activist-hedge-funds-ramp-up-campaigns.

In South Korea, numerous large, listed companies are managed by a controlling family. The family ownership in *chaebol* firms on average amounts to over 25 per cent, allowing them to maintain control over member firms.[99] Controlling families often engage in tunnelling by way of related party transactions, issuance of undervalued stocks and unfair mergers to siphon off the value of group companies.[100] Institutional investors have generally been too weak or rationally inert to effectively monitor the controlling shareholders.[101] Companies targeted in Korea have primarily been those with limited ownership by founding families. For instance, activist campaigns against KT&G are feasible because KT&G was a former government monopoly and hence had no controlling shareholders, giving activists the opportunity to amass larger positions.[102]

Notwithstanding the fact that companies in China, Japan and South Korea generally have a concentrated shareholding structure, the three jurisdictions have different regulations of foreign funds, which have arguably contributed to different levels of shareholder activism, as the following section will show.

14.3.2 Regulation of Foreign Funds

Foreign institutional investors play a crucial role in increasing hedge fund engagement. Marco Becht et al. observe a strong positive correlation between foreign institutional ownership and the level of hedge fund engagement at the firm level in countries such as the UK.[103] They also observe that foreign hedge funds, and US hedge funds in particular, played active roles in a significant proportion of cases in North America, Europe and Asia. Out of the 53 activist events in Germany between 2000 and 2010, all of them were engaged by foreign hedge funds and more than half of them were US hedge funds.[104]

Wary of the potential detriments brought by hedge fund strategies, a number of Asian countries tend to impose stricter regulatory requirements. This is especially so since most governments tightened their regulations over hedge funds following the Asian Financial Crisis and

[99] See Hyeok-Joon Rho and Kon-Sik Kim, *supra* note 98, at p. 188.
[100] Sang Yop Kang and Kyung-Hoon Chun, *supra* note 75, at p. 6. [101] Ibid.
[102] Josh Black, "Corporate Governance in Asia" (2023), *Insightia*, online: www.insightia.com/asia2023.
[103] Marco Becht, et al., *supra* note 2, at pp. 2947–2948. [104] Ibid., at p. 7.

the Global Financial Crisis. Coupled with the lack of hedging techniques such as the strict limits on shorting, these regulations greatly restrict the role of hedge funds, making it difficult for hedge funds to play an active role in promoting corporate governance.

In China, there is a limited number of foreign hedge funds as a result of regulation. Foreign funds' entry into the Chinese market is tightly controlled. There are two main ways for foreign intuitional investors, including hedge funds, to invest in the Chinese capital market. The first is for foreign parent companies to convert their assets into RMB through foreign exchange and then invest directly in the Chinese capital market, of which there are three main ways: Qualified Foreign Institutional Investors ("QFII"), RMB Qualified Foreign Institutional Investors ("RQFII", raising RMB directly) and Shanghai-Hong Kong/Shenzhen-Hong Kong Stock Connect. The second way is to set up foreign private securities funds directly in China.[105]

Foreign institutional investors and hedge funds must be approved by the China Securities Regulatory Commission (CSRC) as a QFII or RQFII in order to trade Renminbi-dominated "A" shares of Chinese companies on the Shanghai and Shenzhen stock exchanges.[106] To satisfy the minimum requirements for approval, foreign institutional investors must have operated an asset management business for at least two years and managed securities assets of no less than USD 500 million in the latest fiscal year.[107]

Foreign investors qualified for QFII are also required to comply with the shareholding limit for domestic securities investments. That is, the shareholding of a single QFII or any other foreign investor in any listed or quoted company shall not exceed 10 per cent of the total number of shares of that company;[108] the combined shareholding of all QFIIs and other foreign investors in A shares or domestic quoted shares of any

[105] Tricor and Tsinghua PBCSF, "China Hedge Fund Report (中国外资私募证券基金行业研究白皮书)" (23 Mar 2022), online: tricorglobal.com/china-hedge-fund-report-2022.

[106] China Securities Regulatory Commission, *Measures for the Administration of Domestic Securities Investment by Qualified Foreign Institutional Investors* [合格境外机构投资者境内证券投资管理办法] Order No. 36, Art 2.

[107] China Securities Regulatory Commission, *Provisions on Issues Concerning the Implementation of the Measures for the Administration of Domestic Securities Investment by Qualified Foreign Institutional Investors* [关于实施《合格境外机构投资者境内证券投资管理办法》有关问题的规定], Item 1.

[108] Ibid., Art 7, Item 1.

company shall not exceed 30 per cent of the total number of shares of that company.[109]

Moreover, foreign investors, including hedge funds, have to comply with the Catalogue of Encouraged Industries for Foreign Investment before they make investments in Chinese markets ("the FI Encouraged Catalogue").[110] The FI Encouraged Catalogue sets out a list of specific industries where foreign direct investments are welcome. Foreign hedge funds can only make foreign investments if specific types of industries fall within the catalogue. Simultaneously, China has a set of Special Administrative Measures for Foreign Investment Access ("the Negative List"), which sets out a list of industries where foreign investments are restricted or prohibited. The 2021 Negative List currently prohibits foreign investment in areas such as editing, publishing and production of books and newspapers. The FI Encouraged Catalogue and Negative List combined limit the industries that hedge foreign funds are able to invest in, and accordingly, lower the levels of shareholder activism that these foreign hedge funds can undertake in China.

Unlike China, there is no such approval system for foreign hedge funds in Japan and South Korea. Foreign hedge funds that find it difficult to make their way into the Chinese markets to pursue opportunities for activist interventions play a major role in catalysing activism in South Korea and Japan. In South Korea, the regulations on foreign hedge funds have been relaxed since the 1990s, when it opened up its stock market to foreign investors, beginning with the Tiger Fund.[111] Foreign hedge funds, such as Sovereign Asset Management and Hermes Investment Management, were active in South Korea in the 2000s,[112] while Elliott Management has been involved in high-profile corporate battles in recent years.

Although foreign shareholders have been subject to various regulations, they play an important role in Japanese capital markets.[113]

[109] Ibid., Art 7, Item 2.

[110] On October 28, 2022, the National Development and Reform Commission (NDRC) and the Ministry of Commerce (MOFCOM) released the *Catalogue of Encouraged Industries for Foreign Investment (2022 Version)* (hereafter the "2022 FI Encouraged Catalogue), which will come into force on 1 January 2023. Encouraged Catalogue includes two sub-catalogues – one covers the entire country ("national catalogue") and one covers the central, western, and northeastern regions ("regional catalogue").

[111] Hyeon Deog Cho, et al., *supra* note 18. [112] Ibid.

[113] Hidefusa Iida, "Foreign Shareholders and Corporate Governance in Japan" (5 Mar 2019), at p. 3.

Shareholding by foreigners took up 30 per cent of the market capitalisation in 2016 in Japan, making them the largest among the investor categories in the Japan Exchange Group.[114] There are two types of regulation of foreign investment in Japan, namely, the Foreign Exchange and Foreign Trade Act (FEFTA) and the laws regulating a specific industry.[115] The FEFTA was amended in 2020 to require foreign investors to file a report with respect to acquisitions of just 1 per cent or more shares. In addition, the amendment has also included a new requirement for foreign investors holding 1 per cent or more of the shares of a listed company engaged in any of the designated business sectors to issue a prior notification when they consent to a proposal to either transfer or dispose of the investee company's business activities.[116] This new legislative change may hinder shareholder activism in Japan moving forward.

14.4 Conclusion

This chapter has collected data on hedge fund activist events across China, Japan and South Korea, and compared the data sample with those reported in the US and the UK to identify and understand the unique features of hedge fund activism in East Asia. The results show that hedge funds in East Asia pursue similar objectives and adopt similar strategies as their counterparts in the UK and the US. Nevertheless, there are distinct differences in the patterns of hedge fund engagements within the three studied markets. In particular, the frequency of activism in China is much lower than Japan and Korea over the years, due to the controlled entry of foreign hedge funds in China and its government-centred approach towards corporate governance.

It is also found that hedge fund activism is on a growing trajectory in these countries, especially in Japan and South Korea. The promulgation

[114] Ibid., referring to Japan Exchange Group, 2016 Shareownership Survey.

[115] Ibid., at p. 8.

[116] In the past, foreign investors were required to report in advance if they intended to acquire 10 per cent or more of the shares of a listed company engaged in any of the designated business sectors covered under the Foreign Exchange and Foreign Trade Act (FEFTA) and the relevant regulations (which includes more than 150 industries, such as weapons, aircraft and nuclear facilities, among others). See Yoshinori Aoyagi, Anderson Mori and Tomotsune, "Shareholder Activism In Japan: Overview" May 2022, https://Uk.Practicallaw.Thomsonreuters.Com/W-028-8547?Transitiontype=Default&Contextdata=(Sc.Default)&Firstpage=True.

of the Japanese Stewardship Code and the Korean Stewardship Code have catalysed a rapid increase in activism in Japan and South Korea as institutional investors are encouraged to play a more active role in corporate governance.

However, the future trajectory of hedge fund activism in China remains uncertain as the heavy state control on institutional investors makes it more challenging for hedge funds in China to gather momentum and effectively carry out their activist campaigns. In this aspect, the Japanese and Korean markets have been and will likely continue to be more receptive towards aggressive hedge fund activism as compared to China.

15

Board-Shareholder Engagement and Directors' Appointments

ANNA CHRISTIE

15.1 Introduction

In 2014, the activist hedge fund Starboard Value made history by succeeding in its campaign to replace the entire board of an S&P 500 company, Darden Restaurants.[1] Described as the 'ugliest shareholder revolt of 2014',[2] Starboard's strategy for Darden was contained in a public 294-page white paper, which explained in intricate detail how the hedge fund planned to execute a turnaround of the company, particularly with regard to deficiencies in strategy and operations at the underperforming Olive Garden restaurant chain.[3] Starboard's campaign began following the vocal frustrations of other Darden shareholders, who had contacted the hedge fund to persuade it to invest in and target the company.[4] Despite holding less than 10 percent of the shares in Darden, Starboard's campaign culminated in the activist hedge fund securing sufficient shareholder votes to replace Darden's entire incumbent board with twelve new board nominees. Ten of

I would like to thank the editors, Luca Enriques and Giovanni Strampelli, for their extremely helpful comments on this chapter, as well as John Armour and Paul A. Davies for valuable feedback on earlier versions of this work. I am also very grateful to the participants in the Assogestioni Corporate Governance Conference in Rome in October 2022, and to Massimo Menchini as the discussant of my chapter, for their enthusiastic engagement and feedback on this project.

1 Stephen Foley, 'Starboard Sweeps Away Entire Darden Board' *Financial Times* (New York, 10 October 2014) www.ft.com/content/1be89158-5086-11e4-9822-00144feab7de accessed 5 September 2022.

2 Lex team, 'Darden Restaurants: Back for Seconds' *Financial Times* (New York, 25 March 2015) www.ft.com/content/50d307f2-d260-11e4-9c25-00144feab7de accessed 5 September 2022.

3 Starboard Value, 'Transforming Darden Restaurants' (Shareholder Forum, 11 September 2014) www.shareholderforum.com/dri/Library/20140911_Starboard-presentation.pdf accessed 5 September 2022.

4 Owen Walker, *Barbarians in the Boardroom: Activist Investors and the Battle for Control of the World's Most Powerful Companies* (FT Publishing 2016) 49.

the nominees were seasoned executives who had expertise in the food and drinks industry or in corporate turnarounds, who were not affiliated with the hedge fund. The elected slate also included two representatives from Starboard – its founder, Jeff Smith, and its head of research. The change in leadership at Darden resulted in a very effective turnaround, with the company's share price rising by nearly 60 percent in the 18 months following the hedge fund's intervention.[5]

Boardroom coups initiated by shareholders, such as Starboard's campaign at Darden, are extremely rare events. Indeed, this campaign was the first and last time (to date) that an activist investor took complete control of an S&P 500 company's board in the United States. However, less extreme examples of minority board representation by activist hedge funds are much more common. Despite being most prevalent in the US, activist board representation campaigns also take place in many other jurisdictions around the world, including the UK and continental Europe. There is also evidence of a recent change in the focus of some activist hedge fund campaigns. While Starboard's campaign at Darden was motivated solely by profit, activist campaigns increasingly also focus on environmental, social, and governance ('ESG') considerations, and a number of bespoke ESG hedge funds have formed in order to conduct such campaigns.[6] A prominent example is Engine No. 1 and its proxy contest at ExxonMobil in 2021, which was the first boardroom battle to focus on the issue of climate change.[7] Here, the hedge fund succeeded in replacing three of Exxon's incumbent directors with their own independent director nominees who had expertise in energy transition and renewable energy. This campaign was supported by various influential institutional investors, including major US public pension funds. It also attracted the pivotal voting support of the Big Three asset managers (BlackRock, Vanguard, and State Street).[8]

[5] Michael J de la Merced, 'Starboard Value's Rise to Activist Prominence' *New York Times DealBook* (New York, 27 April 2016) www.nytimes.com/2016/04/28/business/dealbook/starboard-values-rise-to-activist-prominence.html accessed 5 September 2022.

[6] Some examples include Impactive Capital, Inclusive Capital Partners and Engine No. 1 in the US, and Clearway Capital in Europe.

[7] Anna Christie, 'The Agency Costs of Sustainable Capitalism' (2021) 55(2) UC Davis Law Review 875, 920–921, 924–927; Anna Christie, 'Battle for the Board: Climate Rebellion at Exxon Marks a New Era of Shareholder Activism' (*Oxford Business Law Blog*, 12 July 2021) www.law.ox.ac.uk/business-law-blog/blog/2021/07/battle-board-climate-rebellion-exxon-marks-new-era-shareholder accessed 5 September 2022.

[8] *See* Chapter 5 in this volume by Dorothy Lund and Adrianna Z Robertson.

These examples are notable activist campaigns that form part of a broader trend. Activist hedge funds have increasingly secured minority board seats at US companies by campaigning to improve corporate strategy and operations or advance ESG goals. Unlike the cases involving Darden and ExxonMobil, the board seats gained by activists are most commonly secured through negotiated settlements, rather than proxy contests culminating in full shareholder votes. The success of activist hedge funds in these bold campaigns may partly be due to activist directors being particularly well suited to overcome some limitations of the current dominant board model. The independent 'monitoring board' may be ill-suited to proactively proposing value-enhancing strategic and operational change or to advancing ESG goals to the extent that investors and other stakeholders now demand. Directors appointed by activist shareholders are much more likely to be proactive in this regard.

This chapter, first, examines current trends in the practice of shareholders appointing directors to corporate boards. Several questions are considered to explore this phenomenon. What types of shareholders appoint minority directors to corporate boards? What are their incentives and motivations for doing so? How easy is it for shareholders to appoint minority directors, and what obstacles might there be? The first part also discusses the distinction between affiliated directors and non-affiliated directors. Next, this chapter explores how current trends in shareholder-appointed directors can shed light on, or challenge, accepted wisdom regarding the appropriate role of the board. More specifically, it argues that activist directors appointed by hedge funds may expose some deficiencies of the independent monitoring board model and provide insights into potential alternative models. This part re-imagines the role of the board to reflect upon how the board can actively contribute to sustainable value creation and be better equipped to address the corporation's role in societal challenges such as climate change. The current board model was advanced and developed during a time when mitigating agency costs through monitoring was seen as the primary function of the board. However, today, creating sustainable value, together with reducing the harmful effects of corporate behaviour on the environment and communities tend to be viewed as much more urgent priorities for the modern board. The second part therefore discusses ideas for facilitating a move towards a more sustainable or enlightened board model. Would the current sporadic interventions of shareholders – where activist hedge funds appoint minority directors and institutional investors adjudicate on their appointment – be more effectively supplemented with, or replaced by, a broader range of shareholders systematically appointing board members? Various academic theories, policy proposals, and law reforms – including the Italian slate voting system – are considered to explore potential improvements to the current practice of director appointments.

15.2 Shareholder-Appointed Directors: Current Practice

In many jurisdictions around the world, the standard practice for director appointments is for candidates to be nominated by the incumbent board of directors, on the recommendation of the nominating committee. In countries such as the US and the UK, most often board elections will be uncontested. Although shareholders will technically vote on director appointments, there will generally be no alternative candidates proposed. However, in certain circumstances, shareholders may propose their own nominees as alternatives to, or in addition to, the directors nominated by the incumbent board.

15.2.1 Directors Appointed by Activist Hedge Funds

15.2.1.1 Activist Hedge Fund Board Representation Campaigns in the US

In the US, the major shareholder protagonists that appoint minority directors to boards are activist hedge funds, to the extent that in recent years board representation became the most common activist hedge fund campaign strategy.[9] Board representation campaigns are not limited to smaller companies. In fact, some of the biggest companies in the US have become targets for activist board representation. Since 2010, more than 100 S&P 500 companies have become the target of such campaigns.[10] These campaigns are almost always successful, especially when the campaign involves a major activist hedge fund.[11] More than 85 percent of board representation campaigns at S&P 500 companies have resulted in

[9] Anna L Christie, 'The New Hedge Fund Activism: Activist Directors and the Market for Corporate Quasi-Control' (2019) 19 Journal of Corporate Law Studies 1, 9.

[10] Hand-collected dataset analysing hedge fund activist board representation campaigns at S&P 500 companies since 2010. Data on file with author.

[11] *See generally* C N V Krishnan, Frank Partnoy, and Randall S Thomas, 'The Second Wave of Hedge Fund Activism: The Importance of Reputation, Clout, and Expertise' (2016) 40 Journal of Corporate Finance 296 (discussing how top activist hedge funds have succeeded in part due to establishing a reputation for 'clout and expertise').

one or more activist-nominated directors being appointed to the board.[12] As was the case in Starboard's intervention at Darden,[13] campaigns for board representation are commonly accompanied by the activist hedge funds submitting extremely detailed business plans and proposals for long-term strategic and operational improvements at target companies.

Although there have been some high-profile proxy battles between activist hedge funds and companies in the US, in recent years almost all activist board representation campaigns at large companies have been resolved via a settlement agreement rather than a shareholder vote. Indeed, since 2010, there have only been ten activist board representation campaigns at nine S&P 500 companies that culminated in a shareholder vote, out of over 130 campaigns.[14]

Activist director nominees can either be affiliated directors who work at the activist hedge fund or non-affiliated directors who are independently selected by the hedge fund, often due to their depth of business acumen in a particular industry or due to an impressive track record in executing corporate turnarounds. Studies on hedge fund activism in the early 2000s revealed that it was much more common for affiliated directors to be appointed. For example, in a dataset of activist campaigns from 2002 to 2006, it was noted that when activists gained seats on the board, 81 percent of those joining the board were activist hedge fund principals with only 19 percent of appointed directors being non-affiliated.[15] However, there have been shifts in recent years, at least at S&P 500 companies. From 2010 to 2019, only one third of appointed activist

[12] Hand-collected dataset analysing hedge fund activist board representation campaigns at S&P 500 companies since 2010. Data on file with author. This not only includes directors that are formally nominated by activist hedge funds but also directors that are co-opted on the board or elected via the company's board slate that are favoured by the activist hedge fund.

[13] *See* Introduction text to n 3.

[14] The companies were Forest Laboratories (Icahn Enterprises) in 2011 and 2012, International Game Technology (Ader Group) in 2013, Darden Restaurants (Starboard Value) in 2014, DuPont (Trian Fund Management) in 2015, General Motors (Greenlight Capital Management) in 2017, Procter & Gamble (Trian Fund Management) in 2017, Automatic Data Processing (Pershing Square) in 2017, ExxonMobil (Engine No. 1) in 2021, and McDonald's (Icahn Enterprises) in 2022. Data on file with author. *See generally also* Lucian A Bebchuk, Alon Brav, Wei Jiang and Thomas Keusch, 'Dancing with Activists' (2020) 137 Journal of Financial Economics 1 (quantifying the upward trend in activist settlements and noting that settlements are more likely when the activist has a credible threat to win board seats in a proxy fight).

[15] William W Bratton, 'Hedge Funds and Governance Tactics' (2007) 95 Georgetown Law Journal 1375, 1412.

board members at such companies were affiliated with the activist hedge fund.[16] The clear trend, therefore, is towards non-affiliated director nominees as opposed to hedge fund principals themselves securing seats on boards. The approach taken does, however, vary considerably by the specific activist hedge fund involved. Some activist hedge funds, such as Trian Fund Management, are atypical in terms of recent trends, as they exclusively appoint affiliated directors to the boards of target companies.[17]

The average activist hedge fund holding in activist board representation campaigns at S&P 500 companies is just over six percent.[18] As a result, support from institutional investors who hold a much larger proportion of the shares is inevitably necessary for campaigns to succeed. When activist hedge funds secure board representation they generally hold shares for longer periods compared to campaigns where no board representation is involved. Therefore, activist board representation as a campaign strategy may appeal to longer-term institutional investors. This longer-term commitment may mitigate some of the common concerns associated with the perceived short-term 'hit-and-run' motives of activist hedge funds.[19] Activist hedge funds are also quite unique in pursuing this form of firm-specific activism, which involves proposing strategic and operational improvements to the company's business model. Other investors are much less likely to have the capacity or the incentives to initiate firm-specific activism or to appoint directors who focus on strategy, operations, and turnaround.[20]

The prevalence and relative success of activist hedge fund board representation campaigns varies considerably by jurisdiction. While board representation campaigns are very common in the US, even at large S&P 500 companies, they are less common in the UK and continental Europe. By way of comparison, in the past decade in the UK less than ten FTSE 350 companies have been the target of activist hedge fund board representation campaigns.[21] Campaigns in continental Europe can be even more complex, especially if there is a two-tier board structure or

[16] Data on file with author.
[17] In each of the successful campaigns initiated by Trian Fund Management at S&P 500 companies from 2010 to 2019, the appointed directors were fund principals at Trian. These individuals included Nelson Peltz (Trian's CEO and Founding Partner), as well as other Partners of Trian. Data on file with author.
[18] Data on file with author. [19] Christie (n 9) 27. [20] Christie (n 7) 915.
[21] Targets include National Express Group (Elliott Management) in 2011, Vesuvius (Cevian Capital) in 2012, Rolls-Royce (ValueAct) in 2015, Alliance Trust (Elliott Management) in

if companies have controlling shareholders. Recent analysis by Activist Insight has shown that in 2021 there were 86 campaigns for activist board representation[22] in the US compared to 47 campaigns in the whole of Europe (including the UK).[23]

15.2.1.2 Incentives for Activist Hedge Funds to Pursue Board Representation

There is some evidence to suggest that in the 2000s, activist hedge funds may have focused on 'low-hanging fruit', for example by targeting cash rich companies to redistribute cash to shareholders.[24] These types of campaigns are now much less common, which could indicate that such opportunities are no longer readily available to activist hedge funds or that other longer-term shareholders may be reluctant to support such tactics. Instead, activist hedge funds have generally gravitated towards pursuing board representation campaigns, accompanied by proposals for strategic and operational change.[25]

In addition to increased support from institutional investors, there may be many other reasons why activist hedge funds choose to pursue board representation campaigns. Without board representation, it may be difficult for activist hedge funds to ensure that their value-creating strategies are being effectively implemented. It may be possible to execute some types of activist campaign strategies from outside of the boardroom – the primary example being financial or balance-sheet activism involving increased dividends or share buybacks. However, some other types of corporate change, especially change that focuses on strategy and operations, is much more difficult to achieve without a board seat and the associated access to inside information that such a board seat will afford the activist. Board representation can also result in activist directors

2015, Barclays (Sherborne Investors) in 2019, and FirstGroup (Coast Capital) in 2019. Data on file with author.

22 That either resulted in a settlement or went to a shareholder vote.

23 Activist Insight, 'The Activist Investing Annual Review 2022' (*Activist Insight*, 2022) www.activistinsight.com/aiar_22 accessed 5 September 2022. These numbers are considerably lower than in 2018 where there were 172 activist board representation campaigns in the US and 74 campaigns in Europe.

24 Bratton (n 15) 1394–1395.

25 *See* Christie (n 7) 913–915 (documenting the evolution of hedge fund activism from 'Activism 1.0' to 'Activism 2.0'). The other type of activism that is still very popular with activist hedge funds is M&A activism which is outside the scope of this chapter.

holding positions on key board committees which can give them a role in choosing the next CEO of the company.

15.2.1.3 Obstacles to Pursuing Activist Board Representation

There are various reasons why activist hedge funds remain the primary instigators of activist board representation campaigns. It is often more challenging for other types of shareholders to nominate directors to corporate boards due to the high costs involved. In the US, running a proxy contest for board representation can prove to be incredibly costly (both for the activist and the target company). Indeed, more than ten years ago the average cost of a proxy fight in the US was estimated to be in excess of $10 million.[26] Of course, it has already been noted that most activist hedge fund board representation campaigns – at least when they involve major hedge funds targeting S&P 500 companies – are settled rather than requiring a proxy contest or full shareholder vote. However, that tends to be the case only for established players who already have a reputation for running successful activist board representation campaigns. The high costs associated with activist board representation mean that there is a very small group of activist hedge funds that can successfully pursue such campaigns. Between 2010 and 2019, only 13 activist hedge funds initiated more than one board representation campaign at an S&P 500 company and seven activist hedge funds (Icahn Enterprises, Elliott Management, Trian Fund Management, ValueAct Capital Partners, Starboard Value, JANA Partners, and Pershing Square Capital Management) were responsible for more than 72 percent of all activist board representation campaigns at S&P 500 companies.[27] Therefore, this strategy is somewhat restricted to the largest and most formidable activist hedge funds. New entrants or other investors may have to conduct a full proxy contest in order to establish a reputation and to have future campaigns taken seriously by large corporations. An example of this was Engine No. 1's campaign at Exxon, which involved the newly established activist fund reportedly spending approximately $30 million on their inaugural proxy contest.[28] These costs are prohibitively

[26] Nickolay Gantchev, 'The Costs of Shareholder Activism: Evidence from a Sequential Decision Model' (2012) 107 Journal of Financial Economics 610, 611 (noting that '[a] campaign ending in a proxy fight has average costs of $10.71 million').

[27] Data on file with author.

[28] Jennifer Hiller and Svea Herbst-Bayliss, 'Exxon, activist spend over $65 mln in battle for oil giant's future' Reuters (Houston, 15 April 2021) www.reuters.com/business/

expensive for most investors, who may therefore have to pursue different strategies if they are seeking a refresh of the board. It is much more common for other investors (including non-governmental organisations, public pension funds, labour unions, religious organisations, or individual 'gadfly' investors) to pursue their activist campaigns through the shareholder proposal mechanism, rather than by nominating directors to corporate boards.[29]

Why do activist hedge funds still pursue board representation despite the high costs involved in these types of interventions that prove to be a major impediment for other types of investors? Activist hedge funds have stronger incentives to pursue costlier forms of activism because their concentrated holdings in a small number of portfolio companies and their compensation structure mean that they can effectively capture a significant proportion of value generating strategies.

15.2.2 Directors Appointed by Institutional Investors

15.2.2.1 The Role of Asset Managers in Director Elections

As discussed above, activist hedge funds are the protagonists of minority board representation campaigns in most jurisdictions around the world. Mainstream institutional investors may, however, play an important role in these activist campaigns. During proxy contests, it is crucial for activist hedge funds to appeal to the interests of mainstream institutional investors as they tend to be the key players who will adjudicate on the merits of the activist hedge fund's campaign. Particularly relevant in this context are the large asset managers that are most often the pivotal voters in proxy contests involving large companies.[30] In settlements between

energy/exxon-activist-spend-over-65-mln-battle-oil-giants-future-2021-04-15 accessed 5 September 2022.

[29] Christie (n 7) 934–943 (explaining the role of other investors in activism via shareholder proposals).

[30] This is especially the case with the rise of index investing. *See* Jill Fisch, Assaf Hamdani and Steven Davidoff Solomon, 'The New Titans of Wall Street: A Theoretical Framework for Passive Investors' (2019) 168 University of Pennsylvania Law Review 17, 19 (noting that '[p]assive investors . . . are the new power brokers of modern capital markets'; and Lucian Bebchuk and Scott Hirst, 'Index Funds and the Future of Corporate Governance: Theory, Evidence, and Policy' (2019) 119 Columbia Law Review 2020, 2033 (noting that 'the proportion of equities held by index funds has risen dramatically over the past two decades and can be expected to continue growing strongly').

companies and activist hedge funds, the views of large shareholders are also likely to be relevant to whether a settlement is concluded.

Further, if there is any discontent among the broader shareholder base, this could prove to be a catalyst to an activist hedge fund getting involved.[31] For example, Engine No. 1's historic campaign at ExxonMobil was initiated following public displays of institutional investor discontent. The world's largest asset manager, BlackRock, had voted against key directors at Exxon.[32] Major pension funds such as the New York State Common Retirement Fund and the Church Commissioners for England (who led the Climate Action 100+ engagement with ExxonMobil) had also urged investors to vote against the entire board.[33] Institutional investors have reportedly made 'requests for activism'[34] in various cases (similar to the requests made of Starboard with respect to a campaign at Darden Restaurants) and have provided support to activist hedge funds seeking board representation.

Even in the 1980s and 1990s, before institutional investors became as large and as powerful as the major global asset managers are now, it was observed that institutional investors on occasion sought to directly influence the selection of directors for their portfolio companies. Two examples were given by Gilson and Kraakman. The first is Carl Icahn's 1988 proxy contest at Texaco for five seats on the oil giant's board. In order to win institutional investor support for the incumbent management, Texaco agreed to select one board member from a list provided by the public pension fund CalPERS.[35] Similarly, in a 1990 proxy fight at Lockheed Corporation, the company agreed to allow institutional investors to influence the selection of three board members in order to gain

[31] *See* Christie (n 9) 12–13 (citing Walker (n 4) 49, 70, 147–148 (noting that several investors in Darden contacted Starboard Value to persuade the hedge fund to target the company; that investors in Yahoo had urged Carl Icahn to launch an activist campaign; and that some of the largest investors in Microsoft encouraged ValueAct Partners to seek a board seat).

[32] Christie (n 7) 926 (citing Ross Kerber, 'BlackRock Withheld Support from Two Key Exxon Directors: Filings' Reuters (Boston, 29 August 2016) www.reuters.com/article/us-exxondirectors-blackrock-idUSKCN11417F accessed 5 September 2022.

[33] As investor leads of the Climate Action 100+ engagement with ExxonMobil, these two pension funds wrote an open letter to ExxonMobil shareholders asking for support at the annual shareholders' meeting to vote for Engine No. 1's director nominees. *See* SEC 'Notice of Exempt Solicitation' (24 April 2020).

[34] Christie (n 9) 12.

[35] Ronald J Gilson and Reinier Kraakman, 'Reinventing the Outside Director: An Agenda for Institutional Investors' (1991) 43 Stanford Law Review 863, 872.

their support against the billionaire activist investor Harold Simmons.[36] These cases involved institutional investors supporting the company's position in exchange for input into director appointments. What is much more common nowadays is for institutional investors to work collaboratively with activist hedge funds, rather than companies, to elect new directors. One example already discussed is Starboard's campaign at Darden. There, it was reported that the mutual long-only fund Capital Research 'work[ed] hand and glove' with Starboard throughout the intervention.[37] Another high-profile example is Engine No. 1's proxy contest at ExxonMobil. There, the fledgling hedge fund's campaign was significantly bolstered by the crucial support it received from one of America's largest pension funds – the California State Teachers Retirement System (CalSTRS). Engine No.1 worked together with CalSTRS on the campaign and the pension fund was vocal in its backing of the dissident slate of board members from the day the campaign was officially launched.[38] The early support of such a prominent pension fund also helped to generate much needed public support from a range of other institutional investors.

15.2.2.2 Asset Managers Nominating Directors

By contrast, examples of asset managers themselves nominating directors to company boards appear to be extremely rare. There are no instances of the largest American asset managers – BlackRock, Vanguard, State Street, and Fidelity – nominating directors to corporate boards. There are various reasons why asset managers choose not to nominate directors to boards. The rational reticence of institutional investors has been well documented, with Gilson and Gordon noting that institutions would only 'respond to proposals but are unlikely to themselves create them.'[39] It has also been argued by Lund that asset managers typically only engage

[36] Ibid, 872–873.

[37] William D Cohan, 'Starboard Value's Jeff Smith: The Investor CEOs Fear Most' Fortune (New York, 3 Dec 2014) https://fortune.com/2014/12/03/starboard-capitals-jeff-smith-activist-investor-darden-restaurants accessed 5 September 2022.

[38] Svea Herbst-Bayliss and Gary McWilliams, 'Exxon faces proxy fight launched by new activist firm Engine No. 1' Reuters (Boston, 11 December 2020) www.reuters.com/business/energy/exxon-faces-proxy-fight-launched-by-new-activist-firm-engine-no-1-2020-12-11/ accessed 5 September 2022.

[39] Ronald J Gilson and Jeffrey N Gordon, 'The Agency Costs of Agency Capitalism: Activist Investors and the Revaluation of Governance Rights' (2013) 113 Columbia Law Review 863, 867, 899.

in low-cost governance interventions (rather than strategy and operations) and may lack a financial incentive to ensure that their portfolio companies are well-run.[40] Additionally, although asset managers are consistently bolstering their stewardship teams, commentators have argued that they still 'underinvest in stewardship',[41] given the vast number of portfolio companies held by large asset managers. In this vein, we might expect that institutional investors may be willing to support (or oppose) activist director elections but would be unlikely to nominate directors themselves. There are additional legal and other reasons why asset managers may be especially reluctant to become involved in the nomination process. Hamdani and Hannes have argued that doing so would 'critically change the role of institutional investors as relatively passive investors with a limited say over company affairs.'[42] The information sharing that generally occurs in the US once a shareholder-appointed director is on the board would also create insider trading concerns for institutional investors.[43]

Although there do not seem to be any examples of American asset managers nominating directors to corporate boards, there are some limited instances of European asset managers becoming more involved in the nomination of directors, especially to advance ESG goals. The legal rules in some jurisdictions make this an easier task to accomplish than in others. A well-publicised example of a European asset manager influencing the nomination of a director to improve the board's climate expertise is the Dutch asset manager Robeco's involvement in the nomination of Samuel Leupold to the board of the Italian energy company Enel in 2020. Here, Robeco had highlighted the board's lack of expertise in climate and energy transition, and on that basis had joined a group of asset managers tasked with submitting a slate of directors under the coordination of the Investment Manager's Committee, with the support of Assogestioni, the representative association of Italian investment managers.[44] The Head of Active Ownership at Robeco, Carola van Lamoen,

[40] Dorothy S Lund, 'The Case Against Passive Shareholder Voting' (2018) 43 Journal of Corporation Law 493, 495.

[41] Bebchuk and Hirst (n 30) 2029, 2050–2059, 2076–2080.

[42] Assaf Hamdani and Sharon Hannes, 'The Future of Shareholder Activism' (2019) 99 Boston University Law Review 971, 973.

[43] Ibid.

[44] Sophie Robinson-Tillett, 'Board Senseless? The Investor Fight Against Climate Incompetence' (*Responsible Investor*, 11 June 2020) www.responsible-investor.com/articles/board-senseless-the-investor-fight-against-climate-incompetence accessed 5 September 2022 (noting that

joined the nomination committee, noting that 'Italy actually has a great system because it allows minority shareholders like us to nominate members of the board'.[45] However, she also stressed that '[t]hese moves may be difficult to achieve at a large scale because not all jurisdictions make it possible.'[46] These statements by the asset manager suggest that introducing legal rules to facilitate the election of directors by minority shareholders in other jurisdictions could result in more board elections by asset managers. The result at Enel was made possible by what Belcredi and Enriques describe as a 'peculiar feature of current Italian corporate governance regulation',[47] where minority shareholders can submit a slate (or list) of candidates to Italian companies and have the right to have at least one candidate appointed to the board, even where another slate gains a higher number of votes.[48] The Italian slate voting system is considered in more depth in Section 14.2.3 of this chapter, to analyse how practical examples of different systems of director elections can inform a rethink of the board.

Outside of the Italian system, which has a specific process devoted to enabling minority shareholders to nominate directors, there is an earlier example from 2020 of Robeco (collectively with a group of other investors) nominating an independent director to the board of CCR, a Brazilian company which is one of the biggest infrastructure companies in Latin America.[49] Following a proposal by the group of investors (featuring Robeco, Franklin Templeton Investments, Leblon Equities, British Columbia Investment Management Corporation, Comgest, Safari, and João Lanza) to add an additional independent director to

'Samuel Leupold was CEO of Wind Power at DONG Energy, which stood for Danish Oil and Natural Gas, during its transformation into one of the world's largest pureplay offshore wind developers, now named [Ø]rsted').

45 'Investors' engagement and Enel: a success story' (*Robeco*, 4 April 2022) www.robeco.com/uk/insights/2022/04/investors-engagement-and-enel-a-success-story.html accessed 5 September 2022.

46 Ibid.

47 Massimo Belcredi and Luca Enriques, 'Institutional Investor Activism in a Context of Concentrated Ownership and High Private Benefits of Control: The Case of Italy' in Jennifer G Hill and Randall S Thomas (eds), *Research Handbook on Shareholder Power and Activism* (Edward Elgar 2015) 386, 393–395.

48 Giovanni Strampelli, 'Institutional Investor Stewardship in Italian Corporate Governance' in Dionysia Katelouzou and Dan W Puchniak (eds), *Global Shareholder Stewardship: Complexities, Challenges and Possibilities* (Cambridge University Press 2022) 130.

49 'Open Letter to CCR S.A. Shareholders' (*CCR*, 20 March 2020) https://ri.ccr.com.br/en/noticia/open-letter-to-the-shareholders-of-ccr-s-a accessed 5 September 2022.

the board, CCR's nomination committee recommended the proposal and agreed to nominate a new director with expertise in sustainability. The candidate, Eliane Lustosa, was then added to the company's nomination slate.

Although there are very limited examples of asset managers nominating directors, it seems clear that when asset managers are involved in director elections, the aftermath of this involvement is quite different to what materialises after many of the director appointments by activist hedge funds. For example, in the Enel case, the CEO's position was never under threat at all. Again, Carola van Lamoen of Robeco noted that 'Enel had just the right man at the helm . . . if you already have top management with that conviction [to renewable energy], then that really helps our engagement, because you have a company that is open to discuss these topics'.[50] Strampelli has noted that this corporate governance mechanism in Italy generally does not have the aim of forcing major changes in corporate strategy or of replacing management.[51] On the other hand, with activist board representation campaigns by hedge funds there is a strong possibility that the CEO is quickly replaced. Data from activist board representation campaigns at S&P 500 companies from 2010 to 2019 show that in 46 percent of companies where hedge fund activists were successful in securing board seats, the CEO stood down either shortly before the board seats were granted to the activist, or within one year of the board seats being granted.[52] Therefore, board representation by activist hedge funds tends to lead to much more dramatic change compared with the nomination of independent directors by other institutional investors such as asset managers.

The increasing attention of asset managers to ESG matters potentially does hold some promise for a change of approach in the future, as institutional investors are collaborating with each other both directly and through investor organisations to improve climate expertise on boards and to ensure that boards focus on energy transition and deliver sustainable value. For example, coalitions such as Climate Action 100+ explicitly foster asset manager coordination.[53]

[50] Ibid.

[51] Strampelli (n 48) 142. There are, however, prominent exceptions, *see* references in n 83 below.

[52] Data on file with author.

[53] Madison Condon, 'Externalities and the Common Owner' (2020) 95 Washington Law Review 1, 64; *See* Chapter 9 by Peter Mülbert and Alexander Sajnovits and Chapter 12 by Tim Bowley, Jennifer Hill, and Steve Kourabas in this volume.

15.3 Re-imagining the Board

Section 15.1 considered current examples of shareholders appointing directors to corporate boards. Activist hedge funds were identified as the most likely protagonists in such an endeavour. At present, activist hedge funds are the only type of investor that consistently has both the incentives and resources to effectively run board election campaigns. By contrast, there are various obstacles which may prevent asset managers or other institutional investors from putting forward their own director nominees. Section 15.3 explores what these current trends in director appointments may reveal about the limitations of the current independent monitoring board model, and how the board may need to evolve to meet investor expectations. In particular, the role that activist-appointed directors may play in analysing and changing corporate strategy and operations provides some insight into an alternative model where boards proactively contribute to sustainable value creation. This part also discusses academic theories that have previously been advanced to increase institutional investor participation in the director appointment process, and a practical example of an alternative legal model that is followed in Italy.

15.3.1 The Current Board Model: The Monitoring Board

It has been widely accepted that the role of boards of directors is to reduce agency costs associated with the separation of ownership and control.[54] Indeed, the principal corporate governance response to the shareholder-manager agency problem is the independent director,[55] whereby boards dominated by independent directors monitor managers to avoid 'stealing'[56] or the mixed motives and cognitive biases of the CEO

[54] Jeffrey N Gordon, 'The Rise of Independent Directors in the United States, 1950–2005: Of Shareholder Value and Stock Market Prices' (2007) 59 Stanford Law Review 1465, 1468.

[55] Lisa M Fairfax, 'The Uneasy Case for the Inside Director' (2010) 96 Iowa Law Review 127, 137.

[56] On 'self-dealing' or 'stealing', Jensen and Meckling note that the agency conflict '[derives] from the manager's tendency to appropriate perquisites out of the firm's resources for his own consumption'. *See* Michael C Jensen and William H Meckling, 'Theory of the Firm: Managerial Behavior, Agency Costs and Ownership Structure' (1976) 3 Journal of Financial Economics 305, 313.

and other executives[57] which can be detrimental to the interests of shareholders.[58] The rationale for the monitoring board and independent directors is simple – these directors do not have connections to management and so can ensure that the company is run in the best interests of shareholders.

There are, however, considerable shortcomings associated with the monitoring board, both in terms of composition and function. Back in the early 1990s, Gilson and Kraakman argued that 'the traditional corporate solution of introducing outside directors to bridge the separation between ownership and control has dramatic limitations'.[59] That statement may be even more true today, given the increased expectations and demands on boards of directors particularly with regard to environmental, social, and governance issues.

The 'monitoring board' tends to be comprised largely of part-time independent directors.[60] In the US, the percentage of public company directors who are independent has grown to 86 percent in 2021.[61] The UK similarly has a high percentage of independent directors, at 72 percent, with continental European jurisdictions having lower percentages around the 50 percent mark.[62] Although independent directors may be better able to objectively monitor management, one major drawback of their role is the part-time nature of their appointments which severely limits the time and attention they can invest in their role.

[57] The other traditional agency problem identified by Jensen and Meckling was 'shirking', however that is not a problem in practice. *See* Jensen and Meckling (n 56) 313.

[58] Indeed, much of corporate law is best understood as a mechanism for constraining agency costs. *See* John Armour, Henry Hansmann, Reinier Kraakman, and Mariana Pargendler, 'What is Corporate Law?' in Reinier Kraakman and others (eds), *The Anatomy of Corporate Law* (3rd ed, Oxford University Press 2017) 29 (highlighting the purpose of corporate law as an attempt to control conflicts of interest or 'agency problems' among corporate constituencies). *See also* Stephen M Bainbridge, 'Responses: Director Primacy and Shareholder Disempowerment' (2006) 119 Harvard Law Review 1735, 1746.

[59] Gilson and Kraakman (n 35) 876.

[60] *See* John Armour, Brandon Garrett, Jeffrey Gordon, and Geeyoung Min, 'Board Compliance' (2020) 104 Minnesota Law Review 1191, 1221 (noting that 'to be classed as "independent," a director must not have an employment relationship with their company, meaning that they are of necessity a part-timer').

[61] SpencerStuart, '2021 UK Spencer Stuart Board Index' (SpencerStuart, 2021) www.spencerstuart.com/research-and-insight/boards-around-the-world?category=all-board-composition&topic=independent-directors accessed 5 September 2022.

[62] Ibid. France has 57 percent independent directors, while Italy has 55 percent.

By virtue of their outsider status, independent directors are unlikely to have direct access to information about the company, so they are heavily dependent on corporate managers for information. Kastiel and Nili have described the problem facing independent directors as 'informational capture', noting that '[a]s part-time employees who often sit on multiple boards, outside directors lack the time, adequate resources, and the industry-specific knowledge to properly obtain, digest, and analyse the extensive and complex information that modern boards are tasked with evaluating'.[63] An information asymmetry problem arises where corporate managers are much better informed than the independent board that is tasked with monitoring their behaviour. A problem related to the necessary reliance of independent directors on management for information is their lack of resources to critically analyse the information they actually receive. Kastiel and Nili argue that 'outside directors suffer from information overload and they often lack the appropriate resources to properly process and analyse the voluminous information they are often presented within a timely manner.'[64] As a result of these challenges, independent directors have been described by Gilson and Gordon as 'thinly informed', 'under-resourced', and 'boundedly motivated'.[65]

Overall, what can ultimately materialise is a situation where outside analysts may be better informed about the company than the independent monitoring board. The above factors can result in a board that may be fundamentally reactive rather than proactive.[66] The limitations of the monitoring board are exposed when activist hedge funds seek to nominate directors to corporate boards. As activist hedge funds invest significant time and resources in analysing the strategy and operations of companies they target, independent directors on the incumbent board may be less well informed about the company than the activist hedge fund or the activist director(s).

[63] Kobi Kastiel and Yaron Nili, '"Captured Boards": The Rise of "Super Directors" and the Case for a Board Suite' (2017) Wisconsin Law Review 19, 23.

[64] Ibid 28.

[65] Ronald J Gilson and Jeffrey N Gordon, 'Board 3.0: An Introduction' (2019) 74 The Business Lawyer, 351, 353.

[66] *See* Jill E Fisch, 'Corporate Governance: Taking Boards Seriously' (1997) 19 Cardozo Law Review 265, 282 (noting that the monitoring board is properly characterised as a safety valve for crisis situations); Gilson and Gordon (n 65) 365; Gordon (n 54) 1541–1543 (noting that independent directors react to stock prices).

15.3.2 Beyond Monitoring: The Enlightened, Sustainable Board

While monitoring is still a useful board function, investors and other stakeholders now often expect more from boards and companies. Hart and Zingales highlight that '[c]orporations are larger, more complex, and more powerful than they were in the 1970s and early 1980s ... the importance of externalities has also greatly increased ... [t]he preferences of investors have changed too'.[67] Stevelman and Haan argue that we are already witnessing a shift away from the monitoring board.[68] In their view, a serious deficiency of the monitoring board is that it 'failed to empower boards to assume a robust role in vetting and advising on strategy'.[69] That is a gap that shareholder appointed directors have often been able to fill, by scrutinising in detail the strategy and operations of a target company in order to implement changes or execute a successful turnaround. If activist board nominees continue to challenge the strategic vision or operational competence of incumbent managers, then the current board model may be forced to change. As the success of activist board representation campaigns – and more recently ESG activist campaigns – illustrates, investors increasingly expect boards to engage in strategic value creation and to address negative externalities by advancing ESG goals. Similarly, there is greater pressure from other stakeholders for boards to play a key role with respect to ESG issues.

Is a change to the focus of the board feasible? While a vision of a more proactive board may be appealing in theory, actually creating such an engaged and involved board in practice presents more of a challenge. It has been emphasised by Gilson and Gordon that 'there are plainly observable reasons to think the present public company board model is hardly the "end of history" for corporate governance' and that 'governance has to evolve to match the radical changes in the markets in which public companies operate'.[70] In practice, activist-appointed directors can mitigate many of the shortcomings of the monitoring board, and so can highlight the potential for new board models. First, counteracting the problem of part-time directors, activist directors tend to invest much more time and energy in their role as directors (especially when the director is affiliated with the activist hedge fund). Second, activist

[67] *See* Chapter 1 by Oliver Hart and Luigi Zingales in this volume.

[68] Faith Stevelman and Sarah C Haan, 'Boards in Information Governance' (2020) 23 University of Pennsylvania Journal of Business Law 179, 181.

[69] Ibid., 185.

[70] Gilson and Gordon (n 65) 354.

directors can both generate and seek additional information that helps to reduce the informational asymmetries that afflict independent directors on the monitoring board. Third, activist directors go beyond monitoring and become involved in strategic analysis and a management function of the board. Therefore, they encapsulate many of the advantages of insider directors on the old-style advisory board, but they also have the benefit of separation from the company, its executives, and importantly the CEO, as they are appointed by an investor rather than being hand-picked by the CEO for their loyalty. The combination of these factors could considerably improve the effectiveness of the corporate boards on which activist directors sit.[71]

If the activist board can result in such beneficial changes, should we be content with the current system whereby activist hedge funds sporadically initiate campaigns and institutional investors adjudicate upon them? Or might we want a broader range of investors to actively nominate directors to boards? One downside of relying on activist hedge funds to initiate campaigns is that such activism cannot provide a systematic solution for all corporate boards. Hedge fund activists will only ever intervene in a small proportion of companies. Even in the US, where hedge fund activist board representation is most significant and most prevalent, 101 S&P 500 companies were targeted between 2010 and 2019, out of 700 companies that were part of the S&P 500 at any point since 2010.[72] This represents just over 14 percent of S&P 500 companies. Relying solely on activist hedge funds to initiate director election campaigns also means institutional investors adopt a purely reactive role, rather than having any incentives to be more proactive.

15.3.3 *Re-imagining the Board: Theories and Practice*

Throughout corporate law scholarship, there have been continuing debates and proposals for institutional investors to become more involved in director election processes. Some of these theories are considered here, to identify useful aspects of these proposals that would help to move towards a more sustainable, value-enhancing board model. Essentially, if we accept that directors appointed by activist hedge funds can add value to boards and change the nature of the board in a beneficial

[71] Conversely, an activist-appointed director may feel more loyalty to the activist fund manager than to the company.

[72] Data on file with author.

way, it is helpful to think about proposals that could involve a scaling up of the value that activist directors contribute, by involving a wider array of investors in the process.

15.3.3.1 Facilitating Director Appointments by Shareholders

In the early 1990s, Gilson and Kraakman proposed an agenda for institutional investors, envisaging that they could collectively nominate professional outside directors who would actively monitor public corporations in the shareholders' interest.[73] They advocated that 'an ideal mechanism for delegating monitoring would seem to be the expert director, chosen cooperatively by institutional investors', while also acknowledging that 'the system of outside directors itself is in need of reform'.[74] At the time, the proposal was still squarely premised on the idea of the monitoring board, rather than envisaging a more substantive and strategic set of responsibilities for directors. Essentially, it was thought that introducing a new class of high-quality professional directors who were outsiders and independent of management would improve the incentives for directors to monitor effectively and their ability to do so. To some extent, this model has become the norm particularly in the US, where many independent directors are professional directors whose main occupation is to sit on corporate boards. However, the proposal for institutional investors to collectively nominate these directors has not materialised.

More recently, Coffee proposed that investors such as the Big Three asset managers 'could form (with other similarly minded institutions) a steering committee and assemble a team of outside directors (who were not their employees) that they could seek to place on corporate boards'.[75] Coffee's suggestion was prompted by the idea that asset managers may fear being disenfranchised by private settlements between activist hedge funds and target companies. The proposal also provided a basis for distributing the costs among the multiple institutions participating in such a committee. Here, it might be argued that institutional investors could adopt this approach even in the absence of disenfranchisement.

However, if the aim is to fully mirror the value added by directors who are nominated by activist hedge funds, there are still missing puzzle pieces.

[73] Gilson and Kraakman (n 35) 883–884. [74] Ibid., 880.

[75] John C Coffee Jr, 'The Agency Costs of Activism: Information Leakage, Thwarted Majorities, and the Public Morality' (2017) European Corporate Governance Institute Law Working Paper 373/2017, 26 https://ssrn.com/abstract_id=3058319 accessed 5 September 2022.

Even if there were a ready market for professional directors who institutional investors could collectively nominate to corporate boards, the problems associated with those directors potentially being underinformed and underresourced may still persist. After all, the activist director appointed by a hedge fund (certainly in cases where the director is affiliated with the hedge fund and perhaps also in cases where the appointee is non-affiliated) often has regular access to a 'back-office' in the form of a team of analysts who work for the hedge fund itself. This can provide much needed support, information, and resources to the director to overcome problems of information asymmetry and lack of resources.

It is clear that there is scholarly appetite for shareholders – especially large institutional investors – to collectively nominate directors, or at least become more involved in director recruitment and nomination. Therefore, some combination of proposals could provide a mechanism to scale up the value that activist directors can generate. However, the practicalities associated with overcoming rational reticence on the part of institutional investors may still prove to be particularly challenging. If these practicalities are not proactively addressed, it would seem likely that the role of minority shareholders nominating directors will continue to primarily be filled by activist hedge funds, at least in the near future. Given that there would be considerable collective benefit from institutional investors taking a more proactive role in the nomination of directors to corporate boards, it is helpful to also consider a practical example where legal reform was implemented to overcome some of these practical impediments and enable institutional investors to be more directly involved in the nomination of directors to corporate boards – the Italian slate voting system.

15.3.3.2 The Italian Slate Voting System

When considering proposals for reform, it is helpful to consider practical examples of different models for director elections, alongside the various academic theories outlined above. Italy provides an interesting example of the adoption of voting rules for director elections which reserve some board seats for minority shareholders.

The slate voting system – which reserves at least one seat on the board for directors nominated by minority shareholders – was introduced in Italy in 1994 for privatised public companies and is now set out in the Consolidated Law on Financial Markets[76] after having been extended to

[76] Law 474/1994. Belcredi and Enriques (n 47) 386; and Massimo Belcredi, Stefano Bozzi, and Carmine Di Noia, 'Board Elections and Shareholder Activism: The Italian

all public companies in 2005.[77] Shareholders holding a minimal threshold of share capital (currently varying between 0.5 percent and 4.5 percent, depending on the company's market capitalisation)[78] are entitled to submit slates.[79] In Italy, individual institutional investors tend not to choose candidates themselves. Instead, a Corporate Governance Committee was set up by Assogestioni (the non-profit Investment Management Association representing most Italian and foreign asset managers in Italy) to select candidates from lists prepared by executive search consultants.[80] Assogestioni plays a coordinating role, facilitating collective action by institutional investors, who then formally and collectively submit the slate. In the Enel example highlighted earlier, Robeco noted that 'our collaboration with Assogestioni made the nomination possible, as they facilitated the entire process, helped reach the number of shares needed to file the nominee list thanks to its investor network, and provided legal advice'.[81]

This process tends to operate very differently from activist situations in the US, when activist hedge funds identify and propose their own alternative director candidates and may use much more confrontational campaign tactics. On occasion there has been a 'showdown between two rival lists'[82] in Italy, which more closely resembles a proxy fight in the US. However, that is the exception rather than the norm. In an interesting reversal of roles, activist hedge funds have not been particularly active in director elections in Italy,[83] preferring to support other investors rather

Experiment' in Massimo Belcredi and Guido Ferrarini, *Boards and Shareholders in European Listed Companies* (Cambridge University Press 2013) 367, 380.

[77] Law 262/2005 (the 'Protection of Savings' Law). *See* Belcredi, Bozzi, and Di Noia (n 76) 367, 381.

[78] Strampelli (n 48) 139.

[79] Belcredi and Enriques (n 47) 386; Belcredi, Bozzi, and Di Noia (n 76) 380.

[80] Belcredi and Enriques (n 47) 393; Belcredi, Bozzi, and Di Noia (n 76) 390.

[81] Robeco (n 45).

[82] *See* Giovanni Strampelli, 'Italian slate voting and semi-dispersed corporate ownership: Lessons from the Generali case' (*The ECGI Blog*, 21 June 2022) https://ecgi.global/blog/italian-slate-voting-and-semi-dispersed-corporate-ownership-lessons-generali-case accessed 5 September 2022, describing a recent battle for elections to the board of Generali, one of Europe's leading insurers.

[83] There are exceptions. *See*, for example, Strampelli (n 82) describing the campaign at Telecom Italia in 2018, where Elliott Management (a nine percent shareholder) secured the majority of board seats by submitting a long slate and winning with 33.47 percent of votes cast, compared to 31.68 percent for the list submitted by Vivendi, the company's largest shareholder.

than submitting their own slates.[84] Data analysing the Italian process has shown that minority shareholders used the opportunity to submit a slate of nominees in around 40 percent of sample firms. In the remaining 60 percent of cases, they chose to remain passive.[85]

Corporate ownership and control in Italy is considerably different to the US and the UK. Family-controlled firms are of considerable importance and firm ownership tends to remain concentrated, with many companies having a controlling shareholder.[86] Despite this, it is still helpful to analyse how the Italian system could potentially inform reforms to director nomination processes in other jurisdictions. Moreover, most asset managers operate globally so if European asset managers such as Robeco have praised the Italian slate voting system and have been eager (at least on occasion) to make use of the particular legal rules to nominate experts in sustainability to the boards of Italian companies, then there may be reason to expect that similar reforms in other countries could result in comparable outcomes to those seen in Italy. As a counterpoint to this argument, preparing and submitting minority slates is a costly endeavour. Given that rational reticence of asset managers is still dominant (especially in a firm-specific context),[87] this would likely realistically limit the number of slates that would be submitted by asset managers even in other jurisdictions such as the US.

Proposals resembling the Italian slate voting system have been advanced by academics in the US in decades past. For example, in 1976, Eisenberg recommended that shareholders holding more than five percent of a corporation's shares be permitted to nominate directors on the company's proxy statement; in 1988, Lowenstein proposed that shareholders collectively be given the exclusive right to nominate one-fifth to one-quarter of the board; and in 1989, Dent advocated that a committee of the company's ten or 20 largest shareholders should be directly responsible for nominating all of the company's directors.[88]

[84] Belcredi and Enriques (n 47) 394.
[85] Belcredi, Bozzi and, Di Noia (n 76) 414.
[86] Belcredi and Enriques (n 47) 384.
[87] Christie (n 7) 898–907, 915; Luca Enriques and Alessandro Romano, 'Rewiring Corporate Law for an Interconnected World' (2022) 64 Arizona Law Review 51, 62–64 (noting that large asset managers hold the entire market and have been shown to display a preference for maximising the value of their portfolio as a whole rather than the performance of individual companies).
[88] *See* Melvin A Eisenberg, *The Structure of the Corporation: A Legal Analysis* (Beard Books 1976) 117–121; Louis Lowenstein, *What's Wrong with Wall Street: Short-Term Gain and the Absentee Shareholder* (Addison Wesley Longman 1988) 209–211; and George W Dent

Therefore, in addition to the academic proposals outlined above, it also seems that there may be at least academic support for a system in the US that resembles the Italian slate voting system.

There are several interesting aspects of the Italian system that can be helpful in considering alternative models for other jurisdictions. The first is the formalisation of the minority shareholder's right to elect directors and the ease with which they can do so. This process is less costly than running a proxy contest at a US company. The second is the unique coordination role that Assogestioni performs, which could be used as a model for other countries in terms of overcoming collective action problems, reducing costs for investors, and enabling shareholders to collaborate without fear of acting in concert.[89]

15.4 Conclusion

In 2019, Gilson and Gordon argued that 'the current 1970s conception of the monitoring board and its surrounding regulatory structure, however well-meaning and responsive to an earlier set of governance shortcomings, is no longer sufficient to meet twenty-first century governance challenges'.[90] At present, the nomination of directors by activist hedge funds is the best, market-generated, solution that exists to address some of the problems that arise with the independent monitoring board. A range of academic and practical proposals that focus on enhancing the role of institutional investors in director elections have also been considered. The key question is how to replicate the role played by value-enhancing activist directors on a broader scale. At first sight, this may seem difficult to replicate as activist hedge funds have unique incentives and play a role that other investors are only very rarely willing to fulfil in terms of initiating director election campaigns. Despite numerous

Jr, 'Toward Unifying Ownership and Control in the Public Corporation' (1989) Wisconsin Law Review 881, 907–908. All cited in Gilson and Kraakman (n 35) 880.

89 CONSOB (the Italian SEC) has confirmed that cooperation between investors in connection with submitting lists of candidates for election to corporate boards will not be classified as concerted action. *See* Strampelli (n 48) 144. *See also* Gaia Balp and Giovanni Strampelli, 'Institutional Investor Collective Engagements: Non-Activist Cooperation vs Activist Wolf Packs' (2020) 14 Ohio State Business Law Journal 135, 185–191 (noting that collective engagements favour the redistribution of engagement costs and lower the free-rider problem and that the presence of a third-party entity coordinating engagement initiatives can work as an effective tool for reducing potential regulatory risks).

90 Gilson and Gordon (n 65) 364.

proposals envisaging a more active role for institutional investors (either individually or collectively), these proposals have not materialised through market forces. Is there any reason to think that some combination of these proposals could be effectively implemented now?

One reason for optimism may be the increasing focus on ESG activism and stewardship by shareholders and other stakeholders. Asset managers face considerable pressure from other shareholders in the investor ecosystem to be proactive in mitigating climate change and addressing other environmental and social issues. Additionally, a key priority for asset managers has always been the quality of portfolio company board members. Combined, these factors might push asset managers or other institutional investors to become more involved in director elections, or even to nominate directors themselves. There are of course some limited precedents of European asset managers already doing so. Barriers to collective action are also being eliminated in some respects, particularly with regard to ESG campaigns and stewardship. It is worth remembering that many organisations (such as Climate 100+) have already been set up in order to lead and coordinate the engagement of institutional investors. More generally, many different types of investors are collaborating on ESG issues in ways they have not done in the past.[91] If some of the legal concerns surrounding collective action (such as antitrust law and acting in concert provisions)[92] were to be alleviated, and some of the informational challenges were to be overcome, it is not beyond the realms of possibility that a wider group of shareholders might become more involved in director elections in the future.

[91] *See* Chapter 8 by Wolf-Georg Ringe and Chapter 9 by Peter Mülbert and Alexander Sajnovits in this volume.

[92] *See* Chapter 9 by Peter Mülbert and Alexander Sajnovits in this volume.

16

Shareholder Proposals and the Debate over Sustainability Disclosure

JILL FISCH AND ADRIANA Z. ROBERTSON

16.1 Introduction

Issuers and regulators around the world are confronting investor demands for increased attention to corporate sustainability.[1] With those demands comes an increasing focus on sustainability disclosure. Transparency about the sustainability of an issuer's operations and the sustainability risks it faces is necessary for the capital markets to price the issuer's securities accurately, to enable investors to make investment decisions that may be informed by both economic and non-economic considerations, and to enable investors to attempt to address sustainability issues through engagement.

Regulatory action is one tool for improving sustainability disclosure. The European Union has taken a regulatory approach through the adoption of the Sustainable Finance Disclosure Regulation, the Taxonomy

We are grateful to Heidi Welsh at the Sustainable Investments Institute (Si2) and Esgauge for generously providing access to their data. We thank Bob McCormick, Adam Pritchard, and Jessica Strine for valuable comments and suggestions. We also thank workshop participants at the Penn Institute for Law & Economics Corporate Roundtable, the Wharton Financial Regulation Conference, and the IOC Annual Forum & Auxiliary Corporate Governance Conference. Levi Haas and Ryland Ploeger provided exceptional research assistance. All errors are our own.

[1] The terminology in the debate over sustainability disclosure is fraught. Although the term ESG (environmental, social, and governance) disclosure has achieved widespread recognition in the popular press, the term encompasses a potentially broad range of issues, including issues that may or may not be material to a specific corporation or corporations generally from an economic perspective. See generally, Elizabeth Pollman, *The Making and Meaning of ESG*, 2022, https://papers.ssrn.com/sol3/papers.cfm?abstract_id=4219857. Some of these issues involve the impact on a corporation from societal developments such as climate change; others involve the corporation's impact on society, such as through its carbon emissions. In an earlier article, one of us used the term sustainability which, in her view, focuses the debate on disclosures that are relevant for investors in evaluating a corporation's business model, management quality and risk exposure. See Jill E. Fisch, Making Sustainability Disclosure Sustainable, 107 Geo. L.J. 923 (2019).

Regulation and the Corporate Sustainability Reporting Directive.[2] In March 2022, the U.S. Securities & Exchange Commission took a similar but more limited step, proposing a rule requiring public companies to make certain climate change disclosures as part of their securities filings.[3] The rule generated substantial controversy, with some commentators arguing that it exceeded the scope of the SEC's rulemaking authority and others criticizing the rule as too limited. Business groups announced their intention to mount litigation challenges. Whether or not the rule is adopted in its current form, climate change is only one of a number of important sustainability issues that firms currently confront. The SEC faces substantial political and practical obstacles, however, in extending the mandate to other environmental, social, and governance (ESG) issues.

This chapter considers an alternative mechanism for sustainability disclosure – private ordering. Companies regularly make voluntary sustainability disclosures on a variety of issues. They may include these disclosures in their securities filings,[4] sustainability reports, third-party tools for ESG reporting such as Nasdaq's OneReport,[5] or stand-alone disclosure documents. In some cases, the company itself initiates the disclosures. In others, the disclosures respond to requests that investors communicate through informal shareholder engagement or formally through the shareholder proposal rule. Recent years have seen tremendous growth in the number of shareholder proposals requesting issuers

[2] See Holly Pettingale, Stéphane de Maupeou, & Peter Reilly, *EU Taxonomy and the Future of Reporting*, Harv. L. Sch. Forum on Corp. Gov., Apr. 4, 2022, https://corpgov.law.harvard.edu/2022/04/04/eu-taxonomy-and-the-future-of-reporting/ (describing EU's sustainability disclosure requirements as part of an effort by the EU "to become the 'first climate-neutral continent.'").

[3] As this book went to press, the SEC adopted a modified version of its climate risk disclosure rule. The Enhancement and Standardization of Climate-Related Disclosures for Investors, Sec. Act Rel. No. 11275 (March 6, 2024), https://www.sec.gov/files/rules/final/2024/33-11275.pdf.

[4] See, e.g., Zabihollah Rezaeea & Ling Tuo, Voluntary Disclosure of Non-financial Information and Its Association with Sustainability Performance, 39 Advances in Acct'ing 47 (2017) https://fardapaper.ir/mohavaha/uploads/2019/03/Fardapaper-Voluntary-disclosure-of-non-financial-information-and-its-association-with-sustainability-performance.pdf (examining nonfinancial information voluntarily disclosed in 10-K filings by public companies).

[5] Nasdaq OneReport, *ESG Reporting, Purpose-built for ESG and simplifies the process of ESG data capture, engagement, oversight, and disclosure*, www.nasdaq.com/solutions/corporate-esg-solutions/nasdaq-onereport-esg-reporting?utm_medium=ppc&utm_source=google&utm_term=esg%20sustainable%20reporting&utm_campaign=SG_IR_US_SUSTAINABILITY_NB&gclid=CjwKCAjwi8iXBhBeEiwAKbUofQtHYkk-daZsPKMHR44xx4U2C8EabsKWJPVw-oRwD_6QG7sZkpqUgBoCpfAQAvD_BwE.

to prepare reports or disclose statistics on a variety of sustainability issues, and issuers are responding to these proposals by disclosing an increasing amount of information.

The chapter surveys these developments. After providing a brief historical context of investor demands for sustainability disclosure, the chapter briefly introduces the EU's sustainability disclosure mandates. The chapter then summarizes the SEC's proposed climate disclosure rule and situates that rule within the context of the existing U.S. reporting framework for public companies. The chapter identifies several key objections to the rule by commentators, focusing in particular on the claim that private ordering is superior to regulation in addressing investor need for climate-related information.

The chapter goes on to consider one specific and important mechanism by which this private ordering occurs – the shareholder proposal rule. After providing an overview of the rule, the chapter offers data on recent shareholder proposals seeking sustainability disclosure, including the information sought, the support such proposals receive when they go to a vote, and subsequent issuer responses. The data reveal several key findings. First, during both the 2021 and 2022 proxy seasons, shareholders submitted hundreds of proposals seeking additional sustainability disclosure. Second, a substantial percentage of these proposals were withdrawn, many in connection with a settlement in which the issuer agreed to provide some or all of the requested disclosure.[6] Because many such settlements were likely generated by the issuer's perception that the proposal was likely to receive substantial voting support, analyses of proposal outcomes that consider only proposals that are submitted to a shareholder vote likely understate the shareholder support for requested sustainability disclosures. Third, the information requested through shareholder proposals differs both from that contained in the SEC's proposed mandates and across shareholder proposals. While some proposals appear to be targeted to companies for which the requested disclosure is highly relevant – such as a request that Exxon report on its full carbon footprint, others appear less so. For example, Dollar General,

[6] See Ceres, *Record number of negotiated agreements between investors and companies in 2022 proxy season*, Aug. 1, 2022, www.ceres.org/news-center/press-releases/record-number-negotiated-agreements-between-investors-and-companies-2022 ("The 2022 proxy season wrapped up with a record-smashing number of agreements reached on climate-related shareholder resolutions, as companies came to the table with shareholders and accepted terms in exchange for resolution withdrawals.").

Macy's, and Zillow were all targeted with requests for information relating to GHG emissions.[7]

The data provided in this chapter suggest an important new insight into the relationship between mandatory disclosure and private ordering. At least within the context of sustainability disclosure, the two appear to function as complements rather than substitutes. In particular, shareholder proposals offer greater flexibility than an SEC rule, enabling shareholders to seek information on a current "hot issue." The frequency with which shareholders sought disclosure of EEO-1 reports[8] and the results of racial equity audits are two examples.[9] Shareholder proposals also facilitate targeted requests of information that would likely not be relevant to the vast majority of issuers, such as the request that Yum Brands provide disclosure on the social costs of antibiotic resistance, or that Pepsi report on sugar and public health.

At the same time, the scope of disclosure available through private ordering is more limited than what a mandatory disclosure regime can provide. A specific shareholder proposal can only seek disclosure on a discrete topic at a single company. Although it is common for shareholders to submit the same or similar disclosure requests at multiple companies, the process of navigating issuer objections to the proposal and mobilizing shareholder support does not readily scale. As a result, the number of companies targeted by any given proposal is extremely limited, and the disclosures produced by private ordering do not allow investors to compare information on a market-wide basis.[10] As a result, mandatory disclosure may be valuable for information that is likely to be relevant to evaluating the business risks and opportunities of a wide segment of the market.

[7] Often, these requests for disclosure are framed as a request for a report related to the company's emissions-related goals or commitments.

[8] The EEO-1 report "is a mandatory annual data collection that requires all private sector employers with 100 or more employees, and federal contractors with 50 or more employees meeting certain criteria, to submit demographic workforce data [to the U.S. Equal Employment Opportunity Commission], including data by race/ethnicity, sex and job categories." U.S. Equal Employment Opportunity Commission, EEO Data Collections, www.eeoc.gov/data/eeo-data-collections

[9] See, e.g., Lydia Beyoud & Andrew Ramonas, Shareholders Up Demands for Workplace Diversity Data Seen by Few, Bloomberg, June 7, 2021, https://news.bloomberglaw.com/esg/shareholders-up-demands-for-workplace-diversity-data-seen-by-few.

[10] See, e.g., Proxy Preview, Amazon – Worker Rights and Safety – Retirement Funds – Plastics Pollution – Climate Lobbying – Political Spending, 2023 Proxy Voting Alerts, Week Four, www.proxypreview.org/esg-proxy-voting-alerts ("Most companies never receive a shareholder resolution.").

16.2 Investor Demands for Sustainability Disclosure

Investor demands for ESG disclosure are not a recent phenomenon. Indeed, as early as 1971, the Natural Resources Defense Council (NRDC) and the Project on Corporate Responsibility filed a petition with the SEC asking it to mandate specified types of ESG disclosures.[11] The SEC was not generally receptive to requests for ESG disclosure for several reasons. First, the SEC has historically viewed sustainability disclosure as categorically different from disclosure on economic or financial matters. Indeed, the SEC explicitly phrased its request for public comment as a "Public Proceeding on Disclosure of Certain Environmental, Equal Employment and other Matters of *Primarily Social Rather than Financial Significance*."[12] The SEC reasoned that such disclosures were not within its core expertise and questioned their materiality to investors.[13] Second, the SEC questioned whether there was an existing methodology for making ESG disclosures, reasoning that, in the absence of such a methodology, the disclosures "would not lend themselves to comparisons of different companies."[14] Third, the SEC identified the difficulty in determining the scope of an ESG-disclosure mandate. As the SEC explained in its response to the 1971 petition by the Natural Resources Defense Council (NRDC) and the Project on Corporate Responsibility, for example:

> [P]articipants in the proceeding suggested more than 100 topics concerning which they desired disclosure. A disclosure document which incorporated each of these suggestions would consist of excessive and possibly confusing detail, whether provided directly to investors or filed with the

[11] See generally, Natural Res. Def. Coun., v. Securities Exch., 389 F. Supp. 689 (D.D.C. 1974) (describing the petition's requested disclosures. In particular, the petition requested that a corporation be required to disclose "(1) the effect of its corporate activities on the environment, and (2) statistics about its equal employment practices." Ibid. at 692. The petitioners explained that "investors now have no available and reliable means of assessing the environmental impact of the particular corporation." As a result, they stated that, "it is difficult and perhaps impossible for investors to make either socially responsible or financially sound investment decisions." They urged the SEC to adopt standardized disclosure requirements to remedy the situation.

[12] Supplemental Information Regarding Public Proceeding on Disclosure of Certain Environmental, Equal Employment and other Matters of Primarily Social Rather than Financial Significance, 1975 SEC LEXIS 1900, *1 (Apr. 4, 1975) (emphasis added).

[13] The report of the Advisory Committee on Corporate Disclosure, led by then-former SEC Commissioner A. A. Sommer, Jr. formalized the position that social and environmental matters were not generally material to investors. Advisory Comm. On Corp. Discl., 95th Cong. Rep. to the Sec. & Exch. Comm'n 391–99 (Comm. Print 1977).

[14] Nat. Res. Def. Council, Inc. v. SEC, 196 U.S. App. D.C. 124, 606 F.2d 1031, 1040 (1979).

> Commission for inspection by interested persons. Thus, certain types of disclosure might be so voluminous as to render disclosure documents as a whole significantly less readable and, thus, less useful to investors generally. In addition, disclosure to serve the needs or desires of limited segments of the investing public, even if otherwise desirable, may be inappropriate, since the cost to registrants, which must ultimately be borne by their shareholders would be likely to outweigh the resulting benefits to most investors.[15]

The SEC refused to adopt the disclosure requirements sought by the petitioners, and the DC Circuit upheld the SEC's decision.[16] Specifically, the DC Circuit held that the SEC "was necessarily given very broad discretion to promulgate rules governing corporate disclosure."[17] Holding that a "narrow" review was appropriate, both because the SEC's decision was not to adopt a rule and because of this deference, the court concluded that "the Commission was wholly justified in rejecting the proposed rules and choosing, for the present, to rely on the existing materiality disclosure standard."[18]

The NRDC litigation was not an isolated effort. Investors continued to urge the SEC to require ESG-related disclosures. In 2007, twenty-two institutional investors petitioned the SEC asking it to issue guidance on climate change disclosure, asserting that "the risks and opportunities many corporations face in connection with climate change fall squarely within the category of material information that is required to be analyzed and disclosed in many corporate filings." In light of that concern, the investors argued that existing disclosures were both inadequate and inconsistent.

[15] Notice of Commission Conclusion and Rulemaking Proposals in the Public Proceeding Announced in Securities Act Release No. 5569 (Feb. 11, 1975), 1975 SEC LEXIS 624, *17–18.

[16] The petitioners were successful in the district court, which concluded that the SEC's actions were arbitrary and capricious in violation of the Administrative Procedure Act. Nat. Res. Def. Council, Inc. v. SEC, 389 F. Supp. 689, 701 (1974). Following the trial court's initial decision, the SEC opened a more extensive public proceeding. Supplemental Information Regarding Public Proceeding on Disclosure of Certain Environmental, Equal Employment and other Matters of Primarily Social Rather than Financial Significance, 1975 SEC LEXIS 1900, *1 (Apr. 4, 1975). The proceeding included the broad dissemination of a release requesting comment and 19 days of public hearings. The SEC received 54 oral presentations and 353 written comments, amounting to 10,000 pages of documents. 1975 SEC LEXIS 624, *8; 1976 SEC LEXIS 1727.

[17] Nat. Res. Def. Council, Inc. v. SEC, 196 U.S. App. D.C. 124, 606 F.2d 1031, 1050 (1979).

[18] Ibid. at 1062.

In 2016, the SEC undertook an initiative to overhaul the reporting requirements in Regulation S-K and, as part of that initiative, issued a concept release "seeking public comment on whether our business and financial disclosure requirements continue to elicit important information for investors and how registrants can most effectively present this information."[19] A number of commentators urged the SEC to incorporate ESG or sustainability disclosures as part of that overhaul.[20]

The SEC did not ignore these requests entirely. In 1973, the SEC adopted rules requiring disclosure of the material financial effects of corporate compliance with environmental laws.[21] In 2009, the SEC issued a rule requiring issuers to disclose "whether, and if so how, the nominating committee (or board) considers diversity in identifying nominees" for the board of directors.[22] In 2010, the SEC issued an interpretive release advising "issuers that they were required to disclose material information about their exposure to risks resulting from climate change, explaining that this requirement was based in several existing provisions of Regulation S–K, including the MD&A, the required disclosure of legal

[19] Concept Release on Business and Financial Disclosure Required by Regulation S-K, Securities Act Release No. 10,064, Exchange Act Release No. 77,599, 81 Fed. Reg. 23,916 (Apr. 22, 2016).

[20] See Natalie Nowiski, Rising Above the Storm: Climate Risk Disclosure and its Current and Future Relevance to the Energy Sector, 39 Energy L. J. 1, 8 (2018) ("The SEC received comments from a number of NGOs and investor groups, such as the CDP, the SASB, Ceres, and the SEC Investor Advisory Committee, advocating for mandatory climate risk disclosure and increased enforcement by the SEC."). See also Heather Slavkin Corzo, Dir., Office of Inv., AFL–CIO, Comment Letter on Concept Release Regarding Business and Financial Disclosure Required by Regulation S–K (July 21, 2016), www.sec.gov/comments/s7-06-16/s70616-305.pdf ("[G]iven the clear and growing demand from investors for environmental, social and governance ('ESG') information, the Commission must begin requiring ESG related line-item disclosures as well as a process to incorporate emerging ESG metrics into disclosure in the future."); Che Odom, Investors Want Sustainability Disclosures in SEC Overhaul, Bloomberg (July 21, 2016), www.bna.com/investors-sustainability-disclosures-n73014445099 and https://perma.cc/8AB2-LTH7 ("Investor advocates are making a strong push for the SEC to require annual, uniform sustainability reporting from public companies as part of the overhaul of the agency's disclosure regime."). At the same time, many industry groups opposed further regulation of climate risk disclosure. Nowiski, this note above, at 8–9.

[21] Securities Act Release No. 5386 (Apr. 20, 1973), 38 Fed. Reg. 12100 (1973).

[22] Proxy Disclosure Enhancements, Securities Act Release No. 9089, Exchange Act Release No. 61,175, Investment Company Act Release No. 29,092, 74 Fed. Reg. 68,334, 68,364 (Dec. 23, 2009).

proceedings, and the section on risk factors."[23] Notably, in 2021, the SEC issued a "Sample Letter" to issuers regarding their climate-related disclosures.[24] A report by the Congressional Research Service suggested that issuers were not disclosing in accordance with the 2010 guidance.[25]As one commentator explained, "The Sample Letter was issued in part due to the concern that many companies were seemingly not adhering to the 2010 Guidance in their disclosures."[26] In addition, the SEC adopted rules regarding conflict minerals and resource extraction disclosure in response to congressional mandates in the Dodd-Frank Act, although that requirement no longer has any practical effect.[27]

Nonetheless, a number of investors continued to view the existing rules as inadequate.[28] In 2018, petitioners representing $5 trillion in assets signed a petition calling for the SEC to require comprehensive

[23] Fisch, *supra* note 1, at 937, citing Commission Guidance Regarding Disclosure Related to Climate Change, Securities Act Release No. 9106, Exchange Act Release No. 61,469, 75 Fed. Reg. 6289, 6290 (Feb. 8, 2010).

[24] SEC, Sample Letter to Companies Regarding Climate Change Disclosure, Sept. 28, 2021 (the "Sample Letter"), www.sec.gov/corpfin/sample-letter-climate-change-disclosures.

[25] Rena S. Miller, Gary Shorter, & Nicole Vanatko (Feb. 17, 2022), Climate Change Risk Disclosures and the Securities and Exchange Commission, at 3 (CRS Report No. R4677) Retrieved from Congressional Research Service website: https://crsreports.congress.gov/product/pdf/R/R46766.

[26] Michael Ruder, Made for TV: The SEC's Regulatory Posture on Climate Risk, Cadwalader Clients-Friends Memos, Mar. 1, 2022, www.cadwalader.com/resources/clients-friends-memos/made-for-tv–the-secs-regulatory-posture-on-climate-risk#_ftn9. See also SEC Chair Gary Gensler, Prepared Remarks Before the Principles for Responsible Investment "Climate and Global Financial Markets" Webinar, July 28, 2021, www.sec.gov/news/speech/gensler-pri-2021-07-28 ("a review of S&P 500 issuers' filings after the SEC's 2010 guidance found filers generally did not engage in 'quantifying risks or past impacts' with respect to climate [and] tended to use 'boilerplate language of minimal utility to investors.'").

[27] Fisch, *supra* note 1, at 939. Prior to the changes, the conflict minerals rule went into effect, and more than 1,000 companies made filings in accordance with its requirements. See Jeff Schwartz, The Conflict Minerals Experiment, 6 Harv. Bus. L. Rev. 129 (2016) (analyzing disclosures pursuant to the rule). The DC Circuit invalidated the conflict minerals rule in 2015, holding that it compelled commercial speech in violation of the First Amendment. Nat'l Ass'n of Mfrs. v. SEC, 800 F.3d 518 (DC Cir. 2015).

[28] See David Gelles, *SEC Is Criticized for Lax Enforcement of Climate Risk Disclosure*, N.Y. Times (Jan. 23, 2016), www.nytimes.com/2016/01/24/business/energy-environment/sec-is-criticized-for-lax-enforcement-of-climate-risk-disclosure.html (stating that in April 2015 an alliance of 62 institutional investors wrote to the SEC "calling for greater scrutiny of climate-related disclosures from energy companies in particular."); Virginia Harper Ho, From Public Policy to Materiality: Non-financial Reporting, Shareholder Engagement, and Rule 14a-8's Ordinary Business Exception, 76 Wash & Lee L. Rev. 1231, 1238 (2019) ("Survey evidence confirms that the vast majority of institutional

ESG disclosure.[29] Although the SEC did not respond to this petition under SEC Chair Jay Clayton, the prospect of SEC rulemaking requiring sustainability disclosure gained traction with the election of President Joseph R. Biden and the shift to a Democrat-controlled SEC. In addition, views on both the importance and the feasibility of sustainability disclosure, particularly climate-related disclosure, continued to evolve. Climate change reached heightened prominence in the public discourse. A variety of organizations developed standardized metrics for climate reporting, particularly the calculation of greenhouse gas emissions. And an increasing number of issuers were making voluntary disclosures in accordance with these metrics.

Developments in the European Union have reinforced the feasibility of increased climate-related disclosure.[30] The EU has adopted a suite of disclosure requirements, focusing primarily but not exclusively on environmental disclosures. The Sustainable Finance Disclosure Regulation (SFDR), adopted in 2019, requires issuers of financial products to report on the extent to which their products are "green." The regulation classifies financial products as Article 9 (dark green) (products which have sustainable investment as their objective), Article 8 (products which promote environmental or social characteristics (light green), and Article 6 (all other financial products). In addition, the SFDR requires disclosure of the weighted average of a product's greenhouse gas emissions on a portfolio-wide basis.

The Taxonomy Regulation, adopted in 2020, established a classification system based on consideration of both whether a firm's economic activity makes a substantial contribution and whether it does significant harm, across a number of environmental objectives, including climate change mitigation, climate change adaptation, sustainable use of water, pollution prevention, and preservation of biodiversity. The classification includes industry-specific objective thresholds defining when a company is considered sustainable. The classification system also requires that, to

investors now believe that companies should disclose material ESG information to investors, but that critical ESG information gaps exist.").

29 See Cynthia A. Williams & Jill E. Fisch, Petition for SEC Rulemaking on Environmental, Social, and Governance Information Disclosure (Oct. 1, 2018), www.sec.gov/rules/petitions/2018/petn4-730.pdf and https://perma.cc/YTA2–8L7L.

30 An overview of these developments is provided by Gaia Balp & Giovanni Strampelli, Institutional Investor ESG Engagement: The European Experience, 23 Eur. Bus. Org L. Rev. 869 (2022).

be classified as sustainable, a fund avoid violation of minimum "social safeguards." In other words, the Taxonomy makes a determination, based on designated criteria, whether a company or product is "green," and organizations must report in accordance with that determination. All financial market participants, all large companies, and listed SMEs will need to make disclosures in accordance with the Taxonomy.

Subsequently, the European Council adopted the Corporate Sustainability Reporting Directive (CSRD),[31] which became effective in December 2022 and will require many large companies, including listed companies, to disclose a variety of E, S, & G information. Among the required disclosures will be a company's climate change risks and its impact on both the climate and society. The CSRD will also require issuers to identify sustainability targets and to report their progress toward meeting those targets.

16.3 The SEC's Climate Rule

On March 15, 2021, then-acting SEC Chair Allison Herren Lee announced a request for public input on climate change disclosures.[32] Stating that investor demand for such disclosures has grown, Commissioner Lee identified 15 categories of information that would be helpful to the Commission in considering and formulating new disclosure requirements. The request for public input generated a substantial response. According to Chair Gensler, three quarters of the unique comment letters submitted in response to Commissioner Lee's request for input on climate-related disclosures "support[ed] mandatory climate disclosure rules."[33] Gensler too supported mandatory climate disclosure, reasoning that "[c]ompanies and investors alike would benefit from clear rules of the road."[34]

On March 21, 2022, the SEC proposed rules to enhance and standardize climate-related disclosure by public companies.[35] The proposed rules would

[31] The CSRD replaced the EU's Non-Financial Reporting Directive (NFRD), which had been launched in 2014 and required firms above a certain size (500 employees) to "map and report climate risks." Fredrik N. G. Andersson & Susanne Arvidsson, Understanding, Mapping and Reporting of Climate-Related Risks among Listed Firms in Sweden, 1 Climate Pol'y 2 (2022).

[32] Allison Herren Lee, Public Input Welcomed on Climate Change Disclosures, U.S. Sec. & Exch. Comm'n (Mar. 15, 2021), www.sec.gov/news/public-statement/lee-climate-change-disclosures.

[33] Gensler, *supra* note 26. [34] Ibid.

[35] The Enhancement and Standardization of Climate-Related Disclosures for Investors. Sec/Act Rel. No. 11042, www.sec.gov/rules/proposed/2022/33-11042.pdf.

require public companies to make a variety of climate-related disclosures in their registration statements and annual reports. If adopted, the rules would amend Regulation S-K to require issuers to disclose:[36]

1. The oversight and governance of climate-related risks by an issuer' s registrant's board and management;
2. The material impact of any climate-related risks on an issuer's business and financial statements;
3. How any climate-related risks have affected or are likely to affect an issuer's strategy, business model and outlook;
4. The issuer's process for identifying, assessing and managing climate-related risks and the extent to which that process is integrated into the issuer's risk management systems;
5. Scopes 1 and 2 GHG emissions in both absolute and intensity terms, with a requirement that large issuers obtain external assurance of those emissions;
6. Scope 3 GHG emissions if material or if the issuer has set a scope 3 emissions reduction target or goal;
7. The issuer's climate related targets, goals and transition plan, if any;[37]
8. The issuer's internal carbon pricing, if used.

The proposed rules on climate-related disclosure were not the only prospect for SEC rulemaking in the ESG space. In August 2020, the SEC began requiring companies to disclose more information about their human capital management.[38] Many have viewed these requirements as too limited or confusing.[39] In 2021, SEC Chair Gary Gensler stated that he had asked the SEC staff to put together recommendations for "mandatory company disclosures on climate risk and on human capital."[40] On June 7, 2022, a group of former SEC officials, academics and market

[36] Ibid. at 41–42.

[37] Companies that have set climate-related targets would have to disclose information on the scope and time horizon of such targets and their pathways and progress toward reaching such targets.

[38] Jessica Mach, Will New SEC Disclosure Rules on "Human Capital" Further Befuddle Companies?, Corporate Counsel, Mar. 15, 2022, www.law.com/corpcounsel/2022/03/15/will-new-sec-disclosure-rules-on-human-capital-further-befuddle-companies/.

[39] See, e.g., Alison Omens, Aleksandra Radeva, & Kavya Vaghul, *The Current State of Human Capital Disclosure*, Harv. L. Sch. For. On Corp. Gov., Oct. 31, 2021, https://corpgov.law.harvard.edu/2021/10/31/the-current-state-of-human-capital-disclosure/ (criticizing the "low overall rate of human capital disclosure we see from companies").

[40] SEC Chair Gary Gensler, Prepared remarks at London City Week. June 23, 2021. www.sec.gov/news/speech/gensler-speech-london-city-week-062321

participants filed a rulemaking petition asking the SEC to require greater disclosure on human capital management.[41] Members of Congress have also encouraged the SEC to adopt improved disclosure requirements regarding human capital.[42]

The SEC's proposed climate disclosure rule generated considerable controversy. The SEC received thousands of comments from issuers, investors, individuals, and trade associations.[43] While investors largely supported the SEC's objective of implementing a climate disclosure regime for public companies, even investors expressed concern about several of the disclosure requirements, including the requirement that issuers disclose scope 3 emissions, the requirement that emissions disclosures obtain external assurance, and the requirement that issuers disclose the financial impact of transition activities.[44] Investors also sought greater alignment with existing market disclosure frameworks such as the TCFD and GHG protocol, which many issuers were already using voluntarily.[45]

Issuers and other commentators were less supportive of the proposed rule. Issuers raised a variety of concerns that the new rule would be costly and burdensome and that it would subject issuers to heightened risk of securities fraud litigation.[46] The rule has also drawn political fire. Among the objections were claims that the SEC lacks the competence to determine the appropriate scope of environmental disclosure,[47] that the rule exceeds the scope of the SEC's rulemaking authority,[48]

[41] Petition for Rulemaking, Working Group on Human Capital Accounting Disclosure, June 7, 2022, www.sec.gov/rules/petitions/2022/petn4-787.pdf.

[42] Mark Warner Press Release, Warner, Brown Urge SEC to Implement Improvements to Their Human Capital Disclosure Rules, June 16, 2022, www.warner.senate.gov/public/index.cfm/pressreleases?id=B4AFB502-0289-4539-9FF8-9DEAE153B900.

[43] Martha Carter, Matt Filosa, Sean Quinn, & Sydney Carlock, *Too Soon? An Analysis of Major Investor Comments on the SEC's Proposed Climate Disclosure Rule*, Teneo, July 8, 2022, www.teneo.com/too-soon-an-analysis-of-major-investor-comments-on-the-secs-proposed-climate-disclosure-rule/.

[44] Ibid. [45] Ibid.

[46] Mark Maurer, Companies Skewer SEC's Climate-Disclosures Plan in Comment Letters, Wall St. J., June 21, 2022, www.wsj.com/articles/companies-skewer-secs-climate-disclosures-plan-in-comment-letters-11655834912.

[47] Benjamin Zycher, *The SEC's Climate "Disclosure" Gambit*, Nat. Rev. Capital Matters, Oct. 29, 2021, www.nationalreview.com/2021/10/the-secs-climate-gambit/?gclid=Cj0KCQjw1bqZBhDXARIsANTjCPLkt3suphN5949UQAv9n68b3Zl1M86f4wTzzdHgvWo39QIYcDUzsBkaAl5GEALw_wcB.

[48] This concern was heightened by the Supreme Court's decision in West Virginia v. EPA, 142 S. Ct. 2587 (2022), which struck down an environmental regulation as beyond the scope of the EPA's regulatory authority. See Bill Flook, Republicans Lean on Supreme Court's EPA Decision to Attack SEC Climate Disclosure Proposal, Thomson Reuters,

and that it constitutes compelled speech in violation of the First Amendment.[49]

This chapter does not address those concerns. Rather, the chapter focuses on yet another argument made by opponents of the SEC's rule proposal: that mandatory climate risk disclosure is unnecessary because climate disclosure can be adequately addressed through private ordering. There are two components to this argument. First, some commentators argue investors can and are obtaining sufficient disclosures about issuer climate risk through private ordering, obviating the need for regulation. Commentators point, in particular, to the fact that a substantial number of issuers voluntarily file sustainability or ESG reports,[50] although the quality and accuracy of the information disclosed in those reports is unclear.[51] Second, other commentators argue that private ordering demonstrates limited investor demand for additional ESG information. In particular, a high-profile comment letter written by Professor Larry Cunningham and signed by a number of law professors (the "Cunningham letter") states that "few [shareholder proposals demanding climate information] are made, being limited to a minority of public companies; most lose; and many are made not by traditional investors but by political activists taking advantage of the shareholder proposal process."[52]

This chapter takes up the challenge posed by the Cunningham letter and examines ESG-related shareholder proposals both for evidence of the extent to which shareholders support climate-related disclosure and for

Aug. 10, 2022, https://tax.thomsonreuters.com/news/republicans-lean-on-supreme-courts-epa-decision-to-attack-sec-climate-disclosure-proposal/.

49 See Sean Griffith, *What's "Controversial" About ESG? A Theory of Compelled Commercial Speech under the First Amendment*, 101 Nebraska Law Review 876 (2023). For a response, see Sarah Haan, *The First Amendment and the SEC's Proposed Climate Risk Disclosure Rule*, June 23, 2022, https://papers.ssrn.com/sol3/papers.cfm?abstract_id=4138712.

50 See, e.g., Lucy Pérez, Dame Vivian Hunt, Hamid Samandari, Robin Nuttall, & Krysta Biniek, Does ESG Really Matter – and Why?, McKinsey Quarterly, Aug. 10, 2022, www.mckinsey.com/capabilities/sustainability/our-insights/does-esg-really-matter-and-why ("More than 90 percent of S&P 500 companies now publish ESG reports in some form, as do approximately 70 percent of Russell 1000 companies.").

51 See, e.g., SEC, Brazilian Mining Company to Pay $55.9 Million to Settle Charges Related to Misleading Disclosures Prior to Deadly Dam Collapse, Press Release, March 28, 2023, www.sec.gov/news/press-release/2023-63 (reporting settlement of SEC enforcement action against Vale S.A. for false and misleading statements in its sustainability reports).

52 Lawrence A. Cunningham, Comment Letter on SEC Climate Disclosure Proposal by 21 Law and Finance Professors, 2022, https://ssrn.com/abstract=4109278.

potential guidance as to the shape that an SEC mandate should take. In the next part, the chapter briefly describes Rule 14a-8, the shareholder proposal rule. It then provides data that are inconsistent with the assertions in the Cunningham letter on shareholders' use of the rule, in 2021 and 2022, to seek greater sustainability disclosure.

16.4 The Shareholder Proposal Process: ESG Disclosure through Private Ordering

16.4.1 Overview of the Shareholder Proposal Process

SEC Rule 14a-8, the shareholder proposal rule, allows shareholders who meet the specified criteria to introduce a proposal for inclusion in a company's proxy statement and to have shareholders vote on that proposal at the annual shareholders meeting. Shareholder proposals have been described as a tool for enabling shareholders to communicate their views to each other and management, with one recent article analogizing the shareholder proposal rule to a "corporate town square."[53] The focus of shareholder proposals has evolved over time, as has the identity of those who sponsor such proposals.[54] In recent years, shareholder proposals have increasingly focused on ESG issues, including proposals that challenge corporate practices, seek to have corporations adopt specified targets or goals, and those that seek additional disclosure.[55] To avoid interfering with the board's authority, under state corporate law, to manage the corporation, most shareholder proposals are framed in precatory terms – as requests for the board or the corporation to take action. Even precatory proposals, however, have been shown to have an impact on board behavior when they are supported by a majority of shareholders.[56]

[53] James D. Cox & Randall S. Thomas, The SEC's Shareholder Proposal Rule: Creating a Corporate Public Square, Colum. Bus. L. Rev. 1147 (2021).

[54] See Jill Fisch, Purpose Proposals, 1 U. Chi. Bus. L. Rev. 113 (2022) (describing emergence of ESG entrepreneurs who play a substantial role in sponsoring and co-sponsoring ESG-oriented shareholder proposals).

[55] We do not take a position in this chapter as to whether the use of shareholder proposals to address ESG issues is normatively desirable. Compare Paul G. & Julia D. Mahoney, The New Separation of Ownership and Control: Institutional Investors and ESG, Colum. Bus. L. Rev. 840, 877 (2021) (suggesting that the SEC could repeal Regulation 14A to reduce the extent to which investors vote on "shareholder proposals designed to advance public policy goals").

[56] Ibid.

One of the limitations of Rule 14a-8 is that a shareholder proposal cannot address a company's ordinary business operations.[57] The rationale is that state law authorizes a company's directors and officers to manage the corporation, and shareholders do not have the right to interfere with that authority. As one commentator observes, "the ordinary business exception is [] one of the most important substantive bases for the exclusion of environmental and social proposals."[58] The SEC's interpretation of what constitutes ordinary business has evolved over time. In particular, the SEC has been increasingly expansive in allowing proposals that address important social policy issues. At the same time, however, the SEC's guidance has encouraged proponents to focus on the societal implications of their proposal rather than the firm-specific economic consequences.

Rule 14a-8 requires a shareholder to submit a proposal by the deadline specified in the company's proxy statement for the prior year.[59] A shareholder may only submit one proposal at a given issuer. There is no requirement that the shareholder or the issuer file the proposal or any notice to the SEC or the public that a proposal has been submitted. If the issuer includes the proposal in its proxy statement, the first public notice of the proposal occurs when the issuer files its preliminary proxy statement with the SEC.[60] If an issuer believes that a proposal can be excluded from its proxy statement on either procedural or substantive grounds, rule 14a-8 requires the issuer to file its reasons with the SEC at least 80 days before filing its definitive proxy statement.[61] Both the preliminary proxy statement and the notice of intent to exclude a proposal are publicly available through Edgar. If, however, a proponent withdraws its proposal prior to the filing of the issuer's proxy statement, there is no requirement that either the proposal or the decision to withdraw it be reflected in a public filing, although some proponents appear to make a practice of publicly disclosing at least some of the instances in which they have withdrawn or settled a proposal.

Several recent developments have affected the availability of the shareholder proposal process to promote ESG disclosure. In 2020, the SEC amended the criteria that a shareholder must satisfy to have a proposal

[57] See Ho, *supra* note 28 at 1246 (discussing the "ordinary business exception" and how it serves as a limit on the scope of permissible shareholder proposals).

[58] Ibid. at 1247. [59] Rule 14a-8(e).

[60] Shareholders can of course publicly report their submissions on their websites or blogs. See, e.g., As You Sow, Current Resolutions, www.asyousow.org/resolutions-tracker.

[61] Rule 15a-8(j).

included in the proxy statement.[62] While previously a shareholder was only required to hold $2000 or 1 percent of a company's stock (whichever was less) for at least a year prior to submitting proposals, the new rule increased the ownership requirements. Under the new rule a shareholder must now hold $2000 worth of stock for at least three years, $15,000 worth of stock for at least two years, or $25,000 worth of stock for at least one year.[63] An additional component of the amended rule, which has received relatively little attention, encourages shareholders and issuers to resolve proposals voluntarily without the need to bring the proposal to a vote. Rule 14a-8(i) requires the proponent to state that he or she is available to meet with the company between 10 and 30 days after submission, to provide contact information and to provide the company with a "written statement that includes business days and specific times that you are available to discuss the proposal with the company."[64]

In November 2021, the SEC staff eliminated the requirement that sponsors of a social policy proposal demonstrate that the policy has a significant economic impact on the corporation.[65] This change had the effect of broadening the scope of permissible proposals that address sustainability issues. Finally, in July 2022, the SEC proposed amendments that would reduce a company's ability to exclude a shareholder proposal on the ground that it had been substantially implemented, was duplicative of another proposal or constituted the resubmission of a previous proposal.[66]

16.4.2 Data on ESG Disclosure Proposals

To explore the extent to which investors are using the shareholder proposal process to seek sustainability disclosure, we obtained data on

62 Sec. & Exch. Comm'n, Procedural Requirements and Resubmission Thresholds under Exchange Act Rule 14a-8: A Small Entity Compliance Guide, Dec. 28, 2020, www.sec.gov/corpfin/procedural-requirements-resubmission-thresholds-guide.

63 The amendments also increased the levels of support required for a shareholder to resubmit a proposal that had previously been included in the company's proxy statement. Ibid.

64 The Rule instructs a proponent that "You must provide the company with a written statement that you are able to meet with the company in person or via teleconference no less than 10 calendar days, nor more than 30 calendar days, after submission of the shareholder proposal. You must include your contact information as well as business days and specific times that you are available to discuss the proposal with the company." (17 C.F.R. § 240.14a-8(b)(iii).)

65 Shareholder Proposals, Staff Legal Bulletin No. 14L (CF) (Nov. 3, 2021).

66 Brian V. Breheny, et al., SEC Proposes Amendments to the Shareholder Proposal Rules, Skadden Insights, July 15, 2022, www.skadden.com/insights/publications/2022/07/sec-proposes-amendments-to-the-shareholder-proposal-rules.

environmental and social shareholder proposals submitted to issuers during the 2021 and 2022 proxy seasons. At the outset, we note an important limitation of our data analysis. As noted above, when a shareholder submits a proposal to a corporation pursuant to Rule 14a-8, that submission does not trigger a public filing or disclosure. Accordingly, there is no way to determine the entire universe of proposals that are submitted to issuers in any given year. In addition, various databases differ in the universe of issuers that they follow. Because most shareholder proposals are submitted at larger capitalization companies,[67] we focused primarily on those companies.

The shareholder proposal data that form the basis of the analysis in this chapter come from Esgauge, a commercial data provider focused on corporate ESG practices.[68] Esgauge provided us with data on environmental and sustainability-related shareholder proposals at 313 large U.S. public companies in 2021 and 2022. The database contains proposals that were submitted to the shareholders for a vote, as well as proposals that proponents voluntarily withdrew and proposals that issuers received SEC permission to omit pursuant to a no-action request.[69] The full dataset contained 909 proposals across the two years (400 in 2021 and 509 in 2022).[70] We excluded 145 proposals that did not request a report, disclosure, or audit, since they did not directly implicate sustainability disclosure.[71] We also excluded a further 159 proposals related to political spending and lobbying, since we felt they were, although related to the debate about sustainability disclosures, too far from the scope of the SEC's proposed rule. For the same reason, we excluded 12 proposals that requested a report

67 See note 70, infra. 68 Esgauge, https://esgauge.com/ (last visited Jan. 26, 2023).

69 See Gibson Dunn, Shareholder Proposal Developments During the 2021 Proxy Season, Aug. 19, 2021, www.gibsondunn.com/wp-content/uploads/2021/08/shareholder-proposal-developments-during-the-2021-proxy-season.pdf. Using the ISS database of Russell 3000 companies, Gibson Dunn reported that, in 2021, over 29 percent of shareholder proposals were withdrawn, a number reflecting almost twice as many as in 2020. See Ibid. ("This increase is largely attributable to the withdrawal rates of both social and environmental proposals, which rose markedly in 2021 compared to 2020 (increasing to 46% and 62%, respectively).") Gibson Dunn also notes that the number of requests for SEC exclusions increased from prior years, and that the success rate for no-action requests held steady at 71 percent. Ibid.

70 We note that, although our data consist of a far smaller number of companies than those analyzed by Gibson Dunn, the 313 companies in our data received more than half the proposals submitted to Russell 3000 companies.

71 Examples of these proposals include adopting diversity candidate search policies, adopting policies promoting employee representation on the board, and converting into a public benefit corporation.

related to corporate purpose.[72] For each proposal, our database contains data on the issuer, the proponent, the nature of the proposal, and the voting outcome, if applicable. In some cases, we also researched whether the "ask" was satisfied; that is, whether the information requested by the proposal was disclosed by the issuer in whole or in part. Our final database consists of 243 proposals for the 2021 proxy season and 350 proposals for the 2022 proxy season relating to a total of 242 companies.[73] Fourteen of the proposals from 2022 were listed as "Filed, not yet voted." Because this does not represent the final disposition of the proposal, we also exclude these 14 proposals from the analysis that follows, bringing the total number of issuers down to 239. We present the breakdown of proposals in Figure 16.1.

As Figure 16.1 demonstrates, a substantial proportion of proposals were withdrawn, indicating that issuers and shareholders reached a settlement without putting the proposal to a vote.[74] This may be due to the amendments to Rule 14a-8.[75] In 2021, 41 percent of proposals were withdrawn without going to a vote; in 2022, 36 percent of proposals were withdrawn.[76] We also observe that the number of omitted proposals fell substantially between 2021 and 2022.

[72] Nine of these proposals invoked the report based on a review of the BRT Statement of the Purpose of a Corporation. The other three were primarily focused on a change of form to a public benefit corporation. For an analysis of these "purpose proposals" see Fisch, *supra* note 54.

[73] 172 of these companies (71 percent) were constituents of the S&P 500 at some point between 2020 and 2022. The most common sectors represented by companies in our data are Consumer Discretionary (21 percent of the companies in the sample), Consumer Staples (13 percent) and Financials (12 percent). Health Care, Industrials, Information Technology, and Utilities each represent between 8 percent and 9.5 percent of the sample. The remaining sectors are Communication Services (6 percent), Energy (5 percent), Materials (5 percent), and Real Estate (2 percent).

[74] See, e.g., Brigid Rosati, Kilian Moote, Rajeev Kumar, & Michael Maiolo, A Look Back at the 2022 Proxy Season, Harv. L. Sch. For. On Corp. Gov., Oct. 23, 2022, https://corpgov.law.harvard.edu/2022/10/23/a-look-back-at-the-2022-proxy-season/ (reporting that, with respect to proposals requesting scope 3 disclosures, 36 of the 55 proposals submitted during the 2022 proxy season were withdrawn and, of those, "24 specifically reference withdrawal due to an agreement being reached, a commitment being made, or general constructive dialogue").

[75] See discussion *supra* note 65 and accompanying text.

[76] See also Matteo Gatti, Giovanni Strampelli, & Matteo Tonello, How Does Board-Shareholder Engagement Really Work? Evidence from a Survey of Corporate Officers and from Disclosure Data (Oct. 24, 2022). *Board-Shareholder Dialogue: Policy Debate, Legal Constraints and Best Practices* (Luca Enriques & Giovanni Strampelli eds., 2024, Cambridge University Press) (reporting that during the 2022 proxy season, institutional investor "engagement resulted in the withdrawal of a shareholder proposal for 44.3 percent of companies in the whole sample, for 41 percent of Russell 3000 companies, and for 44.3 percent of S&P 500 companies").

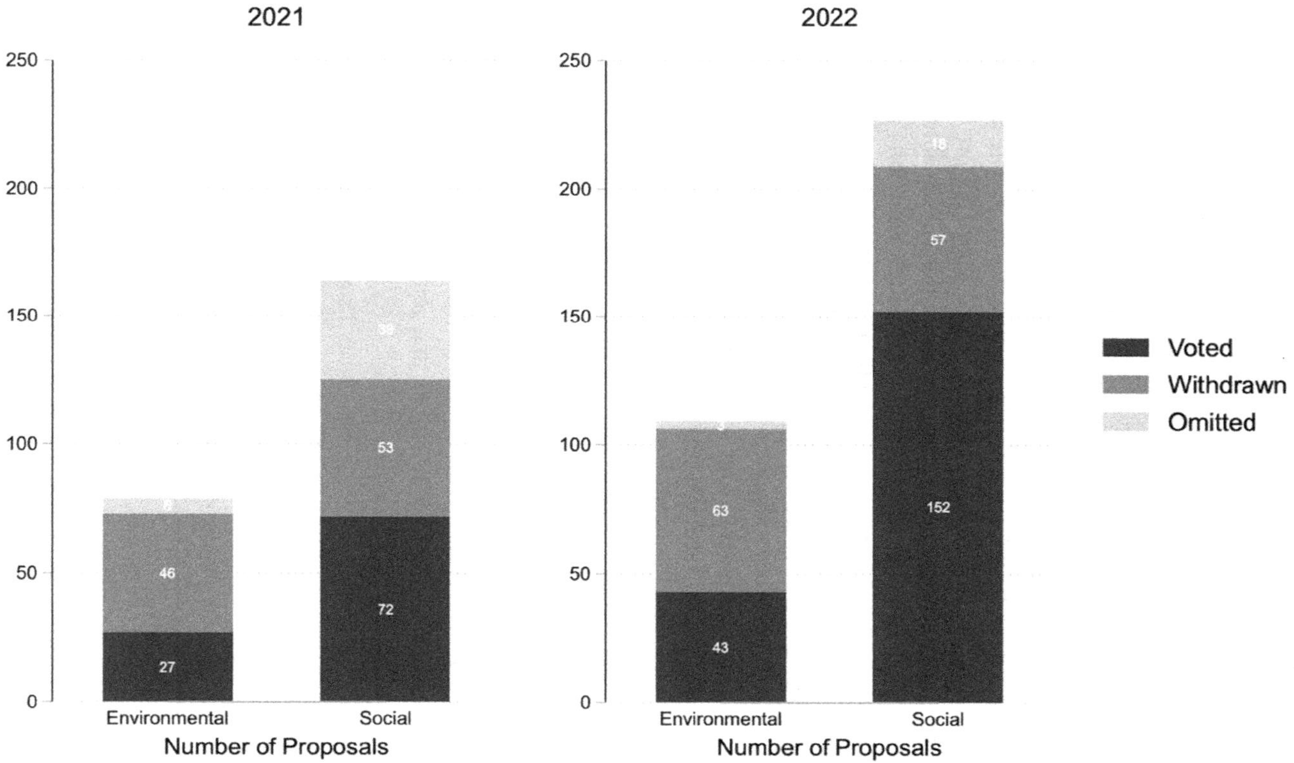

Figure 16.1 Number of environmental and social shareholder proposals

Of the proposals in our data, the environmental ones are substantially more likely to be withdrawn (58 percent compared to 28 percent, a difference that is statistically significant at the 99.9 percent level). It is reasonable to posit that these withdrawals were influenced at least in part by the prospect that the proposals would receive substantial voting support if they were submitted to shareholders. During our time period, a substantial number of large institutional investors increased their voting support for ESG proposals and environmental proposals in particular. BlackRock, for example, voted in favor of 47 percent of environmental and social proposals that came to a vote in 2021.[77] Further, large institutions have publicly stated their support for certain types of disclosures such as "'quantitative' information about a company's scope 1 and 2 emissions and a company's emissions reductions plans."[78] Notwithstanding this, we caution that our data on withdrawn proposals, while extensive, is not complete. As discussed in Section 16.4.2, there is no systematic repository of withdrawn proposals. As a result, it is possible that there are systematic unobservable differences between the environmental and social proposals that made it into our database. We stress, however, that this also implies that our data are likely to understate the number of withdrawn proposals.

Proponents may, of course, withdraw shareholder proposals for a variety of reasons, but one common reason for withdrawal is that the issuer has agreed to provide some or all of the information requested by the proponent.[79] If a proponent accepts the issuer's proposed voluntary disclosure, the proposal is settled without ever being submitted for a shareholder vote.[80] One reason that issuers are willing to settle shareholder proposals is that they anticipate that some of these proposals will

[77] Catherine Clifford, Blackrock to Vote for Fewer Climate Shareholder Provisions in 2022 than 2021, CNBC, May 11, 2022, www.cnbc.com/2022/05/11/blackrock-to-vote-for-fewer-climate-provisions-in-2022-than-2021.html. This number was up from the 9 percent of environmental and social proposals that BlackRock supported in 2020. Christine Williamson, BlackRock Won't Back Climate Shareholder Proposals It Considers Too Prescriptive, Pens. & Inv. May 10, 2022, www.pionline.com/esg/blackrock-wont-back-climate-shareholder-proposals-it-considers-too-prescriptive.

[78] Clifford, *supra* note 77.

[79] See, e.g., New York City Comptroller Brad Lander, Shareholder Initiatives Postseason Report 2022 (Dec. 2022), at 4, https://comptroller.nyc.gov/reports/shareholder-initiatives-postseason-report/ (explaining that "[t]he [five New York City pension funds and retirement] Systems withdrew approximately 85 percent of their shareholder proposals after the companies receiving the proposals agreed to take steps to implement the request.").

[80] See Sarah C. Haan, Shareholder Proposal Settlements and the Private Ordering of Public Elections, 126 Yale L. J. 262, 282–83 (2016) (describing and criticizing the process of settling shareholder proposals as reducing transparency and increasing agency costs).

receive substantial shareholder support.[81] If issuers are correct in this perception and proposals that are likely to receive substantial shareholder support are settled, support levels for proposals that go to a vote are likely to be depressed. Indeed, given the extensive information available to issuers about how investors are likely to vote on ESG proposals, it is somewhat surprising that issuers allow any proposals to go to a vote that are supported by a majority of shareholders.[82] Nonetheless, as Figure 16.2 indicates, some voted proposals receive majority or even supermajority support. Within our data set, 20 proposals received majority support in 2021, including proposals seeking information on GHG emissions, plastic pollution, and diversity in the workforce. In 2022, 26 proposals received majority support.

The average level of support for environmental proposals was 37 percent. Social proposals fared worse at 27 percent, a difference that is statistically significant at the 99 percent level. More importantly, however, Figure 16.2 demonstrates the substantial variability in the level of support that these proposals received. For convenience, in each histogram below, we report the proportion of the proposals in each year and category (environmental vs social) that were withdrawn. If we treat a withdrawn proposal as being, for practical purposes, equivalent to a proposal that passed with majority support, the picture changes dramatically. Using this alternative measure of success, about two thirds of environmental proposals were successful (67 percent in 2021 and 68 percent in 2022), along with over 30 percent of social proposals (40 percent in 2021 and 32 percent in 2022).[83]

[81] See Ibid. at 294 ("it is reasonable for corporate management to conclude that social and environmental proposals pose a real threat at the shareholder ballot box").

[82] Although ESG shareholder proposals are generally precatory, and directors are not required to take action in response to a proposal that receives majority support, precatory proposals that receive majority support frequently lead boards to take the requested action. Fisch, *supra* note 54 at 122. This response is due, in part, to the policy of proxy advisor Institutional Shareholder Service to recommend against the election of directors who fail to respond to a shareholder proposal that has received majority support. Ibid.

[83] We further note that investors may support the disclosure contemplated by a shareholder proposal even when they do not vote to support it. Common reasons include proposals that are too prescriptive or where an issuer is already making sufficient progress toward providing the requested disclosure. See, e.g., Jamie Smith, Four key takeaways from the 2022 proxy season, Ernst & Young Board Matters, 2022, www.ey.com/en_us/board-matters/four-key-takeaways-from-the-2022-proxy-season ("some investors may have voted against specific shareholder proposals (e.g., because they thought the proposal was too prescriptive or that the company is making sufficient progress under the current circumstances) even if the broader underlying cause or concern (e.g., achieving net zero emissions globally by 2050) is generally aligned with the investors' priorities").

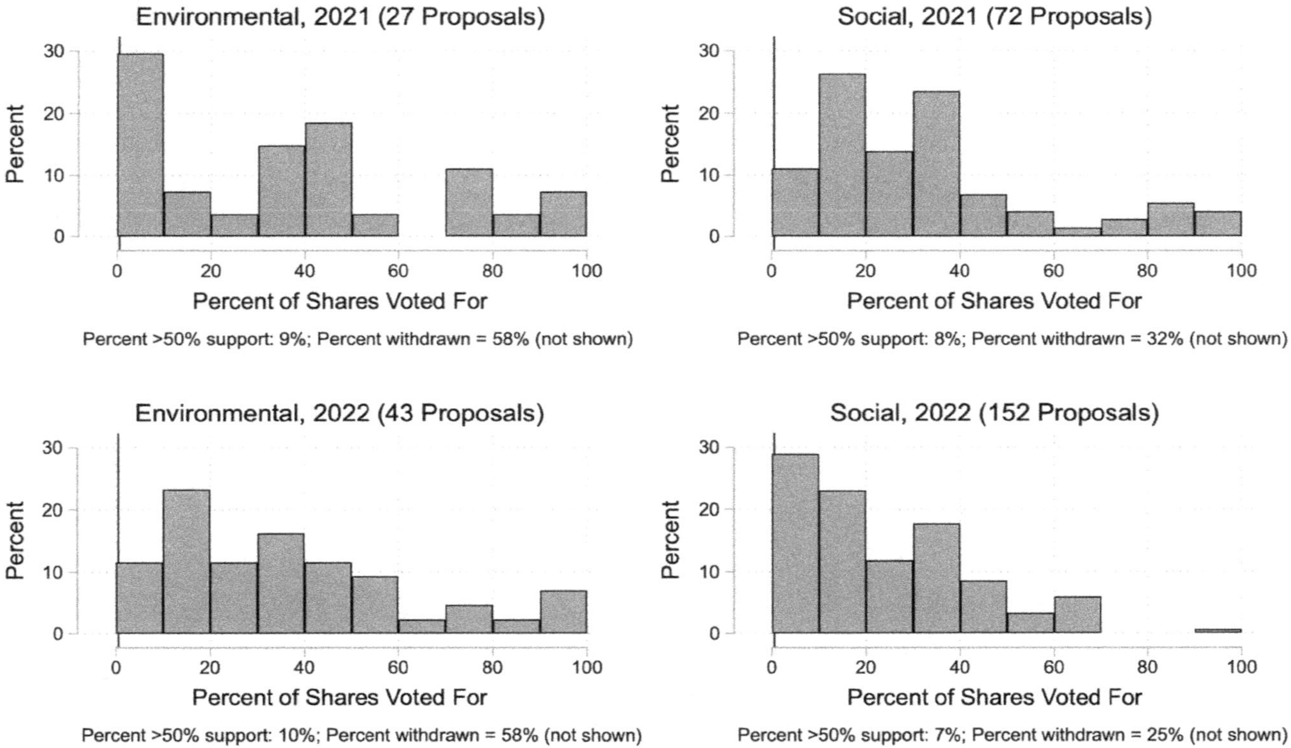

Figure 16.2 Distribution of votes in favor, by year and category

Moving beyond the general statistics, our data provide a detailed window into the types of information investors are seeking through shareholder proposals.[84] Popular topics for shareholder proposals included emissions and pollution data. Shareholders also sought information on issuers' transition plans and the governance structure by which issuers managed their environmental risks. Social proposals often focused on EEO-1 disclosures and racial equity audits. A number of proposals straddled the line between social and governance proposals, including requests for information on board diversity.

Our data contain several environmental proposals directed at issuers in the energy sector, including proposals seeking information on GHG emissions, transition plans and the impact of climate change on business operations. CalPERS, for example, asked ExxonMobil to provide "annual public reporting of the company's greenhouse gas (GHG) emissions across its full value chain, so as to include scopes 1, 2 and 3 emissions." Three different energy issuers were the targets of proposals – from three different proponents – asking for reports relating to flaring, including a request that the Board of Hess "report on if, and how, Hess will curtail its impact on climate change from routine flaring and venting, beyond existing efforts."[85] All three of these proposals were withdrawn. At the same time, environmental proposals were also introduced at a wide range of issuers in other industries, including issuers such as Monster Beverage, Public Storage, and Twitter. The proposal at Twitter, for example, asked the company to disclose its "climate policies, performance, and improvement targets responsive to the indicators set forth in the Net Zero Benchmark, or any rationale for failure to adopt such metrics."[86]

One thing that our data do not speak to is the success of settled proposals or those that received substantial voting support. While we do not have systematic data on this, our ad hoc review yielded mixed

[84] See also Gatti et al., *supra* note 76; Lisa Fairfax, "The Perils and Promise of Shareholders as Stakeholder Advocates," Chapter 7 in this volume.

[85] The proponent was the Vermont Pension Investment Committee. The other two issuers (proponents) were Marathon Oil (the Minnesota State Board of Investment) and PDC Energy (Trinity Health).

[86] The proponent withdrew the proposal at Twitter "given the Company's efforts towards sustainability, including announcing its pledge to set a target validated by the Science Based Targets Initiative and publishing its first Global Impact Report." As You Sow Withdraws its Shareholder Proposal Submitted to Twitter, MarketScreener, May 18, 2021, www.marketscreener.com/quote/stock/TWITTER-INC-38965267/news/As-You-Sow-Withdraws-its-Shareholder-Proposal-Submitted-to-Twitter-33383252/.

results. Some companies do seem to have provided the requested disclosures. For example, the New York City Comptroller's Office reports that eleven corporations agreed to annual public disclosure of their EEO-1 reports in response to the New York City Employees' Retirement System's 2022 shareholder proposals, all of which were settled without going to a vote, and at least some have already made those reports available.[87] Proponents withdrew a proposal that the board of Abbott Laboratories adopt a policy requiring that the company disclose its annual Consolidated EEO-1 Report on its website. Consistent with this proposal, the company's 2021 report is available on its website.[88] Companies have varied, however, in the speed and extent to which they comply. For example, although proponents withdrew an analogous proposal at Netflix, requiring the company to disclose its EEO-1 Report no later than 60 days after the date of its submission to the EEOC, as of mid-February 2023, only the reports through 2020 were available, although by April 2023, Netflix had posted the 2021 report.[89]

Issuer responses to climate-related requests appear to be more mixed. Although US companies appear to lag behind European peers with respect to disclosure of Scope 3 greenhouse gas emissions, and "investors report that Scope 3 estimates are useful for informing their financial decisions,"[90] issuers have resisted investor efforts to obtain greater climate-related disclosure. Both Chubb and Travelers' Insurance Co., for example, sought to exclude proposals asking them "to report whether and how each intends to measure, disclose, and reduce [their greenhouse gas emissions]."[91] In both cases, the SEC required that the proposals be submitted to a shareholder vote and the proposal was supported by a

[87] NYC Comptroller Brad Lander, Shareholder Initiatives Postseason Report 2022, Dec. 21, 2022, https://comptroller.nyc.gov/reports/shareholder-initiatives-postseason-report/. The NYC Comptroller votes the proxies and implements shareholder initiatives for five New York City pension funds and retirement systems including the New York City Employees' Retirement System.

[88] Abbott Labs., 2021 Consolidated EEO-1, https://dam.abbott.com/en-us/documents/pdfs/abbott-citizenship/2021-Consolidated-EEO-1.pdf (last visited Feb. 14, 2023).

[89] Netflix Investors, EEO-1 Reports Section, https://ir.netflix.net/resources/EEO-1-Reports/default.aspx (last visited Apr. 10, 2023).

[90] Shannon M. Lloyd, Maida Hadziosmanovic, Kian Rahimi, & Pankaj Bhatia, Trends Show Companies Are Ready for Scope 3 Reporting with US Climate Disclosure Rule, World Resources Institute, June 24, 2022, www.wri.org/update/trends-show-companies-are-ready-scope-3-reporting-us-climate-disclosure-rule#:~:text=Companies%20from%20other%20Global%20North,CDP%20reported%20Scope%203%20emissions.

[91] As You Sow, SEC Upholds Landmark Shareholder Proposals to Chubb and Travelers Seeking to Reduce Company's Scope 3 Climate Emissions, Mar. 5, 2022, www.asyousow

majority of shareholders.[92] Given the fact that climate-related disclosures may require issuers to collect new information, it is unclear how to determine the appropriate timeframe by which to evaluate issuer responsiveness.[93]

16.5 Lessons from Shareholder Proposals

Although our examination of the data continues, a preliminary analysis suggests several lessons for the SEC in formulating a mandating disclosure policy. First, shareholder demand for greater disclosure of environmental and social information is substantial. In each of the last two years, shareholders submitted hundreds of proposals seeking this information. Second, and perhaps more significantly, many shareholder demands for information are not being met, even when a proposal is withdrawn pursuant to a settlement. This suggests that private ordering is not a perfect substitute for mandatory sustainability disclosure.[94] Rather, this chapter argues that private ordering through shareholder proposals can play a complementary role to SEC-mandated disclosure in addressing the informational needs of shareholders with respect to sustainability issues.

Notably, the information sought by shareholders through the shareholder proposal process differs dramatically across proposals and issuers. Recent proposals have focused on events such as the Business

.org/press-releases/2022/4/5/sec-upholds-shareholder-proposals-chubb-travelers-scope-3-climate-emissions.

92 Ibid. 72.2 percent votes cast supported the proposal at Chubb. Ben Maiden, Chubb shareholders vote for GHG report, Corporate Sec., May 25, 2022, www.corporatesecretary.com/articles/esg/33030/chubb-shareholders-vote-ghg-report. The Travelers' proposal was supported by 55.8 percent of shares voted. As You Sow, Investors Send Greenhouse Gas Reduction Message to National Insurance Companies, June 1, 2022, www.asyousow.org/press-releases/2022/6/1/investors-greenhouse-gas-reduction-message-insurance-companies. See also Vanguard Investment Stewardship Insights – Valero, June 2022, chrome-extension://efaidnbmnnnibpcajpcglclefindmkaj/https://corporate.vanguard.com/content/dam/corp/advocate/investment-stewardship/pdf/perspectives-and-commentary/voting_insights_valero.pdf (noting that, although Vanguard did not vote to support shareholder proposal at Valero, Vanguard encouraged such disclosure during its private engagement "given the apparent materiality of Scope 3 emissions to Valero").

93 See also Haan, *supra* note 80, at 322 (warning of the difficulties in enforcing privately negotiated settlements of shareholder proposals).

94 For a more extensive analysis of the reasons why a disclosure mandate may, in some cases, be preferable to a system of voluntary disclosure, see Lisa M. Fairfax, Dynamic Disclosure: An Exposé on the Mythical Divide Between Voluntary and Mandatory ESG Disclosure, 101 Tex. L. Rev. 273, 304 (2022).

Roundtable's statement on stakeholder governance or the nationwide attention to racial justice following the murder of George Floyd. To a degree, these shareholder proposals appear to serve the function of communicating shareholders' views on current issues of importance. It is less clear whether these issues will remain salient for an extended period of time. As a result, the fact that a large number of shareholder proposals are seeking the same information may not, without more, indicate that a sustained change to issuer disclosure policy through an SEC mandate is warranted.

On the other hand, many proposals seek information consistent with that reflected in the SEC's proposed climate disclosure rule, including information on GHG emissions, issuer transition plans, and the effect of climate risk on operations. Here, shareholder proposals may serve an information-generative function for the SEC as it seeks to formulate disclosure policy.[95] The proposals highlight areas in which common metrics or existing documents facilitate disclosures. The ability of issuers to respond to these requests suggests that the cost of doing so may not be unduly burdensome. And shareholders' supporting statements can provide the SEC with evidence as to how the requested information is relevant from an investment perspective. On the other hand, the burdens of this and other disclosures are likely to differ by issuer size, with larger issuers better able to bear the costs of collecting the relevant information and preparing reports than smaller ones. While our data suggest that there is substantial shareholder demand for sustainability disclosures at large issuers, it does not necessarily follow that the same shareholders think these disclosures are cost-justified at smaller ones. In formulating its mandatory disclosure rules, the SEC could make better use of the information generated through the shareholder proposal process including these important subtleties.

At the same time, the fact that not all issuers comply with these proposals is consistent with two different (not necessarily mutually exclusive) interpretations. On the one hand, it could indicate that producing these reports *is* burdensome to the issuers, or at least, that in the judgment of the board of the issuing company, the cost outweighs any benefit. On the other hand, it may also suggest that shareholders cannot rely on private ordering to obtain the information that they need, or at least want. These alternative interpretations highlight the challenges of

[95] Lisa Fairfax describes voluntary disclosure more broadly as providing a "feedback loop" in which demands identified through voluntary disclosure provide the basis for mandatory rules. Ibid. at 325. She terms this process "dynamic disclosure."

drawing inferences from a complex system in which a large number of players are balancing many competing interests.

These two roles – highlighting new and timely issues and identifying areas in which increased disclosure is becoming mainstream and practical – also have different implications for SEC regulation. Because shareholder proposals can identify and target new issues, there is no reason for SEC regulation to be out ahead of the market and to seek, through mandatory rules, to require disclosures that are not currently being produced, to some degree, through market forces. At the same time, SEC regulation can provide a valuable baseline – standardizing existing disclosure policies and extending those policies to the range of issuers that are not targeted by, or do not comply with, shareholder proposals. Indeed, disclosure mandates are likely necessary to achieve universal and uniform disclosure. The variability in information sought by shareholders suggests that such mandates should be limited to a core set of data, with voluntary disclosure continuing to provide flexibility and responsiveness for a broader range of issues. Both voting support and issuer responses to shareholder requests offer insights into which information is most likely to be valuable and cost-justified.

16.6 Conclusion

Issuers are facing growing demands for sustainability disclosure. In the EU, such disclosure demands are increasingly the product of regulatory mandates. Whether such regulatory mandates will succeed in the U.S. remains to be seen. The SEC has taken the first step to adopting such a mandate through its proposed climate disclosure rule.

Critics of mandated disclosure have argued that regulation is unnecessary because shareholders can obtain adequate sustainability disclosure through private ordering. As evidence that shareholders are not demanding such disclosure, they point to the limited use of the shareholder proposal rule. This chapter demonstrates, contrary to that assertion, that shareholders are making extensive demands for sustainability disclosure through the shareholder proposal rule, that shareholder support for these demands is substantial, and that the demands are successful, in at least some cases, in generating the requested disclosure. At the same time, the data reveal the limitations to the use of shareholder proposals, including the difficulty in extending even apparently successful disclosure demands, to the entire universe of public companies. In modifying the mandatory disclosure regime, the SEC should seek to complement these private ordering efforts.

17

Board-Shareholder Engagement and Disclosure Obligations under Corporate Governance Codes

ANA TALESKA

17.1 Introduction

Corporate governance codes have become widely popular in the last thirty years. Since the adoption of the first set of corporate governance recommendations in the United Kingdom (UK) with the 1992 Code of Best Practices,[1] the introduction of corporate governance codes as self-regulatory, non-binding instruments has expanded across all major corporate governance systems[2] and corporate governance codes have been credited with converging important corporate governance aspects across the Member States of the European Union (EU).[3]

Corporate governance codes typically operate on a comply-or-explain basis. Companies can either follow the code recommendations or explain any departures therefrom. In this manner, it is argued, companies are able to develop optimal governance structures without the rigidity of mandatory rules.

This chapter evaluates board-shareholder engagements within and outside shareholder meetings through the lenses of eleven European corporate governance codes and critically assesses the role and relevance of code recommendations in encouraging and facilitating

[1] *Report of the Committee on the Financial Aspects of Corporate Governance* (London: Gee Publishing, 1992) (1992 Cadbury Report).

[2] See *Study for the European Commission, Comparative Study of Corporate Governance Codes Relevant to the European Union and Its Member States* (Brussels 2002) (Comparative Study on Corporate Governance), 8 (reporting on the wave of adoption of first European corporate governance codes) at https://ecgi.global/code/comparative-study-corporate-governance-codes-relevant-european-union-and-its-member-states (all URLs were last accessed on 7 May 2023, unless otherwise stated); see generally Ruth V. Aguilera and Alvaro Cuervo-Cazura, 'Codes of Good Governance Worldwide: What is the Trigger' (2004) 25 Organization Studies 415. For a comprehensive international database of corporate governance codes, see also https://ecgi.global/content/codes last accessed on 9 September 2002.

[3] Comparative Study on Corporate Governance (n 2), 6.

board-shareholder engagement. The corporate governance codes surveyed herein have been selected to cover codes adopted in jurisdictions with a common law origin (UK), French civil law origin (France, Italy, Belgium, Luxembourg and the Netherlands), German civil law origin (Germany and Austria) and Scandinavian civil law origin (Sweden, Denmark and Norway).

This chapter makes several contributions. First, it provides a structural analysis of the European corporate governance codes surveyed herein and finds that they include different categories of recommendations which vary in important ways in terms of compliance and disclosure by listed companies.

Second, this chapter surveys code recommendations for engagement with shareholders within and outside shareholder meetings. With respect to code recommendations on shareholder engagement within shareholder meetings, it finds that these are largely repetitive of the rights shareholders can exercise in the context of shareholder meetings under EU law and the implementing national laws. As a result, such comply-or-explain recommendations are mostly irrelevant.[4] With respect to code recommendations on shareholder engagement outside the shareholder meeting, this chapter finds that the majority of code recommendations surveyed herein simply recommend that companies and/or boards of directors, engage with shareholders – a best practice that is already widely acknowledged and accepted by listed companies.[5] I argue that due to their generality, these code recommendations have no important effect on the quality or frequency of board-shareholder dialogue and produce suboptimal public information on the company's approach to engagement.

Several European corporate governance codes, however, recommend adoption of a policy on bilateral engagements with shareholders.[6] This chapter argues that such recommendations are a step in the right direction as such policies, on one hand, can convey important information to investors about companies' approach to shareholder engagement (provided such policies are publicly disclosed) and, on the other hand, can help companies and directors develop an approach towards shareholder engagement that is tailored to the needs of the respective company and its investors.[7]

[4] See notes 26 to 49 and accompanying text.
[5] See notes 50 to 55 and accompanying text.
[6] See notes 56 to 70 and accompanying text.
[7] See notes 71 to 93 and corresponding text.

Third, this chapter also contributes to the ongoing debate on the desirability and relevance of European corporate governance codes. In a recent paper Brian Cheffins and Bobby Reddy argue inter alia that the recommendations included in the UK Corporate Governance Code[8] are largely irrelevant and impose net costs on premium listed companies. The authors propose that the UK Corporate Governance Code is abolished and some recommendations are included as disclosure requirements under the Financial Conduct Authority's Listing Rules.[9] Consistent with Brian Cheffins and Bobby Reddy's contribution, this chapter finds that some European code recommendations on shareholder engagement suffer from irrelevance by way of duplication of mandatory legal provisions or by recommending best practices on shareholder engagement that, as a matter of general principle, European-listed companies already widely acknowledge and accept.[10]

17.1.1 Disclosure Requirements under European Corporate Governance Codes

For European-listed companies, code-compliance has been integrated into financial reporting as a matter of EU law. With Directive 2006/46/EC a new requirement was introduced, requiring listed issuers to prepare a corporate governance statement as a separate section in the management report, which should include at least a reference to the corporate governance code to which the issuer is subject, and the corporate governance code, if any, which the issuer applies voluntarily, as well as all relevant information about corporate governance practices that the issuer has implemented and are exceeding the statutory requirements applicable under the relevant national law.[11]

[8] FRC, The UK Corporate Governance Code (London: FRC, 2018) (the UK Corporate Governance Code).

[9] Brian C. Cheffins and Bobby V. Reddy, 'Thirty Years and Done – Time to Abolish the UK Corporate Governance Code', Journal of Corporate Law Studies (2022), available at: https://doi.org/10.1080/14735970.2022.2140496 (Cheffins and Reddy, Thirty Years and Done) (for a response see Piergaetano Marchetti and Maria Lucia Passador, 'Thirty Years and Far from Being Done – Is it Truly Time to Abolish the UK Corporate Governance Code?', Bocconi Legal Studies Research Paper No. 4269661, available at: https://papers.ssrn.com/sol3/papers.cfm?abstract_id=4269661).

[10] Cheffins and Reddy, Thirty Years and Done (n 9), 26–44.

[11] Directive 2006/46/EC of the European Parliament and of the Council of 14 June 2006 amending Council Directives 78/660/EEC on the annual accounts of certain types of companies, 83/349/EEC on consolidated accounts, 86/635/EEC on the annual accounts

Considering the comply-or-explain nature of corporate governance codes, Directive 2006/46/EC further asks issuers that depart from a corporate governance code recommendation, to make detailed disclosures about such departure, including the reasons for non-compliance.[12] Issuers making no reference to any corporate governance code in their corporate governance statement should also explain the reasons therefor.[13]

Interestingly, most of the corporate governance codes surveyed in this chapter include not only comply-or-explain provisions, but also (high-ranking) principles in relation to which listed issuers have to report how they have been complied with[14] or with which listed issuers are simply expected to comply.[15] The comply-or-explain recommendations are then aimed at achieving compliance with these high-ranking principles.[16] However, in some jurisdictions these high-ranking principles are legal requirements, which inherently contradicts the idea of corporate governance codes as a non-statutory instrument operating on a comply-or-explain basis.[17]

and consolidated accounts of banks and other financial institutions and 91/674/EEC on the annual accounts and consolidated accounts of insurance undertakings, Art 46a.

[12] See Directive 2013/34/EU of the European Parliament and of the Council of 26 June 2013 on the annual financial statements, consolidated financial statements and related reports of certain types of undertakings, amending Directive 2006/43/EC, Art 20(1)(b).

[13] Ibid.

[14] Listing Rules Sourcebook, as published by the Financial Conduct Authority pursuant to Financial Services and Markets Act 2000 (FSMA 2000) (UK Listing Rules), rule (LR) 9.8.6 (stating that UK issuers listed on the Premium segment of the London Stock Exchange must include a statement in their annual financial report setting out "how the listed company has applied the Principles set out in the UK Corporate Governance Code, in a manner that would enable shareholders to evaluate how the principles have been applied").

[15] See e.g. Corporate Governance Committee, The 2020 Belgian Code on Corporate Governance (2020) (Belgian Corporate Governance Code) 5. See also, Luxembourg Stock Exchange (LSE), The X Principles of Corporate Governance of the Luxembourg Stock Exchange (Luxembourg: LSE, 2017) (Luxembourg Principles of Corporate Governance).

[16] Ibid.

[17] See Government Commission for Corporate Governance (*Regierungskommission*) (GCCF), German Corporate Governance Code (*Deutscher Corporate Governance Kodex*) (GCCG: 2020) 1, 2 (German Corporate Governance Code) (providing that 'the principles reflect material legal requirements for responsible governance, are used here to inform investors and stakeholders'); see also Austrian Working Group for Corporate Governance, *Austrian Corporate Governance Code* (2021) 11–12 (Austrian Corporate Governance Code).

To add to the complexity of the structure of corporate governance codes, certain codes, in addition to legal requirements and comply-or-explain provisions, also include a third category of non-binding, voluntary 'suggestions' or 'recommendations' in relation to which no compliance or disclosure applies, that is, companies may depart from these provisions without any disclosure or explanation.[18] Even if voluntary, the inclusion of these recommendations in the respective codes may nonetheless result in increased investor and proxy advisor compliance expectations, additionally increasing the compliance and disclosure cost of reporting companies.[19]

In addition to the increased complexity of the structure of European corporate governance codes, the number of principles, comply-or-explain recommendations and voluntary provisions is significant and has grown over time.[20] As illustrated in Table 17.1, the codes adopted in the countries with Scandinavian civil law origin include the lowest number of recommendations, followed by the UK Corporate Governance Code and the codes adopted in German civil law origin countries, whereas the codes adopted in countries with French civil law origin include the highest number of recommendations[21] (for example, the Belgian and Dutch code feature the highest overall number of code recommendations with 10 principles and 123 provisions, and 25 principles and 136 provisions, respectively).[22]

[18] See Luxembourg Principles of Corporate Governance (n 15); German Corporate Governance Code (n 17); Austrian Corporate Governance Code (n 17).

[19] It is reasonable to surmise that this is indeed the desired effect of the introduction of voluntary recommendations in corporate governance codes.

[20] Cheffins and Reddy, Thirty Years and Done (n 9), 5–6 (showing that the number of code provisions and principles has expanded from 19 provision under the Cadbury Code of Best Practice to 18 Principles and 41 Provisions under the 2018 UK Corporate Governance Code (n 8). Another example of expanding number of code recommendations over time is the Belgian Code on Corporate Governance which featured 9 Principles and 87 Provisions under the 2004 version of the Belgian Code on Corporate Governance and 10 Principles and 124 Provisions under the (current 2020) Belgian Code on Corporate Governance.

[21] See the Italian Corporate Governance Committee (ICGC), Corporate Governance Code (ICGC: 2020) (Italian Corporate Governance Code), which is an exception in this respect with (only) 20 principles and 37 recommendations.

[22] Belgian Corporate Governance Code (n 15); Monitoring Committee Corporate Governance Code (MCCG), Corporate Governance Code (CGCM: 2022) (Dutch Corporate Governance Code).

Table 17.1 *Overview of corporate governance codes' characteristics*

Country	Name of code	Year of current (first) version[a]	Issuing body of current version of Code	Code structure (Reporting standard)	Scope
United Kingdom	UK Corporate Governance Code	2018 (1992)	Financial Reporting Council	18 Principles (Mandatory reporting under FCA Listing Rules) 41 Provisions (Comply-or-explain)	Issuers listed on the Premium segment of the London Stock Exchange
France	AFEP-MEDEF Corporate Governance Code of Listed Companies	2020 (2008)	*Association Française des Entreprises Privées* (AFEP) and *Mouvement des Enterprises de France* (MEDEF)	101 Recommendations (Comply-or-explain)	French companies whose shares are admitted to trading on a regulated market in France
Italy	Corporate Governance Code	2020 (1999)	The Italian Corporate Governance Committee	20 Principles 37 Recommendations (Comply-or-explain)	Companies whose shares are listed on the Italian main market, with some recommendations applicable specifically either to large companies with market cap >EUR 1 bn and/or companies with controlling shareholder
Belgium	The 2020 Belgian Code on Corporate Governance	2020 (2004)	Corporate Governance Committee	10 Principles (Listed issuers expected to be in compliance) 123 Provisions (Comply-or-explain)	Belgian companies whose shares are admitted to trading on a regulated market in Belgium

Table 17.1 (*cont.*)

Country	Name of code	Year of current (first) version[a]	Issuing body of current version of Code	Code structure (Reporting standard)	Scope
Luxembourg	The X Principles of Corporate Governance	2017 (2006)	Luxembourg Stock Exchange	10 Principles (mandatory) 96 Recommendations (Comply-or-explain)	Luxembourg companies whose shares are admitted to trading on a regulated market in Luxembourg
The Netherlands	Dutch Corporate Governance Code	2022 (2003)	Corporate Governance Code Monitoring Committee	25 Principles 136 best practice provisions (Comply-or-explain)	Companies whose registered office is in the Netherlands and whose shares are admitted to trading on a regulated market and all large companies with a balance sheet > EUR 500m whose shares are admitted to trading on an MTF
Germany	German Corporate Governance Code	2022 (2002)	Government Commission on Corporate Governance	26 Principles (Mandatory/legal requirements) 61 Recommendations (Comply-or-explain) 6 Suggestions (Voluntary)	Listed companies and companies with access to capital markets pursuant to section 161 (1) sentence 2 of the German Stock Corporation Act

Austria	Austrian Code of Corporate Governance	2023 (2002)	Austrian Working Group for Corporate Governance	43 Legal requirements (L-Rules) (Mandatory) 43 Comply-or-explain (C-Rules) (Comply-or-explain) 4 Recommendation (R-Rules) (Voluntary)	Austrian exchange-listed companies
Sweden	The Swedish Corporate Governance Code	2020 (2004)	Swedish Corporate Governance Board	49 Rules for corporate governance (Comply-or-explain) Explaining provisions	Swedish companies whose shares are listed on a regulated market in Sweden
Norway	The Norwegian Code of Practice for Corporate Governance	2021 (2004)	Norwegian Corporate Governance Board	15 Recommendations (Comply-or-explain) Commentary to recommendations after each recommendation	Norwegian companies that are required by the Norwegian Accounting Act to report on their policies and practices of corporate governance (mainly companies whose shares are listed on regulated markets in Norway)
Denmark	Danish Recommendations on Corporate Governance	2020 (2001)	Danish Committee on Corporate Governance	40 Recommendations (Comply-or-explain) 30 General principles (unnumbered) (explaining the recommendations) 28 Comments to recommendations	Danish companies whose shares are admitted to trading on a regulated market in Denmark

[a]On information of the year of first code adopted in the respective jurisdictions as reflected in Table 17.1 (*Overview of corporate governance codes' characteristics*), see Ruth V. Aguilera and Alvaro Cuervo-Cazurra, 'Codes of Good Governance' (2009) 17(3) Corporate Governance: An International Review 376, 380.

17.2 Board-Shareholder Engagement Under Corporate Governance Codes

Shareholder engagement came to the centre-stage of the European academic and policymaking debate after the 2008 financial crisis and in particular, with the revision of the EU Shareholder Rights Directive. The revision was meant to address the lack of institutional investor engagement with, and monitoring of, corporate management by introducing comply-or-explain obligations for institutional investors and asset managers to adopt and disclose an engagement policy with respect to their investee companies. Such engagement policy should include information, inter alia, on how institutional investors conduct dialogues with investee companies and vote their shares at shareholder meetings.[23]

In carrying out the 2017 reform of the EU Shareholder Rights Directive, however, the European legislator did not consider – in spite of the bilateral nature of engagements – the need to encourage or include reciprocal comply-or-explain recommendations for companies (or their boards) to engage with shareholders.[24] As Sections 17.2.1 and 17.2.2 demonstrate, corporate governance codes have attempted to fill this gap by introducing recommendations for companies or their boards (where applicable), to engage with shareholders within and outside the shareholder meeting as a matter of good corporate governance practice.

17.2.1 Corporate Governance Codes and Board-Shareholder Engagement Within *Shareholder Meetings*[25]

In theory, shareholder meetings provide a useful opportunity for corporate boards to engage with shareholders. Compared to other forms of engagement, however, annual meetings have been viewed as overly scripted, controlled by management, inflexible, and overall, an

23 Directive (EU) 2017/828 of the European Parliament and of the Council of 17 May 2017 amending Directive 2007/36/EC as regards the encouragement of long-term shareholder engagement (EU Shareholder Rights Directive), Article 3(1).

24 The 2017 revision of the EU Shareholder Rights Directive dealt with companies' access to shareholders holding shares via intermediaries by way of introducing rules aimed at improving company access to, and communications with, these shareholders. See EU Shareholder Rights Directive (n 23), Chapter Ia (*Identification of shareholders, transmission of information and facilitation of exercise of shareholder rights*).

25 See Chapter 12 by Bowley et al. in this volume.

inadequate forum for a meaningful and open discussion between the board and shareholders.[26]

Nine of the eleven European corporate governance codes surveyed in this chapter include recommendations relating to the exercise of shareholder rights at shareholder meetings and the information to be provided to shareholders in connection with, and ahead of, meetings.[27] For example, the Luxembourg Principles of Corporate Governance recommend that companies guarantee shareholder participation by way of entering into a dialogue with the board and the executive management of the company and entrust the chairman of the board to ensure that relevant questions raised by shareholders are appropriately answered at the shareholder meeting.[28] In the same vein, under the Belgian Code, companies are expected to provide all relevant information to shareholders for the exercise of their rights and to encourage their participation in shareholder meetings.[29]

A similar picture is presented under the corporate governance codes adopted in the three countries with Scandinavian law origin. The Danish Code provides that the board of directors, when organizing shareholder meetings, should facilitate shareholder participation, voting and raising questions for management at the meeting via proxy (and webcast or other digital transmission).[30] The Norwegian Code of Practice for Corporate Governance provides that the board should ensure shareholder participation at shareholder meetings and, more broadly, that shareholder meetings are organized so as to facilitate dialogue between

[26] See H.S. Brikmose and T. Strand, 'Institutional Investors: The Way to Active Ownership' (2012) Nordic & European Company Law LSN Research Paper Series No. 10-30, 3–4 at: https://papers.ssrn.com/sol3/papers.cfm?abstract_id=2151206 (arguing also that the institutional investors are partly to contribute to this trend as they sidestep the shareholder meetings and prefer to enter into private engagements with investee companies); see also, Lisa M. Fairfax, 'Mandating Board-Shareholder Engagement' (2013) 2013(3) University of Illinois Law Review 821, 844–845 (analysing the reasons why annual shareholder meetings are not more widely used as forums for constructive dialogue with shareholders).

[27] The exceptions are the UK Corporate Governance Code (n 8) and the Italian Corporate Governance Code (n 21).

[28] Luxembourg Principles of Corporate Governance (n 15), recommendation 10.7.

[29] Belgian Corporate Governance Code (n 15), provisions 8.2, 8.3. Provision 8.4 also recommends the chair of the board to provide adequate answers to shareholder questions raised at shareholder meetings.

[30] Danish Commission on Corporate Governance (DCCG), Danish Recommendations on Corporate Governance (DCCG: 2020) (Danish Corporate Governance Code), recommendation 1.2.1.

shareholders and the officers of the company[31] and that sufficiently detailed information in relation to any resolution tabled at the meeting is provided to shareholders so as to enable them to form an informed view on the relevant matter.[32]

The German Code similarly contains recommendations of a general nature relating to the corporate governance role of shareholder meetings and the resolutions the shareholder meeting is typically called to vote upon[33] whereas the Austrian Code includes legal requirements relating to the organization of shareholder meetings, which include, inter alia, the statutory deadlines for calling the meeting, submission of director candidate slates and publication of voting results.[34]

The aforementioned code recommendations on shareholder engagement within shareholder meetings, however, are largely duplicative or even narrower in scope and content than the legal rules on shareholder rights and shareholder engagement at shareholder meetings set out in the EU Shareholder Rights Directive and the national laws implementing the EU Shareholder Rights Directive. In fact, the EU Shareholder Rights Directive already goes much further in terms of guaranteeing shareholder participation in shareholder meetings than the code recommendations surveyed in the preceding paragraphs. First, it provides that the convocation notice and the agenda of the meeting are circulated no later than on the 21st day prior to the day of the meeting[35], thus guaranteeing an adequate time for shareholders to familiarize themselves with the agenda items and plan their attendance. Second, the Directive ensures that a single record date applies to all companies in each EU Member State and that no transfer restrictions are applicable in the period between the record date and the date of the meeting and that the shareholder right to participation in the meeting is not conditioned on their shares being deposited prior to the meeting.[36] Third, the Directive provides that convocation should include at least a prescribed set of information on the venue, agenda and relevant documents for the meeting, description of procedures that have to be observed for shareholder participation and vote at the meeting (including proxy voting, voting by correspondence or

[31] Norwegian Corporate Governance Board (NCGB), The Norwegian Code of Practice of Corporate Governance (Norwegian Corporate Governance Code) (NCGB: 2021), recommendation 6.

[32] Ibid. [33] German Corporate Governance Code (n 17), principle 8.

[34] Austrian Corporate Governance Code (n 17), section II (*Shareholders and the General Meeting*), rules 1–8.

[35] EU Shareholder Rights Directive (n 23), Article 5(1). [36] Ibid., Article 7(1).

by electronic means), and the rights pertaining to shareholders in the context of a shareholder meeting that are deemed to enable an informed shareholder participation at the shareholder meeting.[37] Fourth, the catalogue of shareholder rights that can be exercised at shareholder meetings under the EU Shareholder Rights Directive, such as, amongst others, the right to put items on the agenda of the shareholder meeting[38], individual and collective submission of shareholder-sponsored resolutions,[39] the right to ask questions[40] in relation to the agenda of the meeting and the right to participate digitally,[41] is significantly broader and more comprehensive than corporate governance code recommendations on engagement within shareholder meetings.

One of the main avenues for board-shareholder engagement at shareholder meetings are shareholder-sponsored proposals included in the agenda and voted at shareholder meetings. Shareholder proposals in Europe are binding on the company (if passed) and can be submitted by a holder of a qualifying position which – as a matter of EU law – may not be higher than 5 percent of the share capital of the company.[42] The grounds for exclusion of shareholder-sponsored proposals are very limited and importantly, shareholder proposals may also relate to sponsoring director nominees for election at shareholder meetings.[43]

The binding nature of European proposals coupled, where applicable, with more stringent ownership requirements lead to shareholder proposals being tabled much less frequently in Europe than in the US, where the respective proxy rules on submission of shareholder proposals

[37] Ibid, Article 5(3). Relevant information as set forth in the EU Shareholder Rights Directive should also be disclosed on the company's website, including the number of shares having the right to vote at the relevant shareholder meeting.

[38] EU Shareholder Rights Directive (n 23), Article 6. [39] Ibid. [40] Ibid., Article 9.

[41] Ibid., Article 8. [42] Ibid., Article 6(2).

[43] Under section 338 of the UK Companies Act, a resolution may be properly moved at an annual shareholder meeting, unless (i) it would, if passed, be ineffective (whether by reason of inconsistency with any enactment or with the company's constitution or otherwise) (ii) it is defamatory of any person or (iii) it is frivolous or vexatious. Under Luxembourg law, no specific grounds for exclusion of shareholder proposals are set out in the law implementing the EU Shareholder Rights Directive. The board of directors has a competence on all matters not reserved to the shareholders pursuant to the law or the articles or association and has the power to carry out and approve all acts and operations consistent with the company's corporate object. The directors, however, will incur personal liability for taking actions that are inconsistent with the law or the company's articles of association (see section 441-9, §2 of the Luxembourg law of 10 August 1915 on commercial companies, as amended) and therefore, one may expect ineffective proposals to be excluded by the board of directors.

"emphasize shareholder participation and protection rather than empowerment".[44]

Corporate governance codes have increasingly come to call for early engagement with shareholders on issues on which a (potential) shareholder-sponsored proposal is or may be tabled.[45] Corporate boards are also expected – as a matter of best corporate governance practice – to engage on proposals which, while not reaching the required majority to pass at a shareholder meeting, have received significant shareholder support or dissent. For example, the UK Corporate Governance Code provides that the board should explain how it intends to consult with shareholders in relation to a management recommendation for a resolution for which at least 20 percent of shareholder votes were cast against the recommendation, in order to understand the reasons for such voting outcome. The board should also publish an update on the shareholders' views and any actions taken by the board in relation thereto within six months after the relevant shareholder meeting.[46]

The Dutch Corporate Governance Code recommends that shareholders consult with management, before they can exercise their right to put items on the agenda of the shareholder meeting. If the item to be put on the agenda by one or more shareholders may result in a change in the company's strategy, by way, for example, of removing supervisory or management board members, the Code envisages that, save for certain limited exceptions, a reasonable response time is first given to the management board which may not exceed 180 days.[47] During the response time, the management board should engage and consult with the relevant shareholders and at the end of such response time, the management board is expected to report to the shareholder meeting on the engagement with the shareholders, including the consideration and exploration of alternative approaches with the relevant shareholders.

In summary, the European code recommendations relating to shareholder engagement within shareholder meetings are duplicative of the more elaborate statutory rights and organizational requirements for shareholder meetings set out under the EU Shareholder Rights

[44] Bonnie Buchanan et al., 'Shareholder Proposals and Practice: Evidence from Comparison of the United States and United Kingdom' (2012) 49(4) American Business Law Journal 739, 741.

[45] See Chapter 11 in this volume by Gatti et al. on this point.

[46] UK Corporate Governance Code (n 8), provision 4.

[47] Dutch Corporate Governance Code (n 22), recommendations 4.1.6, 4.1.7.

Directive and the respective implementing national laws of EU Member States. As such, these code recommendations are of no relevance for the engagement of companies and corporate boards with shareholders. The bodies entrusted with the issuance and updating of European corporate governance codes should consider removing these recommendations and replacing them with best practice provisions that will encourage shareholder engagement beyond legal requirements or general well-accepted best practices. A good example in this respect is the UK Financial Reporting Counsel's Good Practice Guidance for Company Meetings which can be voluntarily applied by companies and includes seven principles that companies can apply that go beyond the statutory rules applicable to holding shareholder meetings.[48] For example, under the FRC Guidance, companies may report at the annual shareholder meetings on matters raised by shareholders and stakeholders throughout the year and explain how such matters have been taken into account by the board or influenced its decision-making.[49]

17.2.2 Corporate Governance Codes and Board-Shareholder Engagement Outside *Shareholder Meetings*

Meaningful and effective engagement has become synonymous with (private) meetings in which boards and shareholders discuss corporate affairs of shareholder interest in a candid and open manner. All 11 European corporate governance codes analysed in this chapter recommend that the company or the board of directors encourages (and seeks) engagement with shareholders. There are generally two approaches that codes follow in terms of formulating recommendations on shareholder engagement outside the shareholder meeting.

Under the first, more common, approach, a best practice provision is included in the respective code providing that the company or the corporate board (as applicable) should engage with shareholders.

For example, the UK Corporate Governance Code recommends, as a (high-ranking) principle, that the board should ensure effective engagement with, and encourage participation from, shareholders and stakeholders so that the company would meet its responsibilities towards these parties. The task of regular engagement is delegated to the chair of the

[48] FRC, Good Practice Guidance for Company Meetings (London: FRC, 2022), principles 1, 2, 4.
[49] Ibid., principle 3.

board who should seek engagement with major shareholders in order to solicit their views on governance and strategy and is expected to convey the shareholders' views to the board as a whole.[50] Committee chairs are also expected to seek engagement with shareholders "on significant matters related to their areas of responsibility".[51]

The French AFEP-MEDEF Corporate Governance Code of Listed Companies recommends that relations with shareholders can be assigned to the chair of the board or to the lead independent director, who then reports on this matter to the board of directors.[52] Similarly, under the Swedish Corporate Governance Code, the chair of the board is entrusted with board-shareholder engagement and with reporting on exchanges with shareholders to the board.[53] Under the Belgian Corporate Governance Code, the board should ensure an effective dialogue with shareholders and potential shareholders via adequate investor relations programs so as to understand their objectives and concerns.[54] In light of the predominantly concentrated ownership structure of Belgian companies, the Code further recommends that corporate boards encourage controlling shareholders to communicate their strategic objectives in a timely manner to the board and to discuss whether to enter into a relationship agreement with the company.[55]

Under the second, less frequently used approach, a recommendation that the company or the corporate board adopts a corporate policy on shareholder engagement is included in the respective code. For example, the Luxembourg Principles of Corporate Governance recommend that listed companies "define a policy of active communication with shareholders and establish a related structured set of practices".[56] Similarly, the Dutch Corporate Governance Code recommends that companies develop an outline policy on bilateral contacts with shareholders and that such policy is disclosed on the company's website.[57]

[50] UK Corporate Governance Code (n 8), provision 3. See also FRC, Guidance on Board Effectiveness (London: FRC 2018), 3.

[51] Ibid.

[52] Association *Française des Entreprises Privées* (AFEP) and *Mouvement des Enterprises de France* (MEDEF), AFEP-MEDEF Corporate Governance Code of Listed Companies (AFEP, MEDEF: 2020), section 4.2.

[53] Swedish Corporate Governance Board, *Swedish Corporate Governance Code* (2021) (Swedish Corporate Governance Code), subsection 6.3.

[54] Belgian Corporate Governance Code (n 15), provision 8.1.

[55] Ibid., provision 8.5.

[56] Luxembourg Principles of Corporate Governance (n 15), principle 10.

[57] Dutch Corporate Governance Code (n 22), provision 4.2.2.

Norwegian-listed companies are also required to develop guidelines for communication with shareholders outside the shareholder meeting, specifying if the dialogue with shareholders is delegated to the chair of the board, the CEO or any other executive member.[58]

The Danish code recommends allocating the primary role for shareholder engagement to management, which engages in an "ongoing dialogue and interaction" with shareholders and stakeholders whereas the board must be given the possibility of getting acquainted with, and taking into consideration, shareholders' views.[59] It further recommends that that the company adopts policies on the company's relationship with its shareholders and that such policy is made available on the company's website. From the commentary to this recommendation, however, it appears that the company's investor relations policy may also satisfy this requirement by describing "the type of information the company must publish and in which languages, and how, when and to whom publication takes place".[60]

The Italian code recommends that the board of directors promotes a dialogue with shareholders[61] and adopts a policy on shareholder engagement, upon proposal of the chair of the board and in consultation with the CEO.[62] The policy on engagement with shareholders should be described in the corporate governance report and should take into account the engagement policies adopted by institutional investors and asset managers.[63]

Codes in the jurisdictions of German-legal origin, however, shy away from recommending that (supervisory) boards facilitate dialogue. Yet, they encourage shareholder engagement on a comply-or-explain basis and include voluntary recommendations – which do not require disclosure or an explanation in the event of non-compliance[64] – relating to the company's communications with shareholders. For example, the Austrian Corporate Governance Code sets out a voluntary recommendation that the company regularly holds conference calls or similar information events for analysts and investors but does not articulate a separate

[58] Norwegian Corporate Governance Code (n 31), recommendation 13.
[59] Danish Corporate Governance Code (n 30), recommendation 1.1.1.
[60] Ibid., recommendation 1.1.2 and comment thereto.
[61] Italian Corporate Governance Code (n 21), principle IV.
[62] Ibid., recommendation 3. [63] Ibid.
[64] Austrian Corporate Governance Code (n 17), 12.

comply-or-explain recommendation for the (supervisory) board to engage and facilitate dialogue with shareholders.[65]

Similarly, in the 2017 edition of the German Corporate Governance Code, a 'suggestion' was included recommending that "the supervisory board should be available – within reasonable limits – to discuss supervisory board related issues with investors".[66] This same provision was initially proposed as a recommendation on a comply-or-explain basis, but in the final version of the Code was 'recharacterized' as a 'suggestion' (the compliance with which is entirely voluntary and does not require disclosure or an explanation in the event of non-compliance). The same voluntary suggestion is set out in the current 2022 version of the German Code.[67] A lack of consensus in Germany on the merits of recommending supervisory boards to engage, and facilitate dialogue, with investors may explain the voluntary nature of the recommendation on board-shareholder dialogue under the current German Code.[68] Nonetheless, a working group consisting of representatives of the business community, investors and academia subsequently adopted voluntary Guiding principles for the dialogue between investors and German supervisory boards, which include principles setting out the issues that can be discussed between German supervisory boards and shareholders (such as board composition and nomination and remuneration of supervisory and management board members, matters relating to the internal organization of the supervisory board and oversight etc).[69]

[65] Austrian Corporate Governance Code (n 17), R-75.

[66] German Corporate Governance Code (n 17), suggestion A.6.

[67] Klaus J. Hopt, 'The Dialogue between the Chairman of the Board and Investors: The Practice in the UK, the Netherlands and Germany and the Future of the German Corporate Governance Code under the New Chairman' (2017) ECGI Law Working Paper N 365/2017, 5; see also *Guiding principles for the dialogue between investors and German supervisory boards* (2016) 2 (German Guiding Principles).

[68] See Wolf-Georg Ringe, 'Stewardship and Shareholder Engagement in Germany' (2021) 87 European Business Organization Law Review 96–106 (surveying the reasons why no stewardship code has been put in place in Germany and generally, the reluctant approach towards corporate engagement in Germany); see also Eddy Wymeersch, 'The Enforcement of Corporate Governance Codes' (2006) 113 Journal of Corporate Law Studies 114 (explaining in note 4 the governmental involvement in the development and adoption of the corporate governance codes in Germany, the Netherlands and Sweden).

[69] German Guiding Principles (n 67). Under the Guidance, the supervisory board may also involve the management board in the dialogue with shareholders and when deciding upon the "basic principles of the content and format of the dialogue with investors"; see principles 7 and 8.

In summary, code recommendations on shareholder engagement under European corporate governance codes include either a general best practice provision that the corporate board (or the company, more generally) should engage with shareholders or recommend the adoption (and disclosure) of a corporate policy on shareholder engagement.[70] The first approach gives flexibility for boards and companies to decide on adequate forms and timing of exchanges with shareholders but recommendations simply providing – as a general principle – that corporate boards should engage with shareholders without further specifying when and how engagement with shareholders shall occur and/or suggesting the adoption of a corporate policy of shareholder engagement to deal with the relevant aspects of shareholder engagement would be fairly easy for companies to comply with, even if the engagement practices of such companies and their respective communication channels with shareholders are suboptimal. Further, under this approach, no information is disclosed to shareholders in terms of how the company or the board, as applicable, intends to engage or has engaged with shareholders. In light of the foregoing, several European codes go one step further and recommend the adoption and disclosure of a corporate policy on shareholder engagement as a best practice in the context of shareholder engagement.

Another line of differentiation between code recommendations relating to shareholder engagement outside shareholder meetings is the level of involvement of corporate boards in shareholder engagement. As illustrated in this part, while some code recommendations – as a matter of best practice – explicitly entrust (and call on) the board of directors to engage directly with shareholders and/or to adopt a policy on shareholder engagement, other code recommendations envisage a leading role of management in the engagement with shareholders. Since the central function of the board in the corporate governance of modern corporations is to monitor management and the overall strategy of the company, having the board of directors in the lead on engagements (and direct contact) with shareholders is justifiably considered best corporate governance practice. This is in contrast to the more traditional approach where management was responsible for engagement with

[70] See on this Giovanni Strampelli, 'Knocking at the Boardroom Door: A Transatlantic Overview of Director-Institutional Investor Engagement in Law and Practice' (2018) 187 Virginia Law & Business Review 187–241 (Strampelli, Knocking at the Boardroom Door).

shareholders primarily via investor relations programs, and shareholders had no direct access to directors. As illustrated in this part, a few corporate governance codes have in recent years been reversing this trend by recommending either that the chair of the board and/or the (lead) independent director are designated as responsible for shareholder engagement or that the board of directors adopts a policy on bilateral engagement with shareholders.

In the next part, I analyse the case for adopting a corporate policy on shareholder engagement. I also discuss how the corporate policies on shareholder engagement already adopted by European listed companies in compliance with the applicable code recommendations differ with respect to the internal structuring of the engagement process and more generally, the delegation of the engagement function between corporate leaders (directors and management).

17.3 The Cafe for a Corporate Policy on Shareholder Engagement

There can be numerous benefits for corporate boards from a constructive and open dialogue with shareholders. First, the board of directors can educate investors on their views, policies and processes with respect to business strategy, performance, governance and sustainability considerations. Second, shareholders can themselves educate boards via engagement on the approach they take in evaluating the strategy, performance and risk, capital structure, sustainability matters and the governance of the investee company as well as on any concerns they may have in relation thereto. The board can then take the shareholder views into consideration as part of its decision-making process. Third, engagement opens lines of communication and ongoing dialogue which can build a relationship between boards and shareholders, enhance trust among them and, ultimately, be critical for the long-term success of the company.

Since the 2008 financial crisis, institutional investors are facing an increasing pressure from policymakers and their own beneficial owners to overcome apathy, step up engagement and exercise their stewardship duties in alignment with their investment strategy and the long-term interests of beneficial owners. The extensive comply-or-explain obligations imposed on institutional investors and asset managers under the EU Shareholder Rights Directive and the voluntary stewardship codes adopted in several European Member States are illustrative of this trend. Albeit grudgingly at the start, more and more institutional investors and asset managers are taking their stewardship roles seriously and demand dialogue with companies.[71]

Even though – as outlined above – companies may themselves, at least in theory, benefit from engagement, they (and their board members) also face various costs, risks and limitations if they are to engage with shareholders. For instance, non-executive directors often lack sufficient time to regularly meet and engage with shareholders, considering their part-time role on the board and the monitoring tasks they are otherwise entrusted with. Director engagement with shareholders is also not a risk-free exercise as directors should not only be well-prepared on the topics to be discussed with shareholders so as to be able to engage appropriately on the issues on the (pre-agreed) agenda, but should navigate shareholder communications carefully so as not to violate the transparency and disclosure obligations of public companies. These arise primarily under the EU Market Abuse Regulation[72,73] for European listed companies. More importantly, engagement allows shareholders to exercise their monitoring function over management more effectively, which may result in increasing managerial accountability. As such, opposition from management on the grounds that boards are overwhelmed with other tasks and should not be overburdened with shareholder engagement, that the presence of board members at meetings with shareholders is unnecessary, or that engagement efforts with shareholders are overly risky from the

[71] In the U.S., the 'Fifth Analyst Call' initiative is one example of a group of shareholders asking for a separate annual call with the company, the chair and the independent lead director, in advance of the general meeting to discuss corporate governance issues and any questions they have in connection with the proxy statement. See Scott Hirst, 'Fifth Analyst Call: Investors Seek Greater Communication with Directors' Harvard Law School Forum on Corporate Governance (20 March 2011), at: https://corpgov.law.harvard.edu/2011/03/20/the-fifth-analyst-call-investors-seek-greater-communication-with-directors/. Some U.K. companies also already hold so-called 'Annual Governance Meetings' where investors have the opportunity to engage on various corporate governance-related matters with the board. See GlaxoSmithKline, Annual Report 2021, Corporate Governance, www.gsk.com/en-gb/investors/shareholder-information/annual-governance-meeting/ (providing details about the Annual Governance Meeting it held with investors in 2021).

[72] See the charter by Klöhn.

[73] Regulation 596/2014 of the European Parliament and of the Council of 16 April 2014 on Market Abuse (Market Abuse Regulation) and Repealing Directive 2003/6/EC of the European Parliament and of the Council and Commission Directives 2003/124/EC, 2003/125/EC and 2004/72/EC, 2014 O.J. (L 173/1).

perspective of disclosure and insider trading rules may be overstated and reflective of a self-serving managerial behaviour.[74]

True, there are reasonable constraints in terms of board availability to engage with shareholders and board members cannot be expected to accommodate every request for a private meeting without making its own assessment of the purpose and utility of such engagement. However, requests from large long-term shareholders or a group of major shareholders interested in discussing corporate governance or strategy-related issues would most likely merit boards' time and attention. Second, there are matters on which shareholders – in accordance with the exercise of their stewardship duties – would more appropriately engage and such engagements would be more informative if held with executive management, unless wider presence from directors and senior executives that have participated in the development and implementation of the policies and plans discussed at the meeting would also be warranted.[75]

From this perspective, shareholders can certainly better manage their engagement efforts and expectations if companies have a clear policy on shareholder engagement. Such policy may include the communication channels between companies and shareholders, such as the type of events to be held with investors during a financial year (e.g. events open to all shareholders, private meetings, meetings and events limited to a certain type or size of shareholders), and the instances when one-way or two-way communications would be more adequate.[76] Shareholder engagement policies can also set out the matters that can be discussed, relative to the type of engagement and the time of the financial year when the meeting takes place, that is, within, or outside of, the proxy season, and ensure consistency across the messages the company communicates with shareholders and market participants. The policy can also extend to shareholder engagement efforts that companies may take during or after the shareholder meeting, including the company approach on inquiries and questions from shareholders, engagements in relation to shareholder proposals that receive significant support from shareholders but are not

[74] See Fairfax (n 26) (analysing the objections that have been put forward for increased board-shareholder engagement).

[75] See Strampelli, Knocking at the Boardroom Door (n 70), 225–239 (offering a proposal for a practical framework for board-shareholder dialogue).

[76] Ibid., 206–225 (analysing the legal restrictions on director engagements with institutional investors arising out of disclosure and insider trading laws from a U.S. and European perspective and finding that such legal restrictions do not prevent altogether director-investor dialogue to occur).

passed and management proposals that receive significant opposition votes from shareholders, engagements with activist investors, controlling, significant and minority shareholders, and engagement with proxy advisors.

As previously described, some of these matters are already covered in various voluntary guidance instruments developed by coalitions of executives and associations of businesses and investment management firms, academic members and/or government-supported bodies. These initiatives can be critical in developing and promoting good corporate governance standards for corporate polices on shareholder engagement. In their absence, there is a risk that corporate policies on shareholder engagement, even if mandated by a comply-or-explain code recommendation, will continue being nothing more than a collection of general statements on the value of board-shareholder engagement with little to no informative value for active shareholders seeking a dialogue with the company. Good examples are the Shareholder-Director Exchange (SDX) Protocol, and its adaptation to the Italian civil law system, and the Italian Shareholder-Director Exchange (I-SDX), which are particularly informative for Italian companies willing to develop a sound and comprehensive shareholder engagement policy.[77] The I-SDX recommends that the corporate procedures for organizing a dialogue with investors include: the criteria for establishing board-shareholder dialogue, issues on which companies and boards have an interest in engaging in dialogue, practical aspects as to how investors can express their interest and initiate a dialogue, criteria for determining the participants to the dialogue, instructions on how to prepare for a dialogue, internal reporting processes in relation to engagements with shareholders, annual/biannual or other periodic programs for engagement with particular categories of investors and procedures for updating the corporate policy on shareholder engagement.

The corporate policies on shareholder engagement of some of the largest Italian-listed companies seem to implement most of the principles set out in the I-SDX protocol. Firstly, these policies seem to clearly differentiate between investor relations programs conducted by the investor relations departments (and management) and the engagement

[77] I-SDX Italian Shareholder Director Exchange *Principi italiani di shareholder-director engagement* (Assogestioni: 2022), at: www.assogestioni.it/sites/default/files/docs/isdx-principi.pdf.

of directors with shareholders.[78] On the latter type of engagement, the individual corporate policies of Italian-listed companies typically set out the topics on which the company has an interest to engage with shareholders (typically within the competence of the board of directors)[79] and the type of interaction that the board intends to have with shareholders, that is, one-way or two-way engagements and bilateral or collective engagements.[80] The overall responsibility for engagement with shareholders is entrusted to the chair of the board and the CEO,[81] who decide on whether to accept or reject an engagement and handle the dialogue with shareholders. Some engagement policies designate specific directors to directly engage with shareholders, typically the directors performing also the functions of CEO or CFO.[82] The investor relations department typically assists the chair of the board and the CEO in the management of the engagement and in setting up meetings and events with shareholders.[83] The engagement policies also include provisions on the internal reporting process with respect to shareholder engagement,[84] monitoring and updating of the corporate policy on shareholder engagement as well as timing of engagements and closed periods.[85]

78 Amplifon, Investor Relations & Shareholder Engagement Policy (2020), available at: https://corporate.amplifon.com/content/dam/amplifon/archive/en/governance/other-corporate-documents/2021/Engagemnt%20Policy.pdf, section 2 and section 3 (Amplifon Policy); see also Gruppo Mondadori, Management Policy for Engagement with Shareholders and Other Interested Parties (2021) available at: www.gruppomondadori.it/content/uploads/2022/01/Management-policy-for-engagement-with-holders-and-other-interested-parties.pdf (Mondadori Policy), 5. Some corporate policies deal with board-shareholder engagement only and a separate policy is adopted with respect to investor relations. See Banca Popolare di Sondrio, Policy for the Dialogue between Directors and Shareholders (2022), available at: https://istituzionale.popso.it/en/investor-relations/dialogue-directors-shareholders (Sondrio Policy), 5.

79 See e.g. Mondadori Policy (n 78), 6; Sondrio Policy (n 78), 9.

80 See e.g. Mondadori Policy (n 78), 10; Sondrio Policy (n 78), 9.

81 See e.g. ACEA Group, Policy for the Management of Dialogue with Institutional Investors and with the Generality of Shareholders and Bondholders (2021), available at: www.gruppo.acea.it/content/dam/acea-corporate/acea-foundation/pdf/en/company/governance/engagement-policy.pdf (Acea Policy), 7; AEFFE, Policy for Managing Dialogue with the Shareholders of Aeffe S.p.a, available at: https://aeffe.com/documents/001_HeaderMenuDocuments/021_Governance/004_Statuto%20Aeffe/Inglese/01/010_Policy%20for%20managing%20dialogue%20with%20Shareholders.pdf, 3; Sondrio Policy (n 78), 8.

82 See e.g. Mondadori Policy (n 78), 11.

83 See e.g. Acea Policy (n 81), 7; Amplifon Policy (n 78), 7; Mondadori Policy (n 78), 7.

84 See e.g. Amplifon Policy (n 78), 10.

85 See e.g. Acea Policy (n 81), 7; Amplifon Policy (n 78), 10; Mondadori Policy (n 78), 14–15; Sondrio Policy (n 78), 11.

Unlike the Italian Code, which recommends that the board of directors (upon the proposal of the board chair in agreement with the CEO) adopt a policy for managing the dialogue with the shareholders, the Dutch Code does not set out a specific role for the board in the engagement with shareholders as it recommends that companies should formulate an outline policy on bilateral contacts with shareholders and that it is up to the management board (which in a two-tier board structure is entrusted with performing the executive functions of the board and is appointed and monitored by the supervisory board) to draw up such policy. The company is expected to facilitate the dialogue, unless, in the opinion of the management board, this is not in the interest of the company.

Consequently, the corporate policies on bilateral engagement with shareholders adopted by some of the largest Dutch-listed companies in compliance with the Dutch Code are effectively investor relations policies rather than policies on the engagement of directors (supervisory board members) with shareholders. The task to engage with shareholders is typically assigned to the investor relations director, management board members and/or the CEO.[86] Express requests from shareholders to meet with board members are in principle also dealt with (and decided by) the CEO[87] and exceptionally, by the chairman of the board in consultation with the CEO.[88] In limited instances the policy provides that the

[86] See e.g. Adyen, Disclosure and Bilateral Dialogue Policy (2022), available at: https://investors.adyen.com/governance#documents (Adyen Policy), section 2.9; Argenx, Policy on bilateral contacts with shareholders (2021), available at: www.argenx.com/sites/default/files/media-documents/argenx_bilateral_shareholder_contact_policy.pdf (Argenx Policy), section 3 (providing that "it is the policy of the company that only the CEO, the VP Investor Relations and any persons authorized by (one of) the aforementioned persons specifically [. . .] are authorized to have substantive discussions about any aspect of the company's business, or speak on behalf of the company"); Pepco Group, Policy on Bilateral Contacts with Shareholders and other Investors (2021), available at: www.pepcogroup.eu/wp-content/uploads/2023/10/Bilateral_Contacts_with_Shareholders_and_other_Investors.pdf (Pepco Policy), section 2.4; ASM, Policy regarding Communications and Bilateral Contacts with Shareholders (2021), available at: www.asm.com/investors/corporate-governance-documents, 1.

[87] See e.g. Adyen Policy (n 86), section 3.6; Argenx Policy (n 86), section 3 (providing that "a request of a shareholder to meet with one or more members of the board shall be assessed by the CEO, with the exception of matters that relate to the integrity of the CEO or a (potential) situation of a conflict of interest, in which case the assessment will be referred to the chairperson of the board).

[88] See e.g. JDE Peet's, Policy on Bilateral Contacts with Shareholders (2022), available at: www.jdepeets.com/contentassets/775a0693629f4e8985f1c7c8d50c2f6e/jde-peets—bilateral-contacts-policy-march-2022.pdf (JDE Peet's Policy), section 1.7; Universal Music

management board should inform the supervisory board on the process and content of any bilateral dialogue with shareholders.[89] Further, the policies typically provide that the company will decide at its own discretion whether to accept engagement requests from shareholders and in so doing may ask the requesting shareholder to provide additional information in writing on the purpose and the topics to be covered during the meeting with the company so that the company can make an informed decision on whether to engage.[90] Several policies provide that no bilateral engagements with shareholders will take place during closed periods.[91]

Interestingly, in Dutch companies with major shareholder(s) where a separate agreement is entered into between the major/controlling shareholder(s) and the company, the policy explicitly mentions that communications between the company and these shareholders shall be carried out in accordance with the respective relationship agreement that is put in place, and that the corporate policy on shareholder engagement shall not apply to communications with these shareholders.[92]

The aforementioned differences between the policies adopted by the Italian and Dutch companies in compliance with the respective code recommendations, show that code governance (and in the Italian case, voluntary instruments developed by institutional investor associations such as the I-SDX) can be of critical importance for the structuring of the dialogue with shareholders outside shareholder meetings.[93]

Group, Policy on Bilateral Contacts with Shareholders (2021), available at: https://investors.universalmusic.com/governance/ (Universal Music Group Policy), section 3.2.

89 See e.g. Adyen Policy (n 86), section 3.7.

90 See e.g. Ahold Delhaize, Policy on Communications and Bilateral Contacts with Shareholders (2009), available at: www.aholddelhaize.com/media/qhylhmkr/ahold-delhaize-policy-on-communications-and-bilateral-contacts-with-shareholders.pdf, 3; Signify, Policy on Bilateral Contacts with Investors and Sell-side Analysts (2021), available at: www.signify.com/static/shareholder-info/bilateral-contacts-policy.pdf, section 4; Adyen Policy (n 86), section 3.4; Argenix Policy (n 86), section 3, JDE Peet's Policy (n 88), section 1.5.

91 See e.g. Fugro, Policy on Bilateral Contacts (2022), available at: www.fugro.com/investors/shares/policy-on-bilateral-contacts; Adyen Policy (n 86), section 2.10.

92 See Pepco Policy (n 86), section 4.1; Universal Music Group Policy (n 88), section 5; Signify Policy, section 5 (providing that "[t]his policy does not apply to the contacts between the Company and Koninklijke Philips N.V").

93 For completeness, see also Association of Italian Joint Stock Companies (Assonime), Principles for Listed Companies' Dialogue with Investors (19 July 2021), available at: www.assonime.it/_layouts/15/Assonime.CustomAction/GetPdfToUrl.aspx?PathPdf=https://www.assonime.it/attivita-editoriale/studi/Documents/cir023021.pdf.

17.4 Conclusion

This chapter has reviewed 11 European corporate governance codes and posited that comply-or-explain recommendations on engagement with shareholders generally have no important effect on the quality or frequency of board-shareholder dialogue and produce suboptimal public information on the company's approach to engagement.

This is because code recommendations for board-shareholder engagement *within* shareholder meetings are largely duplicative of the shareholder rights already set out in the EU Shareholder Rights Directive and national implementing legislation, whereas the majority of the code recommendations on board-shareholder engagement *outside* shareholder meetings reflect only the well-accepted notions on the desirability for companies and/or corporate boards to engage with shareholders.

Considering the heightened institutional investor focus on engagement with investee companies stemming from their own comply-or-explain engagement obligations under the EU Shareholder Rights Directive, the forms, format and content of the board-shareholder dialogue have become increasingly important for both companies and shareholders. In recognition of this reality, a few European corporate governance codes recommend the adoption of a corporate policy on shareholder engagement as a best practice with respect to engagements between companies and shareholders. The bodies entrusted with issuing and updating the national corporate governance codes should consider, where applicable, the introduction of such comply-or-explain recommendations for adoption of a corporate policy on shareholder engagement so as to improve the transparency of the company's engagement efforts within and outside the shareholder meeting, and to allow companies to optimally structure their engagement practices.

18

Board-Shareholder Engagement and Insider Regulation

LARS KLÖHN

18.1 Overview

When institutional investors engage in behind-the-scenes talks with the boards and top management of publicly listed firms, they might ask questions, which are highly relevant for the valuation of the firm's securities: What are management's expectations about sales, growth or revenue in the next quarter? Who will replace the chair of the board after her retirement? What about the rumour that one of the key employees is going to quit his job and work for the competition? What is the board's position on Hedge Fund *X*'s campaign to make the company sell off a substantial part of its business?

To respond to those questions in a meaningful way, management might have to selectively (privately) disclose nonpublic and material (price-relevant) information, that is, *inside information*, to those investors. Therefore, the question arises whether insider regulation curtails the board-shareholder dialogue in a significant way and – if the answer to this question is "yes" – whether we should get rid of those constraints by introducing new regulation.

To answer these questions, I will first assess how relevant the selective disclosure of inside information in practice really is (Section 18.2). I will then describe and compare the applicable insider regulation in the US, the EU, and the UK (Section 18.3). As the result of the comparative analysis will be that EU (and UK) law is much stricter than US law, I will finally address the question whether the EU should introduce a safe-harbour rule, which would allow the private disclosure of inside information to institutional investors to facilitate shareholder engagement (Section 18.4).

I am grateful to Luca Enriques, Jill Fisch, Matteo Gatti, Marco Maugeri, Giovanni Strampelli and other participants in the Auxiliary Corporate Governance Conference in Rome on October 12–14, 2022 for helpful comments. All errors and omissions are mine.

18.2 Practical Relevance

18.2.1 No Ban on Listen-Only Sessions

The practical relevance of insider regulation as a constraint on board-shareholder dialogue seems to be rather low. First, insider regulation does not prevent so-called "listen-only sessions", in which the management does not disclose any information at all to investors but merely listens to what they have to say.[1]

18.2.2 Lower Need to Inform Anchor Investors

Second, majority shareholders and other "anchor investors", which are present in many publicly listed firms in EU countries such as Germany, France or Italy, often do not need to be informed about anything that is going on in the company. If they are not present themselves personally, they usually have representatives on the management board or – as the case may be – on the supervisory board and thus know the information anyway.[2] Of course, those representatives usually owe a duty of confidentiality to the company subject to the applicable national corporate law. But it does not seem far-fetched to assume that this duty does not always stop them from passing on sensitive information to the controlling shareholder because enforcing the duty of confidentiality is notoriously difficult, especially amongst private parties (i.e. outside of criminal or other state-administered proceedings).

18.2.3 Investor Preferences for Immaterial Information; Mosaic Information

Third, institutional investors such as the managers of hedge funds, pension funds or index funds often do not want to acquire inside information.[3] Perhaps not surprisingly, there does not seem to be much empirical evidence on this topic because "informal contact between institutional investors and firms is by its very nature private and difficult

[1] Strampelli, 12 Va. L & Bus. Rev. 187, 205 et seq (2018).

[2] On the selective disclosure of inside information under the German *Konzernrecht*, see *infra* 18.2.3.2.

[3] Strampelli, 12 Va. L & Bus. Rev. 187, 206 (2018); Mosca, 15 Eur. Company & Fin. L. Rev. 805, 812 (2018).

to quantify".[4] Some studies suggest that the focus of behind-the-scenes-talks between investors and managers is more about "framing and making sense of public domain information, rather than introducing new information"[5] or that "management meetings provide information that is useful, but not price-sensitive".[6] On the other hand, there is some evidence indicating that private meetings with the management of publicly listed firms enable investors to make more informed trading decisions,[7] but it is unclear whether this is because the investors participating in those talks are better at interpreting information or because they receive material information.[8] Anecdotal evidence suggests that large shareholders often explicitly request that advance checks be carried out to ensure that they do not receive inside information in private meetings with management.[9]

From a common-sense perspective, it seems plausible that institutional investors do not wish to receive material information because they would risk being barred from trading until the information has been disclosed to the public even if it remains disputed whether the information has caused any of their trading decisions.[10] In the US, the Supreme Court decided in *O'Hagan* that insider trading must be "on the basis" of material nonpublic information.[11] In 2000, the SEC adopted Rule 10b5–1 which clarifies that a person trades "on the basis" of inside

[4] Bebchuk/Weisbach, 23 Rev. Fin. Stud. 939, 942 (2010); along the same line Mallow/Sethi, 12 N.Y.U. J.L. & Bus. 385, 396 (2016); Strampelli, 12 Va. L & Bus. Rev. 187, 191 (2018).

[5] Barker/Hendry/Roberts/Sanderson, 37 Acct. Org. & Soc'y 207, 214 (2012).

[6] Cascino/Clatworthy/García Osma/Gassen/Imam/Jeanjean, 11 Acct. Eur. 185, 192 (2014).

[7] Solomon/Soltes, 58 J. L. & Econ. 325 (2015); Bushee/Jung/Miller, 2 J. Fin. Reporting 31 (2017); see also Green/Jame/Markov/Subasi, 114 J. Fin. Econ. 239 (2014), finding that brokers who host investor conferences issue more accurate earnings forcasts on participating firms than non-hosting brokers (who are typically not invited) and that recommendations by hosting brokers generate abnormal returns for investors.

[8] Solomon/Soltes, 58 J. L. & Econ. 325, 352 (2015): "Overall, our analysis indicates that private meetings convey information to investors who are present and that these effects are concentrated in hedge funds who attend such meetings. This variation across investor types is consistent with two possible interpretations. First, investors may be receiving the same information, but it is not equally valuable to all investors. Hedge funds may be better at parsing out the meaning of ambiguous information conveyed by management, or the information conveyed may be valuable only in conjunction with other information that investors have. This would be consistent with the mosaic theory of investing. The second hypothesis is that hedge funds are being given different and inherently more valuable information."

[9] Strampelli, 12 Va. L & Bus. Rev. 187, 209 (2018) with further references.

[10] Strampelli, 12 Va. L & Bus. Rev. 187, 206 (2018); Klöhn, 185 Zeitschrift für das gesamte Handels und Wirtschaftsrecht 182, 205 (2021)

[11] US v. O'Hagan, 521 US 642, 652-653 et passim (1997).

information if the trader is "aware" of the information when making the purchase or sale.[12] In the EU, under the so-called Spector Rule,[13] it is generally presumed that an investor "uses" inside information within the meaning of Art. 8(1) of the EU Market Abuse Regulation (MAR)[14] when he or she is in possession of inside information at the time of the trade.[15]

The ideal scenario from an information trader's[16] point of view seems to be the management disclosing some piece of information which, by itself, is immaterial to the *reasonable investor* but which helps the *recipient* to "complete a 'mosaic' of information that, taken together, is material".[17] Receiving such information – sometimes referred to as "mosaic information"[18] – does not trigger the insider trading ban since the materiality (= price relevance) of inside information must be assessed from the *reasonable investor's* perspective.[19] Thus, if the recipient of the information is better at analysing information than the reasonable investor and then trades on this analysis, the recipient does not exploit his or her privileged access to nonpublic information to beat the market but merely reaps the benefits of his or her superior analytical skills.[20] This

[12] 17 CFR § 240.10b5–1.

[13] This terminology was first suggested by Klöhn, 7 Eur. Company & Fin. L. Rev. 347, 351–353 (2010).

[14] Regulation (EU) No 596/2014 of the European Parliament and of the Council of 16 April 2014 on market abuse (market abuse regulation) and repealing Directive 2003/6/EC of the European Parliament and of the Council and Commission Directives 2003/124/EC, 2003/125/EC and 2004/72/EC, OJ L 173, 12.6.2014, p. 1.

[15] ECJ, Case C-45/08, Spector Photo Group NV, Chris Van Raemdonck v. Commissie voor het Bank-, Financie- en Assurantiewezen (CBFA), EU:C:2009:806, para. 62. The EU legislator incorporated this presumption into MAR, as can be inferred from Art. 9 MAR and recital 24 of MAR; see Hansen in Ventoruzzo and Mock (Eds.), Market Abuse Regulation, 2nd ed. (OUP, 2022), para. B.8.66 (stating that *Spector* must be considered valid case law under MAR); Veil in Veil (Ed.), European Capital Markets Law, 3rd ed. (Hart Publishing, 2022), § 14 para. 73.

[16] Information traders are traders who look for and analyse potentially price-relevant information to gain an informational advantage vis-à-vis other traders (to identify an arbitrage opportunity), cf., e.g., Black, 41 J. Fin. 529, 531 et passim (1986); Goshen/Parchomovsky, 55 Duke L.J. 711, 714 (2006); Klöhn, 10 Cap. Mark. Law J. 162, 172 (2015).

[17] SEC Release No. 33-7881, 34-43154, Aug. 24, 2000, 65 Fed. Reg. 51,716 at 51,722.

[18] See, e.g., Corporate Counsel's Guide to Insider Trading and Reporting (Westlaw 2022 ed.), § 8.4 with n. 21.

[19] In the EU: Art. 7(4) MAR, in the US: TSC Industries, Inc. v. Northway, Inc., 426 U.S. 438, 449 (1976) (with respect to Rule 14a-9); Basic, Inc. v. Levinson, 485 U.S. 224, 232 (1988) (with respect to Rule 10b-5).

[20] Cf. SEC Release No. 33-7881, 34-43154, Aug. 24, 2000, 65 Fed. Reg. 51,716 at 51,722: "The focus of Regulation FD is on whether the issuer discloses material nonpublic

is not at odds with any insider trading regulation, regardless of whether this regime conceptualizes insider trading as fraud or as a violation of the principle of equal access.[21]

To see why, imagine that the issuer publicly discloses the information conveyed at the private meeting. If we assume that this information is immaterial to the *reasonable investor*, the *recipient of the information* would be able to reap the same benefits from analysing and then trading on the information as in the aforementioned scenario in which the information remained nonpublic. The public disclosure of the information would not change anything precisely because the information was immaterial to the reasonable investor. Thus, there is no need to ban trading on this information even if it has not (yet) been made public. The real question in this case is if and to what extent it really is possible to be better at analysing information than the reasonable investor, that is, whether we should conceptualize the reasonable investor as an "average human being" or as a personification of an efficient securities market.[22]

18.2.4 Reasons Why Insider Regulation Still Might Be Relevant

Although institutional investors thus generally prefer not to receive material information, this does not mean that insider regulation is completely irrelevant in the "real world" of board-shareholder talks.

18.2.4.1 Involuntary Disclosure of Material Information and Chilling Effect

First, at least in the EU, the unlawful disclosure of inside information is actionable even if it occurs without intent or certain knowledge of the person disclosing the information.[23] Given the vagueness of both the

information, not on whether an analyst, through some combination of persistence, knowledge, and insight, regards as material information whose significance is not apparent to the reasonable investor."

21 In the US: SEC v. Bausch & Lomb Inc., 565 F.2d 8, 14 (2d Cir. 1977); Elkind v. Liggett & Myers, Inc., 635 f.2d 156, 165 (2d Cir. 1980); the SEC adopted the "mosaic theory" in SEC Release No. 33-7881, 34-43154, Aug. 24, 2000, 65 Fed. Reg. 51,716 at 51,722; in the EU Klöhn, Marktmissbrauchsverordnung (Beck 2018), Art. 7 paras. 186–189.

22 On this issue see Klöhn, 177 *Zeitschrift für das gesamte Handels- und Wirtschaftsrecht* 349, 377 (2013).

23 See, e.g., § 120(14) of the German *Wertpapierhandelsgesetz* (gross negligence). In France, administrative sanctions for violating the ban on private disclosure of inside information under Art. L621-15 al. II lit. c) n° 3 do not require any state of mind, the objective breach of the law suffices; see AMF Commission des sanctions, 21 avril 2005, SAN-2005-12 sub.

concept of inside information and the "normal course of business" test under Art. 10 MAR,[24] insider regulation may thus chill the board-shareholder dialogue even in situations in which no inside information is involved. Managers might simply refrain from engaging in any discussion about a sensitive topic because they fear that they might later be held responsible for unlawfully disclosing inside information to investors.

18.2.4.2 Trading Plans; Rebalancing Portfolios

Second, not all trading in possession of inside information violates the ban on insider trading. In the EU, it is commonly assumed that traders can rebut the presumption that trading in possession of inside information constitutes the "use" of inside information within the meaning of Art. 8 MAR[25] by showing that there is no causal link between the possession of inside information and the decision to trade.[26] This is why the mere rebalancing of portfolios according to previously defined criteria such as the composition of a stock market index would not violate Art. 8 MAR even if the portfolio manager is in possession of inside information. In those cases, (passive) investors might have no objections against receiving inside information.

18.2.4.3 Insider Abstention

Third, neither US nor EU insider trading regulation bans insider abstention, that is, the decision *not* to trade in a publicly listed security, even if this decision is due to the possession of inside information.[27] In the US, Rule 10b-5 bans trading on material nonpublic information under certain circumstances,[28] but it does not prohibit insiders from abstaining from trading based on such information.[29] In Europe, refraining from trading in a publicly listed security violates the ban on insider trading

III.1.: "*Considérant qu'il est peu important de savoir si M. A a transmis l'information privilégiée à M. E de manière intentionnelle ou maladroite dans la mesure où les éléments constitutifs du manquement, qui est objectif, sont réunis.*"

24 *Infra* 18.3.2.1. 25 On this presumption see *supra* 18.2.3.

26 Hansen in Ventoruzzo and Mock (Eds.), Market Abuse Regulation, 2nd ed. (OUP, 2022), para. B.8.162 ("not motivated by the inside information"); Klöhn, Marktmissbrauchsverordnung (Beck 2018), Art. 8 para. 139; Kumpan/Schmidt in Schwark and Zimmer (Eds.), Kapitalmarktrechts-Kommentar, 5th ed. (Beck 2020), Art. 8 para. 61; Winner in Kalss, Oppitz, Torggler and Winner (Eds.), EU Market Abuse Regulation (Edward Elgar 2021), para. 8.066.

27 On this issue see Fried, 113 Yale L.J. 455 (2003). 28 *Infra* 18.3.1.

29 Manne, 4 Cato J. 933, 933–935 (1985); Fried, 113 Yale L.J. 455, 456 (2003); Anderson, 2015 Utah L. Rev. 339, 363–364 (2015).

only if the trader cancels or amends an order which he or she placed before learning of the inside information.[30]

Institutional investors contemplating buying (or selling) a company's shares might therefore have a *clear preference to receive inside information* if it indicates that they should stop carrying out their plan. They could use this information to abstain from their trades without the risk of breaking any insider trading law. Moreover, management has a *clear incentive to disclose inside information* to investors in order to avoid having to deal with a disgruntled shareholder who regrets having built, increased or reduced its stake in the company.

18.2.4.4 Example: The FCA's Action Against Sir Christopher Gent

As a real-life example, take the action by the UK Financial Conduct Authority (FCA) against Sir Christopher Gent from 5 August 2022.[31] Sir Christopher was the non-executive Chairman of ConvaTec Group Plc, a medical products and technology company, whose shares were listed at the main market of the London Stock Exchange. On 10 October 2018, Sir Christopher, in his capacity as Chairman, privately disclosed to two investors that the company was expected to publicly announce that it would be revising financial guidance and that the CEO was going to retire.[32] One of the recipients of the information was the senior executive of Company A, one of the largest shareholders of ConvaTec, which had a relationship agreement with the company that imposed confidentiality and no-dealing obligations on Company A.[33] The other recipient was a director at Company B, another shareholder of ConvaTec, which had instructed its brokers two days earlier to make enquiries with potential block sellers in order to facilitate a purchase of a minimum of 20 million ConvaTec shares,[34] that is, to significantly increase its stake in the company. After learning about the information conveyed by Sir Christopher, an employee at Company B called its stockbrokers and instructed them to "pause" and "wait for (ConvaTec's) earning announcement", stating that "[w]e are sort of at a risk off moment and it may last for a while and so I think we might be able to get a bigger

[30] Sentence 2 of Art. 8(1) MAR.

[31] FCA, Final Notice to Sir Christopher Gent, 5 August 2022, www.fca.org.uk/publication/final-notices/sir-christopher-gent-2022.pdf.

[32] Ibid paras. 4.54 and 4.62. [33] Ibid para. 4.55. [34] Ibid para. 4.33.

block, cheaper, if we just wait".[35] On 15 October 2018, the company publicly announced that the expected revenue growth in the fourth quarter would be only 1.0 per cent instead of the 2.5 per cent to 3.0 per cent previously expected and that its CEO had informed the board that he wished to retire and would step down and cease to be a director with immediate effect. After this announcement, the stock price fell by 33.1 per cent. When asked why he disclosed the information to the two investors, Sir Christopher claimed, among others, that he was not aware that the information was inside information[36] and that he did not want to "surprise shareholders of scale with announcements" given the intention of Company B to build a more significant shareholding in ConvaTec.[37] The FCA imposed a fine on Sir Christopher for illegally disclosing inside information to both Company A and Company B.[38]

18.3 The Law

18.3.1 USA

18.3.1.1 Case Law on Tipping

The US case law conceptualizes insider trading as fraud. The legal basis of the ban on insider trading is Rule 10b-5,[39] the general antifraud rule, which states that

> [i]t shall be unlawful for any person . . . to engage in any act, practice or course of business which operates or would operate as a fraud or deceit upon any person, in connection with the purchase or sale of any security.

An important consequence of this conceptualization is that the private disclosure of inside information – *tipping*, as it is usually called in the US literature – is, *by itself, not prohibited* but sanctioned as aiding and abetting to the insider trading of the person to whom the information was disclosed. Thus the tipper (and subtipper) cannot be held liable as long as the tippee (or subtippee) does not trade.

In its seminal *Chiarella* decision of 1980, the US Supreme Court refused to recognize the equal-access-principle as the foundation of the US insider trading prohibition by stating that the mere possession of inside information does not trigger a duty to disclose that information

[35] Ibid. para. 4.68. [36] Ibid. para. 4.66. [37] Ibid. para. 4.65.
[38] For more details on the FCA decision see *infra* 18.3.2.3. [39] 17 CFR § 240.10b-5.

when trading on the open market.[40] Instead it required that there be a breach of some (usually, fiduciary) duty that makes the trade fraudulent. Three years later, in *Dirks*, the Supreme Court held that a tippee, that is, an outsider receiving inside information from an insider, could be held liable for insider trading only if the tippee assumes an insider's duty to the shareholders not to trade on this information.[41] In line with *Chiarella*, it held that outsiders assume such duty not merely because they receive inside information, but rather because such information was made available to them improperly.[42] Thus,

> a tippee assumes a fiduciary duty to the shareholders of a corporation not to trade on material nonpublic information only when the insider has breached his fiduciary duty to the shareholders by disclosing the information to the tippee and the tippee knows or should know that there has been a breach.[43]

According to *Dirks*, this test "requires courts to focus on objective criteria, i.e., whether the insider receives a direct or indirect personal benefit from the disclosure, such as a pecuniary gain or a reputational benefit that will translate into future earnings."[44]

After *Dirks*, there was some dispute among courts and scholars over the question under which circumstances the selective disclosure of inside information to analysts and investors was improper.[45] In line with the wording in *Dirks*, market participants viewed such disclosure as permitted as long as the person disclosing the information gained no personal benefit.[46]

18.3.1.2 Regulation Fair Disclosure

As selective disclosure became frequent in the US, the SEC became concerned.[47] These concerns grew during the tech bubble of the late 1990s when it was common for managers of publicly listed firms to disclose inside information to analysts in exchange for favourable reviews and buy-recommendations. The SEC had essentially two options: the first

[40] Chiarella v. United States, 445 U.S. 222, 232 (1980).
[41] Dirks v. SEC, 463 US 646, 660 (1983) (by implication).
[42] Dirks v. SEC, 463 US 646, 660 (1983). [43] Dirks v. SEC, 463 US 646, 660 (1983).
[44] Dirks v. SEC, 463 US 646, 663 (1983).
[45] Brountas, 92 Colum. L. Rev. 646, 660 (1992) with further references.
[46] SEC Release No. 33-7787, 34-42259, Dec. 28, 1999, 64 Fed. Reg. 72,590 at 72,593.
[47] Strampelli, 12 Va. L & Bus. Rev. 187, 206 (2018). On early attempts by the SEC to connect selective disclosure to the reputational personal benefit covered by *Dirks*, see Bengtzen, 33 Fordham J. Corp. & Fin. L. 33, 71 et seq. (2017) with further references.

was to extend the reach of insider trading law to selective disclosures that "personally" benefited the *company* instead of the insider. The SEC opted against such extension because it feared that the high sanctions for insider trading would not only deter unwanted selective disclosure but chill legitimate corporate communication as well.[48] Instead, it enacted an extended disclosure regime called Regulation Fair Disclosure ("Regulation FD"),[49] while making clear that this approach neither altered *Dirks* nor considered selective disclosure fraudulent.[50]

Unlike the US case law on insider trading, Regulation FD is based on the notion of equal access, that is, the notion that all market participants covered by Regulation FD should be placed "on equal footing with respect to competition for access to material information".[51] However, Regulation FD does not ban the private disclosure of inside information. Instead, it requires that whenever an issuer, or any person acting on its behalf, discloses any material nonpublic information regarding that issuer or its securities to certain named recipients, the issuer shall make public disclosure of that information simultaneously, in the case of an intentional disclosure, and promptly, in the case of a non-intentional disclosure.[52] This rule applies to disclosures made to brokers, dealers, investment advisers, institutional investment managers, investment companies and holders of the issuer's securities "under circumstances in which it is reasonably foreseeable that the person will purchase or sell the issuer's securities on the basis of the information".[53] Regulation FD does not apply to disclosures made to a person who expressly agrees to maintain the disclosed information in confidence.[54]

18.3.1.3 Constraints on Board-Shareholder Dialogue

Case Law on Tipping US case law on tipping does not seem to limit behind-the-scenes talks between managers and shareholders in a significant way. Managers usually do not breach their fiduciary duty towards

[48] SEC Release No. 33-7787, 34-42259, Dec. 28, 1999, 64 Fed. Reg. 72,590 at 72,595; see also Anderson, 6 Fordham J. Corp. & Fin. L. 273, 279 (2001) (citing former SEC Commissioner Harvey Goldschmid).

[49] 17 CFR Part 243.

[50] SEC Release No. 33-7787, 34-42259, Dec. 28, 1999, 64 Fed. Reg. 72,590 at 72,594; see also Bengtzen, 33 Fordham J. Corp. & Fin. L. 33, 73 (2017).

[51] SEC Release No. 33-7881, 34-43154, Aug. 24, 2000, 65 Fed. Reg. 51,716 at 51,734: "This regulation will place all analysts on equal footing with respect to competition for access to material information."

[52] 17 CFR § 243.100(a). [53] 17 CFR § 243.100(b)(1). [54] 17 CFR § 243.100(b)(2)(ii).

shareholders when talking to selected shareholders because such talks are beneficial to the company, for example by facilitating long-time support of investors. Moreover, the Supreme Court's *O'Hagan* decision suggests that selective disclosure can be authorized by the firm.[55] This is why tipping liability under *Dirks* seems to apply only in cases in which managers talk *behind the back of their colleagues* to shareholders with the goal of gaining some personal benefits or earning an outright bribe.[56]

Regulation FD Thus, the decisive question under US law is: does Regulation FD curtail the disclosure of inside information[57] during behind-the-scenes talks between managers and shareholders? Again, the answer is "no"[58] due to the following considerations[59].

- First, Regulation FD does not apply to disclosures made to a person who expressly agrees to maintain the disclosed information in confidence.[60] In the words of the SEC, this means that any conversation

[55] US v. O'Hagan, 521 US 642, 655 (1997); on this see Coffee, 218 N.Y.L.J 5 (1997); Bengtzen, 33 Fordham J. Corp. & Fin. L. 33, 71 (2017).

[56] In these cases, issuers are under no duty to publicly disclose the inside information that the manager passed on to the investor because Regulation FD does not apply, see 17 CFR § 243.101(c) excluding from the term "person acting on behalf of an issuer" persons who disclose material nonpublic information "in breach of a duty of trust or confidence to the issuer".

[57] The literature stresses that Regulation FD does not prohibit the disclosure of immaterial information to shareholders; see, e.g., Strampelli, 12 Va. L & Bus. Rev. 187, 205 (2018). This is true but not really remarkable at least from this chapter's perspective, since any insider regulation applies to price-sensitive (= material) information. If the disclosed information is not material, any insider regulation is simply irrelevant. What is more important is that due to its laxity, Regulation FD does not seem to provide a significant chilling effect on the selective disclosure of immaterial information. In this regard, Regulation FD differs from EU and UK law.

[58] Yockey, 61 S.C. L Rev. 171, 210 (2009); Fairfax, 2013 U. Ill. L. Rev. 821, 836 (2013); Rock, 97 Cornell L. Rev. 849, 871, 898 (2012) (noting that "Regulation FD is beside the point"); Bengtzen, 33 Fordham J. Corp. & Fin. L. 33, 74–78 (2017) (listing features of Regulation FD that may cause it to fail to restrict selective disclosure as intended); Strampelli, 12 Va. L & Bus. Rev. 187, 207–208 (2018) ("corporate concerns related to Regulation FD should not be exaggerated"); others view Regulation FD as an obstacle for the board-shareholder dialogue, see, e.g., Bainbridge, Constraints on Shareholder Activism in the United States and Slovenia (15 May 2000), https://ssrn.com/abstract=228780, p. 16; Lund, 43 J. Corp. L. 493, 503 n. 42 (2018).

[59] For more reasons Bengtzen, 33 Fordham J. Corp. & Fin. L. 33, 74–78 (2017).

[60] *Supra* 18.3.1.2.

between the board and a shareholder "would not present Regulation FD issues if the shareholder provided such an express agreement.[61]

- Second, even if shareholders do not provide such an agreement, for example because they want to remain free to trade on the information, issuers can circumvent Regulation FD by having investors talk to firm employees not covered by Regulation FD,[62] that is, employees who do not qualify as "persons acting on behalf of an issuer" within the meaning of Regulation FD.[63]
- Third, even if Regulation FD applies to selective disclosures of inside information made to investors, it merely mandates public disclosure of the selectively conveyed information. It does not ban the recipient from trading on this information.[64] By selectively disclosing the information the issuer violates Regulation FD only if it does not make simultaneous or prompt public disclosure depending on whether the selective disclosure was made intentionally (which includes recklessly not knowing that the information disclosed is both material and nonpublic[65]). In this regard, it is noteworthy that the SEC declared that it would take into account the circumstances surrounding a selective disclosure event in determining whether a manager's materiality assessment was reckless.[66] Thus the SEC assesses recklessness more leniently in a private setting, which seems to be the typical situation of behind-the-scenes talks between managers and shareholders.[67] If the violation of Regulation FD occurred without recklessness, the selectively disclosed information must be published "promptly", which Regulation FD defines "as soon as reasonably practicable ... after a senior official of the issuer *learns* that there has been a non-intentional disclosure ... of

61 SEC, Compliance and Disclosure Interpretations on Regulation FD, June 4, 2010, Answer to Question 101.11.

62 Soltes, 52 J. Acct. Res. 245, 268 (2014); Bengtzen, 33 Fordham J. Corp. & Fin. L. 33, 74 et seq. (2017).

63 See 17 CFR § 243.101(c) defining person acting on behalf of an issuer as "any senior official of the issuer ... , or any other officer, employee, or agent of an issuer who regularly communicates with (recipients covered by Regulation FD)".

64 Bengtzen, 33 Fordham J. Corp. & Fin. L. 33, 75 (2017); Strampelli, 12 Va. L & Bus. Rev. 187, 210 (2018).

65 17 CFR § 243.101(a).

66 SEC Release No. 33-7881, 34-43154, Aug. 24, 2000, 65 Fed. Reg. 51,716 at 51,722: "a materiality judgment that might be reckless in the context of a prepared written statement would not necessarily be reckless in the context of an impromptu answer to an unanticipated question."

67 Along the same line Bengtzen, 33 Fordham J. Corp. & Fin. L. 33, 75 (2017).

information that the senior official *knows, or is reckless in not knowing*, is both material and nonpublic".[68] Regulation FD explicitly provides that such disclosure can take place up to 24 hours after a senior official learns of the non-intentional selective disclosure and that the information disclosed was both material and nonpublic or is reckless in this regard.[69] These provisions of Regulation FD justify the suspicion that (1) *intentional* selective disclosures in the context of board-shareholder behind-the-scenes talks are rare and that (2) *unintentional* selective disclosures can be fixed rather easily, thus avoiding violations of Regulation FD.

- Both suspicions are confirmed by the SEC's enforcement history. After the introduction of Regulation FD, the SEC indicated that it would seek to enforce only "clear violations" of the new rules.[70] Since Regulation FD came into force in October 2000, there have been only 15 cases of SEC enforcement.[71] The accumulated issuer penalties amount to 3.2 million USD[72] and the accumulated officer penalties were 325,000 USD.[73] None of these enforcement actions were based on communications or disclosures associated with board-shareholder engagement.[74]
- Finally, Regulation FD explicitly states that "no failure to make a public disclosure required solely by (Regulation FD) shall be deemed to be a

[68] 17 CFR § 243.101(d) (emphasis added).

[69] 17 CFR § 243.101(d); see also Bengtzen, 33 Fordham J. Corp. & Fin. L. 33, 76 (2017).

[70] SEC, Written Statement Concerning Regulation Fair Disclosure, May 17, 2001, www.sec.gov/news/testimony/051701wssec.htm: "These remarks, and similar ones by other Commission officials, have indicated that Commission enforcement of the regulation will be focused on clear violations."

[71] Bengtzen, 33 Fordham J. Corp. & Fin. L. 33, 82–83 (2017) found 13 cases in the period between October 2000 and 10 February 2017. Since then, there seem to have been only two more cases, namely Therapeutics MD, Inc. (File No. 3-19362 August 20, 2019) and AT&T [SEC v. AT&T, Inc., et al., No. 1:21-cv-01951 (S.D.N.Y., filed March 5, 2021)].

[72] For the period between October 2000 and 10 February 2017, Bengtzen, 33 Fordham J. Corp. & Fin. L. 33, 82–83 (2017) calculated a total issuer penalty of 3 million USD. After that, the issuer fine in the case of Therapeutics MD, Inc. (*supra* n. 71) was 200,000 USD (www.sec.gov/enforce/34-86708-s). In the case of AT&T (*supra* n. 71) the SEC did not fine the issuer but sought civil monetary penalties against the issuer before the court (www.sec.gov/litigation/complaints/2021/comp-pr2021-43.pdf). As of the time of writing, the case is still pending.

[73] For the period between October 2000 and 10 February 2017, Bengtzen, 33 Fordham J. Corp. & Fin. L. 33, 82–83 (2017) calculated a total officer penalty of 325,000 USD. In the two cases mentioned *supra* n. 71, the SEC did not fine any individuals.

[74] For the period of 2000–2017 see Strampelli, 12 Va. L & Bus. Rev. 187, 209 (2018) with further references. In the two cases after 2017 (*supra* n. 71), the recipients of the information were analysts.

violation of Rule 10b-5".[75] Regulation FD thus bars private plaintiffs from bringing civil lawsuits for violations of Regulation FD.[76]

Considering all this, Regulation FD "can reasonably be regarded more as a 'crutch' for issuers to avoid engagement with shareholders than an actual impediment on director-shareholder dialogue".[77]

18.3.2 EU

18.3.2.1 Prohibition of Private Disclosure of Inside Information

Although the notion of inside information is comparable to the US concept of material nonpublic information, EU insider trading law is conceptually very different from the US case law on insider trading after *Chiarella*. It is based on the notion of equal access, that is, "on the assurance that investors will be placed on an equal footing and protected from the misuse of inside information".[78] In line with this principle, Arts. 8 and 14 lit. a) MAR prohibit anyone in possession of inside information from using that information by trading in publicly listed securities that the information relates to, regardless of whether trading is conducted by an insider or an outsider and without regard to how precisely the trader obtained the information.[79] All that is required is that outsiders know or ought to know that the information they are trading on qualifies as inside information.[80]

The same principle applies to the private disclosure of inside information. Arts. 10(1), 14 lit. c) MAR, such disclosure is generally prohibited regardless of whether it is made by an insider or an outsider and regardless of whether the person disclosing the information obtained the information improperly.[81] Of course, a strict prohibition of private disclosure of inside information could severely hamper legitimate communication within the firm and with external advisors who often rely on inside information to do their jobs – think about lawyers, accountants, bankers. This is why Art. 10 MAR exempts private disclosure of inside information "where the

[75] 17 CFR § 243.102.

[76] Bengtzen, 33 Fordham J. Corp. & Fin. L. 33, 73 (2017): "private enforcement is not possible".

[77] Strampelli, 12 Va. L & Bus. Rev. 187, 211 (2018).

[78] Sentence 3 of Recital 24 of MAR.

[79] Gilotta, 13 Eur. Company & Fin. L. Rev. 631, 636 (2016); Strampelli, 12 Va. L & Bus. Rev. 187, 213 (2018).

[80] Art. 8(4) MAR.

[81] Mosca, 15 Eur. Company & Fin. L. Rev. 805, 823 (2018).

disclosure is made in the normal exercise of an employment, a profession or duties".

As the ECJ has recently decided in the case of *A v. AMF*, the "normal course of business"-exception contained in Art. 10 MAR must be interpreted strictly.[82] The disclosure of inside information is lawful only "if it is strictly necessary for (the exercise of an employment, a profession or duties) and complies with the principle of proportionality".[83] Thus, in order to be made "in the normal exercise of an employment, a profession or duties" the disclosure must meet four requirements.[84] It must

- be intended to serve a *legitimate purpose*,
- be *suitable* to achieve this purpose,
- be *necessary*[85] to achieve this purpose and
- comply with the principle of *proportionality*.[86]

18.3.2.2 Duty to Publicly Disclose Selectively Disclosed Information

Although Art. 10 MAR curtails the selective disclosure of inside information much more severely than the US Supreme Court's adjudication on tipping, EU law also contains an equivalent rule to Regulation FD. Under Art. 17(8) MAR,

[82] ECJ, Case C-302/20, M. A v. AMF, Judgment of the Court of Justice (Grand Chamber) of 15 March 2022, EU:C:2022:190 para. 78 with reference to ECJ, Case C-384/02, Grøngaard and Bang, EU:C:2005:708 para. 34.

[83] ECJ, Case C-302/20, M. A v. AMF, Judgment of the Court of Justice (Grand Chamber) of 15 March 2022, EU:C:2022:190 para. 78. By this decision the ECJ applied the same test to Art. 10 MAR that it had developed with respect to the old Insider Dealing Directive in Case C-384/02, Grøngaard and Bang, EU:C:2005:708 para. 34.

[84] Klöhn, Marktmissbrauchsverordnung (Beck 2018), Art. 10 para. 44; Kulenkamp/v. Bonin in Beck'scher Online-Kommentar Wertpapierhandelsrecht (Beck, 2022), Art. 10 MAR para. 14; Kumpan/Grütze in Schwark and Zimmer (Eds.), Kapitalmarktrechts-Kommentar 5th ed. (Beck 2020), Art. 10 MAR, para. 28.

[85] On the question whether there is a difference between "strictly necessary" and "necessary" and on the position of the ECJ in this regard, see Klöhn, 60 CMLR 547, 566 (2023).

[86] The disclosure is *suitable* if it promotes the purpose, i.e., if it increases the chance of achieving the purpose. The disclosure is *necessary* if there are no other means which are equally suited to achieve the purpose and pose a lesser threat to market integrity. The disclosure is *proportionate* if the disclosing party's interest in selectively conveying the information outweighs the market's interest in containing the inside information. Thus, the aspect of necessity relates to the appropriateness of the *means*, i.e., the action, while the aspect of proportionality relates to the appropriateness of the *ends*, i.e., the effect, of the disclosure.

> [w]here an issuer . . . or a person acting on (the issuer's) behalf or for their account, discloses any inside information to any third party in the normal course of the exercise of an employment, profession or duties as referred to in Article 10(1), they must make complete and effective public disclosure of that information, simultaneously in the case of an intentional disclosure, and promptly in the case of a non-intentional disclosure. This paragraph shall not apply if the person receiving the information owes a duty of confidentiality, regardless of whether such duty is based on a law, on regulations, on articles of association, or on a contract.

Thus, EU law contains a two-tier system for containing selective disclosure of inside information:

- First, under Art. 10 MAR any selective disclosure of inside information is prohibited unless it is made in the normal course of the exercise of an employment, profession or duties.
- Second, if an issuer or a person acting on behalf or for the account of the issuer lawfully discloses inside information to a third person, they must publicly disclose this information (simultaneously or promptly) if the recipient of that information is under no duty of confidentiality, Art. 17(8) MAR.

As clear as this structure seems, it should be pointed out that the disclosure obligation under Art. 17(8) MAR does not seem to have any practical relevance in the EU.[87] This follows from the simple fact that, if the recipient of a selective disclosure is under no duty of confidentiality, the disclosure usually does not occur in the normal course of business and is thus prohibited by Art. 10 MAR. Moreover, if the recipient is under no duty of confidentiality, the issuer can, by definition, not ensure the confidentiality of the information and therefore loses the privilege to keep the information confidential under Art. 17(4) MAR. The issuer must therefore publicize the information under the general continuous disclosure obligation under Art. 17(1) MAR regardless of whether the requirements of Art. 17(8) MAR are met.

18.3.2.3 Constraints on Board-Shareholder Dialogue

Lack of Guidance by the Legislator, the ECJ and ESMA The ECJ has never decided on the application of Art. 10 MAR in the context of board-shareholder dialogue. Likewise, the European Securities and Markets

[87] Klöhn, Marktmissbrauchsverordnung (Beck 2018), Art. 17 para. 453.

Authority (ESMA) has not issued any guidance on the application of Art. 10 MAR in this context. For the sake of completeness, it should be noted that recital 19 of MAR states that

> [t]his Regulation is not intended to prohibit discussions of a general nature regarding the business and market developments between shareholders and management concerning an issuer. Such relationships are essential for the efficient functioning of markets and should not be prohibited by this Regulation.

However, this statement seems to be rather redundant since "discussions of a general nature" usually do not involve the disclosure of any inside information, which is defined by Art. 7(1) MAR as "information of a precise nature", that is, as information, which "is specific enough" to enable a conclusion as to its price relevance (Art. 7(2) MAR).[88]

In addition, the EU Shareholder Rights Directive[89] encourages and facilitates the board-shareholder dialogue. However, it does not govern the question of under which circumstances issuers or persons acting on their behalf may selectively disclose inside information to investors.

In summary, to what extent Art. 10 MAR restricts board-shareholder dialogue is to a large extent an open question. However, as will be shown below, two points can be made with sufficient certainty. First, selective disclosure to controlling shareholders is generally permitted if the applicable national corporate law recognizes that the controlling shareholder has a legitimate interest in receiving the information (*infra* "Selective Disclosure to Controlling Shareholders"). Second, selective disclosure to non-controlling (institutional) shareholders may not be based on rather generic considerations such as "promoting shareholder loyalty" but require that they serve a specific goal which is in the interest of the company (*infra* "Selective Disclosure to Institutional Shareholders for the Sake of Shareholder Engagement"). Of course, in both situations, the

[88] Along the same lines, FCA, Final Notice to Sir Christopher Gent, 5 August 2022, para. 5.21(c): "although Recital 19 to EU MAR provides that discussions of a general nature regarding the business and market developments are permissible between shareholders and management concerning an issuer, Sir Christopher's disclosures of inside information were outside the scope of that type of discussion".

[89] Directive 2007/36/EC of the European Parliament and of the Council of 11 July 2007 on the exercise of certain rights of shareholders in listed companies, OJ L 184, 14.7.2007, p. 17, last revised by Directive (EU) 2017/828 of the European Parliament and of the Council of 17 May 2017 amending Directive 2007/36/EC as regards the encouragement of long-term shareholder engagement, OJ L 132, 20.5.2017, p. 1.

selective disclosure must meet the requirements of suitability, necessity and proportionality, which must be decided on a case-by-case basis.

Selective Disclosure to Controlling Shareholders As the ECJ stated in its *Grøngaard and Bang* judgment on the old Insider Dealing Directive,[90]

> [w]hat is to be regarded as coming within the normal ambit of the exercise of an employment, profession or duties depends to a large extent, in the absence of harmonisation in that respect, on the rules governing those questions in the various national legal systems.[91]

This adjudication is still valid under MAR.[92] Thus, within the limits of EU company law, it is up to the Member States to define the corporate governance role of (significant) shareholders and accordingly to facilitate or suppress the private disclosure of inside information under Art. 10 MAR. To be clear, member states cannot change Art. 10 MAR or regulate how Art. 10 MAR must be interpreted by national courts. They can, however, define legitimate purposes which management may pursue by selectively disclosing inside information and thus influence the way Art. 10 MAR operates.

For example, in Germany, disclosing inside information about a subsidiary to controlling shareholders within a group of companies is relatively easy due to the notion that German *Konzernrecht* not only permits but actually facilitates the management of a group of companies as a single entity (*einheitliche Leitung*), a notion which in German is called *Konzernermöglichungsfunktion*,[93] that is, the enabling function of German groups of companies' law.[94] The same is true for Danish law, as the Danish Supreme Court decided in the matter of *Vase*.[95] The European Court of Justice might have accepted the general notion that

[90] Council Directive 89/592/EEC of 13 November 1989 coordinating regulations on insider dealing, OJ L 334, 18.11.1989, p. 30.

[91] ECJ, Case C-384/02, Grøngaard and Bang, EU:C:2005:708 para. 40.

[92] Klöhn, Marktmissbrauchsverordnung (Beck 2018), Art. 10 para. 38.

[93] On this notion, see Mülbert, Aktiengesellschaft, Unternehmensgruppe und Kapitalmarkt, 2nd Ed. (Beck 1996), p. 16, 452; Verse, Der Gleichbehandlungsgrundsatz im Recht der Kapitalgesellschaften (Mohr Siebeck 2006), p. 340. The High Court of Justice (*Bundesgerichtshof*, BGH) has also recognized this notion, cf. BGH Neue Zeitschrift für Gesellschaftsrecht 2008, 831, 833 para. 18 (Züblin/Strabag).

[94] See, e.g., Klöhn, Marktmissbrauchsverordnung (Beck 2018), Art. 10 paras. 133–136.

[95] See Højesteret (Danish Supreme Court) Ugeskrift for Retsvæsen 2006.3359; on this decision see Hansen, 14 Eur. Company & Fin. L. Rev. 367, 375 (2017); Strampelli, 12 Va. L & Bus. Rev. 187, 222 (2018).

subsidiaries may selectively disclose inside information to parent companies to enable them to manage their subsidiaries in its *Verdonck* judgment[96] – a rarely cited judgment on the old Insider Dealing Directive.[97]

Selective Disclosure to Institutional Shareholders for the Sake of Shareholder Engagement

General Principles In the light of the ECJ's mandate that the exception under Art. 10 MAR must be interpreted "strictly",[98] that is, narrowly, a prudent interpretation would suggest that management might not disclose inside information to investors for *rather generic purposes* such as increasing shareholder loyalty,[99] securing long-term support of shareholders, the avoidance of an unpleasant surprise to a major shareholder or of an "ex post public display of dissent, which would harm the issuer's reputation and share price".[100] If information could be selectively disclosed for such purposes, the exception in Art. 10 MAR would easily swallow the rule contained in Art. 10 MAR, which is that selective disclosure is prohibited. Moreover, such interpretation could potentially justify the selective disclosure of almost any inside information, including highly price-sensitive information like financial data and forecasts that almost anyone agrees should not be eligible for selective disclosure to investors.[101] Finally, such broad interpretation of the "normal course of business" – exception would allow management to justify almost any disclosure even if it was primarily made for management's personal reasons such as "schmoozing" with investors. Put differently, it would make it much easier for managers to collude with selected investors to the detriment of all other shareholders, by selectively disclosing inside information to some shareholders as compensation for their toleration of management's self-serving behaviour.

[96] ECJ, Case C-28/99, Criminal proceedings against Jean Verdonck, Ronald Everaert and Edith de Baedts, EU:C:2001:238.

[97] This point has been made by Mosca, 15 Eur. Company & Fin. L. Rev. 805, 842 n. 137 (2018).

[98] ECJ, Case C-384/02, Grøngaard and Bang, EU:C:2005:708 para. 34; ECJ, Case C-302/20, M. A. v. AMF, Judgment of the Court of Justice (Grand Chamber) of 15 March 2022, EU:C:2022:190 para. 78.

[99] *But see* Strampelli, 12 Va. L & Bus. Rev. 187, 214, 224 (2018) (with regard to the principle of equal treatment of shareholders).

[100] *But see* Mosca, 15 Eur. Company & Fin. L. Rev. 805, 841 (2018).

[101] In the EU, Mosca, 15 Eur. Company & Fin. L. Rev. 805, 839 (2018); Strampelli, 12 Va. L & Bus. Rev. 187, 222 (2018); in the US, Rock, 97 Cornell L. Rev. 849, 903 (2012).

Rather, Art. 10 MAR must be interpreted as allowing managers to selectively disclose inside information to investors only if such disclosure is not only *in the interest of the company* but also necessary and proportionate to achieve *specific short or medium term goals*, such as soliciting support for management proposals in upcoming shareholder meetings, securing investor demand for an upcoming increase of capital, seeking support if the firm faces a crisis, debunking/clarifying rumours that are detrimental to the company's interest or discussing management positions on activist investor campaigns (when doing so with a public announcement would be itself harmful to the company). In particular, if approval by the shareholder meeting is necessary, it may be appropriate for directors to explore how shareholders are planning to vote and to convince them of the option that, in management's view, is the most beneficial to the company by disclosing inside information to investors.[102]

The question of whether selective disclosure in those cases meets the requirements of necessity and proportionality can only be answered on a case-by-case basis. Some criteria that need to be considered are the importance of the shareholder to the company, the relevance of the inside information for the shareholder's decision (the more relevant the information, the more justified the disclosure, other things being equal), the price-sensitivity of the information (the higher the price-sensitivity, the less justified its selective disclosure) and the availability of alternative information which does not qualify as inside information and therefore can be disclosed without risking a violation of Art. 10 MAR.[103]

In contrast, Professor Giovanni Strampelli has stated that under EU law any inside information may be disclosed to investors selectively as long as the recipients agree to keep the information confidential and abstain from trading financial instruments to which the inside information relates.[104] Professor Strampelli bases this notion of a

[102] Along the same lines, Mosca, 15 Eur. Company & Fin. L. Rev. 805, 841 (2018).

[103] For further general criteria and guidelines on the "normal course of business"-exception under Art. 10 MAR see Klöhn, Marktmissbrauchsverordnung (Beck 2018), Art. 10 paras. 43–90.

[104] Strampelli, 12 Va. L & Bus. Rev. 187, 215 (2018): "Thus, . . . when institutional investors agree to keep the information received confidential, and not to trade on the basis of such information, directors are allowed to freely engage in dialogue with them and to disclose material non-public information."

"confidentiality-based exemption under Article 10"[105] on Art. 17(8) MAR,[106] a rule which he interprets as allowing managers to selectively disclose inside information to shareholders if they sign a confidentiality agreement.[107] However, by its explicit wording, Art. 17(8) MAR *requires* a disclosure, which is thus lawful under Art. 10 MAR. It does not *make* the selective disclosure lawful simply because the recipients sign a confidentiality agreement. Article 17(8) MAR merely states that, if a selective disclosure is lawful under Art. 10 MAR, the issuer still has to publicize the information conveyed if the recipient is under no duty of confidentiality. It does not state that any disclosure is deemed lawful under Art. 10 MAR as long as the recipient is under such duty. As can be inferred from its position within MAR, Art. 17(8) MAR merely introduces an additional duty to publicly disclose inside information besides the general continuous disclosure obligation under Art. 17(1) MAR. It does not provide an exception to the prohibition of selective disclosure of inside information contained in Arts. 10 and 14 MAR. Moreover, Art. 17(8) MAR does not even require a confidentiality agreement between the person disclosing inside information and the person receiving it. As sentence 2 of Art. 17(8) MAR explicitly states, any duty of confidentiality suffices, "regardless of whether such duty is based on a law, on regulations, on articles of association, or on a contract." If Professor Strampelli's interpretation were correct, the ban on private disclosure under Art. 10 MAR would be widely irrelevant because most typical recipients of inside information are under a duty of confidentiality within the meaning of Art. 17(8) MAR – think about lawyers, accountants, bankers, members of the management board, members of the supervisory board and the like.

In contrast, Professor Strampelli backs his interpretation of MAR by invoking recital 19 MAR,[108] but, as stated before, this recital merely clarifies that board-shareholder talks on *general issues* are not in conflict with MAR, that is, talks on issues that do not involve the disclosure of inside information which, by definition, must be "specific enough to enable a conclusion to be drawn as to (its price relevance), Art. 7(2)

[105] Strampelli, 12 Va. L & Bus. Rev. 187, 215 (2018).
[106] On the wording of Art. 17(8) see *supra* 18.3.2.2.
[107] Strampelli, 12 Va. L & Bus. Rev. 187, 215 (2018).
[108] Strampelli, 12 Va. L & Bus. Rev. 187, 215 (2018). Strampelli Ibid at 215 n. 129 (2018) also cites recital 36 of MAR as support for his interpretation, but this recital concerns the market sounding exception of Art. 11 MAR, not the general rule of Art. 10 MAR.

MAR.[109] Under EU law, it is not uncommon that even legal rules contain redundant statements that are inserted for the sake of clarification.[110]

Application to the FCA's Action against Sir Christopher Gent If we apply the aforementioned principles to the case of Sir Christopher Gent,[111] we can see that the FCA was right in finding that he violated the prohibition of private disclosure of inside information under Arts. 10 and 14 MAR. First, the fact that the recipients of the information had agreed to keep the information confidential and not to trade does, by itself, not make the disclosure lawful – despite the wording of Art. 17(8) MAR.[112] Second, the general objective of "fostering good relations with shareholders" was not sufficient to allow the private disclosure of inside information since such interpretation of MAR would be in conflict with the ECJ's mandate to interpret the "normal course of business" exception in Art. 10 MAR "strictly".[113] The same goes for Sir Christopher's wish not to "surprise shareholders of scale".[114] If this objective could justify the selective disclosure of inside information, almost any inside information could, in principle, be disclosed to significant shareholders, especially information that is highly price-relevant. Under such a broad reading of the law, the "normal course of business" exception would swallow the general rule of non-disclosure.

18.3.3 UK

In the course of Brexit, MAR was "onshored", that is, adopted into UK law on 31 December 2020 by the European Union (Withdrawal) Act 2018.[115] The onshored act is now referred to as "UK MAR".[116] Changes to EU MAR were made by the Market Abuse (Amendment) (EU Exit)

[109] *Supra* 18.3.2.3 "Lack of Guidance by the Legislator, the ECJ and ESMA".

[110] As an example, consider the requirement of "relating, directly or indirectly, to one or more issuers or to one or more financial instruments" in Art. 7(1) lit. a) MAR. This requirement does not limit the concept of inside information. There is no information which is price-relevant and does not also relate, directly or indirectly, to one or more issuers or to one or more financial instruments. It is therefore redundant.

[111] *Supra* 18.2.4.4.

[112] The FCA did not address this point explicitly.

[113] FCA, Final Notice to Sir Christopher Gent, 5 August 2022, para. 5.21(b) (without reference to the ECJ case law).

[114] FCA, Final Notice to Sir Christopher Gent, 5 August 2022, para. 5.21(e).

[115] www.legislation.gov.uk/ukpga/2018/16/contents/enacted.

[116] www.fca.org.uk/markets/market-abuse/regulation.

Regulations 2019[117] to ensure that UK MAR operates effectively in the UK. Most of these changes are of a rather formal or editorial nature such as the replacement of references to EU legislative acts with references to UK (onshored) legislative acts. Therefore, the core insider regulation of EU MAR continues to be effective in the UK despite Brexit. This goes especially for the definition of inside information (Art. 7 MAR), the insider dealing prohibition (Art. 8 MAR), the ban on private disclosure of inside information (Art. 10 MAR) and the safe harbour for market soundings (Art. 11 MAR).[118] Thus, at least for now, everything we have said with respect to EU law applies in the UK as well.

18.3.4 Comparison

Comparing US and EU/UK law, it becomes clear, that – at least on paper – the MAR curtails the disclosure of inside information in the context of board-shareholder dialogue much more severely than US law.

- Under Art. 10 MAR, disclosure of inside information is *allowed* only if it occurs "in the normal course of business" of the company. In light of the ECJ's mandate to interpret the exception contained in Art. 10 MAR "strictly", that is, narrowly, selective disclosure made in behind-the-scenes talks between managers and investors is lawful only if the disclosure serves a concrete objective in the company's interest, if the disclosure is necessary to achieve that objective and if it complies with the principle of proportionality. Thus, management cannot disclose inside information to investors for the sole purpose of "improving investor relations" or "avoiding to (unpleasantly) surprise shareholders".
- In contrast, in the US, disclosure of inside information is *illegal* only if managers breach their fiduciary duties to the company when selectively disclosing inside information to investors. This usually requires that managers talk with investors in order to gain some monetary or reputational benefit for themselves. Regulation FD has the potential to prevent selective disclosure of inside information to investors but it can be avoided rather easily, especially by making investors sign a confidentiality agreement or by having them talk to firm employees not covered by Regulation FD.[119]

[117] www.legislation.gov.uk/uksi/2019/310/contents/made.
[118] On this issue, see Jennifer Payne, Chapter 19 (in this book).
[119] For more reasons for the failure of Regulation FD to curtail selective disclosure see *supra* 18.3.1.3 "Regulation FD".

From a practical perspective, the decisive question is whether those differences of the law in the books have real-life consequences, that is, whether board-shareholder talks in the US more often involve the disclosure of inside information than in the EU/UK. To the best of my knowledge, there is no empirical evidence on this issue.

From a theoretical perspective, we should not expect much difference because, as was pointed out earlier, institutional investors usually do not want to receive inside information.[120] If this is true, that is, if there is no *demand* for inside information, the fact that EU/UK law restricts the *supply* of inside information more severely will not have any effect. Put differently, to the extent that the *market* regulates and actually restricts the selective disclosure of inside information in behind-the-scenes-talks with investors, *differences in insider regulation* have no effect in the real world.

If that is correct, the major difference we should see is that investors in US companies benefit more often from selective disclosure of inside information *by abstaining* from trading.[121] Because investors have a clear preference for receiving inside information for the purpose of abstaining from trading,[122] and because issuers/managers have an incentive to provide such information when they are aware that significant shareholders are contemplating to trade in the issuer's shares,[123] supply of such information should be higher in the US than in the EU/UK because US law allows such disclosure more leniently than EU/UK law. Unfortunately, it seems very hard to test this hypothesis empirically because both the disclosure of inside information in behind-the-scenes talks and insider abstention are hard to observe. In this regard, the FCA action against Sir Christopher Gent is quite a spectacular outlier.[124]

18.4 Policy Options

From a policy perspective, the main question is whether legislators should introduce a safe harbour rule allowing the selective disclosure of

[120] *Supra* 18.2.3.

[121] Likewise, we should see more selective disclosure in the US in other situations in which investors have a preference for receiving inside information because they do not have to fear breaking insider trading law, such as when exercising pre-defined trading plans.

[122] *Supra* 18.2.4.3. [123] Ibid.

[124] Cf. FCA, Final Notice to Sir Christopher Gent, 5 August 2022, paras. 4.55 and 4.63 noting that "[n]o audio recording nor any contemporaneous written record was made" of the two conversations in which Sir Christopher disclosed the inside information.

inside information to investors for the purpose of facilitating shareholder engagement if certain pre-defined conditions are met. Such proposals have been made or encouraged in both the US[125] and the EU.[126]

The main argument in favour of such proposals is the promise of shareholder engagement to enhance corporate governance and increase the long-term firm value for all constituents of publicly listed companies. This notion has been embraced by regulators around the world, most prominently, perhaps, in the revision of the EU Shareholder Rights Directive[127] which states in its recital 14 that

> [e]ffective and sustainable shareholder engagement is one of the cornerstones of the corporate governance model of listed companies, which depends on checks and balances between the different organs and different stakeholders.

However, as we have seen, most institutional shareholders want to engage *without* receiving inside information. Consequently, guidelines for board-shareholder meetings generally indicate that price-sensitive information should not be disclosed during meetings between managers and investors.[128] As argued above, if we hypothesize that there is only little demand for inside information by engaging shareholders, the law curtailing the supply of inside information is rather insignificant.[129] On the other hand, any safe harbour rule might be used for purposes the legislator did not foresee, in our context perhaps for selective disclosures which primarily serve management's personal goals at the expense of shareholders as a group.[130]

Moreover, from the mere fact that shareholder engagement is beneficial to society, it does not follow that *selectively* disclosing inside information to *some* investors is also beneficial to society. Instead, there seem to be good reasons to mandate more transparency with respect to the board-shareholder dialogue that puts all shareholders on equal footing, a point which has already been made by Professors Bebchuk and Hirst.[131]

[125] Rock, 97 Cornell L. Rev. 849, 903 (2012).

[126] Strampelli, 12 Va. L & Bus. Rev. 187, 214, 230 (2018).

[127] *Supra* 18.3.2.3 "Lack of Guidance by the Legislator, the ECJ and ESMA" with n. 90.

[128] Cf. SDX, The Shareholder-Director Exchange, Introduction and SDX Protocol, February 2014, p. 13 ("clearly inappropriate").

[129] *Supra* 18.3.4.

[130] *Supra* 18.3.2.3 "Selective Disclosure to Institutional Shareholders for the Sake of Shareholder Engagement", "General Principles".

[131] Bebchuk/Hirst, 119 Colum. L. Rev. 2029, 2125 (2019): "In our view, it would be reasonable to interpret Regulation FD as requiring companies to disclose the existence

Finally, a safe harbour would make regulatory sense only if one believed that selective disclosure to investors is *generally* beneficial to the company and to society as a whole.[132] Under this assumption, designing a safe harbour rule would be mostly about defining the topics that management would be free to talk about, the eligible recipients of disclosure and the administrative measures to be taken by the issuer if it wants to make use of the safe harbour rule (for example documentation).[133] In the end, a safe harbour rule might look somewhat like Art. 11 MAR.[134]

If, however, one believed that such disclosure should be made *only in specific situations* and with a view to a specific purpose, a safe harbour would be primarily about defining those situations and purposes. The appropriate form of such regulation is not a *rule* but a *standard* because the costs of *making* such a rule, that is, defining the circumstances under which selective disclosure would be allowed in advance, would greatly outweigh the costs of *applying* it ex post.[135] Within this framework, any attempt to design a safe harbour regulation would be futile because such regulation would have to be a *rule* that creates legal certainty for issuers and investors and not a *standard*, which necessarily leads to some degree of legal uncertainty. This is exactly why the most important safe-harbour

and contents of all of their significant engagements with major investors. That Vanguard believes information from its private engagements with a company to be material is highly suggestive that other investors would regard it as material as well, and the information should therefore also be considered material to the company. Vanguard knows what demands it has communicated and how the company has responded; Regulation FD should require the disclosure of this information to all investors."

132 Along this line Strampelli, 12 Va. L & Bus. Rev. 187, 224 (2018) "engaging in dialogue with relevant shareholders, especially with institutional investors, is per se consistent with the interests of the company, since sound investor relations are crucial for listed companies", citing Hirt/Hopt/Mattheus, Die Aktiengesellschaft (2016), 725, 737 and Hopt, The Dialogue Between the Chairman of the Board and Investors: The Practice in the UK, the Netherlands and Germany and the Future of the German Corporate Governance Code Under the New Chairman (European Corp. Governance Inst., Law Working Paper No. 365/2017, 2017), https://ssrn.com/abstract=3030693, pp. 8–9.

133 See the framework proposed by Strampelli, 12 Va. L & Bus. Rev. 187, 225–239 (2018) under the headlines of "Identifying topics for dialogue", "Selecting participants in dialogue (on behalf of the company)", and "Adopting and disclosing a policy on director-shareholder meetings"; see also Rock, 97 Cornell L. Rev. 849, 903 (2012) who proposes "a safe harbour from Regulation FD for a defined set of 'high level topics' . . . with the exclusion of price-sensitive information like earnings".

134 On this topic see Jennifer Payne, Chapter 19 (in this book).

135 On the economics of choosing between rules and standards, see Kaplow, 42 Duke L.J. 557 (1992).

regulations contained in MAR are rules, not standards (see Art. 5 MAR on price-stabilization and buy-back programmes, and Art. 11 MAR on market soundings).

Moreover, even if we assume that a safe harbour rule would be desirable and that investors would generally be interested in receiving inside information to better engage with management, it remains doubtful whether a safe harbour rule would be used in practice. In this regard, the EU's experience with Art. 11 MAR is helpful. Although this safe harbour applies both to issuers and persons acting on behalf of issuers, issuers rarely conduct market soundings under Art. 11 MAR by themselves because complying with Art. 11 MAR is simply too costly. Instead, they rely on banks as repeat players to provide the service of conducting market soundings. Such intermediation does not seem feasible with respect to conducting management-shareholder dialogue because investors want to talk directly with the top management of the issuer. Second, market soundings under Art. 11 MAR work because investors receive inside information only for a relatively short period, usually for a couple of hours before the accelerated book building starts. In contrast, inside information disclosed in board-shareholder meetings would have to be kept confidential for a much longer period since the topic of the talk, that is, the circumstances to which the inside information relates, would typically not vanish in the ensuing weeks – think about soliciting support for the next shareholder meeting or during an activist's campaign. Such a "no trade" period seems to be unacceptable for most institutional investors, even assuming for the sake of argument that they would generally be interested in receiving inside information for engagement purposes.

Overall, it therefore seems that a safe harbour rule would be of little benefit and come at a great cost. Proposals to enact such rules should thus not be supported.

19

Market Soundings Rules

The Challenges and Opportunities for Board-Shareholder Engagement

JENNIFER PAYNE

19.1 Introduction

The potential value of effective board-shareholder dialogue for companies, shareholders and participants in the market more generally is well understood. Interest in this issue has risen in recent years, driven in part by a demand for more board-shareholder dialogue from activist shareholders, particularly on environmental and social issues,[1] as well as increasing expectations placed on institutional shareholders to engage with their investee companies.[2] Such a dialogue between boards and shareholders faces a number of potential difficulties, however, depending on the nature of the relevant legal regime and, in particular, the attitude of that regime to the regulation of corporate information. The ability of a board to disclose selectively sensitive and valuable information about the company and its plans to a subset of shareholders, and the ability of the recipients to utilise that information, varies from jurisdiction to jurisdiction. This chapter examines the restrictions placed on such a dialogue by the EU market abuse regime and the solution offered by the market soundings rules for one particular category of board-shareholder engagement. It then considers whether the solution offered by the market soundings regime can provide a valuable template for board-shareholder engagement more generally.

[1] Iain MacNeil, "Activism and Collaboration among Shareholders in UK Listed Companies" (2010) 5 Capital Markets L J 419; Wolf-Georg Ringe, "Shareholder Activism: A Renaissance" in Jeffrey N Gordon and Wolf-Georg Ringe (eds) *The Oxford Handbook of Corporate Law and Governance* (Oxford University Press, 2018); Oliver Hart and Luigi Zingales, "The New Corporate Governance" in Chapter 1 of this volume.

[2] See eg FRC, UK Stewardship Code 2020, Principle 10. See also Shareholder Rights Directive, Directive (EU) 2017/828, Art 9(c).

The EU market abuse regime imposes a number of significant challenges on board-shareholder dialogue.[3] First, the Market Abuse Regulation imposes a continuous disclosure obligation whereby issuers must disclose inside information to the market as soon as possible.[4] The information being disclosed in the course of board-shareholder dialogue may well be inside information if it is precise, has a direct or indirect relation to one or more issuers or financial instruments, and has not been made public but if made public would have a significant effect on the prices of financial instruments.[5] At the core of the EU regime is an assumption that corporate information in publicly traded companies is a public resource, which belongs to the market rather than the company and that the information needs to be made available to all investors within the market simultaneously, in other words that there should be equal access to information for all investors within the market. There is accordingly a constraint on selective disclosure: an issuer or a person acting on behalf of an issuer which discloses any inside information to any third party in the normal course of the exercise of an employment, profession or duty must make complete and effective public disclosure of the information.[6] From the perspective of the person who wishes to disclose the inside information to an investor, the Market Abuse Regulation prohibits the unlawful disclosure of inside information.[7] There is an exception where the disclosure is made in the normal course of an employment, a profession or duties,[8] but this exception has been interpreted narrowly.[9] From the perspective of the person who would receive the information, they will find themselves unable to engage in certain behaviour, such as buying or selling securities of the issuer, without breaching the insider dealing provisions within the Market Abuse Regulation.[10] This ensures that those with privileged access to information are not allowed to obtain any undue economic advantage by trading or by transmitting inside information to third parties. However,

[3] For discussion, see G Strampelli, 'Knocking at the Boardroom Door: A Transatlantic Overview of Director-Institutional Investor Engagement in Law and Practice' (2018) 12 Va L & Bus Rev 187.

[4] MAR, Art 17(1). The opportunity for the issuer to delay disclosure is extremely limited: Art 17(4).

[5] MAR, Art 7(1), 7(2). [6] MAR, Art 17(8). [7] MAR, Art 14(c).

[8] MAR, Art 10(1).

[9] Case C-384/02 *Grøngaard and Bang* [2005] ECR I-9939. This approach was followed in Case C-302/20 *MA v AMF*, 15 March 2022.

[10] MAR, Art 8(1). See also Arts 8(2) and 10(1).

these constraints may be unwelcome to recipients who do not wish to be wall-crossed in this way.[11] This regime stands in stark contrast to other jurisdictions, such as the US, which manage the issue of inside information disclosure very differently,[12] although the selective disclosure regime is somewhat similar.[13]

The EU provisions appear to constrain significantly the opportunities for board-shareholder dialogue. However, the benefits of board-shareholder disclosure are recognised within the Market Abuse Regulation which provides that:

> This Regulation is not intended to prohibit discussions of a general nature regarding the business and market developments between shareholders and management concerning an issuer. Such relationships are essential for the efficient functioning of markets and should not be prohibited by this Regulation.[14]

Accordingly, the Regulation incorporates an EU-wide market soundings regime which is designed to protect the communication of certain information (effectively inside information) by firms and other actors.[15] The focus of the regime is on creating a safe harbour for disclosures made where issuers/offerors and their advisors or brokers are gauging investor interest in a potential capital markets transaction such as IPOs, rights issues, debt

[11] For an example of a shareholder being found to have violated insider dealing provisions when he sold shares following conversations with the issuer about potential future fundraising transactions, see FSA, David Einhorn, Decision Notice, 12 January 2012. This was despite the shareholder specifically refusing to be "wall-crossed".

[12] See *Chiarella v United States*, 445 US 222 (1980); *Dirks v SEC*, 463 US 646 (1983). See E Greene and O Schmid, 'Duty Free Insider Trading' (2013) Columbia Business Law Review 369; M Ventoruzzo, 'Comparing Insider Trading in the United States and the European Union: History and Recent Developments' (2014) 11 European Company & Fin Law Rev 554; L Klöhn, 'Board-Shareholder Engagement and Insider Regulation', Chapter 18 in this volume.

[13] See Regulation FD (Fair Disclosure), 17 CFR Part 243. For discussion see Edward B. Rock, 'Shareholder Eugenics in the Public Corporation' (2012) 97 Cornell L Rev 849; M Bengtzen, 'Private Investor Meetings in Public Firms: The Case for Increasing Transparency' (2017) 33 Fordham J Corp & Fin Law 33; G Strampelli, 'Knocking at the Boardroom Door: A Transatlantic Overview of Director-Institutional Investor Engagement in Law and Practice' (2018) 12 Va L & Bus Rev 187.

[14] MAR, recital 19.

[15] MAR, Art 11. This Article is supplemented by Commission Implementing Regulation EU 2016/959, Commission Delegated Regulation (EU) 2016/960 and by ESMA guidelines (ESMA, Final Report Guidelines on the Market Abuse Regulation – market soundings and delay of disclosure of inside information 13 July 2016, ESMA/2016/1130). As discussed in Section 19.2 the regime also encompasses non-insider information.

issuances or secondary market sales of equity or debt. Notably, therefore, the market soundings regime attempts to facilitate the second benefit of board-shareholder engagement outlined above, namely the benefit to the board of eliciting information about future plans from investors, rather than the first, namely the potential corporate governance benefits attached to any such engagement.[16] The explicit goal of the market soundings regime within the Market Abuse Regulation is market-focused, namely "the proper functioning of financial markets",[17] rather than company-focused.

The introduction of the market soundings regime can therefore be seen as a means of facilitating certain types of board-shareholder engagement within the framework of an insider trading regime that otherwise discourages selective disclosures. It is clear that not all forms of such engagement are covered, only those within the scope of the regime, and also that the regime is aimed at board-investor engagement rather than board-shareholder engagement as such. The regime seeks to balance the benefits of dialogue with the benefits of the market abuse regime more broadly. In Section 19.2 of this chapter, the EU market soundings regime is examined in detail. The regime is subject to a number of conditions and restrictions which are central to its operation, and the trade-offs created within the regime are assessed. It is argued that while the regime can be regarded as broadly successful in its aim of creating a safe harbour for board disclosures within its ambit, it does so at a significant cost to those seeking to utilise it. In Section 19.3 the question of whether this regime could provide a template for board-shareholder dialogue more generally is explored. It is argued that the market soundings regime as currently constructed maps poorly onto a broader vision of board-shareholder dialogue and is unlikely to operate as a useful model. However, for the reasons explored in Section 19.4, it is argued that this is unlikely to be unduly problematic.

19.2 The Operation of the Market Soundings Regime

19.2.1 Rationale for the Regime

The market soundings regime was introduced into the EU for the first time in 2016. No such regime existed at EU level prior to the Market

[16] According to MAR, recital 32, market soundings "are a highly valuable tool to gauge the opinion of potential investors, enhance shareholder dialogue, ensure that deals run smoothly, and that the views of issuers, existing shareholders and potential new investors are aligned".

[17] MAR, recital 32.

Abuse Regulation. The Market Abuse Directive[18] did not contain any equivalent provision although some Member States, such as the UK, sought to deal with this issue within their national regimes.[19] The Market Abuse Directive prohibited insiders from disclosing inside information to third parties unless such a disclosure was "in the normal course of exercise of an employment, profession or duties"[20] and with a requirement that the insider must make "complete and effective public disclosure" of such information unless the recipient was bound by a duty of confidentiality. No safe harbour for any forms of issuer-investor dialogue existed and accordingly the question arose whether disclosure by the issuer to selected parties regarding a planned operation was acting in the "normal course of an employment, profession or duties". In *Grøngaard and Bang*[21] the ECJ decided that a piece of information is deemed to be disclosed in the normal course of the exercise of employment, profession or duties when there is a close link between the disclosure and the exercise of employment, profession or duties and the disclosure is necessary for the exercise of that employment, profession or duties. This strict approach apparently left little room for market soundings to occur, and yet market soundings had become a common practice in the market due to the benefits that they are deemed to provide. Accordingly, this was something the Market Abuse Regulation sought to address.

The Market Abuse Regulation provides the following policy justifications for the introduction of the market soundings regime:

> [Market soundings] are a highly valuable tool to gauge the opinion of potential investors, enhance shareholder dialogue, ensure that deals run smoothly, and that the views of issuers, existing shareholders and potential new investors are aligned. They may be particularly beneficial when markets lack confidence or a relevant benchmark, or are volatile. Thus the

[18] Directive 2003/6/EC.

[19] The Handbook of the national regulator in the UK specified the factors that should be taken into account when assessing whether a disclosure was made in the proper course of the exercise of an employment, profession or duties (FCA Handbook, MAR 1.4.5) in order to clarify the circumstances when an issuer could discuss a future transaction with an investor without falling foul of the unlawful disclosure provision in the market abuse regime. In particular any disclosures were required to be accompanied by the imposition of a confidentiality requirement, should be reasonable and should aim to facilitate a "commercial, financial or investment transaction".

[20] Directive 2003/6/EC, Art 3(1)(a).

[21] Case C-384/02 *Grøngaard and Bang* [2005] ECR I-9939. This approach has been followed subsequently by the ECJ, see Case C-302/20 *MA v AMF*, 15 March 2022.

> ability to conduct market soundings is important for the proper functioning of financial markets and market soundings should not in themselves be regarded as market abuse.[22]

The first benefit identified is therefore to the issuer. Market soundings can assist issuers in checking the likely investor interest in a planned transaction. Specifically, given the scope of the EU market soundings regime, it can enable issuers to receive feedback from investors on the size and price of a planned offer of shares or securities to the market or to selected investors. This can provide issuers with a valuable sounding board and allow then to cross-check their assumptions about the likely interest of investors ahead of a new issue. It can therefore be a useful tool for issuers and can assist price discovery. This can help to ensure that the planned transaction is acceptable to the market once announced and is ultimately successful. As the quote above makes clear, this can be particularly valuable for issuers where the market price is difficult or impossible to gauge. This could be because the shares are not yet publicly traded. Even where the shares are publicly traded and there is a market price available to act as a yardstick for the pricing of the intended transaction, there may be some uncertainty about the market response to a planned transaction, such as where markets are unstable.[23] In keeping with this market-focused justification, the market soundings regime is not limited to dialogue between the issuer and its existing shareholders but covers issuer-investor discussions more broadly.

There is also a potential benefit to those receiving the market sounding. This will generally be a selected group of investors, and within the EU market sounding regime the person disclosing the information seems to be free to select the recipients of the disclosed information. For those being sounded, the information provides early notice of a transaction and the ability to influence its structure and price. Crucially, the justification for the market soundings regime set out in the Market Abuse Regulation focuses not on the benefits to the individual investor-recipients of the information but on the benefit to investors generally via the "proper functioning of the financial markets". Gauging investor interest in a planned issue so as to ensure that it is priced correctly can benefit the smooth operation of the securities market and thus investors

22 MAR, recital 32.

23 Alternatively, the issuer may wish to issue shares not to the public generally but rather to a subset of investors via some form of placing.

generally. This focus on the benefit to investors fits with the core objective of the regulation of market abuse more generally.[24]

The basis of the EU approach to prohibiting insider dealing is that such behaviour causes investors to lose confidence in the market, believing that the market is rigged against them. A significant component of this approach is market egalitarianism, that is, that investors should have equal access to information in the marketplace.[25] This idea of market egalitarianism has been influential in forming the EU regime,[26] and requires that investors should have equal access to information and should not be unfairly disadvantaged by insiders dealing in the market on the basis of non-public information.[27] The market soundings regime therefore seeks to balance the benefits of board-investor dialogue in certain circumstances with this core ideal of market egalitarianism.

19.2.2 Content of the Regime

The market soundings regime creates a safe harbour for a limited range of board-investor interactions from the difficulties they would otherwise face under the Market Abuse Regulation, provided certain conditions are fulfilled.

The limited range of board-investor interactions within the ambit of the regime involve the communication of information prior to the announcement of a transaction to one or more potential investors by an issuer, a secondary offeror of financial instruments, an emission allowances market participant or a third party acting on behalf of these persons. The regime only covers communications to gauge the interest of

[24] MAR, recital 2.

[25] This is not the approach that is adopted in all jurisdictions. In the US, for example, the parity of information approach has been rejected by the courts as too broad in scope given that the US insider trading provisions are based on an anti-fraud provision: *Chiarella v United States*, 445 US 222 (1980), 234. For further discussion of the US approach see E Greene and O Schmid, "Duty-free Insider Trading?" (2013) *Columbia Business Law Review* 369.

[26] N Moloney, *EU Securities and Financial Markets Regulation*, 4th edn (Oxford University Press, 2023) 682.

[27] It is clear that absolute parity of information is not required by the regime. While the Market Abuse Regulation seeks to prevent insiders trading on the information to make a gain or avoid a loss, it does not seek to prohibit information traders such as analysts trading on the information that they have acquired in the course of their roles. For discussion see J Payne, "Disclosure of Inside Information" in R Veil and V Tountopoulos (eds) *The Transparency of Stock Corporations in Europe* (Hart Publishing, 2019).

potential investors in a possible transaction and the related conditions, such as size and pricing. The transactions within the scope of the regime include situations where a company decides to go public and list on a regulated market and secondary offerings such as rights issues. The regime also covers the disclosure of inside information by a person intending to make a takeover bid for the securities of a company or to engage with a merger of the company, if that information is necessary to enable the parties entitled to the securities to form an opinion on their willingness to offer the securities and the information is reasonably required for the decision to make the takeover bid or engage in the merger.[28] However, given the focus of this chapter on board-shareholder disclosures, this form of bidder-shareholder dialogue will not be discussed further.

There are three particular difficulties created by the Market Abuse Regulation for board-shareholder disclosures which the market soundings regime seeks to address: (i) the person disclosing the information may be liable for unlawfully disclosing inside information contrary to Article 14(c); (ii) the recipients of the information are provided with information which may be inside information and which they are then potentially able to use to buy or sell securities, recommend that another person engages in insider dealing or induce them to do so, or disclose that inside information and (iii) issuers are generally prohibited by Article 17(8) from selectively disclosing information to a subset of investors and not to the market generally.

19.2.2.1 Unlawful Disclosure of Inside Information

Article 14(c) of the Market Abuse Regulation prohibits the unlawful disclosure of information to third parties. Unlawful disclosure of inside information arises where a person possesses inside information and discloses that information to any other person, except where the disclosure is made in the normal exercise of an employment, a profession or duties.[29] As discussed in Section 19.2.1, prior to the market soundings regime there was considerable uncertainty regarding whether information provided by the board to selected shareholders about the price or size of a planned capital raising exercise in order to gauge the likely interest in the transaction would fall within this exception.[30] The solution adopted by the market soundings regime is that where such a disclosure

[28] MAR, Art 11(2). [29] MAR, Art 10(1).
[30] See Case C-384/02 *Grøngaard and Bang* [2005] I-9939.

is made "in the course of a market sounding" then, as long as the relevant conditions are complied with, the disclosure is deemed to have been made in the normal course of the exercise of a person's employment, profession or duty.[31] Accordingly such a market sounding will not constitute an unlawful disclosure of inside information for the purposes of the Market Abuse Regulation.

The conditions are as follows. First, before conducting a market sounding the person intending to disclose the information (the disclosing market participant) must specifically consider whether the market sounding will involve the disclosure of inside information and make a written record of its conclusion and its reasons.[32] This obligation applies to each disclosure of information throughout the course of the market sounding. These written records must be provided to the competent authority upon request. Second, where the information is deemed to be inside information, before making the disclosure the disclosing market participant must obtain the consent of the person receiving the market sounding to receive the information and provide that person with specified pieces of information about the obligation on the recipient to keep the information confidential and not to use the information in ways that would breach the provisions of the Market Abuse Regulation, such as using the inside information to buy or sell securities in the issuer.[33] The disclosing market participant must keep records of all information given to the person receiving the market sounding, the identity of the investors to whom the information has been disclosed, and the date and time of each disclosure.[34] Again, these records must be provided to the competent authority upon request.[35] Next, the disclosing market participant must establish a procedure for conducting market soundings.[36] Although it seems to be left to the disclosing market participant to select to which investors they disclose, once they are selected there is an obligation to disclose the same level of information to each recipient.[37] Finally, where information that has been disclosed in the course of a market sounding

31 MAR, Art 11(4).

32 MAR, Art 11(3) and see Article 3 of Commission Delegated Regulation (EU) 2016/960.

33 MAR, Art 11(5). Discussed further at Section 19.2.2.2.

34 MAR, Art 11(5) and see Articles 3 and 4 of Commission Delegated Regulation (EU) 2016/960.

35 The records referred in in Article 11 must be kept for at least five years: Art 11(8) and Article 6 of Commission Delegated Regulation (EU) 2016/960.

36 Article 2 of Commission Delegated Regulation (EU) 2016/960.

37 Article 3(5) of Commission Delegated Regulation (EU) 2016/960.

ceases to be inside information according to the assessment of the disclosing market participant, they shall inform the recipient accordingly as soon as possible, and keep a record of this information which will be provided to the competent authority upon request.[38] Detailed templates are provided for the records of communications with recipients for the purpose of the market soundings regime.[39]

These conditions set out in the market sounding regime are mandatory, and time-consuming.[40] There is a significant cost attached to them. The onerous and costly nature of these conditions can perhaps be justified given the aims of the Market Abuse Regulation and the strong emphasis on market efficiency and investor confidence. In the market soundings regime, the importance of preventing unlawful disclosure of inside information to third parties is balanced with the market efficiency gains that may arise from boards being able to accurately price capital raising measures. However, it is notable that the market soundings regime extends to situations where the disclosing market participant deems that the information is not inside information, in which case the time and costs involved in complying with the regime (albeit at a reduced level) are less easy to justify, particularly in light of the mandatory nature of the regime; it is not possible for the parties to weigh the relative benefits and costs of the regime and opt out if need be.[41] Whether these costs can be justified in any broader board-shareholder dialogue regime is also doubtful, as discussed in Section 19.3.

19.2.2.2 Use of Inside Information by the Recipients

The next issue for the market soundings regime is the fact that the disclosure by the disclosing market participant may result in the

[38] MAR, Art 11(6).

[39] Annexes I–III to Commission Implementing Regulation (EU) 2016/959.

[40] Although the mandatory nature of the regime is not set out in the Market Abuse Regulation, this point was emphasised by ESMA in its review of the Market Abuse Regulation in 2020: ESMA, MAR Review Report, 23 September 2020 | ESMA70-156-2391, 74.

[41] At that point the disclosing market participant still has obligations under Art 11 of the MAR. A procedure for dealing with the communication still applies, albeit a slightly simplified one. For example, there must be a statement that the communication is for the purposes of a market sounding, a statement that the recipient will receive information which the discloser considers not to be inside information and the recipient must agree to receive the market sounding. As with communications deemed to involve inside information, there is a record keeping requirement imposed on the person disclosing the information.

investor-recipients being in possession of inside information which they might then be in a position to (mis)use in various ways. Of course, if the information that is disclosed is inside information then the recipient of the information will be subject to the obligations within the Market Abuse Regulation that relate to those that come into possession of inside information. Accordingly, they are prohibited from using that information by acquiring or disposing of financial instruments to which that information relates[42] or recommending that another person engages in insider dealing or inducing another person to engage in insider dealing[43] in the circumstances described in Article 8. They will also be caught by Article 10 if they unlawfully disclose that inside information to any other person, except where the disclosure is made in the normal exercise of an employment, a profession or duties.[44] However, it is possible that the investor may not know that the information is inside information when it is disclosed to them by the issuer. For certain categories of person, including shareholders of the issuer,[45] this is irrelevant, but otherwise the Market Abuse Regulation provides that the person must know, or ought to know, that it is inside information.[46] It is also possible that they do not want to receive that information and thus be prohibited from these various forms of behaviour.

The market soundings regime attempts to deal with this issue. The regime requires issuers to specifically identify the information which they deem to be inside information and ask for the investors' consent to be "wall-crossed" in order to make clear to investors that they have a choice.[47] If they still want to trade in the securities of the issuer or otherwise be unencumbered by Articles 8 and 10 of the Market Abuse Regulation they can refuse to be wall-crossed and for some investors this will be an option they want to exercise. If, however, they receive the information, the regime requires the person disclosing the information to make clear the consequential restrictions that the Market Abuse Regulation places on the recipient. It is important to recognise, however, that investors cannot rely on the designation placed by the discloser of the information as to whether it is inside information or not. The regime provides that "[n]otwithstanding the provisions of this Article, the person receiving the market sounding shall assess for itself whether it is

[42] MAR, Art 8(1). [43] MAR, Art 8(2). [44] MAR, Art 10(1).
[45] MAR, Art 8(4)(b). [46] MAR, Art 8(4), 10(1). [47] MAR, Art 11(5).

in possession of inside information".[48] The difficulties facing recipients in this situation are amply demonstrated by the facts of the *Einhorn* decision.[49]

David Einhorn was the portfolio manager of a company (Greenlight Capital Inc) that held approximately 13 per cent of the shares of Punch Tavern plc. Punch decided to raise new capital via an issue of shares and entered into discussions with potential investors, including Mr Einhorn, to gauge their interest in subscribing for these shares. While other investors that were approached agreed to be wall-crossed and signed non-disclosure agreements, Mr Einhorn refused to be wall-crossed in any discussions between himself and Punch and specifically asked not to receive inside information. Nevertheless, in the course of those discussions, reference was made to the possible issue of new shares by Punch and the intention to use the capital to repay convertible bonds. Mr Einhorn subsequently decided to sell part of Greenlight's shareholding in Punch. After Punch's announcement of its intention to issue new shares the share price fell by 30 per cent so that by selling Greenlight's shares when he did Mr Einhorn avoided a loss that he would otherwise have suffered if he had retained all of Greenlight's shares in Punch. The UK regulator determined that both Mr Einhorn and Greenlight were in breach of the insider dealing provisions and imposed a penalty on them. Despite Mr Einhorn's request not to be wall-crossed the regulator found that given his experience it should have been apparent to him that the information he received was confidential and price sensitive. The lesson is that the protection provided to recipients of information by the market soundings regime is by no means absolute.

19.2.2.3 Selective Disclosure

The EU market egalitarian approach to market abuse regulation discussed at Section 19.2.1 militates against selective disclosure of information. Article 17(8) of the Market Abuse Regulation requires an issuer

[48] MAR, Art 11(7). Similarly, the market soundings regime requires the person disclosing the information to inform the recipient as soon as possible after the discloser deems that the information has ceased to be inside information (Art 11(6)) but in this regard also the recipient cannot rely on this designation and must decide this for themselves.

[49] David Einhorn, FSA Decision Notice, 12 January 2012. Although this decision pre-dates the Market Abuse Regulation the approach adopted in *Einhorn* remains relevant for the EU regime given the explicit reference in the market soundings regime to the need for recipients to assess for themselves whether the information received is inside information and not to rely on the assessment of the issuer in this regard.

(or a person acting on behalf of an issuer) which discloses any inside information to any third party in the normal course of the exercise of an employment, profession or duty, to make complete and effective public disclosure of the information, simultaneously in the case of intended disclosure and promptly in the case of unintended disclosure. This creates a challenge for the market soundings regime since by definition this regime envisages the disclosure of information to a selected subset of investors which may well constitute inside information, concerning as it does a planned future issue of the issuer's securities.

Article 17(8) is subject to a carve out, however. Where the person to whom the information is disclosed is bound by a duty of confidentiality then disclosure to that individual will not trigger a general duty of disclosure.[50] This covers those who automatically owe a duty of confidentiality as a result of their profession, such as the issuer's lawyers and accountants. It also covers those who are placed under a duty to keep the information confidential. The market soundings regime places such a duty on the recipients of the information that agree to be wall-crossed; thus, market soundings fall within the carve out to the selective disclosure requirement. In this way the regime seeks to balance the benefit to the issuer of engaging in selective disclosure with a subset of investors with the overarching goal of facilitating market efficiency and investor confidence.

19.2.3 Assessment of the Regime

Judged narrowly, the market soundings regime can be regarded as a successful mechanism for dealing with a particular and limited issue, namely facilitating issuers wishing to engage with investors about the size and pricing of a limited number of capital raising transactions by creating a safe harbour within the market abuse regime. Early uncertainties regarding the possible scope of the regime seem to have been resolved and the review by ESMA of the Market Abuse Regime in 2020 made only minor tweaks to the market soundings regime.[51] However, the safe harbour provided by the regime comes at a price; the regime is undoubtedly onerous and costly for issuers and leaves investors potentially exposed in *Einhorn*-type scenarios. The question arises as to whether

[50] For further discussion see L Klöhn, 'Board-Shareholder Engagement and Insider Regulation', Chapter 18 in this volume.

[51] ESMA, MAR Review Report, 23 September 2020 | ESMA70-156-2391, Part 6.

this successful, albeit narrow and costly, regime can operate as a model for other forms of board-shareholder engagement.

19.3 Can the Market Soundings Regime Act as a Model for Other Forms of Board-Shareholder Engagement?

While the EU market soundings regime is in many ways successful at performing the task it has been set and some elements of the market soundings regime may be valuable, the regime as a whole maps poorly onto a broader board-shareholder dialogue regime and is unlikely to operate as a useful model.

The EU market soundings regime is formulated to deal with a very specific set of issues which arise from the operation of the EU market abuse regime and is intended to facilitate only a narrow set of board disclosures. Specifically, one of the key aims of the regime is to enable boards to effectively set the terms of forthcoming capital raising measures, to the benefit of the board and to investors generally via increased market efficiency. It is a market-focused regime. This has important implications for the structure of the regime and creates significant challenges when attempting to map this regime onto a broader vision of board-shareholder dialogue which is rooted in potential benefits to shareholders and a corporate governance focus.

The market-orientated model of the market soundings regime makes it both broader and narrower than would be needed for a more general board-shareholder dialogue mechanism. It is broader in that it covers not only interactions between the board and shareholders, but also between the board and investors more generally.[52] It is narrower in that the ambit of the market soundings regime is only a subset of matters about which boards and shareholders may wish to engage.[53] It covers only communications to investors in relation to a limited number of possible capital-raising transactions, and only insofar as it seeks to gauge their interest in

[52] The EU market soundings regime also covers not only interactions between the board and shareholders, but also dialogue between bidders or those intending to engage in a merger with a company and the shareholders of that company.

[53] It only relates to financial instruments within the scope of Article 2 of MAR: see ESMA, Questions and Answers on the Market Abuse Regulation (MAR), ESMA70–145-111 Version 16 (last updated on 23 June 2022), 35. These are, broadly, financial instruments admitted to trading on EU-regulated markets, MTFs or OTFs and other financial instruments whose price or value depends on or has an effect on the price or value of these EU-admitted securities (MAR, Art 2(1)(d)).

the relevant transaction and its terms and not for any other purpose.[54] It is notable therefore that the market soundings may take place only a short time before the anticipated capital raising activity so that the period during which the recipient has the information, but the market does not, may be relatively short. A broader board-shareholder regime may involve disclosures where this period is much longer. The market soundings regime focuses only on disclosures made by the board in the course of the board-shareholder dialogue; it is confined to the communication of information from issuers and those acting on their behalf to investors. It is about board disclosures (monologue) rather than dialogue. Further, this regime deals with only a limited set of issues. It does not, for example, deal with any company law issues that may arise where boards disclose information to a sub-set of shareholders. Company law issues are on the whole jurisdiction-specific and some regimes may require the equal treatment of shareholders in some circumstances, which may in turn create difficulties where the board dialogue is only with selected shareholders.[55]

There are two questions to consider regarding whether some form of safe harbour based on the market soundings regime should be developed. The first is the compatibility of such a safe harbour with the current design of the EU market abuse regime. The justification for the market soundings regime is that it facilitates market efficiency and can be accommodated within the overall aims of the market abuse regime. By contrast, the benefits of facilitating a dialogue between shareholders and the board about directors' pay, or about ESG concerns, for example, are not first and foremost founded on market efficiency, but on corporate governance concerns. While corporate disclosures can of course be viewed as beneficial both in market efficiency and corporate governance terms,[56] this latter goal is not emphasised within the market abuse regime. Similarly, while the EU is starting to recognise the importance

[54] It does not extend to communications after the announcement of such a transaction.

[55] See S Lombardo and F Mucciarelli, 'Market Soundings: The Interaction Between Securities Regulation and Company Law in the United Kingdom and Italy' (2019) 16 European Company & Fin Law Rev 310.

[56] For discussion of the benefit of corporate disclosures from a corporate governance perspective, see eg MB Fox, 'Required Disclosure and Corporate Governance' (1999) 62 Law and Contemporary Problems 113; P Mahoney, 'Mandatory Disclosure as a Solution to Agency Problems' (1995) 62 University of Chicago Law Review 1047; R Kraakman, 'Disclosure and Corporate Governance: An Overview Essay' in G Ferrarini et al (eds) *Reforming Company and Takeover Law in Europe* (Oxford University Press, 2004).

of broader ESG goals[57] these are still in the early stages of development. At present there is therefore no mechanism within the market abuse regime to balance these goals against the overarching market efficiency rationale. Reform in this regard seems unlikely at present. While another safe harbour within the Market Abuse Regulation, that involving legitimate interests in Article 9, does encompass some scenarios that seem potentially to extend beyond activities that might be viewed as beneficial to the market, those extensions are narrowly focused on the policy goals associated with the ban on insider dealing.[58] This does not seem to provide any basis for the much more expansive exception that would be needed to extend the market soundings regime to accommodate a broad set of corporate governance goals. There was no suggestion in the recent ESMA review of change of this nature and such a reform of the Market Abuse Regulation seems unlikely any time soon given its focus on market efficiency and market egalitarianism.[59]

The second question is the extent to which such a safe harbour would be beneficial for boards and shareholders. Within the EU, communications between the board and shareholders need to consider the market abuse regime and the issues discussed in Section 19.2 that arise around selective disclosure and for disclosers and recipients where the information is inside information.[60] As discussed in Section 19.2, the market soundings regime is not vital for this purpose, since board disclosures to

[57] See eg Regulation (EU) 2019/2088 (EU Sustainable Finance Disclosure Regulation); Communication from the Commission to the European Parliament, the European Council, the Council, the European Central Bank, the European Economic and Social Committee and the Committee of the Regions Action Plan: Financing Sustainable Growth, COM/2018/097 final.

[58] See eg Article 9(3) which involves the situation in which a person engages in an acquisition or disposal in order to discharge an obligation that has become due in good faith and not to circumvent the prohibition on insider dealing. While there may be some benefit to the market in allowing a person to conclude an agreement that was agreed prior to the acquisition of inside information, equally there may not. More generally this provision seems based on the fact that such a person is not utilising the information to make a gain or avoid a loss and would have dealt in the securities in any case. There is no unfair advantage being obtained in such a situation as the terms of the deal are agreed before the inside information is acquired. Article 9(5) seems to have a similar rationale.

[59] See ESMA, MAR Review Report, 23 September 2020 | ESMA70–156-2391.

[60] Other jurisdictions tackle these issues in different ways. In the US, for example, the issue of selective disclosure is similar to the EU position under Article 17(8) of the Market Abuse Regulation as a result of Regulation FD but the position regarding insider dealing and the potential liabilities of discloser and recipient are distinct (see eg M Ventoruzzo, 'Comparing Insider Trading in the United States and the European Union: History and Recent Developments' (2014) 11 European Company & Fin Law Rev 554).

selected investors were, after all, possible before the 2016 regime. Rather, what the regime is intended to provide is certainty for the parties, but at a (significant) cost. Unless any extended regime were made voluntary rather than mandatory so that the parties could themselves weigh the costs against the expected benefits and opt out if need be, the costs of providing this mandatory safe harbour are likely to be simply too high. This raises the question whether the certainty sought by boards could be provided in other ways.

Even without a specific market soundings regime, the discloser of inside information will be protected from liability for unlawful disclosure if they can demonstrate that the disclosure is strictly necessary for the exercise of an employment, a profession or duties and complies with the principle of proportionality,[61] and will be able to avoid the prohibition on selective disclosure as long as the recipients are placed under a duty of confidentiality.[62] Of these two issues it is the first that brings the greatest potential risk to boards wishing to disclose inside information to shareholders. As long as recipients are fully informed and consent to wall-crossing, and a duty of confidentiality is imposed, it is the application of the *Grøngaard* test that seems to create the greatest risk for boards.[63] The boundaries of the concept are strictly policed by the ECJ as the recent decision in *MA v AMF* confirms.[64]

These decisions by no means prevent disclosure by the board, however, and there will clearly be circumstances where disclosure of inside information by the board to certain shareholders can be regarded as strictly necessary for the exercise of an employment, a profession or duties. Equally, however, some disclosures of inside information will not, and should not, be regarded as falling within this exception. The disclosure of highly sensitive information to certain shareholders to ensure their support or loyalty, such as the forthcoming financial results of the company, would be incompatible with the fundamental principle of equal access to information at the heart of the market abuse regime. Take the example of the recent action by the UK regulator against Sir Christopher Gent.[65] Sir Christopher Gent, the non-executive chairman of a company listed on the main market of the London Stock Exchange, disclosed inside information to two key investors because he wanted to foster good relationships with those shareholders. He was found liable for

[61] MAR, Art 14(c) and Case C-302/20, *MA v AMF*, 15 March 2022. [62] MAR, Art 17(8).
[63] See n 21 and accompanying text. [64] Case C-302/20 *MA v AMF*, 15 March 2022.
[65] FCA, Final Notice to Sir Christopher Gent, 5 August 2022.

unlawfully disclosing inside information and fined £80,000. While this may seem surprising when viewed through the lens of the US regime (after all there was no evidence that he intended to make a personal gain or avoid a loss from making these disclosures) it is entirely in keeping with the policy rationale of the EU regime.

Within the EU, the policy goal should not be to allow boards to selectively disclose inside information to shareholders whenever they like, but rather to provide clarity as to when boards can do so without falling foul of the Market Abuse Regulation provisions. Notably this is not an area on which ESMA has sought to provide guidance in its Q&As.[66] Instead this is regarded as a company law issue and it is for Member States to determine the legitimate purposes for which boards may selectively disclose inside information.[67] It is therefore for Member States to provide this clarity. This is something that some Member States did before the market soundings regime.[68] Within the context of the current regime it would be beneficial for Member States, while being mindful of the CJEU's narrow interpretation of the Market Abuse Regulation in this regard, to provide guidance to boards around these issues, including when the disclosure of inside information to certain shareholders might be regarded as necessary for the exercise of the normal course of business and what might be regarded as proportionate. This might include, for example, the disclosure of information by a subsidiary to a parent company in some circumstances. This may well vary by jurisdiction, according to national norms and corporate governance structures, and may well vary over time. While this is predominantly an issue for Member States, it is possible that EU-level developments might affect this in the future. The introduction and expansion of the EU Shareholder Rights Directive is a first step in this direction and it may be that corporate governance developments at EU level in the future might shape the norms around when disclosures of inside information by boards to shareholders may be regarded as being strictly necessary for the exercise of an employment, a profession or duties. Of course, in all circumstances, any disclosure would need to be accompanied by clear communication to the shareholder about the fact

[66] ESMA, Questions and Answers on the Market Abuse Regulation (MAR), ESMA70–145-111.

[67] See J L Hansen, 'Market Abuse Case Law – Where Do We Stand With MAR?' (2017) 15 European Company & Fin Law Rev 805.

[68] See eg FSA Handbook MAR 1.4.5.

that the information is inside information, agreement with the investor that they will be wall-crossed, and the imposition of a duty of confidentiality.

19.4 Conclusion

The market soundings regime is a response to a very specific set of problems created by the operation of the EU market abuse regime. It creates a safe harbour for disclosures to investors regarding a limited number of planned capital-raising activities in order to enable the size and pricing of the planned activity to be more accurately assessed, the justification being that this will result in the more efficient operation of the capital markets, an aim which is in line with the overall goal of the market abuse regime. The market soundings regime is successful within its narrow compass, providing certainty to issuers but at a considerable cost in terms of the burdensome nature of the process, and without providing protection to investors in all circumstances. It has been suggested in this chapter that it does not provide a helpful model for a broader board-shareholder dialogue regime. However, this should not be regarded as unduly problematic. There is little evidence that institutional investors want to receive inside information, since this then constrains their behaviour in the markets very significantly.[69] Decisions such as *Einhorn* support this view. To the extent that shareholders want to receive disclosures that do not comprise inside information, this is not constrained by the market abuse regulation and no safe harbour of the kind described in this paper is needed. If shareholders want to receive inside information that the directors can disclose within the ambit of the *Grøngaard* test, and they consent to be wall-crossed and agree to a duty of confidentiality, then such disclosures are not prohibited by the market abuse regime. Only those that fall outside the ambit of that test are prohibited by the regime, and it is suggested that there are many board-shareholder disclosures that *ought* to be prohibited, particularly those involving highly price sensitive information where the primary intention is to bolster shareholder loyalty. More clarity around the boundary of the *Grøngaard* test would be valuable as described above, but this chapter is not making any claims for an enlargement of the ambit of this test which would undermine the aims of the market abuse regime.

[69] G Strampelli, 'Knocking at the Boardroom Door: A Transatlantic Overview of Director-Institutional Investor Engagement in Law and Practice' (2018) 12 Va L & Bus Rev 187.

Ultimately, if the board has concerns about these issues, the solution is either not to disclose at all or to disclose the information to the market as a whole, so that all shareholders receive the information. This latter approach would be in keeping with enhancing transparency about a range of corporate issues, including ESG, while maintaining the principle of equal access to information.[70]

[70] L Bebchuk and S Hirst, 'Index Funds and the Future of Corporate Governance: Theory, Evidence, And Policy' (2019) 119 Columbia Law Review 2029.

Printed in the USA
CPSIA information can be obtained
at www.ICGtesting.com
CBHW051311311024
16557CB00016B/276

9 781009 36076